DAVID LLOYD GEORGE

DAVID
LLOYD
GEORGE

THE POLITICS OF
RELIGIOUS CONVICTION

Jerry L. Gaw

THE UNIVERSITY OF TENNESSEE PRESS

KNOXVILLE

FRONTIS: David Lloyd George, c. 1911, the year the House of Lords' veto power was stripped, and the National Insurance Act was passed. National Library of Wales.

Library of Congress Cataloging-in-Publication Data
Names: Gaw, Jerry L., 1952– author.
Title: David Lloyd George : the politics of religious conviction / Jerry L. Gaw.
Description: First edition. | Knoxville : The University of Tennessee Press, [2023] |
Includes bibliographical references and index. | Summary: "Unlike available
biographies of David Lloyd George, Jerry Gaw's study focuses on the popular
British statesman's religious convictions and his lifelong adherence to Churches
of Christ. Gaw explores the way Lloyd George applied Christian principles to the
socioeconomic and diplomatic crises he encountered beginning with his time in
the British legislature. Gaw's interpretation of Lloyd George is largely based on the
latter's twelve diaries and more than 3,200 letters written to his brother from 1885 to
1943. These diaries and letters have been little explored by modern biographers.
Gaw's deep analysis presents an entirely different perspective on Lloyd George
and explains, in part, how he came to the decisions now enshrined in the
annals of political history"—Provided by publisher.
Identifiers: LCCN 2022042524 (print) | LCCN 2022042525 (ebook) |
ISBN 9781621907640 (hardcover) | ISBN 9781621907657 (pdf)
Subjects: LCSH: Lloyd George, David, 1863–1945—Religion. | Prime ministers—
Great Britain—Biography. | Churches of Christ—Great Britain—Biography. |
Great Britain—Politics and government—1901–1936. | Great Britain—
Politics and government—1837–1901.
Classification: LCC DA566.9.L5 G39 2022 (print) | LCC DA566.9.L5 (ebook) |
DDC 941.083092 [B]—dc23/eng/20220912
LC record available at https://lccn.loc.gov/2022042524
LC ebook record available at https://lccn.loc.gov/2022042525

CONTENTS

Acknowledgments
xi

Introduction
1

1
Religion and Democracy,
1796–1923
9

2
Church and Convictions,
1875–1945
31

3
Temperance and Licensing,
1878–1921
63

4
Ireland and Home Rule,
1880–1914
87

5
Easter Rising and Anglo-Irish War,
1914–1922
109

6

Land and Pensions,
1880–1910

127

7

Insurance and Housing,
1911–1922

169

8

Disestablishment and Disendowment,
1883–1920

197

9

Tithes and Education,
1886–1922

225

10

Imperialism and the Second Boer War,
1878–1902

247

11

Diplomacy and World War,
1902–1916

269

12

Victory and Peace,
1916–1922

299

Conclusion
315

Notes 323
Bibliography 375
Index 389

ILLUSTRATIONS

Following page 154

Penymaes Chapel

Lloyd George's Foster Father

"Highgate" and Shoe Shop

Band of Hope Certificate, 1870

"Blue Ribbon" Pledge, 1887

Good Templars in Denbighshire, c.1885

Berea Chapel, Built 1886

Margaret Lloyd George

Miss Frances Stevenson

Gladstone and the Irish Land League

William O'Brien's Land War Poster

Parnell and the Home Rule Bill

Dominion Status for Ireland

Too Much Social Legislation

Old Age Pension Postal Order

National Health Insurance Flier

National Health Insurance Stamp

Suffrage League Postcard

Tithes Payments for 1836

Siege of Mafeking Bank Note

Leading Opponent of Balfour's Education Bill

Lloyd George Rescued by Constables at Birmingham

Boer Camp of Women and Children

Women Munitions Workers in WWI

British Tank at the Battle of the Somme

Lloyd George's WWI Cabinet, 1917

Uncle Sam Entering WWI

Sinn Féin Election Poster

The Heroes' Reward

Big Four in Versailles

ACKNOWLEDGMENTS

NUMEROUS PEOPLE have contributed of their much appreciated interest, time, expertise, suggestions, and financial support to make the completion of this endeavor possible. The David Laine Memorial Award at Lipscomb University, generously funded by Dr. Alton and Mary Baker in honor of his classmate there, initially enabled it. Another gracious amount from ten members of the Mr. and Mrs. W. L. George family aided continued research at the House of Lords Record Office or National Library of Wales. Furthermore, three Faculty Development Grants facilitated by Dean James T. Arnett and Provost W. Craig Bledsoe of Lipscomb provided additional funding for three of the four trips necessary to finish searching the archives in England or Wales. Three sabbaticals and two summer grants were also crucial to revise the manuscript for publication.

In addition to the very efficient Assistant Archivist K V Bligh at the Record Office as well as the extremely knowledgeable Robert Evans, Ann Francis Evans, and Rhiannon Michaelson-Yeates at the National Library who translated Welsh phrases, many more libraries gave access to their holdings through interlibrary loans to Lipscomb's library. Immediately willing members at a few copied pages of non-circulating sources for email attachments and even direct mailings to me. Janet Claridge, a part-time Special Collections Librarian at The University of Birmingham, printed nine pages of a tightly bound typescript diary that she had to ultimately mail me twice; Shelley L. Jacobs, the Disciples of Christ Historical Society's Archivist, was particularly helpful in emailing pictures of articles from eleven bound volumes of one nineteenth-century periodical; David W. Kiger, Theological Librarian for The Seminary Library at Milligan College, verified all of the publication months from his same eleven volumes; and his predecessor, John Mark Wade, emailed me a copy of an entire short book. Sara Harwell, Chief Archivist for the Disciples' Society when it was in Nashville, made several British Church of Christ journals available for me to research also. Carolyn T. Wilson, Marie P. Byers, Eunice F. Wells, Elizabeth C. Heffington, Julie Harston, Anna Leta Moss, and Elizabeth H. Rivera at Lipscomb's Beaman Library were especially valuable in assisting my frequent campus needs.

Three peer reviews, one from the University of Tennessee Press Board, plus copyediting offered excellent advice for improving the organization and conciseness of the manuscript, but any mistakes are entirely those of the author. Press director Scot Danforth was the first to see the project's potential, and acquisitions editor Thomas Wells has masterfully steered it to its fruition. Editorial assistant Jonathan Boggs, marketing assistant Linsey Perry, and publicist Tom Post have also expertly performed their important functions. Several close colleagues as well as students over the last twenty-eight years showed genuine interest in or encouraged the work's progress, including professors Tim Johnson, James McDonough, Robert Hooper, Dwight Tays, Richard Goode, Don Cole, Guy Vanderpool, Howard Miller, Neal Allison, Marc Schwerdt, Caleb Clanton, Paul Turner, Secretary Jennie Johnson, Librarian Myrna Perry, and former graduate Dave Talbert.

Authors' families make sacrifices of their time, attention, interests, plans, and money for such an undertaking to reach realization, especially after so many years. It is with heartfelt love and sincere gratitude that I thank my wife Vicki and my son David for all of the above and more. She always inspired me to keep going, and he was never resentful of my absence from home for long hours at a time. The effort was never required for career security and was certainly not for monetary gain, but it was absolutely essential for my personal as well as academic self-respect.

Introduction

DAVID LLOYD GEORGE, the last Liberal Prime Minister of the United
Kingdom, resigned a century ago this fall, after sixteen-and-a-half continuous
years in various government posts, but neither he nor his party ever returned
to office. He is most often associated in the collective memory with two enduring perceptions, that he started a welfare state in Britain and that he won
the First World War, neither of which is entirely true. However, in his position
as Chancellor of the Exchequer, he did implement old age pensions and national health as well as unemployment insurance, but then as the first Minister
of Munitions, he increased arms production enough for victory on the western
front. After serving as Secretary of State for War next, he became prime minister the last month of 1916, and a very small part of his political leadership
acumen during the last half of the war was to order a re-implementation of
naval convoys, the system he was most responsible for employing to counter
submarine warfare.[1]

One political scientist has described Lloyd George as a conviction politician
whose "clearest convictions" were the Welsh causes he championed, "land reform always" composing "one of his central convictions," suffrage for women
as well as men a "firm and consistent conviction" from which "he never wavered," and his opposition to the Second Boer War a "pure conviction." The
author elaborates that he "never proved doctrinaire," was "the least dogmatic"
of such politicians, and was forced to "maneuver" more than the others because of war. Like them, he "possessed a sense of mission." He even showed
press magnate Lord Riddell a psychic's letter, predicting he would fulfill a
huge mission and be kept safe by guardian forces, "a remarkable statement"
he also accepted "because I am myself convinced that nothing will be allowed
to happen to me until I have accomplished some great work for which I have
been singled out." However, he had to be "pragmatic" and "practical" in order
to maintain power over a coalition of mostly Conservatives, not changing convictions in his own eyes, though exercising "extreme flexibility," only to return

to those beliefs more radically after he resigned. Though the author does not note Lloyd George's religious conviction *per se*, she does stress that from the "traditional practices of the Welsh preacher," he did develop "a distinctive oratorical style."[2]

Lloyd George remains the only prime minister of Welsh descent in British history, but he was actually born in Manchester, England, on January 17, 1863, living there for just two months. He held the highest office in the land, from 1916 to 1922, six of his fifty-five years as a member of Parliament, having first been elected to the House of Commons in 1890, at the age of twenty-seven, and accepting a peerage in the House of Lords a little over three months before dying on March 26, 1945. His social and economic achievements started as soon as he became a Liberal Cabinet Member, President of the Board of Trade, in December 1905, but mostly were realized from 1908 to 1915, while he occupied Number 11 Downing Street, residence of the Chancellor of the Exchequer, the second highest position in the government. Then, after finishing thirteen months as Minister of Munitions, followed by six as Secretary of State for War, he was finally able to move into Number 10 Downing Street thirty-eight days shy of his fifty-fourth birthday and twenty-six years, eight months after he first occupied his seat in the Palace of Westminster.[3]

My interest in Lloyd George was piqued in 1979, upon discovering in sources for a master's thesis on the history of British Churches of Christ in the nineteenth century that he was a member of that religious tradition. Focused research on him then began in 1994, to uncover how his particular spiritual heritage influenced the convictions he developed and pursued once he became a member of the English legislature. Having experienced the same doctrinal upbringing led me to twenty-eight years' study and writing on the socioeconomic policies he furthered and the way he applied Christian principles to the diplomatic or military crises he encountered. The result is an entirely new analysis of why he did what he did as a representative of the masses in the British Isles.[4]

A religious interpretation of Lloyd George's political motivations must begin by discussing the distinct precepts and practices of the church in which he held membership his entire life. Next, his experiences in that fellowship and either positive or negative reactions to them are critical to an understanding of the course of his faith. The faith that evolved informed why he decided to tackle the legislative challenges he did and what he hoped to accomplish for the government but more importantly for the people of the United Kingdom. Those laws pertained to licensing alcohol, influenced by the temperance movement; addressing home rule with the two parts of Ireland, the Easter Rising, plus the Anglo-Irish War; reforming land ownership along democratic lines, with old age pensions, national health insurance, national unemployment insurance as well as housing made possible by taxation of the wealthy to protect the poor; ending payment of tithes in support of the Church of England schools so educational opportunities could be provided on an equitable basis for every nonconformist; disestablishing in addition to disendowing Anglicanism in Wales; and securing justice for the small nations in empires, or Christian minorities under non-Christian rule, through international diplomacy, or, if absolutely necessary, war—even a world war.[5]

Though he never wavered from his firmly held conviction about the right to vote for all, neither his writings nor speeches specifically relate those beliefs to religious tenets from his upbringing like those previously mentioned. As early as 1879, though, he privately noted during a speech by a woman defending female suffrage, "As for myself, I do not see why single women and widows managing property should not have a voice in the adjustment, etc., of the taxes." Interestingly, he later told his only female secretary that Henrik Ibsen's 1879 *A Doll's House* "converted him to woman suffrage." Also, his Criccieth Debating Society discussed the franchise in 1885, a year after the lowest paid male householders got the vote in the Third Reform Act, resolving to favor female suffrage. As a franchise bill was going through the House of Commons from July 1912 to January 1913, he was interrupted in his native village of Llanystumdwy, as suffragettes stormed a platform that had been built for the dedication of an institute financed with money he had won in a libel suit three years earlier. Ironically, as his brother bequeathed the property and buildings purchased with the money, he also presented two stipulations for their use: no alcohol and no religious or political discrimination to join. Lloyd George reiterated the second in his keynote speech, including the words "without distinctions of creed." Clearly, he was still opposed to creeds or sectarianism, which he so often expressed in private correspondence and public addresses because of the egalitarian, democratic religious teaching he received growing up. In 1918, his government passed the Representation of the People Act, granting all males at twenty-one and women householders at thirty the vote. Christabel Pankhurst, a suffragette, converted to Christ in 1918 also. She then began ministering in writing or speaking, and even shared London's Castle Street Welsh Baptist Chapel pulpit with Lloyd George in 1931.[6]

David Lloyd George: The Politics of Religious Conviction is based heavily on twelve diaries Lloyd George kept from 1878 until 1892 and over 3,200 letters he

wrote to his brother from 1885 to 1918, the latter the most significant collection
of his personal correspondence. Then, for almost twenty-one years, they did
not write. Archival letters to his uncle, wife, mistress, and two Parliament
colleagues are also important primary sources as are entries from diaries of a
childhood friend, two secretaries, and a fellow Cabinet member. He ceased
writing his mistress on diplomacy from October 1918 to August 1921, due to
her being where he was or to pressing issues. The diaries and letters to his
brother have been available since 1989, and this book makes the most extensive
use of them. Even his brother, oldest son, middle daughter, and a nephew who
have written biographies of him have no more than ten pages on the religion
in which he spent his life. The dozens of other books about him contain three
or less.[7]

This volume is not a biography but an effort to finally understand reasons
Lloyd George fought contests that in some cases could have easily brought an
end to his chosen vocation and in others pitted him against his own religious
tradition or political party to achieve what he thought was best for the disadvantaged in British society as well as for the empire. Multiple overseas trips
to the National Library of Wales and the House of Lords Record Office were
necessary to examine private diaries, letters, or collected papers on his public
religious utterances, but fortunately his diaries and the letters to his brother
were also online. Parliamentary debates and Welsh newspapers are online too,
helping this project come to fruition. Interestingly, the senior archivist at the
National Library of Wales wrote that in their sources "references to Lloyd
George's religious experiences are few and far between, although he does occasionally refer to his philosophy and beliefs."[8]

Upon hearing the subject I had set out to research, the first cabdriver hired
in South Wales quickly voiced that Lloyd George was a womanizer. A North
Wales bed-and-breakfast owner privately shared that Welsh people exclusive
of her think Lloyd George was a compulsive liar but are proud it was for them.
A candid visitor to the cemetery where Lloyd George's family is interred volunteered that his great-grandmother became pregnant in 1880, suggesting
possibly by Lloyd George when he was seventeen. She was fourteen years older,
was sent away, had a child who looked like him, and he along with his relatives
moved from Llanystumdwy to Criccieth. The woman's descendant conjectured that these events might explain why Richard Lloyd and the Georges
left their village home. Obviously, the length of this effort proves the senior
archivist's estimate inaccurate, and the evidence within should convince

seriously objective readers that Lloyd George was neither a philanderer nor a pathological liar.[9]

Having unequivocally stated the above, it is true that he lied to his uncle about articles he wrote pseudonymously for a Welsh newspaper and a Church of Christ periodical because of their harsh criticism of local girls or brotherhood elderships in the principality. It is also a fact that he often flirted, was invited to wives' homes socially, usually for meals, and loved female company at leisure times, particularly holidays abroad with couples. For seven and a half years, beginning when he started keeping diaries, he had many entries about adventures with girls, but two weeks after his twenty-third birthday, he wrote a very telling one that reflected on such times because of another girl with whom he was tempted to flirt: "felt strong inclination to decide upon a plunge—but felt chary of placing myself in an inextricable position." Looking back, he added, "Previous experience of my own fickleness makes me distrust myself to enter upon a 7 or 8 year's trial of my fidelity," indicating he had regularly flirted but was reluctant to continue it, which his further diary entries verify. He was already seeing the girl who would become his wife, Margaret Owen, proposed to her seven months later, and ten months after promised her he would flirt no more. It is known, though, that he had a thirty-year affair with his secretary, Frances Stevenson, but it did not begin until after more than two decades of begging Margaret to live with him in London instead of staying in Wales for their children. He married Frances two years after Margaret died, and no proof of any other sexual infidelity before or after either marriage exists, despite an ever-growing number of accusations to the contrary by some. Four years before his only affair started, he even won thirteen-hundred pounds from two libel suits against newspapers that implied he was the adulterer in a divorce case, accusations from which he had been absolved eleven years previously.[10]

Lloyd George's oldest daughter, Mair, who died of appendicitis at age seventeen, six years before his infidelity began, looked a lot like Frances. Mair was two years younger than Frances, but they had attended the same school and knew each other. In 1911, Frances was also a teacher where Mair's youngest sister, Megan, went to school, and Lloyd George employed her as a tutor for the summer. As early as August 1, 1911, he told his brother he would like to know Megan's opinion of her governess, and she taught her until the winter was over. Frances then lived with the family in Criccieth the next summer, after which Lloyd George asked her to be one of the secretaries for the Chancellor of the Exchequer "on his own terms." She agreed to his offer on Christmas Day and became his mistress on January 21, 1913, having joined J. T. Davies in the Treasury Office. She was also the first female principal private secretary in any government office after he became the prime minister. He had talked with her about his grief over Mair's death by at least late February of 1913 because she wrote a poem on the back of his first dated extant letter calling on the spirit of Mair to still light the way for him. Ironically, he also wrote his brother just two months after she passed, "my dear little Mair came to me last night in my sleep to tell me how pleased she was with my success." According to Frances's diary, he even told her on the second anniversary of the day they "married" that she had "taken the place somewhat of Mair, 'my little girl whom I lost' as he always calls her." He never fully coped with Mair's death, and his second extant, undated letter to Frances plus others have greetings such as, "My darling little girl," or "My own sweet child."[11]

The best example of Lloyd George's pleading with Margaret was in a letter he sent to her seven years after taking up residency in London. "I have more than once gone without breakfast. I have scores of times come home in the dead of night to a cold, dark & comfortless flat without a soul to greet me. I am not the nature either physically or morally that I ought to have been left like this," he confessed. "You have been a good mother. You have not—& I say this now not in anger—not always been a good wife." His plea ended, "You may be a blessing to your children. Oh, Maggie dear, beware lest you be a curse to your husband. My soul as well as my body has been committed to your charge & in many respects I am as helpless as a child." Forty years later, he confided in A. J. Sylvester, his final secretary, that some wives sacrifice everything for husbands but others for their children. The year he fell from power, one biographer wrote of him what could be said of many Christians. He possessed "the strangest capacity for dividing his life, his mind, and his soul into watertight compartments." His best-known biographer's initial assessment of him, based on sources too inadequate for such an analysis, is, "Prayer meant nothing to him, and his belief in God was only a vague belief in Destiny, which gave a semblance of meaning to history and, therefore, to his own career." Based on those inaccurate interpretations, he wrongly asserts that Lloyd George was spiritually lightweight and simply fooled nonconformists into supporting him for a long time. The last evaluation is an insufficient explanation for the subsequent decrease of non-Anglican participation in politics, which had begun after Liberals were unsuccessful in getting a new education act passed following their 1906 victory and should be attributed even more to evangelists using fewer expositions of scripture, higher criticism, middle-class wealth, and socialism.[12]

Lloyd George definitely compartmentalized the various aspects of his multifaceted adult existence and carried a lot of baggage like everyone else, but he took nothing spiritual about himself or physical about the needs of others lightly. Indeed, he pondered religious beliefs much more than most teenagers or young adults to determine what he accepted or rejected, and he followed through on the convictions he internalized with a tenacious consistency externally. He spoke of that consistency to Sylvester, being unabashedly honest on the difference between his words and actions, expressing his desire for everyone to listen to the former and ignore the latter. This book aims to honor his first wish.[13]

1

Religion and Democracy, 1796–1923

"I learned all my democracy from
Alexander Campbell and Abraham Lincoln."

BEST KNOWN AS Great Britain's prime minister during the last half of World War I and its representative at the Paris Peace Conference, David Lloyd George had also become a Christian on February 7, 1875. He had just turned twelve years old on January 17, and his uncle, Richard Lloyd, baptized him in the Afon Cwrt stream flowing by Penymaes Chapel in Criccieth, North Wales. Today the stone structure is a private residence, but the baptistery can still be seen, complete with rock steps leading down into the babbling brook.[1] Uncle Lloyd had been a foster father to David, his older sister, and his younger brother for over a decade as well as an elder and unpaid preacher for the congregation since 1859. Penymaes had begun as a Particular Baptist church in 1796 but identified with Scotch Baptists in 1801. Forty years later, it became part of the Churches of Christ fellowship. David Lloyd, Richard's father, had preached at the chapel from 1830 to 1839, during which he became familiar with the teachings of Alexander Campbell, a leader of Christians in America who simply called themselves "disciples of Christ." Some have suggested that the elder Lloyd was favorably disposed toward Campbell's doctrines, while others insist he vigorously opposed certain ones. Regardless, two years after David Lloyd's pulpit tenure ended due to his untimely death, the congregation affiliated with other churches that agreed with Campbell's plea to restore the New Testament church. By 1870, the annual gathering of representatives from such churches in the British Isles, which started in 1842 and became known as cooperation meetings, recommended each congregation be named "Church of Christ" with members called "Christians" only. Church of Christ had also been a common designation for dissenting churches since the 1600s.[2]

The leading scholar of the history of Churches of Christ in the United Kingdom, David M. Thompson, emeritus professor of Modern Church History at the University of Cambridge, has astutely observed that the nineteenth century "saw the development of a number of groups who rejected the idea of denominationalism and sought to recreate primitive Christianity on a New Testament basis outside the existing denominations." Including "the Churches of Christ" among them, he elaborated, "These groups were not all alike, and they were not without some sympathisers in the established denominations, but they represent an interesting byway from the main nineteenth-century road." In the most succinct analysis of the path the Churches of Christ followed, he later wrote, "By the end of 1842 therefore, Churches of Christ as they are known today were recognizably in being. The name as such was not yet widely used," he contrasted, "but by meeting together at Edinburgh in 1842 the churches had taken a step towards a corporate existence which the Scotch Baptists never took. Their cooperation for evangelistic purposes also indicates that they had broken with the largely non-evangelical tradition of the Scotch Baptists." Anachronistically, congregations in Scotland and Wales dating from 1809 identified as "Church of Christ" after Campbell's teachings were accepted by some there, but it was also capitalized as a name by his father, Thomas, in his *Declaration and Address* of the same year. Alexander also used the upper case in 1830, *The Millennial Harbinger*'s first year, but then wrote "the particular congregations" where he had been "for many years" were known by no other name. In that same year, Barton W. Stone, whose followers began uniting with Campbell's in 1832, put "church of Christ" in lower case like the New Testament, describing who built and heads it, not the name of it.[3]

The legacy of Campbell and Stone's union, which spawned what has been labeled the Restoration or Stone-Campbell Movement, includes the Christian Churches (Disciples of Christ), Christian Churches\Churches of Christ (Independent), and Churches of Christ, though no official distinctions were published until 1906. Rational arguments in Campbell's writings had a direct impact on Lloyd George, and Stone's emotional revivals may explain his support of the 1904–05 Welsh Revival. However, to understand the formation and evolution of his religious upbringing, it is important to discuss the doctrinal differences that led the Penymaes congregation through three religious identities in less than half a century. The influence of these changes on his grandfather and uncle informed what he was taught, and how he responded to that instruction helped shape his Christian world view. Both of the Lloyds were engaged in their community and well read, especially Richard, who acquired from friends or publishers almost all the Welsh journals that pertained to the religions of his day. The Particular Baptists who founded the Penymaes church were hyper-Calvinists and subscribed to the 1689 Confession of Faith, which was not translated into Welsh until 1721. They only ordained one ruling elder, though the minister exercised more power and was often called a teaching elder. Furthermore, they chose at least one deacon, gave church membership to immersed believers, practiced closed communion, and paid preachers.[4]

The two most notable Particular Baptist preachers in northern Wales were Christmas Evans in Anglesey and John Richard Jones in Merionethshire. They worked together briefly, but in 1798 the latter parted company with the Particular Baptists, vehemently objecting to paying ministers and entitling them Reverend. In addition, Jones had come to believe in a plurality of elders and thought non-members should not be given communion, hymnbooks, or the collection plate. Knowing his chapel's history, Lloyd George insisted on handing people songbooks as they entered Penymaes, and closed communion infuriated him.[5] Jones angrily denounced his former associates, calling them "Babylonian Welsh Baptists." After his bitter departure from the Particular Baptists, Jones eventually joined forces with Archibald McLean, the recognized leader of Scotch Baptists, with whom he had corresponded for two years. He had become familiar with Scotch Baptists as early as 1790, and a friend in Wrexham loaned him McLean's *The Commission given by Jesus Christ to his Apostles* in 1795, published nine years earlier, to explain his understanding of first-century Christianity. The Scotch Baptist denomination had begun in 1765, but none of the correspondence between the two men suggests that McLean encouraged Jones to separate from the Particular Baptists. Clearly, though, he wanted Jones and his followers to accept his views. Jones's first letter to McLean was written on September 2, 1796, and mainly expressed agreement with his teachings but requested additional explanation of his thinking on having more than one elder and foot washing.[6]

Since McLean was in England at the time, one of his co-elders, William Braidwood, answered Jones, stating that his words had been read to the whole congregation, that none of them was aware of Scotch Baptists in Wales, and that a copy of a song they had sung at their love feast would be mailed to him. He even used a similar phrase, "captives of Babylon," to describe Christians in error and asked numerous questions to determine if they agreed on those errors. He also addressed three queries from Jones, explaining that foot washing was performed if needed but not only to demonstrate humility, that several passages in scripture refer to multiple elders, and that miracles through human hands had ceased. Finally, he noted that he would send a William Jones, "bookseller in Liverpool," three copies of McLean's book, apparently due to his correspondent's urging.[7] McLean ultimately wrote Jones three months afterward, giving a short account of the origins of Scotch Baptists, concurring with Braidwood's answers, and adding he believed an elder having one wife meant at a time. He also invited Jones or some of his fellow teachers to visit him in Edinburgh as well as William Jones in Liverpool. He ended by asking him what he thought of getting a Welsh translation of his book done and expressed hope to be at Chester or Wrexham in the summer, where they might also meet.[8]

The Scotch Baptists began at a time when there were no Particular Baptists in Scotland, but they actively supported the Particular Baptist Foreign Missionary Society after its inception in 1792. J. R. Jones never embraced foreign missions or Sunday schools, and an 1803 letter to him from McLean also indicates that he did not accept believers worshipping in error as true converts or tolerate Christians who served in the military during war, "whether offensive or defensive." McLean believed they could, as long as they did not enlist before first trying to avoid going to war "by insurance and substitutes." Also, unlike McLean, Jones did accept premillennialism, the teaching that Christ will return to earth for a thousand years prior to the final judgment. An 1805 missive from McLean to Jones confirms the latter's belief in it. Nonetheless, he had led five Particular Baptist churches of North Wales into the Scotch Baptist fold. With a combined membership of 155, they were located at Ramoth, his church home, Harlech, Dolgelley, Criccieth, and Glyn Ceiriog. Since other Baptist preachers in Wales stopped going to those services, Jones had to minister to them all but only went to Criccieth on week nights. He died in 1822, and David Lloyd was in attendance at Penymaes the last time he spoke there.[9]

McLeanist and Church of Christ congregations in nineteenth-century Britain shared several doctrines but also differed in a number of very significant ways. Their mutual beliefs included that the Bible was the only rule of authority in precept and practice; the teachings and examples of Jesus, as well as the apostles, were binding; every congregation should have elders, but more than one whenever possible; only immersed believers should be asked to commune; the Lord's Supper should be observed every Sunday; an offering for expenses and "poor members" should be collected weekly; and justification through faith was "an intellectual act." Unlike the McLeanists, the Church of Christ did not believe in original sin and total depravity, taught free will instead of Calvinism, rejected the Mosaic law as binding on Christians, claimed conversion came through the word without a separate preparation of the heart by the Holy Spirit, and held immersion as the method by which one was baptized to receive remission of sins and enter the kingdom instead of being just an outward manifestation of inner salvation with its promises already.[10]

Though the congregation in Criccieth had been a Church of Christ for over twenty years when Lloyd George was born, he was very much aware of its religious roots. Harold Spender, one of his childhood friends and biographers, was quoted as saying that Lloyd George "calls himself a Particular Baptist." Spender made the comment while touring the United States for the three-hundredth anniversary of the Mayflower's landing.[11] Lloyd George also referred to himself as a Scotch Baptist on at least one occasion, while traveling in Wales with Alfred Milner, who had served in his War Cabinet and was one of his colonial secretaries. Milner asked Lloyd George what religion a certain chapel was. He answered that it was the one to which he belonged, "Scotch Baptists." When queried about its difference from "an ordinary one," he replied, "Oh, a world of difference, Milner; I cannot tell you what it is, but I am prepared to go to the stake for it!" Another version of this exchange in a 1923 *Methodist Monthly Greeting* published in Newfoundland, Canada, has Lloyd George asking, "Do you know I belong to a branch of the church that holds deep convictions on the question whether baptism is for the remission of sins or on account of the remission of sins? And I would go to the stake for my convictions in the matter; but for the life of me I cannot now tell which side I am on."[12]

Elaborating on his own religious experience at Criccieth, Lloyd George told a large assembly of Presbyterians in Scotland, "We thrived on controversy in my home church. We were sticklers for sound doctrine. I can not now recall what it was about on any one of the different story occasions, but I well remember that we had jolly times arguing." Eventually, though, Criccieth became less conservative than many Churches of Christ in the British Isles, exhibiting a spirit of greater liberty, according to one visitor from America. This shift was especially true after 1890, when an effort known as the Forward Movement opened the minds of some in the churches to greater opportunities for showing the love of Christ. These included more evangelism along with social consciousness at home, foreign missions, programs for youth as well as women, and even aid for the care of workers' children or orphans, but also biblical criticism. Three in the movement had direct contact with the Criccieth church, Lloyd George, or one of its elders. William Webley, a fellow Welshman, visited Criccieth in 1891 as his first assignment on behalf of the cooperation's General Evangelist Committee. Sydney Black, minister for the biggest Church of Christ in Britain by 1900, London's Fulham Cross, befriended Lloyd George. He asked him to address a session of the 1898 cooperation meeting, and Lloyd George told his brother that Black was "a fine chap." Black also preached at Criccieth during a 1902 evangelistic tour, and within a year there were nine congregations in London, three of them in Fulham. Thomas Ainsworth personally knew William Williams, Richard Lloyd's co-elder for fifty-four years, and eulogized him in 1913 as "one who was in every way sound as a rock upon the New Testament principles."[13]

Returning to the years before the Criccieth congregation affiliated with the Churches of Christ, it is clear that even Jones and McLean did not agree on all matters. In a rare extant letter from the former to the latter in 1806, arguments concerning who is really a Christian, whether true Christians can marry those such as "Papists, Socinians, and Swedenborgians" who worship in denominations, as well as a lengthy ongoing disagreement over the millennium were included. Tellingly, Jones began by not only reporting that McLeanist congregations in North Wales were united but also lamenting, "Our profession is too simple, unindulgent and self-denying to attract many followers, nor yet many hearers. However the few churches in our connection are upon the whole increasing, though slowly." He announced an appendix to a hymnal he had published in Welsh too, including songs from collections by McLean.[14] An 1812 missive from Braidwood to Jones relayed McLean's death, but by 1818, he was expressing regret that Jones's church had split over disputes concerning who should be disfellowshipped and whether they could be restored if they were withdrawn from twice.[15]

On the subject of baptism, the Scotch Baptists taught an Independent Scottish missionary to Ireland that the only acceptable mode of it was immersion of believers. In 1808, that missionary for the Haldane brothers debated Alexander Carson, an ordained Presbyterian minister who had left the Ulster synod three years earlier, and Carson started investigating adult baptism by immersion only. Robert and James Haldane, founders of numerous Scottish Independent churches who had taught infant baptism, were both immersed as adults that year but did not make it a litmus test of fellowship. A split also occurred among Haldaneans in 1808, but the road to division had begun over two other issues on which the brothers refused to compromise. Like McLean, they believed in a plurality of elders and mutual exhortation, all men having the responsibility to teach in worship assemblies as opposed to listening to one designated teacher. Unlike McLean, however, the Haldanes became convinced that both aspects of church polity were requirements, not suggestions. They reached these conclusions after reading William Ballantine's *Treatise on the Elder's Office*. Ballantine had cast his lot with them in 1807, two years after his book appeared. He eventually moved to London and then America, where he identified with Scotch Baptists and Churches of Christ, respectively.[16]

Lynn McMillon, an historian of Scottish origins of Churches of Christ in the British Isles and America, has noted, "Ballantine's own experience helps to demonstrate the close relationship of the various groups." Even some members of the main Edinburgh church of the Haldanes looked into worshipping with the McLeanist church in the capital the year of the division. Another letter from Braidwood to Jones in February 1808 mentions how James Haldane "entertains serious doubts about baptism, and cannot now sprinkle infants," how "Some of his people have gone back to the National Church," and how "a few of his people are inquiring after us." Only eight months later, though, Braidwood informed Jones that Haldane and most of his congregation of two hundred or so had been baptized, but "There are still things which prevent his union with us, though in many respects we are agreed." Regrettably, a division also occurred among the Glasgow McLeanists in 1810. It split 168 who thought no elder had to be present at worship services for communion to be scriptural from those who did; two years prior, fifty Independents who believed the former had joined the Glasgow congregation. Additionally, some McLeanists who emigrated to Canada and America became so legalistic that they opposed association with other Scotch Baptist churches, any nonchurch group doing the church's work, or all other societies.[17]

The preacher for the Haldanean church in Glasgow, Greville Ewing, was Carson's friend since they were classmates at Glasgow University. Also, Carson and James Haldane were two of many visiting ministers at the Independent congregation in Rich Hill, Ireland. Thomas Campbell and son, Alexander, occasionally attended there. The Presbyterian congregation where the elder Campbell preached was only two miles away, and he eventually moved to Rich Hill to establish a public school. He and his son ultimately taught there. The interconnectedness of these different religious communities is obvious, but regardless of these links, Carson, the Haldanes, Ballantine, and Ewing are more important here because of their influence on Alexander rather than for whatever contact they had with Scotch Baptists. He was acquainted with all of these individuals, and the republicanism they shared had a particularly profound impact on him. Writing of Independents in general, Robert Richardson, Campbell's son-in-law and biographer, stated their emphasis on "the right of private judgment" in religious matters captured Campbell's imagination. "Opposed as well to Presbytery as to Prelacy and Popery, and regarding each congregation as independent and supreme in its jurisdiction, their views naturally made them republican in civil affairs."[18]

Campbell exhibited the temporal as well as spiritual republicanism he learned from men like the Haldanes or Ewing, in actions and words. He also attended the University of Glasgow, which "was still seething from the effects of the French Revolution, the new sciences, the issues of revealed versus natural religion," and Thomas Reid's Scottish "Common Sense philosophy."[19] Among other philosophical writings he studied were those of Francis Bacon, Isaac Newton, John Locke, David Hume, William Godwin, and Jean Jacques Rousseau. Ewing introduced the young student to his professors and invited him to his home on many occasions for a cup of tea or meal. Campbell also came under Ewing's doctrinal influence, specifically on how often to observe the Lord's Supper. Ewing was the first to practice weekly communion in Scotland, where the custom was to take it only twice a year.[20] The eminent religious historian, Sydney Ahlstrom, may have been indicating the influence of Ewing on Campbell concerning this observance when he wrote, "Even in Glasgow Campbell was so far estranged from his traditional church allegiance as to walk out of a Presbyterian communion service."[21]

During that service, Campbell had gone to the presbyters to secure the token that was required of everyone who wished to commune. They asked him for papers proving he was a member of the denomination, and he told them his membership was in Ireland. Consequently, they inquired into his religious beliefs, and persuaded to extend fellowship, gave him a token. When they served communion, though, he refused to partake, and when handed the collection tray, he contributed the token. In very dramatic prose, Richardson later stated, "It was at this moment that the struggle in his mind was completed, and the ring of the token, falling upon the plate, announced the instant at which he renounced Presbyterianism forever the leaden voucher becoming thus a token not of communion but of separation." This reads entirely too much like what influenced Martin Luther to start his Reformation, the sound of an indulgence coin hitting the bottom of a receptacle to free a soul from purgatory according to Catholic teaching. Even Richardson added that Campbell not only did not reveal his change of heart at the time but also willingly accepted a letter of reference from the church's leadership. A three-volume biography of Campbell by Eva Jean Wrather stresses that he did not consider the decision to be courageous but simply another step on the road to truth. His most recent but only critical biography explains he afterward viewed it as figuratively refuting sectarian practice and preparing for spiritual change.[22]

Campbell later applied that same independent-mindedness to the topics of religious and political liberty. In his periodicals, he equated the two and asserted "the rights of Christians are just as clear and as inferrable [sic] as the rights of man from the same stock of common sense, enlightened by religion." Relating rights and responsibilities, he philosophized, "Whatever the natural rights of men are, they belong to all men naturally; consequently the natural rights of men are equal rights. For whatever belongs to all men naturally, must equally belong to all. To give to others what belongs to them," he elaborated, "is a duty we owe them; to withhold from them what belongs to them, is a sin. There can be no favor, donation, or gift, in conferring natural rights upon others," he added, "for natural rights cannot be conferred; they belong to man merely because he exists. Now if it be duty to give to others what belongs to them, it is our duty not to invade the rights of others, but to protect and guarantee them." According to Lloyd George's nephew and biographer, churches influenced by Campbell instilled in their members, "a love of religious liberty and the freedom to worship . . . unhampered by the surveillance of any external organization." He goes on to assess that "one effect" of his uncle's "upbringing was to transform this influence into a passion for political independence, unhampered as far as possible by a rigid adherence to a party line." Worship at Penymaes left a particularly enduring mark on his memory because of "the extreme simplicity of the service, the complete lack of pomp and ostentation and the reiterated theme that all were equal in the sight of God."[23]

Campbell's views on natural rights and his spirit of forbearance affected Lloyd George. While serving as Chancellor of the Exchequer in 1913, he commented, "A very large part of the economic and social principles I am pressing upon the English people I obtained from reading the writings of Alexander Campbell." He made the statement to a representative of the American Christian Missionary Society, then exclusively sponsored by the Christian Church (Disciples of Christ), the other part of the Stone-Campbell Movement. It was formally recognized in the 1906 religious census, and Churches of Christ disagreed with it because it used an organization outside local congregations to do mission work and had adopted instrumental music in worship. The society's emissary, Z. T. Sweeney, "after the exercise of a good deal of red tape," had found Lloyd George in Parliament and invited him to the society's next meeting, in Toronto. Sweeney also preached at Criccieth and stated that Lloyd George and his family "were highly interested listeners." Presumably due to other pressing matters, the chancellor did not travel to Toronto, but a religious historian from the Churches of Christ, in an error-riddled article, charged without foundation, "He always resisted attempts to pull him into a service of the churches of Christ."[24]

In 1913, Lloyd George began a land campaign to provide farm laborers a minimum wage and security of tenure to tenant farmers, which he had to abandon the very next year because of the advent of World War I. He had already distinguished himself as a socioeconomic reformer, though, by improving the working conditions of those in the merchant navy, gaining concessions for railroad employees, establishing the Port of London Authority, procuring old age pensions, implementing national health as well as unemployment insurance, and stripping the House of Lords of its power to veto legislation for such things. Becoming prime minister during the First World War, he gave women the right to vote, argued against unfair punishment of the Germans at the Paris Peace Conference, disestablished and disendowed the Church of England in Wales, and negotiated dominion status for the Irish Free State. He fell from power in October 1922, and while touring the United States the next year proclaimed, "I learned all my democracy from Alexander Campbell and Abraham Lincoln." He uttered the statement to a Christian Church elder during a St. Louis "dinner party, at which there were only ten present." He also called Campbell great but referenced James A. Garfield as a member of the Church of Christ before mentioning the others. He was not only familiar with his Particular and Scotch Baptist roots but also knew of his Church of Christ heritage from Campbell's teachings and Garfield's example.[25]

Campbell's writings first entered the British Isles in 1825 at Newry, Ireland, near where his father was born, and ten years later reached Wales. William Jones, the former bookseller in Liverpool, began disseminating them in March 1835. He now ministered for a Scotch Baptist chapel in London, where Ballantine had been a co-elder. This Jones had heard of Campbell from one who lived near him in Bethany, Virginia. Jones was from Wales, but John Roberts translated Campbell's first reprinted article into Welsh. It dealt with the discussion Jesus and Nicodemus have in John 3. An elder of the Scotch Baptist church in Bryndeunydd, Roberts was from Llannefydd, Denbighshire, which borders Carnarvonshire on the east.[26] J. R. Jones had also corresponded with him more than once, addressing him as "Very Dear Brother" in 1806 to share that fourteen members had left "Popular Baptists" on the Lleyn peninsula and wanted to join his "connection." Another letter, dated 1819, addressed a mutual friend's death.[27]

One Particular Baptist and two Welsh Baptist ministers, respectively, translated more of Campbell's writings into Welsh. John Evans of Bangor translated part of the 1823 debate on baptism between Campbell and W. L. McCalla, a Presbyterian preacher. Also, some from Evans's congregation separated to follow Campbell's teachings. John Williams, from Rhos of Wrexham, rendered "Remission of Sins" out of Campbell's *The Christian System* in 1839 and *The Living Oracles*, Campbell's New Testament, in 1841. Most notably, Robert Ellis, first of Glyn Ceiriog, Tredegar, but then Carnarvon, converted five of Campbell's lectures on baptism into Welsh and put portions of *The Christian System* in the 1845-46 *Seren Gomer*, the first weekly in Welsh. As editor of *Y Tyst Apostolaidd* (The Apostolic Witness) in 1851 and *Y Greal* (The Grail) in 1852, he spread Campbell's beliefs too. He was forced to resign from the latter.[28] Both Welsh Baptists worked together to oppose landlords and church rates in Denbighshire, with Williams also calling an assembly at which he spoke on universal suffrage. All of those issues became extremely important to Lloyd George years later. *The Christian System*, Campbell's only book to formulate his views of scriptural doctrines all Christians should accept, first appeared in 1835 as *Christianity Restored* and was the equivalent of a faith statement, but he did not try to compel readers to agree with him. *Seren Gomer* started giving his writings significant press in 1839.[29]

For sixteen months, William Jones published a paper entitled *The Millennial Harbinger and Voluntary Church Advocate*. Half of the first eight issues and a third of the second eight were composed of Campbell's works. Though Jones discontinued his monthly in 1836, another periodical known as *The Christian Messenger and Reformer* began the next year. Its editor was James Wallis, who had just established a congregation in Nottingham from a small group that left the Scotch Baptists. His journal was also translated into Welsh and continued the reprinting of Campbell's articles under its various names or editors throughout Lloyd George's life, one of the names being *The British Millennial Harbinger*. Lloyd George's initial exposure to those articles must have started at an early age because he told an American missionary that he had heard "his uncle read the writings of Alexander Campbell by candlelight in the shoeshop."[30] Campbell's own first periodical was *The Christian Baptist*, published from 1823 to 1829, and his second was *The Millennial Harbinger*, which ran from 1830 to 1870. Jones and Wallis adopted the use of "millennial" from Campbell, whose type of millennialism was basically postmillennialism, but his expressions about unscriptural religions and unethical political systems were at least as negative as some premillennialists. The former taught that there would be progress for a figurative thousand years leading up to the return of Christ for the final judgment, while the latter proclaimed that Christ would return to establish His Kingdom on earth after things reach their worst. Campbell lived until a year after the American Civil War, after which most Church of Christ members in the United States became amillennial, believing that Christians have been in a thousand-year reign with Christ since His church began. World War I had the same impact on a majority of British members.[31]

Postmillennialism apparently influenced Lloyd George because while privately criticizing Neville Chamberlain's inaction on April 10, 1939, he made reference to believers in the victory of Christian principles, literally but also humorously interpreting that it "is perfectly honest and has the greatest example in the world, though it has taken a damned long time for it to succeed over 1,000 years." Three American presidents from the "disciples of Christ" heritage came under the influence of postmillennialism and endeavored to improve their society. Garfield initiated civil service reform, Lyndon Johnson founded the Great Society, and Ronald Reagan often spoke of the United States as a shining city on a hill. George Marsden, the dean of American religious historians, states, "Postmillennialists typically were optimistic about the spiritual progress of the culture. They saw human history as reflecting an ongoing struggle between cosmic forces of God and Satan, each well represented by various earthly powers, but with the victory of righteousness ensured." A future Lloyd George biographer posited that, as early as 1912, his subject defined politics as a tool to make "a new earth wherein dwelleth righteousness" (II Peter 3:13, KJV).[32]

Lloyd George's maternal grandfather was a contemporary of William Jones, and Jones not only corresponded with David Lloyd but also visited Criccieth, where he espoused Campbell's views. The reprinted articles from Campbell's publications were available to the elder Lloyd too. One tangible result of Campbell's teachings, particularly the equality of all Christians, was that no distinction should be made between clergy and laity. Once Penymaes identified with Churches of Christ, a special pew for deacons, called a *Sêt Fawr*, was removed. Lloyd not only became the preacher at the McLeanist church in Criccieth eight years after J. R. Jones expired but also, as a very bright dialectician, helped found an eclectic society there in 1823. The year the elder Lloyd died, the ongoing disagreements between Campbell and William Jones over whether the first covenant's moral law was binding on those under the second, whether the Holy Spirit works on sinners' minds apart from God's word to convert them, and whether baptism saves or faith only started separations in several North Wales' Scotch Baptist congregations. Ramoth, Harlech, Criccieth, and Rhos of Wrexham divided, but all at Penmachno sided with Campbell. Particular Baptists in Rhos of Wrexham, Bangor, Llanfair Caereinion, and Llanidloes also split.[33]

At Ramoth, ten who accepted Campbell's views were expelled, at Harlech six were, but at Criccieth a majority agreed with him and were able to keep the building. One of the eleven who left Penymaes cited as the reason for departing "that it was *as impossible to believe the Gospel, without some direct influence, as to create a world!!*"[34] Those severing ties with William Jones grew closer to combining with Churches of Christ. Two years following Lloyd's death, Penymaes made the transition, and two decades after he perished, his son became its minister, diligently preaching Campbell's plea for the restoration of the primitive church. It had seventy-one members when Richard Lloyd started and remained in that fellowship for eighty more years. Therefore, the religion in which Lloyd George was reared considered principle to be paramount to personal opinions, instilling republicanism in him and making him a most effective proponent of democracy not only in Wales but also in the United Kingdom.[35] Before it merged with Welsh Baptists in 1939, Penymaes, then known as Berea, expressed its liberty in Christ, making it clear that it would "adhere" to taking communion "every Lord's Day" as well as keep other "distinctive tenets" it had espoused as a Church of Christ.[36]

As noted before, the first cooperation meeting of congregations identifying as Churches of Christ in the United Kingdom convened in 1842, one year after Penymaes became part of that fellowship. It met in Edinburgh with twenty-two "messengers," a dissenter term, and almost as many visitors, but no one from Criccieth was there. Two men from Wrexham made the trip, and ninety-five members in Wales were verified, though another two hundred were believed to be in the principality. Fifteen out of fifty-five congregations listed had delegates, and eleven more sent letters, but the total number of members could only be determined for forty-three churches, 1233 souls. Three men from the Nottingham congregation, the largest by more than twice, were picked as a

General Evangelist Committee to choose itinerant evangelists and collect as well as dispense any church contributions earmarked for them. James Wallis was one of the three.[37]

A second cooperation meeting was not convened for five more years, and Campbell was touring the British Isles at the time. He visited Wales, and when he spoke to the representatives who had gathered just across the border in Chester, England, two men from Penymaes were there. This time, twenty-six churches sent forty-two delegates, and two forwarded letters. Presiding by unanimous vote, Campbell talked about the "inalienable duties and obligations; rights, immunities, and privileges" of "every church of God." He was asked to choose an evangelist from the United States who could work effectively with the British churches, and £100 was designated for his college in Bethany. The delegates from Penymaes said their church could probably give £5 of £180 pledged by fourteen congregations for general evangelization in 1848. One from Penymaes was another William Jones, originally from Tremadoc, a relative of J. R. Jones who had been a co-elder with David Lloyd and then followed him as the minister at Criccieth; the other was David Williams, but Jones was the only recognized leader for the church. When Jones left to start another congregation in Portmadoc, Penymaes's members chose Richard Lloyd along with William Williams to be co-unpaid ministers and elders.[38] At sixteen, Lloyd George became an articled clerk in Portmadoc and eventually opened a law firm there, which is still in practice. He occasionally worshipped where Jones preached and commented on him a number of times in his diaries. Jones once defended Campbell's teaching on immersion following a "bitter attack" in *The Act of Baptism*, an 1882 work by the president of Llangollen Baptist College, Hugh Jones.[39]

Campbell had been a Baptist for several years after leaving Presbyterianism, but he now differed with them on a number of teachings, including how to become a Christian. Primarily, he became convinced one was not a Christian until immersion, communion should be taken every Sunday, instrumental music was not authorized by the New Testament, and no sectarian names should be worn. Members of British Churches of Christ and Campbell did not concur on every topic either, though. There was an ongoing discussion in their respective magazines on whether communion should be closed or open. During Campbell's life, the question was not answered to the satisfaction of congregations native to British soil, but the two sides remained cordial. Campbell died in March 1866, and five months later, at a Nottingham cooperation meeting, delegates adopted an official stance of closed communion, even resolving, "we hereby decline to sanction Evangelistic cooperation with any brother, whether from America or elsewhere, who knowingly communes with unbaptized persons, or who, in any way, advocates such communion." However demonstrably Campbell left a Seceder Presbyterian worship service in Glasgow, it was not due to being afraid of partaking unworthily but because he strongly opposed staid preaching and closed communion. The latter excludes unknown and unverified Christians from observing it.[40]

The cooperation meeting for 1867 was held in Birmingham, and David King was now editor of Wallis's journal. As an unyielding foe of millenarianism, though, King renamed the publication *The British Harbinger*. The conference recommended evangelistic efforts for Wales be put "in the hands of Edward Evans." Evans had originally been hired by the General Evangelist Committee six years earlier but had accompanied Joseph Bryant Rotherham on preaching trips in Wales soon after the latter had left a Particular Baptist pulpit in Shropshire and moved there as a new Church of Christ member in 1854. Both lived in Montgomeryshire, Rotherham in Newtown and Evans in Llanidloes, but Evans spoke in Welsh, followed by Rotherham in English. Rotherham transferred to Scotland in 1859, assisting works in Manchester and Birmingham, but King proposed Evans as a located evangelist for Wales. However, some congregations like Penymaes had started their own funds for evangelism instead of contributing to the General Evangelist Committee, the former having planned as early as 1858 to support an evangelist "in the locality of Merthyr Tydvil." Some doubted Evans's ability, probably because he stammered, but he remained in the committee's employ until 1886. He ministered mostly in Wales but also in Bath, Birkenhead, and Northumberland, England, as well as Scotland. By 1883, he had moved fifteen times.[41]

Evans visited Criccieth frequently and became quite well known to Lloyd George. They wrote each other, traveled together, and even slept in the same hotel room once. Lloyd George also supported Evans monetarily, buying him reading materials and supplementing his expenses for transportation. The comments recorded in his diaries about the Sunday or Wednesday night lessons Evans brought varied widely over the period from 1878 to 1884, when he was fifteen to twenty-one years old: "long & middling," "desultory & pointless," "splendid," "short & sweet," "really effective," "long & dry," and "long & windy." Length was clearly his biggest objection, the longest sermon noted by Evans being forty-five minutes. He particularly elaborated on one midweek pontification he considered too long, describing it as "a 40 minute *tir*ade against sin," his emphasis on tiring.[42]

Lloyd George also made reference to cooperation meetings twice, one at Liverpool in his first diary and the other at London twenty years later in a letter encouraging his brother to attend. Like Campbell, he was a firm believer in free will and considered his religious temperament to be latitudinarian and rationalistic. He recorded in his 1883 diary, "Man however indifferent he may seem ordinarily to religion is very sensitive in that part of his temperament." However, D. R. Daniel, a friend and confidant since 1887, told him around 1908 that "his 'religious position' would become a field of contention," quoting Lloyd George's words. "He seemed to be struck with the remark and there was a quizzing flash in the eye," Daniel wrote. Lloyd George then responded, "I know I have the *religious temperament*," and Daniel remembered his next words being, "but if an angel from heaven came to demand it I could not write down what my religious convictions are." Daniel then cited his final statement definitively, "I know not."[43]

Lloyd George was not partisan in his religious thinking either, going as far as to say to his brother, co-elder, deacon, and later to Baptist preachers that baptism was not absolutely essential for salvation, contrary to what was taught in the Churches of Christ. Furthermore, to oppose the state church, in 1909, he renounced what he called "undenominationalism" and alleged that one should remain "faithful to his own denomination."[44] This did not mean that he was ecumenical, but practical, realizing he could not defend the concept of one New Testament church and at the same time refute an established religion, even though the doctrine of only one scriptural body of Christ, founded by Him, was taught in the Churches of Christ. Also like Campbell, however, Lloyd George obviously believed his fellow church members were Christians only, but not the only Christians. Not surprisingly, he carried a similar lack of party loyalty into politics. In 1935, he told his final secretary that his uncle "was very broadminded. Very friendly with the village curate, who lent him books of reference. Thus, I myself was brought up very broadly and that is why I have never been a good party man." An article in *The Liverpool Daily Post and Mercury* commented on the example Richard Lloyd set for his nephew, stating the former's shoe shop "was the forum of the village, wherein would gather the deacons of the chapel and the politicians of the country side, hammering out questions of land tyranny, social oppression, and that curious aggression practised by the exclusively-termed 'Church' people of Wales."[45] One Lloyd George biographer claims debates there were mostly on "the rights and wrongs of the religious sects."[46]

Campbell was one of the greatest religious and philosophical influences on Lloyd George, but another John Roberts was a leading political example and mentor. This Roberts was a radical republican, active in the political arena and as a member of the Church of Christ. The first entry on politics in Lloyd George's diaries indicates he had gone for a walk with Roberts, talking about "Gladstone Eastern Question Republic aristocracy." Roberts got Lloyd George to become more active in both arenas by honing his debating skills and putting his religion into practice, the latter by helping the Penmachno church, all of the members having been McLeanists until they finally identified as a Church of Christ in 1851. Throughout his political career, Lloyd George proceeded to reiterate repeatedly the theme of combining belief and action. During the 1880 election, ending with William Gladstone becoming prime minister a second time, he recorded concerning the contest in Carnarvonshire, "on the whole taking the potency of the cry of Race & Religion I think we have every cause for congratulation—Am satisfied myself." Just three days afterward, though, he observed that, "Electioneering makes you neither a cool statesman nor a profound lawyer—nor an ardent religionist (!)" Race referred to minorities like the Welsh in the British Isles.[47]

After President Garfield was assassinated in 1881, Lloyd George wrote, "for myself I could not feel so much for any public man—Such is the influence of a good man—Can not be emulated?" Then he stated, "It is worth trying at any rate—The failure would not be ridiculous because the intention wd be good—Who would not be good to excite such commiseration." Eight months afterward, he started writing an article for the *Cambrian News* titled "on Social Revolutions." In 1931, George Lansbury invited him to join the Labour Party, to which he responded, "Like yourself I am now merely concerned with spending the remainder of my life and strength in advancing ideas and causes which I was brought up to believe in. . . . I have always sincerely striven to do my best for the class from which I sprang." The following year, Lansbury became the leader of the Labour Party. Initially elected to the House of Commons as a Liberal in 1890, Lloyd George was in opposition for twelve of his first fifteen years but was still instrumental in abolishing mandatory tithing to the Church of England by nonconformists, fighting required rate payments for the support of state education in the Anglican schools, and proposing legislation in favor of the temperance movement.[48]

Only two years into his fifty-five consecutive in the House of Commons, Lloyd George distinguished the Established Church, "whose bishops are nominated by English kings," from the "ancient British Church," in which the "officers were elected by the people." He affirmed the one could "claim no continuity" from the other. Being more emphatic in 1898, he stated, "The Bible condemned the priesthood and said that every holy and good man was a priest." This was the kind of democracy taught by Campbell, who believed in the priesthood of all believers and pleaded for the restoration of the "ancient" or primitive church. In fact, Campbell achieved his united movement of "Christians only" in America during the Jacksonian era of the common man. Lloyd George, writing his younger brother, William, in 1901, congratulated him on being elected chairman of the Criccieth School Board, and discussing himself stated, "Am getting strong hold on English democracy." Just two months previously, he had informed William that the London County Council chairman had described him as "the only man whom the British democracy trusted."[49]

In correspondence with his brother, several times, Lloyd George also referred to the "people" in democratic ways. In regard to his first budget, he told him in 1908, "It was time we did something that appealed straight to the people." From Balmoral Castle in 1910, where he was a guest of the new king, George V, and his wife, he wrote that he had made "two powerful friends," and, "They both like me & take on pains to conceal it. This may be of some use to the millions of poor people, who are still sitting in the darkness of a great social wretchedness. If it is not, then it will not be my fault." The following month, Eleftherios Venizelos became prime minister of Greece, and while touring London two years later, Lloyd George shared with William that Venizelos had hailed him at a breakfast as "the champion of the new democracy." In 1914, he conveyed that his budget formed part of his policy for "improving the conditions of life for the people." Miss Frances Stevenson, his only female secretary, recorded one year later that Seebohm Rowntree, who had authored a study on the extent of poverty in York, begged him "not to forsake democracy, for if he did so, then they could see no hope for democracy in the future." He replied, "How could I forsake democracy? It is not merely that I have taken up the cause of the people, but I am one of them. How could I leave them." In 1916, he ruminated to William one more time: "Without vision the people perisheth" (Proverbs 29:18, KJV).[50]

Lloyd George not only pointed out the religious, political, and socioeconomic problems but also proposed solutions. At a 1903 meeting of Calvinistic Methodists in northern Wales, he issued a challenge to each member to be accountable for the actions of the government, since it "was a democratic one." He concluded, "Every Christian man was responsible for every wrong in the land," and the pulpit should marshal the forces of society against injustice. He also voiced his conviction again that people should not "exclude the claims of Christ from politics" as well as his dissatisfaction with the funding of Anglican schools by the government, trafficking in alcoholic beverages, and the plight of the indigent. These were concerns the church militant should attack. In his respect for "the unfortunate poor, the downtrodden and submerged masses of the land," he called passionately for "the Christian Churches . . . to pick them up out of the gutter, and to place them in a position where they would appreciate the benefits of our common religion." He talked to all the nonconformists who invited him, seeing himself as having taken up Gladstone's mantle on their behalf, but to keep support for causes he championed and himself, not to be identified as part of a universal, interdenominational Christian effort.[51]

In addition to charging pulpits with the duty of mobilizing armies to alleviate social and economic ills, Lloyd George insisted in a speech at Fulham Cross Church of Christ that Sunday Schools had instilled the rank and file with consciences for the task. He gave credit to the Bible classes he had attended in his youth with enabling him to do his job as President of the Board of Trade from 1905 to 1908. Having just left that post to become Chancellor of the Exchequer, he elaborated five months later that "the noblest battles" fought by these legions of soldiers, "trained almost from the cradle" in the nonconformist chapels, were being waged "against intemperance, ignorance, vice, everything that lowers and debases the human mind." He contended that religion supplied people with basic necessities, strengthened "their hearts to bear the inevitable sorrows of life," and presented "some idea or system or scheme of things that will light up the valley of the shadows, and will swallow death in victory, as the religion of Christ has done in the experience of untold myriads." He chose the Christian "system," to which Campbell's words helped open his eyes, and after only one year as the chief economic officer in the British government, he decided that, politically, he "saw no hope for the democracy except in Jesus of Nazareth."[52]

While presiding at the annual afternoon floral service for London's Castle Street Welsh Baptist Chapel in 1911, Lloyd George revealed that he was still struggling to realize his desired goal of marrying religion and politics but rededicated himself to "bring religion into the realms of statesmanship. Why? The responsibility was that of religion, and the disgrace was religion's if things went wrong." He went on to stress "for the sake of the good name of religion, religion must be the inspiration of politics." He maintained that, "Sacrifice was the basis of the Christian religion," and reasoned, "that was why people should interpret political principles in the light of Christian principles." Interspersing all of these maxims with two references to poverty, he then observed that its eradication "was really at the door of religion" and also "the first thing that the Christian Church had done when she was established . . . was to look after the poor, to sell her goods, and to see that there was no single poor man in her midst." Lastly, he opposed "political reformers who believed conscientiously that they would never be able to save the people until they had destroyed religion. There never was a greater or more destructive mistake than that." Positive changes in history had proven just the opposite, he argued: "But for the spirit of religion and self-sacrifice, reforms would never have been brought about. If they destroyed the Christian Churches, they would turn the country into a burned up wilderness." Without religion, the masses would become victims of, "The spirit of cruelty, the spirit of despotism, the spirit of self-seeking! There was nothing between the people and tyranny but the spirit of the Christian Churches."[53]

This declaration elaborated almost verbatim on a proposed novel Lloyd George considered writing at nineteen, revealing in his 1882 diary, "Idea struck me that it would not be a bad 'spec' sometime to write a novel demonstrating how the poor are neglected in religion & politics and inculcating a principle, or 'cry' of 'religion & politics for the poor' Bravo! A really *brave* (Oh!) Design." Three days before, he had recorded, "Reading 'Democracy' the popular novel which exposes American politics." Speaking about poverty again in December 1911, he told a South Wales conference of Anglicans and Free Churchmen that it "is not the fault of Providence. Providence has provided an abundance," but "millions" were still "suffering." Churches "guide, control, and direct the conscience of this community. The Church is the greatest permanent force in the land today." These statements, three decades apart, manifest phenomenal consistency and religious motivation in one who has often and unfairly been accused of being "unprincipled," even "Beyond hope of appeal, it seems."[54]

Lloyd George spoke of his consistency to his last secretary, explaining, "I don't claim to be logical, but I do claim to be consistent. I am consistent in all things, and I want you and other people to take heed of what I say and not what I do." He also talked about providence in relation to himself at a Carnarvon gathering on the fortieth anniversary of his first election to Parliament. Stating he had wanted to be a sailor, he added, "But Providence had ordered otherwise. Every person born into this world starts with 'sealed orders.' He may attend to a few small errands at this port or that," he continued, "but presently a wireless message comes from above and then a man discovers his real mission and destiny. Who dares disobey that heavenly call?" That view of providence was generally the same as Campbell's and most in the Churches of Christ. Kenneth Morgan, the distinguished historian who surmised in 1963 that Lloyd George seemingly stood "arraigned as an unprincipled and ruthless adventurer, convicted of the destruction of British nineteenth-century radicalism," expounded on his egalitarianism in 1974. "In personal terms," he stated, based on his own family experience, "he was essentially the great democrat, perhaps most able to relax in the company of self-made businessmen and press lords, but readily approachable to Welsh working men whom he met at Castle Street chapel or in his constituency."[55]

Some of Lloyd George's opponents even came to respect and admire him in his lifetime for the way he stuck to his principles. William Abraham, known as Mabon, thought that he was too radical, that he wanted to control all of Wales, and that he had betrayed Liberals to become prime minister. Mabon wielded considerable political as well as economic power as a member of Parliament and leader of the largest miner's association in South Wales, respectively, but by 1921, he told a Welsh newspaperman that, "He is a man of ideas and principles. I felt very sorry when Asquith resigned, but I have come to my place long ago. There are two sides to the story. I have not the least doubt that George is a man sent from God as truly as John."[56] Admittedly, both statements Lloyd George made about Campbell were to his fellow church members, and most of his utterances about religion were spoken at religious gatherings of one sort or other. However, his original commitment to incorporating religious principles into the political arena occurred when he was still in his teens, and his consistency in pursuing that purpose was amazing. Only a world war temporarily deterred him from his socioeconomic program, and during it he insisted he was championing the relatively defenseless Belgians as he had the Boers in 1898. After the armistice, he wasted no time returning to prewar questions that had not yet been completely solved.

2

Church and Convictions,
1875–1945

"God is all wise—he knows what is best for us—
God is all good—he'll do what is good for us."

NUMEROUS ACHIEVEMENTS in David Lloyd George's fifty-five-year political career were motivated by Christian convictions he first learned at home and church as a very young child. Two days after his death on March 26, 1945, Prime Minister Winston Churchill addressed the House of Commons, praising him and his compassion for the masses:

> There was no man so gifted, so eloquent, so forceful, who knew the life of the people so well. His warm heart was stirred by the many perils which beset the cottage homes: the health of the bread-winner, the fate of his widow, the nourishment and upbringing of his children, the meagre and haphazard provision of medical treatment and sanatoria, and the lack of any organized accessible medical service of a kind worthy of the age, from which the mass of the wage earners and the poor suffered. All this excited his wrath. Pity and compassion lent their powerful wings. He knew the terror with which old age threatened the toiler that after a life of exertion he could be no more than a burden at the fireside and in the family of a struggling son.[1]

Lloyd George was reared in a cottage, "Highgate," in the village of Llanystumdwy, North Wales, rented by his widowed grandmother Rebecca Lloyd and her son Richard. He lived there from twenty months old to age fifteen because his father, William, had expired, and his mother, Elizabeth, had moved back home. He returned two years later, the family acquired a house in Criccieth, and he remained there until he married at twenty-five. Criccieth is a mile and a half east of Llanystumdwy, and the church building, Capel Uchaf, Penymaes, was utilized until 1886, when the congregation moved into a new chapel named Berea. Berea continued as a Church of Christ until 1939 but then joined the Welsh Baptist Union. Richard Lloyd was a cobbler, like his mother, who maintained the attached shoe shop after his father died when he was five. Also like his father, he became an elder and minister at the chapel, serving in both capacities from twenty-four until his death at eighty-two in 1917.[2]

Lloyd George began his formal education at age three, and for the next twelve years studied at the only school in Llanystumdwy, a "national" school administered by the Anglican Church in Wales. He was instructed in the Catechism as well as the Apostles' Creed and had to participate in festival days such as Ash Wednesday. Upon reaching adolescence, though, he boldly decided to lead rebellions against those practices, persuading his classmates not to state either of the first two at an annual inspection by local landowners and school managers. The revolt only lasted until his younger brother, William, could no longer resist the beloved teacher's admonition. During another year's forced processional from the school to the Church building for the third observance, the students hid among the trees. His brother later stated that none of these conventions was ever required of the non-Anglican children at that school again. These events occurred roughly two years prior to Lloyd George's departure from school, so after he was baptized by his uncle, a sequence that looms large in the following discussion of his convictions.[3]

Exactly three weeks after his twelfth birthday, Lloyd George became a Christian by being immersed in the name of Jesus Christ for the remission of sins as a penitent, confessing believer, and he considered himself to be a member of the Church of Christ for the rest of his life.[4] He was not always faithful to all tenets he was taught, however, and numerous biographers have stated he either became an atheist, agnostic, deist, or at the very least, lost faith in Jesus for a number of years.[5] In his diary for 1918 to 1923, George Riddell, the leading go-between for representatives of the United Kingdom and the British news media in Paris after World War I, expounds upon what Lloyd George told him about his religious development. Riddell often transcribed days later whatever he remembered hearing on a given occasion but did eventually enter that, in his youth, Lloyd George believed that God and His angels constantly watched for anyone who intentionally missed worship services, which was "a horrible nightmare" for him. Also, Lloyd George, according to Riddell's recall,

almost went "mad" at the thought of a conventional heaven with angels singing continually, an idea that caused him to become "an atheist for ten years."[6]

Another account of Lloyd George's religious views by one of his closest
friends has been interpreted by his most eminent biographer to mean that he
experienced a "loss of faith" commencing the very night he was baptized. In
reply to this writer's inquiry, the biographer wrote, "I am sure that 'of yore' in
the passage . . . refers to the Nonconformist theology in which he had been
bred."[7] The friend, D. R. Daniel, who had initially grown acquainted with
Lloyd George in 1887, had many conversations with him on a variety of subjects, including religious ones. Recollections of their conversations, which
took place at the end of 1908 and the beginning of 1909, were transcribed
by Daniel in preparation for a biography he never finished. At roughly the
same juncture, Lloyd George divulged his concepts to another acquaintance,
Herbert Morgan, minister for London's Castle Street Welsh Baptist Chapel
from 1906 to 1912, but Morgan never put down in writing anything about
their discussion.[8]

Pertaining to Lloyd George's spiritual experiences and ideas, Daniel recorded in his diary:

> Tens of times we talked on these questions, and he described to me the
> dramatic history of the ruin of the temple of his faith, like the shaking of
> an earthquake, the night he was baptised. He had met difficulties before
> as far as I could gather, but a mind as fast as his was sure to find holes in
> the armour he was taught to wear. But that unforgettable night he lay
> awake at the bottom of his bed. The great happening of his day and age
> had probably driven sleep from him. He meditated on what he had done
> and confessed, his eyes staring into darkness, he saw all the heaven of his
> doctrine and his religious imagination of yore being closed (shut) before
> him . . . his metaphor was of a building collapsing in a heap leaving a pile
> of shapeless ruins, before the eye of his mind. He got up to sit on the bed,
> in depths of darkness, and he witnessed by tongue and words 'None of
> these things are anything but baseless imaginings—all that I've been
> taught, all I've confessed. God and all things taught to me is a dream.'
>
> I cannot be sure in detail of the words used, but the idea is right in
> detail. . . . I remember him telling of his memory of praying. An odd
> strangeness came over him in closing his eyes, he heard his own voice
> echoing in the void, himself addressing nothingness. I believe this was a

little after the night mentioned above if not earlier, for I recall him saying he stopped this rite at that time almost, and he has never since restarted.[9]

That some sort of faith was ruined is indisputable, but one must be very careful not to presume that Lloyd George was saying he stopped believing in God the same day he professed he did. The key phrase in Daniel's remembrance of Lloyd George's descriptions is "of yore." Clearly, he was talking about "all that" he had "been taught" or "confessed," spanning considerably more distance than the immediately preceding hours. The only explanation for a "temple" that had been erected and collapsed "before the eye of his mind" at that age would be religious instruction he received at home, Penymaes congregation, other chapels he visited, or the Church of England school.

In 1911, Lloyd George relayed the same basic memory to Charles Masterman, his fellow member in the House of Commons and also later in Prime Minister H. H. Asquith's Cabinet. Masterman related the story to his wife, Lucy, and annotated her typescript account of the event. She records that Lloyd George was eleven when "he woke up one night and as he lay awake he realised in a sudden flash that he did not believe one word of all the religion that was being taught him either in church or chapel, that he regarded it all as fiction." To this, her husband added that "It had not been produced by any special reading but like the sudden breaking of something in his brain. Revealed this to his uncle at 14. Old man not angry, commented he would come back to it all again. 'And so I have—in a way,' L. G. said to me." After the word "fiction," though, her diary immediately quotes the following statements from Lloyd George: "From that time on," he said, "I was in a Hell. I saw no way out!" Another entry about his mostly positive view of the local parson is followed by her remembrance of what he shared with her husband about the clergyman. He had offered "to pay for his education as a teacher if he would join the Church of England, a big opportunity for a poor boy. 'He meant kindly,' George added, 'but he could not see that he was asking me to sell my soul.'" Her next and last sentence of that paragraph reads, "Atheist he might become, but Church of England never."[10]

When Lloyd George was nineteen, though, he composed an essay on the purpose of life to be read at the Portmadoc Debating Society's Christmas meeting in 1882, dealing with his view of atheism and his desire to do good. He wrote that atheism "is a mistaken attitude concerning the true purpose of life, and what lies at the root of this misconception," he continued, "is the incorrect belief that life consists only of our short-lived existence in this world." Then, he argued that atheism has caused man's spirit to suffer and "has deeply wounded his spiritual personality." Lastly, he asserted that Christians, not atheists, attain "real happiness," contrasting the Apostle Paul and Voltaire as his examples. As he ended, he stressed, "The greatest glory the great Creator of the Universe can receive from man is for man to grow to maturity in beauty of mind and body." Elaborating on the "Father in heaven," he suggested that one reflects His glory "by diminishing man's misery in every respect and by promoting his happiness. In this respect Jesus Christ is the *great model*."[11]

Elaborating on Lloyd George's attitude toward God two years later, however, Lucy Masterman relates the description he gave to her husband of his despair following his daughter's death. He was "turning over the leaves of a book on poisons with a view to their use. 'Then' he said 'I felt no; before it comes to that I must do something for the poor. I felt I was destined for that.'" She goes on to express, "One of the strongest elements in him is this conviction that he has a destiny, and that he is being used by the Lord for a great purpose. 'He was making me for what he wanted,' he said thoughtfully on another occasion. 'It was a cruel process,'" she quotes him, still in the context of his child's passing. "'But that was what he was after.' The thing of course was said half in joke, or he could not have said it at all. But it was absolutely genuine. It is at the basis of a great deal of his courage, and of course what his enemies would call his recklessness." Two years later, when his brother also lost a child, he elaborated on his loss, empathizing with no hint of jocularity: "When the blow fell, it all seemed so wantonly cruel. Fate seemed to me to have inflicted torture without any purpose ... it all seemed to me to be a piece of blind fury. I know now what it was for. It gave me a keener appreciation of the sufferings of others. It deepened my sympathy." He went on to write, "God alone knows" what both children "have been saved from by their early flight."[12]

In spite of his way of coping with the subject, Lloyd George's comments regarding his spiritual *raison d'être* should again be analyzed with gravity because they were some of his most intimate reflections. Whether crisis occurred when he was eleven or on the day he was baptized really does not matter, as he was responding to religious issues that had been raised years earlier, and he did not mention baptism to Masterman or his next confidant. The particular teachings he considered fiction were not enumerated by the Mastermans, but to suggest that he renounced the ordinance of baptism the same day he submitted to it, using the references to indoctrination that plainly took place beforehand, is irresponsible. In actuality, it stands to reason that if he was eleven when he experienced a turning point in his spiritual awareness, it could explain why he decided to be baptized shortly thereafter.

Significantly, Lloyd George divulged his religious ordeal to a third person who wrote it down in a diary, this time including enough additional information for certain conclusions to be drawn. Frances Stevenson, his secretary, mistress, and second wife, was the last confidant to keep a private version of his very personal emotions on the topic. Even before sharing feelings about his youth, he reiterated for her his conviction to aid those in poverty and compared leaving Parliament before he could to treason. In the context of scripture, he let her know it had just been the past several years he had fathomed the biblical quote, "Woe be unto me if I preach not the gospel!" Repeating the same passage five months later, on Valentine's Day, 1915, he elaborated on how it applied to him: "But I know in the end I should never be able to give up this job I have taken up of bettering the lives of the poor. . . . I see my way so clearly," he added, "that I should be full of reproach for myself if I turned to anything else, or devoted myself to making money, which would be easy for me now." He also explained that the poor he was talking about were not those in Llanystumdwy but those like Victor Hugo describes in *Les Misérables*, the book he recalled motivating him to take action for them. "The people in the village where I lived were poor," he noted, "but there was no real want or privation. Our little cottage was humble enough, but we had enough to live on. There was no wretchedness in our district." He added that it was after he departed Wales that he "realised what poverty really meant and what a need the poor have of someone to fight for them."[13]

Nine months later, he reflected considerably further on his childhood and teen years, which she analyzed as follows:

Religion too troubled him. When he was eleven years old, he suddenly came face to face with the fact that religion, as he was taught it, was a mockery & sham. He says he remembers the exact moment—he was in bed—when the whole structure and fabric of religion fell before him with a crash, and nothing remained. The shock to him was so great that he leapt out of bed. From then onwards for years he was in mental distress on the subject of religion—he felt like a man who has been suddenly struck blind, and is groping for the way but can find no support. He says the thought was horrible to him that the universe should be under no direction, with no purpose, no supreme control, and at last he confided to his uncle the state of mind that he was in. Strangely enough, old Richard Lloyd was not in the least shocked, but seemed to understand perfectly well. But D. says that the religious meetings and services were a source of unhappiness to him for years. There was a prayer meeting which was held every week on a Thursday to which D. used to look forward with loathing—the same prayers, the same set phrases, the same talk week after week (D. gave me reproductions of some of the happenings at them). In fact, it was in the main religion which made his life so hard to bear and so full of boredom. He could not feel that he had a part in it, and yet he was unable to get away from it. This state of mind continued for years & saddened his whole outlook.[14]

Stevenson also dates this incident as taking place in his bed the year before Lloyd George was baptized. To the contrary, though, fifty-two years later in *The Years that are Past*, she states that he took her to an "exact spot on a road" at which the break occurred, probably the one connecting Llanystumdwy and Criccieth. Earlier in the diary passage, she also pinpoints his unhappiness as beginning when he was three, the age he started attending the Anglican school. Furthermore, her allusion to what he had been taught about the universe sounds as if the instruction was from a teacher who had been influenced by higher criticism's attacks on miraculous creation. Lloyd George was familiar with the new higher criticism of the late nineteenth century because one of his favorite anecdotes dealt with it. Recounting a tale from Welsh preaching, like he often did, he said "perhaps" the best pulpit illustration he had ever heard was pictured by Herber Evans, minister of Salem Congregationalist Chapel in Carnarvon from 1865 to 1894 and principal of the denomination's theological college in Bangor. Evans analogously compared the Bible to a small, torn, tattered lamp. Directed at those espousing "higher criticism," he defended the inspiration of scripture against critiques of its historicity. "It is full of holes," Lloyd George quoted Evans as portraying, "there are even rents in it, the five Books of Moses may be said to be all wrong, the dates may be wrong, the geography may be wrong, I myself may even have had my doubts about it, but although they pick it to pieces, the little light still keeps on." Evans ended his lesson, "Thy word is a lamp unto my feet, and a light unto my path," but Lloyd George cited Psalm 119:105.[15]

Lloyd George had possibly heard Evans's illustration on May 5, 1885, penning in his diary that he had listened to him preach, and "Never heard anything more eloquent than this sermon. I was quite overwhelmed. Just like uncle when at his best," his praise continued. "He has a marvelous power of pathos. Undoubtedly the greatest pulpit orator in Wales of public men." Whether Lloyd George had been exposed to higher criticism at school, especially a liberal theology concerning the universe, is unknown, but it definitely would not have been taught at his home or church. When he was twenty, the age Stevenson records him saying his sadness ended, he prepared an undelivered speech, entitled "Helping Each Other," emphatically refuting higher criticism. He started by asserting, "God has meant us to do this. Taught us this in His arrangement of the universe." That comparison would illustrate that "the greatest should afford some assistance to the smallest, and that the smallest in his turn may do something for the greatest." Churches of Christ did not teach theological liberalism, though higher criticism was discussed in publications and at cooperation meetings. Some of its assertions influenced a few younger members, but even they did not agree with everything it claimed because it denied miracles, including—among other truths—the virgin birth, bodily resurrection, ascension, and the Second Coming. Catechisms, creeds, prayer books, and religious festival days were not part of Church of Christ precepts or practices either.[16]

Yet, Lloyd George was accustomed to repetitious religious rituals. At the beginning of school each day, a set of prayers out of the *Book of Common Prayer* was read by the students, and before being dismissed they recited a like set. His own words, quoted by one of his first biographers, extol his talent in the entirety of another school ritual that had to be repeated every time a student reached the age of advancement to the next level. "I was especially strong," he said, "in the Catechism, in which I usually got the first place." He had to state, write, and answer questions from it at the annual inspection by board managers, local squire, as well as rector, the same inquiry he famously rebelled against around age thirteen.[17] The rote Thursday recitations he detested, however, were almost certainly those he experienced at Band of Hope meetings. In fact, having to verbalize the same prayers over and over would cause one to get to the point where, "he heard his own voice echoing in the void, himself addressing nothingness." No wonder he "stopped this rite," and feeling like he could not escape was likely because he was required to go. He asked his first son if he believed in prayer, and when he answered yes, fervently for a miracle in times of trouble, Lloyd George confessed, "There have been times when I prayed—prayed desperately, but there seemed to be no one at the other end of the telephone." The son also specifically recalled his father's negative comments on Anglican liturgy: "He despised parrot-like incantations, mere conditioning of faith. Religion had to be a potent, a living thing, humanly demonstrable; and if not always explicable, its mystery had to excite the mind and the emotions."[18]

Lloyd George's last secretary also remembered his employer inquiring of him, "Do *you* say your prayers?" Receiving another affirmative response, he told him that his youngest daughter's prayers were quick, kneeling in distress like his uncle, having previously mentioned all of hers were private and not demonstrative. "I could not do that.... There is none of the mystic in me that there was in my old uncle, or even in Megan. I feel I have no contact." After laughing, he elaborated, "I do not know which way to look to get hold of him. I am more of a Pagan." Both Sylvester's diary and Stevenson's book unequivocally maintain that Lloyd George never did pray, but how could they possibly know of any private ones he had, with or without physical manifestations? He may have laughed due to nervous energy because his wife had just died, heavy snows kept him from getting to her in time, and she was buried three days earlier. His official biographer also astutely observed, "he could jest about creedal quarrels" and shock with "heretical views."[19]

In addition to school and Band of Hope meetings, Lloyd George was expected to attend all his own church assemblies, but where he worshiped had its midweek services on Wednesday nights. Band of Hope meetings, called seiat, were conducted Thursday nights at the Llanystumdwy Calvinistic Methodist chapel. The method of singing known as tonic-sol-fa was taught, but participants also said prayers, orally read scriptures, shared personal experiences, and learned about abstaining from liquor.[20] The Church of Christ in Criccieth did not establish its Band of Hope until 1896, and two years later, the Temperance Conference of the Churches of Christ reported it was sending the *Band of Hope Chronicle* to congregations on a monthly basis. It was also distributing 1,400 copies of R. M. Hyslop's *The Band of Hope: An Aid to the Sunday School.* Thirteen years hence, though, a visiting evangelist worshiping at Berea reported that their services needed "to be conducted with greater emphasis, and the evident restraint hampers the full play of the deeper spiritual emotions." He singled out that "leaders of the meeting wanted a little more dramatic force," and that praying was "inefficient through inaudible presentation."[21]

Consequently, it must have been emotionalism exhibited at the aforementioned Thursday evening Band of Hope sessions that Lloyd George was acting out for Stevenson. Also, Richard Lloyd probably did not respond with anger or shock at his nephew's revelation because it pertained to circumstances years in the past, because Lloyd George admitted being horrified by the prospect of what he had been taught then, and because the uncle was confident he would again come to fully appreciate God as a personally involved creator. After all, the teachings discussed were not those he learned at home or his congregation. His uncle definitely would have been distressed had Lloyd George disclosed losing his faith the day he was immersed and would have been devastated had he conceded going through with baptism a year after becoming an unbeliever. Maybe the teenager expected a more impassioned reaction, since a teacher at the same school had hit his uncle for speaking Welsh, and the blow left one ear deafened. Richard Lloyd even refused to speak at a Liberal Committee meeting in 1882 because of his hearing loss.[22]

Of Lloyd George's own admission, he did return "in a way" to the understanding of God he had received from Uncle Lloyd and remained a member of the Criccieth church until he died. Recounting his elaboration, Sylvester's diary reads: "He held no great belief in their doctrines, but he had been brought up amongst them and, having progressed amongst them, he would never have it thought that, once he had made his position, he had let them down by transferring to some other faith." Lloyd George even spoke at Penymaes and Berea in the 1930s, the only occasions his nephew remembered hearing him give public presentations in Sunday worship services. The first was in the evening and ended almost immediately due to emotions getting the best of him as he specified where his uncle or the other leaders of the congregation had sat. He talked for about ten minutes during a morning assembly at the second, discussing "So your light is to shine before men, that they may see the good you do and glorify your Father in heaven" from James Moffatt's translation and repeating numerous times they should never let the light go out. Gatherings he unfailingly supported for decades at Berea were those for young people every New Year's Day, mailing letters to encourage his family's participation in them and sending baskets filled with oranges for the children. He personally attended the one in 1945, slightly less than three months before his death, sharing tea with them and then struggling to his feet long enough to comment on how very joyful they appeared.[23]

Indeed, Lloyd George did not always believe each biblical interpretation he was taught at home or in the Church of Christ, but even closer to death, he told a nonconformist preacher who visited him at Ty Newydd, his last house in Criccieth, "I wish I could have the blind faith of the Catholic." Uttering that merely revealed that his faith was not the blindly accepted beliefs of family or church, but his own personal faith in God and Jesus. In his surviving diaries, he scrutinized three scriptural observances more closely than others: baptism, communion, and prayer. His thoughts on each practice must also be carefully examined. On May 8, 1881, he worshipped at the sister congregation in Portmadoc. The morning began poorly, with a doctrinal disagreement in Sunday school, and he described the sermon as being "full of hackneyed arguments." After the service was over, five people were baptized, but he even complained about that because he could not see very well due to the crowd and "the inconveniences of the submerging arrangements. All I know is that I had to stand out under a scorching sun . . . waiting with the purposes of waiting & after waiting with the prospect of not waiting & getting free of sun, people & enforced sanctity." Returning for its second assembly led him to record that William Jones "again harangued us as to the Celestial and Tartarian prospects of the neophytes and of us all indeed. Then comes that ceremony they call the sacrament or breaking of bread or what you will. This imposing farce having been gone through or dragged through . . . we sang an anthem & filed out."[24]

Later in the evening, Lloyd George was back in Criccieth and attended the gathering at Penymaes. Arriving half an hour late, he found them "at it praying," but he also contrasted his uncle's "genius" to the "wish-wash" and "would-beism" of what he saw and heard in Portmadoc. He closed his account of that difficult Sunday, noting that he went for a walk, "enjoying the only worship (real) I partook of today—the worship of a god of nature. It is better than all the cant & rant, delusion illusions & hallucinations of the whole much abused & overdone Xian system." This remark does not indicate atheism or deism on his part but the desire of an eighteen-year-old to be outdoors instead of indoors. Another unseasonably nice Sunday the following March, when he had to study for a law exam, he wrote about his "extent of sacredness for the day, that it being a day set apart for a much needed rest it should be so respected—Believed in my heart of hearts," he shared with his brother, "that a good walk on such a beautiful day would have shown far greater appreciation of the blessing than sticking in a musty hovel to listen to the mumbling of musty prayers and practices."[25]

Lloyd George's favorite place to walk was by the Afon Dwyfor River flowing through Llanystumdwy. After one such stroll, he again irreverently commented on worshipping inside: "Nothing convinced me more than this walk of the scandalous waste of opportunities involved in a chapel—huddling religion of pseudos—the calm & beauty of the scenery breathed far more divinity than all the psalmodies & prayers of a million congregated Churches." When his wife chastised him for doing the same thing in London after he was elected to Parliament, he scoffed, "There is a great deal of difference be-tween the temptation to leave your work for the pleasure of being cramped up in a suffocating malodorous chapel listening to some superstitions I had heard thousands of times before & on the other hand the temptation to have a pleasant ride on the river in the fresh air with a terminus at one of the loveliest gardens in Europe." During the last six months of his life, he still walked to the river in the mornings, with his second wife, and he is also buried by it.[26]

To spoil Lloyd George's entire day on May 8, 1881, would have taken much more than the debate in Sunday school because he had experienced other dif-ferences of opinion at churches without becoming vitriolic. His opinion of William Jones, who had ministered at Criccieth for twenty years before es-tablishing the congregation in Portmadoc in 1859, does not explain his harsh comments either. There might have been some resentment of Jones by those who still worshipped at Criccieth because "five or six" of their number had gone to Portmadoc with him, and he reported that "about twenty joined us from the Scots Baptists." Lloyd George was critical of him at other times he visited the Portmadoc congregation, describing his sermons as "utter chaos, apparently designless—or perhaps design apparentless" and "vociferous inan-ity." He even grew frustrated when Jones did mission work in South Wales instead of his uncle, enviously penning news, "Hear today that 28 have joined us at Llanelly—That fellow Jones will get all the praise—he deserves none of it—only wish uncle had gone there."[27] Whatever personal feelings he had about Jones's preaching or evangelistic efforts, however, would not account for such caustic language as "enforced sanctity," "imposing farce," and the final sentence of that day's diary entry.

The sanctity that Lloyd George thought was being enforced was not bap-tism because a person had to willingly submit to that act. What bothered him was the heat, his poor vantage point, and having to wait so long. He also repeatedly referred in his diaries to his dissatisfaction with being required to assemble for three services on Sundays. After one Sunday in 1886, when he only went once, he wrote, "Enjoyed chapel much more than if I had been there twice before." Another entry two years later started with emphatic language denoting his disgust, "In Chapel thrice." To remain even longer under oppres-sive conditions for some immersions he could not personally see irritated him. Being inconvenienced by attending a baptism prompted another derogatory response when it delayed a rendezvous with Margaret Owen, who eventually became his first wife. He grudgingly let Maggie know he would "be later than usual coming from Chapel this afternoon owing to the ducking." Another letter to her ten months before they wed lamented that in going "to chapel both morning & afternoon," she was acting "like a Covenanter," a pejorative reference to Presbyterians in Scotland because she was a Welsh Calvinistic Methodist.[28]

Lloyd George eventually argued in favor of the position that baptism was not absolutely imperative for salvation. He initially brought the subject up in the presence of the co-minister at Penymaes, its song leader, and William, after tea one Sunday. It was "rather a momentous (for me) disputation," he excitedly entered in his diary, "as being the 1st time I ever ventured or rather had an opportunity of asserting my latitudinarianism & rationalism in society of my religious friends—They were all taken aback—The old man especially," he triumphantly stressed. "I went so far as to doubt the essentiality or even expediency of stickling for baptism. The discussion was brot about by my defending the welcome reception given by the Leicester Baptists to Page-Hopps the Unitarian." William Williams was the old man, and his cousin, G. P. Williams, was the song leader as well as the host of the afternoon tea. John Page Hopps had been educated at a Baptist college in Leicester before becoming a Unitarian minister. It took another seven months for the twenty-one year-old to become confident enough to argue in Sunday school that Christian ordinances "were mutable necessarily if not in their causes certainly in their effects— The effect of baptism in this country & age was not the same as in Canaan in the land & age of formalities so that whatever the effect desired for baptism on its institution it did not exist now—Forms changed principles only were eternal." A month later, reading F. W. Farrar's *Early Days of Christianity*, he wrote assuredly, "so far it confirms me in the rationalistic philosophy I have deduced from the New Test:" Farrar was archdeacon at Westminster Abbey and later dean of Canterbury.[29]

Expressing a similar theology after two more years, outside the relatively safe confines of his Sunday school and teas after church, Lloyd George proudly noted a "long discussion with preachers as to baptism being indispensably necessary—I said it was not." He was in Blaenau Ffestiniog at the time and had gone to a Baptist preaching meeting earlier the same day. W. S. Jones from Llwynpia, South Wales, had spoken, "a thorough orator tho' not much otherwise in him," he judged. Presumably, Jones was one of the discussants engaged in the exchange, which occurred at the house of R. D. Evans, a doctor who treated Lloyd George as a boy while studying medicine at the University of Edinburgh when Joseph Lister taught there. Evans also became an ardent political supporter who facilitated connections for Lloyd George on land reform, and the future father-in-law of his daughter, Olwen. Lloyd George was a frequent guest in Evans's home and during another visit saw baptisms in a river without obstruction. He depicted them as "very striking" and expressed pleasure when an individual standing next to him was "much impressed with baptism & fraternity of Baptists." Of the latter, the other person elaborated "appear to be a regular freemasonry," and Lloyd George recorded "liked this last remark."[30]

Why Lloyd George labeled the Lord's Supper as an imposition and a farce is much harder to explain, though. He was probably upset with the practice of closed communion, when anyone who had not been baptized was not allowed to partake and had to leave in order for the members to have exclusive access. He sarcastically recorded the practice once, after being late for another worship service, stating he arrived at chapel in time to hear the last portion of his uncle's sermon and "went in after the 'unwashed' came out." Something about the manner in which the Lord's Table was administered made him feel it was hypocritical, for he also described it as "partaking of that mummery." Since he obviously included himself as a partaker, the pretentiousness to which he so vehemently objected must have been its discriminatory nature. Another of his comments concerning communion sheds additional light on an even more particular aspect of the practice. During his first visit to London, he saw Parliament and wrote, "I will not say but that I eyed the assembly in a spirit similar to that in which William the Conqueror eyed England on his visit to Edward the Confessor as the region of his future domain. Oh, Vanity." He also worshipped at the Hope Chapel Church of Christ, which had a "Very simple way of carrying on—they have curious juice there—unfermented I suppose." For the evening service, he attended Fetter Lane Chapel, a Moravian church, and noted that some of the singing was performed by a choir, as opposed to Churches of Christ, where all singing was congregational. Obviously, the use of unfermented grape juice was not yet common in the observance of communion, even in congregations of only teetotalers.[31]

The last sentence in Lloyd George's diary for May 8, 1881, is not associated with any specific doctrine. He frequently used the terms "cant & rant" to refer to a style of preaching he did not like, especially the intonation and peroration of English as opposed to Welsh sermons. "My impression," he had already decided, "is that so far as speaking is concerned the Welsh are incomparably superior to English." For example, after Peter Stephen, a member of the General Sunday School Committee of the cooperation of Churches of Christ, had discussed his work and preached at Penymaes the month before, Lloyd George colorfully described him as well as his presentations: "Altogether a nice sort of a fellow appears to be zealous earnest and an all round 'Christian dupe,'" he wrote. "Every English orator I have as yet heard has some confounded rant about him & the same miserable intonation & Stephen's was no exception. I take it it would not be very difficult to shine as an English preacher especially so for one who has had the advantage of listening to Welsh preaching. As far as the matter of the sermon went," he added, "it was not altogether despicable—rather a hickledy pickledy sort of composition void of any design but not of sense." He thought Uncle Lloyd was the best speaker ever and compared all others to him.[32]

Following one Sunday morning lesson by his uncle, Lloyd George recorded, "all through his sermon there were the most striking hits & the peroration swept everything before." He then logged the text his uncle used, Luke 16:19–31 about the rich man and Lazarus, and explained that he "asked outsiders not to go to hell if it were only for the sakes of those who were already there, that it added to the misfortunes (if possible) of the unhappy watchers." He also watched as "The audience feelings drowned in tears." Later, even he admitted crying after his uncle's concluding remarks in another sermon on King David and his reliance on God, which, in his words: "Melted me into tears." His uncle could simply quote scripture "in such a way as to melt me at any rate into tears in spite of myself." By comparison, when John Roberts gave a sermon at Criccieth the same day his uncle had "striking hits," his verdict was "improving but this intonation or cant of his spoils him," describing Roberts's cant five months afterward as "disagreeable" in addition to a "disgusting stoop." Roberts was a deacon at the Portmadoc church, occasionally spoke there or for sister congregations, and often hosted political debates in his candle house, which Lloyd George regularly attended. The latter's first debate, however, was with the local blacksmith on adult versus infant baptism.[33]

The mournful tone of prayers also affected Lloyd George negatively, particularly when the extent of their dolefulness reached the point of absurdity. In one of his prenuptial letters to Maggie, written while at chapel, he observed, "some fellow is on his knees close by my elbow telling in lugubrious intonation all sorts of funny things to the Omniscient—I am trying to amuse myself as I best can by surveying the landscape." He had been even more critical of prayers in her church. After going there with others on a Monday six years earlier, he denounced, "They prayed on & thanked Divine mercy (of which the fact that they were alive after such words & supplication was the surest indication) in a manner which excited our disgust & as we suspected good displeasure or contempt—The rant of wouldbeism and the cant of hypocrisy alike sickening and truly contemptuous." Each aspect of public prayer that struck him as delusive, illusive, and hallucinatory is unclear, but between his comments on the practice at both chapels, he recorded a view of its efficacy he had broached in Sunday school: "I maintaining boldly that the notion that it had any effect in changing the predetermined schemes of the All Wise was a thoro' absurdity—This was my argument—God is all wise—he knows what is best for us—God is all good—he'll do what is good for us—If he changes his schemes at our dictation or petition he is wrong erratic either in intention or consummation."[34]

One aspect of Lloyd George's ideas on worship is abundantly clear, though. He did not reject the "Xian system" *per se*. On the contrary, in diaries and public addresses, he defended pure Christianity against those who attempted to bind or loosen more than scripture authorized. After reading speeches given at the Positivist Society, for example, he found the group lacking. Its leader, he construed, "believes positivism is the gospel of regeneration of humanity whereas I believe all these grand truths are taught in a far grander way & in a mode which more powerfully appeals to man's heart by Xianity. This *is* Xianity & Xianity is this & I mean to teach so one day." Frederic Harrison, historian, jurist, and president of the English Positivist Committee had done the speaking. His faction had left a larger organization started by Richard Congreve, the first such society in London. Congreve had adopted Auguste Comte's philosophy. Harrison's thoughts were "wonderfully in accord with my own," Lloyd George admitted. "He gave vent to many of the ideas which have been puzzling me for many a day. The only real difference is this," he conscientiously acknowledged, Harrison is proclaiming another gospel than that of Jesus. It is worth reemphasizing here the title of Alexander Campbell's book on the beliefs all Christians should share, *The Christian System*, and that the phrase "Christian system" has never been common in religious history.[35]

A year to the month after Lloyd George was so critical of one Church of Christ worship service, he started the singing, led a prayer, and preached at another. He had invited Roberts to go to Penmachno in Denbighshire, where the congregation had only one elderly male member to direct services. He decided to go primarily because of an attractive young lady who lived along the way. His diary contains his opinion of his first and last formal Sunday sermon: "Spoke for 4 or 5 mins—Did not feel a bit nervous. Delivered it fluently but rather hurriedly." Concerning his praying, however, he wrote, "I was dreadfully nervous in doing this I scarcely knew what I said." Prayer was undoubtedly more difficult for him than other aspects of public worship, but he was still willing to try. A sister in the congregation was "very troubled" by some of the words he used and told him so in a letter. His response was that "no one had more scorn poured on him than I. I had been *one only* amongst all the young men of my profession—as you know it's a profession which is not noted for its piety," a clear reference to law. "But I believe—rather I hope— I would feel happy, not miserable, when I'm subjected to contempt because I'm given an opportunity to do some small work for Jesus who has done so much for me. This is no boast—I would be ashamed to boast about so small a contribution as mine."[36]

Bible readings and song leading were talents Lloyd George was called on to perform at his congregation. Teaching a Sunday school class of infants once also, he contrasted, "Didn't care much for it but prefer it to moping in my own class." He even engaged in "spouting" a few Wednesday nights, some which he detailed. In March 1883, he began "rather trembling at first but it was a sort of nervousness that gave strength," and after a "few opening sentences," he "got on swimmingly—rather solemnly." As he started "looking around," he "got into the spirit of the thing." When he finally did speak again three months later on Revelation 22, however, he "felt rather nervous," but learning that an old man cried caused him to write "Bravo!" A talk in July 1884 made him feel "less abashed than usual," and he, "looked the congregation right in the face," but then disclosed in his diary, "I really cannot speak effectively in chapel—the subjects I must necessarily speak on are not those upon which I feel deeply & earnestly & you are ashamed somehow of appearing to be so awfully good." He had read James 2 "in earnest" two years prior, though, and recorded a speech entitled "Faith without Works" in April 1885.[37]

Lloyd George not only manifested strong emotions verbally but also expressed them powerfully in writing and started submitting pseudonymous letters as well as articles to Welsh papers when he was only seventeen. They were published over the next two years, and then he authored an address to Welsh Churches of Christ signed "By a Welsh Brother." This piece appeared in *The Christian Advocate,* one of the periodicals that reprinted articles by Campbell and was still advertising *The Christian System* the year Lloyd George died. In a scathing rebuke of the churches for doing nothing evangelistic, he tried to provoke them to jealousy by reporting the English were "sowing the truth and garnering into their churches rich harvests of repentant souls." He ruefully included himself: "We are not so notorious for evil deeds—the dead work no evil. In good works we abound not—we are dead. There is neither work nor device in our living grave." Decrying the fact that Churches of Christ were relatively obscure in Wales, he nevertheless exhibited a very mature understanding of their distinction, emoting, "It strikes me that our existence as a religious body is hardly known. When known, we are not recognised, we are always confounded with the Baptists and other denominations. . . . So mock religions are worshiped, whilst the worshipful religion is mocked." He also demonstrated knowledge of the restorationist plea of the Churches of Christ, portraying, "When it bubbled forth on the day of Pentecost, it was a pure, limpid stream, which reflected the divine love and revived a parched earth." However, he was pleasantly surprised to learn there were a million and a half members in the United States when he toured it in 1923.[38]

Near the end of what he described as his "epistle," Lloyd George even chided his Welsh brethren with this regret: "You see men a-hungering, and praying for the 'crefydd wir' (the true religion), and yet you allow them to gather in and consume the wild gourds which poison their mess, without even remonstrating with them." As far as the wild, poisonous teachings of the other religious bodies were concerned, he was especially critical of "the darkness of priestcraft and sectarianism." Particularly, he bemoaned those "led by the *ignis fatuus* lights which swarm on the horizon into the infernal swamps of Calvinism (which are nigh unto the atheistic slough) and wallow deeper and more inextricably at each effort made to extricate themselves. Voices rend the darkness in imploring shrieks, 'Am I saved?' 'What shall I do to be saved?' 'Is there no one in Wales who will make an effort to save the sinking wretch?'" Interestingly, Campbell had employed the same Latin phrase, also directed at Calvinism, in a letter to the editor who became the first to publish his writings in Welsh.[39]

The anonymous blasts against Calvinism were leveled by Lloyd George two years before he met Maggie, though he warned her about the snares of it too. Hearing about her attendance at "preaching meetings" three days after proposing to her, he queried, "Who raved most deliriously about the agonies of the wicked's doom & about the bliss of every true Calvinist's predestination? I hope you have sunk no deeper in the mire of the Cyffes Ffydd & other prim orthodoxies—Believe me." Cyffes Ffydd is Welsh for the Confession of Faith drafted in 1823 by Calvinistic Methodists in Wales. Changing topics to his law practice in the same letter, he mixed in religion twice: "I have done pretty well at Portmadoc & am consequently inclined to take a rather hopeful view of the ways of Providence just now. That is why I have for the present set aside the true orthodox gloom." He finished the missive by bringing up his offer of marriage and asking her for a written reply. "Do, that's a good girl. I want to get *your own* decision up on the matter. The reason I have already given you. I wish the choice you make—whatever it be—to be really yours & not anyone else's."[40]

After four more weeks, Lloyd George invited Maggie to attend a lecture, telling her to persuade her mother to let her go and stating the subject "was an eminent Methodist divine who flourished before Christ & in fact initiated him into the true principles of Calvinism. That ought to propitiate her." Over twenty years later, he was still fussing to his uncle about her church and how she gave short shrift to anything pertaining to his. Referring to an enjoyable annual event at his church, he griped, "M. dismisses the Berea tea & meeting in one line. But that is natural. No place has a right to be successful except Seion. The best of these Methodists has all the arrogance & intolerance of their sect. Congratulate all the Bros from me." Capel Seion was her congregation, where three of their children, Mair, Gwilym, and Megan, became members. Their first, Richard, and third, Olwen, were immersed at Berea. Uncle Lloyd baptized Olwen, but her father read a lesson for the joyous Sunday night occasion and "remarked that the five candidates were direct descendants of the founders of the church at Criccieth over 100 years ago."[41]

Lloyd George first planned to send his article to all Church of Christ elders in Wales and wrote it because he was angry at his uncle for not doing mission work in Llanelly. It expounded in hypocritically glowing terms, though, "the eminently satisfactory results which have followed the teaching of our venerable Brother Jones of Portmadoc at Llanelly demonstrates that whenever an earnest effort is made to forward the cause of truth in Wales, that effort will not be without its success." Roberts had been daring enough to assert, as Lloyd George put it, all of the Portmadoc brethren had "deplored my uncle's inactivity. . . . They believe he would create a sensation down south." Confronting his uncle about Llanelly, Lloyd George "made a violent attack upon him," but "He was absolutely impervious." The article was never mailed as "heatograph" copies like intended, but within four days, "28" Llanelly Baptists "joined" the Church of Christ because of a "schism." He finished his "epistle" the day he learned the news, but his brother "persuaded" him "to send it to Xian Advocate." Ironically, the year before Jones left Criccieth, Penymaes reported to the cooperative meeting that it could not send money for the general mission work. Instead, it was going to earmark its funds "for Wales, which highly calls for our support, as there is a large field opened for us in South Wales, whence we are about sending an Evangelist to proclaim the things pertaining to the kingdom of God in the locality of Merthyr Tydvil." It may have been a disagreement over financing evangelism there that led to Jones's departure from Criccieth.[42]

When the article finally appeared, Roberts figured out Lloyd George was the author and informed him it was available. The finished product was slightly different from what had been submitted, a sentence "left out," "two phrases" changed, and "modifications of rather too violent expressions," Lloyd George noted. William Williams "attributed the authorship of the *Christian Advocate* article to him" as well, but was "easily persuaded" that an "English brother" had written it. Uncle Lloyd was not as quickly deceived, being only "½ persuaded." He was "very suspicious that it very like my style" and "seemed rather troubled at the exposure contained in the article." The next day, however, Lloyd George gloated, "Uncle rather confirmed in his opinion today that it is written by an English brother." He did not tell him he wrote it until four months later. The editor who altered the text was Gilbert Y. Tickle, but its writer complained the statement omitted "was a good one & I am sorry he has left it out." Nevertheless, he sent a letter of thanks to Tickle for inserting his article in the journal.[43]

Tickle not only edited *The Christian Advocate* but also presided at cooperation meetings seven times, chaired the General Evangelist Committee for thirty-three years, composed songs, and compiled a hymnal. In his capacity as a committee chair, he visited Penymaes seventeen months before Lloyd George's article appeared, both elders met him at the train station, and he attended a full assembly conducted in Welsh. There "with mail" from Portmadoc, he preached on a Sunday night. In Lloyd George's estimation, "He delivered us an English oration," adding, "If it be the average of Anglican public spoutings, goodness alone what the worst specimens are like. The matter of the sermon was good—nothing extra, no brilliant ideas, cogent arguments etc. But the delivery—it was monotony itself—yes monotony—grim and bare." In a subsequent report of his trip, Tickle extolled Jones for years of traveling weekly to work with the Criccieth church, giving him more credit than the current leaders for its growth. The bad critique by Lloyd George might have been because Tickle had voiced that when he was there.[44]

Lloyd George started his journalistic endeavors a year after his religious convictions had taken shape in his mind. In Lucy Masterman's account, he told her husband that he was around seventeen when he read Thomas Carlyle's *Sartor Resartus*, and "His deliverance came to him." Specifically, one sentence in a chapter entitled "Church Clothes" affected him. He interpreted it as, "Let us take these outworn vestments to bind the sore and bleeding wounds of humanity." A direct quote from another chapter, "The Everlasting Yea," is clearly reflected in Lloyd George's epiphany about his own religious mission: "conviction, were it never so excellent, is worthless till it converts itself into conduct." In that chapter, Carlyle is favorably disposed toward those who have a definite faith as opposed to the hostile atheists he decries in "The Everlasting No." Lloyd George also mentioned to Masterman that Charles Spurgeon significantly affected him at about the same age. "Not the eloquence," Masterman annotated, "but the personality gripped out the heart of this young uncertain spirit." He was twenty-one when he first heard Spurgeon, while in London to take the law exam, but he started reading his *John Ploughman's Talk* at seventeen and described his writing as, "Interesting full of sound philosophy keen observation—a clearness & simplicity of style which is almost unique— Sometimes the character of ploughman is forgotten & Mr. Spurgeon shows himself."[45]

In 1881, Uncle Lloyd "analysed the report of the Metropolitan Tabernacle in illustrating" a statement from one of his sermons. It had been built twenty years earlier to house the growing number listening to Spurgeon. He preached there until his death in 1892, and it seated roughly six thousand. Lloyd George also noted reading one of Spurgeon's sermons in 1883, "'Supposing Him to be the Gardener' a very striking one—he is a fine study." He finally saw Spurgeon preach eight months later and depicted him as "a capital speaker" but "not an orator." His "real strength," he concluded, "lies in his great earnestness—& his voice is undoubtedly magnificent—it sounded every word clearly throughout the extensive hall." Concerning the topic, "He discoursed faith—unbounded faith—ad nauseam—His orthodoxy is fanaticism himself—infinite credulousness," but its delivery, "His talk is exactly like the old Welsh congregational singing—the words containing the same superstitious notions of religion." After making all those observations and objections, Lloyd George ended his diary entry by examining himself: "He almost galvanized my dead faith into something like a transient somnolence if not life."[46]

Stevenson's diary indicates that Lloyd George was *circa* eighteen when he read Carlyle, "which helped and comforted him" due to its description of "a man who went through the same phases as he was going through. When he had finished it," she recorded, "he felt strengthened in his mind, for the purpose of things had been revealed to him to some extent, and his vision was cleared." She also mentions "Renan's 'Life of Christ,'" which was given to him by a Methodist preacher and had the same effect on him, "for he was able to see things from a broader point of view." Lloyd George had voiced amazement to her that a Methodist in rural Wales would give him "the work of an atheist, but the work of a man to whom Christ was a living being, a hero, a perfect *man*." An inference of God's providence can be seen in his expression of astonishment. Even she deduced that once he had read both of these books, he "felt much happier, but there is no doubt that the mental struggle which he went through during those years left a mark upon him, and helped to form his character." In his diaries, it is evident that he had read Carlyle's book by age eighteen because he bought his brother a copy of it only a month after that birthday. Five years later, a day following his twenty-third, he also entered, "Reading Renan's Jesus." Ernest Renan was a leading promoter of higher criticism, but even before he wrote that book, he delivered an opening address as professor of Hebrew for a French university, in which he described Jesus as "an incomparable man." He lost that appointment two-and-a-half years later, accused of upsetting the peace of the people with his teachings. Other beliefs he arrived at from his study of philology included some standards of higher criticism, that *Isaiah* was authored by more than one man, that Moses lived before the Pentateuch was written, and that Daniel's prophecy was apocryphal.[47]

The diaries of the other D. R. Daniel, the Mastermans, and Stevenson have been used by numerous historians and biographers of Lloyd George since the 1970s to interpret his faith or the lack thereof. Three other accounts of his reflections on his religious past have not been, though, and they definitively clarify the context of what he was talking about. Of Carlyle's book, Lloyd George revealed the same thing in an interview with William T. Stead four years prior to Daniel, seven before the Mastermans, and eleven earlier than Stevenson. The only exception was what he told his uncle at fourteen. In Stead's rendering, it was "his orthodox moorings" he discarded, leaving him "all at sea" once he released the cables tying him to them, his comparison to *Sartor Resartus*. If Stead knew anything else, he did not elaborate, and of course, his revelations were for public consumption. A departure from orthodoxy for Lloyd George, however, would mean what he was taught in the Anglican school and would not necessarily include a loss of faith in God. Stead was an editor of *Pall Mall Gazette* and *The Review of Reviews*, the latter of which he started. Lloyd George and he shared an interest in the media, namely newspapers, but when Stead perished on the RMS *Titanic*, he wrote Maggie, "Poor old Stead. His last regret must have been that he could not survive to describe so horrible a catastrophe. Extraordinary mixture of humbug and nobility of character."[48]

Next, in January 1908, also before Daniel was told anything, an editorial in *Current Literature* reported that Lloyd George, "confessed that he was inclined to irreligion, but Carlyle, whom he devoured, made him spiritual, rebellious, and a Christian of the most fervent type." It becomes ever more clear that his concept of religion is what changed, not his belief in Jesus. He now understood that the most effective way to serve Christ was by loving one's neighbor as himself. *Current Literature* also described how he applied that way in his speeches after he was elected to Parliament, comparing his oratory to Salvation Army street corner assemblies: "It was a loud and gesticulating mode of speechifying filled with references to the law of God." The editor inserted then, "Once in a while the orator and his audience burst simultaneously into a hymn that reechoed among the surrounding hills." Unhesitatingly, the piece condescended into, "His methods, like his antecedents, were thought vulgar in London," but in South Carnarvonshire, it just as freely granted, "his gestures, his allusions to the fortitude of Job and his confidence in God's eternal justice, set forth in the ornate Welsh of which he is a master, made him an uncrowned king." His confession to his uncle is not contained in this article, either, which was for the American public.[49]

Three years later, four months before the Mastermans' trip to Criccieth, Lloyd George was quoted by another journalist, Harold Begbie of *The Daily Chronicle*. Begbie simply began his story, "He had discovered religion" while reading Carlyle's work. "Religion is service to humanity," his subject thought. "Christ is the minister and servant of mankind." After making those salient points, he told Begbie, "he had purpose in his mind, faith in his soul, and a God to serve and a heaven to strive for." He specifically listed for Begbie what had caused him to feel "himself suddenly stripped of all confidence in his religious instruction. The catechism, the Anglican services to which he was forced to go, the theology of his pastors and masters, all, indeed, that these servants of an organized Christianity had to tell him of God and His universe—rang suddenly false in his soul." He even unequivocally dated the sudden ringing inside him that their teachings were false as having occurred at age eleven. The enumerated negative influences were only connected with the school he attended and the religion sponsoring it. Neither pastors nor masters were titles used for preachers in Churches of Christ, and their congregations did not consider themselves part of organized Christianity. In fact, the Evangelical Alliance, established in 1846, did not include them in its membership because it considered insisting on immersion for salvation a human works doctrine. Lastly, Lloyd George told Begbie he found *Sartor Resartus* in his father's library at age sixteen. It "brought the full light" to him by asserting all dogmas should "be torn up to make bandages for the bleeding wounds of humanity." Historian Don M. Cregier insisted that Lloyd George "experienced 'conversion' at a revival meeting" as a teen, but his and all other sources fall miserably short of proving any other salvation experience than his baptism.[50]

Begbie's article not only came out prior to Lloyd George telling Charles Masterman his story but also four years earlier than Stevenson heard it, the point being that it, too, was already public knowledge decades earlier than their diaries were published, 1939 and 1971, respectively. Once more, the revelation to Richard Lloyd three years later was not in Begbie's account, so it must have been far less important to Lloyd George than other sadnesses. It is simply inconceivable, therefore, that he would proclaim in published interviews a loss of faith in God at the very moments he was becoming the recognized leader of nonconformists by opposing Balfour's Education Act in 1904, or while holding two Cabinet posts in 1908 and 1911. In 1904, he had even shared with John Herbert Lewis, one of his best friends and a Liberal MP for Flintshire, that "he regretted that he had not become a preacher. The pulpit, dealing as it did with every phase of human life, offered infinite opportunities for influence, and it dealt with matters of eternal consequence."[51]

As detailed earlier, Lucy Masterman's diary for 1913 noted Lloyd George's conviction to accomplish something for those in poverty, and Stevenson pointed out the same after telling of Carlyle and Renan. Referring to his "convictions" as also being "ideals and principles," the latter stressed that they "are *part of him*, always have been and always will be." Then, she remembered a speech he delivered directly after he entered the House of Commons, and wrote, "he predicts the great Armageddon which is to be waged against poverty and human suffering. This horror of all the needless suffering which human beings are called upon to endure, is the keynote to his career." Concerning biblical interpretation, though, Lloyd George told Daniel that he believed "the ministry in Wales is becoming more and more sensible and rationalistic," later claiming "that all sensible men have long ago shed the old fashioned views of the Bible." He had also put the last comment on the back of his summary of an article about Charles Darwin by H. N. Brailsford, published in *The Daily News* on February 12, 1903. His summation included the observation that those who do not understand evolution should return to the Dark Ages.[52]

Evidently, Lloyd George accepted a liberal interpretation of Genesis by about 1908, and even in his diaries, he had referenced not only reading it in Sunday school but also suggesting, "that it clearly proved the human origin of the book as representing every phase of the human character." Then, he emphatically professed that "all scripture is profitable for convicting, etc." While discussing Joseph's dreams and interpretations a week later, however, he controversially conjectured that "the whole thing could be attributed to Joseph's exceptional shrewdness," adding the more shocking parenthetical caveat, "when the exaggerations of the tradition of a superstitious age were deducted." He liked Old Testament study "to trace the moral development of man." Morgan, Lloyd George's confidant around 1908, like Daniel, was both his new preacher and a proclaimer of "the new Biblical Liberalism." He had been chosen by Castle Street due to "his liberal theology rather than someone fired by the Revival," which had started in Wales in 1904 and was "marked" by "emotionalism." He was a Christian Socialist who "had a profound belief in the need to save society as well as the individual." Lloyd George chaired his 1906 induction, and he wrote a book entitled *The Church and the Social Problem* in 1911. The belief he shared with Daniel about the state of Welsh ministry was probably against the backdrop of the revival.[53]

Lloyd George's convictions, once his concept of religion had changed, must be examined in connection with William and Maggie, too. Later in the year that he bought his brother a copy of *Sartor Resartus*, he composed two very interesting diary entries five days apart. In one, he raised "religious difficulties" and in the other "sceptical vagaries." At first glance it would be easy to speculate that both pertained to his faith in Christ or doubts about doctrines he had been taught in the Church of Christ. A closer look, though, reveals that he was addressing social or moral concerns in the context of his relationship with Maggie and her religion. The first entry was on a Sunday and logged his having received a letter from her saying he could not see her until two o'clock the next day. Immediately afterward, he "felt miserable in Chapel— can't stand this sort of nonsense much longer." He then recorded having had a "walk with W. G. discussing these religious difficulties W. G. inclined to concur in many points," adding, "his ambition appears to be to become a moral reformer mine to be a social reformer."[54]

W. G. was Lloyd George's brother, and it would be a gross exaggeration to conclude that he agreed with his sibling's notions on subjects like baptism, communion, or prayer. As a matter of fact, William George later composed a summary of the teachings in the Church of Christ for the Welsh Church Commission Report in 1911, which affirmed in the strongest possible terms their most intrinsic beliefs: "the restoration of primitive Christianity," communion on "every first day of the week," a different "purport or effect of baptism" than taught by "the particular Baptists," adult baptism, no creed or ministerial titles, and local church autonomy. He concluded with the perception that the "Welsh people are daily becoming more conscious of" the "twin evils" of "creeds and priestism in all its forms," which "the position taken up by the Churches of Christ" was "a standing protest against." His last sentence is very curious as an appeal to others after what he had just written: "The gain in this respect is, I would submit, a great deal more than what is lost by apparent lack of unity." The talk Lloyd George had with William that night was apparently about the turmoil created in his courtship of Maggie because of her parents' religious and social expectations for her. Obviously, his hope to oppose injustices in society was explored in that context, too, while his brother desired to improve people's morals.[55]

The "sort of nonsense" that had thoroughly perturbed Lloyd George was not being able to have "Maggie" at his beck and call. Less than two months earlier, he had chided her for her proclivity to "manufacture excuses by the score" and "difficulties by the myriad," including that she had "infringed many" appointments with him. After enduring these snubs for another four months, he seethed so much that he "felt grievously—savagely in fact—annoyed disappointed & wounded." He remedied the circumstance by writing a "fierce letter—too high tempered perhaps & calculated to put her on her mettle, but something had to be done." It is untenable to think he was depicting the aspects of worship as "nonsense," as the entry was on the same day he saw "very striking" baptisms, and there would have been no communion service for him to ridicule because it was the evening assembly. Two days after he wrote, they met, and he frankly told her, "I lost whatever dignity I had in taking by stealth what ought to be afforded to me as a right." Although "she concurred & promised that something should be done," he reiterated his worry thirteen days later, penning, "I somehow feel deeply that it is unmanly to take by stealth & fraud what I am honestly entitled to. It has a tinge of the ridiculous in it."[56]

Letters between Lloyd George and Maggie had to be secreted through a pasture wall on her farm, and she had to lie, sneak out of the house, or wait until her parents left in order to see him. Before they married, she was hard on him, protesting encounters he had with other girls. Following one, she had given him a, "Rather strong rebuke—for having condescended to gabble at all with Plas Wilbraham girls—I foolishly let out somehow that I had done so— she let me off—dismissed me—in disgrace." This happened on an occasion when he rendezvoused with her at a "trysting place," and she wanted him to "hide" so her escort would not see him. Unexpectedly it seems, he saw her two days later, "overtook her and induced her to come for a stroll & managed to bring her over nicely—In fact we parted on most friendly terms." The extent of her jealousy can be seen from a promise he made to her: "I swear by the pen which I now hold in my hand that I shall not flirt nor even wink improperly at a girl."[57]

Maggie was so concerned about Lloyd George socializing with other girls that he had to press her for a decisive commitment to get engaged. His daily chronicle reads,

> she at last admitted that her hesitation was entirely due to her not being able to implicitly trust me—she said that sometimes she did, at other times she didn't—She then asked me very solemnly whether I was really in earnest—I assured her with equal solemnity that I was as there was a God in Heaven—'Well then' she said 'if you will be as true & as faithful to me as I am to you it will be allright'—She said nothing about her mother's frivolous objection to my being a Baptist nor as to her own objection to my sceptical vagaries—for I told her emphatically the other day that I could not even to win her give them up & that I would not pretend that I had—they were my firm convictions.[58]

Whatever Lloyd George's skeptical idiosyncrasies were, which even his brother did not know, Maggie still married him. She would not have hesitated because of his complaints about immersion or weekly communion, which her church did not practice, and as previously noted, he was as critical of prayers at hers as his own. The opposite would have been true of others in her position. They would have endeavored to capitalize on any religious struggle he might have had to persuade him to leave his church and join theirs. Also, he would not have to pretend about his doctrinal views when he was with her, since she did not share them, and if he was telling her that he no longer had faith, she would have reacted much more negatively, with no consideration at all of becoming his wife. After they wed, he even defended his faith when her folks were "very anxious she should go to her own" Sunday school. He then was the one who "strongly objected on ground of ante-nuptial arrangement & said it was more important for her to keep faith with her husband than to please her S.S. scholars."[59]

The only things Lloyd George would have to watch mentioning when talking to Maggie were his meetings with other girls to talk, walk, sing and his "ribaldry or tendency thereto." Her nagging about those popular pastimes led him to retort that two of the females in question were a "fishwoman's daughters," members of his chapel, and one a client of his law firm. He went on to pen, "one of the few religious dogmas of our creed I believe in is—fraternity with which you may couple equality." Then, sermonizing, he chastised her, proclaiming, "My God never decreed that farmers & their race should be esteemed beyond the progeny of a fishmonger & strange to say Christ—the founder of our creed—selected the missionaries of his noble teaching from amongst fishmongers." The kind of religious exclusivity that had caused him consternation about closed communion also made him furious with anyone who thought himself better than others socially. "If proof were required of the utter hollowness of what is known as respectable Christianity let him but study the silly scorn of classes for their supposed inferiors. The barbarous castes of the Heathen Hindoo are but a faint imitation," he lectured her. In spite of his pontificating, he was genuinely convinced of the need to be social, particularly in light of his career as a lawyer.[60]

Having stressed this about his wish to socialize with girls, however, Lloyd George's "firm convictions" did not pertain only to completely innocent recreational pursuits. At age seventeen, after his older sister had scolded him about flirting, he grasped, "This I know that the realization of my prospect, my dreams my longings for success are very scant indeed unless I am determined to give up what without mistake are the germs of a 'fast life.' Be staunch and bold and play the man." He then reflected, "What is life good for unless some success some reputable notoriety be attained—the idea of living merely for the sake of living is almost unbearable—it is unworthy of such a superior being as man." His aspirations were unalterable, but personal and professional recognition would also further him politically. He reaffirmed his love for Maggie but conveyed his resolve to achieve prominence as well. "To this end I shall sacrifice everything—except I trust honesty. I am prepared to thrust even love itself under the wheels of my Juggernaut if it obstructs the way," he warned. "Believe me—& may Heaven attest the truth of my statement—my love for you is sincere & strong. In this I never waver. But I must not forget that I have a purpose in life. And however painful the sacrifices I may have to make to attain this ambition I must not flinch—otherwise success will be remote indeed."[61]

Lloyd George did not sacrifice his relationship with Maggie until twenty-five years after he married her, when he began an illicit affair with his new secretary, Stevenson, whom he met at Megan's school in the summer of 1911 and hired to be her tutor. His attendance at Castle Street in London, after he was elected to Parliament, has caused some members of the Church of Christ to dismiss him as a faithful Christian, and others than his fellow believers have questioned whether his policies were motivated by religious convictions due to his immoral behavior. A legalistic member went so far as to unequivocally declare in 1938, "Lloyd-George is not a member of the church of Christ," but twenty years earlier had written that he "worships with the Welsh Baptists, not because he has changed the religious convictions of his youth, but because of their use of the Gaelic language in their services." Morgan, who moved to a church in Bristol after his tenure at Castle Street, explained to another member, self-described as a Disciple-Baptist, that Lloyd George "did not want to remove his membership" and that one of his elders, William Williams, would not have agreed to provide a letter of "transfer to any church outside their own fellowship, not even to a Church of Christ of the American type." Those churches had open communion.[62]

Despite a definitive statement like Morgan's, disputes raged in both Church of Christ and Baptist periodicals over claims to Lloyd George. One noted American preacher, T. B. Larimore, wrote Lloyd George personally to ask if he was a member of the Church of Christ. He answered in the affirmative but also said that in Wales it was called "the Campbellite Baptist Church." Again, though, regardless of how many times it was verified, the most doctrinaire members would not accept it. When Lloyd George died, the editor of the most influential Church of Christ paper in America stated as fact that he did "place his membership" with the Welsh Baptists but "should have stood uncompromisingly by his convictions." Other interpreters who view him as disingenuous in the religious rhetoric he used to promote his political policies have usually been biographers. They seem to have been negatively affected by his infidelity, and as demonstrated, some of his closest associates had doubts about his religious sincerity. Even his mistress countered T. P. O'Connor's assessment of him as a mystic, entering in her diary that he was a realist: "What religion he has is purely emotional, and not spiritual." O'Connor was a writer and member of Parliament as an Irish nationalist. Malcolm Thomson, who collaborated on the official biography of Lloyd George with Frances Stevenson, after she became his second wife, stated that he inhaled air during his childhood that "was saturated with the conviction that defence of the humble against the mighty was the heart of the Gospel," clearly more than just emotionalism on his part.[63]

In 1951, Thomas Jones, Deputy Secretary of Lloyd George's Cabinet, dismissively and sweepingly arraigned: "His mind was neither speculative nor devout, and the deep spirituality which is the texture of the finest characters would not be attributed to him at any period of his public life." Kenneth Morgan also minimized his devoutness in 1973, concluding in an edited volume of family letters that he was "not a religious man at all in the conventional sense—he veered between a deistic worship of nature and a stern rationalism worthy of his Unitarian father." Not being able to research Lloyd George's diaries and letters to William, though, Morgan's analysis appeared to be a plausible interpretation, but the weight of evidence in those sources renders it too simplistic. In 1988, Martin Pugh confidently asserted that his religion "was neither spiritual nor doctrinal," citing from Morgan's work his letter to Maggie on "the agonies of the wicked's doom" as proof but taking it out of context. Plainly, he was not as conservative as most in Churches of Christ, but he was always spiritually minded, even quietly "murmuring the words of the Psalmist" right before delivering his "People's Budget" speech: "Turn unto me and have mercy upon me. Give thy strength to thy servant and save the son of thine handmaiden" (Psalm 86:16, KJV).[64]

Of the multivolume biographers, John Grigg made the same premature judgment the same year as Morgan for the same reason in his initial volume, though he tried to get permission from Lloyd George's nephew to study the archival materials. Grigg wrote, "It is no wonder that a man whose spiritual luggage was so light should have failed to hold the allegiance of British Nonconformists to the end of his days. The wonder is that he ever succeeded in becoming, as he did for a time, their acknowledged leader and champion." Eight years later, however, possibly because of the nephew's very adamant objection to his statements, Grigg did concede: "Though certainly no saint, he excelled many saints in the amount of benefit that he brought to his fellow men." In a telephone conversation with this author in 1995, Grigg simply characterized Lloyd George as "a secularist rather than a sectarian," so he still insisted wrongly that his subject was not spiritual. He is correct, however, about him not being sectarian. Bentley Brinkerhoff Gilbert wrote two volumes, the first also published two years before access to the sources, but his insights on Lloyd George were more astute. He surmised that "nothing in his journals substantiates any claims of agony of soul, or more easily checked, any detestation of religious services." The emotions he vented in them, Gilbert went on to elucidate, "are not the writings of one whose framework of externally founded morality has been shattered and who is struggling for a personal system of belief." They are "fairly non-religious in tone," he opined, deducing, "What the evidence seems to point toward is a gradual diminution of

David's unquestioning childhood religious conviction" to the extent that he lost "most of the old religious faith in which he had been raised."[65]

Undoubtedly, Lloyd George strongly disliked how certain aspects of worship were conducted, questioned how his religious convictions should be put into effect, and left many of the dogmas he was taught behind him. His faith in God and Christ endured, however. He convincingly echoes in diaries as well as published words that he was always a member of the Church of Christ, and his religious utterances should not be dismissed casually. Though he did have an extramarital affair for three decades, he also married Frances Stevenson two years after Maggie died. The historical archives are also replete with references to his spiritual awareness and resoluteness in improving the lives of the masses by employing Christian principles.

3

Temperance and Licensing, 1878–1921

"Drink. What a reckoning that monster is piling up!"

THE FIRST REFERENCE in Lloyd George's diaries to any activism he undertook in a socioeconomic cause pertained to licensing the establishments that sold alcoholic beverages. In July 1878, he distributed notices of and attended a meeting to discuss the subject in Portmadoc, six and a half miles east of Llanystumdwy. The household in which he was reared was one of teetotalers and nonsmokers, but he would ultimately rebel against both restrictions. Eighteen months later, he entered "Sunday Closing Petition" in his diary, indicating he was staying abreast of attempts to stop all trade in spirits on the day of worship. He also continued going to licensing meetings, even accompanying Randal Casson and his wife on one occasion. Casson was the youngest member of a Portmadoc law firm, which had hired Lloyd George as an articled clerk when he turned sixteen. Though Lloyd George remained active in public discussions concerning the sale of liquor and refrained from imbibing intoxicants himself until he was nineteen, he apparently began rejecting the notion of teetotalism fairly early on. Commenting on a particular speaker he heard address the subject of abstinence, for example, he disparaged the "Chief Templar" because he was "spouting total abstemiousness" and was "to the point in neither the illustrations used by him nor in their applications."[1]

Drunkenness was another matter entirely, though, and Lloyd George staunchly fought against it throughout his life. During a parliamentary election in late 1880, he wrote, "The public as well as private individuals are very gullible when intoxicated and thus they always are in election times." Two days later and just one month before his eighteenth birthday, he was offered a drink at the home of a committeeman who was working for one of the candidates.

He turned it down and then noted that his host, "upon my declining a glass advised me tho' he was no teetotaler himself to adhere to my abstemiousness and neither to smoke drink nor gamble." The man obviously thought Lloyd George's refusal meant he was a teetotaler. Interestingly, the latter introduced the topic of smoking in his diary only two months later, and cited four times in 1881 that he had a cigar. One of those days was a Sunday when he went walking with some friends, "smoking cigars all the way (!)" The day, his last three words, and especially an exclamation mark probably indicate unbridled rebellion against his strict upbringing. Entries referencing competitive games followed after another five months, namely quoits and drafts, but wagering is not suggested. Seven more months passed before he first recorded drinking alcohol, though he qualified it by stating, "Got a good glass of Port . . . for my cold."[2]

Distinguishing good wine from bad implies that Lloyd George may have tasted it before. Regardless, he soon tried it again, noting that he had a glass of wine while working ballot boxes in Carnarvon. He then immediately added, "Toothache troubling me." Whether the two were also connected in this case is uncertain. When he "was given some brandy" by Casson on another occasion, it was specifically for a palpitation. It is certain, though, that Lloyd George enjoyed alcohol for other uses than medicinal purposes, the latter undeniably allowed by the Bible (I Timothy 5:23, KJV) but not by total abstinence. Casson was also the one who introduced him to the drinks as well as light meals available in pubs. Lloyd George once had two glasses of port before relaxing at a temperance hotel and attending a weeknight Wesleyan revival, another possibly rebellious act. He frequently met male as well as female friends for tea at temperance hotels, however, staying overnight in one, and even more often assembled with other churches, as long as their services did not conflict with his. He also attended temperance lectures, describing a particularly moving speaker as "fearfully sensational," adding: "Almost everybody's eyes filled with tears." The address was given by H. J. Williams, United Kingdom Alliance Secretary for the region, also known as "Plenydd." After hearing him again the next year at Criccieth's Wesleyan Chapel, Lloyd George portrayed him as "horribly rakingly sensational." They became friends, though, and Williams started carrying the teenager to temperance gatherings to make his own presentations.[3]

By the end of 1881, the "Sunday Closing Petition" Lloyd George had alluded to the previous year culminated in the Welsh Sunday Closing Act. It was the crowning achievement by temperance workers for the principality, a precedent because it emboldened the Welsh to pursue other laws regarding causes distinctive to them. Disestablishing the Church of England in Wales, stopping land tithes for the support of Anglican schools, and securing tenure for tenant farmers were some. After the second reading of the closing bill, one particular "house to house canvas" in North Wales produced a seventy-six to one vote in favor of it. Lloyd George had attended a General Licensing Meeting in late August 1881, and the number of applicants indicated that the purveyors of spirits expected a vote against them. "Only 29 out of the 62 publicans called for their licenses," he calculated, prompting him to speculate, "Are they waiting to see what will be done with the Sunday Closing?" Intriguingly, he first confessed to drinking on a Sunday, shortly after the prohibitive act was passed, and *"Signed the Blue Ribbon Pledge"* not to drink only ten days before consuming his second, more possible indications of rebelliousness. He also honed his rhetorical skills as a devil's advocate two days later by accepting the challenge of opposing closure at a meeting of the Portmadoc Debating Society, but defending the opposite of what one believes is common practice for debaters.[4]

In addition to gaining speaking experience at debating societies, Lloyd George preached once, on a Sunday morning at Penmachno, for approximately five minutes, and occasionally made speeches at Penymaes on Wednesday nights. He went back to Penmachno with Edward Evans, but Evans preached, and they spent Sunday night at the White Horse Inn, sharing a bed. Before parting company the next day, Lloyd George "ordered some Welsh newspapers" for Evans and "Gave him 2 ozs of tobacco & a glass of beer." One day after buying the evangelist a beer, he had some "ginger beer" himself, usually but not always nonalcoholic. Before that summer was over, however, he was definitely drinking beer that contained alcohol. He recorded having two while playing cards, and just six days later had three more along with two glasses of wine over a period of several hours, adding, "so that's keeping blue ribbon pledge grandly!"[5]

The very next day, Lloyd George "stopped for a glass of beer" on his way to a Sunday evening worship service at Penymaes, for which he was late. He also enjoyed beer with bread and cheese but continued to attend annual licensing as well as temperance meetings, specifically preparing for and delivering speeches at the latter. One December night he "had a drink" before he was scheduled to speak at a temperance gathering that "was called off." He did speak at one later that month and called for an act of Parliament to squelch the evil, noting in his diary the person who had chaired the meeting "said he expected that I would soon be in Parlt myself to pass such measures—My

Lord, to what! And fancy me working myself up to anything thro' my industry! It is easy to deceive the public." After being complimented on his talk four days later, he wrote, "If I shall be able to make that impression upon the neighbourhood, my speechifying will not be labour in vain."[6]

Lloyd George's nephew suggested he embraced the temperance movement to garner as much support from Welsh nonconformists as possible, especially among Calvinistic Methodists, who were the largest. He also stated that his uncle "first made his reputation as a public speaker" addressing temperance meetings. Lloyd George may or may not have gambled on games of chance, but he certainly took chances by drinking alcohol publicly at the same time he was making a name for himself opposing it. As his nephew so ably put it, "He was really running an appalling political risk in frequenting pubs, particularly on a Sunday!" Trying to imagine the conflicting emotions such behavior would engender, he goes on to relate that his uncle "must have been frightened by his audacity in visiting local inns for the occasional drink." He then added, "he had probably taken a tight hold on his Blue Ribbon pledge of total abstinence once more when he addressed" the December temperance meeting mentioned above because it was held in Llanystumdwy. As far as his drinking on Sunday was concerned, Lloyd George was less likely to see fellow churchgoers in pubs that day and might have been trying to relate to other segments of society for political reasons. Again, he was probably rebelling against his family's moral rules, but he also could have been experimenting with a vice they had forbidden to simply familiarize himself with its effects, either as a trial of faith or for future insight in speaking on temperance.[7]

Whatever hold Lloyd George had on his promise to abstain temporarily slipped three months later when he drank some ale. The following year, at the age of twenty-one, he also bought a friend "a glass of Port & took a glass of claret myself—this drink, I believe, is non-intoxicant." The remaining diaries contain no further references of his purchasing alcohol for himself or anyone else. They do, however, include many comments on his ever-increasing opposition to the liquor trade, his decision to join the Good Templars, and his additional speeches dealing with temperance as well as local option. His strong feelings about licensing the sale of alcohol had come close to costing him his job as an articled clerk in the fall of 1883. Casson asked him to accompany a Henry Roberts and "explain to the people" why they should sign a petition to support a new Criccieth hotel that had applied for a liquor license. An earlier petition against it, only signed by the "five publicans" already in the town, had been rejected, despite their having hired a lawyer. Lloyd George wrote what "a nice story it would be to spread about me that I was doing my utmost to obtain a license for another shop to sell the stuff which I am convinced banes mankind & corrodes its happiness & prosperity! No, not if I am ruined."[8]

Fortunately, Lloyd George was able to persuade his boss that he should not get involved because it would make Ellis-Nanney hostile. Nanney was squire of Llanystumdwy, justice of the peace, as well as landlord of twelve thousand acres in three counties: Carnarvonshire, Merionethshire, and Montgomeryshire. He also happened to have been a guest at the school when Lloyd George led a rebellion against quoting the catechism and Apostles' Creed. One day after thinking he might be fired, a greatly relieved Lloyd George wrote, "So I am rid—Thank goodness, of a very dirty job." Roberts and two other men got nearly every businessman along the Criccieth Marine Terrace to sign, "including 3 or 4 prominent—chief teetotalers," Lloyd George recorded, causing him to also quip, "the opposition of the publicans has almost converted it into a Temperance party hotel—but I did not care about going round for signatures—I had scruples."[9]

Only eight days before his last diary reference to personal involvement with alcohol, Lloyd George became a member of the Good Templars, "in order to get opportunities now so rare—to learn public speaking." He had attended one of their meetings three days before, and no sooner had he enlisted than he started recruiting others. He proposed making the meetings more interesting, was appointed to a committee to that end, and became its secretary in a little over two weeks. A community picnic to publicize the organization, a club room for games at the Criccieth Board school, and singing during meetings were all implemented by him, plus he started making speeches at their assemblies only two weeks after joining. When he was asked to give a speech at the picnic, in English as opposed to Welsh, he recommended John Lloyd-Jones, the local Anglican vicar, instead,. However, he did print thirty-six circulars in English and seventy more in Welsh to be distributed by "young templars." He had planned to provide more for the prospective visitors, penning, "I believe there are a few Blue Ribbonists amongst them," but was not able to when the time came because "my paper was used up."[10]

The vicar refused to be the keynote speaker of the picnic because it was going to include entertainment and be held at a chapel. He agreed to participate if it was in the town hall, but two guest speakers, T. Jones-Lewis of Menai Bridge and Alexander Balfour of Liverpool, addressed the crowd in an English chapel built for Methodists or other nonconformist visitors to Criccieth. Jones-Lewis was a clergyman, and Balfour owned a shipping firm. "Plenydd" was there also and spoke, as did Lloyd George after all, in English. He went after the first guest, maybe because the latter "was very unfortunate in his speech for he began by deprecating the extreme temperance advocates who insisted that intoxicants even in a moderate degree were injurious—he said the ground of example was a far better one." Afterward, Lloyd George told one of the attendees he wanted to see a Temperance Society "of all sects without any ritual or formula belonging to it," an application of his egalitarian religious thinking to other organizations. In what must surely be considered more than coincidence, he started a Young Men's Society at the Board school shortly before 1884 ended, and the first topic discussed was "Moderation and Total Abstinence." Just a week prior to proposing that the society should meet at the school, he had opined that he "clearly scored another success" in a temperance address there. The building was full, but he was unaffected by it, stating, "Strange to say I did not feel nervous at all." Later, the Chief Templar of Portmadoc told him his speech was "grand" and "the best by far they ever had in numbers & enthusiasm." He even tried to pay for Lloyd George's expenses, but any remuneration was refused.[11]

In January of 1885, Lloyd George gave two temperance speeches at Blaenau Ffestiniog, which were anything but grand. The first was on his twenty-second birthday to what he depicted as a "Rough audience. Had good hearing. Spoke with much fire and impetuosity. Bench broke just at beginning of my speech. Only one cheer in the course of address." The second, only two-and-a-half weeks later, did not have an auspicious beginning either, "especially as the audience marched away in troops during the proposer of my resolution's speech." He "got up" regardless, and as soon as he "had delivered two or three sentences several who had started out sat down and listened. . . . Much cheered once or twice." Two who stayed tried to put as good a spin on the presentation as possible, one elaborating, "His features wore an expression of great earnestness, but withal there was a pleasant smile." The other, in a backhanded compliment, said he "had a kind of tremor in his voice," but it was "very effective in describing the evils of intemperance."[12]

The first mention of local option by Lloyd George was in his 1882 diary, and he merely recorded that he had heard an English member of Parliament speak on it. He addressed it himself in 1885, at a full town hall meeting in Portmadoc. Obviously, he spoke in favor of communities having the right to restrict or even prohibit the sale of liquor, and according to the newspaper, he "was simply unanswerable, and no doubt succeeded in convincing many people of the necessity for local option." Prohibition bills had been presented to the

House of Commons by members of the temperance movement's primary political advocate, the United Kingdom Alliance, since before Lloyd George was born. When the bills repeatedly failed, the tactic changed in the 1880s to proposing resolutions that would grant communities a number of methods for controlling or stopping alcoholic beverages from being sold. He had read the "Alliance News especially all reports of Licensing meetings," and determined "we ought to do something in this district." One biographer mistakenly claimed he served as "secretary of the local branch of the United Kingdom Alliance," apparently confusing that organization with Good Templars or the Anti-Tithe League, for which he was secretary of South Carnarvonshire.[13]

Lloyd George did attend a temperance conference at Carnarvon in 1885 and exploited his association with the movement to build support for his law practice, which he had begun on New Year's Day. He started eating lunch and renting rooms at the temperance hotels "to try to catch a little business there on market days." His practice grew to such an extent that he had offices at Portmadoc, Criccieth, Blaenau Ffestiniog, and Pwllheli. In a very ironic case at a police court, he even applied for the transfer of an inn's license and was "refused on temperance grounds." Just six months earlier, at his first appearance in a session's court, he had opposed such a transfer, but regardless of the legal ramifications of licensing, he remained adamantly opposed to drunkenness and was particularly outraged at doctors who had an "obvious addiction to drink." When a new physician opened a practice in 1886, Lloyd George wrote, "We've had too many drunken doctors already." By the fall of 1887, he was in the inner circle of the temperance movement, attending an executive meeting of the North Wales Temperance Association. He also now even refused to drink when companions did. Three days after his twenty-fifth birthday, four days before he wed, he was with friends whose behavior upset him: "Either I was in an extra serious mood owing to coming events or the company indulged in a hilarity which I did not appreciate for I did not enjoy myself—they drank smoked & played billiards & flirted with giddy barmaids ad nauseam."[14]

Lloyd George made only one more diary entry about the drink issue before he was elected to the House of Commons, simply noting that he had attended a "Temperance Festival" at Pwllheli. He entered Parliament as its youngest member twenty-two months later, representing his fellow Carnarvon Boroughs's constituents. Less than a month after he took the oath of office, Richard Lloyd started prodding him to address Parliament. He assured Uncle Lloyd that he intended to oppose using liquor taxes to reimburse sellers of alcohol who lost their licenses but also explained why he was waiting for his first talk: "Let the cry against compensation increase in force & intensity—then is the time to speak. I can do better myself then. The steam is hardly up yet." Predicting an uphill battle, he added, "The House did not seem at all to realise or to be impressed with the gigantic evils of drunkenness. Later on there will be more of that spirit as the country gets aroused."[15]

Lloyd George had done his part to awaken the masses to those evils nine days before he addressed Parliament, delivering what he considered to be his most effective public speech. He very skillfully motivated a crowd at a United Kingdom Alliance rally in Manchester's Free Trade Hall. He was the last speaker in what was by then only a half-full hall, but both he and the press assessed his effort in glowing terms. The subject of the speech was compensation of those who sold liquor, and he turned their cry for equity against them, personifying "Equity" as a judge who would punish them for having unclean hands. Those hands would not receive taxes from alcohol sales because the dirty business "reeks with human misery, vice and squalor, destitution, crime and death." Good Templars also opposed any compensation of publicans, arguing that dispossessed sellers should get no money until those who were negatively affected by alcohol were paid for the harm it did. When Lloyd George finally delivered his maiden speech, the bill being debated also pertained to compensation. It offered too little money to entice a sufficient number of owners to sell their pubs and made no provisions for rescinding the licenses of superfluous establishments. He voiced that the bill "delays the great work of temperance reform . . . I believe in this great question of temperance reform. It removes inducements to evil and substitutes incitements to good." His comments came while he was supporting an amendment to provide budgeted liquor taxes to technical schools instead of publicans. The amendment failed, but so did the provision for "whiskey money" to be used to pension the purveyors of spirits. The funds were ultimately earmarked for technical schools, with the stipulation that county councils oversee the money.[16]

The drink issue did not come up again until the following spring, but as soon as the 1891 session began Lloyd George's uncle started pressuring him once more. At the end of January, he vented to his brother: "Tell our G. O. M. at home that he must exercise his soul in patience. *I* must not overdo it . . . I have to speak on Disestablishment & also on the Direct Veto (Wales) Bill. . . . *That* is my opportunity. You must learn to labour & *to wait*. I am not idle you can assure the Governor." The upcoming legislation that he specifically named was more accurately known as the Liquor Traffic Local Veto (Wales) Bill, and it pertained to the local option he had wanted for some time. Debate on it began in March, and it passed on its second reading, though it never became statute law. He stated that "the disorder that arises in connection with public houses" made the turmoil over the collection of tithes look like nothing in comparison. He recommended one pub for every fifteen-hundred people up to three thousand and then one for every additional one thousand inhabitants. He called for passage of the bill for Wales and referred to "the contaminating influence of the public house. This is a great and momentous social question which touches the very root and fabric of society." He concluded his remarks by envisioning a time in the near future when "the people will no longer allow their intellects to be enfeebled and their moral senses to be blunted by the demoralizing influence of strong drink."[17]

The United Kingdom Alliance had asked that the veto bill get an impartial hearing, and a sufficient number of Conservatives voted for it. Conservatives needed the support of Liberal Unionists to stay in power, many of whom identified with the temperance movement. Liberal Unionists, under the leadership of Joseph Chamberlain, had split off from the Liberal Party five years earlier over Gladstone's attempt to give Ireland home rule. They wanted to keep the United Kingdom intact. Even though the veto bill never took effect, Lloyd George told Thomas E. Ellis that its passage was a "splendid victory" and was "Quite unexpected," since the "staunch teetotalers" were the only Welshmen present for the vote. Ellis had missed the debate because of illness, but the following year he became the only Welsh member in Gladstone's fourth ministry as a Junior Lord of the Treasury and Deputy Whip. A month after writing Ellis, Lloyd George joked with a London temperance assembly, telling them that Wales had "no ranting, humbugging moderate drinkers" because they were "either teetotalers or right down jolly tipplers."[10]

Lloyd George had to concentrate on a reelection campaign of his own in 1892, and early that year his brother reminded him, "You always were anti-Beer." In June, he wrote several diary entries on the temperance issue: "Pamphlets on Church defence in one stall & alcoholic liquors on another both of them too often active as stimulants to zeal in the same cause. A revival more spirituous than spiritual," he punned. Waxing more serious, he accused, "In this strife between alcohol & civilization this national Church refuses even to preserve a decent nationality." Then, he concluded that month's tirades with an even stronger contrast: "*Moral* attitude on temperance question more halting than even the Eisteddfod—where men meet for merriment." His second victory at the polls was all the more important because the Liberals only had two more members than the Conservatives, and the latter could count on forty-seven Liberal Unionists to side with them. Welsh and Irish support were absolutely crucial for Gladstone to have any effectiveness. One way to garner Welsh approval was through more liquor legislation because they still wanted local option. The election was over in early July, and the next month Lloyd George chaired the first meeting of the Baptist Union of Wales, where he discussed temperance. Approximately 240 clergy and laity attended the inaugural session in Carnarvon.[19]

Throughout the following year, Lloyd George remained comparatively quiet but did get energized when a Welsh member introduced another bill for local option. On the Ides of March, an opponent of the new bill argued that teaching against temptation was needed but not laws, to which Lloyd George responded that not having moral laws leads to anarchy. He then castigated pub owners, contrasting them to former slave owners in the British Empire and bringing up compensation in reference to the £20,000,000 slave owners had received. Yet, "slaves were the absolute legal property of their owners," he countered, and were provided with clothing as well as food. On the other hand, those enslaved by liquor were "Stripped" and "despoiled." Drink "destroyed them body and mind" and "reduced them to beggary and starvation." He bolstered his argument with statistics that half of all the paupers and nine-tenths of all the criminals were produced by the deleterious effects of alcohol. He concluded his remarks by appealing last to nationalism: "Let the Welsh people grapple with this evil, which had been the despair of the past, and which casts a gloom over the future of democracy." The bill was the initial attempt by a political party in the House of Commons to overtly provide for prohibition, but it never became law. The Alliance expended approximately £17,000 to influence legislators, temperance workers received over six-hundred thousand signatures on a petition, but the liquor industries got in excess of one million names and funneled £21,000 into opposing the bill.[20]

Gladstone had afforded the Welsh people some leeway in liquor control during his second ministry, but in March 1894, his last government resigned without accomplishing anything for Wales because the House of Lords vetoed his Irish home rule bill. Lord Rosebery became the next prime minister, made Tom Ellis his Chief Whip, and quickly announced, "if the State does not soon control the liquor traffic, the liquor traffic will control the State." In a meeting with Welsh members called by Lloyd George, however, the Leader of the House of Commons and Chancellor of the Exchequer, William Harcourt, refused to give an ironclad pledge to champion issues distinctive to Wales. The pledge Lloyd George wanted most of all was for an upcoming bill that would disestablish and disendow the Anglican Church in Wales to be steered through every phase of the legislative process, extending the session through the fall if required. The bill was presented by H. H. Asquith, the Home Secretary, on April 26. During his speech on it four days later, Lloyd George stressed that the principality had enjoyed independence in the past and some measure of it had been acknowledged during his lifetime in the Welsh Sunday Closing Act.[21]

The disestablishment and disendowment bill was pulled in July due to furious opposition from the Anglican clergy. Rosebery pledged that there would be another bill in the following year, and it was again presented by Asquith on February 25, 1895. However, Rosebery's government lost a vote on an entirely different matter and resigned in June. The resulting election brought the Conservatives under Lord Salisbury back to power for the next seven years, in a coalition with Liberal Unionists. Lloyd George won his seat again, but the size of his party's defeat meant that disestablishment and other distinctively Welsh issues would have to wait even longer. Finding himself a backbencher once more, he nevertheless continued to talk about temperance, and as a social issue of particular importance to the Welsh people, it actually provided him with more opportunities to assert himself on their behalf than disestablishment had during Salisbury's last ministry from 1886 to 1892.[22]

Outside Parliament, Lloyd George advised people to be moderate if they chose to drink, and in worst cases he advocated closing pubs altogether. A particular village in Monmouthshire was so bad that every pub "was packed like a sardine-box with 'boosers,' and there was a large amount of that heavy, solid, sodden drunkenness that is produced by beer." He judged it was a place of "perfect pandemonium and a blot on civilisation." Inside Parliament, he proposed an amendment to a bill for increasing customs duties on beer in 1896, recommending that they be removed from light beers "in the interests of temperance." People would then supposedly drink less of the more intoxicating heavy beers. He even used obstructionist tactics on bills for land reform as well as education in 1896 and 1897 because he wanted to get the government to pay attention to Welsh causes.[23]

Lloyd George began 1898 by attending a conference in Manchester to discuss the attitude of the Liberal Party toward yet another bill for local option. Herbert Gladstone, son of the former prime minister, had given a speech against it the previous November because he thought it would not be implemented even if it passed. He had totally opposed it earlier in the decade but because a majority of the Liberals wanted it he had publicly altered his stance, while still privately considering it controversial. Second only to home rule, he blamed local option for the defeat of the Liberals in 1895 and felt that the party was too wedded to the methodology for limiting the drink traffic, rather than in tackling drunkenness itself. He compared his party to a ship that needed to throw local option overboard after running aground in bad weather and also advocated stiffer punishments for drunkards as well as allowing fewer establishments to sell alcohol.[24]

In his speech at Manchester, Lloyd George said that the Welsh would demand some version of local option from the party and chastised the leadership for not properly explaining what it was. He clarified its meaning, stating, "The majority might refuse to have any gin-palaces or dram shops at all; or they limit their numbers. But the bill did not give the power to any majority, however great, of entirely suppressing the sale of alcoholic drinks in any district whatever." In addition to exempting brewers, distillers, and wine merchants, the bill excluded hotels serving food, lunch bars, dining halls, and railroad refreshment areas. Unable to resist a dig at the landed class, Lloyd George ended his comments by contrasting their power to what local option would give voters. "In fact," he said, "the Bill did not give to the ratepayers anything like the control enjoyed by great landowners, who can, and sometimes do, make the purchase of a glass of ale impossible over square miles of territory," thus monopolizing the trade.[25]

Liberals had portrayed brewers, squires, and bishops as an "unholy trinity" but remained divided on whether to sponsor another local option bill in 1898. Lloyd George fumed to his brother, "I am inclined to believe a self denying ordinance would be a good thing for Wales." Six months following, at the inaugural meeting of the National Liberal Council for Wales and Monmouthshire, he specifically attacked the Anglican clerics and reiterated that the principality as well as the other parts of the United Kingdom should each be given authority over its area's internal matters. He even leveled the charge, "If the priest were asked to go to a temperance meeting in a Nonconformist Chapel, it would be quite a shock for him. The Chapel people were not registered practitioners; if they saved life, it was only by a fluke. That then was the theory of the priesthood."[26]

Lloyd George was also inclined to play a more active role in his own religious fellowship in 1898, writing his brother in June, "I preside over the Temperance meeting" at London the first of August, and expressing his hope that William could attend the cooperation meeting the same week. Sydney Black, minister of Fulham Cross Church of Christ, whose Twynholm Assembly

Hall was the venue for the meetings, sent Lloyd George a letter confirming the assignment but chaired the session himself. Lloyd George was a no-show, possibly because he had only been "advertised as one of the speakers" or because W. S. Caine was also on the list and had played a major role in splitting the Liberals twelve years prior. Lloyd George had been Black's friend before entering Parliament, gave addresses in the Fulham Cross building many times, frequently saw Black's family at their home or his, and at his funeral eulogized his sacrifice for social as well as civic justice. The Temperance Conference, which convened earlier the same day as the meeting Lloyd George was supposed to join, neither officially part of the cooperation that gathered the next day, was very united and active, sending 2,450 copies of the United Kingdom Alliance's budget to "each officer of churches and each Sunday school teacher" in October. The Alliance recognized Churches of Christ as "amongst its foremost fellow workers in temperance reform." Not all in the churches thought the association was good, but after Lloyd George became prime minister, the leading publication of the fellowship reported that he had been "regarded as" one of "the chief orators and the most promising politicians on the United Kingdom Alliance platform."[27]

Lord Salisbury had made it clear in 1896 that he would not entertain legislation for local option, though he did agree to establish a royal commission to look into how liquor licensing had evolved. It met for three years and was led by Viscount Peel, Robert Peel's son, who had earlier served as Speaker of the House of Commons. It consisted of three equally represented groups, the liquor industry, temperance workers, and those who were neutral. Majority and minority reports were issued, sellers of alcohol and neutrals signing the former, Peel and protemperance members the latter. The majority report recognized that a huge wrong needed to be corrected and the number of places selling alcohol should be greatly reduced by licensing justices. It also called for compensation for those who lost licenses. The minority report agreed with reduction as well as compensation, but stipulated the first by statute, allowing one licensed establishment for every 750 people in towns or four hundred in other areas, and limited the second to seven years. Local veto was also to be granted to Wales in five years, Scotland in seven, and England eventually. As the new leader of the opposition party in the House of Commons, Henry Campbell-Bannerman accepted the minority report as his party's policy, but his new Chief Whip, Gladstone, convinced him to avoid its specifics. Most Liberals, even those wanting prohibition, accepted Peel's report, but not all were happy with it. The United Kingdom Alliance remained neutral, but the

Good Templars continued to oppose any compensation and created the Prohibition Party to try and unseat all who favored it. Lloyd George continued to voice strong feelings, especially in private, and remained active behind the scenes to counter the liquor trade.[28]

In June 1899, Lloyd George told William about the death of Robert Wallace, a radical Scottish MP representing East Edinburgh for the previous thirteen years who convulsed and collapsed on the floor of the House of Commons as he stood to make a speech. He just simply wrote, "Poor old Wallace. A sad end to a brilliant intellect. Drink. What a reckoning that monster is piling up!" By the end of the year, he was even attending a Church of England temperance meeting because of his concern over alcohol. The Anglican clergy usually sided with Conservatives, but many of them also worked to get the consumption of alcohol regulated more strictly and especially to restrict licensing. In fact, Frederick Temple, Archbishop of Canterbury, in his previous post as Bishop of London had influenced Salisbury to found the royal commission to study licensing. Temple and ten other members of the Church of England Temperance Society met with the prime minister and insisted on closing public houses on Sunday and granting fewer licenses. However, the society wanted nonlicensed establishments to be allowed to sell beer for two hours on Sunday for people's meals, and it also favored compensation, on moral grounds if not legal. The society was the biggest of its type in Britain, seven thousand chapters and almost two hundred thousand members. Temple also served as president of the National Temperance League, a nonreligious organization that included many United Kingdom Alliance men, and he was a staunch teetotaler. Some nonconformists in the temperance movement took heart when he became archbishop.[29]

The day after Lloyd George attended the Anglican meeting, he went to the annual nonconformist conference of the National Council of the Evangelical Free Churches. Also present was Alfred T. Davies, a friend of over a decade. Davies read a paper on the relationship between municipal activity and morality, which the Church of England Temperance Society later printed. In his remembrances of Lloyd George half a century later, Davies wrote "from an early stage" in their careers each of them did "a close study of a particular branch of law—the Liquor Licensing Acts and their Administration, along with its ally, the 'cause' of Temperance." He claimed they either took or assisted in taking "leading cases" relating to the liquor trade "to the highest courts of the land," making "legal history." He quoted from a speech given by Lloyd George during his first campaign, in which he exaggerated his influence on Liberals before he was elected. "I have always been a consistent advocate of Temperance, and had the privilege of being largely instrumental in bringing about the adoption of the 'Direct Veto' by the party," he had asserted. "If returned to Parliament, I shall do all in my power to support measures which have for their object the removal from our midst of the disastrous temptations of strong drink." Six months after that election, Wilfrid Lawson, United Kingdom Alliance President, heard him speak at an alliance meeting, referring to him "in very handsome terms. Said he wished they had more such 'boy members,'" Lloyd George told Maggie. Direct veto and local option were terms used synonymously, as were local option or local veto, but local veto called for an up or down vote on allowing alcohol, while local option either outlawed it or restricted issuing licenses.[30]

What influence Lloyd George had on his party and others down to 1899 suffered when he opposed the Second Boer War. Nonetheless, he won his biggest majority in the election of 1900, and two years later regained any political influence he had lost, plus more, by opposing an education bill drafted by Arthur James Balfour, Salisbury's nephew and Leader of the House of Commons who succeeded his uncle before 1902 ended. A new licensing bill was also proposed and passed with little resistance because it was limited. One enacted a year earlier had outlawed selling alcohol to children, paving the way for more legislation even though *The Christian World* had editorialized that prohibition would hardly be needed if it passed. Indeed, during the first two decades of the new century, the amount of beer purchased fell by nearly a fourth. The negative attention drawn to the problem of children in pubs, diminishing revenues, wanting to reduce drunkenness to stem the tide of hostility against them, and a desire to restore public reputations contributed to brewers reinventing the pub as a more family-friendly place where nonalcoholic beverages, food, music, games as well as reading materials were provided. The 1902 law improved governing licenses' effectiveness, brought off-licensed businesses such as grocery stores under licensing justices, and required that clubs be registered. Most licensed grocers were loyal to the Liberal Party, in spite of its anti-liquor policies, because licensing helped keep their illegal competitors in check and alcohol prices higher. More may also have lived in areas dominated by Liberals, supporting them to keep their licenses. Lloyd George still hated alcohol's toll, noting a second colleague's death from it: "E. J. C. Morton. Another victim of drink. Chamberlain killed him. He made a mistake once in a speech & C wiped the floor with him. M never recovered & took to drink. Tragedy."[31]

Joseph Chamberlain was not responsible for Morton's death but did split the government of Arthur James Balfour. On New Year's Eve 1903, Lloyd George had a meeting with Winston Churchill, in which the latter said he and thirty other Unionists were willing to join the Liberals. Unionist had become the accepted term for the coalition of Conservatives and Liberal Unionists, many of whom were upset with Chamberlain for his abandonment of free trade in favor of tariffs. This time the division caused by Chamberlain benefited the Liberal Party. Lloyd George relayed to his brother two non-negotiable terms that he laid down to Churchill, insisting, "I told him that on Education & Temperance we were inexorable." Churchill, elected as a Conservative only three years earlier, agreed to accept those terms. The Unionist ranks divided over another licensing bill introduced the following spring, which said that licenses could not be revoked except in instances of misconduct, and that the violators still had to be compensated from taxes paid by all licensed establishments. Any new licensees would now be ineligible for compensation and would be heavily taxed for their licenses. Nonconformist Unionists and Anglican leaders opposed the 1904 bill, and it was temporarily postponed. "There are powerful influences in their own party," Lloyd George observed for William, "working against the shameless surrender to the drink interest which was undoubtedly contemplated by Balfour." Others considered the bill to be a massive reversal of government authority and a financial boon to brewers, but 50 percent of Balfour's Cabinet also reaped financial rewards from their shares in the industry.[32]

On the day the licensing bill was finally introduced, Lloyd George attacked it as well as Balfour, stating it was "fettering the discretion of the magistrates most materially" and thus increasing the value of "the worst type of house . . . which ought to be destroyed," whereas Balfour was attacking the licensing authorities "for unduly favouring temperance" in his constituency of Manchester. "Tories furious," Lloyd George gloated to William, "Temperance men delighted." The government had taken over the regulating of how long a licensee could sell alcohol thirteen years earlier, but licensing magistrates had been particularly aggressive over the last few, and brewers had been engaging in cutthroat competition to buy as many licensed properties as possible. They drove up the cost of land, created public companies in which investors owned shares, and argued that when licenses were not renewed, stockholders such as homemakers as well as thrifty widows were hurt. The bill passed its first reading, at which point the leading periodical of Churches of Christ ran articles opposing it. A prominent itinerant preacher for the fellowship warned it would "seriously curtail the power of the local Licensing Justices," plus "radically alter the nature and duty of the Licensing body." He further alleged, "While it professes to facilitate the reduction of licenses, it really endows the public-houses, making that which is only a yearly holding into a vested interest, thus establishing the right to compensation whenever any license is refused on the ground of non-requirement." He concluded that passage of the bill would "render temperance reform well nigh impossible, and it will saddle the country with an enormous financial liability."[33]

Liberals and temperance workers, of course, also fought the bill, and Lloyd George made special preparation to challenge it. Describing the government's intentions as "iniquitous," he alerted his brother, "Debate on tomorrow. I am off to rake up my choicest adjectives." He had already used colorful language to lambast the bill in a speech at Cardiff: "The cry of the orphan has risen against it, the wild plea of the poor maniac is against it; the moans of the myriads to whom it has brought sorrow and shame have ascended to the Throne against it; the arm of the Most High is uplifted against it." Then he chastised the sponsors by saying "woe to the Party, woe to the statesman, woe to the Government that intervenes between the recreant and its doom." The bill was enacted nevertheless, and for that and other reasons Lloyd George anticipated the return of the Liberal Party to power. As year's end neared, he discussed a temperance bill for the next session of Parliament at a private conference called by the Anglican Bishop of Hereford.[34]

Indeed, Liberals did regain power by the end of 1905, when Balfour quickly resigned his office instead of dissolving the House of Commons on December 4. He believed that Liberals were so disorganized they could not form a government, but six days later one was declared and a general election was set for the next month. Lloyd George became a Cabinet member for the first time, appointed President of the Board of Trade by Prime Minister Henry Campbell-Bannerman. He was offered the Board of Trade "to defend Free Trade" against the attacks of Chamberlain, and at the Alliance meeting the following year asserted that the traffic in alcohol was "a greater handicap to our trade, commerce, and industry than all the tariffs of the world put together." He told William he was "delighted" with his new post, adding he had "asked for pledges about Education & the extension of self-government for Wales—& got both." The two promises had come directly from the prime minister, and in a conversation with John Morley, Secretary of State for India, Lloyd George clarified one aspect of the second pledge: "Told him, I must see Wales right. That I would stand by my people whatever happened—self government including power to deal with temperance." Though now in the Cabinet, he still championed Welsh nationalism.[35]

Lloyd George won reelection in January 1906 and did address the drink issue that year. Calling it "the most urgent problem of the hour for our rulers to grapple with," he assured all of the British people it soon would be. He blamed it more than anything else for individual poverty and the reduced consumption of manufactured goods. Increasing the production of goods would put three times as many people to work as the drink industry, he also contended. In actuality, no licensing bill was agreed on by the Liberal Party in 1906 or 1907, even though Lloyd George had promised swift action and chaired the Alliance meeting the latter year. Herbert Gladstone, Home Secretary after the election, chaired a Cabinet committee on licensing, but as already stressed, he did not want local veto and pushed for almost nothing except a limit to how long compensation would be paid to those who lost their licenses. Temperance workers voiced their opposition to such a watered down bill, and the Chancellor of the Exchequer, Asquith, chaired the committee. He also opposed a forceful measure, but the Cabinet ultimately strengthened the planned bill.[36]

The licensing bill of Campbell-Bannerman's government did not see the light of day until February 27, 1908, and it called for the reduction of both the number of licenses and the amount of compensation. The former was to be decreased by roughly a third, based on the population, and the latter was to be restricted to fourteen years. Now, only one pub was permitted for every one thousand city dwellers, and no women were allowed to work in them. Lloyd George informed his brother that he had "fought out claim of Wales to separate treatment on Licensing Bill—carried it! Count that in to run for righteousness." After the bill's introduction he shared, "I want education out of the way to fight the publicans." He then received a letter from Stuart Rendel, Welsh Party head from 1888 to 1894 and now a peer, asking him to lead the licensing fight in the country. The religious fellowship of Lloyd George got involved in the battle again, too, specifically the North Wales and Cheshire Conference of Sunday school teachers who passed a resolution in favor of the bill.[37]

Even though 75 percent of the 1906 Liberal candidates had campaigned for the amending of Balfour's licensing law, and the United Kingdom Alliance got a resolution for local option passed in the House of Commons by a margin of over six to one, Unionist opponents of the new licensing bill couched it in confiscatory terms. They warned that landlords and owners of industry would be next. Balfour led the opposition, practicing the same obstruction-ism that Lloyd George had, but Anglican leaders supported the bill. Those in the industry who contributed to Anglican charitable causes therefore talked of ceasing, poor priests and widows who had stock in breweries were trotted out in the front lines of demonstrations, and a mass rally of 130 trainloads of drink workers was held in Hyde Park in September. The number of oppo-nents reached almost 250,000, compared to 100,000 who had publicly shown support two months preceding. Through limiting debate, the bill passed the House of Commons but was defeated in its second reading by the upper house in November, despite amendments made by Asquith to extend compensation for up to twenty-one years and ease restrictions on clubs.[38]

Asquith had succeeded Campbell-Bannerman as prime minister in April and appointed Lloyd George to be his Chancellor of the Exchequer. After the bill was vetoed by the House of Lords, where Unionists outnumbered Liberals by more than five to one, the new chancellor told his brother, "Peers very sorry for themselves. . . . Debate all on our side & the Lords feel they have made fools of themselves." Balfour and Lord Lansdowne, the upper house Unionist leader, agreed to counter the huge Liberal majority in the lower house by com-bining forces. Then, Lloyd George depicted the Lords as Balfour's poodle. "It fetches and carries for him. It barks for him. It bites anybody that he sets it on to," R. J. Q. Adams quotes him. In public, however, he uttered belligerently, "The Government has started, and it is not going to turn back. If we knew that a fortnight hence, when the division on the Licensing Bill comes, we should be beaten, we should be driven out of power, we would rather fall, and from that fall stand up to begin the fight again. We have been beaten, beaten badly, but it is only the first skirmish. The war has but begun, and we must see it through." As it turned out, the veto was among the final power plays made by the upper house before it was stripped of its power, except in financial legislation, three years later.[39]

Lloyd George was Chancellor of the Exchequer from 1908 to 1915, and in April 1909, he proposed his first budget. It was known as the "People's Budget" because it provided funding for socioeconomic reforms. One way he intended to get £2,600,000 for social programs was with license and liquor taxes tied to land rates, which Irish Nationalist MPs opposed because their greatest con-tributors were alcohol sellers. He reasoned, "when a country requires revenue to provide for the defence of its shores and to supply the urgent social need of its people, that seems to be just the moment when, before imposing fresh taxes on its citizens, it ought to look round and see whether it has farmed its property to the best advantage." The tax started out as three pence on each pound's worth of liquor sold at clubs but ended up being either that or as much as six pence on each they purchased. He even claimed the "representatives of the trade," with whom he had negotiated, "do not object to pay the share I have allocated them."[40]

A month after Lloyd George introduced his budget, he was cautiously optimistic with William: "Up to present no signs of a serious revolt against the Whiskey Tax." In September, though, he wrote his uncle, "Getting on very slowly with Licensing provisions. Not enough 'drive' behind." He was undoubtedly affected by the death of his sister, Mary Ellen, less than a month earlier. News of her passing, submitted to the foremost Church of Christ periodical by a member from Berea, stated she "was a very earnest and enthusiastic Temperance worker, and the cause of sobriety has lost one of its most energetic supporters in this district." Less than three years later, when the evangelist who started his itinerancy at Criccieth in 1891 visited it, he reported that many women there were "active in Temperance service." By September 28, Lloyd George was up to speed again, informing his brother that a majority of Irish Nationalist MPs would back everything in his budget but tobacco and whiskey. Finally, after the 1910 spring session began, it got the nod from Edward VII on April 29, whiskey tax and all, one year to the day since its introduction.[41]

Shortly before giving up his chancellorship to become the Minister of Munitions, Lloyd George tackled the issue of drink once again in order to improve worker productivity during the First World War. On March 29, 1915, he spent forty-five minutes trying to persuade George V to give up alcohol for the duration of the war and then met with representatives from the shipping industry, "all Tories & drinkers—pressing for total prohibition! Whilst I have been engaged all day on this gigantic problem I suppose my Welsh teetotal friends have been occupied in nagging at me at Rhyl. God help the country that is under their care." The shipbuilders told him there were hundreds of repairs on warships delayed because riveters were drinking. He referred to the issue as "this gigantic problem" and filled the next two days with Cabinet and brewers' meetings. He ended March by telling William, "I hope to do more for temperance in a fortnight than your Rhyl bletherers can do in a century." Abstainers there were clamoring for more liquor legislation.[42]

The monarch issued a letter on April Fools' Day, vowing to abstain until the war ended, and Lloyd George described it as "a stunner" sure to herald a successful temperance campaign. George V wanted the chancellor to head up the campaign, but Lloyd George did not have time. "Doesn't Rhyl look small—petty by the side of this gigantic move," he smugly wrote his brother. Only one week later, Asquith asked him to take responsibility for munitions. Lloyd George had just finished the entire Easter holidays working on his temperance "big scheme" and had more to do. In letters to his wife, he first simply stated, "Up to the eyes in Liquor," and later elaborated, "Endless difficulties about Drink. He is the toughest of all foes. But I am getting at him." His mistress agreed, writing that he was "steeped in drink" and "drink mad," able to "talk and think of nothing else. . . . It must be about the biggest & most difficult thing he has tackled." By the end of April, he was telling his brother that he expected his temperance bill to be achieved but it was "going to be overlooked in the howling hatred of taxes."[43]

Lloyd George's temperance scheme was enacted as one of the amendments to a Defence of the Realm Bill, which permitted the military to restrict pub hours where troops were stationed and supervise all purchases of alcohol for the armed forces. He repeatedly used extreme rhetoric to get his measure approved, making statements such as "Drink is doing more damage in the War than all the German submarines put together" or "We are fighting Germany, Austria and Drink, and, as far as I can see, the greatest of these deadly foes is Drink." He also tried to secure more taxes on alcohol in his last budget as chancellor. He asked for extra revenue from heavy beers, six times as much from champagne, four times as much from wine, and twice as much from liquor, and intended to dilute spirits from 25 to 36 percent. Ultimately, he withdrew the taxes and suggestions that the government purchase all breweries and pubs in addition to completely prohibiting liquor. Nationalization would cost in excess of £225,000,000, not counting the distilleries, and even the United Kingdom Alliance opposed it. Conservative leaders and Labour backed it, but temperance organizations defeated it. Lloyd George told George Riddell, a wealthy newspaperman, that he favored buying out the trade but not total prohibition, shrewdly adding "that the threat would make the trade easier to deal with."[44]

Before the defense bill was passed, though, Lloyd George reached an agreement with the liquor trade to prohibit all spirits under three years old. "That is quite useful," he explained to his brother, "as it puts out of the market all the cheap fiery whiskey." The day Parliament enacted it, however, he wrote, "Still some trouble over the raw whiskey." The defense bill authorized the establishment of an autonomous Central Liquor Control Board, which could regulate the industry wherever it saw fit without the trade having any recourse and could operate pubs and breweries. The Board reduced the number of hours drinking establishments could be open to only five and a half hours a day, a third of what they had been. To lessen drunkenness further, the operating hours were from noon to mid-afternoon and early evening hours. Purchasing alcohol with credit and buying rounds for others were prohibited. The Board's chairman told Lloyd George that pubs under his auspices, eventually numbering about four hundred, set new standards for how establishments should look and be run. In addition to the pubs it controlled, the Board established 840 canteens at industries so workers could opt for a nourishing lunch instead of just drinking. Some beer was occasionally included to keep them coming. When Lloyd George became prime minister a little over a year and a half later, having served as Secretary of State for War the last third of that time, pubs were open fewer hours than they had ever been. The percentage of alcohol in beer was also less. By the end of 1918, the amount of alcohol imbibed declined over 50 percent, 37,000,000 gallons the last year of the war compared to 89,000,000 the first. The number of arrests for being drunk was under 20 percent of the prewar figure.[45]

Lloyd George's coalition government discussed lowering the amount of imports needed for the beer industry only days after he became prime minister. It agreed to reduce the percentage of beer produced by half because of the lack of grain for food. It also considered state purchase again, planning to make 10,000,000 barrels of beer a year instead of the 36,000,000 to which the brewers were accustomed. Lloyd George even rationalized it as possibly becoming prohibition's closest supporter in a lot of places, a speculation that was borne out in Scotland three years later when only 3 percent of the places involved chose to ban licenses. Both he and the brewers ultimately balked at state purchase, he because of the expense and they because of the fear the government would return the trade to them after the war in a far less lucrative condition in light of the limitations it was going to impose. In spite of Lloyd George's inflammatory rhetoric, he never said that drunkenness was the only reason for the critical deficiency in ammunition but that it was mostly the cause. He expressed to Christopher Addison, a doctor who had been his chief aide at the Ministry of Munitions, that it was the government's fault there were too few artillery shells and warships: "The idea that slackness and drink, which some people talk so much about, are the chief cause of delay, is mostly fudge." In any case, the production of sufficient munitions no longer lagged.[46]

In 1915, R. P. Weston and Bert Lee had written a song entitled "Lloyd George's Beer" to poke fun at the weakening of the popular beverage. Two years later, after Lloyd George became prime minister, Ernie Mayne sang his rendition of it, which became a hit on the home front:

Lloyd George's Beer

We shall win the war, we shall win the war,
As I said before, we shall win the war.
The Kaiser's in a dreadful fury,
Now he knows we're making it at every brewery.
Have you read of it, seen what's said of it,
In the Mirror and the Mail.
It's a substitute, and a pubstitute,
And it's known as Government Ale (or otherwise).

Lloyd George's Beer, Lloyd George's Beer.
At the brewery, there's nothing doing,
All the water works are brewing,
Lloyd George's Beer, it isn't dear.
Oh they say it's a terrible war, oh law,
And there never was a war like this before,
But the worst thing that ever happened in this war
Is Lloyd George's Beer.

Buy a lot of it, all they've got of it.
Dip your bread in it, Shove your head in it
From January to October,
And I'll bet a penny that you'll still be sober.
Get your cloth in it, make some broth in it,
With a pair of mutton chops.
Drown your dogs in it, pop your clogs in it,
And you'll see some wonderful sights (in that lovely stufo).

Lloyd George's Beer, Lloyd George's Beer.
At the brewery, there's nothing doing,
All the water works are brewing,
Lloyd George's Beer, it isn't dear.
With Haig and Joffre when affairs look black,
And you can't get at Jerry with his gas attack.
Just get your squirters out and we'll squirt the buggers back,
With Lloyd George's Beer.[47]

Whiskey and rum were also sometimes rationed, the former for officers but the latter for the rest, with the possible exception of when the leader in charge was a teetotaler. Lloyd George was prime minister from December 1916 to October 1922, and the year before he left office, the 1921 Licensing Act was passed, which was clearly influenced by the regulations from the war but did not reduce the number of licenses awarded. Pubs could only be open for nine hours between eleven and eleven, preventing immoderate drinking before lunch, overindulgence throughout the day, and after hours inebriation. One stipulation, that pubs had to close for a couple of hours in the afternoon, remained in effect in England until 1990. Indeed, Adams considers these rules to "among the most long-lived alterations to British life which stemmed from the First World War." After all, as another historian astutely observed, no restrictions on the production, distribution, and consumption of alcohol would have been "as far-fetched an idea as complete prohibition." Lloyd George even acknowledged, "Every government that has ever touched alcohol has burnt its fingers in its lurid flames." As previously detailed, he drank alcoholic beverages himself, and on occasion bought beer for others, including a preacher with whom he traveled as a teenager. Once he became an adult, he did enjoy wine with evening meals, a liqueur with a smoke, or late in life some Irish whiskey before bed on the advice of his physician, but the author of an article in 1944 nonetheless confidently stated, "He is still a tee-totaler."[48]

That Lloyd George consistently and sincerely denounced the abuse of alcohol, however, is clear. Contrary to what some of his biographers have claimed, he neither used the temperance issue solely for political advantage nor discarded it when it no longer served him as a politician. He saw what drunkenness does to society, and his anti-drink policy was one of the many ways he improved life for the British people.[49]

4

Ireland and Home Rule,
1880–1914

"Look at this ill-fated island!"

WRITTEN COMMENTS by David Lloyd George on Irish home rule first appeared eleven days after his seventeenth birthday. His 1880 diary records that the Irish Home Rule Party members in the House of Commons were, "as usual," holding on to an "obstreperous & obstructive policy," and Liberals were "indifferent as to their attitude and not truckle much to them." He entered nothing else about it for over a year but noted on February 4, 1881, that "33 Irish homerulers were suspended," and the next day wrote "we had a hot disputation about coercion & suspension of Irish members" at John Roberts' candlehouse. Those present were "hot mad hot agst Gladstone's 'despotism' as they call it." Two weeks later, he referenced an essay he submitted to *The North Wales Express* concerning Ireland, the "truculence" of which his uncle "condemned" because "violence even when justifiable is not profitable." It was his third article for the paper, all pseudonymous and mentioning oppression of the Irish by Tories, oppression of Irish landlords as a cause of rebellion Gladstone had to address, or crime incited by the Irish National Land League, respectively. The timing of his entries as well as articles correspond to the Land War in Ireland from 1879 to 1881, when the league was established and home rule Irishmen in Parliament were recognized by their electors as having distinct independent party status to pursue Irish demands. Other agreements it proposed were that landlords who intended to sell be forced to sell to tenants and that the Irish Republican Brotherhood's right to exist as well as use arms to achieve its goals be acknowledged.[1]

Gladstone had also disestablished the Church of England in Ireland in 1869 and enacted a land law for the island the next year. The former resulted in the

selling of state church properties to six thousand tenants who had been working them, while the latter added over eight-hundred to that total and stipulated that landlords could no longer reap financial gains from improvements
made by their tenants. Lloyd George clearly expected more from Gladstone's
second ministry, and the league, co-founded by Michael Davitt and Charles
Stewart Parnell but presided over by the latter, had tried to bring down rents
by peaceful activism. When the league began advocating boycotts, though,
and Davitt motivated intimidated tenants to employ illegal tactics to oppose
evictions, a coercion law was passed in March 1881 to suppress criminal acts.
However, a second land act was implemented six months later, providing fair
rent determined by judges with no change until 1896, fixed tenure as long as
rent was paid, and free sales to reimburse the tenants for their improvements
if the land was sold. Obviously, resolving the first of the so-called "Three Fs"
in courts was the hardest for both tenants and landlords to accept. Mandatory selling to tenants was rejected and small landowners in western Ireland,
who had started the league, received almost no relief, while large ones and the
Protestants in the north reaped rewards. No benefits were offered to leasers,
those owing back rents, or farm workers who had no land. The law effectively
divided and conquered the league.[2]

In October, the league's most prominent members in Parliament were arrested, and it was outlawed later the same month. The Irish MPs incarcerated included Parnell, for treason against the land law, John Dillon, William
O'Brien, and William Redmond. Parnell led the nationalistic Irish Parliamentary Party (IPP) to strive for Ireland's home rule. Gladstone intervened
in April 1882, and all were freed in May, along with Davitt, who had been in
prison the previous fifteen months for inciting lawlessness. He was also jailed
from 1870 to 1877 for his participation in a Fenian assault on Chester Castle.
Fenians, the Irish Republican Brotherhood, were a clandestine organization
formed in 1858 mainly by Irish cohorts in America, which Davitt had joined
before adulthood. While behind bars, Irish leaders had called on tenants to
refuse rent payments, prompting the government to outlaw the league. They
were let out because of an agreement with Gladstone to rein in hostilities in
exchange for ending coercion and revisiting giving some assistance to leasers
of land or tenants overdue in their payments. Four days later, though, Lord
Frederick Cavendish, newly appointed Chief Secretary for Ireland on his first
day in office, and T. H. Burke, the Under Secretary, were stabbed to death in
Phoenix Park by Fenian extremists. Coercion was then quickly reinstated, but
three years after the first league was created, another one known as the Irish

National League was instituted, allying itself with Catholicism instead of Fenianism. A period of relative calm followed, due more to rents decreasing in excess of 20 percent by 1883 and potato harvests increasing over fifty the next three. While tenant complaints were lessening, however, landlords' objections grew as they lost revenue from lower rents.[3]

Three thousand landlords, most of them English, had met in Dublin on January 3, 1882, to call for the British government to compensate them. Later that year, an arrears act indirectly did so to some extent and assisted tenants as well. Exactly a month after the Dublin meeting, *The North Wales Express* reported that a speech delivered by Lloyd George at the Portmadoc Debating Society, "shook the very foundations of the landlords claim to compensation." It was entitled "Should Irish landlords be compensated on account of the working of the Land Act?" He argued that their tenants were in worse condition than Britain's slaves had been. "The slave was hard worked—the Irish tenant was also ill-fed." He had shown his uncle a copy of his intended remarks two days before delivering them and received "a censure," with Richard Lloyd pointing out that his nephew's opinions were different from his own. The foster father even expressed disappointment in his hopes for the nineteen year-old but was especially "anxious" to know how his "maiden speech" had gone two days following the event. The night he addressed the society, Lloyd George noted that he was nervous and glad when it was over. By the end of that year, he had bought A. M. Sullivan's book, *New Ireland*, and stated "it may be of use in Debating Society." After finishing it, he added, "it has made me more Irish than before even." His nephew explains this shift in his thinking about those who wanted home rule, observing that he referred to Michael Davitt as his "most admired character in real life" but that he esteemed Charles Stewart Parnell as much as he did Gladstone or Chamberlain.[4]

Davitt had persuaded Parnell to be the league's president as a show of unity on the issues, and even though Parnell denounced the assassins, many believed he approved of their actions. In 1883, W. E. Forster, the former Chief Secretary for Ireland who left Gladstone's second ministry because coercion had ceased, went so far as to claim that Parnell knew the murderers and what they were going to do. In his diary, Lloyd George called these "terrible charges against Parnell" but added that he did "firmly believe that he in a way connived at or rather palliated murder in some instances—and rightly so, as I believe." Some murders, he went on to assert, were justifiable for "political justice and expediency of the highest order." Finally, he acknowledged that "it would not do for Parnell publicly to admit this—It would bring him within the power of the law—and most important of all, it might be construed by both fanatics and villains as a justification and incitement for all murder."[5]

In early January 1886, Davitt spoke in Wales, where a land league was being formed and farmer discontent was mounting over tithes. When Lloyd George learned the Irishman was going to speak, he wrote, "Glad to hear it—I do earnestly hope this agrarian agitation will succeed—The notion is to my hearts delight." As it turned out, he also spoke at the meeting and, that same day, put down his impressions of Davitt, describing him as calm and quiet "except when reference is made to the Irish landlords then he fired up—talks in fierce accents." He then met with him the next day and discussed the "future of agitation—Feel that I am in it now." Not only referring to the agrarian movement but also to his political future, he recorded the belief that his presentation had "gone like wildfire—going to make me M.P." In fact, after hearing how Lloyd George ended the meeting, Davitt had suggested he pursue a career in national politics. In publicly thanking him for coming to Wales, Lloyd George had chided those local Liberals who did not attend because home rule was not yet an official policy of their party. He said "Davitt was a man who had not only done much for humanity, but had also suffered much for humanity," and opposing "a man because he did not belong to their nation was most narrow-minded and contrary to the principles of their religion." Noting the parable of the good Samaritan, he described Davitt as "the stranger . . . who had come there to bind up their wounds." Turning to the second Irish league, he saw a "need for that movement. There was the greatest misery existing in the country. Working men were starving. The aristocracy were squandering the money earned by the sweat of the working man's brow. . . . The people only wanted union. They had now the power."[6]

Three-and-a-half months after he met Davitt, Lloyd George was speaking in favor of home rule throughout Wales, and Gladstone championed a bill to that effect in Parliament. Gladstone was defeated in the House of Commons, and the Liberal Party split over the issue. Chamberlain and ninety-two members of the party sided with Conservatives against the bill, becoming known as the Liberal Unionists. When the bill was introduced, Lloyd George had a heated debate with John Roberts over whether Gladstone or Chamberlain was right. Roberts, he entered, was "a hot Gladstonian—believes Chamberlain to have been moved entirely by selfish aims in the matter—I did not agree with him—for my part I believe Chamberlain to be right in the main." Chamberlain addressed the House of Commons on the second reading of the home rule bill, and argued against a separate parliament in Dublin because it would undermine the empire's legislature. He claimed that he favored the principle of home rule but wanted Northern Ireland to be left out of any agreement reached. Lloyd George called his speech "a thorough masterpiece—very convincing & clear," and a month later wrote he "wd like to see Joe holdg the balance between the parties." In a speech of his own at Cardiff in February 1890, he offered as reasons for home rule in Ireland that the empire was too large to properly care for each of its parts and that Parliament did not understand each locality as well as provincial legislators. He stated the same reasons were just as true for Wales, but that those who feared "Rome Rule" taking control of Ireland, the island separating from the realm, or its lawful being dominated by its lawless had no such worries about Wales. The principality had never threatened to depart from the United Kingdom, and no politically-motivated murders were being committed by the Welsh. "There is no bloodstain on its whole political record," he asserted.[7]

If Lloyd George was conflicted at all by the two views on the Irish issue, he clearly made his choice by the end of the year he was elected to Parliament. Writing to Ellis on November 27, 1890, he concluded, "For Wales I see but one way out of the difficulty & that is to fight the next election on Disestablishment & practically ignore the Irish question." The difficulty he referred to was the growing controversy surrounding Parnell's adultery with Katherine O'Shea, the wife of Captain W. H. O'Shea. An uncontested divorce was granted to Captain O'Shea only ten days before Lloyd George's letter, but Irish home rule members of Parliament remained loyal to their leader. On the same day that he wrote Ellis, he wrote his wife, stating, "If Parnell sticks & his party stick to him it is generally conceded that Home Rule is done for. Isn't he a rascal. He would sacrifice even the whole future of his country too." He had told her of his "idiotic misconduct" earlier but added regret: "Here is quite a young man having attained the greatest career of this century, dashing it to pieces because he couldn't restrain a single passion. A thousand pities."[8]

A day before Lloyd George sent his letters to Ellis and Maggie, Gladstone recommended that Parnell be replaced for the good of the Liberal Party as well as for his own leadership of it. Parnell responded with a manifesto to his own people on November 29, rejecting cooperation with the party and its leader's suggestion. Two days later, the party met, and by the end of the week, forty-four of seventy-two Irish members ended their allegiance to it, a hostile division between home rulers that lasted until 1899. Because Parnell withstood the party and Gladstone, Lloyd George castigated him further in his correspondence with his wife and prophesied concerning Ireland's future.

"He must be a base selfish wretch. By sticking to his post he is doing incalculable injury to the Irish cause—whatever happens eventually. He is dividing the Irish people into two parties & the schism will not be bridged over in a hurry." Nevertheless, he admired the public coolness of Parnell under political pressure and ended by writing, "He is a bad lot but undoubtedly clever."[9]

The day Lloyd George wrote Ellis, he mailed a letter to his brother too, observing that Parnell "is an exceedingly cunning chap. You see him today talking to fellows in his own camp whom he would disdain hardly to look at a few weeks ago. He now chats freely with them. He means to get a favorable vote Monday next." It was favorable but came following heated disagreement until Friday of that week. In an earlier letter to William, he confided "we are all correspondingly depressed. Anger & despondency reign supreme on the Liberal benches. A gloom has overcast our late jubilance. The Tories on the other hand can hardly restrain their joyousness. Confound it all." The letter then ends with a much more trenchant description of Parnell: "He marched into the House defiantly & even fiercely. He is a terrible man." The jubilance had concerned Liberal gains in the latest election, but the growing strife between Irish members threatened to undo them in the future. Halfway into the week's contentious debate, however, he was cautiously optimistic that "the chances" for the Liberals had "improved," though Parnell was just as tenacious. "Parnell's fight is simply sublime," he observed. "It shows what a leader he is and the stuff he is made of. He is a grand fighter." During the following year, those opposed to Parnell gained the advantage, winning the first three of four bye-elections in Ireland. Parnell then died before the fourth, which coincidentally unseated Michael Davitt, and the anti-Parnellites even claimed his constituency.[10]

Lloyd George blamed controversy over Parnell for his refusal to address disestablishment in the waning weeks of 1890. "There will be a set debate on Welsh Disestablishment in February or March," he informed his brother. "The Parnell scare, which monopolises the attention of the House & the Country will be over then." Also, more members would be present, they would be more attentive, and Gladstone would be speaking. He went on to elaborate that Parnell and his supporters were "playing a very bold game," obstructing the early December party meeting with "motions for adjournment" that could "go on ad infinitum." He then labeled the Irish leader "an utter desperado" and drew his missive to a close by noting, "the old man has repudiated Parnell." Just because Gladstone renounced Parnell did not stop him from creating more controversy. He tried to muster enough support from his countrymen in Parliament to remain in control but ended up dividing their ranks. Even their rejecting him in 1891 did not relegate home rule to obscurity, though. In fact, Lloyd George revisited the issue with Ellis shortly after 1893 began, rededicating himself to it by asserting: "I shall confine myself to attacking at large the men who would truck and starve Home Rule." It should be stressed that this was after Gladstone had returned to power for a fourth time, during which he ultimately succeeded in getting the House of Commons to pass an Irish home rule bill, only to be defeated by the House of Lords.[11]

Twenty days after Lloyd George's letter to Ellis, a second bill for Irish home rule was put forward by Gladstone's government. His first one stipulated that Ireland should have a limited parliament, with no Irish representatives seated in London. The second bill simply reduced Irish representation by approximately 20 percent because of the decrease in the island's population after the famine and emigration. However, they were only allowed to vote on matters pertaining to Ireland or the empire. The details of the latter could not be worked out to the satisfaction of a majority and the voting clauses were eventually discarded. The third reading of the bill occurred the first day of September, but the upper house voted it down by a margin of ten to one. Lloyd George did not speak on the bill, and his most eminent biographer maintains that his views on home rule were more akin to those of Joseph Chamberlain than to those of Gladstone. Chamberlain favored the granting of national councils to the various parts of the United Kingdom, a concept that became known as Home Rule All Round. Grigg insists that Lloyd George thought Welsh MPs should have joined Liberal Unionists, which would have potentially resulted in a three-fold positive outcome: Gladstone would have been forced to compromise on his first home rule bill, Parnell would have accepted a more agreeable one, and Chamberlain would not have cast his lot with Conservatives. Grigg's supposition may be accurate, but Lloyd George's comments on Chamberlain's speech in opposition to the bill were not complimentary. In a letter to a Welsh newspaper, he described it as "poor and limp indeed. His speech was without substance, and his delivery thoroughly bad."[12]

Gladstone decided to retire after losing his second bid for Irish home rule, and the Cabinet passed the baton to Lord Rosebery. Both Rosebery and William Harcourt, Liberal leader in the House of Commons, considered the issue to be detrimental to the party. The new prime minister told the House of Lords that England as the largest member of the United Kingdom would have to approve any decision on home rule, after promising Liberals that he was bound by and would honor it. He consequently lost half of an already tenuous majority in the lower house, gave the upper house an excuse for defeating the home rule bill, and squandered an opportunity to return Liberal Unionists to the Liberal fold. In hindsight, he should have remained silent or ambiguous about it, instead of being dismissive, Grigg explains. An amendment decrying the veto power of the House of Lords was quickly proposed by the Irish who were now upset with Rosebery. Lloyd George and several other Welsh as well as English Liberals sided with them, and the amendment narrowly passed. Both Parnellites and anti-Parnellites were angry at the prime minister, and his government was humiliated by the amendment. Relishing their slim victory and presumed new clout, Irish MPs pushed for and got a bill passed to protect evicted tenants in their homeland. It suffered the same fate as the home rule bill. When Rosebery's government resigned over another issue the next summer, Lloyd George had to run for a third election. During the campaign, only he and four other Liberal candidates in Wales addressed Welsh home rule. He was accused of joining the followers of Parnell and the Conservatives to bring down Rosebery. He was even characterized by a member from his own party and shire as the Parnell of Wales.[13]

In his approach to home rule for Wales, and for that matter, universal devolution, Lloyd George had made no bones about the fact he wanted to emulate the Irish model, namely working with whichever political party was in office to realize his objectives. From June 1895 until the end of 1905, it was the Conservative Party, and he attributed his party's loss to England's fear of Irish home rule, which had been incited by Liberal Unionists. His solution to what he considered an illogical anxiety was a federal system in which there was home rule for all parts of the United Kingdom. Joseph Chamberlain had since rejected Home Rule All Round, and his own party now showed no inclination toward it. However, he soon got the opposition leaders' attention with his masterful strategy in obstructing the Agricultural Rating Act in 1896. As a result, he was invited to dine with Rosebery and other influential Liberals to make plans for the party, during which he took the opportunity to reiterate the need for devolution. Harcourt was so impressed with how he maneuvered in the House of Commons, he said that Lloyd George's "little finger" was better in a parliamentary battle than all of the Liberal members from Scotland. One reporter stated that due to his tactics in opposing the bill, "the Parnell of Wales became the Chamberlain of England." A newspaper published in London acknowledged that Lloyd George had begun 1896 with less than total confidence from most of his party but now he could not be lauded enough for his efforts. Part of the praise he got was for energy he also expended against an education bill to benefit the Church of England schools, which was withdrawn by the government though reintroduced and passed in 1897 over repeated amendments he proposed. It finally prevailed when separate financial aid legislation was promised for nonsectarian schools, winning Chamberlain's support.[14]

In addition to being against the Agricultural Rating Act and special consideration for the sectarian schools, he opposed an amendment that would authorize a Catholic university for Ireland as well as the Irish Local Government Bill in 1898. It was the first time he had rejected the wishes of the Irish for their homeland, but the former was also sectarian and the latter would have enriched the landlords even more. The anti-Parnellites, led by John Dillon, had sided with Lloyd George on the agriculture legislation but not on the education bill, infuriating the Liberals, especially nonconformists. Parnellites, led by John Redmond, criticized Dillon for helping delay the agriculture act and accused him of forsaking home rule by siding with the government on the education bill. So there was not only a continuing split among the Irish, though Parnellites were outnumbered seventy to eleven, but also now a rift between the Irish and the Liberals. When one Irish MP exhorted Lloyd George to permit Ireland to handle its own affairs, he retorted, "it is time that British Members were beginning to take care of themselves," another appeal for a universal devolution. His refusal to acquiesce obviously hurt his relationship with them, and for some time when they saw him they acted like they were looking right through him. Gilbert even goes so far as to assert that Lloyd George incited them into arguing to garner favor with the English, and he was publicly proclaiming by November that Wales would pursue its own course in the future. He had expressed to William the concerns of some in Parliament about Irish sensitivity to devolution for all instead of just their country; "I think it is time Liberals should define their position on Home Rule generally. It is more honest—& more in the interests of the highest expediency to do so."[15]

From 1899 to 1902, the Second Boer War raged in South Africa, and from 1902 to 1904, lengthy parliamentary battles were waged over sectarian education. Since Lloyd George was the most vehement opponent of both, other issues like home rule received less of his attention, even though Dillon worked with him against the war and Parnellites boisterously praised his assertion that the education initiative allocated resources from faithful nonconformist supporters of home rule to assist Catholicism's leaders in opposition to Ireland. Dillon had equated Great Britain's actions in South Africa to Spain's in Cuba, those of barbarians who raised the ire of all cultured peoples, but he and Redmond voted for the 1902 education bill on its second reading because it provided financial support to Anglican or Catholic schools in England and Wales. Irish MPs did abstain at the final reading of the bill, though. Conservative Party sops to the Irish from 1896 to 1902, for Catholic schools and local government, were conscious attempts to destroy home rule through bribery. After losing the education fight, most of the Liberals also lost their enthusiasm for Irish home rule in the next ten years.[16]

Coincidentally, the same year that Liberal excitement for Ireland started waning, Conservative Chief Secretary for Ireland, George Wyndham, proposed a land purchase bill in hopes of solving that thorny Irish issue. He was secretary from 1900 to 1905, following Gerald Balfour, who had held the position the previous five years. However, coming on the heels of the bill's introduction was the implementation of the crimes act to quell any potential Irish agitation, and when the two were linked in the first legislative session of 1902, the bill had little chance of being enacted. In fact, it was withdrawn before the session ended, violence ensued, and approximately two-thirds of the Irish were coerced into submission under the terms of that crimes act. The law stipulated immediate judgment and imprisonment up to six months for anything from preventing evictions to boycotts. In addition to others, eleven sitting and two former members of the Parliament were jailed. Ironically, that Criminal Law Amendment Bill was the first introduced by Arthur James Balfour, Gerald's older brother, after he had become Chief Secretary for Ireland in 1887, and he became the prime minister on July 12, 1902. He and Wyndham, who was his personal secretary in Ireland, were friends, and they worked together to propose another land purchase bill for the following year. Another coincidence occurred when a centrist attempt at conciliation on the land issue among the various Irish factions began that fall. Moderate landlords and the organizations representing tenants in the north and south decided to compromise, leading to the Wyndham Act of 1903, providing bonuses for landlords who allowed voluntary purchases by tenants. Tenants got sixty-eight and a half years to pay and an annuity of three and a quarter percent, but landlords got a grant of 12 percent. No Irish voted against it, and Liberals backed it half-heartedly.[17]

Dillon was never on board with centrism, even though both northern Irish Presbyterians and southern Catholics were, and by the time Conservatives fell from power in December 1905, his influence renewed a more general division among the Irish. Compromise subscribers formed the Irish Reform Association, endorsing the politics of conferring as well as conducting business, but they also fed Dillon's home rule fervor by embracing a limited

Irish devolution. Wyndham agreed and lost his position in the Conservative government as a result, Dillon being among his leading detractors. Limited devolution was more along Lloyd George's line of thinking, and his letters shed light on one consequence of events in Ireland by the time of Parliament's first session in 1904, that the Irish had "no funds to help their men in constant attendance" in the lower house. In fact, he blamed that and lax Liberal whips for not bringing down the ministry. Anticipating an imminent return of Liberals to power, though, he noted renewed importance of home rule to them that summer, telling William, "In order to make sure of Home Rule & Disestablishment we mean to adjourn as soon as we get them through & meet in November to pass Revenue Bill. This suits me much better as you cannot concentrate public attention on anything until Home Rule is out of the way." The next February, an Irish home rule amendment was proposed, and he let his brother know it was "a mistake in tactics," though he delivered a speech about it. On December 5, the Liberals returned to power under Prime Minister Henry Campbell-Bannerman, and Lloyd George was offered the Cabinet post of President of the Board of Trade.[18]

Now that he was in a position to facilitate progress for Ireland as well, Lloyd George took on the Protestants in the northern part of Ireland who stood in the way of it. On July 4, 1906, he informed his brother, "I had a royal time with the Irish last night. Went for the Irish Orangemen hot & strong much to the joy of the Irish Nationalists." He had accused the Orangemen of being bigots because of how Catholic railway workers were being treated by their Protestant employers. The Orangemen "meant to attack" him six days later because of his "stand . . . but they funked it after all—although they were preparing for it." The next February, he went to Belfast, which was the first time in over two decades a Liberal Cabinet member visited Northern Ireland for political reasons. Despite threats of bodily harm, he spoke to a sizable crowd at Ulster Hall, though with extraordinary security precautions. Even troops were confined to their quarters in case they were needed. Talking like a Protestant to other Protestants, which members of Churches of Christ did not consider themselves, he confessed there would still be differences between them. Some who were hearing him would not agree with the extent of devolution he wanted, and others would not concur that state schools supported with public funds should be run by the public instead of by sectarian religious leaders. Consequently, he would speak his mind and let the chips fall where they may.[19]

After an introduction based on the history of the last twenty years, Lloyd

George posed a question for his audience to consider. What had Ireland asked for itself? "What has she asked for centuries, asked when her voice was choked with blood, asked from the prison, asked from the scaffold, asked on the battlefield, asked when she was dying from starvation? She asks but one thing—the freedom to govern herself." Qualifying emotive rhetoric, he added, "I do not mean to say that when Ireland asks for bread, England now gives her a stone. England has done that in the past. I do not mean to say that when Irishmen ask for fish, Englishmen give them scorpions. They do not." He finished the context of his question, however, by acknowledging that the English did "insist upon giving them things which do not suit their palates or their appetites, and the most aggravating form of hunger is to be offered dishes that one does not want." In conclusion, he had one more question for his listeners. Would Ireland's people be magnanimous? "Look at this ill-fated island! What a morass its history is of racial, religious, personal misunderstanding, ruthless oppression, savage vengeance, frenzied crime against the law—yes, and by means of the law—legal wrong, lawless justice." Then, heralding the "myriads of men, women, and children, from generation to generation, sunk and struggling in it, and yet clinging with unutterable devotion to the woe-stricken land which bore them," he finished with this specific sober charge: "The tardy, but true, national conscience of Britain has been awakened, but the responsibility rests primarily upon Ulster. Will the Protestant North rise above prejudice and belief and blood? Will you lead in the rescue? If you will, I as a Protestant tell you that you will add one more laurel to the many that your faith and mine has won in the cause of human progress."[20]

In the spring of 1908, Lloyd George became Chancellor of the Exchequer but spent three years getting his "People's Budget" and the Parliament Act passed, the latter stripping the upper house of its veto power. However, it could delay non-money bills for two years from their second readings. The Irish knew that the battle with the Lords had to be won before another home rule bill would stand a chance, so for the past two years they primarily engaged in fighting the whiskey tax that provided part of the funding for the "People's Budget." Five months into the struggle over various aspects of his budget that lasted from April 1909 until April 1910, Lloyd George anticipated its imminent defeat in the upper house, followed by dissolution and another election. He reported to William there was "an anti House of Lords majority of *208*. Irish will also support all Budget except whiskey & tobacco. It is almost too good to be true. It would be a bigger majority than the Khaki Election. That was only 150." The so-called "khaki election" had been held in 1900, during the Second Boer War, and the pro-imperialist Conservatives won.[21]

After sharing *"quite confidential"* information, he had briefly considered accommodating the Irish because of two surprising developments. They were drinking less, which was personally his most important goal, and money from portions of the budget conditionally implemented prior to full enactment was not sufficient to keep the government from borrowing other resources. The Irish had voted against the budget on its second reading but had abstained on its third, and in the early months of 1910 they had also adopted the slogan, "no veto, no budget." Lloyd George had met resistance in the Cabinet to compromising with them because it would appear Liberals were being dictated to in return for their support. As a result, only two weeks before the reintroduced budget was passed on its third reading, he let his brother know emphatically, "We are not going to give in on whiskey to the Irish." It had been a gamble because the Irish could have brought the government down if they had voted against the budget again, but John Redmond and seventy-one of the eighty-two Irish members voted for it; the other eleven, who were led by William O'Brien, opposed it because they felt betrayed when Lloyd George reneged on whiskey taxes.[22]

In addition to ending the House of Lord's veto power in 1911, Lloyd George successfully implemented national health and unemployment insurance. No sooner had 1912 begun, though, than he stated he was "instigating a move to dish Tories over Ulster." He mailed those words to William on the last day of January, and when he finally played his hand, it laid out home rule for all of Ireland except the six northern counties. One or all of them could choose to be excluded. Churchill was the only Cabinet member who agreed, and it was not permitted to become part of the third home rule bill. Of course, the Parliament Act now prevented the House of Lords from vetoing an Irish home rule bill, but it could forestall it for up to two years. It had also shortened the period between general elections from seven to five years. Thus, with options for preventing home rule until returning to power, Conservatives and Bonar Law, leader since November 1911, made their stand on defending Protestants in the north. Law's father was a Presbyterian preacher born in Ulster, which undoubtedly influenced the fervor with which he opposed Irish home rule. A Cabinet committee was working on the third home rule bill when Lloyd George mentioned his "move" to his brother, but only a week after his assertion, he indicated that the Irish were asking for far too much. The Cabinet had met the day before, deciding to save any possible concessions to Ulster until they were absolutely needed and until the extent of a mounting resistance movement there was known. Less than five months earlier, fifty-thousand opponents of home rule marched in Belfast, and the main speaker, Edward Carson, called for them to create a separate government on the day home rule was passed. Carson was a member of the Parliament and for two years had been the recognized leader of the Irish who wanted to keep their status in the United Kingdom.[23]

Just two days before the third home rule bill was officially introduced, H. H. Asquith, the prime minister since 1908, and his Cabinet found out that the extent of the resistance in Northern Ireland was significantly increasing. This time, eighty-thousand marched in Belfast, and Law told them they would be supported in the heat of their fight by Conservatives, seventy of whom were present. Couching his comments in such belligerent terms seemed to justify the threat to create a separate government for the north if home rule was passed and must have fanned the flames of a resistance movement already procuring permits for militia-type drills to uphold liberty as well as law. In a letter to Maggie on the same day the third home rule bill was "launched," Lloyd George called Law "rude & silly." The bill was presented on April 11, 1912, and passed a second reading early the next month. It provided for the creation of a bicameral legislature in Dublin that would look after Irish affairs, but Parliament would still govern all foreign affairs, including trade. The number of Irish members in the latter would be forty-two, exactly half its existing representation. All laws passed in Dublin could be subject to appeals or amendments by a lord lieutenant and the imperial government. The lord lieutenant would be chief executive for Ireland, would represent the monarchy, and would nominate individuals for the non-elected upper house. The Irish police would continue to serve as part of the United Kingdom's law enforcement. No religion could be endowed, and all tax revenues in Ireland would go to the United Kingdom's coffers until income exceeded spending for three years running. In the meantime, six million pounds a year would be allocated for the island.[24]

The same month the bill passed its second reading in the lower house, an amendment was proposed by a fellow Liberal that would have allowed the northern counties of Antrim, Armagh, Derry, and Down to be exempted from it. Liberal leadership spoke out against the amendment, but both Law and Carson supported it, giving Lloyd George hope that his "move" might one day still have a chance. Law ratcheted up the rhetoric, though, when at the end of

July he argued the inhabitants of Ulster "would be justified in resisting such an attempt by all means in their power, including force." He could, "imagine no length of resistance to which Ulster can go in which I should not be prepared to support them, and in which, in my belief, they would not be supported by the overwhelming majority of the British people." That might help explain why two months later Carson was able to get almost five-hundred thousand individuals, including women, to sign a covenant stating their resistance to home rule. In December, he proposed his own amendment to exclude the nine northern counties where the most Protestants lived, but without success.[25]

By the end of 1912, Lloyd George felt that the best way to get home rule and disestablishment passed would be a veto of his franchise bill by the House of Lords the next summer, followed by another election. "Lingering for 2 yrs will be thoroughly bad," he exclaimed to his brother. Of course, his franchise bill was pulled in January before it could be vetoed, and a new election was not called for by the government. The latter may not have been anyhow because the Conservatives had won five bye-elections in a row at that point and had become the biggest single party in the House of Commons. January also saw the successful third reading of the home rule bill, followed by its quick defeat in the upper house. It was then passed again in short order, only to be thwarted once more by the time of the mid-year adjournment. All the lower house had to do now was pass it a third time, with no changes whatsoever, and the veto would be overridden.[26]

Lingering certainly was bad for home rule because an Ulster Volunteer Force was created soon after 1913 started, and by year's end nearly one-hundred thousand members had joined. In response, but also because home rule seemed to be less and less likely, the Irish Volunteers were formed in November. Anticipating another upper house veto, tantamount to enacting home rule for all of Ireland, and concerned by the founding of paramilitary groups, King George V persuaded Asquith to confer with Law the last quarter of 1913 to hopefully prevent an Irish civil war. Law had tried more than once since May to get the monarch to dissolve the Asquith ministry, and the king had twice informed the prime minister of the Conservative's plea for his dismissal. Asquith reminded the ruler of 1910s elections and that forty more English members voted for the second reading of the third home rule bill than against it, meaning it was not something that only the Celtic fringe wanted. Asquith agreed to talk with Law, nonetheless, and they held three secret meetings. At their second session, Asquith floated a trial balloon to gauge his counterpart's reaction to the possibility of temporary exclusion for the six so-called plantation counties. It would last as long as a decade or so, for any county voting for it in a referendum. During their last session, though, Law flatly turned down any exclusion on a temporary basis. In the interim, it was Lloyd George, not Asquith, who presented the prime minister's views to a group of Liberal leaders one day and the entire Cabinet the next. Possibly not aware of the secret sessions, he set the time frame at six years, allowing for two general elections before exclusion ended. Only a new law from London would keep Ulster from rejoining the rest of Ireland after that.[27]

The Irish Nationalists did not want exclusion on a temporary basis either, since they were opposed to any exclusion at all. Redmond and Dillon, who had been working toward that same end for over a decade, believed Carson's threat to establish a new government for Ulster if home rule was enacted was a ruse. When they were approached with the ministry's proposal, Redmond by Asquith and Dillon by Lloyd George, Redmond countered with a plan similar to one Edward Grey first suggested, described as home rule within home rule. It would permit Ulster to have its own limited council but make it answerable to Dublin. Dillon liked the ministry's plan better because exclusion was temporary, but neither he nor Redmond wanted any action until absolutely necessary. When the majority of Irish MPs learned of a possible compromise on home rule, they objected, and, as their leader, Redmond had no choice but to officially state no concessions would be made regardless of his own personal views. Lloyd George spoke to him the next day, assuring him Carson was serious and relaying a report the Chief Secretary for Ireland, August Birrell, had shared with the Cabinet the day before: fifteen-hundred guns had been transported to Ulster from Liverpool with more than sixty rounds of ammunition for every one; ironically, Birrell undercut Lloyd George earlier, telling Redmond not to pay too much attention to the government. Lloyd George went on to warn Redmond that he, Grey, Churchill, and others would resign if force had to be employed to keep Ulster from leaving before it was given the exclusion option. Home rule would stand no chance at all in a new Conservative ministry. As 1913 closed, the ministry took steps to curtail the growing threat of violence, outlawing the movement of weapons to Ireland.[28]

A day before the 1914 parliamentary sessions opened, Lloyd George told William he had spent five or six hours with Dillon the previous weekend and that he as well as others were "dead against proposing terms *now*. So am I. P. M. strongly in favor of unfolding his concessions at this stage. Carried the Cabinet against him. He was very upset. I am sorry. But a quarrel with the Irish at this stage—especially when they are right—would be fatal." In fact, in a meeting with Redmond, Asquith had already broached the subject of Northern Ireland having broad authority to veto after home rule was passed. George V, however, dissuaded him from committing to such a stance publicly because he believed leaders in the north would reject it. Six days after the session began, Lloyd George also wrote his brother, "This morning had long & interesting talk with Irish leaders. P. M. has left it to me to negotiate with them." Twelve days later, he added, "Ministers dined at Buckingham Palace last night. Had a long & interesting talk with the King—re Ulster. Believe the Irish MP's will accept my plan."[29]

On Wednesday, March 4, Lloyd George again wrote, "Settled with the Irish & carried my plan through the Cabinet today. Next step is to submit it to the other side which the P. M. will do Monday." His revised plan now spelled out that for a referendum to be held in a given county, around 10 percent of those able to vote in imperial elections should sign a petition to support it, and the years of exclusion should be reduced to three. Once more, the king got involved and insisted on the original six-year plan. Five days later, the third home rule bill began a final route to passage. Redmond did grudgingly accept the final version, but Carson did not and labeled it a judgment of execution not to be carried out until six years later. However, not to be left completely out of the loop, Carson indicated that he was still willing to talk about exclusion, if no period of years was specified and if the four counties initially listed remained outside home rule until the legislature in London voted differently. Law wanted a referendum held throughout the British Isles on the issue of exclusion and agreed to honor whatever the majority decided.[30]

Between the time of Carson's rejection of the third home rule bill and Law's British Isles plebiscite idea, Churchill called Carson's presumed bluff to create a provisional government in Ulster if the bill passed. Obviously referring to Carson, he threw down the gauntlet, stating, "if all the loose, wanton and reckless chatter we have been forced to listen to these months is in the end to disclose a sinister revolutionary purpose, then I can only say to you 'Let us go forward and put these grave matters to the proof.'" Carson denounced Churchill on the floor of Parliament a couple of days later and promptly left for Northern Ireland, where he claimed he was needed. It occurred to a number of political leaders that he was possibly planning to implement his threat. Lloyd George commented on both of the speeches to his brother, starting with Churchill's. "The fat is in the fire. Winston's speech has enraged the opposition," he recorded, "but it has bucked up our supporters tremendously. It was the right word at the right moment & I am glad that I am largely responsible for it." Moving then to Carson's retort and its future implications, he shared, "No one can quite foretell the course of events. The P. M. is ready for anything. The insolence of Carson's answer today has stung him." Lloyd George was also stung because, on the following day, after communicating to William in Welsh that the ministry was preparing for the worst in regard to Ulster, he lamented, "What a sensational tragedy." Actually, Carson did not put a provisional government into effect at Belfast, but because of that fear and the ministry's possible response to it there was a mutiny in Ireland three days after Lloyd George's expression of sorrow.[31]

Sixty officers from a cavalry brigade at Curragh military base in Kildare, west of Dublin, said unequivocally that they would resign their commissions before they would take up arms against Ulster. Their leader, Brigadier General Hubert Gough, from Northern Ireland, was instructed to come to London, where the Secretary of State for War, J. E. B. Seely, confirmed in writing that the ministry had no such policy. Either still unconvinced, or possibly trying to embarrass Liberals since he was supported by the shadow cabinet of the Conservatives, Gough succeeded in getting John French, Chief of the Imperial General Staff, to write down his belief that Seely's confirmation meant force would not be employed by the army to make Northern Ireland submit to home rule. The same day French signed off on the assurance Gough had been given, Lloyd George reported things were heating up and asserted to his brother, "I am all for fighting." That bold affirmation was followed the next day by, "There is a glorious revolt in our party against the Army. . . . But Jack Seeley [*sic*] is a empty headed jackass & he has made a mess of things." On March 28, he was of the opinion that French would survive the debacle, writing simply, "Think French will stay."[32]

French and Seely tendered their resignations, however, and Asquith revoked their written promises, personally assuming French's duties. The ministry now knew its authority in dealing with Ireland was compromised, and the Irish were emboldened to pursue their ends regardless of what London said. What came after only illustrated both. On April 25, a vessel carrying nearly twenty-five thousand guns and almost three million cartridges docked at three different ports in Northern Ireland. The weapons had been purchased in Germany for Ulster Volunteers, something Carson had encouraged. James Craig, Irish Unionist member of the House of Commons and the organizer of the Belfast march in 1911, seemingly acted as a liaison between the smugglers and the shadow cabinet. Transporting of munitions into Ireland violated ministry prohibition, but the government in London did nothing in response because it was unsure whether troops there would obey an order to confiscate the contraband, and it was afraid of what would happen if they did. George Dangerfield speculated the outcome could have been very different if the order had been given, while quoting Birrell's belief that all Irishmen took pride in London's authority being successfully challenged.[33]

In spite of events spiraling downward, Lloyd George did not give up hope. On May 7, he reported to Richard Lloyd that he was "trying to settle Ireland. Believe I have it now in my hands to do so." Eight days later he also informed William, "King sent for me this morning to the Palace. Had an hour with him. He wanted to talk over the Irish situation. He is anxious I should attend the next conference between the leaders. I had a most pleasant interview & a most useful." His brother was not told he had conveyed the only remaining feasible option for Northern Ireland: it could no longer be temporarily excluded. He even recommended an amending bill, supposed to be passed by the lower house to add temporary exclusion to the home rule bill, be changed by the House of Lords to read permanent. As it turned out, Asquith never joined those two bills but sent another amending bill directly to the Lords in June. It was altered to such an extent that it served no purpose. They not only changed temporary to permanent exclusion but also applied it to all nine counties of Northern Ireland, stipulating no time limit to be imposed or referendums required. Three days before they received the separate amending bill, and due to Asquith's strategy opposed by him as well as by other Cabinet members, Lloyd George said permanent exclusion could not be sanctioned. After the Lords made Asquith's amending bill unrecognizable, it was returned to the lower house for an up or down vote. Approval would kill home rule, but rejection would possibly lead to the formation of a provisional government for a nine-county Ulster by Carson, and likely a civil war. So, Asquith decided another leaders' conference from all sides should try to resolve differences. Knowing the king wanted one for some time, and with his approval, Asquith officially notified him of the proposed meeting so he could invite the participants to meet at Buckingham Palace.[34]

A day before Asquith also secured the monarch's approval for the conference to be at the palace, Lloyd George revealed to William that something was about to happen. "Things coming to a point over Ireland," he exclaimed. "We shall settle or fight within next 2 or 3 days." A day later, he elaborated: "In the thick of the Irish crisis. P. M. sent me to see Bonar Law today. Had a very earnest conference with him. He is hopeless of peace. Next move—a Conference. Secret news. Bonar insists & should be on it. Thinks it is the only chance of settlement." In fact, there had been several behind the scenes meetings in late June and early July, yet another effort to find common ground between the various principals. These less-than-official talks were instigated by Alexander Murray and Lord Rothermere, newspaper tycoon and sibling of Lord Northcliffe, the most influential publisher in the United Kingdom. Territory was debated, and Murray, Baron of Elibank, was able to get the Conservatives to accept the permanent exclusion of the four counties first suggested, without south Armagh but with Tyrone and north Fermanagh added. Also, there would only be one plebiscite for all of them. The most debatable of all the counties was Tyrone, and at the subsequent Buckingham Palace conference, Lloyd George suggested it be divided too. Neither Redmond nor Carson, though, was willing to accept what the Liberals and Conservatives were only hesitantly ready to pursue before the conference. Therefore, an official conference was considered the only remaining hope.[35]

When the Buckingham Palace conference convened on July 21, the Speaker of the House of Commons, J. W. Lowther, acted as chairman, but the king started it, admonishing all involved to strive for a kind give-and-take exchange. The other attendees were Asquith and Lloyd George, the latter specifically requested by the Irish Nationalists; Law and Henry Lansdowne, the leader of Conservatives in the House of Lords and a landlord in southern Ireland; Redmond and Dillon for Irish Nationalists; and Carson as well as Craig for Ulster. Asquith and the king also decided on Lloyd George, though Lord Crewe, leader of the Liberals in the upper house and Secretary for India, was considered too. Three days before the conference, Lloyd George had told his brother, "Crewe is to be left out of the Great Conference & I am to be substituted. Redmond, Birrell & *Bonar Law* insisted upon it! The three said the Conference at best was not a hopeful expedient but without me it would be hopeless. Now I hear the king was of the same opinion—so I am on the List." Asquith did not agree with the desire of the monarch to have Balfour accompany Law because he considered Balfour to be the "real wrecker" of previous compromise attempts on the Irish question. Indeed, among numerous other inflammatory comments Balfour had made since stepping down as leader of Conservatives, he said that, in some cases, "it is justifiable for a population to resist the government . . . and there has never been any question that the coercion of Ulster in the sense of compelling Ulster to leave a free environment under which she is happy, and put her under a government which she detests, is one of those cases." He made the remarks in the lower house after the gun-running occurred in April and concluded, "I hold now, and I held 30 years ago that if Home Rule was forced upon Ulster, Ulster would fight and Ulster would be right."[36]

The conference lasted for three days, but no agreement was reached primarily because of two counties neither Irish side could bear to relinquish, Fermanagh, where there were marginally fewer Protestants than Catholics, and Tyrone, where they were roughly equal. Temporary versus permanent exclusion was not formally discussed, but Alvin Jackson notes that nationalists informally indicated the possibility of dropping their objections to limiting exclusion. Talks about territorial boundaries started once again, and both nationalists agreed they could accept Carson's boundary but would have no party to lead. Two days after the conference, yet another gunrunning episode occurred. This one was north of Dublin, and the rifles were for 160,000 Irish Volunteers. One-fourth were reservists from the imperial army, and a third lived in Ulster. These weapons were also German and were purchased in Belgium by Protestants favoring home rule. Most were not new and were far fewer than those acquired by Ulster Volunteers funded by industrialists from Belfast or wealthy Englishmen like Lord Rothschild, who contributed no less than ten thousand pounds. Fifteen-hundred rifles and forty-five thousand cartridges reached the south by July 26. After some rifles had been offloaded, the local police chief alerted his superior, who contacted Birrell's Under-Secretary. In the ensuing confusion, royal troops were dispatched to disarm seven-hundred Irish Volunteers who were picking up the guns. The superior and two leaders of the Volunteers had a heated argument, and while the exchange dragged on, Volunteers quietly left the scene. On returning to barracks, not having accomplished their mission, the royal troops were harassed by a rabble armed with sticks and stones. At one point, soldiers in the rear opened fire, and when shooting stopped four of the mob were dead and thirty more wounded.[37]

Coercion, not used against the north in spite of repeated violations, now had been used in the south, even though it had not been authorized by London. In fact, a little over two years before the bloody incident, Lloyd George had told C. P. Scott, editor of the *Manchester Guardian*, that he believed the southerners ought to have weapons to offset Ulster. Not only did coercion tie the hands of the nationalist leaders considering compromise but also resulted in Asquith's amending bill being postponed by the House of Commons on July 30. The latter, however, was ostensibly because Austria had declared war on Serbia two days earlier. On September 18, the third home rule bill, which had been given its third reading on May 25, finally received the king's assent.

He was supposed to have bestowed it on June 25 but did not because some questions remained unanswered. Once royal approval was granted, Asquith put the law on the statute book without the amending bill, meaning the future of Northern Ireland would remain unsettled. A suspensory bill was added, postponing implementation of home rule for the duration of the First World War, which Great Britain had officially entered on August 4.[38]

5

Easter Rising and Anglo-Irish War,
1914–1922

"God save Ireland—for if he doesn't—
their leaders will damn him."

AMAZINGLY, OLD IRISH RIVALRIES suddenly seemed smaller compared to the larger threat from Germany. Redmond willingly suggested using Irish troops, and Carson assisted with government mobilization. Ninety members of the House of Commons left their duties to serve in the armed forces, but Balfour used their absence to try and prevent Asquith from putting home rule on the statute book. Redmond, who asked that action be taken, was lambasted by Balfour, and Lloyd George told Austen Chamberlain that such rancor "advertised our differences to the enemy." Son of Joseph, Austen Chamberlain was the leading speaker on finances for Conservatives and had tried to solve the controversy over Ireland in late 1913, proposing federalism or devolution throughout the British Isles once again. Catherine B. Shannon goes further than Lloyd George in criticizing Balfour for repeated attempts to bring down the Liberals and prevent home rule, even stating that he "cannot escape responsibility for exacerbating the crisis that the German and Austrian general staffs hoped would diminish Britain's ability to aid France on the outbreak of World War I." The prime minister told Walter Hines Page, America's ambassador to Britain, that Germany would be pleased with rebellion in Northern Ireland because it would be viewed as civil war, and the world would be alarmed. Page sent the information to President Woodrow Wilson. Asquith's Cabinet had learned by way of a letter to Lloyd George from the editor of the *Daily Chronicle* that the Irish in the United States had considerably bigger impact than Germans politically, and if upset by a crisis over home rule would cause more trouble for the United Kingdom's war concerns.[1]

Germany and Austria-Hungary must have been very disappointed when both northern and southern Irishmen volunteered for service in the British military, ultimately fighting side by side, even though H. H. Kitchener, Secretary of State for War since August 5, failed to aid Redmond's efforts to recruit Irish soldiers or grant the request for a distinctive division of them to be created. Ninety-thousand southern Irish Catholics plus a dozen battalions of Ulster Protestants, supplied and clothed with northern money, fought in the war. Just because the Irish cooperated with the government once the war began, however, did not mean they accepted everything it did. In fact, they continued to oppose licensing or taxing of liquor and especially prohibiting its manufacture or sale during the war. Because of liquor's effect on production, Lloyd George successfully limited its access as the war progressed. In May 1915, shortly before becoming Minister of Munitions, he reflected upon some of the heated criticism he was receiving from the Irish on the issue to William. "Irish fighting hard for their liquor," he noted. "God save Ireland—for if he doesn't—their leaders will damn him." Four days later, Frances Stevenson, his secretary and mistress, wrote a more thorough discussion of his view: "He says that if the question of Home Rule ever comes up again—as it might possibly do—he for one will not give the Irish his support. It would mean now, he says, putting Ulster, which is a fairly sober province, under the heel of the rest of Ireland, which has so clearly shown itself to be dominated by the whisky & beer interests." She also recorded what he told Francis Acland, Under Secretary of State for Foreign Affairs, that day: "'My dear fellow,' said he to Mr. Acland this morning, 'I've *done* with Ireland!'"[2]

Lloyd George was deceiving himself if he truly thought he was through with the Irish. A year to the month after he made that statement, following one visit from Redmond and two from Joseph Devlin on the same day, he mused to his brother, "So the Irish—who have been cool ever since my attack on whiskey are getting more friendly." Devlin, the Irish MP representing West Belfast, was recognized leader of the nationalists in the north and had chided the government for being afraid to assert itself more in talks with Ulster Protestants. Five days later, Lloyd George informed William that both Asquith and Law wanted him "to take Ireland with full powers to effect a settlement. Rather interesting that when there is a special difficulty they always think of *me*!" In another two days, he wrote that Asquith and the Cabinet had asked him "to try & settle Ireland—& to govern it. Last proposition I refused—former I felt bound to assent to. So I shall for the next few weeks be immersed in an Irish bog." He did not want his title to change again, having

been Minister of Munitions for only a year, and to govern Ireland would require his assuming Birrell's responsibilities. Birrell had been relieved of duties
on May 1 because of the "special difficulty." After agreeing to the first request,
and with the understanding no one would be appointed Chief Secretary for
Ireland for a while, Lloyd George also told his brother how hard his task
would be. "Deeper & deeper in the Irish bog. Asquith announced my mission
today. Troublesome crew. O'Brien hates Dillon—Dillon hates O'B. &c&c."
He used the term mission more than one time during his years in the Cabinet,
comparing his assignments to a kind of religious evangelism.[3]

The special difficulty was an uprising a month prior and its aftermath. The
Easter Rising in Dublin began April 24, a Monday of holiday weekend, and
lasted the rest of the week. It started with eight-hundred men but grew to as
many as fifteen hundred. The weapons smuggled into the Dublin area almost
two years earlier were now put to use. Others, namely ten thousand captured
Russian rifles, four-million rounds of ammunition, and ten machine guns,
were coming from the Germans but sank on the ship transporting them. Its
captain scuttled it Good Friday, when it was intercepted by the British navy.
Roger Casement, rebellion organizer who had been in Germany since November 1914 and had recruited a handful of Irish POWs to side with it against
Britain, was also captured that day. Royal police arrested him after a German
submarine had dropped him off. The insurgents had hoped for five-thousand
men in Dublin, twice that throughout the south, and a German troop contingent, but those goals never materialized. The general in charge of Ireland was
not even there when hostilities began, and only one-sixth of his troops were
at their stations. The rebel leader was Patrick Pearse, a teacher and member
of the Irish Republican Brotherhood's military committee, a secret organization advocating violence to gain independence. His second-in-command was
James Connolly, labor organizer and leader of a two-hundred-man Irish Citizen Army. Some of the Citizen Army charged Dublin Castle, headquarters
of Britain's government, but after killing the only policeman guarding it and
subduing half a dozen troops in a guard room, moved to buildings across the
street. The Under Secretary was there, but rebels lost their chance to capture
him. He was preparing to imprison the known rebel leaders, after the events of
Good Friday, but did not get authorization from Birrell until it was too late.[4]

Birrell knew of rebellious acts by insurgents since the war began but
hesitated doing more than force some into Britain and prohibit subver-
sive literature. In addition to publishing antiwar media arguing Irishmen
should not help liberate others until they were freed, they protested in the

street and occasionally brandished firearms as they marched. Before Pearse joined the Irish Republican Brotherhood, he had been a member of a group that split with Redmond because of the latter's support of the war effort. Redmond and his followers became known as National Volunteers and numbered nearly 175,000, while the splinter group kept the original name of Irish Volunteers but consisted of only about fourteen thousand, led by Eoin MacNeill. MacNeill had helped establish the Gaelic League in 1893, mainly to promote the Irish language, had been in Northern Ireland's civil service, and taught the early history of Ireland at University College in Dublin. He did not want violence to achieve his goals, unless it was virtually assured of success, but Pearse and Connolly were willing to become martyrs. They chose the post office as the center of operations, taking possession of it with roughly 150 men by overcoming seven guards not armed. From it, they proclaimed a provisional republican government. Others took a judiciary complex, workhouse, factory, mill, bridge, park, and small fort housing munitions. The one guard outside and eleven others inside were easily subdued, but its main weapons cache was not taken because the soldier with the key was enjoying his holiday. Eamon de Valera, professor of mathematics and future president of Ireland, commanded 130 men at the mill. In response, Britain proclaimed martial law and sent nearly twelve thousand troops to counter the insurgency. Two very bloody clashes occurred, outside the judiciary complex and at the bridge.[5]

Casualty totals vary, but the highest recorded is four-hundred and fifty dead, with twenty-six hundred plus wounded. More than half were civilians, and British regulars had greater losses than rebels. Within two weeks, fifteen, including Pearse and Connolly, were shot, but Casement was hanged in August. Both a son of parents who participated and Grigg have claimed that Pearse's brother was shot just because of his sibling ties, but William Pearse was obviously involved as well. Seventy-five others, including Eamon de Valera, were given death sentences later commuted, but MacNeill got life for obstructing recruiting efforts and inciting people. Since it was wartime and because some insurgents were involved with Germans, verdicts were meted out by courts-martial. The arrests and convictions without rhyme or reason, combined with military justice, or injustice, heightened resentment for years. About thirty-five hundred were taken into custody, around half sent to jail or a Welsh camp. Redmond asked Asquith to end executions after day one, but he waited five more to tell the general in charge of Ireland that he would wish for no more killing unless absolutely necessary. By then, nine others had been shot, and apparently it was absolutely necessary to execute four more in the next four days. Dillon advised Redmond to request no executions, and on May 11 spoke to Parliament about the rebels' courage, how they could have been loyal troops for the kingdom, and how they fought better than the regular army. Asquith went to Dublin the next day, staying one week to show there was a civilian government still overseeing Ireland and to see the damage. Firing squads stopped the day he arrived. What he saw was a city center devastated and looted. The post office and other buildings had been destroyed by incendiary artillery shells. People were experiencing no food, gas, banking, mail, or transport service and few open shops.[6]

Redmond and Devlin had visited Lloyd George two days prior to Asquith returning from Ireland. The prime minister had three objectives when he got back: replace Birrell, strengthen Redmond's reputation in the eyes of the Irish nationalists, but stem the growing tide of sentiment against Britain in America, not yet in the war but home to many Irish immigrants. Considering a number of people to take over for Birrell, he decided on Lloyd George, who turned secretaryship down but agreed to add Ireland to his duties. Asquith told Parliament that the Cabinet had approved the arrangement unanimously. It responded with enthusiasm, and when asked if he could pull it off, Lloyd George said, "I am that kind of beggar. I always do think beforehand that I am going to bring things off." He began separate talks with the principals the next day, eating with Carson and Craig, issuing a written announcement that agreement had been reached only two-and-a-half weeks later. Their agreement was the Home Rule Act would be implemented right away and an amending act excluding six counties would be enacted as emergency legislation during wartime. All of Fermanagh and Tyrone would join the original four, no change would occur in the number of Irish representatives during the war, and all except those for Ulster would be recognized as the Irish House of Commons. The agreement would last a year after the war, and if the government had not made permanent plans by then, it would continue as long as necessary. A conference to effect a permanent solution to the Irish question would be convened when the war ended. A day before publishing the agreement, Lloyd George already knew there was opposition in the Cabinet that unanimously chose him to solve the problem.[7]

For just more than a year, the Cabinet had been a coalition consisting of eleven Liberals, nine Conservatives, and a Labour member, but Lloyd George made the mistake of thinking if he persuaded Conservatives to accept his plan, most of their cohorts would follow. He confessed to his brother on June 20, "Irish situation getting hotter and hotter. Unionist members of

Cabinet in revolt—except Bonar Balfour & F. E. Carson fine." F. E. Smith was Churchill's friend and had often acted as a liaison between leaders of the major parties but now served as Solicitor-General. Carson, Attorney General from May to October 1915, was now leader of the opposition. Three days later, Lloyd George informed William, "No news yet from Ireland but I am hopeful although I feel certain there will be a stiff fight with the bishops & priests." His difficult struggle was not with the Catholic clerics but with three other Conservative members of the Cabinet who were opposed to his plan, one of them Lansdowne. They were far less influential than Law or Balfour and their resignations would have little or no impact. Another, Lord Selborne, did resign but was quickly and uneventfully replaced. Selborne, a Liberal Unionist who had joined the Conservatives years earlier, was the President of the Board of Agriculture, and his departure was due to a conference of nationalists in Ulster on the same day Lloyd George predicted "a stiff fight." Led by Devlin, the conference convincingly approved Lloyd George's plan. Four-hundred thousand Catholic northerners were represented, but no more than half of their delegates attended. The day after, a newspaper article revealed that Lloyd George had confirmed to Carson in writing that exclusion would be permanent. Once again, a positive sign was followed by a negative sign, and he was personally responsible for this one. He threatened to resign if his plan was not passed, but as on previous occasions he did not.[8]

Privately, Lloyd George defiantly told his brother it did not matter if the Cabinet did split, insisting, "Irish Crisis still boiling. I mean to get my plans through—whoever goes." These harsh comments were made after two days of Cabinet meetings filled with contention. The other two malcontents, Lansdowne and Walter Long, were threatening to resign too. Lansdowne now held the title of Minister without Portfolio, meaning he could vote in the meetings but had no specific responsibilities. Long served as President of the Local Government Board, another minor office, but had more seniority than any other Conservative. Ironically, the most supportive Conservative Cabinet member was Balfour, the First Lord of the Admiralty since Churchill's dismissal, and he persuaded the remaining Conservatives in the Cabinet to work with Lloyd George to bring about home rule. Ten days later, he, Carson, and Law, Colonial Secretary in the coalition government, tried to get the members of their party to accept Lloyd George's plan as a war necessity, but the majority refused. Balfour discontinued his efforts for the year, but after four days, Lansdowne stated emphatically northern Irish Unionists insisted on nothing short of permanent exclusion.[9]

Lansdowne made his demand in the House of Lords, reaffirming Britain's enforcement of law in Ireland and its support for the general in charge too. Less than two weeks later, he proudly told Selborne that any resolution of the problem in Ireland was mired by internal pressures. The path for another plan to end its troubles had been blocked. Redmond and his followers had now been spurned by a representative of the Cabinet, and Asquith would endanger its survival if he pursued implementation of the Home Rule Act. Indeed, eight days after Lansdowne's intransigent words, the Cabinet voted to do what he said Ulster Unionists wanted, and to not allow the same number of nationalists in Parliament as before. Redmond found out three days later, when Lloyd George, now the Secretary of State for War, told him. He had agreed in writing over two years earlier to accept the idea of exclusion with a plebiscite for three years, and his letter to that effect had been read to the Cabinet by Asquith, who then commended it to the king. All he wanted in return was that nationalist members not go on record in support of the third home rule bill and that no last minute changes be made to it. Since then, Asquith as well as Lloyd George had made more than one such change, and Redmond was humiliated by their broken promises. Five days after, he was left with no choice but to reject the revised plan, the Cabinet ended discussion of it, and Asquith told King George V it had been shelved. The next day, Asquith sent a letter to Redmond, in which he refused to talk about blame but stressed how important it was for a willingness to compromise to continue. He declared on July 31 that attempts to reconcile the Irish had momentarily collapsed and a new Chief Secretary had been selected. He was obviously not giving up on a settlement because a law authorizing it had been passed.[10]

However, Lloyd George became prime minister in December with more authority than he thought. Less than five months after he assumed the office, Frances noted, "I think he himself is amazed at the power that now lies between his hands, and he is certainly losing no time in using this power beneficently. If only he can settle the Irish question! I feel that everything hangs on that." She had reason to be hopeful because he had talked to Carson about conceding on county option, "for the sake of the Empire." He thought America would have entered the war sooner if the Irish crisis had been solved in 1916 and there would have been "many hundreds of thousands of recruits from Australia." Wilson had asked Congress for a war declaration just nineteen days before Stevenson's comments. After a second "long talk with Carson," Lloyd George "joyfully" told her, "I think I am going to settle the Irish question." He also announced he was going to see the nationalists for "the first time since last year." He tried to get them to reconsider the previous year's proposal, but they would not. His power was not great enough to make them do what they did not want to do. He then took the advice of an old friend and retired general, J. C. Smuts, who recommended a convention of only the various Irish factions should be held. Such a convention, even if it failed, would make the Irish crisis less of a distraction from the bigger problem of war. When it did convene in July, the republicans, now led by a group known as Sinn Féin, refused to attend, even though the government released all remaining prisoners from the Easter Rising. An agreement to grant Ireland the same relationship as Canada and Australia was reached, passed by the nationalists along with Southern Unionists, but all Ulster Unionists voted against it because it did not give them the option of excluding themselves from the new dominion.[11]

Consequently, the two most extreme factions either did not attend or rejected the wishes of the majority who did. It was meaningless to continue without both, and when the convention ended a year after his joyful prediction, Lloyd George held all the Irish accountable but especially the nationalists, observing, "They are not satisfied with getting self-determination for themselves, without depriving others of the right of self-determination." Again, he was not powerful enough to enforce his will and made matters worse on April 9, 1918, four days after the convention's end, telling the House of Commons that Ireland would now be included in the conscription of soldiers for the war. He added that a portion of the dominion status recommended by the convention, which he personally did not want, would begin at the same time as the Irish draft, but the former did not lessen the uproar from the latter. He had discussed conscription for Ireland with Law, his new Chancellor of the Exchequer, three months before, stating, "This is the opportunity for Ulster to show that it places Empire above everything. If the little Protestant community in the South, isolated in a turbulent sea of Sinn Feinism and Popery can trust their lives and their property to the majority there," he said, "surely the powerful community of the North might take that risk for the sake of the Empire in danger."[12]

Redmond, who gradually saw his influence dwindle after actively supporting the empire's war, died in March 1918, and the same month Lloyd George told the House of Commons that Ulster Unionists "are as alien in blood, in religious faith, in tradition, in outlook, as alien to the rest of Ireland in this respect as the inhabitants of Fife or Aberdeen." Nonetheless, he wanted a solitary legislature for the entire island, especially while the war continued, and he insisted that London control law enforcement as well as trade. Only one week after Lloyd George announced his plan for an Irish draft, it passed the House of Commons, but before the roll was taken, Dillon marched out of the legislature with his followers, casting his lot with Sinn Féin and the Catholic hierarchy in Ireland. It may have looked like Home Rule was going to become "Rome Rule" in the south, but the former was actually being eclipsed by this much more separatist movement. Ironically, after vehemently resisting it for decades, the north would ultimately get home rule to an extent through partition from the south. Sinn Féin, which means "We Ourselves," was founded in 1907 by Arthur Griffith, who was not in favor of a republic, and his organization did not officially participate in the Easter Rising. Afterward, however, Sinn Féin joined the Irish Volunteers and capitalized on the unrest caused by the executions that followed the rising. Its greatest growth occurred after joint campaigns against conscription, with Dillon and the Roman Catholic bishops, which made it look more legitimate.[13]

Two days after Dillon walked out of Parliament, he and de Valera held a Dublin meeting of other Irish Party members, Sinn Féin, bishops, and trade union representatives. They pledged to resist conscription and called a twenty-four-hour strike in five days. Except in Belfast, public transport, stores, industries, presses, and pubs discontinued service. Because of the increasingly radical anti-conscription demonstrations and a concern for Southern Unionists, Lloyd George sent French to assess the situation and reestablish order. French, commander of home forces in 1916, underestimated the extent of resistance and recommended force to put down what he thought was a vocal minority appearing to exercise leadership. He was made Lord Lieutenant in May, and by month's end nearly all Sinn Féin leaders were imprisoned, accused of conspiring with Germans against Britain. Most of the charges were based on connections with Germans during the rising, just used as excuses to incarcerate the troublemakers. In June, the sixth member of Sinn Féin in sixteen months was elected to Parliament, one of them from prison. None chose to be seated, but the growing influence of the movement was obvious to all. Eight months earlier, de Valera had been unanimously elected president of the organization and twice publicly proclaimed Sinn Féin was the political arm of the movement, while the Irish Volunteers were the military branch of it. Griffith served as vice-president. De Valera was elected president of the volunteers also, but he ended his membership with the less and less significant Irish Republican Brotherhood. Because French thought the republicans were only a loud few with no real power, he called for one more voluntary recruitment to raise an army of fifty-thousand men by the first of October. All talk of conscription ended a little over a month later due to the armistice, no action having been taken.[14]

On December 14, 1918, the United Kingdom held its first general election for eight years, and Sinn Féin got 48 percent of Ireland's votes. More importantly, republicans captured 73 of 105 seats in Parliament but did not claim them. Dillon's Irish Party received 23 percent of the electorate but only seven seats, including one occupied by a home rule member living in Liverpool. Dillon even lost his seat to de Valera, after serving three decades. Irish Unionists won 29 percent of ballots cast, giving them twenty-five seats. In spite of challenging all but two of the seats, Sinn Féin did not win a majority of the more than one million votes registered, representing an average turnout of 73 percent of eligible voters. Forty-eight Sinn Féin candidates were actually in jail when polls were open, including de Valera whose name was submitted for four different constituencies. Insisting on Ulster's rights and security was just one issue Lloyd George had to stand firm for to maintain support from Irish Unionists and Conservatives. Sinn Féin and the Irish Party drafted policy statements two months before the election, and with 70 percent of the representatives chosen, the former proceeded to implement its manifesto. The Irish Party had gone beyond home rule to home rule along with dominion status, but Sinn Féin stressed a separate republic with its own legislature to govern the island. After the armistice was signed and prior to the election, though, the coalition government issued its own manifesto, ruling out two things: the departure of Ireland from the empire and the coercion of Ulster under a Dublin parliament. Ronan Fanning argues that the papers of Lloyd George indicate nothing in the way of concern about the electoral outcome in Ireland or how quickly the policies of Sinn Féin were put into practice.[15]

For the next year, no new agenda for Ireland was put forward by Lloyd George's government, but Sinn Féin also wasted no time taking the initiative for independence. On January 7, 1919, just eleven days before the Paris Peace Conference began, Sinn Féin delegates who were not in prison or had otherwise been unable to vote met to create an assembly for all of Ireland, which they named Dáil Eireann. A constitutional committee was commissioned, and anyone elected was invited to attend the first meeting of the assembly two weeks later. Only Sinn Féin members accepted the invitation, but almost two-thirds of their delegates were absent. Thirty-four names were recorded as imprisoned by the foreign enemy, Britain. The provisional constitution was read, followed by a declaration of independence from the kingdom. The declaration proclaimed that the Irish Republic began on Easter Monday, 1916, Dáil

Eireann as National Assembly was ratifying it, and it would be implemented by whatever means necessary. An appeal was also sent to nations attending the Paris Peace Conference, to recognize an independent Ireland and to deal with it on an equal basis with England. A domestic program presented referenced Patrick Pearse as the first president and emphasized total economic control by the republic, including all exports or imports. A five-man government was established, including Eoin MacNeill and Michael Collins but headed by Cathal Brugha, a hero of the Easter uprising who was given the title of Priomh-Aire or first minister.[16]

Within two months of the National Assembly's first meeting, de Valera had escaped from prison with the help of Collins, and the others incarcerated the previous year were released by the coalition government. As a result, on April 1, almost twice as many attended its second meeting and elected de Valera to replace Brugha. Brugha was now defense minister and Collins was finance minister, but Collins was also president of the Irish Republican Brotherhood. Working with the splinter Irish Volunteers, he began a guerrilla war so serious that by the end of the summer the coalition government had outlawed Dail Eireann, which went underground. Chief Secretary, Ian Macpherson, had taken the same action inside Ireland four months earlier and had labeled Sinn Féin illegal. A month later, a Cabinet committee was commissioned to determine a policy for Ireland that was consistent with a federal framework for all the United Kingdom, which Lloyd George and Long, chairman of the committee, still preferred. The Home Rule Act was to take effect a year after all the peace treaties were signed but required county option in the north. Implementation would cause a crisis with Ulster, which wanted guaranteed exclusion, but rescinding it would cause more problems in the south by removing a law keeping it in the United Kingdom. Long's committee made changes to protect the six counties and reassert the realm's priorities for the south. It recommended home rule parliaments for both north and south too. A Council of Ireland, with equal representation for both, would try to bring about unity and be recognized as Ireland's legislature if both parliaments agreed. The coalition government would retain certain powers, particularly over defense and military bases. If agreement was reached on one legislature, everything else would be turned over to it as long as Ireland remained at least a dominion.[17]

Craig was willing to have a home rule parliament in Belfast, as long as Ulster was limited to the six counties Protestants could effectively control. He requested a boundary commission to clearly define the demarcation line and suggested that the council be a House of Lords, with power to veto certain types of laws. Home rule parliaments were included, and the north was restricted to Ulster, but other opinions Craig offered were not added to a bill recommended by the committee. On December 22, 1919, Lloyd George introduced the Government of Ireland Act, which passed a year to the month later. He said that any attempt by the south to secede would be treated like the civil war in America, hoping for its approval of his government's handling of Ireland. He also made a plea for Ireland and Britain to finally bury the hatchet, reasoning from his many years of working with both that "There is a path of fatality which pursues the relations between the two countries and make them eternally at cross purposes. Sometimes Ireland demands too much; sometimes when Ireland is reasonable England offers too little; sometimes when Ireland is unfriendly England is sulky; sometimes when England has been friendly, Ireland has been angry; and," as he intuitively observed, "sometimes when both Britain and Ireland seem to be approaching towards friendship, some untoward incident sweeps them apart and the quarrel begins again. So the fitting time has never been and never will be. But it is always the right time to do the right thing; and Britain can afford now more than ever, and better than ever, to take the initiative." Prophetically, above his bed at the prime minister's official residence in London, "There is a path which no fowl knoweth and which the eye of the vulture hath not seen" (Job 28:7, KJV), was embroidered with silk.[18]

Wilson's government had pressured Lloyd George to solve the southern issues peacefully. Between the introduction and passage of the law, the Irish Republican Army, the official name of the guerrillas, killed 230 troops as well as constables. Another 369 were wounded. Beginning in March 1920, auxiliary forces composed of unemployed veterans known as the Black and Tans were sent to reinforce British firepower, but they were at least as brutal as the guerrillas. At the end of the year, there were about ten thousand constables and twelve hundred auxiliaries. By March 1921, there were roughly forty-thousand soldiers in Ireland, but their general in charge wanted sixty thousand more. The month the Black and Tans began arriving, constables killed Cork's mayor in retaliation for fallen comrades. Another act of counterterrorism by constables, and especially the auxiliaries, was the indiscriminate killing of a dozen Dubliners at a sporting event after the Irish Republican Army murdered eleven intelligence officers there. Sixty more were wounded, and November 21 became known as Bloody Sunday.[19]

Earlier that same month, Lloyd George called the guerrillas "a small nest of assassins" and "a murder gang." Their number was considerably smaller than those they opposed, no more than fifteen thousand total and only three to five thousand at any one time, but they were protected by a majority of the population, particularly in rural areas. Their cumulative casualties over the two-and-a-half years of the war numbered seven-hundred and fifty-two killed as well as eight-hundred and sixty-six injured. Three months before the murders of intelligence officers, all at home or in hotel rooms, two with their wives, the coalition government had passed the Restoration of Order in Ireland Act, dispensing with habeas corpus writs and permitting courts-martial without benefit of defense attorneys unless it was a capital case. None was found guilty of murder before the law was enacted, but two dozen were executed between then and the end of 1921. Four months after it passed, Lloyd George boasted that his government had "murder by the throat." Clearly, he did not understand how widespread Sinn Féin's support was or the ability of its military arm to continue war, but he knew they might attempt to assassinate him. He had told his wife not to worry about herself and their youngest child, writing, "There has never been a case of assassination of wives & daughters. Of course, they will try to kill me & may succeed. I must do my duty." Just over a week later, he reported, "Ireland is a hell's broth. . . . I dare say there is a good deal of damnable business on both sides. This is inevitable & may end in forcing the moderate men on both sides to seek a settlement."[20]

It is not coincidental that the Government of Ireland Act passed the month Lloyd George had boasted, and it called for parliamentary elections the next May. The south would be designated a colony unless it took electing a parliament seriously and less than half the delegates attended its first session. Guerrilla attacks increased from three to five hundred a week that May, and over the next two months, British casualties amounted to 25 percent of their losses in the war of independence, or Anglo-Irish War. Elections were held in the north and the south, resulting in forty of fifty-two seats in the north going to Irish Unionists, 128 in the south going to Sinn Féin, with four others won by Southern Unionists. No members of Sinn Féin showed up for the first legislative session, so the parliament was disbanded and the south became an imperial colony. The northern parliament was convened by the king in June, and James Craig became its first prime minister. Craig had met with de Valera in Dublin the month before to see if they could find common ground, endangering his own life by traveling to the southern capital, but no agreement was reached. The Cabinet had begun talking in May about a truce, and before the king opened the legislature in Belfast, Smuts advised him to be conciliatory toward the south. Smuts wanted dominion status mentioned, but after consulting Lloyd George, who opposed it for the south and a truce, backed off. When the king got home, he wanted to capitalize on a positive response to his speech, and a day later the Cabinet proposed sending de Valera a letter, inviting him to a conference. The north was also invited, and in Dublin, Smuts urged de Valera to accept. He did and did not definitively rule out dominion status. The way was cleared for two-party talks when the north rejected its invitation, and the Cabinet offered a truce to start on July 11, 1921.[21]

Lloyd George then acted as if he had been given marching orders and met with de Valera three days later. Stevenson noted the two met alone for almost three hours, Lloyd George pacing the floors beforehand. To impress de Valera to reconsider crown allegiance, he put a map of the British Empire up, saying, "The B.E. is a sisterhood of nations—the greatest in the world. Look at this table: There sits Africa—English & Boer; there sits Canada—French, Scotch & English; there sits Australia," he continued, "representing many races—even Maoris; there sits India; here sit the representatives of England, Scotland & Wales; all we ask you to do is to take your place in this sisterhood of free nations. It is an invitation, Mr. De Valera: we invite you here." De Valera did appear somewhat persuaded but balked "as if frightened and timid." At that point, the Welshman predicted darker days ahead if his invitation was refused, which de Valera interpreted as a threat. He also insisted that the south do three things: officially recognize the northern legislature, put no taxes on products from the realm, and allow military bases for the imperial navy and air force. Other dominion colonies were permitted to tax kingdom goods, so this was even more restrictive. Again, de Valera did not reject limited dominion out of hand when he balked but made a counter offer the next month, stating he wanted a treaty of association with the kingdom and its colonies, would recognize the king as over the commonwealth but not Ireland, but would not take an oath to him. Lloyd George replied, emphasizing there had to be allegiance. He wrote Maggie on August 13, predicting de Valera would refuse: "These Irishmen are once more most troublesome."[22]

Lloyd George then summoned the Cabinet to a meeting in Inverness, Scotland, where he was vacationing. At the town hall, the only place a Cabinet ever convened other than in London, he contended allegiance to the crown must be insisted upon but was outvoted. Again acting like he was taking instructions from the coalition, he wrote de Valera, extending the offer for further discussions in order to determine the most effective way to bring Ireland's nationalistic goals and its relationship to the remaining realm in line. The response he actually sent to the southern Irish president contained what the

Cabinet had overruled, and Lloyd George told Maggie, "Threw all the Cabinet over on De Valera & sent my own reply which they had rejected." He went on to tell her de Valera accepted. However, the Irishman decided not to attend additional talks himself but sent Griffith, Collins, and three others, along with a secretary, requesting that Dail Eireann give them full power to negotiate a settlement independently. The second elected assembly, which actually met in August, elected de Valera president and honored his wishes. It was also understood there would be no signing of a treaty until it was voted on by Dail Eireann. Before the second one had assembled, the coalition government had set all remaining incarcerated members of it free.[23]

The new talks began October 11, and the Irish were told they should accept a designation of free state, Saorstatt, instead of republic as well as acknowledge the king's supremacy over the commonwealth with which they were willing to be happily associated externally. They were also willing to grant the north considerable autonomy, if it submitted to Dublin's oversight instead of London. They staunchly refused to swear allegiance to the king, and Craig unequivocally refused to put Ulster under the southern legislature. To strengthen his hand in negotiating with Griffith's committee, Lloyd George decided to go to Parliament, explain his position on allegiance, and put it to a vote of confidence. The result on October 31 was a resounding endorsement, 439 to 43 in his favor. Griffith had agreed to write a letter indicating that his group would be reasonable in the matter, but his cohorts amended it twice before accepting on November 4. They intended for it to stress external association and Ireland's fundamental oneness, but it also allowed for the British navy to use southern ports and the south's willing participation with those still in the Commonwealth of Nations.[24]

Lloyd George interpreted the letter's words to be tantamount to allegiance, informing the Cabinet six days later that the Irish delegation was no longer flying its standard of republicanism but imperialism. In exchange for these real and imagined concessions, he agreed to push for an all-Ireland parliament to be elected by the island's entire population. Because of their compromises, he also decided not to use force against them, telling Lord Riddell, owner and editor of a Sunday paper that had more than two million subscribers, "I have made up my mind that I will not coerce Southern Ireland. I may lose everything but I shall know I have saved my soul anyway." An idea of a legislature for all of Ireland held no appeal for Craig, now wanting the north to get dominion status. Therefore, Lloyd George went to another plan based on what Craig himself had proposed earlier, a boundary commission. Griffith also accepted creation of a commission to ascertain the precise boundary be-tween north and south but in the process actually recognized the partition of Ireland. Lloyd George persuaded Collins that a boundary commission would so limit Ulster that it would have to join the south to survive economically.[25]

Progress was being made in mid-November, and Lloyd George spoke very respectfully to Stevenson about the southern Irish representatives. She quoted him saying they "have behaved splendidly all through this fight," and that supporting him "whole-heartedly & loyally, they have given nothing away to the press, & have shown great courage in the face of difficulty and even danger, for they have plenty of extremists on their side." By November 23, however, Stevenson recorded that talks were "not going too well" because the Irish "have got scared." One day prior, they had back-pedaled on almost all their concessions, but Lloyd George had told them he would stop negotiating if they reneged. The next day he wrote his wife, stating, "The Irish negotiations have taken a turn for the worse—seriously. This time it is the Sinn Feiners. Last week it was the Ulsterites. They are both the sons of Belial."[26]

One more day passed, and three of the Irishmen, including Griffith and Collins, returned home, only to come back to England within days completely opposed to an oath of allegiance. A week after, the whole delegation went to Dublin to confer with de Valera's Cabinet. Delegates, including the secretary, were divided evenly, but de Valera sent them to London two days later with the same refusal to take an oath. On that day, December 4, Lloyd George told them that their refusal could not be permitted and would mean war. Their response essentially amounted to accepting that fate. Individual discussions then began with Griffith and Collins, Griffith agreeing to dominion status if Craig assented to the idea of one Ireland, no matter how vaguely, and Collins willing to consider the boundary commission again. Mysteriously, however, the wording of guidelines for the proposed boundary commission had evolved at some point from insisting any future changes should coincide to the ex-tent feasible with the public's desires, to accepting them as long as they geo-graphically and economically suit existing circumstances. Griffith, Collins, and the third delegate who had returned to Dublin ten days earlier, met the following afternoon with Lloyd George, Churchill, F. E. Smith, and Austen Chamberlain. Before going further, Griffith and Collins waited for Craig's response to a new proposal he had received from Lloyd George after his initial rejection of an all-Ireland parliament. It would let Ulster join the legislature, along with the option to depart twelve months after a treaty was ratified.[27]

Lloyd George argued there was no point in waiting to sign a treaty as Craig's decision made no difference. If Ulster refused to join an all-Ireland parliament, the boundary commission would take effect. Griffith was then reminded of his earlier agreement to accept the commission and indicated his willingness to proceed. Once he conceded, Lloyd George agreed to let southern Ireland have complete control of its finances. If it remained separate, Ulster would have to keep paying the kingdom taxes. When none of the other Irishmen said they would sign a treaty, Lloyd George threatened war again "in three days." Geoffrey Shakespeare, one of his secretaries, somewhat nervously delivered the threat to Dublin, writing in his memoirs, "The ultimatum conjured up before their eyes further years of bloodshed and reprisals on a vaster scale. . . . Lloyd George had reached the limit of his patience. He threatened war, he looked war, and he intended war, unless they signed."[28]

At nine that night, a copy of a treaty was taken to the delegates at their premises, and after minor changes were made, a final draft was signed by three of them in the early morning hours of December 6. The other two official delegates signed later in the day, and the Irish Free State was born. Lloyd George had agreed to inform Craig of the outcome by then, who rejected any official link with the south. Two days later, the southern Irish Cabinet passed the treaty by a vote of four to three, with de Valera, Brugha, and one other opposed; on December 16, Parliament followed suit. When the treaty was voted on by Dail Eireann a month later, it was approved by sixty-four to fifty-seven, after which de Valera resigned. A motion was made to reelect him, but he lost by two votes and led his supporters out. Griffith was then elected president by representatives still present, but London did not recognize him or the smaller legislature. The coalition government sanctioned a provisional administration under Collins, which was chosen by a reassembled home rule parliament with more than four members attending. Collins and Griffith, though, cooperated in forming the new state. They also attempted to get de Valera to work with them, but a civil war ensued in June 1922, following a split in the general election for the legislature of the new state. The main campaign issue was the treaty. Those in favor won by almost five to one, twenty-three more seats than their opponents. The treaty had been ratified by Parliament on March 31 in the Irish Free State (Agreement) Act but did not take effect until the state constitution received the king's proclamation on December 6, exactly six years after Lloyd George was chosen prime minister.[29]

6

Land and Pensions,
1880–1910

"Feudalism is the enemy."

SHORTLY AFTER TURNING seventeen, Lloyd George started addressing a second socioeconomic cause that became a priority of his political career: land reform. In his 1880 diary, he referred to the reelection of a Liberal MP for Carnarvon Boroughs as both "a great blow to landlord terrorism &—as great triumph for the ballot." Gladstone was also chosen to be prime minister again because his party won the general election too. Following his first victory in 1868, many tenants who voted for Liberals were evicted by their Conservative landlords, a reaction that was largely responsible for his passage of a secret ballot four years later. Lloyd George was five when those evictions occurred but referenced the ones in his village while leading a tour of it for Charles and Lucy Masterman in August 1911. In her diary, she recorded his comments as they passed the grave of John Parry, steward of the largest landlord in the area: "'He was a terror,' George remarked. 'My word! He was a terror. He was the man of the 68 evictions.'" He went on to say that some evicted children were his classmates, and returning to Parry, he judged, "'Oh, he is learning now what he did then. My word! We ran in the woods if we saw him coming.'"[1]

On February 2, 1883, after three articles plus a debate on Irish land issues the three years prior, Lloyd George bought Henry George's *Progress and Poverty* and "read a few pages" of it that day. It was January 14 of the next year before he cited the book again, writing he disagreed with its "scheme—appropriation of the rent so nothing but aimless plunder." He agreed "the great object is to get the control of the *land itself* into the hands of those whose interests are so vitally affected by it," but also reasoned, "it strikes me that almost every argument applicable to such confiscation is also an argument for state appropriation of personal property. My own idea is the devolution to the State of deceased owners' properties so that all alike may have an equal chance of starting life." What the American socioeconomic philosopher proposed was a single tax on the value of land to replace all other taxes: "This is the secret which would transform the little village into the great city. With all the burdens removed which now oppress industry and hamper exchange, the production of wealth would go on with a rapidity now undreamed of. This, in its turn, would lead to an increase in the value of land, a new surplus which society might take for general purposes." George's reader was not opposed to all land taxes because fifteen days after starting the book, he helped a friend "to post notices of poor rate," a parish land tax administered by the Local Government Board in England and Wales to provide for the needs of total indigents. However, a week later, he vehemently denounced unjust landlords. After justifying the murder of "wretches" as "an act of political justice," he included "an evicting landlord," rationalizing that one in that position "would otherwise escape punishment & as an act of political expediency it served to call attention to the corrupt & atrocious social system."[2]

By August 1885, Lloyd George was speaking on behalf of Liberal candidates running for a general election to begin three months later. On November 19, the week before voting began, he spoke on leasehold at a Liberal meeting in Talysarn because the lowest paid agricultural workers could now vote following passage of the Third Reform Act in 1884 by Gladstone's government. After the election, twenty-five of thirty-four Welsh parliamentary seats had representatives other than landlords, a downward trend since 1880, when six lost. Gladstone's third ministry did not begin until February of 1886, but the previous month Lloyd George recorded hearing that Davitt was going to address a meeting in Blaenau Ffestiniog. On February 12, Davitt spoke to a crowd of working men about Irish home rule in a venue capable of holding fifteen-hundred people, but because land leagues were also already being established in Wales, he was asked to give his advice on how to organize the various efforts that were springing up individually throughout the principality.[3]

Two Welsh shires had leagues, a third was planning for one, the city of Aberystwyth was proposing a political union to that same end for two more, and tenants in one district of a sixth were withholding rents they considered exorbitant as well as demanding that they be lowered. The meeting with Davitt was chaired by Michael Jones, the leading advocate for Welsh land reform, and he asked Lloyd George, who had earlier recommended the creation of a league in Criccieth, to speak after Davitt. Because there were two Michaels on the stage, Lloyd George then decided to compare them to the one in the Bible, stating the archangel "being single-handed, was unable to dispose of Old Nick" (Jude 9, KJV), but "he trusted" these "would be able to bring the cause of the farmers and the working man to a successful issue." Defining the land league as broadly as possible, he called on all male laborers to unite against landlords who were flourishing, "feeding their game with food that ought to go to the people," whereas the former were in misery. The next day, he wrote that his speech had "gone like wildfire–going to make me M.P.," and Jones was for him becoming one.[4]

Lloyd George used another scripture in regard to owners of land wasting its bounty on the wild animals while human beings were going hungry, quoting "the bread of the children is given to the dogs" (Matthew 15:26, KJV). In his comments, he also targeted the Anglican clergy, who sided with landowners, because tenants had to pay tithes to support Anglican schools. Drawing an analogy from the parable of the Good Samaritan (Luke 10:25–37, KJV), he said, "The farmers of Wales had fallen among thieves, but the Welsh priests were a great deal worse than the priest referred to in the parable. The priest in the parable merely passed by without taking notice of the man, but the Welsh priests had joined the robbers." Gladstone had begun a third ministry eleven days before Davitt's meeting, but sixteen days earlier, Lloyd George had noted what brought Lord Salisbury's first government down.[5]

Recording he was rejoicing over the defeat of the Conservatives, Lloyd George attributed it to "a Gladstone-Chamberlain combination" in defense of an allotments proposal introduced by Jesse Collings, which would have provided three acres and a cow to dispossessed rural laborers for a very reasonable amount of rent. "May the rent develop," he continued, "It will be like the famous Waverley pen 'a boon & a blessing to men.'" Collings was born into a family of farm laborers, formed the Rural Labourer's League, and was most responsible for the part of Joseph Chamberlain's 1885 "Radical Programme" stressing allotments and smallholdings of three acres for agrarian workers, one arable but two for pasture. Allotments would make them renters while smallholdings would turn them into proprietors. A day after Salisbury lost the vote on the issue of allotments, Lloyd George promoted participation in a conference to establish one Welsh land league and was told by John Hugh Davies "farmers require but a start to join it." He then "tried to induce him to get delegates from his district." At a Liberal Committee meeting the next day, he proposed sending delegates, it carried unanimously, and being chosen one of two, he wrote: "I was surprised at the alacrity with which it was passed. I had anticipated some opposition."[6]

On the first of February, Lloyd George had a talk with John Bryn Roberts, the recently elected Liberal member to the House of Commons for a new South Carnarvonshire constituency, Eifion, a district that included Criccieth. Roberts was staying aloof from the proposed land league because of his belief that it would fail from a lack of farmer support. "My own belief is," Lloyd George recorded, "& I told him so—that the farmers would join provided the leaders took the movement in earnest." He and Roberts differed on certain political actions, but they were both opposed to evicting tenants who voted for Liberals and reserving land for wild game at the expense of farmers. The conference finally convened in Blaenau Ffestiniog several weeks following Davitt's visit there, and on March 20, Lloyd George referenced winning a legal decision for Richard Hughes, as a "case which will do me a great amount of good amongst the farmers."[7]

Gladstone fell from power four months later in an attempt to get Irish home rule enacted. After another month, a tithe war began in Wales, preoccupying the land movement on one aspect of reform. It was officially abandoned by the end of the following year in favor of a Welsh Land, Commercial, and Labour League because only one of the Welsh parliamentarians still supported it, Thomas Edward Ellis. Ellis had been largely responsible for the creation of a farmer's league in Merionethshire, but Thomas Gee, publisher of *Baner ac Amserau Cymru*, the influential North Wales newspaper that motivated the formation of an anti-tithe league, established and chaired the new organization. One of Gee's sons forwarded a preliminary version of the constitution for his father's new league to Lloyd George, who suggested in addition to farmers it include agricultural laborers, urban leaseholders, miners, and quarrymen. Lloyd George also alluded to an allotments compensation act that Salisbury's second ministry passed in 1887, labeling it "a sham and a delusion" that "falls far short of Chamberlain's scheme which was a really great idea." He had added city renters because "Conservatives seem to have a stronger hold upon the town than the counties."[8]

Lloyd George concluded his letter by strongly recommending success for the new league depended on its being for all of Wales so farmers would not be alone in their battle. Only three months later, he noted what "a very sensible" friend said "on agrarian questions. Says farmers are gradually opening

for a revolt—gettg desperate seeing they haven't much to risk." Indeed, clashes
between farmers and those who auctioned off their stock at the bidding of
the clergy to pay for tithes occurred regularly into 1889 as well as sporadically
until 1896. In 1890, however, Salisbury's government introduced the Tithe
(Rent-Charge Recovery) Bill, which passed in 1891 and eased tensions by making landlords, not tenants, pay the tithes. A year later, Gladstone was back in
power for his fourth and final term, but he put Irish home rule first on his
agenda again. He agreed to put disestablishment of Anglicanism in Wales
second, but when its progress lagged, he reluctantly formed a royal commission on Welsh land in 1893. Certain Welsh party members, including Lloyd
George and Tom Ellis, the Second Whip, had asked for it, claiming landlords
in Wales were more oppressive than English ones.[9]

Though Gladstone got the House of Commons to pass a home rule bill, he
resigned when the House of Lords vetoed it and handed the party's baton to
Lord Rosebery in 1894. Rosebery served from March of that year until June
of the next and is credited with what Chancellor of the Exchequer William
Harcourt achieved in the budget of 1894. It assessed duties on inherited land
the way property exchanges of all sorts were, instead of the smaller amount
required according to the terms of the previous duty on succession. The royal
commission lasted throughout 1896, and Lloyd George's brother gathered information from South Carnarvonshire for its findings, which were recorded
in seven large volumes. His report included testimony concerning a preacher
and his family who were evicted from a farm of Hugh Ellis-Nanney one day
after voting for a Liberal in 1868. When the commission's work was published,
the Conservatives were back in power for a decade with Salisbury's third ministry and that of his nephew, Arthur James Balfour.[10]

In a Friday night letter to Richard Lloyd in 1896, Lloyd George expressed
one particular grievance with the commission he intended to address in Parliament. "I am waiting my turn to bring on the question of intimidating Welsh
witnesses on the Land Commission," he specified. "I fear it cannot come on
tonight. If it doesn't then I must keep them until the small hours of the morning on Thursday about it—because bring it on I will." As it turned out, he got
to introduce the subject at 2:30 on Tuesday morning, and the discussion lasted
two hours. He claimed that "about a dozen cases" had been reported, naming
three tenants and an unnamed fourth who were evicted, their rents going up
because of their testimony. Relating facts on three more anonymous ones, he
included a widow and asserted that forty others "who offered to give evidence

were afraid to come forward" because of what had happened to those who did. He then charged that the Public Prosecutor should have protected the farmers and asked that funds provided for the Home Office be accordingly reduced by £500.[11]

The Home Secretary, Sir Matthew White Ridley, responded that his Liberal predecessor, H. H. Asquith, had already dealt with those cases. However, he also stated he had been asked to investigate allegations of intimidation and had consulted with both the Treasury Solicitor as well as the Attorney General. They concluded that no formal accusations could be brought against the landlords involved. The next month, Lloyd George attacked the Agricultural Land Rating Bill, introduced by Henry Chaplin, President of the Local Government Board. Chaplin had been made chairman of the royal commission Gladstone established to offer suggestions on coping with the ongoing agrarian depression, but because he was a Conservative, he delayed publishing any findings until after the Liberals fell from power. Now, under Salisbury, the resulting bill proposed to decrease rates on cultivated land by 50 percent. Liberals opposed it, nonetheless, because it would help landowners and increase taxes. Taxes would have to go up because the national treasury had to make up the difference for poor relief. The reduction in rates was to last half a dozen years.[12]

More than anyone else, Lloyd George forestalled the passage of the bill for three months, and a speech on its second reading brought him considerably more recognition. That night, he exulted to William that he had, "scored the greatest hit of my life. Immense success. House in a ferment." On another especially contentious night three weeks later, as he continued the fight on the bill in committee, he informed Richard Lloyd, "I have just been doing a little bit of obstruction which ought to satisfy you." After mentioning that he and John Herbert Lewis had proposed amendment after amendment for two-and-a-half hours, he elaborated, "I put 15 amendments tonight, so you will perceive that as usual your rowing has done some good. For all that I must beg of you to be reasonable. I must not throw my reputation away." He ended the letter by noting that John Clifford was with him and that he "was delighted with the business." Clifford became the best-known Baptist preacher in England after Charles Spurgeon died, and he romanticized rural life. He preached for Paddington's Westbourne Park chapel, where his sermons extolled the virtues of the countryside. "The landscape of the farm is full of Divine feeling," he proclaimed, "and rich in suggestions that inspire calm and quicken industry. It throbs with the tender heart of God. It is alive." He served as the president of the Christian Socialist League also, from its inception in 1894 until 1898, and then led the Christian Socialist Brotherhood which superseded it.[13]

Lloyd George, Lewis, and half a dozen others were suspended early the next morning for refusing to end discussion on the bill and leave their seats to join their party for a vote on one of its clauses. Instead of the suspension causing his reputation to be overthrown, however, he was ultimately courted by Harcourt, now the Liberal leader, and other Liberal principals. Harcourt specifically asked him to speak when the bill came up for its third reading on July 1. The next day, both Lloyd George and the newspapers were singing his praises. He shared with his brother that *The Standard* had hailed him as "the acknowledged leader of the obstructives," and *Westminster Gazette* acclaimed, "It is doubtful if a private member has ever done greater service to his Party in Parliament." Opposing the bill was tricky for Liberals, as it resulted from a commission Gladstone authorized and because it would presumably benefit tenant farmers.[14]

Lloyd George characterized the bill as a boon to landlords, attacking Chaplin and other members of Salisbury's Cabinet. He figured that the rate decrease would save the former £700 annually and the latter collectively £2.25 million. Referring to the £1.5 million the treasury was going to have to pay to supplement local rates, he also contrasted the government's willingness "to relieve the landlord who had had to dispense with a few luxuries" such as his carriage, half of his six gamekeepers, and "one or two of his men in buttons" with an unwillingness to "vote a single crumb for the industrious and honest" workers who were "starving at the present time." In his biography of Lloyd George, Ian Packer, noted historian of the land issue in England, concluded that he was rewarded by the Liberal leadership for shaming Conservatives with statistics. After the bill finally passed, a Conservative in the House of Commons acknowledged the validity of Lloyd George's castigation. Thomas Usborne of Chelmsford said nobody had refused to admit the bill relieved landlords instead of tenants and he wished nobody would. Of Lloyd George's debates, biographer Bentley Gilbert asserted that they "gave him his first opportunity in the House of Commons to enunciate his beliefs about the nature of property and wealth, which were the nearest he ever came to a social philosophy." The first part is undoubtedly true, but he had developed his world view from his mid-teens through early twenties, and it remained consistent as a socioeconomic philosophy for numerous political issues during his career, rooted in his religious convictions.[15]

On land reform, Lloyd George distinguished two kinds of property in terms of rates that the bill would assess equally: one, personalty, "was the creation of the industry of its owner," he said, but the other, land, "was not so." It "had not been improved materially by the owners of the soil," but since poor relief started coming from the local rates "the value of land had enormously increased. That was owing to nothing done by the owners or occupiers of the land, because the land was no more productive now." Instead of reducing rates on land by half, lower rents 50 percent because they were twenty-five shillings per acre as opposed to three shillings two pence for rates. Testimony at the commission hearings had revealed that those who farmed land and were responsible for the improving of it "were making no profit." They were even "paying their rents out of capital" and applied "the wages of their farm servants" to them. In spite of that, landlords were not lowering rents until their lands were vacated, were taking "their land in hand themselves because they did not wish to lower their rents," and were still asking for relief, supposedly "for the distressed farmer. It was the old professional beggar's trick," Lloyd George charged, "they pretended to beg for others, and the moment the charitable person's back was turned the stalwart ruffians spent the money in the nearest public-house. The taxpayers of this country ought to put an end to this shameful practice." Landowners were leeches, wanting not only the land but also "the capital value" of it by "seeking to bleed the taxpayers." Farmers and townsmen, who both increased the value of land by their improvements, paid landlords who added nothing to it.[16]

Speaking less on the third reading of the bill, Lloyd George nonetheless made contrasts in the assessing of land for rates and other investments like stock as well as rate reductions for land as opposed to decreases in rents, or the lack thereof. Land speculators were charged rates based on the amount required for the poor, which had gone down the previous decade from fifty-nine to forty-three thousand pounds and were now to be cut in half. Rents, though, remained the same or went up after land was vacated, prompting him to scoff "the Government were making hay while the sun shone for their friends and making it in a hurry as if they anticipated an early break up in the weather. But they meant to be assured that when the time came the landlords' hay should not be left out in the wet." They were confident when the bill passed 292 to 140, and ultimately, it was extended beyond the initial six-year limit. While chastising them, Lloyd George reminded them of their promise to introduce other legislation dealing with matters like "the encouragement of freehold occupancy, the amelioration of the lot of the aged poor, the protection of agricultural tenants in their improvements, the preservation of Voluntary Schools, compensation for injured working men," and better housing for all members of the working classes.[17]

To their credit, Conservatives passed an Agricultural Holdings Act in 1900 before calling for another election to try and increase their majority that October. It decreased the costs of and streamlined compensation settlements for paying the tenants who had made improvements, while lessening the landowners' authority to seize as well as sell the personal property of tenants in lieu of unpaid rent. As far as encouraging freehold occupancy, it should be stressed that there were fewer agricultural laborers in the 1880s and 1890s, which discouraged those left from launching out on their own in a waning vocation. Even acreage of smallholdings had only grown by slightly more than two hundred from the time of Harcourt's budget until 1902. Interestingly, Liberals did not make land reform a priority in their campaigns for the 1900 election. The Second Boer War was the primary foreign issue by then, and old age pensions surpassed agrarian concerns as the salient domestic one. Gladstone had sanctioned another commission in 1893 to research the viability of the government financing pensions, instead of mutual friendly societies. Chamberlain served on the commission and was the dominant voice in favor of government aid, five shillings a week for workers aged sixty-five on their voluntary participation basis. Previous recommendations for government-backed pensions had required compulsion. Chamberlain had used his influence two years before as the third party's power broker to create and oversee an unofficial parliamentary committee that studied the subject. In his 1892 election bid, he ran on not only pensions but also compensation for workers injured on the job. Therefore, he was qualified to sit on the Gladstone commission, though he had not been successful in getting pensions passed and would not be, mostly because Conservatives did not trust him as an ally.[18]

Lloyd George entered the arena on pensions during his 1895 reelection campaign, stating his support for them but that he had seen a pamphlet purporting it would necessitate £5 million a year to fund them. He further pointed out that tithes had been used in the past to provide for the poor but were now being given to the clergy, while indigents lived in workhouses. Taxes on inheritance, which Harcourt's 1894 budget had increased, royalties' taxes, and taxes on the rents of land, not the improvements to it, should also be used to pay for pensions, he asserted. Because of his interest in the issue, he was put on a select old age pensions committee to represent Wales in 1899, begun by Salisbury and, ironically, chaired by Chaplin. However, he used that position to embarrass the government with a quandary, proposing more funding than could be allocated during the Second Boer War. After telling William he had "been placed" on the committee, he cautioned him nine days later, "There's going to be fighting & consequently fire."[19]

Four days following his warning, Lloyd George chronicled some specifics for his brother: "We spoiled Chaplin on the Old Age Pensions Committee today. He wanted to thrust the inquiry on to Poor Law. After two hours fight we carried a resolution that we were to consider Old Age Pensions *first*." The "we" consisted of seventeen men, including Davitt and William Redmond for Ireland. Before summer, Lloyd George was expressing doubt that England would go to war with the Boers, but as uncertainty later turned to apprehension, he made the connection for William, "If we go to war with the Transvaal there will be no pensions." This remark clearly shows that he truly wanted them, though he used the issue for political advantage as the likelihood of war continued looming larger. Nine days after sharing his uneasiness with his brother, he wrote that he and Lionel Holland, another committee member, were going to see Chamberlain that evening "in his private room on Old Age Pensions. Joe is getting restless & means I think to kick over the traces." So he would not be misunderstood, he plainly declared, "He won't do it over Transvaal but over the other."[20]

Chamberlain, the Secretary of State for the Colonies in Salisbury's last government, had selected a committee to avert a pensions bill proposed by Holland. "The Chamberlain interview was most interesting," Lloyd George reported two days after they had visited. "It lasted ¾ers of an hour & was only then broken up by a division." A division meant a vote was forthcoming on a bill. He concluded with gracious words for Chamberlain as well as for himself. "He was very amiable. One idea of mine to get over a difficulty which had rather baffled most of those who have gone into this question, struck him immensely." Passing on Chamberlain's response to his brother, he quoted, "'By Jove,' he said, 'that is very clever.' 'I never thought of it before.' He was quite enamoured of it. He told me to come & see him any time I liked about the business." The committee's final report advised pensions of five to seven shillings, depending on the cost of living, be provided for everyone earning less than ten shillings weekly, except for those who had been convicted of crimes or given poor relief.[21]

District guardians were to distribute the pensions, but the committee did not speculate on the total costs involved, leaving that for economic authorities to determine. Nonetheless, Lloyd George, who not only got the committee to agree to the exceptions noted but also listed ways for previous beneficiaries of poor relief and criminals to qualify for pensions, purposefully inflated the expense to the government. He first intimated as much to his wife on July 21, penning, "Old Age Pensions has reached the most critical stage. We are now considering the report & if we carry our point we can place the Government in a most awkward fix." Referring to it again five days later, he detailed, "I have added some millions on to this Bill for them. I am sure I put on 2 or 3 millions yesterday & a similar sum today. Never mind, it goes all to the poor who really need it. It has the additional advantage of putting these bandits who are now in power in a nice fix. They can neither carry out these recommendations nor drop them—not without discredit." He started his final paragraph with, "Chaplin told me today that the Chancellor of the Exchequer is already swearing at him."[22]

Lloyd George also told Maggie and William that Conservatives on the committee sided with his plans, presumably because he used humor to sway them. "Carried two most important points," he shared with his brother. "Quoted Lecky against himself. He & Committee roared." The famous Whig historian was obviously one of the seventeen. Lloyd George then relayed to William the first "two millions" he had tacked on to expenses were in his "amendments against the Government," and then frankly mused, "it is curious how two or three of the Tories voted for me." According to one Lloyd George biographer, Chamberlain even admitted he "carried with him the progressive Conservatives" and won over Chaplin to his way of thinking. The persuader wanted pensions kept entirely separate from the poor law, desiring to support a lawful life with providential care, instead of with a system based on the belief that sins cause one's poor lot in life.[23]

Nearly three months later, a week after the Second Boer War began, Lloyd George wrote his brother about the select committee. Referencing Chaplin, whom he had seen earlier in the day, he remarked, "He was very nice. Said 'Well I do things for you that I wouldn't do for any other member.' The old boy is quite touched by the open & straightforward way I dealt with him on Old Age Pensions Committee. Opposed him openly but was quite loyal to him as Chairman." Though the committee's work had ended and no action was taken by the House of Commons, two months later Lloyd George again stressed that the war would delay passage of pensions for an unknown period of time. The following fall, he campaigned for a fourth parliamentary term in the "khaki election" and assured his hearers that he would champion pensions when Parliament met again. Actually, another bill to that effect was not introduced until the spring of 1903, after the war was over, and it was not Lloyd George who sponsored it.[24]

Lloyd George did use the 1903 bill, however, which also wound up in a select committee going nowhere, to attack Chamberlain, who had spent so many millions on the war and was now advocating tariffs. Indeed, Chamberlain split the Balfour coalition on tariffs in 1905 and caused its fall from power like he had the Liberal Party on Irish home rule nineteen years before. When Lloyd George began his assault on Chamberlain, the Colonial Secretary was absent but came in immediately after he was mentioned as being "too busy taxing the bread of the poor to have any thought of old age pensions for them." Further, "He was formulating great schemes for taxing the raw material of the industrial classes and had no time for such things as old-age pensions." Waxing sarcastic, Lloyd George then added, "The right hon. Gentleman had seen the beauties of the illimitable veldt, and he had forgotten all about temperance, finance, education, and old-age pensions. Those insignificant things were not to be put into the same category as the illimitable veldt." He even leveled Chamberlain's labors, "causing an expenditure of £250,000,000 for the war in South Africa," had "brought the question of old-age pensions to its present low estate."[25]

Noting comments by Chamberlain in 1894, "that the deserving poor were impatient for this reform," Lloyd George inquired, "Had the poor become less impatient? Or was it that they were less poor or less deserving?" It appeared Chamberlain was now asking, "deserving poor, are you clamouring for your pensions still? Turn your thoughts from these worldly, insignificant affairs, and contemplate the illimitable veldt." Interestingly, Lloyd George also revealed that the treasury had figured the cost of pensions to be £10 million annually, but "it was very little use" for the government "having a free hand" with the war over, "unless they had a full purse." Since 1899, "the Government had added £30,000,000 to the taxation of the country, but not for the deserving poor in the way of providing old-age pensions. They could not find one-third of that amount for the deserving poor." He suggested that a penny tax on sugar would cover the first year's expense.[26]

After a member of the House of Commons raised concerns about negative reactions to the ten shilling a week income ceiling to qualify for pensions, Lloyd George argued there had to be a limit to prevent fear on the part of taxpayers, who "would pay if they knew that it was for a kind of insurance fund. As to the age limit," he added, "somebody had said something about seventy.

That had been tried in Germany, and what happened was this. The rural population had benefited to some extent, but in the towns the seventy limit was perfectly useless." He remained convinced that pensions should start at sixty-five, and there should be a cap on income. However, he expressed the belief that a scheme by Charles Booth, the philanthropist who recommended pensions for all, "might be found ultimately to be the only workable one, but they could only bring the ratepayers up gradually." Nothing workable was found that year, but when Balfour resigned to capitalize on disputes among Liberals and increase his majority, the Liberal Party won the required election of 1906 by a landslide, many of its new members promising to deliver on pensions.[27]

Henry Campbell-Bannerman, leader of the Liberals, was asked to form a government the day after Balfour resigned, and Asquith became Chancellor of the Exchequer. Lloyd George was given a Cabinet post as President of the Board of Trade. Asquith did not address pensions in his first budget but included a £1.5 million for them in his second, characterizing them "as the most serious and the most urgent of all the demands for social reforms." Regardless of the priority he placed on them, and to the chagrin of many in his own party in addition to Labour members, he projected that pensions would become reality "before the close of the next session of this Parliament, if we are allowed to have our way—it is a large 'if'—to lay firm the foundations of this reform." He offered no details of how the reform would be implemented, but as it turned out, Campbell-Bannerman resigned in April 1908 because of ill health, and Asquith became the prime minister as well as First Lord of the Treasury.[28]

Asquith presented his third and final budget on May 7, as Lloyd George had just been promoted to chancellor, but handed pensions off to the latter the next day. They had been pulled out for solitary enactment. "Budget over," Lloyd George informed William, "Asquith spoke for over 2 hours—a very fine performance. Old Age Pension's at 70—5/-: a week & half the sugar tax off. Very great satisfaction on our side," he thrilled, "& it leaves the coast clear for me to initiate my own schemes. It was time we did something," he then insisted, "that appealed straight to the people. It will I think help to stop the electoral rot & that is most necessary. If it failed it might react in the House & bring us down prematurely." Two days later, a letter to his brother started by simply stating, "Sugar deputations. I am up to the neck in sugar." Beginning four days after Asquith "put the old age Pension Bill in my charge," Lloyd George also told William, "I mean to cut down Army Expenditure . . . I am not going to increase taxation to pay old age Pensions until I have exhausted all means of reducing Expenditure." It helped that Asquith had already lowered the empire's debt £47 million.[29]

Returning to his plans for the finances of the realm, which he thought were "the salvation of the party," Lloyd George shared with William, "I have great schemes fermenting in my brain." Twelve days later, he was "Settling details of Old Age Pensions scheme," but "Found that the calculations upon which Asquith & the Cabinet Committee appointed to consider the question had based their scheme were all wrong." Then, obviously breathing a sigh of relief, he observed, "If the opposition had any gumption at all they would have wormed it out in one or other of the many debates on the subject. But they have talked about everything except our estimates." On June 3, he sent his brother a copy of the bill, and six days later lamented being "so choked up with this Pensions scheme" that he could not see him in Carnarvon. He was busy arranging "the procedure rules" for pensions. The bill's second reading, June 15, he wrote, "Delivered myself of my old age pension speech.... Got the grip of the thing thoroughly now & can see my way clearly."[30]

The following day, Lloyd George elaborated on the impact of his address, stating it "has settled things in our party & my difficulties over Old Age Pensions are now much less than they looked a week ago." His presentation finally laid out the schemes that were causing his brain to ferment, pensions as well as national health and unemployment insurance, the former to be noncontributory but the latter to be contributory through taxation. Concerning pensions, those who made over twenty-six pounds a year, vagabonds, the insane, felons, or poor relief beneficiaries of the previous year were to be excluded. Married couples who did not earn more than thirty-nine pounds annually were to be provided with seven and a half shillings per week. He also informed William about husbands and wives on June 25: "My capture of the party yesterday over Married Couples was quite the best thing I have ever done in the House," he estimated. "I was prepared to give away £400,000," he then confided, "but was afraid of being rushed on the pauper clause which would have cost me £900,000. The married couples cost £334,000 only, & I have rallied all the party with that concession to resist further pecuniary demands."[31]

Conservatives attempted to do to the 1908 Old Age Pension Bill what Lloyd George had done to their select committee endeavor nine years before, by proposing amendments that would increase the costs to the point it would be economically unfeasible. He accepted one of the many amendments they proposed, that when more than one pensioner shared a dwelling, husbands and wives or siblings, all should receive the full amount, not prorated couples' pension. An adjusted rate for annual incomes of twenty-one to thirty-one pounds, ten shillings, he wanted but refused to pay for in full from the minimum starting point, was also accepted. He had told his brother in the communiqué for June 25, "Sliding scale I fought for inside the Cabinet but too late as I was not on the Committee dealing with Old Age Pensions. Now I get my way on it." Five days later, he wrote, "Got on rippingly yesterday through much the most dangerous country," and a "coup" the previous Wednesday "settled it." That Wednesday was when he referred to his "capture" of fellow Liberals, uniting them in opposition to any more financial amendments.[32]

The following day, he expressed great satisfaction in outfoxing Conservatives on one of their amendments, penning William, "Got the opposition into a hopeless tangle & then escaped from one of the most troublesome & dangerous amendments yet moved." He also conveyed on July 2 that he had "just finished a two hour Conference on the Report stage of Old Age Pensions." One week later, though, opposition leader Balfour raised an interesting point about how to determine who in Ireland would receive a pension, as births had not been legally recorded there by civil authorities prior to 1865. Lloyd George suggested consulting trade union applications, probably accurate, but clearly proving an Irishman's age was going to be problematic. The percentage in Ireland who became pensioners was thus more than twice that in England, one reason there were nearly seven-hundred thousand recipients by the spring of 1910 as opposed to the predicted half million. The expense also grew to around £12 million after two more years, almost a 100 percent higher than the original estimate.[33]

On Monday and Tuesday of the third full week in July 1908, Lloyd George let William know successively that "Old Age Pensions in the Lords," then "Old Age Pensions will go through," and finally that "The Peers ran away from the Pensions Bill." It became an Act of Parliament with Royal Assent on August 1. After only six weeks off, which included a visit to Germany so he could study its insurance system, he was actively pursuing his next social reform measures. "I am engaged deeply in a talk with Winston about our plans for the future of unemployment &c.," he wrote his brother. He had actually learned nothing about unemployment insurance on his trip but did talk extensively to administrators for invalid insurance and to Bethmann-Hollweg, Vice-Chancellor who oversaw the social insurance program. To get opinions of leading government outsiders, he also spent hours with the evolutionary socialist Edouard Bernstein and a political operative for trade unionists. Six months before Lloyd George met with Churchill to coordinate their agendas, the latter had sent correspondence to a weekly, in which he predicted that the Liberal Party would cease to exist if it did nothing about unemployment. Having followed Lloyd George as President of the Board of Trade in April, Churchill had started work on a plan that would lead to government acquisition and expansion of labor exchanges to keep those without jobs informed of employment opportunities as well as to help defray their transportation costs.[34]

Two weeks after the meeting with Churchill, Lloyd George made a speech at Swansea, in which he stated that there would be further socioeconomic legislation by Parliament, using a new phrase, new Liberalism, to describe his party's platform for the amelioration of unemployment, infirmity, and sickness. New Liberalism intended to tactfully employ government intervention to solve the problems caused by a hands-off approach, instead relying on the individual to do so. It was attractive to a lot of nonconformists because it countered the desire of some for socialism to be implemented by the state. He also castigated the House of Lords for vetoing bills that would have helped the people. One of his earliest biographers insisted that Lloyd George "declaimed against the old Liberalism" for promises that brought political gain but no change and that he had a "settled conviction" that the land issue was "at the root of the social evil." He quotes him saying, "Feudalism is the enemy," and thinking that the House of Lords was its "great stronghold." The day after his Swansea speech, Lloyd George told William, "Insurance success in spite of suffragettes. Never had such a reception in my life. Streets crowded with cheering multitudes who could not get in either to meeting or overflow."[35]

On October 12, the Cabinet appointed Lloyd George as chair of a committee "to deal with the whole question of unemployment," he informed his brother, but not all favored government-provided insurance for those out of work. The day before, he had mentioned seeing John Burns, the President of the Local Government Board, who was "very obdurate about the unemployed." Calling him stubborn again five days later, he grumbled about having to be "off now to see the Prime Minister about it." That morning he had eaten breakfast with Churchill, Richard Haldane, Harold Cox as well as Sydney and Beatrice Webb to discuss the "insurance scheme." Haldane was Secretary of State for War, and Cox was a staunch supporter of laissez-faire. The latter had proposed an amendment to reject the Old Age Pensions bill prior to its second reading and was the sole Liberal to oppose it on its third. The Webbs were the leading voices of socialism in the United Kingdom, and they objected to insurance because it was going to be compulsory. They viewed Lloyd George as underhanded, Churchill as detrimental, and Burns as arrogant because, having led labor unrest, he seemed to sell out the working classes once he entered the Cabinet.[36]

There was enough opposition from both sides on insurance that, three days later, Lloyd George told William it was "still unsettled," and he feared the government was "going wrong." Calling his budget "a gigantic business" on October 25, he communicated, "Had a fresh idea this morning. The Prussian budget helps me enormously. I am now on the track of land values. If there is any money in it I mean to collar them." A debate about the unemployed "went off rather badly" two days later. Burns was "at his worst & the P. M. not as effective as usual." He shared confidentially that the prospects for a settlement on education were good, adding, "Glad. Want it out of the way," showing how focused he now was on his national insurance policies. Less than one month after he starting tracking land values to find monies to help finance what he referred to in November as his "Compulsory Insurance Scheme," he spent three hours working with the Inland Revenue Department and also announced to his brother, "Going with Estate Duty. Found we are done out of hundreds of thousands of pounds every year."[37]

Lloyd George received more good news when a group of British trade unionists, who had gone to Germany to investigate its social insurance system, returned to state it had no deleterious consequences on the trade unionists there, confirming his "impression," he enlightened William. That same day, he related that he had hosted a "Great breakfast of Friendly Society leaders" at 11 Downing Street for the second time in as many weeks. On the first occasion, "representatives of all the leading friendly societies" had joined him "to discuss contributory scheme. Had 4 hours of them. Got on well, although they were most hostile at first." No hostility was mentioned in connection with their return visit, which, "Went off very well." Friendly societies were private insurance companies that served over four-million clients, who for weekly payments of from four to eight pence received a network physician, ten shillings every week they were sick, and fifteen pounds toward their funeral if they perished.[38]

Large urban areas had voluntary hospitals, but rural communities only had infirmaries set up under the 1834 Poor Law, and the stigma associated with relying on that or any other form of charity dissuaded many lower-class workers from seeking their services. Because longevity was on the increase, and the number of births was decreasing, the thousands of friendly societies had a cash flow problem and were willing to meet with the Chancellor of the Exchequer. He assured them that national insurance would not be in competition with their organizations, since it was only for the ill, injured, pregnant, and widows who were not currently being served by them. In fact, every worker now had to join a friendly society at the lowest liability level, and its cost would be deducted from his pay but offset by employer as well as government contributions. Obviously, Lloyd George also wanted to meet because of their influence. They had defeated Chamberlain the decade before when he tried to implement contribution-based old age pensions and had opposed the 1908 bill, even though it reduced their disbursements. Their agreement allocated 50 percent less for new enrollees, five shillings a week, plus one and a half more per child.[39]

Both sides also concurred in sending their plan to actuaries for an expense estimate, but the societies refused to promise they would endorse the findings. No figures were forthcoming for fifteen months. Lloyd George was so busy trying to get his first budget passed during those same months he could not have effectively devoted himself to insurance anyhow. In regard to his "People's Budget," he did begin talks on local taxation at the end of February 1909, which would later help fund his national health and unemployment insurance schemes. He attended a private banker's dinner early the next month also and corresponded with his brother the following day, "Completely captured old Rothschild." The financier Lord also "gave me a topping idea for a tax that will bring in £800,000," he added. Interestingly, the only Jewish peer vehemently opposed the budget three months later because he felt his wealth would be taxed unfairly, referring to it as socialism and collectivism. He did not offer other options for financing it, but later congratulated Lloyd George warmly on the way he funded the First World War.[40]

In June, Baron Nathaniel Mayer Rothschild even chaired an anti-budget gathering of financiers in London. Lloyd George had expressed to William just over one month earlier, "Luckily for me there is a great boom in the City so they don't mind extra taxes." A day before the gathering, he also stated, "I have decided to divide the land taxes & give half to the local authorities towards reducing the rates. So that if they throw these taxes out they will have the ratepayer at them." "They" were budget opponents in Parliament. Twenty-seven years later, he admitted to his last secretary he "had not cared very much personally about land values" in 1909, "but he had known that it was the best question on which to attack the Lords." Three days after the gathering, he let his brother know about his "trouncing of Rothschild" in the

House of Commons and that all the Liberals were "delighted." He not only confronted the monied interests in the legislature but also landed ones in private. During a deputation of the latter in his chambers, he "scrubbed the floor with Lord Hugh Cecil & the great landlords," according to what he shared with William. Then, he informed the public and, indirectly, possible foreign foes in one of his best-known speeches.[41]

On July 30, Lloyd George spoke to four-thousand people at a mission hall connected to a former pub that had become a coffee house in the East End of London. Because it was very hot, every window was opened and loud demonstrations by suffragettes outside could be heard, but all ears and eyes on the inside were fixed on the "bounder" from Wales. He began by sharing the recent report of funding being approved for four more dreadnoughts to be built and stressed how important the safety of the kingdom was to all, even though the wealthy had been recalcitrant in agreeing to pay their part. He quickly moved to the significance of his social agenda, for which the rich did not want to contribute enough either. He used three dukes as examples of landlords who had reaped benefits from land they had done nothing to appreciate in value, were paying the same rates as the land's original worth, and had been helped by Conservatives to recoup half the cost. He told people his budget included proposals for unemployment relief and financial help to friendly societies so they could ameliorate the sufferings of former uninsured sick, widows, and orphans.[42]

Lloyd George credited Providence with blessing the rich but stated that, in the future, 20 percent of their land value increases would go to benefit the community, who were the ones truly responsible for improvements to it, both rural and urban, agricultural, mineral, or industrial. As he drew to a close, he warned the landowners to be good stewards in helping to defend the nation and in relieving its people, not just taking pleasure in their properties, or else the requirements of ownership might be subject to change. In a very personal final statement, he also identified with the plights of the people, voicing that God should forbid him from causing them further distresses by taking any more food from their cupboards or making their lives more difficult. In a missive to William the following day, he rejoiced, "Limehouse was great. The people are at last thoroughly roused." Others were also aroused but not in a positive way. Edward Carson, the Privy Council member and Unionist from Ireland as well as Edward VII accused him of inciting class warfare. Asquith even sent him a fairly strong rebuke.[43]

Before the Limehouse speech, Conservatives thought they could defeat the budget, but their hopes greatly diminished when they "failed to carry a resolution against the Budget at the Central Chamber of Agriculture" in early May, Lloyd George gleefully conveyed to his brother. By mid-July, he told William, "Squared the agriculturists—Liberal & Irish," which "dazed" the Conservatives. The chamber insisted on rate reform, and his land clauses addressed that issue. Also, he dedicated two million pounds of the government's money in 1909 to assist in paying for agricultural improvements, research, and education. It helped his cause that agricultural land was not to be taxed the half pence on the pound rate the capital value of undeveloped land was, a detail stressed in his speech as a specific complaint all the yelling of landowners was directed toward. Within four days of his speech, he let his brother know that a member of Parliament as well as Lord Northcliffe, proprietor of the *Times* and *Daily Mail*, said his land clauses were "very popular."[44]

Northcliffe further claimed Lloyd George's budget "has completely destroyed the Tariff Reform propaganda in the country," the policy the Conservatives were promoting to counter his plans for securing additional revenue. "He said they had all miscalculated the popularity of the land clauses," Lloyd George explained to William. His description was, "it is a 'mighty rushing wind' sweeping before it all opposition. I hear from all parts of the country startling accounts of the change effected by the Budget in public opinion. There is undoubtedly a popular rising such as has not been witnessed for over a generation" (Acts 2:2, KJV). Using two additional biblical references in connection to the House of Lords, he wrote his brother: "What will happen if they throw it out I can conjecture—& I rejoice at the prospect. Many a rotten institution system & law will be submerged by the deluge," like God's flood (Genesis 7:11–24, KJV). "I wonder whether they will be such fools. I am almost wishing that they should be stricken with blindness," like Syrians were (II Kings 6:8–18, KJV). In less than a month, a million and a quarter copies of his speech were sold, he communicated to William, a "Quite unprecedented sale." Expounding, he shared, "Street hawkers go in to newspaper offices to buy in order to resell in streets."[45]

In addition to his proposed taxes on land, which would reap half a million pounds a year, Lloyd George advocated a super tax on incomes greater than five-thousand pounds annually and increased existing taxes on the following: death duties, income not earned, tobacco, alcohol, licenses, and duties on stamps. Combined with three million pounds of the government's sinking fund, they were supposed to garner the estimated £16.5 million to finance his budget. The super tax was six pence on each pound of earnings above three thousand, impacting ten thousand people. Gilbert labeled the contest that ensued as "a war upon the rich" and "class politics." Lloyd George informed his brother as early as January that the taxes on tea and spirits were part of the budget but that they were already being reduced. In March, he stated, "Licenses through & Stamps," followed on May 24 with, "Up to present no signs of a serious revolt against the whiskey tax." A day later he wrote, "Irish tobacco this afternoon. We are on now to petrol." Concerning the status of land clauses and liquor, he shared on September 1, "Jolly glad that P. M. is fagging away at those." He, however, was working "on Death Duties & Income Tax & the rest that I cannot physically get through without assistance. I have had *none* up to the present."[46]

By late September, Lloyd George was much better and credited God for helping him, as he did a number of occasions. "I am the only member who is not a bit tired," he now gratefully acknowledged, and then humbly added, "In that respect Providence has been kind to me & I feel less worn out than I did a month ago." As October began, he was preparing another speech that would target dukes and particularly the House of Lords. He revealed to William that he had "one tip top case of land values" he intended to use, "full of dramatic interest" and "a first rate illustration of my Budget. Got all the original deeds and letters." Two days later, in a posting he couched as "(Very Confidential)," he reported that Edward VII was "angry with the Peers for proposing to throw the Bill out. Doing his best to restrain them." The next day, he noted that the king and the Prince of Wales liked his attack on Philip Snowden, a Labour leader opposing his national insurance plan. "They were delighted most particularly with passage about Liberal Party remedying grievances of all classes & not merely of one." Both would have been even better ammunition, if he had been able to use them more, for his egalitarian policies.[47]

The speech for which Lloyd George was getting ready was delivered in Newcastle on October 9, where the crowd was twelve hundred larger than the one at Limehouse. They heard the dukes compared to two dreadnoughts each in terms of expense, a quarter of a million pounds to maintain annually, surviving more years, and equally as terrifying. Then, in a transparent allusion to the members of the upper house, he referred to the five-hundred unemployed men who were trying to prevent the millions responsible for the kingdom's riches from reaping the rewards of their labor. Attacking the upper class in general, he asked, "Who ordained that a few should have the land of Britain as a perquisite? Who made ten thousand people owners of the soil, and the rest of us trespassers in the land of our birth?" His confidence in challenging the House of Lords and its constituents was growing exponentially, although thirteen days later, after revising the estimated tax on liquor because of a 30 to 70 percent reduction in alcohol consumption, he revealed to William, "The opinion amongst the initiated is hardening in favour of the theory that the Lords mean to 'Chuck' the Budget. If they do there never has been such a delivery of our enemies into our hands since the Syrian army was stricken with blindness," referring to how Elisha overcame his foes. Clearly, Lloyd George was so conversant with the Bible, it was readily at his disposal.[48]

Based on what Lloyd George had written to his brother three days earlier, he was trying to force a battle with the peers, preferring that to their avoiding a struggle. "I deliberately provoked them to fight," he asserted, but he was also strategically preparing himself if the tactic failed: "I fear me they will run away in spite of all my pains." He proudly told William less than a month later, "The Lords are in for it. I am delighted that at last I have succeeded in manoeuvring them into this position," even adding that his "Limehouse & Newcastle speeches & my Nation article more especially were deliberately designed to drive them into this imbecility." All that remained was for Liberals to "act with common prudence & courage," and "the Peers are done for & that barrier to progress will be a ruin." The article mentioned emphatically affirmed a constitutional clash was unavoidable and imminent. One day earlier, he confided in Maggie, "Well the Lords have made up their minds. The Lord hath delivered them unto our hands. That is my feeling." Eight days later, he informed William that "Rosebery advised" Lords "not to throw out the Bill! After of course abusing us all round." The former leader had said the budget was socialism and would end everything, not only property but also monarchy, empire, family, and faith.[49]

In a letter to his brother on November 25, 1909, Lloyd George projected onto the members of the House of Lords his supposition of their sentiments under the circumstances in which they found themselves. "Peers feel very sick. They know now they are in the trap. But they cannot get out." Five days later, the upper house did pitch the finance bill, including the budget, so that his proposals would have to be debated in the country. Subsequently, Parliament was dissolved by the king and another general election had to be called, scheduled for the last half of January 1910. Among his own constituents, Lloyd George won again but by a smaller margin than four years prior, winning a three-to-two ratio of votes over Bangor's mayor, H. C. Vincent. However, the Liberals overall returned to London with ninety-eight fewer members than they had just two months before. Conservatives, or Unionists, came back with only two fewer than Liberals, a gain for them of 117 seats, but forty Labour Party members and eighty-two Irish in the new Parliament were generally expected to side with Asquith's ministry. In less than a month, though, radicals "were openly talking of Asquith resigning & my forming a Govt.," Lloyd George corresponded to William. "I discourage that sort of talk as it is full of mischief," he tersely ended.[50]

Nevertheless, two days later, Lloyd George was wondering, "P.M. quite nerve shattered. Never seen him quite like this. He is decidedly not the man to lead a Revolution." He passed on some good news for the Liberals, too, "that the King was dead against a Crisis & that the Tories are bent on not turning us out just yet." The concerns were over whether the king would create enough new peers to pass a bill to reform the House of Lords and whether the Irish would now support the budget in the House of Commons. The former had not even been requested since the election, Asquith confessed sheepishly four days earlier, and the latter had repeatedly insisted "no veto, no budget," meaning they wanted the veto power of the upper house removed before voting for the finance bill. Tories were hoping, with the help of the Irish of course, to defeat the budget in the lower house this time, bringing the Liberals down and vindicating the November decision of the House of Lords. Asquith may not have led a revolution, but Lloyd George did not hesitate to rebel. One week later, he "gave the Tories fire & brimstone," he bragged to William. "The Irishmen quite forgot they were opposed to the Budget & shouted with the loudest."[51]

During the next month, Lloyd George tried to drive a wedge between nationalist followers of John Redmond, William's brother, and those of O'Brien, who led a new independent minority faction of Irish after the election. His effort to peel away the latter by offering to provide more money for buying land and to do away with the whiskey tax failed. Regardless, a split occurred when the resolutions for the Parliament Bill, to remove the veto from the House of Lords, were approved and the last installment of the finance bill was brought to a vote. King Edward VII had promised to pursue guarantees that new peers would be appointed if the Lords voted the budget down. Before the House of Commons passed the finance bill again, Lloyd George commented to his brother on the Irish rift. Alluding to his unsuccessful attempt to woo O'Brien, he nonetheless diplomatically rationalized, "O'Brien incident useful. Puts the other fellows on my side. They hate each other—but the Redmondites have 70 votes—W. O'B only 9. The more he attacks me the better will they like me & my Budget."[52]

Two days afterward, Lloyd George expressed doubt "whether we can induce the Irish to vote for the Budget," but resignedly added, "we have I think come to a bold & a right conclusion. I submitted a proposal as to guarantees—said I had to go if the Cabinet did not agree. To my amazement it was finally accepted & tomorrow night the P.M. will read my words." He alerted William to "look out on Friday morning for an emotional pronouncement by him." The very day Asquith used Lloyd George's language, the Parliament Bill's resolutions were passed, its full title was initially presented, and it was read. Late that night, Lloyd George anxiously wrote to William, "Asquith gets up to make the momentous declaration in a few minutes." Prior to posting it the next day, he elucidated, "My poor words were a triumph for the government yesterday. Never seen such enthusiasm on our side since the great Gladstone days." Asquith spoke of how crucial it was "to secure safeguards—the safeguards which experience had shown to be necessary for the legislative utility and honor of the party of progress." Since the resolutions had been accepted at every stage of the parliamentary process in the lower house, he insisted that the Parliament Bill should be given "statutory effect," fearing his ministry might fall if the finance bill was defeated. If the government had to resign or was dissolved, he would "secure" the desired effect first.[53]

When the finance bill came up for a vote in the lower house four days later, Asquith did precisely what the Cabinet acquiesced to under pressure from Lloyd George, linking the promise of assurances from the king and a reiteration of the whiskey tax, which forced Redmond's hand but worked masterfully. O'Brien attacked Lloyd George even worse after that position became known, and the day the budget was approved again labeled him a liar who had tried to mislead the Irish into voting for it. All the independents opposed it, but every Redmondite voted in the affirmative. Calling Asquith's ultimatum "momentous," while at the same time describing the words he allegedly borrowed as "poor," reveals Lloyd George's all-too-frequent false humility, especially in his letters to William. Others also often stroked his ego, too, though. For example, twelve days following Edward VII's assent to the finance bill, after the Lords had refused to veto it, the chancellor shared with his brother what the establisher of the *Review of Reviews* told him: "Stead told me he had heard from the King that he was more impressed by his talk with me than with any of the other ministers."[54]

Slightly more than five weeks later, Lloyd George unashamedly compared himself to his most immediate colleagues, professing to William, "I am & always have been the only sanguine member of the Cabinet." He even projected pessimism onto the people four days later. "There is no political excitement in the country for the moment," he lamented to his brother. "That apathy necessarily tells against a Progressive party. But we have held the seat. That is the only thing that counts." The perceived lack of interest may have been because no progress was being made on unemployment or insurance until the money for them had been enacted into law, issues he had been questioned about on the campaign trail six months earlier. Ironically, the following day, he let William know, "Awaiting a debate on the Super tax." Before July ended, he was dealing with metropolitan leaders, and in August he focused on municipal taxation. With September came a renewed concern for the poverty of the masses, and October witnessed new emphasis in the land question. The year closed with treasury officials discussing his insurance scheme.[55]

Lloyd George was definitely not optimistic about the session he had with "enraged city magnates" that summer, frankly telling his confidant, "I don't mind admitting I was somewhat unhappy at the prospect. Complete success. I quite conquered them. I saw they feared me for I had beaten them so I spoke snootily to them but told them straight & salutary things." While on vacation from Parliament, he even asked his brother to aid him with the issue of municipal taxes. "Utilising my motor time to think out problem of local taxation. Will you help me to this extent? I want to find out how mansions are rated compared with shops." He also named several specific "choice places" and requested that "a few luscious premises" be investigated. "See that parks are included & give figures for park if separate." William's mission was in response to members of the House of Commons who wanted land reforms, most in the new Parliament now in favor of a single tax at local and national levels, instead of a value tax assessed for yearly appreciation.[56]

There were two sets of reformers, the Land Nationalisation Society and the Parliamentary Land Values Group, the latter drafting a new statement of its goals less than four weeks prior to Lloyd George commissioning his brother. Like their first document, it stipulated that municipal powers should uniformly put a value tax on a property's undeveloped land, but now added that there should also be a national tax on an entire holding's value. This would thus include improved parts, and similar to the super tax on specific income levels, the revenue gained would be used to assist the poor, pay for infrastructures, finance schooling, provide more constables, build more institutions for the mentally challenged as well as bring an end to taxes on food. In speaking on the budget, Lloyd George had distinguished landowners in the country from those in the cities and believed in the agrarian myth. It became increasingly evident to the people, however, that he opposed the landlords in both places, favoring farm employees in addition to tenants. In Wales the distinction was understood and even supported, but in England it backfired to some extent, as he was viewed more and more as a champion of industrialization over landed interests. To the contrary, though, he desired all of the United Kingdom to be a land of freeholders, without any hereditary pyramid property structure. That, along with other aspects of his budget, seemed to some from every one of the socioeconomic classes in the nation to be socialism.[57]

Having stressed that, it should also be emphasized that only 58 percent of males could vote, and greater suffrage, male and female, would have benefited the Liberals and their policies much more. Lloyd George's love for the masses was unmistakable, though, in correspondences with William and in his public speeches. Edward VII had died three weeks after assenting to the finance bill, but Lloyd George was invited to visit the next monarchs, King George V and Queen Mary, in Scotland that September. He determined to use his friendship with them to alleviate the sufferings of the disadvantaged. The next month, he helped prepare a land conference for which "the gigantic figure of 3,600,000" forms had "come in" and once again took his cause for relief of the poor to churches, addressing the Liberal Christian League at London's City Temple on the "problem of destitution" one Monday night. He informed his brother three days later, "All the Tory papers . . . have had friendly articles on City Temple. Daily Telegraph glowing 'sustained eloquence' &c. British Weekly & Xian World also."[58]

The second paper recorded Lloyd George's most passionate quote: "Some men get their fair share of wealth in a land, and no more; sometimes the streams of wealth overflow to waste over some favoured regions, often producing a morass which poisons the social atmosphere; men have to depend on a little trickling runlet, which," he portrayed, "quickly evaporates with every commercial or industrial drought; sometimes you have masses of men and women whom the flood at its height barely reaches, and you then witness parched specimens of humanity, withered, hardened in misery, living in a desert where even the well of tears has long ago run dry." It also, as well as the third paper, listed his causes for waste, after he unequivocally dismissed waste and laziness as traits of the working class: waste in land, of armaments, and by the idle rich. He then mentioned Form IV, which asked specifics, showing that under two-thousand people accounted for almost half the wealth that remained annually from deaths and that over 80 percent of the deceased left nothing in terms of property but inexpensive clothes or maybe furniture. He ended by advising the masses to have, "unswerving resolve through all difficulties and discouragements until their redemption is accomplished."[59]

As 1910 drew to a close, it went out like a lion instead of a lamb because of the certain refusal of the Lords to pass the Parliament Bill, which led to another dissolution and election to mandate the bill's passage. A Constitutional Conference that had its first meeting on June 17 in an effort to resolve numerous differences between the parties, convened its last on November 10 without agreement on the major issues of Irish Home Rule and what to do about the upper house veto. A week before its twenty-first and final gathering, Lloyd George foresaw the outcome in a letter to William that began "Looks unpromising now. We shall have another meeting tomorrow morning & then—as far as I can see the deluge. I am all against further concessions & I shall not be at all sorry to get back to the fighting line. Trying to settle is a worry—combat is joy if the cause be good." In fact, for about three months, he had been quietly working to form a coalition from the two leading parties, consisting of six of eight conferees but also Churchill, Haldane, and Andrew Bonar Law. Balfour, however, was most responsible for both efforts failing. On the day of the conference's last session, Asquith's Cabinet agreed another election should be held as soon as possible. That day, Lloyd George wrote William, "Well—the fat is in the fire & frizzling," but he did not mail it until the next day because, "Winston came in & once he starts talking it is all over for at least an hour."[60]

The frizzling turned out differently this time, however, because the prime minister got the guarantee from George V to appoint as many new peers as necessary to enact the Parliament Bill, and dissolution occurred on November 28, with the voting beginning on December 3. One week later, Lloyd George won for the second time that year, receiving the second largest vote total of his career against a new challenger, Austen Lloyd-Jones. Both main parties earned exactly the same number of seats for the House of Commons, 272, while the Irish and Labour each increased two. Before the new year began, Lloyd George forwarded to his brother that he had eaten with Sir Rufus Isaacs, Attorney General, and Sir Robert Chalmers, Chairman of Inland Revenue, "to talk over Land Tax questions." Isaacs and Charles Masterman, the number two man at the Local Government Board, also joined him in discussion of "our Insurance Scheme" with the "Treasury officials," he also sent. He was wise enough now to consult with a select few who had legal and administrative expertise to help him accomplish what was left of his socioeconomic agenda.[61]

Penymaes Chapel, Capel Uchaf, where Lloyd George attended from age 1 to 23. Reproduced by permission of the photographer, Howard Richter.

Lloyd George's foster father, a Church of Christ elder and minister for 59 years. From J. Hugh Edwards's *The Life of David Lloyd George,* University of California Digital Library.

"Highgate" and Shoeshop, where the Lloyd family lived and worked until 1880. From Herbert Du Parcq's *Life of David Lloyd George,* University of California Digital Library.

Band of Hope certificate, 1870, which Lloyd George attended at Llanystumdwy's Calvinistic Methodist chapel in Criccieth. National Library of Wales.

"Blue Ribbon" pledge card, 1887, which Lloyd George signed in 1882. University of Washington Libraries, Special Collections, PAM0268.

Good Templars in Denbighshire, ca. 1885, a meeting of total abstainers in the county where Lloyd George had preached. National Library of Wales.

Berea Chapel, built 1886, the new building constructed for Penymaes, where Lloyd George was a lifetime member. Photograph by Alan Fryer.

Margaret Lloyd George, Lloyd George's first wife and the mother of his five children. Library of Congress.

Miss Frances Stevenson, Lloyd George's mistress, secretary, and second wife. *Daily Mail,* August 15, 2019.

Gladstone and the Irish Land League, a rebellious organization he dealt with during his second ministry. National Library of Wales.

William O'Brien's Land War poster, a call to action by an Irish Land League leader to free others arrested. National Library of Wales.

NO RENT!

NO LANDLORDS' GRASSLAND

Tenant Farmers, now is the time. Now is the hour.
You proved false to the first call made upon you.
REDEEM YOUR CHARACTER NOW.

NO RENT

UNTIL THE SUSPECTS ARE RELEASED.

The man who pays Rent (whether an abatement is offered or not) while PARNELL, DILLON &c., are in Jail, will be looked upon as a Traitor to his Country and a disgrace to his class.

No RENT, No Compromise, No Landlords' Grassland,

Under any circumstances.

Avoid the Police, and listen not to spying and deluding Bailiffs.

NO RENT! LET THE LANDTHIEVES DO THEIR WORST!

THE LAND FOR THE PEOPLE!

Parnell and the Home Rule Bill, the Irish leader in Parliament trying to revive Gladstone's 1886 legislation. National Library of Wales.

Dominion status for Ireland, a problem that ties Lloyd George up as De Valera, Carson, and Devlin look on. *The Literary Digest,* August 30, 1919.

PUNCH, OR THE LONDON CHARIVARI.—July 24, 1912.

"OLIVER ASKS FOR" LESS.

John Bull (*fed up*). "PLEASE, SIR, NEED I HAVE QUITE SO MANY GOOD THINGS?"
Mr. Lloyd George. "YES, YOU MUST; AND THERE'S MORE TO COME."

Too much social legislation, a concern for land and other social reforms being implemented by Lloyd George. Mary Evans Photograph Library.

Old Age Pension postal order, the weekly payment to single claimants over age 70. National Library of Wales.

National Health Insurance flier, which encouraged support for the Liberal Party agenda in 1911. National Library of Wales.

National Health Insurance stamp, totaling a week of four pence from a worker, three from an employer, and the state's two. National Library of Wales.

Printed and Published by the Artists' Suffrage League, 259, King's Road, Chelsea.

"Why won't they let the Women help me?"

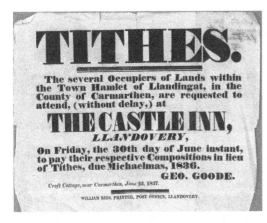

(*Above*) Suffrage League postcard, noting women were needed to help with the government's policy decisions. National Library of Wales.

(*Left*) Tithes payments for 1836, a poster calling on land tenants to pay that year's past dues from their tenants' possessions. National Library of Wales.

Siege of Mafeking bank note, a government bond sold to support the town until the Boer siege was relieved. National Library of Wales.

Leading opponent of Balfour's Education Bill, Lloyd George champions nonconformists in Parliament against it. National Library of Wales.

Lloyd George rescued by constables at Birmingham, which occurred during his anti-Boer War speech that caused a riot he barely escaped alive. From *The Town Crier*, December 21, 1901, Library of Birmingham, England.

WHAT OUGHT TO HAVE BEEN DONE.

Boer camp of women and children, an outdoor camp in the elements used to stop Boer guerrillas. National Library of Wales.

Women munitions workers in WWI, one of many jobs they filled to back the war as the men fought. National Library of Wales.

British tank at the Battle of the Somme, a new weapon first introduced there by Britain in September 1916. National Library of Waless.

EARL CURZON.

VISCOUNT
MILNER.

MR. LLOYD
GEORGE.

MR. ARTHUR HENDERSON.

MR. BONAR LAW.

THE WAR CABINET.

Lloyd George's WWI Cabinet, 1917, whom he chose after becoming prime minister the previous December. National Library of Wales.

Uncle Sam entering WWI, representing America's involvement in 1917 due to unrestricted submarine warfare, not the reasons indicated. Library of Congress.

A. 2.

IS IRELAND
A PART OF
ENGLAND ?

On April 12th, **CAPTAIN D. D. SHEEHAN** said in the
English House of Commons:

"I know all the English arguments. They only
take account of England's position. It is quite
natural they should only take account of England's position, but they are all founded upon the
English delusion that Ireland is a part of
England."

If Ireland is not a part of England, why should Irish
Members attend the English Parliament, especially when
they are outnumbered there 6 to 1?

Vote for Sinn Fein
AND SHOW THE WORLD THAT IRELAND
IS NOT A PART OF ENGLAND.

DUILLEOG PHOIBLIOCHTA SINN FEINEACH, 1918

Sinn Féin election poster, the political arm of Irish republicans who won a majority of Ireland's seats in Parliament that year. National Library of Wales.

THE HEROES' REWARD.

1

The Wealthy of England, they promised a land
 "Fit for Heroes to live in." Oh lor! ain't it grand!
"Rare and Refreshing" should be all the fruit,
 But Heroes find NOW that this stunt doesn't suit!
They gave of their best, that their homes might be brighter,
 But NOW they can starve—whilst the Wealthy sit tighter!

2

The Wealthy of England are hunting the foxes—
 The Heroes of England are shaking their boxes.
The Wealthy of England draw millions in rents—
 The Heroes of England are begging for cents.
They fought for "THEIR" Country, in glorious belief—
 But NOW, in their thousands, apply for relief!

You've been "Had" ONCE —
Don't be "Had again"!

THIS TIME
To Secure Justice—

VOTE for SIMMONS,
The LABOUR PARTY CANDIDATE.

Printed and Published by J. Patrick, Perchurst, Birmingham.

The Heroes' Reward, a Labour Party election leaflet criticizing Lloyd George's promises to veterans. National Library of Wales.

Big Four in Versailles, leaders of Great Britain, Italy, France, and America at the Paris Peace Conference. National Library of Wales.

7

Insurance and Housing,
1911–1922

"Landlordism is doomed."

ARTHUR JAMES BALFOUR thought Lloyd George's first budget was unconstitutional because it included plans to change the value of land. He also considered him unprincipled because he had endeavored to form a coalition while the Constitutional Conference was convening in 1910. In fairness, though, he also told a relative that his political opponent had always been that way, and he regarded it as his weakness as well as his strength. Lloyd George's opinion of his efforts can be gleaned from comments he shared about the death of a man named Carter in early February 1911. "He was my foulest foe in the boroughs," he wrote William. "His zeal outran conscience. Like many a conscience what with party zeal & self interest it was top heavy." As John Grigg has so rightly observed, Lloyd George "was a good patriot, but not a good party man." On a 2010 BBC Radio 3 podcast of Arts and Ideas on Night Waves, Roy Hattersley, Lloyd George's most recent biographer then, described the 1910 coalition as one of conviction, which his subject preferred to the one of necessity in 1916 or the one of convenience in 1918.[1]

By the close of February, Lloyd George's new strategy of conferring with experts yielded fruit. Insurance, not land reforms, now took precedence for more than a year, but he did return to the latter with a vengeance once he secured medical coverage for the British people. The last day of the month, he explained to his brother what he was doing in Parliament: "Been submitting my sickness & invalidity scheme to the Prime Minister. He is very pleased with it. Thinks it a most attractive scheme." He then portrayed it as "a huge scheme" and added, "I propose introducing it before Easter." Now, he utilized the term "invalidity" to encompass widows and orphans because he found out the previous summer that industrial or commercial insurance companies were planning to fight his scheme. They did not want pensions provided for the two specific groups mentioned, something he told the friendly societies that would be included to avoid government competition with them. Collecting insurance "societies," as industrial companies with agents but no stockholders were frequently known, received burial contract payments from forty-million enrollees. Seventy-thousand operatives visited the insured every week for installments of up to two pence. Agents often loaned money to clients, seeing themselves as their friends and advisors. A dozen concerns earned more than 90 percent of the profits, and the totals collected were valued in excess of £300 million pounds, fifteen million plus of which was paid annually.[2]

Lloyd George tried to assure commercial interests at the start of the previous December that his insurance scheme did not contain monies from burial profits or other disbursements at death, and no legislation for invalids or the sick would be presented for vote in the lower house without every insurance provider being asked for input. By March 3, 1911, frustration with complexities of implementing his scheme spilled over into his correspondence with William. "I should like to devote all my time to Insurance until Easter," he wished, "But I can't manage it." The next day, however, he clarified that he was working on his budget proposals, "as long as I can so as to be thoroughly fit for the immense labour of piloting through the shoals & rapids the Insurance Bill." He spent most of the month in what he depicted for his brother as a "nice old Georgian mansion" near Folkestone, owned by Arthur Markham, a coal magnate and Liberal MP. From there, after "another hard day's work" three weeks later, he informed William that his insurance plans were "assuming final shape." He pinpointed the day they were going to be introduced to the House of Commons as "Wednesday after Easter," which would have been April 19. Before the holiday, he further related he had met with "officials & draftsmen" in order "to go through the Bill," had two days of conferences on it, and discussed it with three deputations.[3]

Herbert Samuel, the Postmaster-General, extolled his budget as the "most statesmanlike measure in modern times," and the Chief Medical Officer of Scotland promulgated it even more broadly as "the greatest scheme of medical service in history," Lloyd George eagerly quoted for his brother. The Cabinet "approved of the main lines of the Scheme" two weeks before it was to be read, "which is all they could consider—& approved with admiration. I am now completing the draft Bill." Only two days following the Cabinet's approval, he specifically mentioned F. E. Smith, Bonar Law, and Churchill, stating, "It will make it so much easier to get it through to be on pleasant terms with these men. I shall have to fight vested interests & there is not too much time to spare this Session. So I must do a good deal of 'smoothio.'" As it happened, the bill was not introduced until May 4 because his throat had been giving him fits since the election and had not recovered until then, the reason for his absence from London. Its lengthy, thorough title was, "To provide for insurance against loss of health, and for the prevention and cure of sickness, and for insurance against unemployment, and for purposes incidental thereto."[4]

When he began his explanations of the Insurance Bill, Lloyd George cited a statistic used by Burns, the Local Government Board president, the previous week, that in Great Britain thirty percent "of the pauperism is attributable to sickness." He then enumerated the millions of people insured for death, sicknesses, or unemployment. Forty-two million were for the first; 6,100,000 for the second; and 1,400,000 for the third. He made it clear, "we do not propose to deal with Insurance for death," though a quarter of a million policies with the friendly societies lapsed annually because families needed their money for other necessities. The government as well as employers should aid workers, "for sickness, and, as far as the most precarious trades are concerned, against unemployment." Compulsory and voluntary sickness insurance were stipulated, the former for weekly wage earners or those who were below the £160 income tax limit, the latter for military men or educators. The former's pay withdrawal would be increased by contributions from the state and bosses. Subscribers to the voluntary part could also include casual laborers, like those at docks or warehouses, taxi drivers, hotel waiters, and even golf caddies.[5]

Lumping sickness and invalidity together, Lloyd George then announced the deductions from workers would be four pence a week for men, as opposed to three for women, equating the amount to "two pints of the cheapest beer" or "an ounce of tobacco." A reduction was justified for those earning fifteen shilling a week or less, male or female, but anyone who was given room and board with their pay was "excluded altogether." Every wage earner "up to sixty-five" could be admitted "within twelve months after" the bill was enacted. Beyond that, admission would be on a prorated scale based on age. Sixteen years old was when one could begin, and three pence weekly was to be paid by the employers "for man and woman alike." The state would then also add two pence a week to the sum, regardless of sex. For the voluntary contributors, a distinction was drawn between individuals who had always been self-employed and those who had worked for others prior to going out on their own. The former automatically had eligibility for the plan, but the latter had to "have been contributors" for at least five years. Both categories had to apply within six months, be forty-five or younger, and contribute the employer's portion. Anyone over forty-five would also be prorated, and each voluntary group would receive the state's part.[6]

Once he had explained the general ramifications of the scheme, Lloyd George then dealt with married women, physicians, maternity benefits, tuberculosis, sick pay, unemployment, and administering the system. Based on information from friendly societies as well as governmental actuaries, he estimated compulsory and voluntary contributors in addition to those under sixteen should approximate fourteen million, seven-hundred thousand people. "I do not think it would be advisable to allow married women who are not workers to join," he said, but working women who became pregnant got a thirty shilling benefit for a four-week absence. Before concluding, he extended the perk to housewives of workers and, if both worked, three pounds. The absence was because many women, "work up to the last moment and the maternity is over in a comparatively few days. I believe we ought to make some provision," he added, "in the interests of humanity to prevent that from taking place." As far as consumption, he observed seventy-five thousand died every year from it, and nearly five-hundred thousand suffered with it. Of the four-thousand beds in sanitaria, only half were available for patients with tuberculosis due to others occupying the rest. Consequently, he set aside a capital amount of £1.5 million to "assist local charities and local authorities to build sanatoria throughout the country."[7]

To pay for maintaining such facilities, Lloyd George figured it would take a shilling and four pence a year for every member, the pence coming from the state but the rest out of the total workers contributed. For pay to help the families of ill workers until they recovered, he allotted ten shillings per week for the first three months and half that for the next three. If the sick could still not work, then a permanent disability allowance of five shillings would continue as long as needed. Pay for the loved ones of ill women in such a case was only seven shilling and six pence weekly for the first until the fourth week, when it became the same as for the men. No one could petition for sick pay until six months after joining a society, and disability would not be granted until one had made contributions for two years. Even those who became ill as a consequence of their "own misconduct" were entitled to a doctor but no sick pay. Until they made five-hundred payments, less would be given to those over fifty or under twenty-one, and a discrepancy between the sexes still existed.

Anyone under sixteen received "medical attendance and the benefit of the sanatorium," but no personal financial assistance was provided.[8]

How to collect and distribute the funds contributed and what to do about the unemployed took most of the remainder of Lloyd George's presentation to the lower house. Cards were to be handed out to employees who, at the end of every workweek, took them to their employers for two stamps to be attached. One worth four pence would be the worker's, but the other valued at three would be the boss's, who deducted the employee's part from wages paid. The card would then be returned to the worker, who gives it to the post office for transmission to its central headquarters. Organizations designated as "approved societies" were to dispense any benefits, so those joining the plan had to be members of one. The requirements organizations had to meet included having at least ten thousand members, a constitution prohibiting disbursements of funds for anything but benefits to members, local committees if no branches existed, self-governance from members for electing officers and representatives, no profits "out of this branch of its business" as well as the necessary provisions "for sickness and old age."[9]

Friendly and collecting societies, new departments in commercial insurance companies for the purpose, labor unions, cooperatives, or even clubs established by employers for workers' benefits could handle the task. Lloyd George forecasted, "A good many more societies, I have no doubt, will spring up the moment we have a scheme of this character, and it is far better to leave it to competition amongst them." Men who were rejected by a society, had left one inadvertently, or just refused to join because they were already uninsurable due to a physical or social malady, like drunkenness, were to be assembled in a local post office society. No benefit would be paid them for a year, and then, it would be less than for others. County health committees, composed of nine to eighteen delegates chosen equally from county councils, approved societies, and each post office society, would be founded to supervise the monies of post office contributors as well as funds for maintaining sanitaria. Lloyd George also agreed, "If any approved society chooses to come to terms with the county health committee to do its medical work for it we propose that they shall have power to do so, and to make arrangements for that purpose." The office for administrating national insurance would pick for those approved societies, if agreement could not be reached, and send a fourth again as many delegates to represent the government too.[10]

The government was also willing to add a fourth to the total of unemployment insurance funds collected, but Lloyd George only intended to apply those benefits "to the precarious trades, which are liable to very considerable fluctuations." Those trades, engineering and construction, comprised merely a sixth of the industrial workforce. Participation in this portion of the law was also mandatory, workers and employers contributed two-and-a-half pence each, but compensation could just be drawn for a total of fifteen weeks. Engineers would receive seven shillings a week, but builders, including ship and other vehicle constructors, got six. Anyone losing his job due to personal misconduct, a strike, or a lock-out would not be covered. Insuring the unemployed was viewed as a "distress allowance" by the state, but accidents were "specially excluded" from the employer's liability for workmen's compensation and would not "be treated as sickness." The subject of owner responsibility for injuries in the workplace was raised by Austen Chamberlain, Joseph's son and the shadow chancellor, but Labour Party leader Ramsay MacDonald pursued it. Lloyd George had already officially ended his delivery, though, and it was after 6:00 p.m.[11]

Chamberlain also desired to know if soldiers and sailors would be "excluded altogether" from the legislation. Lloyd George replied that if they had been friendly society members before joining the military, they could continue as such with a wage deduction of two pence and get all the benefits of civilians on retirement. However, certain military pension plans would preclude them. In the final sentence of the bill's formal presentation, he had crescendoed with a scripture. "I think that now would be a very opportune moment for us in the Homeland to carry through a measure that will relieve untold misery in myriads of homes," he challenged Parliament, "misery that is undeserved; that will help to prevent a good deal of wretchedness, and which will arm the nation to fight until it conquers 'the pestilence that walketh in darkness, and the destruction that wasteth at noonday'" (Psalm 91:6, KJV). Even though he had been speaking for over two hours, he still wrote William that night, "Got through. No doubt as to its being a smashing triumph. All parties now engaged in lauding it. It has transfigured politics. Anything is now possible. Voice splendid thanks to likkis ball of Uncle Lloyd."[12]

Lloyd George's "smoothio" also worked, at least on Smith, a Conservative representative for Liverpool. Smith's speech eleven days after the bill's introduction was "very complimentary in reference to Insurance," according to the chancellor's correspondence with his brother. Bonar Law, who succeeded to the leadership of the opposition six months later, never fully accepted the legislation, particularly the arbitrary appointment of unconfirmed bureaucrats to oversee it. His party, though, was smart enough to resist it by stirring up outside interests, not risking themselves being seen as against an increasingly popular bill in the eyes of the people. The most challenging political outsiders proved to be the doctors, and Lloyd George had to negotiate with them for the next year and a half. Only three days after Smith's speech, he lunched with both "the editors of the Lancet & British Medical Journal." Six days later he updated William, revealing, "I am busy outside squaring doctors & Collecting Societies." After twenty-four more hours, he confidently prophesied, "I am busily engaged in squaring diverse interests outside. Believe I will succeed in roping most of them in—all the really formidable ones." That was the day the Insurance Bill was read for its second time, and five days following it he was even more assured in saying, "Doctors & Collecting Society petitions I believe I have smashed. That is the general opinion. Spoke for nearly 2 hours my voice being sharper at the end."[13]

The speech Lloyd George referenced was on May 29, during continued debate pertaining to the second reading. What doctors had objected to was their fee being only four shillings per patient a year and being controlled by the government, though they received two more shillings for prescriptions they often provided at their expense. Addressing them at the British Medical Association's conference three days later, he was able to allay certain grievances by suggesting they ask the House of Commons to let local committees, provided for in the bill, distribute the health benefit. That way there would be no more society contracts but, rather, panels of doctors listed by the insurance companies for patients to select. By June 29, he was even bolder after two more physicians' meetings, first penning his brother, "The doctors just left me after a prolonged interview—got on *well*," and then, "Had great time with Friendly Societies this morning. Never witnessed greater enthusiasm at a small meeting as that manifested at the end. Believe I have squared the doctors."[14]

As July began, Lloyd George was still informing William "although progress will be slow at first," once the bill gets out of the committee stage, "the passage is assured." Further, he also acknowledged, "Concessions I must make here & there as I did on Budget. That I do not mind." Two days later, he shed more light on why things would move slowly at first. "We will not make much progress until the future is clearer—as to Lords & other things we shall then rush through. I am *very* pleased." After disposing "of some very contentious & difficult questions" a day earlier, he had written his brother on July 11, "we are getting on like a house on fire. We will get 3 if not 4 clauses today." As the month ended, a dozen clauses had been accepted, but seventy-five remained. As of August 1, the lower house took the health benefit away from approved societies and gave it to local committees, what physicians wanted because they opposed being under their auspices. Because industrial insurance companies sided with the medical profession against the societies, they won its reciprocity in persuading Parliament to cease mandating local committees. The committees were to be composed of 250 random contributors, to oversee the scheme's management, which would have precluded insurance agents from collecting fees.[15]

In spite of the good news that doctors and insurance companies were cooperating, Lloyd George described his efforts on the bill as "plodding through" in a letter to William the same day. His sense of slow, heavy exertion turned into immense relief and elation ten days later, when he told Maggie what had transpired in the House of Lords. "Veto through. I can hardly believe it. The dream of Liberalism for generations realised at last," he contemplated. "Gladstone, Bright, Bannerman, Harcourt—all looking forward to this day but passed away without seeing their hopes fulfilled. So pleased that I am responsible for it. The Budget did it." The Lords had acquiesced to the Parliament Bill without persisting in attempts to amend it and had then enacted it. He had written his wife the day before, stating, "Fate of Veto Bill still doubtful. Chances are we carry it by a small majority. Rosebery delivered a powerful speech in favour of passing it." He had also relayed to her that he introduced payment for MPs in a speech to the House of Commons, which became part of the final legislation King George V assented to on August 18.[16]

From the royal palace at Balmoral during Parliament's summer recess, Lloyd George also mailed a letter to Maggie saying he had "made great friends" with the king's physicians. He then described Sir Frederick Treves as "a fine fellow" and added, "He is disgusted with the conduct of the medical profession over the Insurance Bill. He wants to help me." During a dozen days prior to Parliament reconvening, he again met with doctors and friendly societies as well as members of the Labour Party's insurance committee. Of the first two, he told his spouse he had been with them "three hours," which was "Most useful. I am in the saddle—well in—& I mean to ride hard over hurdles & ditches—& win." For the third, he elaborated, "They mean to support a time limit for the Bill. That means an enormous lightening of my labours. They are thoroughly friendly . . . They have had an actuarial report which completely supports my scheme." He garnered support for the bill by public speeches as well as private meetings, and as he often did, went to churches where he could comfortably proclaim his views to large audiences.[17]

One week before the House of Commons returned for its autumn session,

Lloyd George spoke at Whitefield's Tabernacle, where the Liberal MP and Congregational preacher, Silvester Horne, chaired the assembly. The chancellor unabashedly alleged that the bill would accomplish more than anything since the repeal of the Corn Law to alleviate wretched unhappiness. He also succinctly summed up the scheme, couching it in terms of ninepence for fourpence, and asserted belligerently he would fight for its enactment into law by the end of the year or fall from office trying. Evaluating his effort in correspondence with his wife two days following, he claimed it had "created an immense impression. The fighting note which I have hitherto rather repressed," he coyly submitted, "has roused the Liberal press to a support which they have not yet given. It has also frightened the others. There has been a great change even in the Mail." After six more days, he renewed written communication with his brother, noting, "Great change in situation last fortnight. Whitefield's Tabernacle did it." He further mentioned a meal that would be attended by ninety journalists, paid for by the Master of Elibank, Alexander Murray, though he insisted it was his idea. "Tomorrow there is a great luncheon to Liberal Editors & leader writers to meet me in order to enlist their active support on the Insurance Bill."[18]

Referring to the luncheon again the next day, Lloyd George interjected for William some gossip he had more than likely learned from one of the newspapermen: "Heard the other side do not mean to fight hard." On October 26, he got his proposed time table for passage of the bill by the end of the session approved and described it to William as his "most difficult and dangerous conquer." November began with his finishing touches on benefits for married women who had been working prior to wedding. If they remained employed they lost no benefits, but otherwise they did until the husband died. Divorce or legal separation were also treated like the death of a spouse. In any event, she had to be at least sixteen and could not become a voluntary contributor. As Conservatives continued their obstructive strategy, he minimized it and gloated to his brother, "In next week there will be a slight flare up. I have got them tight in the vice." He also got some opposition from O'Brien and other Irish members, who did not want the bill applied to Ireland or to have the Irish Parliament pay for it until home rule was assured. He was also smug about the independent Irish leader in another missive to William, exulting, "I trampled him in the mud."[19]

A "busy day . . . visiting tuberculosis institutions in Hampshire" fell between the attacks by Lloyd George's political rivals, as he tried to make certain that free treatment would be available for anyone contributing to the insurance plan, he explained to his brother. Ultimately, however, sanitarium guardians had to fulfill the obligation as they had before. William decided to play a role in aiding his brother, suggesting a Welsh handbook on the scheme his sibling considered "an excellent idea. Drive ahead. It will pay—an incidental advantage." Lloyd George needed every advantage he could gain as numerous clauses of the bill continued to prompt resistance virtually to the end of the year. The inclusion of household servants was the last conflict of 1911, and he had a "Deputation of Masters & Maids" on November 28, which he labeled "a great success. Carried them completely." However, a campaign by mistresses against licking stamps did not peak until the next day, and he told his brother, "The Tory papers—all except Daily Mail—dropped agitation against servants inclusion. The D Mail correspondent in the lobby says he cannot find a Unionist MP who wants to propose their exclusion." Only the upper house could stop passage now before Christmas, but the *Daily Telegraph* stated that the House of Lords did "not intend to attempt any amendment," Lloyd George corresponded to William.[20]

Nonetheless, the last day of the bill's report stage found Lloyd George very contemplative as he corresponded to his sibling, "I am quite ready for smooth or storm. I have had both on this Bill but I am nearing the harbour. There will be a little moaning at the bar when I sail across it." He had adapted "may there be no moaning" from Tennyson's "Crossing the Bar." He also called a final desperate attempt by the opposition to amend the bill, "a feeble thing & in two years' time they will rue it. They are however so divided about it that they had to do something." They tried to delay passage until the first 1912 session but lost by a vote of 324 to 21. H. W. Forster led the way, after saying four months prior that Lloyd George was the most successful at getting difficult legislation enacted because he was a master of compromise. On behalf of Conservatives, Forster objected to the bill's reaching its third reading by use of the guillotine to limit discussion and, in their opinion, its inequity. After the amendment was so convincingly defeated, Lloyd George wrote his brother, "The House rocking with laughter when they refused to vote against the third reading. The bill will now go through." Anticipating the final outcome, the Conservatives had abstained, but he confidentially portrayed them as "furious & cowed."[21]

Debate or the lack thereof in the upper house was "going on quickly," Lloyd George told William five days after Forster's comments. "Insurance Bill received Royal Assent!" was sent in five more. When he knew the bill would become law before the end of 1911 because the House of Lords did not object, he then turned his attention to tuberculosis again, telling William, "In the House last night until 1.15 discussing the sanatorium grant." Indeed, he was still dealing with the issue off and on seven months later, even meeting with doctors at Waldorf Astor's house in May, which led to them passing "a resolution to work the sanatorium benefit" two months afterward. At that juncture, he informed Uncle Lloyd, "That gives me 6 months to manage the other medical benefit. That suits me admirably. Don't care whether they break off negotiations now. In fact it suits me." Collections for the scheme also started that July, and no benefits were scheduled to be paid until the following January. He was not overly concerned with continued rebellion from the official medical organization because of his belief the majority of physicians were ready to begin providing care under the terms of the act.[22]

Less than two weeks after 1912 commenced, Lloyd George wrote his wife while he was vacationing on the French Riviera to let her know that Liberals "mean to have a great campaign throughout the country—some thousands of meetings to explain the Act." He had moved Robert Morant from the Board of Education to chair the National Insurance Commission and informed her that the new commissioner was "getting on admirably" in talks with trade unions about their role as approved societies, in spite of their conflict of interest as collective bargainers. By the end of the first week in March, there were five-thousand meetings "already arranged," he communicated to William, "We aim at 10,000." Two months to the day later, he had a three-hour session with the insurance commissioners, which he described as, "Most satisfactory." Three days following that was when the Insurance Advisory Committee first met. "Doctors & I on best of terms," he guaranteed William. "Made a start with them. It will take time but it is useful to find they were neither hostile nor sulky." Based on that alone, he felt free to return to reforming landownership, at least in "meditating a great land campaign." He cautiously qualified those aspirations, though, adding, "I am keeping it back until it is urgently needed. We want to come back on a great land revolution next time. No playing with the question any longer. Next year would be time enough to start it under ordinary conditions," he explained to his brother, "but a bad slump in Liberalism might force one to start it sooner."[23]

As it happened, Lloyd George had to invest more time on the land question much sooner than anticipated but also put doctors in a "much better frame of mind" after a conference in June. He even contended to William that he was, "Quite satisfied with position so far," when he had a follow-up meeting with them. Toward the month's end, he was more concerned with insurance companies and the women's movement for suffrage. Writing William on June 26, he confessed that he had put "a truculent letter" in the papers, chastising "a firm of solicitors" who "say they won't conform to the provisions" of the law. Two days later, he maintained that a meeting at Lady St. Helens Catholic Church in Essex, "to form a domestic servant society," was "a great success. It will break the passive resistance movement." The movement was instigated by Tory newspapers to convince people not to pay for insurance. Ending Tory opposition took longer than satisfying solicitors. The key to the latter was numbers, and Lloyd George figured for William, "Members pouring in to Insurance approved societies. Prudential 2.000.000!"[24]

Prudential was the biggest insurance company, and of the dozen leading such concerns, it controlled roughly 40 percent of the revenue. Collections from almost ten million insurance plans, written by the major businesses annually, approached 50 percent as much as the financial requirements of the United Kingdom. As Prudential went, the rest of the industry were expected to go, and nine days after the collecting agents began their work on July 15, Lloyd George shared additional encouraging news with William: "We sold 16.000.000 of stamps the first week." He revealed that Wales was leading the way but abruptly ended, "I do not care a scrap about the doctors." His ongoing disagreement with the medical association over what the cap for practitioners should be led to another cessation of talks. The association dickered for eight shillings, six pence, but he remained at six shillings, which included the allotment for prescriptions. The mutually respected accountant William Plender was then commissioned to go and ask doctors what they made, but the answers calculated to a level of four shillings, five pence, confirming Lloyd George's halfway estimate. On July 19, Maggie received word, "It looks now as if the Tories were doing their level best to prevent its coming on! How different it would have been had the Act been in a muddle. They would have insisted on a debate on its administration. Now they are actually obstructing to keep the debate off."[25]

Conservatives had sided with the medical organization but found that their partners were unskilled in mental gymnastics with the chancellor and backed off. Lloyd George had projected that within a month of the mid-July start date, all those who were eligible for coverage would be members of approved societies and making their payments. The accuracy of his predictions also dealt a blow to detractors, when in excess of 90 percent of contributions had been received by the central post office seven days into the venture. Even during vacation in Marienbad, Austria-Hungary, between the summer and

fall sessions of Parliament, Lloyd George still kept his spouse updated: "Insurance news continues good. I dreaded a holiday abroad this year as I pictured
the Daily Mail & Telegraph every day full of letters & articles on the 'Insurance Muddle'. Instead of that they barely mentioned it. I never expected it
to work so smoothly at such an early stage," he admitted, and eagerly shared,
"Lawson [Harry], the proprietor of the Telegraph, is here. He does not think
the Insurance Act unpopular."[26]

More contributions than anyone had anticipated were being paid by October 1, but at "a most important meeting of the advisory committee" four days
after that, friendly societies, trade union leaders, insurance companies, and
employers were "all represented." Lloyd George then expressed astonishment
at their progress, adding for William, "Surprised at the strong feeling in support of a national medical service." Eighteen days later, he revised payment for
the doctors in a speech to Parliament, and wrote his brother, "General opinion
seems to be that the doctors must now come in." The amount to be paid would
now be as much as the British Medical Association had been demanding and
potentially more. In all, the doctors could earn nine and a half shillings, which
broke down into six and a half for care given, one and a half for drugs, and
one and a half for additional prescriptions if necessary. Incidental expenses
like mileage and the mandatory six pence for the sanitaria benefit were also
included in the third disbursement. Even following his announcement, he was
still negotiating with the profession in November, but William learned its representatives were "Quite friendly in discussion. Too early to produce result."[27]

As late as eight days before Christmas, William was furthermore reading,
"Working hard at doctors. My plans are maturing & I feel confident. Would
be rather pleased than otherwise if there were a rejection of our terms. I want
to see the experiment of a medical service tried." On New Year's Day, Lloyd
George was preparing yet again for doctors, and reported four days later,
"Doctors still on the run. County after County coming in." The very next day,
though, they were "tumbling over each other now in their hurry to come in."
Verifying his assessment one day after that, he expounded, "Doctors panels
almost complete. There will be odds & ends to pick up but they will amount to
nothing." Four days before benefit payments were to commence, he included
a pun from his most beloved mentor: "I agree with Uncle Lloyd that some
of the London doctors are taking their physic badly." As chancellor, he was
concerned about the medical block because he commented on it so extensively
and because the British Medical Association had called for a strike six months
earlier. He had tentatively looked into forming state medical forces to run the

scheme, if doctors abstained, but in the end he was victorious, and the association lost influence as well as members over the next decade.[28]

Less than five weeks before insurance collections started, and during a strike by transport workers from the Port of London in which negotiations had "broken off," Lloyd George exhorted William, "All this will help the land campaign I am projecting & waking up to." Five days later, though, he also wrote, "I am not working up my land programme now," only admitting after five more days, "Collected £5500 already for my land campaign." Another week following, he gladly reported, "the Tories are getting frightened over rumours of the new Land policy." By July 3, his port strike mediation had ended without a minimum wage for dockworkers, although coal miners had received one in a law four months earlier. The same day he also conveyed to William that he was "Working hard at my Land Campaign. Had the committee to breakfast with me. Seebohm Rowntree is a treasure. He is working like a nanny at it." Obviously, the group was tasked with exploring the prospects, and Rowntree was one of several who had attached his name to a short brochure proposing a Liberal plan to give all workers a minimum wage, farm laborers first. The plan would also improve local taxation systems, procure additional land in rural areas or housing in urban areas, and nationalize the railroads.[29]

The signers wanted to acquire statistics for the plan, and Rowntree had already published an exposé on the lifestyles of York workers eleven years prior. It did not hurt that his father was a cocoa magnate, had signed the brochure, and helped fund the committee's legwork. Other rich men, like Maurice de Forest, a baron who was a member of the lower house, and William Lever, of soap production renown, financed the investigation that had to be carried out. The former was put over a subcommittee to gain urban numerical data. Both the committee and its subcommittee were recognized by the prime minister five days after the breakfast but never officially authorized to perform their specific functions, mailing inquiries or commissioning inspectors. Lloyd George told William that Asquith had "accepted full responsibility for my land movement," but inserted, "Tories sick. They thought they could split us by representing this as my move against Asquith & the moderates." Naming several moderates, Haldane, Isaacs, Churchill, all of whom he found "quite friendly," he started to strategize, "Winston alone being doubtful, but he has become very reactionary of late. However, Winston is not going to give trouble provided I give him money for his navy. If he keeps quiet he is worth a million or two."[30]

A factor motivating Lloyd George to pursue another land movement in the late spring and early summer of 1912 was three Liberal victories. However, by mid-August he was complaining to Maggie about a loss in Manchester because the candidate "was a poor sort of hedging Liberal. He shunned the Land Question. You wait until I start my campaign." The next month, the land inquiry committee engaged in a number of talks at de Forest's estate over a weekend, but Lloyd George was still not ready to formally begin his last reform battle prior to World War I. He did continue to fight his political opponents, though, and in a lower house debate on the committee's inquiring into land tenure, he had "a glorious row" on October 15, gloating to his wife, "Austen rushed on to the point of a cloaked sword." In guarded optimism, he also revealed to her, "But it has definitely raised the Land Question & it gave the House a glimpse of the savage passions that will be raised by the campaign when it is well on. Home Rule & all else will be swept aside. I ended deliberately on the word 'game'. This produced pandemonium."[31]

Lloyd George had attacked Chamberlain because he asked if the identities of respondents to the inquiries would be published, presumably so Conservatives could find out who witnessed abuses by landlords. He had also made it clear seven days earlier that he did not believe in the single tax on land but that its value when sold should be assessed. Asquith had tried to allay other fears two days before, when he promised that there would be no land confiscated once the campaign fully began. Regardless, Conservatives resisted to such an extent that William read on November 11, "My own first impulse is that we ought to go on until next summer. Get Franchise Bill thrown out 2nd time by House of Lords," Lloyd George argued, "Meanwhile have a roaring campaign on Land—thorough understanding with [leaders] & then go to country." It is apparent his intention was to have another clash with the upper house, which would lead to a new election, resulting in the same kind of success on land reform he enjoyed with his "People's Budget," Parliament Act, and national insurance. In February 1913, he wrote William, "P.M. has given me permission to start my Land Campaign to rouse the public conscience on the evils of the land system. It means that I start with official sanction & you can trust me for the rest."[32]

The month before Asquith permitted him to officially begin the crusade against abuses of landlords, Lloyd George let the editor of the *Manchester Guardian* know he was not planning to start his reform movement until he had £50,000 to pay for informative booklets on land problems that could be mailed to the masses. He anticipated the movement would continue into 1915 but only stressed better wages and better lodgings for agricultural workers to that point. The day following correspondence with C. P. Scott, he turned fifty, writing William, "Telegrams letters & postcards pouring in from all parts of the Kingdom—birthday & Insurance." His efforts to change the system of landownership would not garner such well wishes. Two days following Asquith's carte blanche, he also informed his brother, "Just attended a Land Enquiry Committee. Getting on well with it." In fact, the findings concerning how the populace were living in rural communities were finished the next month and printed. On March 12, he admitted, "We are all so tired that we can get up no excitement as yet. Yesterday I had a good time over land taxation. Awkward question."[33]

Lloyd George gave a reason for his exhaustion a week later when he updated William on the Marconi trial while also relishing, "Rufus & Samuel smashed the Marconi slanders in Court today. Our fellows very pleased. My name was not mentioned in the libel suits. The rascals had been suggesting I had made scores of thousands out of the contract with the British Government. I never had a penny in it. I had a little in another wireless Co/ which had nothing to do with the contract." Then, a letter dated March 21 arrived from George Cadbury, and contrary to Grigg's assessment, its author must have known about the scandal. Cadbury, observed, "Those who hate you and your measures make themselves heard, but the millions who rejoice in your work and in the courage you have shown on behalf of labour, like myself, have no means of expressing their gratitude for what you have done." He went on to write that the word of Christ would "be more fully carried out as to the brotherhood of men, that in His sight the humble labourer is equally as precious as the wealthy millionaire," and added, "Those who are in the advance guard of an army must expect to bear the brunt of the battle. I trust you will not be discouraged by apparent defeat . . . by the ingratitude of those whose cause you are pleading." As he concluded, he stated, "Your fate is only that of every great leader whose names go down to history as the great benefactors of mankind," but also, "It is extremely difficult when falsely accused to remain absolutely calm and collected under a sense of duty done." This sounds very much like Cadbury was not only a well-known Quaker but also a believer in postmillennialism. Seemingly, Lloyd George was too, even as late as the year the Second World War started, as revealed in chapter one of this study.[34]

On March 22, Lloyd George warned, "if Bonar thinks he can make anything out of it he will get the smashing of his life." Anticipating "the witness box" in four days, he asserted, "Not one of them dare even suggest corruption."

On March 31, he was relieved but defiant. "My exam: is over. The atmosphere today was a totally different one. Today I was the accuser. It is over now & utterly smashed & pulverised. I am receiving-still-congratulations from all quarters. They all say it will help strengthen my hold on the people." It was not over, however, and his broker was "in box" on April 9, part of a parliamentary enquiry lasting until June 19. After the investigative select committee's findings were revealed, exonerating all involved but doubting the wisdom of investing in an American Marconi affiliate, a debate began on the eighteenth to address a Conservative motion tantamount to calling the participants liars. Lloyd George told his brother nine days prior that he was expecting it, but chomping at the bit, stated, "Am eager to be let loose on it. I have things to say about my critics." Five days later, he wrote, "Marconi Committee Report is giving great satisfaction to our friends." His defense "will be couched in a moderate tone," William read on the seventeenth. "Hell fire for the Tories will come outside." Once all ended, he still warned, "If the Tories go on I mean to hit out straight from the shoulder. I want to. Burning for an opportunity."[35]

Concerning the "good time" that Lloyd George had on March 11 with local taxes, there was a parliamentary debate during which he agreed with the opposition on site value taxes being used to relieve local authorities of financial burdens. Education, the uninsured who had tuberculosis, police forces, and roads were included, but he defined "local" as where profits are generated, not "necessarily" where the "increment arises." He was not on board with the revenues being raised locally, arguing that the machinery for collecting them should be imperial. However, on the topic of state subsidies to make up the difference needed in municipalities, he retorted, "I cannot conceive a more futile and mischievous method of dealing with the problem." He believed it would cause them to become vested interests and that all of the mentioned burdens would end up national charges, divesting local powers of any say in such matters for their vicinities. He thought it was necessary in some cases to redefine "areas" as geographically larger than before, agreed that a one or two pence rate should be imposed at the local level, recommended that local authorities should pick two or three of the problems to tackle, and insisted that a single tax would not be appropriate since some property owners improved their land while others did not. He concluded by admitting that the corrections required in the local taxation system could not be made until the next year at least and blamed the cost of armaments for the inability to reduce local taxes.[36]

In April 1913, Lloyd George did not increase taxes, but he did again blame armaments for taking funds that could be utilized for more social relief. He also broke his budget proposals into not only a finance bill but also one on revenue because the Parliament Act allowed the House of Lords to delay money bills. Now, he told the lower house that finance bills would be confined to "the renewal of temporary taxes" to avoid being postponed, and that revenue bills would provide "for the general amendment of the law" to include amended or new revenue allocation proposals. By the time of his 1913 budget revelations, ironically, financial support for the land campaign suffered a significant setback when de Forest stopped contributing and even castigated its committee for a lack of commitment to the nationalization of land. He nevertheless told his brother in May that the Land Committee was coming to Walton Heath to "spend a weekend with me preparing some Reports & our plans." More than likely, this remark refers to the urban report, since the rural report was mostly composed and would be done in August, though not published until October. The former would not be finished for nine more months and was not published until April 1914.[37]

To aid in the funding of the urban inquiry, Lloyd George found Joseph Fels, another soap mogul, to replace de Forest, and the nationalization of land became a huge issue at a July conference. Farmers, estate agents, surveyors, and government agricultural officials were represented. Because all agricultural land was exempt from current taxes, they were afraid entire site valuations would lead to a national tax on holdings and alter how their improvements were assessed. As a result, they demanded tax deductions from whole appraisals for improved land maintained by steps like draining, hedging, and fertilizing. That month, Haldane, now Lord Chancellor, recommended a Land Commission of leaders familiar enough with agrarian circumstances to mediate grievances between tenants and landlords, including wage negotiations. By two months later, Lloyd George agreed, though he had ridiculed any interference by Haldane on land issues seven months earlier. He asked Haldane for help, but then requested assistance from other Cabinet members, to draft a memorandum for a commission with authority to declare improvements immune from local rates and award better, minimum wages to agricultural laborers. Immunity, or at least some relief, were now deemed possibly more effective than the valuation of sites.[38]

Before the rural report was finally published and Lloyd George officially began his latest land campaign, he wrote Maggie about another morning's fare to discuss the subject: "We had a most successful breakfast in spite of some ominous rumblings from the Land Taxers—they were as pleasant as they possibly could be. Hemmerde whom we all dreaded was specially helpful.

That is what comes of making troubles in advance." These were members of Parliament as well as others who favored a single tax. E. G. Hemmerde had just won a seat for Norfolk advocating it, something Lloyd George was clearly not going to promote. The rural report's details reflected his preferences, including justifications for raising agricultural laborers' pay and a practical plan for achieving that goal. As a majority was working sixty hours a week for less than eighteen shillings, it was not hard to get general agreement from both parties that something had be done. However, governmental financial support for such things as rent on dwellings was not factored into the report. Boards would be created in local areas to stipulate pay increases, but the amount would not be one for all and would differ according to regions based on economic conditions.[39]

Lloyd George even contributed the preface of a book by Rowntree, *The Labourer and the Land*, published in 1914. There, he credited laws like the one for miners in 1912 with raising pay that helped remove from England's reputation a "blot on its Religion and its Civilization," which was "shameful." Subsidy increases for country lodgings and city dwellings were suggested in the report, but government grants were not typically viewed as favorable by Lloyd George or most of the other Liberals. They thought of them as charity, or worse, doles. The report estimated there were 120,000 too few cottages for the workers. Before publication of *The Labourer and the Land*, Lloyd George had met the committee principals in July, and they determined that additional payments for rents would be added to wage packages. Local councils would also be pressured to provide more housing or lose their government funding for other things. This would hopefully allay fears that landowners would charge more from renters and farmers would lower payments to agricultural workers, if residences were subsidized separately from wage adjustments. Liberals also hoped wage increases would lead to more laborers buying smallholdings, moving Britain from feudal to democratic landownership.[40]

To also relieve the anxieties of farmers, most of whom supported Conservatives but were unsure of their land tenure status, the report unequivocally extended total security adjudicated by a land court specifically appointed for that purpose. Uncertainty made them potential converts to Liberals. Lloyd George did not want farmers to be hurt financially by what was being offered to their agricultural laborers, but the landowners for whom they were tenants. Of course, landlords also rented property in urban areas, though developers often owned apartment complexes or other edifices constructed on the land. The builders were not taxed on the value of the land but on any income their structures accrued, and they naturally expected their occupants to defray their taxes. They would, however, be given financial aid for improvements to dissuade them from adding to the burdens of tenement dwellers. Once again, Lloyd George intended for the landlords to absorb the added costs. To ease the minds of those who were shocked by such socioeconomic changes, Liberals explained that implementation of tenure security would motivate farmers to spend more of their money on the land and dedicate as much fertile soil as possible to growing crops. Fear of landlords evicting them for such things as planting on their wildlife reserves would be gone. To discourage landowners from raising rents to drive tenants off the farms or simply because tenants wages went up, a land court system would determine what was equitable and decrease rents when necessary. Lloyd George and the Liberals desired to distance landowners from tenants and, in the process, take them from controlling land to merely living off of it for considerably less wealth.[41]

The campaign for this ideology, regardless of how well defined or not it was, commenced in Bedford on October 11 with two speeches by Lloyd George. He asserted that some dwellings in Llanystumdwy were still vacant due to evictions of their occupants who had voted for Liberals when he was five, that agricultural workers were able to afford less than when Henry VIII ruled, that those in the upper house owned a third of all English land, and that landlords who used their properties for everything except farming were not subject to the regulations that owners of industries or mines were. Lord Beauchamp, First Commissioner of Works, chaired both presentations, and the assertions were first heard by twenty-five hundred party representatives. Four-thousand more Liberals heard them later the same day. Lloyd George had informed William one day before that Beauchamp "was making arrangements for the meeting."[42]

Two days following his deliveries at Bedford, Lloyd George summed up the foray of his scheme for his brother: "First shot went off even better than I anticipated. The meetings were great—enthusiasm determination—all present. We shall win. Landlordism is doomed. I felt it on Saturday more than ever." Three consecutive Cabinet sessions then convened on October 14 to discuss the campaign's details, and his reasoned perspective for William was, "Most satisfactory Cabinet—Ulster & Land. We are going through the land proposals one by one so that I shall be in a position to place the whole plan before my next meeting at Swindon next week." His letter the next day qualified, "Another excellent Cabinet. Bore down all opposition so far—tomorrow we have another Cabinet to finish off. The P.M. did not want another but one or two Members of the Cabinet are still unhappy about the most drastic of my proposals so we must have another go." Walter Runciman, President of the Board of Agriculture, was the main objector because his post was going to be incorporated under the Land Commission, now called the Ministry of Lands and Forests. He expressed concern about the possibility of a fixed wage for agricultural laborers, saying they would be fired and even more arable soil would be turned into grazing land.[43]

Lloyd George was able to appease Runciman by putting construction of new farmhouses in his hands instead of municipal powers. Burns was another one who voiced opposition, but his objection was to something that was not even brought up: rent subsidies. On the last meeting day of the Cabinet, the chancellor joyfully shared with his brother, "Cabinet over. My plans adopted. Hurrah." Every Cabinet member approved his proposals, and he then made final preparations for a speech at Swindon six days later, where he fleshed out the new ministry's work. It would have multiple land commissioners on a board, and the money for new dwellings would come from the excess capital generated by the national insurance scheme. The board would also be responsible for overseeing land valuation. In his opinion, communicated to William two days later, the delivery "has gone like hot cakes." After three more days, he also conveyed what he was told by Percy Illingworth, the Chief Whip, "the land scheme is going like hot cakes in the North." Two days following that observation, he relayed, "Land going strong" and Lord Chancellor Haldane is "Very pleased with way it has caught on."[44]

William then read from his brother on October 30, "Had a most important deputation this morning of traders on leases of business premises—Tories & Liberals." In his typically optimistic fashion, Lloyd George judged, "They went away delighted with their share in Land programme." Nine days later, his positive mood suffered a reality check in Reading, a stunning blow not only personally but also politically. G. P. Gooch, the Liberal candidate for Isaacs's former seat, lost to his Conservative opponent; but more disturbing was that the Labour Party got numerous Liberal votes. He had run on just insurance and land reforms, which made his defeat rejection of Liberal political policy. Isaacs, now Lord Chief Justice, represented that constituency for more than nine years, making it look like the personal denunciation of a close Lloyd George associate. Two days earlier, the chancellor wrote William about the upcoming election there, insisting, "They started Land Campaign much too late at Reading." After five more days to think about the outcome, he shared that it was "largely due to Larkin. Workmen won't stand this discrimination between Carson & Larkin. I raised the question today." Going further, he stated, "The methods of Larkin's prosecution were an outrage in justice."[45]

James Larkin was an Irish nationalist who had established the Irish Transport and General Workers Union. He advocated violent sympathetic strikes for better jobs and dwellings for urban workers. Just before the Reading election, he had been imprisoned in Dublin on a seditious libel charge, but a lot of workers believed Carson should have been for his comments. There was also a campaign fight over urban versus rural housing interests because Larkin did not feel the plights of the former were being taken into consideration. What Lloyd George had declared at Swindon about insurance monies being used to build lodgings for agricultural laborers caused no small stir among urban renters. Critical placards carried the words "Reading Electors! Do you want your Insurance taxes fooled away on wild-cat country cottage schemes?" He had given his viewpoint at the National Liberal Club but clearly had to share part of the blame too. Larkin was set free on November 13. On election day in Reading, Lloyd George had spoken in Middlesbrough and had made a conscious effort to reach urban laborers. He stated that they and agricultural workers needed one another, as land was central to reforms in society. Authorities in local towns had to have power to purchase properties for a fair price to redress grievances.[46]

Liberals went on to lose three more seats in as many months, but as far as the land reform campaign was concerned, Lloyd George assured his brother after November 21 that "Oxford was the greatest triumph of the Land Campaign so far. The Tories had been whipping up for weeks—sons were brought in to vote." Grigg concurs it was his best land campaign address and points out that it was held at the Oxford Union Society, where somebody hurled a big pheasant, striking his head. Nevertheless, he persevered and won over the hostile crowd so that a motion denouncing his land program lost. Most who attended were lower level students at the university. Eight days later, in Holloway, he indicated that the vote should be extended to the leaseholders, something he had not yet mentioned. His next public proclamations came in Scotland during the first week of February in 1914, the month the urban inquiry was finished. In December, though, he kept William aware of the campaign's status, reiterating that Scott remained "Sound on Land," and interjecting, "Am sending Davies Report for his land observations."[47]

David Davies was the representative for the county seat in Montgomeryshire and was the descendant of a very rich nonconformist mining and shipping family. He was no Liberal lackey, however, but worked with both parties to benefit his constituents. Pro-Conservative newspapers in his shire had published in March 1913 that agricultural laborers were part of a Davies cult, but did not associate at all with Liberalism, which they described as radical socialism. Lloyd George knew he needed Davies's input and support. He told his brother on December 11 that the best way to stay abreast of developments was to read J. A. Spender's weekly letters in the *Westminster Gazette*. "Gives you excellent idea of present position of Land Campaign," he suggested. Spender was its editor and the nephew of the most avid parliamentary single tax advocate from the 1890s, W. B. Saunders. Spender had even double-checked the rural report's introduction to make sure it was consistent with the contents. As 1913 drew to a close, Lloyd George spent his time motivating campaign workers, telling William, "Delivered a long speech to the land lecturers at the N. L. C." There were eighty of them, paid ten pounds each from private sources, plus 150 volunteer workers. He informed them he was willing to include some rating change in his plans and local assistance for any national services.[48]

Asquith had also addressed the National Liberal Club in December and asserted that local powers would be made to acquire land for improvements. Representatives from the English and Welsh associations voted to approve an oversight group to serve as the executive for the national campaign, the Central Land and Housing Council. Rowntree, secretary of the council, stated that the campaign would be more effective if opposition to it were greater. However, approximately one-hundred assemblies were convened daily, a fourth of a million signs were manufactured, and ten million pieces of information were distributed. Before the prime minister spoke, Lloyd George had received a letter from one of the two leading planners of the work the inquiry committee was doing. J. St G. Heath, a university economics lecturer in Birmingham, expressed doubt that the local authorities would get more land for development, whether compelled to do so or not. On behalf of others who still wanted nationalization, he also expressed disappointment with existing proposals. New Year's Day 1914 started with Lloyd George assuring another correspondent that the rating valuation would be employed to make landlords pay their share of taxes. It fell short of specifying the rate amount or of agreeing to a national tax on whole properties. The recipient of his confidence was P. Wilson Raffan, an even-handed member of the lower house. He seemed to want a known rate more than nationalization but was a leading Liberal voice for the latter too.[49]

In a speech given at Glasgow on February 4, Lloyd George finally divulged a value tax on grounds, to be put on top of current rates at the local level. He also said the valuation of the land could not be finished until 1915 and any laws using the statistics could not be enacted until 1919. Then, eight days later, he reiterated for the lower house his statement about when valuation could be completed, but he now specified March 31, 1915. He had been asked for a date certain because on April 1, 1914 half of those funds were to be devoted to benefiting local authorities. Also, he had heard from delegates of the National Farmer's Union by February 6, who told him the funding of local land acquisition was their only objection to the governmental plan. Trying to extinguish so many fires was very difficult, especially when other issues such as Irish home rule, the navy arms race with its attendant expenses, and women's suffrage competed for his attention. On February 19, he wrote his brother about a specific issue he did take time for in Parliament. He was going to make "an important announcement on local taxation."[50]

Lloyd George informed the House of Commons that he intended to offer financial aid to local powers for expenses incurred providing services benefiting the state. Included were education, roads, poor law responsibilities like workhouses for paupers or asylums for lunatics, and police. Again, he blamed increases in naval armaments for delaying action on the need but also promised "that this demand is not merely a serious one, but that it is an urgent one" he would address in the present session. His battle against the Agricultural Rating Act was brought up by Conservatives, who said it only provided temporary relief due to the fight he waged and stressed that laws since then had added to the burden of rural areas. He apologized for not being able to deal with the growth in expenditures at the local level since becoming chancellor, even acknowledging that, indirectly, old age pensions had led to more municipal money being spent "for outdoor relief" as part of the Poor Law, "a fact which is not at all to be deplored or regretted." Defending his opposition to the rating law, he insisted it was not because it lowered local rates. He considered it the worst kind of relief for agriculture, since those making improvements got less proportionally than those who did not and depressed areas less than prosperous ones. He equated it to grants that are "unequally distributed" and charged that they had to be used more efficiently or be withheld, if not removed.[51]

A week after Lloyd George made the commitment to propose action on local taxation in the spring session, he met with a farmers' deputation from Cornwall and then excitedly revealed to William that they, "Looked just like Welshmen—farms all had Welsh names." Tenant farmers were the one segment of rural society who did not jump on the land campaign bandwagon. They wanted tenure security and rent relief but did not want the system of owning land altered because it would potentially create significantly more competition. February was also the month that the urban report was finally composed, but all the Cabinet talked about the next month was the Irish problem. Then came April and the 1914 budget, which started out with clauses for rating relief as well as lowering taxation on improvements. The inequities of the former would be corrected with the future national valuation taxes and the latter redressed by the relaxation of tax rates for construction. On the last day of that month, Lloyd George sent a missive to his brother, calling the budget his "Biggest scheme since 1909." The urban report was also now published.[52]

Since the presentation of the budget in the lower house had to be put off until May 4, the urban report was discussed first. The delay was primarily because of the problems with the Irish but also due to the finance and revenue bills not being ready. Housing for workers was the initial topic, divided into slum, cottage, or parlor dwellings. Up to 10 percent lived in slum dwellings, as many as 75 percent in cottages, and the rest in parlor houses, which were considered sufficient. Those in cottages were compared to agricultural workers in terms of the strong action needed to alleviate their economic distress. At least they were able to improve their rentals, but occupants of slum properties could not. The problem with cottages was too few of them. Those that did exist were frequently constructed improperly, were not as big as they needed to be, had less sanitary accommodation than required, or were not spaced far enough apart. The mandatory purchasing of land by local urban powers was to be the answer, including the providing of urban planning for open spaces, parks, and improved transportation for the workers to get to their jobs. The land bought would be developed and leased to construction concerns. For slum dwellers, the recommendations were to add enough increases to their wages for a justifiable rent or to have urban authorities acquire livable aged houses for the rent the workers could pay. Any who did not have full-time jobs had to find them, but there were no suggestions offered to solve that problem.[53]

Even commercial interests were permitted to participate in compulsory purchases of land leases. First, however, they were also to demonstrate how they would make the properties more profitable than the proprietors had. Businessmen who owned shops on someone else's property were also allowed to take their disputes with the landowners to land courts. In fact, the majority of the workforce, who leased for short periods of time, primarily week to week, could go to court too. By applying these aspects of the rural report to the middle-class urban leaseholders, Liberals hoped to broaden their base. Rating of site values, they believed, would endear them even more to all segments of urban communities except the landlords. A pence of the local rates already in place, therefore, was now to be deducted and recouped from site value taxation. Existing urban rates would also be reduced by a five-million pound state grant. Imposing a site value tax on the landowners, though, kept them from reaping the government rewards.[54]

In his budget address, Lloyd George revealed that he wanted an increase in income taxes to help rural and urban local powers, proposing to achieve that goal by creating a graduated scale for earned incomes above £1000. Earnings from £1000 to £1500 would pay ten and a half pence; £1500 to £2000, a shilling; £2000 to £2500, a shilling, two pence; and £2500 to £3000 or above, one shilling, four pence. It was the last category of the four that raised the most objections, since those over £3000 were also paying the super tax, which along with inheritance taxes, was going up. Since the national valuation of land was not scheduled to be finished until the following year, and the grants would be based on those figures, he decided provisional ones should be given sooner to relieve local authorities from December through March. They would be funded by the immediate collection of graduated income taxes. The special grants amounted to £2.5 million, but the complete calendar year grants would be eleven million. He also made it clear in answering the same question three times that the relief as far as rates was concerned was for improvements and not the land itself. He stressed that the sites had to be rated separately but not "to transfer the whole burden from the composite subject to the site."[55]

Lloyd George went so far as to commend landowners for allowing the valuation of their estates and also stated that the results showed an "extraordinarily high" proportion of improvements. However, the disparity between those who had or had not spent money on their land was obvious too. He added that some landlords were unable to afford improvements, but others had used their land "for other purposes which ought not to be encouraged." He probably was again referring to hunting preserves and uncultivated pastures. Two days following his budget speech, he candidly updated his brother, "Opposition angry but cannot attack—& angriest of all because they cannot." Ending with an elaboration, he calculated, "Support & opposition alike growing as they begin to realise far reaching character of proposals." Members from both parties rebelled, and the reasons were numerous. When the finance bill was finally published in June, it contained the provisional grants. Consequently, being a money bill it was ruled unconstitutional for debate in the ways and means committee. Lloyd George, therefore, removed grant monies so the rest could be approved. However, a law had yet to be passed that would allow those funds to be spent for the grants. The way it stood, the ministry would just accumulate money.[56]

Before May had ended, Lloyd George met again with employees of farmers, sharing with William that it was a "Most interesting deputation of agricultural labourers," but more rebellion loomed large. Almost fifty Liberals in the House of Commons also opposed his budget because, as descendants of vested commercial and industrial interests, they were against the site valuation rating as well as growing weary of radical socioeconomic changes. The day the revenue bill was published, June 19, a letter from them appeared in the *Times*. They wanted fiscal responsibility and stated that the landlords might end up with the grant monies if the Liberals lost a general election before the necessary bills for regulating them could be enacted. The revenue bill that emerged provided neither for the rating of site values nor the reduction of local rates on improvements. It only allowed the acquiring of facts toward those ends. Three days later, land clauses were taken from the finance bill by the Cabinet, its prospect being that a separate bill for finances would be introduced in the fall session. The meanings of the former were that the provisional grants were off the table for the time being, but those supposed to endure were too because of the other funds. The Cabinet also lowered graduated income taxes on the highest earners by a pence, resulting in some radical Liberals and Labour members abstaining or voting against the second reading of the finance bill on June 26. It passed, though, but by a narrower margin of thirty-eight.[57]

As far as the progress of the budget itself, Lloyd George predicted for his brother merely eleven days following, "The millionaires will give us a little trouble but that is to the good as it will accord an impression that we have been bullied by our rich men." After six more days, the Cabinet abandoned its plan for a fall session and tried to bring an end to the summer one quickly to avoid possible dissolution. On the last day of July, however, Lloyd George's finance bill was enacted, a law Grigg equates with that five years earlier. In four more days, the United Kingdom was at war with Germany and her allies. It accomplished socially and economically what Lloyd George desired with his land campaign in terms of democracy, so much so he repealed land taxes once it was over. His speeches on reconstructing Britain, during the "coupon election" of 1918, were about making the land fit for its heroes. "Give back the people, as many as you can, to the cultivation of the soil," he said two weeks after the armistice.[58]

Lloyd George had founded the Ministry of Reconstruction in 1917 and chose Christopher Addison to run it. Addison had served under him in the munitions ministry and had just finished eight months as Minister of Munitions himself. His 1919 Housing and Town Planning Act then followed, and by the time implementation of it ceased in 1922 because of expenditures, 213,800 houses had been constructed. For health reasons, buildings were to allow for lots of air and light, cooler areas for storing foods as well as indoor washrooms. As a result, epidemics and diseases such as tuberculosis or typhoid declined. After overseeing the reconstruction office for eighteen months, Addison served as President of the Local Government Board for six. During that tenure, though, he established the Ministry of Health to eclipse the board, becoming its first leader down to April 1921. Insurance for those who could not find jobs also had to be increased after the war, so the Unemployment Insurance Act was passed in 1920. It brought every wage earner under its scope, except those making more than 250 pounds in nonmanual labor, soldiers, farm workers, domestic and civil servants, or teachers. Its benefits had to be amended twice in 1921 and once in 1922, due to economic decline that left over two million jobless before Lloyd George fell.[59]

8

Disestablishment and Disendowment, 1883–1920

"Anglicanism is now an established failure."

THE FIRST MENTION of the topic of disestablishment by Lloyd George was at age twenty in his 1883 diary. He noted that a conference on the subject was going to be held on November 20 and wanted John Thomas Jones to appoint delegates from Carnarvonshire to attend but added "told him I was too busy." Jones was a landowner in the county and a deacon at the Calvinistic Methodist church in Criccieth. He later vied for the hand of Margaret Owen, who attended there but married Lloyd George. The following month, in a typical Sunday afternoon discussion at the house of a deacon from his congregation, Lloyd George was asked about his feelings on disendowment because of a letter that had appeared in the *Mercury*. He divulged in his diary, but evidently not to the deacon, "3 or 4 all-but-conclusive refutations of anti-liberationist logicisma rushed into my mind." Talks by him on Welsh disestablishment did not begin until 1885, and he only wrote general references in diaries of either praise or criticism he received for the next three years. Concerning his critics, a November entry reveals a "prolonged attack," in which some "were beastly—comparg me to a 'mosquito,' . . . Don't feel much annoyed—Never felt less—In fact felt somewhat gratified that I should be made the chief butt of attack at every Tory meetg we have had since I began spouting—as witness the disestablishment meetings."[1]

Lloyd George's attention had been shifting to the issue of disestablishment from licensing and temperance for quite some time. It had often been discussed at Portmadoc Debating Society and disestablishment gatherings. While publicly debating a Sarn curate in 1887, someone in the crowd stated that those who favored disestablishment should have to stand on the right;

Lloyd George added, "Yes, the goats to the left." On February 13, 1888, he started getting a little more specific in his diaries, reporting that he spoke for ten minutes at a disestablishment assembly in Portmadoc and "raised the wind." His sentiments as well as activism against the Church of England, particularly that it was still the state religion in Wales, were even stronger and certainly more consistent than his feelings about alcohol. Half of his diary entries for 1889, which admittedly ended after only a month, were on Anglicanism, especially its schools in Wales. The broader threat as he viewed it, though, was to Welsh identity. "The history of the English Church in Wales," he insisted, "is one of a persistent & determined series of attempts to crush out Welsh nationality."[2]

The first effort in the House of Commons to disestablish Wales arose when Lloyd George was only seven. Gladstone had opposed a resolution to that effect, which was then rejected by a margin of 164. Another challenge was attempted in 1886, during Gladstone's third ministry, but there was no vote on the resolution. An amendment to reform the state religion, however, failed by only twelve votes. The second resolution finally made it to a vote three years later, which was also defeated, this time by fifty-three. Less than three weeks after Lloyd George was first elected to Parliament, the North Wales Liberal Federation passed a unanimous resolution calling for each Welsh member to demand disestablishment in exchange for his support of Irish Home Rule when Gladstone returned to power. He had defeated Ellis-Nanney by eighteen votes on April 10, 1890, and took the oath of office a week later. He waited until June 13, however, to deliver his maiden speech, but the measure being debated pertained to licensing, not disestablishment.[3]

Though Lloyd George's initial delivery for the lower house was not on disestablishment, his first speech in London was. On May 7, he was the last of several speakers to talk about it at the Liberation Society's annual conference, which convened in Charles Spurgeon's Metropolitan Tabernacle. He had obviously been asked to participate shortly after entering London because he had informed William on April 21, "I must devote my whole mind to preparing for the tabernacle meeting." Even his arrival in the capital had highlighted the priority he was expected to place on Welsh distinctiveness because he was greeted at the train station by some Welshmen carrying the banner of Cymru Fydd, Wales's nationalist movement. Nine days after his tabernacle address, he mailed a letter to his uncle, telling him, "The Western Mail & the Bishop of St. Asaph appear to be enraged. The latter functionally attacked me at some Church meeting here," he incredulously announced. Published at Cardiff, in the more English southern part of Wales, *Western Mail* had the largest daily newspaper circulation in the principality. The Anglican bishop A. G. Edwards was the newest of four in Wales, having just been appointed to the post the previous year.[4]

Lloyd George's detractors argue that he always stressed form over substance, but recognizing that he was the youngest member in Parliament, he understood the need to promote himself and then focus on the controversies at hand. Though he did not speak on disestablishment in either 1890 session, he opposed his party by voting against a Liberal's committee motion, but on August 12 explained to his brother the difference in dealing with fellow politicians and the public. "I can't gain much in this House by my speech," he relayed, "on the contrary I may lose much influence—these MP's are so frightfully nervous & respectable. My audience is the Country." A speech he had prepared for the next day was against funding royal and noble ceremonies like investitures or funerals. Afterward, Queen Victoria made her displeasure with him known to Salisbury. He was mostly, though, contrasting expectations in Westminster to the freedom he felt among the public. His inaugural legislative session ended five days later, and he returned to public forums.[5]

Addressing a Sheffield crowd on November 20, Lloyd George threatened that Welsh Liberals would no longer support the party if English members did not place priority on disestablishment. The threat was all the more significant because Charles Stewart Parnell, leader of the Irish Home Rule or Parliamentary Party, had just been named an adulterer in a divorce case. Liberals needed Irish support to regain power, and they championed home rule, but the numerous nonconformists among their ranks would not tolerate infidelity. The lower house reconvened five days after the Sheffield speech, and the Irishmen chose Parnell as their leader again. Gladstone, however, put home rule on hold until they dealt with Parnell. Near the end of the year, Parnell even appeared once on the same platform with Lloyd George, who stressed for William, "Parnell wants to have *his* say." Another spokesman, "very self-important in his way," was William Abraham, a former miner representing a valley area of Wales known as the Rhondda. Abraham, whose moniker was "Mabon," had established the Cambrian Miners' Federation and became the first president of the South Wales Miners' Federation. He told Lloyd George he would not bother to speak unless they allotted him thirty minutes. Liberals "crammed the programme" with so many "party speakers" that Lloyd George feared having enough time. "Poor me," he also lamented to his brother, "they have relegated to the end of the programme so that the chances are I can only get 5 to 10 minutes. If that be the case I shall positively refuse to speak. I am not going to mangle a good speech."[6]

One thing that made Lloyd George defensive about how often he spoke in the House of Commons, as opposed to public venues, was Uncle Lloyd pressuring him to do so. Resenting it, he vented his frustration to William, instead of to his beloved mentor: "Tell uncle that I hear he is raving about my not taking part in debates. I feel very annoyed with him. Seeing what I have done he might trust me to know when & whether to speak. I can't rush in like a babbling idiot to express my views upon every conceivable topic." He argued he had "exercised a wise discretion in not talking," but Uncle Lloyd should understand, "Unless he restrains himself I'll throw it up in disgust." He had already tactfully tried to convey this to his uncle, telling him that Arthur Acland, who had introduced him in the House of Commons, counseled him not to talk too soon. "Now there is nothing that damages a man in this House more than to speak too frequently," he quoted Acland as saying. "Asquith, who of all the comparatively young men has the highest reputation speaks but once, occasionally, twice during a session," Acland continued. "He has thus acquired a status & always gets an audience."[7]

Regardless of Acland's advice, and to Uncle Lloyd's great pleasure, Lloyd George began speaking often as well as loudly after the new year started. He had stayed silent too long for his own liking, but instead of talking on disestablishment, he used the tithe bill to try and achieve his goals for Wales. Attaching disestablishment lectures to debating about other bills was not all that he had in mind, though. He also told John Herbert Lewis, a landowning lawyer who was one of his best friends and became a member of the House of Commons a year later, that he wanted a new *"Disestablishment* Campaign." He further shared having suggested "a meeting to consider the question of a Liberation Campaign in Wales" to both federations in the principality. By April 11, Tom Ellis was reading, "You may have heard of the new Disestablishment Campaign the Welsh National Council proposes initiating ... & unless the many regrettable jealousies of the North & South Wales Federations upset the business I think it is bound to succeed."[8]

Two months prior, Lloyd George had been upset with his uncle again for prodding him to debate more often. "Tell our G. O. M. at home that he must exercise his soul in patience. *I* must not overdo it more than S. T. E. I have to speak on Disestablishment & also on the Direct Veto (Wales) Bill." G. O. M. stood for Grand Old Man, an affectionate nickname for Gladstone, and S. T. E. were the initials of Samuel T. Evans. Evans, a grocer's son, was the Liberal MP for mid-Glamorganshire and the only Welsh member who opposed the tithe bill as much as Lloyd George did. Lloyd George then closed with William, "So that I shall have to make two pretty good long speeches to the House in the course of a couple of months. *That* is my opportunity. You must learn to labour & *to wait*. I am not idle you can assure the Governor." On February 18, he also let his brother know how hard he thought it would be to speak on disestablishment when the time arrived. "Don't think there will be the remotest chance of getting in a word even edgeways," he predicted. "We all want to speak—especially those who didn't help us in the Tithe fight."[9]

As it turned out, disestablishment did not even come up for discussion until the next year, when a Welsh MP from Flintshire moved a resolution to debate it. Lloyd George's comments on it were of no great importance, and anticlimactically, instead of focusing on the real problem, he chose to zero in on how many Anglicans were in Wales. He and three other Welsh members did, however, take advantage of what were otherwise innocuous discussions on the Clergy Discipline (Immorality) Bill to voice their objections to the Established Church. The bill, first introduced in July 1891, was a progressive measure intended to make it easier to dismiss any clergymen found guilty of misdemeanors and to provide financial assistance for the bishops who had to pay for the prosecutions. Lloyd George, Evans, D. A. Thomas, and Ellis, with two Scotland representatives, one a Welsh native, forced the bill's withdrawal until the following spring. Thomas, Merthyr's representative, was also a grocer's son, though his father became wealthy investing in coal mines. In February 1892, Lloyd George spoke on disestablishment at Birkenhead and leveled the charge, "The present Anglican institution has nothing in common with the ancient Church of the Welsh people," concluding with the sarcastic slur, "except perhaps, its endowments." When the clergy bill was reintroduced in April, Lloyd George was successful in getting himself, Evans, Ellis, and Wynford Phillips, the Welshman who represented Scots, appointed to the committee assigned to review it. To counter their obstructions, Gladstone also got himself appointed. His intimidation was unnecessary, though, because Henry Campbell-Bannerman, the committee's chair, restricted debate on the bill, and it became law in June. Tom Ellis never had any enthusiasm for the tactics of Lloyd George or Evans but had missed the tithe and direct veto battles due to sickness.[10]

Contrasting disestablishment with disciplining clergy, Lloyd George had also written his wife after the bill was initially presented, chafing, "I don't see why we should be bothered with a confounded ecclesiastical bill." A month before its reintroduction, he shared, "a prominent High Churchman" wrote he too preferred the former. Early April 1892, he spoke on disestablishment at an Anglesey and Carnarvonshire nonconformist conference but ran his second campaign in the summer. Winning by 196 votes, a much bigger margin than his first victory, it was, however, the most narrow of any Liberal candidate in northern Wales and the second lowest in the principality. His opponent was Sir John Puleston, an Anglican from Pwllheli, a member of Parliament for two decades, and the governor of Carnarvon Castle. Puleston used what Lloyd George had said in the debate on the disestablishment resolution, and what he wrote in articles to a Welsh newspaper, to label him a republican sympathizer unfaithful to the monarchy. Not only did Lloyd George win, but also the Liberals were able to return to power in a fourth Gladstone ministry.[11]

As soon as it was known that Liberals had regained the House of Commons and also had carried thirty-one out of thirty-four seats in Wales as well as Monmouthshire, Lloyd George once again started calling for Welsh concerns to be placed on the party's agenda. "It is very important that Liberal statesmen should understand clearly why Wales is so overwhelmingly Liberal at the present moment," he told a crowd in Conway. "It has been done," he stated, "because Wales has by an overwhelming majority demonstrated its determination to secure its own progress." Not just speaking for himself, but also the other Welsh Liberals, he threw down the gauntlet, warning the party and its leader, "I do not think that they will support a Liberal Ministry." Contributing a personal opinion only, he then stressed, "I care not how illustrious the Minister may be who leads it—unless it pledges itself to concede to Wales those great measures of reform upon which Wales has set its heart. Wales has lived long on promises," he observed in concluding, but now wanted "prompt cash." Though he did not mention disestablishment as such at Conway, he had given it first priority in his opening campaign speech.[12]

Lloyd George's focus on disestablishment caused it to become "so dominant an issue," J. Hugh Edwards, his parliamentary colleague and biographer years later, asserted, that "people realised that their demand for religious equality was in process of being transformed into the concreteness of a Parliamentary Bill." Optimistically, Lloyd George wrote Maggie, "Tell uncle that Gladstone has given us better pledges on Disestablishment than even we ventured to anticipate." Gladstone endeavored to buy some time, however, in spite of the fact that the Liberal Party program drafted the previous October at Newcastle had listed disestablishment as second to Irish Home Rule. His government stalled by proposing a Welsh Church Suspensory Bill as a sop to the Welsh instead, but it fell miserably short of what they expected. The bill, introduced on February 23, 1893, by H. H. Asquith, the new Home Secretary, would temporarily freeze appointments to vacant Anglican sees in Wales or Monmouthshire. Also, it would stipulate that any clergy who lost benefices because of legislation were not entitled to compensation. Lloyd George and the other Welsh MPs initially looked upon this bill as a first step toward their goals but soon doubted Gladstone's commitment. He told his wife, "we must press him hard. He will try to get out of it if he can." In fact, the bill was removed after seven months without a second reading.[13]

Welsh Liberals were also very disappointed that a major post was not given to one or more of their members in this fourth ministry of Gladstone. George Osborne Morgan, a representative for Denbighshire, who had served in his second and third ministries as Judge Advocate General and Under Secretary for the Colonies, respectively, turned down an offer to return to his initial office. Another Welsh member, Edward Reed, also rejected an insignificant appointment, but Tom Ellis agreed after much thought to become a Junior Lord of the Treasury. That position also made him Deputy Whip, meaning he would no longer be able to side with those who occasionally withheld their support from the government to draw attention to Welsh matters. Indeed, it was now Ellis's responsibility to make them tow the party line. For that reason, Lloyd George and other friends of Ellis had mixed emotions. Evans, Lewis, and Beriah Evans, supervisor of the Welsh National Press Company, tried to talk him out of accepting the job. Lloyd George at first seemed pleased any Welshman was part of the government, but also sorry to lose a fellow obstructionist, he later alleged he had been against Ellis taking the office.[14]

Whether Lloyd George was opposed to Ellis joining the ministry, he did acquiesce to its suspensory bill, even though he proposed his own resolution just over two weeks before its introduction. He updated his uncle, "We have just terminated a long meeting of the Welsh party where we discussed the Disestablishment situation. I proposed a strong resolution & supported it in a strong speech which was cheered at each point. After a protracted discussion we carried it *unanimously*." The leader of Welsh members, Stuart Rendel, congratulated him on putting it so well. Rendel, whose constituency was Montgomeryshire, became their chief in 1888, though he was not Welsh. Regardless, he encouraged them to fight for distinctive Welsh legislation under the auspices of the Liberal Party. He particularly favored disestablishment because it had broad appeal inside the principality, with little serious opposition outside. He considered it a feasible problem to tackle and tried to win religious liberty for the Welsh, while also devoting his time to removing their politics from manipulation by English nonconformists. The Liberation Society was also slowly trying to get it implemented on a national scale, but Rendel got tired of waiting. Having a daughter who was married to one of Gladstone's sons did not hurt his efforts either.[15]

John Grigg stressed that Lloyd George was far less verbal in 1893 than earlier, and not only on the suspensory bill. Though he was more restrained during his fourth year in Parliament, he actively participated in drafting a government bill to not only disestablish but also disendow the state church in Wales. Asquith drew up its initial proposal in November. Immediately after the first draft's completion, Lloyd George updated Lewis, who had been ill too, on the government's plans. Assuring him that he was "very much" missed by all Welsh members, he enthusiastically encouraged, "especially as we stand in need of your valuable counsel & assistance in shaping our proposals for Disendowment. I fully trust, however, that you will be back in the House before the Scheme has been whipped into anything like its final form." An election the following month would give Lloyd George an opportunity to "humble Church insolence," he told William. "They treat nonconformity as if it were a mere footstool to power." He started the next year explaining to his wife his perceived chance at humbling the state religion for its lack of respect.[16]

On New Year's Day, 1894, Lloyd George informed Maggie that H. J. Torr, a Liberal from Horncastle, was running for the district seat of Lincolnshire and was, "against Disestablishment or rather Disendowment & as I consider his victory would be a disaster for Wales I have taken in hand the matter of either bringing him round or punishing him." Having "attended a meeting of the Liberation Society" earlier that day, he told her he had moved "that unless he voted for Welsh Disestab. the Liberationists in the constituency would be asked not to support him." He finished his letter very judgmentally, asserting, "I don't see why these snob Churchmen should be allowed to ride on Non-conformist votes into the House of Commons to oppose Noncon. principles." Two days later, he followed up with Maggie, elaborating that Torr had "positively refused to have anything to do with Disestablishment" and was "very wild about it." After another day, he explained that he as well as others had "induced" the society members "to carry a resolution appealing to the electors to withhold their support," and "with much greater difficulty, persuaded them to pass a resolution to send that to each elector." He even "guaranteed the expense" for mailing it, although he then promptly looked up two other Liberals who agreed "to find the money" and confidently assured his wife, "I knew I would get it." On January 6, he admitted to her he was "engaged in sending out" the resolution by himself. Torr was a leader in the Church but wanted to reform it. He lost, but the resolution must not have been the reason, as more Liberals voted in that election.[17]

Shortly afterward, Ellis wrote a statement on the Cabinet's behalf, which largely endorsed Asquith's proposal for a disestablishment bill. On February 8, he even went so far as to tell the North Wales Liberal Federation that a number of the Church's leaders would soon be astonished. However, just three months later, Lloyd George relayed to Maggie that J. G. Davies, a Calvinistic Methodist preacher in Barmouth, told him at "the most numerous and representative" meeting of the federation "yet held" he had visited at length with Ellis. Ellis, "had utterly failed to convince him that the government were in earnest in their intentions to push the Bill through." A different prime minister was in office then, though, because Gladstone resigned on March 3. He stepped down mainly due to the House of Lords' veto of the Home Rule Bill he finally got passed by the lower house six months earlier but also because his Cabinet refused to dissolve and fight them.[18]

Lord Rosebery was chosen to fill Gladstone's post, but two days after Gladstone resigned, Lloyd George told William that ten Welshmen would withhold their support for the new government if Rosebery refused to give a pledge on disestablishment. "It wouldn't turn them out but it would reduce them to a state of impotence," he pronounced. Ellis became Chief Whip under Rosebery, but that did not stop Lloyd George from fomenting a rebellion when William Harcourt, Leader of the House of Commons and Chancellor of the Exchequer, did not make an ironclad commitment in a meeting with Welsh members called by Lloyd George. Yet, more important in sparking the rebellion was the result of a Montgomeryshire bye-election to fill Stuart Rendel's seat, left empty by his acceptance of a peerage. A Liberal just barely won the election, prompting Lloyd George to interpret the close call as meaning Welshmen wanted more aggressive, nationalistic stances by their representatives. Only three other Welsh members joined him in that assessment, two being Lewis and Frank Edwards. They had been chosen as co-whips of the Welsh party under Osborne Morgan, its new chairman after Rendel. Lewis was hesitant, but Edwards was eager. The last of the three was Thomas, but he was not Lloyd George's minion. He participated as self-appointed champion of South Wales.[19]

Before all four of the men committed themselves to the rebellion, a disestablishment and disendowment bill was introduced, again by Asquith. It was not to take effect until the beginning of 1896, but it would have ended the established religion in Wales, removed Welsh bishops from the upper house, and given Church tithes to county councils. As Lloyd George prepared to speak on it, he informed his wife, "I shall strongly criticise the life interests part of the measure but, of course, I shall avoid anything in the nature of an attack on the Government." However, days later he wrote, "Our game now is an independent party." During his delivery, he noted that Wales had enjoyed independence in the past, a measure of it even being realized in his own life-time with the Welsh Sunday Closing Act and intermediate education. He refuted those who said the number of Anglicans and nonconformists in Wales was roughly the same, also objecting to compensation of clergy who lost their offices. After two days, he then glowingly shared for his brother how many had congratulated him on "a daring performance. Quite the first thing of the kind ever done here. First bold assertion of our separate National existence & first bold attack on the Church right in the front."[20]

Sixteen days before he spoke in the House of Commons, Lloyd George had already taken his nationalistic plea to voters in his district. Addressing a Carnarvon crowd, he professed it was time for independent action to be taken by Welsh legislators to pressure Rosebery's government into making disestablishment a priority. He said the Cabinet was composed of Church-men and added that some of them "were originally Nonconformists, but they left their Nonconformity behind immediately they came in contact with the atmosphere of London society." Another sixteen days following his parliamentary presentation, he won endorsement in Bangor for his obstructionism. He claimed that all he and the other three colleagues wanted was a promise from the government to steer disestablishment through every phase of the legislative process that year, extending their session through autumn, if necessary. They would then be loyal again. Beriah Evans later stated for disestablishment that Lloyd George was willing to sacrifice party loyalty, friendship with Ellis and co-whips as well as a Liberal government in power. He also quoted Lloyd George's response to those who had leveled that if disestablishment was passed, the United Kingdom would eventually have no religions: "The nation will never lose its religion so long as it maintains its reverence for things spiritual; and if a nation ceases to take an interest in religion, the maintenance by law of an official connection with religion in the form of an Established Church, is a piece of loathsome hypocrisy that deceives neither God nor man."[21]

As it turned out, a majority of Welsh members stayed with Rosebery, and

regardless, the bill was pulled in July due to furious opposition from the Anglican clergy. Rosebery did pledge there would be another bill on it in the
following year, and the rebels agreed to start accepting the official instructions
from the Liberal leadership again. That, of course, meant Ellis, their fellow
Welshman. Parliament did not meet in the fall, but the new bill was presented
by Asquith on February 25, 1895. It was essentially the same as its predecessor,
but Lloyd George was determined to see that it did not meet the same fate.
Seventeen days before the bill's introduction, he wrote to his spouse that he
had "read up last year's debate on Disestablishment so as to be well up in their
arguments." He also asked her to send him an article on the national awak-
ening in Wales against Anglicanism by Edwin Jones, Bangor's vicar. Books
by the Bishop of St. Asaph and John Pryce, the former on the Church of England but the latter on the ancient British church, were requested too. He even
guardedly staked his regard on the bill's success, telling William on March 1,
"This week quite establishes my parliamentary reputation so long as I don't
upset it & I don't think I shall." The same day the bill came up for a second
reading, an article by him appeared, pointing out that only one-fourteenth
of Welsh people were communicants in the Church of England and "that
after an adequate test, extending over a period of 350 years, for two centuries
and a-half of which it had practically no competitor, Anglicanism is now an
established failure."[22]

When the bill reached the committee stage in two more months, Lloyd
George succeeded, after two attempts, in getting Asquith to amend it to include a Welsh National Council to oversee tithes, elected by county councils.
It had also taken him two tries to even get the Welsh members to accept it.
Nearly two-thirds of them had not been present for the second meeting. A
day after the bill's approval by the Welsh Party, he alerted his brother that
the London and North-Western Railway "people are moving heaven earth &
the other shop in order to get us ruled out of order." Any rumblings of Welsh
nationalism were viewed as threats to company interests in Wales. The bill
already provided a three-man commission to disperse funds from the tithes,
but Lloyd George pointed out it was quite exceptional for a majority of them
to be from unaffected areas and for an overwhelming non-Anglican majority
in affected areas to have no representation. The opposition saw an opportunity
to split Liberals by endorsing the amendment, at which point he asked for its
removal. Conservatives objected, and when a vote on it came, he was embar-
rassed by having to vote against what he had sponsored.[23]

Ironically, just three days before officially introducing his amendment,

Lloyd George had revealed to William that the "Church party" had decided to support it. He delighted, "This will frighten the Govt." His grandstanding at the expense of his party is clearer in a subsequent letter to his brother eleven days later. He wrote that success on the amendment and victory by Cymru Fydd over the South Wales Liberal Federation would mean "the people will begin to believe that the 'Gods are with me.' They are always apt to judge by result." Of course, the people were the Welsh, and Cymru Fydd was resisting Wales's domination by its most heavily populated counties, Glamorgan and Monmouth. Thomas led the other organization, but for some time there had been a power struggle between him and Lloyd George for official recognition as the spokesman for all Wales. Thomas opposed a Welsh National Council because it would give smaller northern shires more power than he was willing to concede. Outwitting him and also promoting Cymru Fydd as the only confederation for a politically unified Wales busied Lloyd George the rest of 1895, since Rosebery's ministry fell in June. That also meant Lloyd George had to run for reelection again.[24]

The 1895 election brought Conservatives back to power under Lord Salisbury for the next seven years, in coalition with Liberal Unionists. Liberals lost six Welsh seats, including the one held by Frank Edwards, and more than one hundred total. Lloyd George won by two fewer votes than in 1892, defeating Ellis-Nanney for a second time. The margin of defeat for Lloyd George's party meant disestablishment or other distinctively Welsh issues would be delayed yet again, but adding insult to injury, he was blamed by some at the time and later for Rosebery's fall. He was criticized for working in a clandestine way to persuade Asquith to bring his amendment up again and talking to the opposition about it. Asquith had apparently agreed to include some version of it in a ninth clause to the disestablishment bill, but before it could even be presented the ministry had lost a vote on an entirely different matter and was forced to resign.[25]

That Lloyd George had conversed with Conservatives, especially the Churchmen, is clear, because he informed William of a meeting he had scheduled with the Archbishop of Canterbury to talk about "the Welsh Clause. I want him to save even a remnant of it in the House of Lords." Five months later, he was still being attacked by disgruntled Liberals for causing Rosebery's fall, something he would have to live with again after Asquith fell from power as prime minister. He appealed to Ellis for help, upset he was being called "a traitor to Liberalism" due to his "action in reference to the ninth Clause of the Disestablishment Bill" and held responsible for driving "the Earl out of office." Ellis defended him in print, but after a month, Henry Campbell-Bannerman, who had served as Secretary of State for War under Gladstone and Rosebery, gave a speech. He included comments on Wales, and according to a letter from Lloyd George to his brother, "puts self government first, religious equality second." Campbell-Bannerman also succeeded Harcourt as the leader of Liberals in the House of Commons later.[26]

In spite of objections to his Welsh nationalism as well as his overtures to Conservatives, Lloyd George was still being heard and continued to have influence. However, references to the topic of disestablishment are far fewer in his letters after 1895. Julia Neuberger, Chief Executive of the King's Fund and a Jewish rabbi, astutely observed in 1999 that he persisted in pressing so much for it "presumably partly because he believed it so passionately as a cause of unfairness . . . partly because of his own experiences, and partly-perhaps-because the nonconformist conscience needed to push for moneys to be made available to the poor which were still going in tithes." In her memorial lecture, she proceeded to stress the last observation, adding that his "speeches seem to suggest that that question of distribution, and the role of religion in poor relief, was central." Disestablishment did not provide Lloyd George with as many opportunities as some other issues to assert himself as a nationalist leader during Salisbury's third ministry.[27]

Home rule, land reform, and the Second Boer War now took up most of his time. Even though he failed to bring the South Wales Liberal Federation under the auspices of Cymru Fydd, like he had its counterpart in the north, Lloyd George remained determined and pragmatic in his approach to nationalism. Having been forced to stop speaking by a boisterous crowd of Thomas supporters at a Newport Welsh unity meeting in January 1896, he nevertheless expressed a very practical attitude to William just four months later. "No harm in proving that Nationalism means something more immediate and substantial than ideals," he wrote after successfully opposing fare increases on Welsh trains by the London and North-Western Railway Company that were already significantly higher than average costs. The company had also been pressuring quarries in Wales to employ railroads instead of ships to transport slate. Obstructionism once again became Lloyd George's preferred method of getting whichever party in power to focus on Welsh concerns.[28]

Lloyd George spent the remainder of 1896 as well as the early months of 1897 opposing the Agricultural Ratings Act and two education bills proposed by the Salisbury government. By February 1898, he was so extremely frustrated with his party's indecision on certain matters, he fumed to his brother, "I am inclined to believe a self-denying ordinance would be a good thing for Wales." After another week passed, he also shared with William that he "was proposed & seconded but declined" the chairmanship of the Welsh Party. The new session had opened, and he was one of three men nominated to succeed Osborne Morgan, who had died in August 1897. As one of the others was Alfred Thomas, a close friend who had helped him numerous times, he took his name out of consideration. More than one of his biographers has suggested that he knew he could persuade this Thomas to do what he wanted, he could ill afford possible but admittedly not likely defeat, and he desired to concentrate on national instead of regional issues. Two days before the vote, correspondence from his uncle touched on all three points, and five weeks after, he was stressing the importance of the third in a letter to his brother: "I mean to raise the whole Nonconformist position in England & Wales." To achieve the goal, he added, "I am summoning a meeting of Noncon: members of the House to consider & agree upon the line of attack."[29]

Nonconformists convened after nine more days, and Lloyd George proclaimed a victory: "We had an excellent attendance," he wrote William, "& they approved of the line I proposed to take." Just under two months later, he again reported, "Most excellent Noncon: conference this afternoon. Great success." In July, he conveyed that yet another nonconformist conference was "first rate." August witnessed the initial assembly of the National Liberal Council for Wales and Monmouthshire, where he seconded a motion that reforms like disestablishment, temperance, land, and education necessitated "such an extension of self-government as will confer on the four nationalities of the kingdom the power to manage their own domestic affairs." He was definitely expanding his leadership among nonconformists, in and out of Parliament, but he told his wife he was concerned about the Cardiff "Cosmopolitans," who wanted "Church Discipline Acts" when "Disestablishment is the only answer." He continued to speak about it at nonconformist chapels, in particular the one at Lewisham, John Scott Lidgett's hometown, on November 10, 1899.[30]

During the same year, Lloyd George also found himself approving of the many endeavors of the Archbishop of Canterbury, Frederick Temple, to counter ritualists in the Anglican Church. Temple weakened ritualists by outlawing two of six liturgical practices through which they were endeavoring to return Anglicans to their Catholic roots, using candles during processions and the burning of incense. At a meeting of the Congregational Union in October of 1898, Lloyd George had negatively contrasted ritualists to the atheists of the French Revolution: "These poor atheists in the madness of strife, in the smoke of the conflict, saw Christ more clearly than the priests of Christendom with all the candles lit on their church altars." In Nottingham that year, he had also stressed that the ritualists did not fear disestablishment and, like Jesuits in their martyrdom, would suffer similar results from their careless acts. He participated with a committee of nonconformist MPs at a National Liberal Club meeting in February 1899, summoned to agree upon an amendment against ritualists. The next month, he spoke on ritualism at Chelsea Congregational Chapel.[31]

Whatever influence Lloyd George had on nonconformists or other Liberals into the fall of 1899, and whatever national ambitions he had, suffered when he vehemently opposed the Second Boer War. In spite of his antiwar stance, he still felt confident in his constituent's support as the year closed. Pointing out contrasts between him and his voters, he enumerated those distinctions for William: "They have been very loyal to me as a whole—despite individual differences to the contrary. The latter are unavoidable anywhere. In disposition, training, creed, habit of thought I am everything they dread. For all that they have stuck to me with a personal devotion which I believe is quite unrivalled by that shown by any other Welsh constituency to its member." By February 9 of the following year, *The Star* went so far as to describe him as "the undoubted leader of the Welsh people . . . no serious rival in their affections," he quoted to his brother. However, two months later, while contemplating his fourth election, he emphatically insisted for William's eyes only, "They can chuck me out next time if they will—& I have no doubt myself they will—but I won't recant a syllable—no nor even moderate my views even a shade." Contrary to being chucked by voters, he won with his biggest margin, 296. His opponent was Henry Platt, former Bangor mayor, Carnarvonshire sheriff, banker, and militia colonel. All Welsh Liberals won, but only a fifth of them were pro-Boers.[32]

In defending the Boers, a numerically small people like the Welsh, Lloyd George viewed himself and was seen by some others as a champion of democracy. He relayed to his brother that the chairman of a county council he attended in February 1901 described him as "the only man whom the British democracy trusted." That April, he acknowledged, "Am getting strong hold on English democracy." During July, he accepted his uncle's advice on, "the advisability of talking on Education," presumably instead of the war, and in the fall he was already preparing a strategy for the postwar years. Neither he, nor the pro-Boers collectively, who simply numbered thirty in Parliament after the "khaki election" of 1900, can be credited with stopping the war. It dragged on for ten and a half more months, but before 1902 ended, he had regained any political influence he might have lost and more by opposing a new education bill. Arthur James Balfour, Conservative Leader of the House of Commons and Salisbury's nephew had introduced the bill before succeeding his uncle as prime minister that July. At Norwich in the spring of 1903, Lloyd George commented on a unanimously carried resolution there that emphatically condemned the resulting Education Act, calling for disestablishment instead. He prophesied, "Let every sort of doctrine be preached," but the "result would be that, in the long run, the truth would be got at. That was the whole essence of liberty and equality." By July of 1904, he was combining disestablishment and Irish Home Rule in anticipation of his party's return to office.[33]

The people of his own district boroughs stood by Lloyd George again in the January 1906 election, which had to be called because the Conservative ministry had not dissolved. This time, he defeated R. A. Naylor, an Englishman who owned a lumber business and spoke no Welsh, by a margin over 400 percent greater than any of his previous victories. Even the leading Conservatives in Carnarvonshire voted for him. He had campaigned exclusively for himself just one week and spent the remaining two helping other Liberals. The additional thirty-three Welsh seats were won by Liberals too, and they also captured fifty-eight of the seventy Scottish districts. Nationwide, Liberals gained the biggest clear majority since Earl Grey's 1832 Whig government. Balfour even lost his Manchester seat, though he was able to get another one for London the next month. Only three of his Cabinet members got reelected. From all accounts, Lloyd George made reference to disestablishment in general terms only and tried to heal wounds that had been caused by a two-year fight over education. His greatest pleasure, though, was how many nonconformists were elected to fight for those issues.[34]

Lloyd George was forced into dealing with disestablishment before anything else in 1906 as D. A. Thomas, S. T. Evans, and Ellis Griffith were clamoring for it. He feared they would put the party in an awkward position with their unyielding demands. Griffith, the representative for Anglesey, came from an upper-class Welsh family, studied law at Cambridge, and had nominated another person to be chairman of the Welsh Party in 1898. Ironically, Lloyd George commented on his intention to smash Griffith two months before the 1906 Parliament convened, justifying to his brother, "he is too great a coward to fight" on the pledges for Wales. On the opening day for the first 1906 session, he approached A. G. Edwards, the Bishop of St. Asaph, to see if the Welsh Anglican leadership would agree to a moderate, gentle bill on disestablishment that would leave everything intact except endowments collected through tithes. Edwards took that proposal to the Archbishop of Canterbury, Randall Davidson, pointing out it was better than previous offers and that Lloyd George apparently wanted as little controversy as possible.[35]

All of them met the following day, when Lloyd George put something new on the table, a royal commission to investigate not only the Church of England but also all the other churches in Wales. Davidson ultimately consented, and on March 7, a unanimous Cabinet did too. The nine-man commission commenced its inquiry in October, having as its chair a Welsh Lord Justice of the Court of Appeal who was an Anglican. The others were divided equally between Anglicans and nonconformists, Evans being one of the latter. The chairman's assignment was to determine the condition of the churches in Wales, not to redress grievances between the Established Church and non-conformist chapels, or most certainly not to legislate disestablishment. The commission limped along for six months, at which point Evans and two of the remaining nonconformists left. In spite of that, plots, and disagreements, it lasted until the end of 1910. Evans stated as early as February 1907 that he was going to resign, and when he did, Lloyd George also viewed him as a coward: "All the same he is missing his chance of making a great name in Wales," he expressed to William. "Not sorry personally. He is funking Vaughan Williams," the chair. Two months after the resignations, Griffith attempted to prompt Campbell-Bannerman into committing to a disestablishment bill for 1908, but the latter said that it should not be expected and that other bills might be given priority.[36]

The day the prime minister disabused Griffith of hopes for a disestablishment bill, Lloyd George told William, "We are in for a row over the dropping of Welsh Disestablishment for next year. I mean to fight the Croakers. At first they will look like winning but I'll down them in the end." The "croakers" were Lords, whom he blamed for not passing Liberal bills on education and licensing as well as disestablishment. That fall, 1907, the so-called Welsh National Convention was held in Cardiff to speak out against the government's lack of action on the disestablishment front. Every Welsh church was invited to share in the effort, and their members were encouraged to come. Lloyd George was asked to participate, and a few days before it met on October 10, he tried to get a written guarantee from Campbell-Bannerman that the issue would be addressed prior to the current session's close. The prime minister also told him that it could not be put forward yet and gave a more specific reason:

the struggle with the House of Lords. Regardless, Lloyd George assured those who organized the convention that legislation was going to appear in 1909, and his message to the assembly of more than two-thousand nonconformists also defended the ministry. To the planners, he repeated that only having to deal with the upper house would stop a bill from being introduced and reminded the attenders that he had hazarded everything for another small people just seven years prior. He would not abandon his beloved Welsh, but they should not shoot at the ministry from the rear. The potential rebellion was defused, and hearers were clearly moved.[37]

Lloyd George then also talked to Asquith about disestablishment, within three months of the latter becoming prime minister on Campbell-Bannerman's resignation due to illness in April 1908. After a surprising Liberal victory in Pembrokeshire, South Wales, Lloyd George described Asquith to William as "quite choked with emotion" and admonished the former, "Now you must give them Disestablishment." Asquith immediately responded, "Yes they deserve it," and Lloyd George shared with his brother, "The result has exhilarated & heartened the Liberals here & to a corresponding degree depressed the Tories." A new bill for disestablishing the Anglican Church in Wales was introduced in April 1909, and Lloyd George informed William that the prime minister personally gave a "first rate" speech in support of it. "Small House & quiet," he stated, "None of the ferocious excitement that surrounded the controversy in 1894."[38]

The 1909 bill never even got a second reading because of the amount of time required for debate on the "People's Budget." It was withdrawn two months later with the understanding that in the next year top priority would be given to it. It had proposed that Welsh dioceses be disestablished on New Year's Day 1911, and local powers choose a Council of Wales to oversee endowment monies once their secularization started in 1915. Those funds would subsidize such social needs as schools and healthcare, therefore making the Church of England look better to the Welsh. The state church would choose representatives to be in charge of buildings, homes, furnishing, closed cemeteries it owned, and donations contributed from 1662. In preparation for the first election of 1910, to begin in mid-January, Lloyd George told a nonconformist meeting in London's Queen's Hall a month earlier that the ministry was going to have to overcome the House of Lord's veto power or disestablishment in Wales would not stand a chance. The election gave the Liberal Party less power than before, only two more than Unionists, the new term for a combined Conservative and Liberal Unionist coalition.[39]

By mid-October, Lloyd George was penning William that the Tories "don't mind settling Welsh Church question." After some "private talks with Balfour" the next week, he specifically confided that even F. E. Smith was "all for settling Lords Home Rule & Disestablishment. If we can do all that it would be a mighty haul. Asaph breakfasted with me this morning. So there are great things brewing." Smith was a member for Walton in Liverpool and had risen to the highest ranks of the Unionist reactionaries, although he also counted Churchill as one of his best friends. Between the two October letters to his brother, Lloyd George also finished his second coalition memorandum for a concerted effort by the two major parties, which among other things offered Welsh disestablishment on the same favorable basis as the Irish agreement in 1869. Because the parties did not agree and the new king, George V, would not threaten to create enough new peers to persuade the Lords to pass such a bill, the second 1910 election was then called for December as a constitutional referendum on the veto of the upper house. This time, Unionists and Liberals ended up with 272 each, though with Irish and Labour support like before, Asquith's government still had a clear majority. The monarch was now convinced to issue the threat he had been asked to make, and the Parliament Act passed eight months later.[40]

Primarily due to King George V's warning, the bill survived in the upper house by a vote of 131 to 114. Davidson influenced twelve additional bishops to vote for it, Rosebery sided with eighty Liberals, and thirty-seven Unionists clinched passage. Of some four-hundred Unionists in all, 112 others joined forces with two clergy in opposition, but the rest abstained. In George V's diary entry that night, he credited Rosebery's decision for convincing twenty of the Unionists to follow suit, even though Rosebery himself had grown more and more estranged from the party he had once led. Lord Curzon was responsible for successfully refuting the bill's detractors, though. One day after the vote, George V's private secretary, Sir Arthur Bigge, Lord Stamfordham, sent a note to Curzon expressing the monarch's sincere appreciation for the role he played in preventing what the king had referred to in his diary as "any further humiliation by a creation of peers."[41]

A caveat in the Parliament Act provided for the upper house to still have the right to delay passage of a law for three sessions in a row. It used that privilege solely for proposed legislation concerning disestablishment and Irish Home Rule. The process for a new bill on the first started in a Cabinet committee meeting two months after the House of Lords lost its power. Six months later what should be included in a fourth disestablishment measure met with the entire Cabinet's acceptance. Contrasting it to the bill from three years earlier, the prime minister assured George V that it left the Anglican Church with more money. It did stipulate, however, that bishoprics in Wales be distinct and not convoke with English clerics in the upper house. Monies dedicated to the state church before 1662 were also to be available to Welsh county councils for benevolence works, the University of Wales, and the Welsh National Library. The official introduction of the bill occurred on April 23, 1912, and Reginald McKenna, the Home Secretary, opened its reading. When he was heckled by two Lords, Lloyd George chastised them. They were members of some families that became rich by the purchase of Catholic properties once the Reformation began and had no right to oppose disendowment.[42]

Even among nonconformists or Liberals generally, outside Wales, declining identity with the principality's demand for disestablishment was evident as 1911 drew to a close. It was clear when a committee of Anglicans and non-conformists met to discuss the wisdom of disendowing any Christian church as the world became less spiritual. The bishops of two Welsh dioceses, St. Asaph's and St. David's, had invited those who were not Anglicans to help them oppose what the latter, John Owen, portrayed as a broadside against the Established Church. He promised a war the likes of which the state religion had not waged in ages, and its central committee began garnering support at bye-elections through the use of biased information. Thus, when the committee held a conference a month after the disestablishment bill was presented, it recommended concession on the amount of disendowment, but Wales was not represented. Amendments to that effect by English Liberals were added to the bill as it made its way through Parliament. Some in Wales warned the ministry that they would bring it down if the bill did not pass, but Lloyd George was not one of them this time. There were also certain Welshmen less enamored with disendowing Anglicanism in 1912, once they realized the money would go for secular uses instead of godly endeavors. One went so far as to claim that nine of ten would cast votes opposing such, if the matter were referred to them.[43]

Two months prior to the year's end, Lloyd George sent two missives to William dealing with disestablishment, indirectly or directly. Contemplating the use of the veto by the upper house on a franchise bill in 1913, he recommended, "then go to country. We could then put through Home Rule— Disestablishment immediately on our return." Eight months earlier, he also referenced the next two years would be difficult but was more optimistic about those two issues: "We must set our teeth & fight . . . Home Rule & Welsh

Disestab: will be through & we can put forward more attractive fare." A dispute three days after he noted going to the country if another veto happened gave him momentary pause, the context of which he shared with his brother: "I am so glad it has burst out over Home Rule & not over Disestablishment. When someone suggested today that the Welsh Bill shd be dropped McKenna & I had to inform our colleagues we should have to go if it were jettisoned." Certain ministers obviously thought their plate was too full.[44]

Clearly, if Lloyd George was serious about leaving his position as the United Kingdom's second most powerful political leader, in the event the disestablishment bill was dropped, those biographers and historians who suggest his enthusiasm for distinctively Welsh causes had waned are mistaken. As already noted, parliamentary debates on regional bills simply did not give him adequate exposure for establishing his leadership inside or outside the government, and national legislation obviously required considerably more of his attention but was also broadly appealing to the masses. A day after he mentioned his possible ministry departure, William received word, "Disestablishment is alright." It was still doing "well" during the first week of December, and he assured, "I am in reserve—when needed. I do not propose to take a leading part unless called in." In the second week, though, disestablishment was not going as well, and it demanded more of his energies than he anticipated. He was now "addressing Liberal Churchmen in a Committee Room upstairs on the Disestablishment Bill," he informed his brother. "Very useful meeting. Think it will break force of intriguing proceeding against Disendowment."[45]

Again, Lloyd George was hopeful too soon because McKenna upset his party's Anglicans three days later. "Real Crisis in Welsh Bill. Liberal Churchmen's serious revolt," he divulged to William. "McKenna delivered a most unfortunate speech which rasped them a good deal. I have done my best to smooth things down. We shall at best have a small majority." Before he posted the letter, he added an update from later that day, again breathing a sigh of relief, "Pulled through by 50." McKenna was responding to a motion from two Liberals, one of whom was Gladstone's grandson and the other a Methodist, that the Church of England be allowed to keep all its money except what it had received from tithes. The *Manchester Guardian*'s editor, C. P. Scott, had also recommended it. Approximately twenty other Liberal members had informed the prime minister that they planned not to vote for the bill on final reading, if the Church of England had not been given advantageous concessions by then. On the other hand, Lloyd George wrote his brother, five days after surviving the McKenna gaffe, "Welsh MPs dissatisfied with concessions.

Very helpful they should say so for it brought Liberal Churchmen round to support the Bill & thus save it. Much as I dislike one of these concessions it has saved the measure."[46]

The specific concession Lloyd George referenced was almost certainly the commuting of the part of Anglican benefices providing for life interests. In an 1894 letter to Maggie, he singled the same one out from the first disestablishment bill. This compromise was also proposed by W. G. C. Gladstone and received the approbation of the ministry on January 10, 1913. Lloyd George described one of that day's disagreements for William: "Had rather a bad division over curates—only 40. This however is I think our last bad fence." Another amendment, to compensate those assistants to parish priests, had been moved, but was defeated three-and-a-half weeks later. Two days after jumping that fence, the bill's third and last reading succeeded comfortably by a margin of 107. It was overwhelmingly defeated in the upper house eight days later, however, five to one. Two of the eighteen bishops even voted for it, the Bishop of Oxford and the Bishop of Hereford. They had been informed by McKenna that the state church in Wales could not afford to commute life interests. One day before the Lords vetoed the first passage of the bill, a mailing from Lloyd George to his brother included the sentences, "Asaph called today. Very depressed—poor fellow. Cried a good deal."[47]

Presumably, Edwards was concerned about hurting the friendship that had grown between him and the chancellor because he had decided to vote against the bill. Since the House of Lords could only forestall the bill's passage temporarily, Asaph need not have worried so. Another first reading of it was not required under the terms of the Parliament Act, but the second reading again on June 17 and its third once more three weeks later were victorious. The upper house declined a second reading of the bill, which hastened its course through the necessary first steps. In the fall, though, three fresh ideas emerged. First, it was mentioned to Lloyd George that to get Unionists to support Irish Home Rule, disestablishment should be abandoned, an option that went nowhere. The notion of ending Unionist resistance to the bill in exchange for the six northern counties of Ireland being removed from the home rule deliberation was also floated. Lastly, one of the peers and the new leader of Unionists in the House of Commons, Andrew Bonar Law, seemed to prefer to let it pass, assuming they would return to power sooner than later to repeal it. The second and third choices did not develop, either.[48]

Edwards continued to be dejected in 1913, three months before the upper house had even declined the second reading of the bill's second incarnation.

Lloyd George shared with William on April 24, "Bishop of St Asaph just left me. He is still very depressed poor fellow." Edwards had also related, "Hugh Cecil liked me very much & has new sympathy with the attacks on me." Cecil was one of the two peers Lloyd George had chastised after McKenna was jeered, the other being his brother Robert, both of whom were sons of Lord Salisbury. Having asserted that their family's palms had run over with fatty oil as a result of stealing from Catholic altars, almshouses, the poor, and the dead, the younger brother's attitude change toward Lloyd George is all the more astonishing. Regardless of Edwards' depression, in excess of fifteen-thousand nonconformists in his bishopric put their names on a petition for the prime minister to do away with disendowment portions of the bill in February 1914. In all, above 100,000 non-Anglicans in the entire principality did so by the time the bill saw its last second reading in April. The margin of victory this time was eighty-four, and four weeks later, on its third and final reading forever, the margin decreased by only seven.[49]

That night, Lloyd George reported to William, "Dull lifeless debate on Disestablishment. Barely a score of members in the House." Once again, the upper house refused a second reading, and after the third, attempted to delay enactment by forming a special group from among itself on July 2 to investigate certain unclear matters related to Welsh Anglicanism. The United Kingdom entered World War I on August 4, and when the ministry moved to make both disestablishment and Irish Home Rule statute law, Unionists acquiesced to present a united front. Many disagreed more with the former than the latter. As events unfolded, the king's assent was actually delayed until September 18. Also, a suspensory act passed in conjunction put off implementation of both for no less than a year, or until the war had ceased. In the case of Irish Home Rule, the entire law had to wait. Ever so subtly, however, only the time frame for commencing disestablishment was stipulated, not those particulars of the law that could immediately take effect to get ready for full deployment. Edwards was livid, believing the Anglican dioceses in Wales had intentionally been misled and betrayed. A huge Welsh Anglican gathering also objected but started working.[50]

Some work to be done before disestablishment, and particularly disendowment, could be operational when the time came involved choosing representatives to oversee securing as well as dispensing what was left to the Welsh Church according to terms of the law. Cathedrals, church buildings, houses for parish priests, transferable edifices, full cemeteries, and annual funds in the amount of 133,000 pounds had to be accounted for as well as delegated.

The monies were from post-1662 private endowments and English donations of interest from Queen Anne's Bounty and the Ecclesiastical Commissioners. The Bishop of St. David's and the Archbishop of Canterbury strongly denounced the loss of 158,000 pounds worth of yearly endowments for secular purposes because of the additional finances that would have to be expended in providing for all unforeseen consequences of the war. The latter also expressed shock that the Anglicans would have to make needed changes for the legislation's maximum implementation without their most able members, whose service in the military would be required. As previously noted, all current clergy with life interests would continue to receive them, a portion even if they left their posts, but curates would no longer be compensated, and new hires would get neither. If a present bishop's seat was given up, the king, as head of the Church of England, had to put someone else on it, after being provided the candidate's name by the three other Welsh bishops or the Archbishop of Canterbury.[51]

Anglican laws would no longer be enforceable in Wales, all Church businesses were to be shut down, and bestowing of offices would have to stop. Furthermore, Church courts would lose their authority, clerical appeals to England would not be permitted, and Welsh bishops could not sit in the House of Lords but would be able to run for election to the House of Commons. Welsh commissioners would allocate disendowed funds to the county councils, the University of Wales, and the National Library but could only serve for three or at most five years. Councils had to get plans for charitable disbursements approved by McKenna, or whoever was Home Secretary, and all tithes from rent-charges would also form part of their allotment. It was a substantially bigger one than for the other two institutions. Finally, the Welsh Church would be allowed to establish its own organization, with a different government plan if desired, and could conduct synods.[52]

In spite of the Unionist agreement not to protest the Welsh Disestablishment Act because of the war, some leading Anglicans refused to consent. Six months after Britain's declaration of war, Asquith's Cabinet advocated a meeting of the principals involved for the Church of England and Wales to come to a peaceful resolution for the acquisition of the former's holdings in light of the chaos created by it. A month later, one of the nobles presented legislation in the upper house that would subject all parts of the act to deferment until a full year after war's end. The ministry countered quickly, offering a six-month waiting period and life interests for any clergy needing to be installed while the war lasted. Its bill passed every step in the House of Lords that day, was in the lower house the next, but did not get addressed until five more, the Ides of March. McKenna had suggested the six-month stay, which caused so much anger by Welsh MPs that he was driven out of his office, over vehement protests by Lloyd George. The chancellor voted for the bill because it provided valuable time to plan how to rebuild all segments of the society following the war.[53]

Lloyd George wrote Maggie about McKenna and the Welsh members, starting three days after the bill's introduction in the upper house. He acknowledged, "McKenna has sadly muddled the Disestablishment business," but he then recognized, "As a matter of fact he is giving nothing away in his Bill but he ought to have consulted the Welsh M.P.'s. That would have put it right." He spoke for the bill on March 15, and informed her later that day, "Went for the Welsh M.P.'s. They are a poor lot of hounds. They thoroughly misrepresent the Bill. It is a very small concession for the sake of unity." What they had falsely construed probably concerned a verbal commitment by Bonar Law and Asquith for no further effort to change or do away with the 1914 act to happen if both parties did not agree. Lloyd George's secretary and mistress, Frances Stevenson, put in her diary, "half an hour later he was still shaking with excitement, & it was a long, long time before he calmed down." A month later, he was still spewing malice to his wife over, "the machinations of the Welsh members. God help the little scabs." He even went so far as to ask the editor of the *British Weekly*, William Robertson Nicoll, to assist the bill with his leading nonconformist paper. He emphasized "religious equality" would be "an accomplished fact," finally ending "the quarrel between Welsh Nonconformity and this alien Church."[54]

All of Lloyd George's efforts to the contrary, the bill for postponing the consummation of disestablishment was itself first deferred and then pulled altogether on July 25. Even one Welsh bishop, most likely Owen, praised him for the bravery and diplomacy he exhibited in his speech on the bill, despite all the disagreements they had voiced on it for years. Since the war was a year old the next month, George V, through an order in his Privy Council on September 14, declared the official date for full disestablishment to come into effect at the war's conclusion. Two years and a month later, the required representative organization was authorized by a four-hundred-member Anglican congress in the capital of Wales, with equal numbers from each bishopric. Two-thirds of them were not ordained. Edwards was the chair of the convention, which also agreed that the Church in Wales be the designated name of the principality's Anglican denomination. In the first month of 1918, a governing body and the representative one conferred, but a constitution was not adopted until disestablishment became a complete reality. Deciding to receive commutation took another nine months, when the second body formed concurred with the first's advice to take it.[55]

Meanwhile, the commissioners in Wales continued to get ready, particularly determining what nineteen parishes sharing the Welsh and English border desired to do. Using a referendum, which included mailing ballots to military parishioners, it became evident that eighteen wanted to stay with the Established Church. Also obvious, especially as late as commutation got approved, was they would not be able to wrap up their responsibilities before the allotted time specified for them to sit expired on the last day of 1919. Because they needed more time, because the Church was in better shape monetarily than in 1914 due to improved grain prices tithes were based on as well as keeping endowments longer than intended by the act, and because life interests were now considerably less due to the loss of 140 incumbent clergy to death, retirement, or relocation from Wales, the original law had to be amended. The Church's central committee called for the act to be revisited in July 1918, by the next government. In September, though, a notice to their leader included a memorandum against it, signed by 181 Unionists. Edwards then informed Bonar Law in October that he wanted a one-time payment of two million pounds for the Church in Wales, in addition to ten thousand more annually.[56]

Even Lloyd George admitted in a letter to Bonar Law nine days prior to the armistice that conditions surrounding disestablishment had changed financially during the war, and he thought it would be possible to solve issues related to money when philosophical differences over repealing the act ceased to get in the way. He had the next electoral contest in mind but made no promises. For his part, the leader of the opposition did not promise Churchmen in his party anything, either, but also stated addressing their concerns over endowments was needed, while still upholding the status of the 1914 law. The most recent Bonar Law biographer asserts that Lloyd George's letter was actually composed by his subject for Unionists to approve and that the prime minister accepted it without a change. It also dealt gingerly with home rule, but foremost, stressed improvements in dwellings, pay, and workplaces for laborers, with no taxation on foodstuffs as well as protection of industry from unscrupulous competitors. The bishops and three Welsh Unionists were totally dissatisfied, of course, but the elder Cecil was so mad that he tendered his resignation to the Shadow Cabinet. Because Cecil had been busy planning for the establishment of a League of Nations, Lloyd George made sure he was in attendance at the Paris Peace Conference.[57]

The so-called "coupon election" was held on December 14, and the coalition government led by Lloyd George returned to power. Nothing was done to amend disendowment until he left the peace talks in late June of the next year. However, he had talked with Edwards four months earlier, who now wanted only £1.5 million but also all of the lands used to support the parish priests. Further, a Church of England parliamentary committee had decided in April that the nation's treasury should pay all costs for its losses. Before other unreasonable suggestions could be offered, Edwards was told by Bonar Law to have a written proposal for amending the act done for Lloyd George by July 26. The king's assent came less than a month later because it moved fairly rapidly through all stages. The resulting Welsh Church Temporalities Act stated that the Welsh Commissioners would be granted more time, would get tithe rent-charges at the rate of £109, and would receive a million pounds from the treasury to offset the payment to the representative body of the Welsh Church, equivalent to a fourth of what the state religion lost. Many nonconformists felt their loyalty had been misplaced and thought Lloyd George abrogated their beliefs as well as his own radical agenda. His response, according to D. R. Daniel's memoir, was they had reduced "the great problem of his country, that of religious equality and Disestablishment" into merely "a petty sectarian squabble." The act fixed disestablishment day as March 31, 1920, and on April 8, A. G. Edwards was chosen to be the first Archbishop of Wales.[58]

9

Tithes and Education, 1886–1922

"The fat is already frizzling in the fire."

STARTING IN 1886, a conflict that became known as the "Tithe War" erupted in rural Wales. It demonstrated the extent to which nonconformists resented their taxes being used to support the Church of England. Three-fourths of the Welsh worshipped in chapels, not Anglican cathedrals or churches, but tenant farmers were still expected to pay 10 percent of the value of the food grains they harvested to the state church. Valuation was based on a seven-year average of selling prices. Over 95 percent of farms in Carnarvonshire were owned by absentee landlords, nearly all of them Anglican. Hostility began when tenant farmers repeatedly asked for tithes to be lessened due to an agricultural depression that dropped costs for foodstuffs by almost half. They argued even longer and more fervently, however, that the Church of England had no scriptural authority to tax them at all, often bolstering their assertions with selected Bible texts. When they refused to pay, legal action was taken to seize their belongings for auction, especially cattle. This step led inexorably to greater condemnation, from God's words or theirs, and physical manifestations of discontent.[1]

Though most of the tenant farmers ultimately paid what the 1836 Tithe Commutation Act required, in the second year of the resistance, they were forcing the authorities to spend money to carry out seizing and selling their possessions before retrieving them by handing over tithes. The initial attempts at resisting the requirement started in 1881, but it took publicity and financing for the efforts to bear fruit. Thomas Gee, Methodist preacher and editor of *The Banner and Times of Wales*, the utmost Welsh newspaper, supplied both needs. He informed the farmers of their legal rights, when planned

confiscations were coming, and ways to oppose the authorities; he also offered financial help for fines they received. Penalties might be levied for such
things as securing fence hinges, oiling cows, or freeing bulls into the midst
of collectors. Lloyd George is given credit for no altercations occurring in his
part of Carnarvonshire, personally being responsible for defusing one case
of seizure and sale cordially. He, the constable, the bailiffs, and the farmer
enjoyed tea together, provided by the tenant's spouse. His involvement with
the movement, however, ended soon, due to some of its tactics and, possibly,
because only one Welsh MP embraced it.[2]

In Montgomeryshire, two counties southeast of Carnarvonshire, farmers
who had not paid their tithes became victims of attempted distraint in May
1887. Around 250 constables, bailiffs, and police from three other counties
came together, traveling from one farm to another on behalf of the Dean of
Christ Church, Oxford, to collect what was owed. After a long argument with
the lawyer representing the Oxford chapter, the first farmer, whose cows had
already been absconded and sold, reluctantly paid almost twice their value to
get them back. The Established Church had the legal right to seize farmers'
stock or produce, after notification. It had to wait ten days before taking possession and could make no provisions for their sale for five more days. Neighbors started to assemble, and by the time police journeyed to the second farm,
fifteen hundred sympathizers as well as curiosity seekers had gathered. Some of
them engaged in fisticuffs with constables, while others hit them with rotten
eggs. One spectator with a stick was thrown to the ground by the constables,
and a farmer was pulled from his horse as he charged through them. Calm
returned when rainfall helped dampen tempers. Then, Anti-Tithe League representatives spoke for quite a while, led by General Secretary Howell Gee, son
of Thomas, the organization's founder. After that, the second farmer refused
to pay unless the tithe was reduced by 10 percent. His plea was turned down,
and the police marched away.[3]

Similar agitation and some violence occurred in practically every Welsh
shire, especially in Denbighshire, where the league had been established in
1886. In one incident there in June of 1887, eighty-four were hurt, including
thirty-five police, after bailiffs tried to confiscate items in payment of tithes
for the Ecclesiastical Commissioners. Approximately one-hundred constables
from that county plus Flintshire, its eastern neighbor, joined four companies
of the 22nd Cheshire Regiment, a lawyer, appraiser, auctioneer, and drovers.
Yet, only one cow was removed because all of the other farmers paid. Police
nonetheless indiscriminately wielded batons at a large number of locals who

had arrived, even bloodying an elderly, lame turnip farmer. The crowd responded by throwing stones at or hitting the constables with sticks until the Riot Act was finally declared. Shire officials always kept soldiers from engaging the crowds, who were amazed by and amiable to the troops. Also, no one ever died, went to prison, or paid fines above five pounds.[4]

Lloyd George acted as secretary of the Anti-Tithe League in South Carnarvonshire, which borders Denbighshire to the west, and spoke at local meetings. Acknowledging his position in a May 19, 1887 letter to Tom Ellis, Welsh MP of Merionethshire whose father was a tenant farmer, he revealed, "arranging a great demonstration in support of the anti-tithe movement to be held at Pwllheli next Wednesday week." He then invited Ellis to speak at the Whitsun vacation meeting and added that, "The people are looking forward to you for the development of a national policy which they are quite tired & disgusted of waiting for from their own representatives." He ended in the style worthy of a budding politician, asking Ellis, "Do you not think that this tithe business is an excellent lever wherewith to raise the spirit of the people?" On June 27, he also entered in his diary that he spoke at tithe meetings in Garn and Aberdaron, the first one to "some very large farmers" and the second "on top of a beer barrel." Both villages, like Pwllheli, are located on the Lleyn peninsula of North Wales. In his own estimation, he delivered the speeches "with hywl."[5]

That very day, a verbal battle ensued between Lloyd George and a local parish priest at a fair in Sarn Mellteyrn, roughly halfway between the other villages. Their exchange was reported in Welsh by a local paper, but this time it was the parish priest's assistant who positioned himself above the crowd on a wall. He accused his opponent of sowing discord in the neighborhoods and called nonconformity a curse among the Welsh. Lloyd George replied by reminding the curate that a fourth of the tithe was to be used to help the poor but for centuries it "had been swallowed by the parsons." Contrasting them to Zaccheus, in Luke 19:2–9, he said that they could be as just as the publican if they would repay what had been taken from the poverty-stricken by giving all tithes to the indigent, including the fourth actually for the clergy. They then swapped charges of thievery as a cleric and a lawyer, but Lloyd George made two more scriptural references. One was about having to beat the air or fight the wind in responding to empty words, I Corinthians 9:26, and the other on agreeing with one's adversary quickly except when he is a robber, Matthew 5:25. After repeated interruptions by the curate, the growing crowd refused to let him talk anymore. Last of all, a farmer called for those in favor of the tithe to move left and those for disestablishment to go right, at which point Lloyd George recited that the goats were on the left, Matthew 25:33. Only a solitary policeman had not moved to the right.[6]

Two months later, Lloyd George wrote in his diary that he spoke at an anti-tithe meeting in Llan Haiarn, and eight nights after was taking time to "look up some tithe history." During September, he was able to persuade the league's executive committee to hold a conference for all North Wales. Then, learning at a league committee meeting in his own village of Llanystumdwy that thirty were refusing to pay tithes, he recorded in October, "Never thought myself there were 10." In 1888, he asked the elder Gee, who had been attacking the local squire, Ellis Nanney, for threatening a tenant active in the anti-tithe movement with eviction, to speak in Criccieth. Diary notes for January 1889 state that he accepted schools "founded expressly for propagation of Church ideas . . . if this propagation goes on at Church expense" but denounced tithes that were "used for proselytism—teachers drafted from amongst Nonconformist children." According to numbers he produced, "In North Wales 284 schools monopolised by Church teachers 253 other schools (203 Bdg 50 British where Churchmen have a chance)." Anglican Church leaders, like the Bishop of Bangor, countered such criticism by asserting that Welsh Methodists were monopolizing endowments for school boards, a reaction Lloyd George portrayed as a "simple attempt to create dissensions & jealousies between sects— old policy of his church."[7]

A government report on the investigation of tithe agitation in 1887 showed Ecclesiastical Commissioners spent more than £65,000 in Wales, but only got no more than £31,000. In some cases, the situation of parish priests indicated that there was not enough from tithes to provide the basic necessities of life, but they were obviously hesitant to pursue any legal recourse against their neighbors. Vicars, who were not first to receive tithes, were the worst off, and the Bishop of St. Asaph stated in 1889 that they were almost starving. That same year, R. E. Prothero, a senior member of Oxford's All Soul's College who became an MP for the university in 1914 and President of the Board of Agriculture under Lloyd George two years later, told of a rural cleric. He had to repair his dwelling, care for a sick wife who died within months, see two daughters succumb to disease from lack of nourishment, and then received a box of trash labeled food. Prothero's written comments also dealt with the need of more funds for Anglican schools.[8]

Before 1889 ended, Lord Salisbury's ministry, his second as leader of the Conservatives, introduced a bill to recover tithe rent-charges that would make it less inappropriate, complicated, or expensive. County courts would be put in charge of collecting them, the way any late payment owed was recovered. They would take and auction a debtor's property not subject to tithes, such as clothes, furniture, and other household items. When the government added an amendment to the bill, even though it would have required landlords to pay tithes, Liberals objected because it contained special favors for them. Since its second reading had been approved, the bill had to be withdrawn for lack of time remaining that year. It was reintroduced in 1890, when Lloyd George first won his seat in Parliament. Thus, he was present when Conservatives tried again to address grievances of tenant farmers in a second Tithe Rent-Charge Recovery Bill. Reiterating that landlords, not their tenants, were to pay the tithes, the bill did not pass the House of Commons until the next year. Though shifting the responsibility to those better able to pay, it did nothing to change who got the money and how it was spent. In one sense, renters were worse off because they would now have to oppose their landowners, if they wanted to challenge the Church.[9]

Lloyd George did not argue against collection of the funds but that they ought to be at the disposal of all in Wales. He and D. A. Thomas, also Welsh, sided with Conservatives against a Liberal motion that the government's second attempt to pass a Tithe Bill include a provision for rates adjusted according to agricultural prices. If the amendment had succeeded, the bill would have lowered them due to the depression in the late 1880s. When he was attacked for his dissent, he defended himself on the grounds that the money in the coffers of the state church, when it was disestablished and disendowed, would be the Welsh people's one day. He communicated to his uncle that the verbal assaults had "done us more good than harm" because "an impression will remain that we are men with a backbone & a conscience." Also, they show "that we are capable of thinking for ourselves & are not willing to allow . . . anyone else . . . do it for us." One month later, July, the bill was withdrawn yet again, but was now scheduled for 1891. In late November, he told his brother some Welsh MPs were still "on the warpath" about it and were clamoring for more opposition, but he felt he should remain quiet to "have a better chance of being appointed to speak on" disestablishment, "whether or no I don't think it well to speak at this juncture." Six days after, he revealed his strategy regarding a third tithe bill. "We must fight it step by step," he planned, "even to the point of obstruction. But mind you," he granted, "*it is an admirable bill & I hope it will* be passed." Closing with specifics, he then figured, "It adds 25 per cent to the value of tithe & that is no mean thing by the time it is nationalised. We should take care not to fight it except as a protest against the idea of its being a settlement of our grievance."[10]

In another missive to William on January 27, 1891, one day after a committee meeting on the third Tithe Rent-Charge Recovery Bill where he had said, "I think it would be difficult to recall a single case in which a clergyman has thought proper to institute legal proceedings, by distraint or otherwise, when tithe has not been in arrear for more than three months," Lloyd George linked his tithe plan of action to hopes for Welsh disestablishment: "I spoke last night once on Tithe Bill. But I don't sympathise with attempt made to whittle it down. *It will be an invaluable measure for us when we once get Disestablishment* & a measure which no Liberal ministry would be allowed to pass," he acknowledged. "I have however some amendments . . . designed to prevent any reduction in its value & I shall fight strenuously upon those." Four days later, he elucidated his tactics, writing that two of his amendments were "designed to protect the national property in tithe. I also move to omit 'Wales' out of the Bill. But this is only in order," he elaborated, "to hitch on a speech on Disestablishment." Proposing one amendment after another, two of which were finally accepted, and giving as many as seven speeches per night, he pressed to keep tithes in Wales for the benefit of the masses when disendowment came. The "grievance" he referenced was distinctively Welsh as was the "national property" he protected. His resolution to redress Welsh complaints was also to please his constituents, however. He proudly told his brother on February 6 that, "One amendment of mine wasting almost whole of last evening. I have *15* on the paper." He then asked, "Don't you think I am making a very good fight? Give me your candid opinions will you? Is it doing any good down there?"[11]

On February 11, though, Lloyd George confidently wrote that he and S. T. Evans, "indeed have fought hard. We have stuck in our seats day by day from 3 until 12 every night this Tithe Bill has been on. The other Welsh MPs who occasionally spoke immediately they had delivered themselves marched out of the House to enjoy themselves in the Smoke Room. We alone stuck there throughout the whole of the performance." Elaborating for Uncle Lloyd, who had relayed his joy, he added, "I am glad you are pleased with my fight over the Tithe Bill. It is only those who actually took part it can possibly tell how very great a strain & burden the struggle was for those who were always there." Next, he referred to an article he had sent to a Welsh newspaper, in which he pushed "a dig . . . to those who 'fought and ran away' but I don't say as I might that they went for their whiskies and cigars—whilst S. T. E. & I sat

for hours & hours in our places watching. Only getting our ½ hour for chop."
Both suggested many amendments, some finding their way into the bill. The
one Lloyd George described as having the greatest significance was for owners
to cover lawyers' fees, as long as tenants were not giving notice of legal action.
Two of his were rejected, tenants' appeals should be heard by county courts
instead of commissioners, usually landlords, and those defending themselves
against the owners should have trial by jury.[12]

The bill passed on March 26 and did authorize county courts to collect
all past due tithes. They would be considered late when a landlord had been
negligent for longer than three months. Distraint could be ordered, but a
receivership system might be used in extenuating circumstances to prevent
antagonism. Recovery of personal items was disallowed for owner liability,
unlike the first bill. Regardless, anti-tithe disturbances continued, but organized assistance of them stopped. Several farm owners who had been voted
to county offices, notably in Cardiganshire, simply did not authorize confiscations or the security necessary for them. Even as late as 1896, however, the
land commission in Wales was referencing sales for tithes, plus altercations between landowners and constables. Denbighshire experienced demonstrations
by as many as two-thousand in 1894, though turmoil manifested itself more in
South Wales after 1889. That year, the principality got the Welsh Intermediate
Education Act, giving county councils created by the Local Government Act
of the previous year authority over secondary schools. Prices for cereal grains
had also gone up by 1889, and the people as well as more temperate agrarian
leaders were now tired of unrest.[13]

Drawing some conclusions in a speech at Bangor exactly eight weeks after
the passage of the bill, Lloyd George stated, "We as Welsh representatives laid
claim to the tithe as endowments belonging to the whole people, and not to
a mere section." Elaborating on the many purposes for tithes, the value of
which increased by 25 percent under the law, he observed that, "The tithes of
England and Wales were given to the Church upon condition that it should
maintain the poor, repair the highways, and educate the people." Then, comparing the Anglican Church to its predecessor, he added, "I am bound as a
Protestant to admit that as long as the property remained in the hands of the
Roman Catholic Church it faithfully discharged its trust." He crescendoed
in his peroration, alleging, "from the moment the property was appropriated
by the present Anglican Church, her clergy have monopolised its benefits for
their own selfish enjoyment. And what has become of the poor, the highways,
and education?" Almost six months earlier, he had explained for his brother

that the additional fourth in tithe value would be, "no mean thing by the time it is nationalised." Two months afterward, he shared how he succeeded in moving that no lawyers' fees should be paid to landowners at the expense of unrepresented tenants.[14]

Just sixteen days after the bill became law, Lloyd George welcomed Tom Ellis's return to Parliament. Ellis had been unable to attend the tithe debates due to illness, so Lloyd George gave him an appraisal of the contest. Beginning with a deferential regard, he related, "I cannot express to you the regret Evans & I felt at your absence during the tithe fight." Then, he quickly changed its tenor, gloating, "It was such a glorious struggle for Wales. Wales practically monopolised the attention of the House for fully three weeks. To my mind that is the great fact of the Tithe Bill opposition." The same letter indicated Lloyd George's desire to engage in another battle over the Free Education Bill the same year: "I fancy we shall have another Welsh fight over free education. Don't you think so?" That June, the bill was introduced, and he also told William he was going to propose two amendments of "cold steel" but not "diamonds." He insisted that religious affiliation should not be a factor in hiring teachers or renewing contracts, and money left over once a given school had paid expenses should be used for technical training, "so as to prevent its being paid over to the parsons." After speaking, he wrote his brother, "I have delivered my soul." On July 13, he mentioned being attacked at the Carnarvon School Board by the curate and asked William, "Shall I take any notice of it. I say no."[15]

When an amendment to protect Anglican Voluntary Schools emerged because they were deemed more popular than their nondenominational counterparts, Board Schools, Lloyd George referenced his shire where twice as many attended the latter. In his view, Voluntary Schools had "a precarious income dependent upon the pleasure of the squire of the parish." Parsons typically supervised them, equating being good citizens with being good Anglicans, so they hired teachers who were devout Anglicans. Lloyd George claimed that these self-appointed protectors desired "a million of money in order to provide Church organists in every little rural parish." Neither of his amendments was passed, and the protective amendment earned only ten votes. However, the bill survived as the Elementary Education Act and received the Royal Assent of Queen Victoria on August 5. It provided ten shillings for all elementary school students, not just those in Voluntary Schools, as a bribe appeasing Joseph Chamberlain and Liberal Unionists for their support. Lloyd George wrote Uncle Lloyd nine days after the bill became law, telling him that he had "initiated an excellent debate on the Education Act." Liberals were returned to power a year to the month later, and in 1894 he was appointed to "fight against the Diggleites on the London School Board. Quite pleased," he confessed to his brother, "It will bring me into the London Noncon: fight. It will just suit me to go for Diggle as I have for St. Asaph." Joseph R. Diggle was chairman of the board and had been an Anglican curate in the capital. The board's Liberals or Progressives, its minority, believed he intentionally funded secular schools less to have more for Anglican ones, though he had lowered the amount of land rate funds used by the board while still providing an education to greater numbers of students. Sydney Black became a Progressive member in 1900.[16]

Conservatives regained office in June 1895 and proposed education bills in 1896 as well as 1897 to further subsidize Voluntary Schools only. The 1896 bill never got a third reading due to 1335 amendments, some by Liberals that Lloyd George opposed. He just spoke against it two times before the House of Commons adjourned in mid-August. On January 22 of the latter year, though, he corresponded with his uncle concerning the second bill, conveying that Harcourt "wanted me to take in hand the resolution of the Government on the Voluntary Schools. Of course I mean to do that." Ten days later, "amid violent interruption from the Government side," according to *The Christian World*, he proposed an amendment to that bill, which would have limited state aid to "necessitous" Anglican schools. On February 16, during its second reading after midnight, he seized on the term "dogma" and asked Anglicans what it meant. After someone responded, "the religion of the parents," he retorted, "Aye, where nine-tenths of the parents are Nonconformists? Then let them give parental control, and the controversy would be at an end." He concluded that the result would be only Board Schools existing in Wales before very long.[17]

Lloyd George's efforts to defeat the 1897 bill notwithstanding, it passed a second reading by 205 votes. When he and other Welshmen increasingly opposed it during the committee stage, closure was enforced six times to stop their 161 amendments from delaying its passage on a third reading. John Herbert Lewis proposed for Wales to be exempted but was convincingly outvoted, and on March 25 it passed the lower house. The upper house soon followed course, and the bill was enacted on April 8. The final act awarded all Voluntary Schools five shillings per pupil and left Board Schools alone. In return for Liberal Unionist support, though, another law was passed to give some money to any of the latter schools needing help. The same month that the 1897 session ceased, Lloyd George referenced his attack on the bill in a letter to William. Defending himself, he revealed Hugh Price Hughes "complained that the English Noncon MPs didn't back me up." Hughes was the Welsh preacher at the West London Mission from 1886 until his death in 1902 and played a pivotal role in establishing the National Council of the Evangelical Free Churches in 1896. He was its first president and served in the same capacity for the Wesleyan Methodist Conference in 1898. Lloyd George had first heard him preach at St. James Hall ten years earlier, while in London on his honeymoon. Afterward, he wrote in his diary, "he is a remarkably good speaker—no pulpit cant about him 'he only speaks straight on'—Subject 'Christ as a Socialist'—a healthy invigorating sermon—brass band there."[18]

By the end of March 1898, Lloyd George made a motion on public education, which the nonconformists in the House of Commons did endorse. His attempts to get them to agree on how to oppose the government's education policy, though, bore no fruit during the remaining four and a half years of Salisbury last ministry. Undeterred, he spoke in June on nonconformist grievances in day schools, and in September, *The Brecon & Radnor Express* reported on a talk he had given at the initial meeting of the National Liberal Council for Wales and Monmouthshire the previous month. He again addressed the use of taxes for the support of Anglican schools as well as a dual educational system existing in Wales, and Thomas Gee, who died just two days before the article came out, had chaired. The newspaper's correspondent summarized Lloyd George as saying that, "the sectarian system was grossly unfair, because it handed over the control of the schools to one denomination. Two millions of the children of that country had their education handed over not only to one denomination, but, what was worse, to the parsons and clergy of one denomination. Speaking for himself, he would rather trust the laymen of any sect than its priests," rationalizing, "The latter had devoted their lives to the promotion of the principles of one denomination, and he would not trust any man absolutely in the interests of another sect under those conditions. Yet that was what they were doing." Peaking with his first point once again, he now added palpably more bias: "They were placing the interests of two million children in the keeping of the priests of one denomination, who were more than ever bent upon exalting their own creed and making the vanity of a class the creed for all."[19]

Elaborating on the appointment of priests, Lloyd George stated they were "exalted by the imposition of hands by some mysterious process." He compared it to being vaccinated and finally quipped that they "had been inoculated with some lymph called, he believed, apostolic succession." He had used the analogy once before, charging in a bigoted way that "pompous and arrogant clergy" had been inoculated, but it was "with unhealthy apostolic lymph." He juxtaposed their process of being chosen to that of nonconformists: "The virtue which had oozed out of the finger of unholy Popes and wicked prelates surely did not confer greater power upon a minister than that blessing which came straight from Heaven as a result of the prayers of holy men." He also referred to the catechisms taught in Voluntary Schools as "a sham" and objected to their being "at the expense of the taxpayer." Board Schools, on the other hand, "had no definite religious teaching," which Anglicans considered "infidel," "heathen," and "pagan." It was officially reported they "had no religious instruction" at all. He pointed out, though, they were in locales where Sunday Schools existed, where children "held the principles of religion pure and undefiled." Furthermore, he had been a student in a Voluntary School, where he was taught "concoctions of catechism" instead of Bible only, where children were instructed "to be humble and lowly to all their betters, and their betters were explained as being the squire, the parson, and the curate." He ended by sermonizing with, "The Bible condemned the priesthood and said that every holy and good man was a priest. That being so, what became of the mysterious system of priesthood which was costing the nation so many millions of money?"[20]

Pertaining to the two types of educational institutions in Wales, it should be pointed out that the Voluntary Schools included those under Wesleyans, Catholics, or non-sectarian groups like the British and Foreign School Society. Combined, by the mid-1890s, they were educating nearly six-hundred thousand of almost two-and-a-half million children in the principality, plus England. Board Schools, or schools with boards, were first authorized by the Education Act of 1870, and a quarter-century later private administrators oversaw all but a third of the elementary schools. In 1895, that alternative type of school was providing education to just under a 1,900,000 students, who averaged more than three times the amount of government aid as those in Voluntary Schools. In an 1898 letter to Maggie, Lloyd George referred to Gladstone's Minister of Education who had drawn up the 1870 act. Thinking of his own continued influence on the nonconformists, he warned, "I dont want to be a second W. E. Forster to betray his fellow Dissenters." What they considered his betrayal was allowing funds from land rates to be used by boards for the expenses of the poorest pupils at Voluntary Schools.[21]

Less than two months after the initial meeting of the National Liberal Council for Wales and Monmouthshire, the Northern Counties Education

League held its annual conference. At a forum following it, Lloyd George impugned the motives of priests in the Church of England. He asserted un-equivocally, the *Manchester Guardian* quoted, "It was not education that the clergy of this country were thinking about, but annexation. It was not schools that they wanted to set up; it was mission rooms. It was not scholars that they wanted, but proselytes." Also, they wanted to be relieved of some of the taxes they had to pay for tithes considered part of their income, which really angered him. In June 1899, the Tithe Rent-Charge Bill was introduced by the President of the Board of Agriculture to pay roughly eleven-thousand priests a sum of eighty-seven thousand pounds. That would come largely from educa-tion funds, to defray their tax liability. Even many among Conservatives saw how objectionable such legislation would be, but it still passed.[22]

On the second reading of the bill, Lloyd George referred to it as a dole. He acknowledged "that the clergy suffer" but questioned "what about the shopkeeper, the artisan, the lodging-house keeper, and all other sections of the community?" Clerics were only concerned about themselves and were not being their brothers' keepers, he judged. Particularly mentioning old age pensions promised by Salisbury's government on the urging of Chamberlain again, he became even more hypercritical, denouncing them and landowners for being like the "Tammany ring." Even taking what turned out to be just five pounds or less a year, he charged hyperbolically, "Why, the squire and the parson have broken into the poor box, and divided its contents among them." In fact, the owners of cultivated land had received a 50-percent reduction in payments of tithes three years earlier under the Agricultural Land Rating Act. When this Tithe Rent-Charge Bill was enacted, it extended the same per-centage for the vicars, who were suffering because of another downturn in the grain market. Lloyd George had stated that Liberals called upon the wealthier among clergy and their parishioners to support their brothers. Both acts were renewed in 1901 for five years.[23]

From the second half of 1899 until springtime 1902, Lloyd George was more preoccupied with the Second Boer War than anything else, but two more at-tempts to revamp education by the last ministry of Salisbury got withdrawn in 1900 and 1901, respectively. The former was pulled because of insufficient time to address it and more urgent matters like the war or electoral plans. The latter would have done away with school boards and would not have provided for any public control of Anglican schools. It was rescinded, but the National Free Church Council took a step in preparation for its reintroduction by suggesting that the local councils steer public thinking toward accepting the notion of school boards that would oversee all educational institutions. A new bill was proposed in 1902, and it did indeed call for the abolition of all school boards, to be replaced by committees for education authorized by the local powers. Church schools were now included as part of the scheme and were provided funding from land rates to defray monetary deficits. England and Wales had some eight-thousand villages with Anglican schools only, where roughly a million nonconformist children had to go. Since Anglican landowners paid the rates, and only two of every six committee members were chosen by a given community, most nonconformists, especially in Wales, would still not control single-school areas, which just had Church schools.[24]

In May 1902, two English progressives from the Forward Movement within Churches of Christ, John Crockatt and Thomas J. Ainsworth, sent a letter to the editor of the most prominent publication in their fellowship on the Education Bill. It read that, in the bill "the religious liberty and Christian conscience of this country are assailed, for should the Bill pass, the religious teaching of the young would be dominated almost entirely by the Anglican clergy whose teaching," they proceeded to blatantly profess, "is in opposition to the Word of God, and has the effect of shutting the mind in after years against the approaches of Truth. Should we not, therefore, as those who value freedom of conscience and national efficiency," they fervently petitioned, "enter our solemn and emphatic protest against such violation?" They concluded with an even more emphatic challenge for their and Lloyd George's brotherhood: "Non-conformity is arming for the fight; shall we not also prepare to take our part in the conflict, and help to press the battle to the gate?"[25]

Six months later, Ainsworth, who had just finished presiding at the cooperation meeting of Churches of Christ, fired off another missive to the editor, stressing that the bill would impose "religious tests upon the teaching profession." He called for "passive resistance" by drawing up a list of those who refused to pay the rate. Their names would then "be sent to the National Free Church Council in London, with the request that we be allowed to join our forces with theirs." John Clifford, minister of a large Baptist chapel in West London whose status was like John the Baptist to nonconformists, had been the first to champion passive resistance. He was actually a democratic socialist in thinking, two of his speeches, "Socialism and the Teaching of Christ" and "Socialism and the Churches," being published as tracts by the Fabian Society in 1897 and 1908. A passive resistance movement was mounted, but it amounted to little, judging from the reaction by the government. As of January 1904, there were only 7,324 summons executed against those who would

not pay and 329 auctions of seized items. Lloyd George was the leader of re-
sisters in Parliament. He initially liked the 1902 bill but quickly changed his
mind, explaining both to his wife: "Balfour is developing a most revolutionary Education Bill," he admitted. "Sweeps away School Boards. Creates the
County Council the educational authority for the County & puts the Boards
Schools & the Voluntary Schools under it." Contrasting it to the school system he was in as a student, he then stated, "& a very great improvement it is."
He did, though, oppose the new system being optional instead of required,
and in July 1905, his congregation in Criccieth, Berea, was featured in the
Manchester Guardian for taking up a collection to assist the cause. Also, his
brother was elected chairman of the Portmadoc Council that month.[26]

Not all in Churches of Christ agreed with Lloyd George or Ainsworth, as a
debate at one division of the cooperation following the bill's passage showed.
Peter Stephen, a member of the Cheshire and North Wales Division, who had
been on the cooperation's General Sunday School Committee when he visited
Lloyd George's congregation, cautioned, "Undue excitement had led some to
pledge themselves too hastily to a proposition of 'Passive Resistance.'. . . It is
futile for those Nonconformists who voted the Tories into power to protest
that they never authorised the Government to deal with education, and that
they ought not to have done it. The *ballot-box*," he said, "was the medium of
production of this Act with all its injustice and flagrant wrongs, and the same
instrument, properly used by every Nonconformist voter, will amend it. The
schools will not be more distinctly denominational than they have been, but
a greater proportion of the cost is to come out of the public purse. It is not a
question of *principle* so much as of *proportion*."[27]

Stephen went on to emphasize that the new law actually provided for "the
principle of popular control" of schools funded by the ministry, and the response should be "to *increase* the *measure* of this control. We do not pay, either directly or indirectly, for religious teaching, neither does the State." The
government agreed to such control in exchange for the use of school buildings
"for secular education. The rental value of the premises may be set down as
the sum paid by the denomination, through the State, to the teacher for that
part of his time which is occupied in giving religious instruction." According
to Stephen, refusal to pay the "school-rate" would be "neither a constitutional
nor a sensible course to take for effecting an amendment of the law." Edward
Evans, the former cooperation evangelist who had often preached where Lloyd
George worshipped, concurred with obeying God-ordained governments,
"to put down evil and support good." However, he saw no biblical injunction

compelling payment of "this special rate, for if we let it go unprotested against it will mean the re-establishment of Romanism." He contrasted having to pay a specific tax to fund religious education with having to pay general taxes. Under Roman rule, he observed, Christians paid taxes that, to some extent, were used to support idolatry, but they were not targeted for that purpose. Stephen retorted that, if any money from Christians ended up in pagan temples, "it seemed of little consequence how it was collected." The Christians paid tribute regardless, and the government will be held accountable for what happened to it. He then admonished everybody, "instead of wasting funds in making up heavy losses through distraints, give freely to *press* and *platform workers*, who should rouse the country against the iniquities of the Act as it now stands."[28]

Lloyd George started participating as a "platform worker" in 1885, and according to his brother, the 1902 Education Bill "provided Dafydd with his first opportunity to prove his mettle as a parliamentarian." Just like Stephen, William George thought more school control by local people was a positive thing, but using their taxes for one religion's dogma was negative. In June 1902, Lloyd George told him of an "educational quagmire" by the Conservatives, stating that "high income tax for clerical schools will not make them more popular." William couched the debate in the House of Commons as one between his brother and Arthur James Balfour, who introduced the legislation but then succeeded his uncle, Lord Salisbury, as the prime minister in July 1902. It had started in March and lasted long after the bill passed that December. Once it was enacted, even Balfour acknowledged that Lloyd George played a pivotal role and showed first-rate legislative capability. The controversy helped Lloyd George reestablish himself as leader of nonconformity in England and Wales after the Second Boer War.[29]

Utilizing his inimitable rhetorical style again, Lloyd George communicated to a Norwich assembly in April 1903 that nonconformists did not fear allowing the teaching of any doctrine at all: "Let each man preach anything he liked so long as he could get another man to listen to him. The result would be that, in the long run, the truth would be got at. That was the whole essence of liberty and equality." Four months later, at a quarterly gathering of Calvinistic Methodists in Penmount Chapel, Pwllheli, he dealt more adroitly with the funding of religious teaching by the government. For the largest Welsh nonconformists but at a conference open to the public too, he posited, "there was one Church which claimed the right to demand that the State should teach its particular dogma and its particular aspect of the truth at the expense of all. Let them suppose that every other church did the same thing." He saw that outcome being, "instead of having one good school in a community well equipped, well staffed, giving the best education, with plenty of good air and light, there would be a lot of miserable little sheep pens here and there, and there would be no education at all." On December 22, he became president of the Welsh National Council in Shrewsbury and stated, in accepting the office, that its number one job would be to ensure victory in all the upcoming county council elections. Optimistic, he wrote Lewis before the first month of the new year had closed, "I never felt more confident of Wales than I do now. There is a deep tranquil resolution throughout the land that bodes ill for this abominable Rel. North & South—East & West the people are united in their determination to dare all & suffer anything rather than stain their consciences by becoming the instruments whereby priestcraft shall establish more firmly its dread throne in the schools of our country."[30]

All enforcement of the 1902 Education Act was postponed in Wales until February 1904, but because many there continued to talk of refusing to pay the taxes necessary to implement the law, Parliament also passed the Education Local Authority Default Act, known as "coercion act," six months later. It authorized the Ministry of Education to execute the legislation and take from grants to county councils any funds they withheld. Elections for those county councils had been held in March, however, and the result was that all of them now had majorities wanting entire power over funds for maintaining schools in addition to ending exams on the educators' religion. Also, Robert Morant, as Acting Secretary of the Board of Education since the previous November and Permanent Secretary as of April Fool's Day, had all but conceded defeat in the matter of Wales. Lloyd George corresponded with William, after having an interview with Morant on October 30, 1903, penning, "*He has practically given up the fight in Wales.* He is willing now to treat Wales as a separate entity for educational purposes & to grant us educational autonomy." Self-rule was to be facilitated by the creation of a Welsh Education Department, "with offices in Wales."[31]

Despite such assurances from Morant, Lloyd George still advised the councils to invoke a clause in the act he had succeeded in getting added, absolving them of maintaining the schools in disrepair. This was his second resistance strategy, since the option of requiring the law had now been changed to mandatory enforcement. At a September Welsh Liberal Conference in Bangor, he had urged nonconformists not to compromise because the National Society of the Established Church had been informing its school managers "to insist upon their rights under the law of the land, and to turn a deaf ear to all proposals for compromise outside the law." Welsh members of Parliament, emissaries from the county councils, and school representatives were in attendance. Lloyd George showed his true conviction on keeping plain biblical instruction in Board Schools, as stipulated by the Cowper-Temple clause of the 1870 Education Act that had created them. He opposed an amendment to stop all teaching of scripture in state-financed schools. William states that since many Anglican schools were in desperate conditions, when total utilization of his older brother's strategy took place, "the intention of the promoters of the Act was frustrated, and time was gained for the contending parties in the long run to arrive at a fair and reasonable settlement of their disputes." Indeed, a year to the month after the Bangor conference, Lloyd George stayed at Asaph's palace when he presided at the National Eisteddfod in Rhyl. He had been invited one other time but turned him down. His brother also mentions a weekend he spent with the bishop, even worshipping together and receiving communion from him, which nonconformists disliked.[32]

Indeed, by the time Conservatives resigned in December 1905, only five county councils had been penalized for not paying, just one shire had nonconformist parents remove a significant number of their students from Voluntary Schools, and the funds raised to support those in dissent were not exhausted. The National Free Church Council promised to dedicate a hundred thousand pounds for them, but the actual amount it provided is unsure, and only £4137 was left over. The most important term of the settlement concerned who would appoint head teachers for Voluntary Schools. Both Anglican overseers and county councils wanted the right. However, the growing cordial relationship between Lloyd George and the Bishop of St. Asaph led to compromise. The former agreed to school governors choosing the teachers, and his worthy counterpart agreed those selected should be *"subject to confirmation or otherwise of the local authority,* who should only have the right to exercise their veto on educational grounds," not religious. Many of the bishops, especially the other three from Wales and the Archbishop of Canterbury, believed that their colleague was relinquishing too much. Lloyd George was particularly upset with the Bishop of St. David's, John Owen, writing to his brother that he was "a little sneak & he rounded on Asaph for not consulting him." He phrased his assessment of the situation in colorful words, "The fat is already frizzling in the fire," and, "Asaph is inclined to take the bit between his teeth & he wants me to proceed." By January 1905, the bishops changed sides on the issue, and he updated William, "St. David's is eager now & Asaph the reverse!

What is to be done with some farts like this? There's a bit of jealousy between them." He had proceeded, though, the "compromise was eventually accepted," and it "proved itself to be a good working arrangement . . . ever since," wrote William in 1958.[33]

Both brothers went to Italy in November 1905, because Lloyd George had been advised by his physician to take a vacation for quiet recovery from a tonsillectomy that caused excessive bleeding. The older sibling stipulated to William his own reason for going, "so as to be ready in January for the big Education fight in Wales & the bigger fight in the House of Commons." He obviously thought the Conservatives would still be in power at the beginning of the new year but encountered a man in Rapallo who strongly urged him to get back to London as soon as possible. The most recent reports from there indicated a change was coming sooner. William returned on December 2 to determine how urgent his brother's arrival should be, and in a mutually agreed upon secret code, he telegraphed that it ought to be immediate. Lloyd George was there two days later and updated him concerning difficulties on his trip: "After your wire I made up my mind to rush off at once," but "had no ticket from Genoa to Turin. No time to get one." In spite of the stress he had experienced, though, he continued, "Feel very fit & ready for action. . . . Balfour resigned & CB called in. An administration will be formed so I hear but nothing has happened so far. It will take a few days. The Daily Telegraph nominates me for Board of Trade. I wish they would give me L.G.B.—if they mean to give me anything."[34]

Henry Campbell-Bannerman began shaping a Cabinet on December 5, which Lloyd George mentioned to his brother, but he also stated his preference for President of the Local Government Board again. He also communicated, "But if I am offered the Duchy of Lancaster I don't know what I'd do. Salary is same as LGB. It was held once by John Bright. It is intended for men whose help on debate in the House is required. Still it has nothing to do with Wales so on the whole my present feeling is I would rather be out than accept it." Two days later, Campbell-Bannerman's assistant asked him to see the presumptive prime minister the next day and for "the address that would reach me promptly," he told William. "It also means Cabinet I think for that is the first thing they settle." Indeed, the following day's correspondence began, "Board of Trade with a seat in the Cabinet." He was "delighted" with it but also informed his brother, "I asked for pledges about Education & the extension of self-government for Wales—& got both." After just one more day, he seemed to be wondering not only whether his family was delighted but also was the position the best for him to take: "I thought you would all be pleased with the appointment. I confess I had never thought of it as trade is not quite in my line. But there is more to be done in it," he justified, "than in any other department almost."[35]

The very same day, Uncle Lloyd prayerfully reflected in his diary, "He had Wales' Cause guaranteed before undertaking any office. I am so proud of this, secured after all his self-spent life of efforts of all kinds on her behalf. Good Providence protect, help and bless my dearest boy, and crown his service to his generation by Thy blessing." What was apparently also meaningful to Lloyd George was the amount of correspondence he received from the clergymen. "Letters," he informed his brother on December 13, "especially from parsons!—overwhelming." After his initial Cabinet meeting the next day, he reported, "*Education first*," probably because he brought it up. Within four more, he was writing, "Been with the Montgomeryshire Councillors re the Bd of Education arranging the troubles there. Defaulting Act to be withdrawn in the County and all moneys to be paid in future direct to Council. That is a great score. That gives us enough out of grants," he calculated, "to pay all teachers salaries for this quarter. Birrell is doing well. He has already decided Barry & Montgomeryshire in our favour & had those Merioneth poltroons fought they would have shared in the triumph." Those three were the only ones in default when Balfour resigned, and the last was where nonconformist children had been taken out of Church schools.[36]

Augustine Birrell had been appointed President of the Board of Education by Campbell-Bannerman, but Morant remained Permanent Secretary. Even though the Liberal Party was now in power, Merioneth continued to stand its ground. The matter was ultimately turned over to the Board's Welsh Education Department, founded in 1907, but the House of Lords rendered a final decision four years later. Ironically, 1911 was when Morant was reassigned to chair the National Insurance Commission under Lloyd George as Chancellor of the Exchequer. A general election was held in January 1906, and Liberals won just under four-hundred seats, with eighty-three for the Irish in addition to twenty-nine for Labour. Conservatives dropped from 402 in the previous election to 157. Lloyd George regained his seat by more than twelve hundred ballots, giving him a spread four times bigger than his other victories. Improving the Education Act was the number two issue upon which Liberals campaigned, and candidates backed by Labour as well as individual socialists incorporated it in four-fifths of their speeches. Regardless of the numbers that Liberals could now muster, which in their own ranks included 177 nonconformists, they failed three times to get their education bills enacted from 1906 to 1908, like the Conservatives had in the first two consecutive years following their 1900 coalition landslide victory with Liberal Unionists.[37]

In late March, Lloyd George told his brother that he had carried his Welsh National Council at a Cabinet meeting, and on April 9, Birrell presented an education bill later named for him. After many Cabinet debates on it, though, he denied association with it in private. The worst argument was over Clause 4, which specified any local educational authority, urban or rural, having above five-thousand inhabitants might provide after school building use for sectarian teaching on every weekday if 80 percent of parents wanted it, an effort to settle any difficulties with Catholics. A week after the bill's introduction, a conference of Sunday school teachers from the Churches of Christ in North Wales and Cheshire passed a resolution of "hearty approval" as well as "the earnest wish that it may be passed and thus bring to an end the present objectionable and unjust state of affairs." John Clifford and other nonconformist leaders met with Lloyd George about it for two hours on June 11, William was informed, but the Cabinet members eventually decided to only permit it in urban areas. On July 8, Lloyd George wrote his brother that he had interviewed Archbishop Davidson about Part IV of the bill, the Welsh Clause, which the House of Commons approved eighteen days later, passing the bill after four more.[38]

Davidson expressed total disapproval of the bill publicly, but during its second reading he cautioned that serious changes were necessary to render it acceptable, and in the committee stage he announced that he would not suggest or agree with any amendments intended to wreck it. The planned council would be under the Treasury, Lloyd George wrote William, and one of its Junior Lords would become the Welsh Minister of Education. In September, he let his brother know he had lunched with the heads of the Free Church Council to discuss education, and on December 1, he was at an Oxford University club after the House of Lords had chipped away at the bill, adding numerous amendments the lower house would ultimately refuse to accept. There, he very bitterly lamented, "This poor bill left the House of Commons with a good majority to speed it on its way. It has been stripped and wounded and left half dead. I am sorry to say," he then bemoaned, "that the priests and Levites did not even pass by; they joined the freebooters." The veto by the upper house came eighteen days later, and he phrased the bill's defeat for William as "finally destroyed by Lords." If passed, it would have ended the part of the

Balfour Act providing for the voluntary schools to have religious instruction funded by the government.[39]

On December 21, a Private Member's Bill introduced by a new Labour Party MP became the Education Provision of Meals Act as statute law. It allowed the local educational authorities to fund the feeding of children in their schools from rate money if volunteer groups called School Canteen Committees and parents could not provide enough. Financing by local powers was not mandatory, but they were at the very least to make facilities and staff available. Two months later, Birrell was made Chief Secretary for Ireland, and Reginald McKenna, who distinguished himself in opposing the 1902 law, assumed the Board of Education's presidency. McKenna sponsored a bill to take the place of the previous year's failure on February 26. Consisting of only one clause not intended to be permanent, it financed nonsectarian religious education from land rate funds. This time, threats of passive resistance by Anglicans and less than encouraging support from the nonconformists resulted in the bill being removed only three months later.[40]

As noted, 1907 did see the creation of a department for Wales in the Board of Education, with its own permanent secretary and a chief inspector for Welsh schools. McKenna, an MP for North Monmouthshire, was over both. The secretary chosen was Alfred T. Davies, who had also taught Lloyd George how to golf. Owen M. Edwards, a respected authority on Welsh culture and history, became inspector, but demanded equality of status with Davies. Gilbert clearly stated that the establishment of an education department for Wales brought an end to any more defiance on the issue by Lloyd George. Before the year ended, though, McKenna gave the Cabinet a rough draft of a new short education bill to be introduced in 1908. It proposed that all Voluntary Schools, except where there was only one, be financed by government grants and volunteers instead of land rates. They should also be backed by 75 percent of parents and be taken out from under local educational authorities. Lloyd George did not like it and was contentious with McKenna, but he stayed out of it officially, especially after becoming Chancellor of the Exchequer in April 1908.[41]

A second Private Member's Bill was put forward in February of the new year, to provide vacation schools, medical inspection, and treatment for elementary students in the public schools. The introduction of McKenna's new bill followed only eleven days afterward, but the same event that put Lloyd George over the Treasury, Campbell-Bannerman's resignation, put McKenna over the Admiralty and brought Walter Runciman to the Board of Education's presidency. That June, McKenna asked for the private member's measure to be postponed, and Asquith, the new prime minister, decided that only government legislation should be dealt with for the rest of the term. Since McKenna's bill also included provision for medical inspections of students, the other never got a third reading, and Clause X of his became The Children's Act as statute law on August 12. The local educational authorities were responsible for funding it, with a commitment by Runciman's board to found a medical branch to assist them. If the inspections revealed children were abused, they were also protected under the law.[42]

Runciman's tenure as the president of the board ended the same year Morant's permanent secretaryship of it did, and no more educational legislation was enacted until after Lloyd George became prime minister. He handpicked H. A. L. Fisher, a modern European historian, a senior member of an Oxford college, Vice-Chancellor of Sheffield University, and most importantly, a staunch fellow Liberal in his coalition government to be the President of the Board of Education. The year the "Great War" ended, Fisher steered the Education Bill of 1918 to passage, raising the age for leaving school from twelve to fourteen and planning for mandatory continuing education after that, a brand new initiative. It was a component of Lloyd George's determination to resolve unsettled issues after the war, especially for the returning veterans who needed job training, land, and healthcare. Fisher knew he needed to get a law approved before the war was over because of various interests that would engage again soon after it and possibly derail another education bill. More educational opportunities had to be provided as part of the program for rebuilding "a land fit for heroes," though some agricultural, industrial, and business concerns resisted additional years of schooling for workers. Fisher did not renew any old battles, so constituencies like the Church of England, which had finally been won over, could be used as allies against new opponents. He also banked on substantial Labour Party support, which did not materialize, and ministry funding for education was cut in 1922, as it was for other reconstruction endeavors. A Tithe Act in 1918 finally set the value of tithes at 109 pounds for the following seven years also, and the 1936 Tithe Act stopped them in Wales permanently, compensating landowners.[43]

10

Imperialism and the Second Boer War, 1878–1902

"The fizz is out of the Jingo pop."

ONLY FIVE ENTRIES INTO his very first diary, Lloyd George mentioned he had been with John Roberts and discussed William Gladstone in regard to the issue of Turkish policy. The Congress of Berlin ended the next day, but Gladstone was not pleased with the emphasis Benjamin Disraeli and Lord Salisbury had placed on acquiring Cyprus in exchange for British financing for reforms in the Ottoman Empire. He objected because they had refused to hold the Turks accountable for atrocities committed against Balkan Christians. The previous year, he even advocated a holy war to free the southern Slavs from Islamic rule, a goal substantially though not entirely achieved at Berlin. Lloyd George chronicled the issue again when Liberals regained power in 1880, noting the party's successes in general and Gladstone's victorious campaign for the Scottish Midlothian seat in particular. After referencing him, he then recorded on behalf of Wales, "Great enthusiasm here." In a series of speeches over the six months before, Gladstone had reiterated his opposition to territorial expansion primarily for imperialism, stressing once more moral rectitude on the part of imperialists and humaneness for people they assimilated. He wanted continental Europe to get involved in the Balkans as well as places like Cyprus, Egypt, South Africa, and Afghanistan.[1]

On November 1, 1880, Lloyd George noted the first of three pseudonymous letters he sent to *The North Wales Express* within the next four months, which included references to England's international relations since the concert system began. He applauded Tory statesmen like George Canning, who in the 1820s had helped developing European states subdue aggression to achieve national identity and freedom. Conservatives such as Salisbury, though, who as foreign secretary was only concerned about his party and had overseen atrocities against Afghans and Zulus, he did not extol. Then, he praised what Gladstone advocated, cooperating with major nations to defend their sovereignty and liberty, or if necessary as fellow Christians, acting unilaterally to get justice for oppressed peoples like Bulgarians or Montenegrins. In June of 1882, he acted unilaterally by participating in militia drills, even though his religious tradition opposed such. His diary reveals he told his uncle he intended to go "camping." Richard Lloyd objected "strongly," but he went to Portmadoc three days later anyhow, donned a uniform, and drilled with Boston Lodge, ending the exercise with the battalion instead of the recruits. He was nineteen.[2]

In order of importance but unrelated, Lloyd George entered two other observations about his training experience. Even in uniform "respectable girls will not notice you," and he could not keep his trousers up because his "braces" broke. Concerning his pacifist heritage, the Particular Baptist preacher who founded the Penymaes church while the French Revolutionary Wars were being fought, taught that all war, defensive and offensive, was "incompatible with Christianity." Scotch Baptists, with whom the congregation affiliated during the Napoleonic Wars, allowed the protection of one's family and property but withdrew fellowship from any males who voluntarily joined a militia, "when they might have avoided it." After the assembly identified as a Church of Christ, Uncle Lloyd acquired periodicals containing the writings of Alexander Campbell and read them to his nephew from age four. They included the practical ethics of Campbell against war.[3]

Two weeks after Lloyd George took part in the militia drill at Portmadoc, he commented on the British naval bombardment of Alexandria in his diary: "I do not understand this Egyptian question—it seems to be a dubious procedure but I am rather glad of the splendid practice of our guns." He was clearly fascinated with the military despite his pacifist upbringing, and whether he doubted some of the reasons for the empire's foreign policy, Michael G. Fry asserts that he "invariably expressed in religious or moral terms" his attitude toward it. Only sixteen days later, he considered Gladstone's explanation of it concerning Egypt to be "very conclusive." In the fall of 1882, though, he decided that the Egyptian policy was not only dubious but also deplorable because of what prompted it. Gladstone had put down a nationalist uprising there, led by Arabi Pasha, to secure the Suez Canal and Egypt's monetary system for British as well as European interests. He never intended, however, a long military presence to expand British colonialism and imperialism. At a postwar debate in the Portmadoc Debating Society on November 13, Lloyd George said the war was evil, and the domination of Egypt by British forces was unjust. He also stated that the rebels never posed a threat to the canal, and that their leader was no more to blame for rebellion than Tewfik Pasha, Egypt's khedive. In fact, the former was looked upon as a champion of lower-class rights, especially freedom from economic oppression.[4]

Slightly more than two months later, just one week after he turned twenty, Lloyd George revealed his true heart on the subject of war. Regardless of a teenage enchantment with trappings of the military, he wrote the following indictment of war on the back of his entry for the day: "A Good Retort in case you were interrupted in an anti-war speech by a jingo faction in the audience singing 'Rule Brittania [*sic*]—Brittania [*sic*] rules the waves,'" he commenced. "No Gentlemen, you are mistaken—God rules the waves! And that God is a God of Peace and *good will* to men of *all* creeds races & nationalities. I will tell you more about him," he continued. "He is a God who will not forever suffer Brittania [*sic*] to ravage & desolate this fair earth he has created for man's happiness & to bring misery upon that creature for whom his beloved son has suffered so much to make happy."[5]

Less than two months following his severe reprimand of the United Kingdom for imperial wars, Lloyd George was invited by Randall Casson, the lawyer who hired him as an articled clerk four years before, to go to a "Volunteer Dinner." He declined because he "hadn't attended drill," but he ordered the "Handbook to Company Drill" less than two weeks later, and a friend took his uniform to be inspected at a drill the same day. Exactly thirty days hence, he went to a "Compy drill" when his family thought he was going to a religious service. He justified misleading them by stating in his diary that he thought he would benefit more "physically and mentally by getting a good exercise drilling—skirmishing." Over fifteen months passed before Lloyd George noted one final, more involved escapade with "camping." He participated in an overnight "Volunteers' Camp" that started at 6:00 p.m., after he had "first made some sundry purchases such as knives &c at Conway—had tea in sergeants tents." He then accompanied one of the sergeants to Llandudno, returned to the camp around 10:00 p.m., and slept in a lieutenant's tent. Early the next morning, he marched in a parade, after which he "pipeclayed my belt & sling & brightened my buttons." He also had breakfast with sergeants and was subjected to an inspection for over three hours. "Got on better than I feared—However was glad to see it over," were his summations at the end of the two-day affair. Thus concluded his personal experiences with the militia, but once again he was very enamored with military paraphernalia and hob-nobbing with noncommissioned officers.[6]

By May 1885, Lloyd George had a more politically pragmatic attitude about war. In the aftermath of Charles Gordon's massacre at Khartoum three months prior, Gladstone's lame-duck government had averted war with the leader of Sudanese rebels. It also prevented war by moving troops from the Sudan to respond to Russia's incursion on the Afghanistán border. Gladstone's second ministry was doomed to fall, though, since it hesitated to supply reinforcements requested by Gordon, who had been besieged for nearly a year. They arrived two days late. In response to Gladstone's foreign policy accomplishments during his final months in office, Lloyd George very prac-tically interpreted in his diary, "Peace prospect assured. Very glad of it. Wars wd have put an end to Local Option, Disestablishment & the like for another six years." Gladstone did return for a third brief ministry, in 1886, splitting the Liberals by trying to give home rule to Ireland and falling from power again in only six months. It was indeed six years after that before he entered his final term in office as prime minister. By then, Lloyd George had been in Parliament himself for two years, championing Welsh domestic issues such as local option and disestablishment. He did not deal with foreign policies or war again until the 1896 crisis between the United Kingdom and Venezuela over the latter's border dispute with British Guiana. Grover Cleveland insisted on the British agreeing to American arbitration, invoking the Monroe Doc-trine, and Lord Salisbury's government relented. Lloyd George denounced the embarrassing submission of British interests to an outside power, again showing he was not a pacifist.[7]

In the fall of 1898, Lloyd George also supported the British Empire defend-ing its territory in the Nile River Valley against encroachment by the French at Fashoda in Sudan. He counseled peace negotiations instead, however, because the two nations were "the only countries where you have perfect civil and religious liberty in Europe." He also warned if the two began "quarrelling with each other," it would "make sport for the titled and throned Philistines of Europe" and they "will mock" the democracies. H. H. Kitchener was Brit-ain's general at Fashoda, and Major Jean-Baptiste Marchand commanded the French, who ultimately withdrew from the region to ward off war. Kitchener had also secured the Sudan earlier that same year, when he defeated the rebels at the Battle of Omdurman. Referring to the subdued dervishes, Lloyd George commended them to William as "brave men who believe in a cause & are prepared to suffer for it. Men who do that are too scarce in this commercial

materialistic age." Dervishes was the European's name for the fanatical followers of the Mahdi, Sudan's Muslim leader, who had founded an Islamic
theocracy after the slaughter of Charles Gordon and his men at Khartoum but
also died the same year. His successor was the loser at Omdurman.[8]

One year to the month after he acknowledged the courage of the Mahdists,
Lloyd George vociferously expounded on the increasing likelihood of a second
war in South Africa between the British and the Boers, eighteen years after the
first. Announcing that war "now seems inevitable," he also bemoaned, "The
prospect oppresses me with a deep sense of horror. I shall protest with all the
vehemence at my command against this blackguardism which is perpetrated
in the name of human freedom." Those words were for his brother's eyes only,
but he also shared with his wife his "hopes that the English will get a black
eye." His use of blackguardism probably included the way the British government was treating the Boer leader, Paul Kruger, as he compared it to an infa-
mous case of French injustice in an earlier letter to William that month: "The
condemnation of Dreyfus is almost as bad as the coercion of poor old Kruger.
Both wicked. Heard of it on our return to civilisation from the Prince." He
had been in Canada before getting the heir's news.[9]

By the middle of October, Lloyd George was sharing with his brother the
specifics of the fighting that began in the interim, placing the blame squarely
on the shoulders of the imperialists. "In my opinion the way these poor
hunted burghers have been driven in self defense to forestall us aggravates our
crime—there is something diabolical in its malignity cunning & inepti-
tude." In all fairness to the British inhabitants, nonetheless, he also informed
William that the "Boers have invaded our territories & until they are driven
back Government entitled to money to equip forces to defend our possessions." The following day's missive made it crystal clear that he did not despise
the empire itself, when he drew a stark contrast between the Irish's and his
view of it: "The Irish attitude towards the British Empire is one of uncon-
cealed hatred & hostility. That is not ours & it is important we should not be
associated with it."[10]

The day after, Lloyd George wrote to his brother that the Boers were bom-
barding Mafeking, but he continued to sympathize with them, calling them
"poor chaps" when they were defeated near Dundee two days later. He and
the newspapers put the battle at Glencoe, west of Dundee, but it occurred
at Talana Hill, east of the town. Boers had also started that attack, but the
British "sent them flying & are now pursuing with cavalry—you know what
that means. Horrible. . . . Well it may end the war. That is only satisfactory

feature." Actually, the Boers renewed their offensive against Dundee the very next day, with such superior numbers of men and cannon that the British withdrew southwest toward Ladysmith the following night. The latter left their wounded, dying, and dead as well as more than a month's rations for five-thousand combatants. News of victory by fellow troops at Elandslaagte, between Dundee and Ladysmith, had reached them the morning of their departure, but the death toll, according to Lloyd George's count for William, was "much heavier than we anticipated at first. We seem to have lost about 180 men & 35 officers. The Gordon Highlanders lost 13 out of their 15 officers." Expressing sympathy for the dead, but also showing powerful feelings of opposition to the expansion of Britain's empire at the expense of a smaller, weaker people, he continued, "The loss in officers is appalling. But it is all to the good. It will bring it home to the parties who are responsible primarily for this wicked war."[11]

Lloyd George had started the letter to his brother on the heavy losses at Elandslaagte in a scornful way toward those who were blindly nationalistic. "The glorious & brilliant Bretones are not so glorious after all. Just as the Jingoes were crowing over a second & a third victory comes the news that the smashed and demoralised Boer army driven with great slaughter to the frontier had actually attacked us at Dundee." He linked the very sarcastic statements to another battle he recorded two days later. It was an attempt to dislodge Boers at Rietfontein, a hilly ridge between Elandslaagte and Ladysmith. He gloated, "Boers have captured a squadron of Hussars—probably the fellows who were 'pursuing the retreating enemy' 'with great slaughter.' We lost 100 men in yesterday's engagement." Returning to Britain's debacle the next day too, he extolled the Boers: "What a victory. It turns out now that so far from our having captured six Boers guns they took one of ours—they had driven off with theirs before we ever reached them. We pursued like idiots & were caught in the trap."[12]

Two more days after that update, Lloyd George revisited the events at Dundee, revealing that in addition to wounded troops and supplies, the British had "left a good deal of ammunition behind . . . amongst other things we left Dum Dum bullets which the Boers wanted to use upon us but Kruger said they must show they were more humane than the British & he ordered them to be destroyed." Hussars were immaculately, colorfully dressed light cavalry, and the British gun mentioned was a Maxim, an automatic machine gun. A larger test version of it, also known as a Pom-Pom because of the sound it made, was already being employed by the Boers, and it fired a one-pound shell. Ironically, it had been made in England. Dum Dum bullets had been altered by cutting their ends to weaken them so they would expand on contact and do more damage. Their use had just been outlawed by The Hague earlier in the year at the world's first peace conference, but the British only agreed in principle, not on paper. Clearly, some were used.[13]

A party "responsible primarily for this wicked war" was specifically mentioned by Lloyd George in a letter to William on October 21. William had told a third individual he was "hoping Cecil Rhodes would be captured," which that person relayed to Lloyd George. The elder brother, in jest, called such wishful thinking "the treasonable utterances of the President of the Garthcelyn Republic," ending his feigned shock by emphasizing, "Treason this blasphemy." Garthcelyn was the name of William's house, and employing the word republic was a way of identifying with the Boers in the Transvaal, though the province had an oligarchy with President Kruger. Rhodes was the leading diamond as well as gold mining entrepreneur in South Africa and lived in Kimberley, another town being besieged by Boers at the time. He founded the De Beers Mining Company in 1880 and had also served as the Cape Colony's prime minister two consecutive times, from 1890 to 1896. Although not directly by name, Lloyd George was himself referring to Rhodes when he told his brother he would vehemently protest against "blackguardism which is perpetrated in the name of human freedom." Late in 1898, and many times the next year, Rhodes had campaigned on the slogan "equal rights for all civilised men south of the Zambesi." Clearly, he meant white men only, the British and others of European descent, but not the peoples of color.[14]

Less than two weeks after singling out Rhodes, Lloyd George connected the war to public sentiment in London. In four reports to William, he not only conveyed shock at the besieging of and battles for the British town of Ladysmith but also his satisfaction at the negative impact they were having on the British imperialists. "The butchery is horrible," he groaned. "The depression here is patent to any man who walks the street. The fizz is out of the Jingo pop." Just four days earlier, the empire's troops had suffered 1,272 casualties, 954 of them having surrendered at one time when an attempt to finish off the Boers backfired. Thomas Pakenham calls it "the greatest strategic mistake of the entire war." Before associating the bad news with emotions in England's capital, Lloyd George had shared with his brother a portion of the slowly arriving correspondence from the field. Starting with the Boers, who were getting closer to Ladysmith, he speculated, "If they succeed they may nab White & his forces before reinforcements can possibly reach him."[15]

Then, turning once more to the previous battle at Dundee, Lloyd George revised its losses upward: "Another interesting item is the list of the missing. It seems that not merely the Hussars but about 80 of our infantry—the very infantry who stormed the hill were captured by the Boers at the great victory at Glencoe." He again misnamed the battle, though referencing Talana Hill, but words like "captured" and "victory" are too strong for taking wounded troops as prisoners after a town has been evacuated due to shelling by artillery. Boers had used a gun specifically made for sieges to bombard the town from high ground four miles away, continuing after the able-bodied British had left. It was known as a Creusot, or a "Long Tom," was made of steel, was fourteen-feet long, and fired six-inch shells. The same day he noted the missing in action, Lloyd George also agonizingly told his wife, "I wish this war were over. I cannot without the greatest difficulty get my mind on to anything else. Bad headaches trouble me the last 2 or 3 days."[16]

Lieutenant-General George White was the General Officer Commanding in Natal, South Africa. The battles where he might have been nabbed were at Nicholson's Nek or Pepworth Hill, halfway between Rietfontein and Ladysmith, on "Mournful Monday," October 30. He personally led at the latter battle but was not captured because he returned to Ladysmith when things started going badly, leaving two subordinates in charge of regrouping and organizing the retreat. Based on the news he received that day, Lloyd George told William, "Big fight proceeding at Ladysmith but so far it is all a matter of artillery & maneuvering." The following day, however, he gave him details: "What a mess we are making of things in Natal. I wired Uncle Lloyd as soon as I heard it. I knew it would gladden his heart. I rather underestimated the number of men captured. They are now computed variously at 1500 or 2000. If the British troops are driven out of Ladysmith," he surmised, "the Cape Dutch will rise almost to a man & three years butchery will scarcely see the end of it. The glory is already out of the business." He actually overestimated the number of casualties, as he often did with those who opposed him at his antiwar speeches.[17]

In early March 1900, Lloyd George spoke against the war at Glasgow City Hall and then described the chaos for his brother: "A tumultuous experience. Worst public meeting row I ever witnessed. 10,000 people outside trying to break into the meeting." Equating them to "savages" because of their "surging struggling fighting yelling," he continued, "A small Armageddon going on inside. Hundreds of the foe got into the meeting. . . . The fighters in the body of the hall were quite menacing. When tired of fighting the roughs sang Rule Britannia, God Save the Queen & the Soldiers of the Queen." Waiting patiently for over twenty minutes, he "shot out a couple of sentences about the terrible list of casualties in that day's papers. A hush instantly fell upon the whole audience. I took advantage of that to pour shot and shell into the rowdies for their want of fair play," cleverly using military analogies to portray his address. He also noted that he lectured "for forty minutes—got a splendid hearing—said stinging things—especially to interrupters—sat down amid great cheering. I conquered them completely." The speaker who preceded him later wrote an account and was quoted as also stating Lloyd George "got complete control" of "the rowdies." As he left Glasgow, though, his carriage came under attack, and another occupant "had his hand badly cut" from broken glass. "They did not touch me," Lloyd George exulted to William.[18]

Less than a month later, Lloyd George informed his brother that he was "pleading" in public, as he had in private with John Morley, Leonard Courtney, and other pro-Boer Liberals, "for any settlement that fully recognized the nationality of the Boers." He delivered the speech at Bangor on April 11, and a resolution to that effect passed by a sizable margin. However, going into the hall, he had dodged a clod as well as stones, during the meeting windows were broken, and as he departed a disgruntled member of the audience hit him on the head with a blunt object. Addled, though not injured because of his hat, he made his way to a restaurant, where constables protected him. By May 18, British troops had relieved the Boer sieges and were occupying major towns of theirs as well as annexing their provinces. The night Mafeking was liberated, likenesses of Lloyd George, William, and Richard Lloyd were set ablaze in Criccieth because they were pro-Boers. The news made London erupt the day after, and Lloyd George chafed to William, "This to me is right down crazy over Mafeking. Crowds jamming the street shrieking & bellowing— Everything is draped in red white & blue from the bus horse to the less intelligent bifurcated ass that rides behind him." Adding insult to injury, he then observed, "When I got into my office this morning I found all my clerks adorned with the popular ribbon & a penny Union Jack stuck on the typing machine. They all clamoured for a day off which I gave them."[19]

In Lloyd George's insightful opinion, the relief of Mafeking was not as negative for Boers as if it succumbed to them. "It is obviously the best thing that could have happened for the Boer Cause," he reasoned. "Had Mafeking surrendered to hunger & disease these brutes would have been so exasperated that any man who stood up for reason & righteousness amongst them would have been clawed to pieces. We would have entered upon that most horrible of struggles—a war of revenge," he expressed to his brother, "the brutes" being the British imperialists again. Looking to the future prospects of the war, he then speculated, "A long siege of Pretoria ensuing now will do marvels. But that is necessary & I believe highly probable. A nation with such strong men at its head never gives in. Had they been weak or incapable the Boer Cause were lost now. But Kruger Steyn Botha & Olivier are just the men who can hearten a crowd into heroes." One week later, he highly praised the Boers once more, albeit still in private, for avoiding capture after their territory had been invaded. "Roberts crossed the Vaal on the Queen's Birthday," he began. "No Boers met anywhere. Brave Boers! I feared they might be caught between Bobs & the river. . . . Their only danger," as he saw it, "is that local and personal jealousies will prevent their following Botha's counsel. I believe him to be a fine commander." Lloyd George ended that day's sharing of information with William expressing shock at how many of the British casualties were due to illness instead of arms: "Our soldiers are dying of filth diseases—enteric & dysentery—at the rate of 40 per day 1200 per month. The rate is increasing. Another 7 months of this will bring home the horror of it." Marthinus Steyn was the Orange Free State's president, and J. H. Olivier was a general for it. Louis Botha was a general for the Transvaal.[20]

It did not take seven more months for people on the domestic front to realize the extent to which British soldiers were suffering. A report in *The Times* only one month afterward revealed that the troops were experiencing widespread, unchecked diseases. Lloyd George told his brother that the correspondence caused a "sensation" in the capital, further commenting that it had recorded, "20,000 cases of sickness—medical arrangements completely broken down—the poor victims lying out on the damp ground in the rain &c—nothing like it since the great Crimean scandal." On July 18, he also explained for his uncle why he was not speaking out against the war in public anymore: "I am reserving myself for another go for Chamberlain & the war. People are beginning to grumble against Roberts for the delay. It will be time enough April next year to growl. The war will be going strong then. What fools the British public are." Chamberlain was then Colonial Secretary in Lord Salisbury's Cabinet and leader of the Liberal Unionists, who sided with the Conservative Party on imperialism. Frederick Roberts, known as "little Bobs," was the commander-in-chief of imperial forces in South Africa, which over the last five months had rescued the besieged British towns of Kimberley,

Ladysmith, and Mafeking. They had captured Bloemfontein, Johannesburg, and Pretoria from the Boers too.[21]

Actually, Lloyd George had spoken out in public again less than two weeks before trying to justify himself to his uncle, but he had encountered a very unruly group of adolescents. At the event, in Liskeard, Cornwall, they had, "Stormed platform—wouldn't listen to anybody. Simply 100 or 150 young hobbledehoys. The bulk of the meeting was with us. Assured it will do good," he consoled William. Despite the optimistic assessment he gave his brother after it, though, the assembly had been forced to adjourn early because some bad-mannered teenagers were throwing furniture all over the auditorium. Lloyd George waited only a week after his response to Richard Lloyd to growl at Chamberlain. In Parliament, he blamed him for leading "us into two blunders. The first was the war. But worse than the war is the change that has been effected in the purpose for which we are prosecuting the war. We went into the war for equal rights; we are prosecuting it for annexation."[17] No sooner had he started his growling at the government, Chamberlain in particular, than the Boers changed the course of the war in a very unconventional direction, and the British response caused him to roar.[22]

Boers were now waging an all-out guerrilla war, and the British reacted with a scorched-earth policy. Isolated guerrilla tactics had achieved limited success in the west over the previous four months, but from July on Boers employed them much more broadly. Even in his hometown, Lloyd George could not escape controversy for his views on the war or his chances for reelection. "Criccieth is no break in the monotony of politics," he wrote William in September, "I get into the same old whirl of argument about the war & electioneering prospects." Then, Queen Victoria officially dissolved Parliament sixteen days later, primarily because Chamberlain was hopeful to strengthen the government's hand in dealing with the enemy. The resulting "khaki election" the next month, so-called because of the new combat uniform of the British army, saw Lloyd George returned with his biggest majority but the Salisbury coalition ministry reinstated with an increase of six. In a speech at Bangor early in November, Lloyd George revealed that Roberts had written Botha to state the houses of Boer farmers, next to railroad tracks damaged by guerrillas, would be burned and animals as well as foodstuffs in a ten-mile radius removed. To relieve their people's affliction, Boers decided incursions into Natal and Cape Colony were necessary. In a forbidding, prophetic tone, Lloyd George spoke at Conway four days before 1901 began, calling on Britain to end the war, but "there would be years of sniping and guerrilla warfare afterwards." Blaming his own military instead of Boer leaders, though, he roared, "a second war had been started upon—a ghastlier war, a war more expensive, degrading and dishonourable for Britain."[23]

The newly elected Parliament had first met in December, and Lloyd George continued his criticism of Chamberlain, accusing him of profiting from the war through investments, a charge he had first leveled eight months earlier. The day Parliament convened, Roberts left Cape Town, having turned over the command of British imperial forces in South Africa to Kitchener less than two weeks prior. Roberts returned to London the next month to become the commander-in-chief of British forces worldwide. Assuming his new responsibilities on November 29, Kitchener not only continued Roberts's policy of burning houses near vandalized rail lines but also implemented the removal of Boer elderly, women, and children from their houses into concentration camps in March of 1901. On the nineteenth of that month, Lloyd George spoke in favor of fairness for the Boers during a debate on whether to establish a Transvaal Concessions Commission, after initial but unsuccessful negotiations between Kitchener and Botha had finished the last day of February. He said such a commission "would only exasperate the Boers, and lead them to protract the war to the utmost" because they believed it would plan to settle British troops on any land they might cede. "Before we could give the farms to our troops somebody would have to be expatriated," he projected, "and he could only condemn the unwisdom of appointing a Commission which would give the Boers the idea that our object in prosecuting this war was not to give equal rights to all, but to obtain not only the gold mines but the country as well." The war's ostensible cause, after all, was Britons living in Boer areas not being given the same political rights as their hosts.[24]

Lloyd George had addressed the topic the previous month too. In an ongoing debate after Edward VII first addressed Parliament, he noted a provision in the estimated cost of peace would settle fifteen-thousand British yeomen on Boer farms. Concerning the desired object of everyone under Boers having equal rights, he griped, "In every sort of case with a legitimate grievance to redress, with every demand for the extension of freedom in the Transvaal, the Government have so conducted the controversy as to have ranged against them every friend of freedom throughout the world, outside Great Britain." He then acknowledged both parties wanted self-rule for Boers, except Chamberlain planned to impose a crown colony on them. However, the Boers would not trust such an agreement because the same man, as a member of Gladstone's second ministry, had promised Egypt freedom but now proposed to renege on that commitment. Turning to the army, he had even higher criticism of Roberts, Kitchener, and lesser leaders for retaliating against many more Boers than those who carried out acts of "treachery." "It is war not against men, but against women and children," treated unequally also. "All those who surrendered voluntarily were given full rations. All the families whose husbands were on commando were put on a reduced scale. It would be increased to full allowance if the husbands surrendered." His last remarks emotionally pictured the result of such discrimination: "It means that unless the fathers came in their children would be half-starved. It means that the remnant of the Boer army who are sacrificing everything for their idea of independence," he portrayed, "are to be tortured by the spectacle of their starving children into betraying their cause." Military historian Philip Warner has asserted that Lloyd George stressed the similarity between Herod and Kitchener, presumably because of cruelty to children.[25]

In June, emotions in Parliament as well as in the public were stirred to an even greater fever pitch because of a report submitted to the former and then published by Emily Hobhouse. Lloyd George, who had joined the League of Liberals against Aggression and Militarism, had urged her to publish it. She was a short, stout, spinster in her forties who had recently toured concentration camps. Henry Campbell-Bannerman, leader of the opposition who had tried to stay in the middle between pro-Boer Liberals and Liberal Imperialists, was emboldened by her account to compare British concentration camps to those used by Spain against the Cuban guerrillas. At a dinner for Liberals in the National Reform Union, June 14, he asked, "When is a war not a war?", referring to some in the government who said under the current circumstances that there was no war. After the group laughed, he answered, "When it is carried on by methods of barbarism in South Africa."[26]

Earlier in the day, Lloyd George had submitted an inquiry to the Speaker of the House of Commons about the protection of South African blacks affected by the "clearing" of Boer lands. Posed to St John Brodrick, Secretary of State for War, it asked are they "deprived of their cattle, sheep, grain, and agricultural implements; if so, whether any compensation is made to the owners for the loss, and what measures are taken to prevent a famine among the native population in the denuded districts." After receiving assurance that all precautions were being "made to secure natives from any avoidable loss" and reimbursements for stock had "been reported in various instances," he further queried whether they were "taken into refugee camps." The answer was that they were "safeguarded as far as possible from the rigours of the war."

Exactly one week later, he revisited the issue, requesting to know when the leaders of the Boers were asked to assume the feeding of women and children in burned-over areas and if they were promised that British troops would not interfere with food transports. In an even more emotional letter to William, seemingly about this question, he wrote, "I had my fling last night. A most useful intervention. I believe I last night did something to improve the condition of thousands of poor little Boer kiddies in these horrible camps. I felt quite happy over it."[27]

On June 17, 1901, Lloyd George succeeded in getting a post-adjournment debate over the death rate in the camps, claiming it was tantamount to "a policy of extermination against children in South Africa." This time, he diplomatically stressed that he was attacking the policy for which Brodrick was responsible, not troops, officers, or Kitchener, "whose hands are full." His "rough computation" of the mortality figures was based on just one month's accounting and showed that 12 percent were dying, compared to 5.2 for the worst month of the war militarily. From what he heard and read, he detailed deplorable conditions contributing to his tally: "the women herded together, sometimes twelve in a tent; tents leaking; clothes saturated; not much clothing allowed; little children half starved; the food they had, bad; their clothes soaked through with rain and dew." Citing a camp medical officer's report, he said, "Examined samples of the mealies, and of sugar used. Sample one: mouldy and contains mite; unfit for human consumption." Even more grievous in Lloyd George's estimation was a double standard applied to allocate food. Children whose fathers were not guerrillas received half a pound of flour and meal, half a pound of meat, plus a "quarter of a tin" of milk. Those of commandos got no flour and one-third as much meat and milk. In a letter to his brother the following day, he expressed the conviction that he had helped Boer children again: "Think I made a deep impression yesterday & the general idea is that much good will ensue to the poor little Dutch kiddies. What fools these Liberal Imperialists are. They couldn't have chosen worse ground of action than the torture of women & children." In his work on Lloyd George, biographer Herbert Du Parcq discussed his heart in regard to the war and described him as a man of "confirmed convictions."[28]

However, Brodrick objected that Lloyd George's mathematical calculations had been "put forward so hurriedly" because he had not seen "the most recent statistics" of Kitchener. He also blamed what the actual number of dead would end up being on the Boer men for deserting their women, intentionally creating an untenable logistical burden for the British. Even when certain paroled Boers had been permitted by Roberts to return to their houses, "a great blunder" Brodrick now admitted, they used them as recruiting stations and then returned to their hit and run attacks. After the men resumed fighting, some of their women turned the farms into "depots," providing "supplies and stores" as well as "information on the movements of our troops." More than once, Roberts had also tried to get Boer generals to provide for the females and minors, offering them the use of the railroads to deliver food to them, but also to no avail, Brodrick explained, because "they traded on our humanity in the matter." Mothers of the sick did not escape his rationalizing, either. More children would have survived if their mothers had followed the medical precautions during epidemics. Under the best conditions during the war, however, Brodrick acknowledged it was hard to take care of a quarter of a million soldiers, "whom it is our first duty to supply," and sixty-three thousand refugees "by single lines of railway." He concluded by professing his desire for peace, so all could go home, and finally promised, "We will do what we can to preserve them from unnecessary suffering, whether they come to us of their own accord, or through our exercise of force, or through the neglect of their own people."[29]

Two days after the adjournment debate, Lloyd George spoke at the London Queen's Hall, portraying the plight of Boers as a spiritual contrast to the British Empire's worldliness: "I thank Heaven for the spectacle of one little nation of peasants standing against the mightiest Empire in the world, preferring to die rather than prostrate itself with the other nations of the earth at the feet of the vulgar priesthood of Mammon." He offered a resolution deploring the government's war policy, demanding an end to "an unjust and dastardly war," and proposing peace terms that "a brave and freedom-loving people could honourably accept." The attendees went further and amended his resolution to call for total independence, which he had decided would no longer be feasible. Approximately a month later, rough totals for the camp fatalities were released, and the final report was published on August 16, only one day before Parliament recessed for the year.[30]

The overall death rate was 11.7 percent, which rounds off to Lloyd George's average, but almost half of the children perished in one of the camps. Chamberlain accepted the oversight of the camps before year's end and ultimately reduced their mortality to 2 percent. By the end of the war, however, there were almost 120,000 Boers interned at camps, more than a sixth of them expiring, with seven thousand of the dead being children. Prior to the conclusion of the 1901 session, Lloyd George, on his way "to get behind speakers chair to put in a question," passed by Edward Grey and "co-Imperialists holding council" in the lobby. "On my return," he alerted William, "Grey beckons me up & we have a regular set to for an hour. He was very genial & very complimentary to me personally. He wanted my forecast of the future. I gave it frankly. I said that as long as nation was in present mood it was right to call Tories in." By the "present mood," he surely meant the war, and he frankly added, "Liberals could not & would not do the job required by England now. But when social reform & bread needed Liberals would be sent for." He ended, "Imperialist papers foaming at the mouth today & the last several days."[31]

Newspapers favorable to the "Limps," as the Liberal Imperialists were called, were acting like rabid dogs because of another speech Campbell-Bannerman made on July 2 in Southampton. He justified his criticism of the ministry and said it led to promises of redressing two grievances: giving the wives of guerrillas as much food as other women and releasing all females who could be cared for by their families or friends. He also stated his belief that there were plotters among the Liberal Imperialists who were trying to exacerbate conflicts within the party. His preference was for elected members to work out their differences but would reach out to all Liberals if necessary to resolve them. Lloyd George was greatly encouraged by his leader's comments, relating to his brother, "C. B. is doing well. His speech last night was excellent. He is showing his mettle & winning—for first time—the respect of friend & foe. The intriguers," he continued, "have given him his opportunity." A week after his plea to party members, Campbell-Bannerman called for a united effort to rid the party of conspirators, and a vote of confidence followed. He won handily, Grey and other Liberal Imperialists agreeing to bury the hatchet. Among the party notables, only Lord Rosebery, leader of the opposition until choosing to resign the post in 1896, dissented. He called the vote pietistic but stopped short of labeling it pretentious. At the end of 1901, and into the next year, he was positioned to take over leadership of Liberals again but never reascended.[32]

Lloyd George also wanted a reinvigorated Liberal Party but not with Rosebery at its helm. He mentioned a fellow politician to William, who had decided to stop attending "any" meetings because they were "no good." Expressing hatred of them also, "especially of the travelling they involve," he nevertheless added it "does not absolve us of our responsibility to do our best." The meetings were obviously postsession gatherings held throughout the country, and he elaborated on why absenting oneself from them was not acceptable. "If we had only the war to think of this might be sound policy," he wrote. "But the future has to be thought of & this is in my judgment pre-eminently the time to build up or rather rebuild a new party & a policy ready for the day when the nation is penitent & willing to be saved." Two weeks later, he delivered a moving speech at Leigh on imperialism, characterizing magnanimous empires as "fearlessly just," supportive of the less fortunate, and without "racial arrogance." Prophetic of his own and the empire's future, he also proclaimed, "I suspect the call of Empire when it shirks Armenia, but goes straight forward to force freedom on goldfields." In his view, freedom for nations within the British Empire was the only way for it to stay intact. "We ought to give freedom everywhere—freedom in Canada, freedom in the Antipodes, in Africa, in Ireland, in Wales, and in India." When he talked to the members of the National Liberal Federation's governing body on December 4, though, he asked them to recommend peace talks but not specifics, and they agreed.[33]

Six weeks after writing his brother in religious analogies, Lloyd George learned the hard way that some who still favored the war were not in a repenting mood, did not want redemption from their deeds, and were willing to send him to judgment. While visiting Birmingham, the home of Chamberlain, where he had served as mayor from 1873 to 1875, he encountered the most unruly crowd of his assemblies, and it turned deadly. First, some demonstrators went to the train station to confront him, whom he eluded. Then, a mob of thirty thousand were encountered by 350 police outside the meeting place. Next, all who could possibly squeeze in did. Lastly, the rabble hurled dangerous objects toward the stage. The gathering was intended to heal wounds between Liberal Imperialists and other party members. One "Limp" began the program before Lloyd George got up and attempted to be heard above the raucousness. Another one was supposed to start, but he had been threatened and his home encircled by an angry crowd. Liberal Unionist papers loyal to Chamberlain had published there would probably be a disturbance but the Liberal Party would be paying for needed repairs to the building when it was over. It had been made clear, however, by those who planned the function opposition to the war was not on the agenda. Lloyd George had been castigated by those papers as being against Britain and had been advised by the head of the police not to come. He got to mention the Boers in passing, address the charge he was Britain's enemy, express shame at the newspapers, and state Chamberlain had turned the nation's flag into his personal handkerchief before he finally had to give up. As the glass ceiling started to collapse, because most windows were broken by bricks wrapped in barbed wire or rocks people who could not get in threw, officers put him in one of their uniforms and a helmet to safely escort him out.[34]

Lloyd George was not harmed but had to be protected until he departed for the capital the next morning. Nearly two score were injured, and sadly a rioter and a policeman were killed. In a letter to William the day after, he referenced the tragedy, grieving, "all they succeeded in doing was to kill one of their own men & to smash a policeman's skull. Poor fellows. I am sincerely sorry for both. Altho' the young fellow who died had himself alone to blame still I have no doubt he was perfectly honest & disinterested in his action." Actually, the demonstrator had died after being clubbed by a constable and hitting a curb. George Cadbury, the chocolate magnate of Birmingham whom Lloyd George had persuaded one year earlier to buy London's *Daily News* and turn it into an antiwar paper, encouraged him in a letter he shared with his brother on December 20: "He says the meeting has done no end of good." Even Birmingham's Lord Mayor, a Conservative who allowed the opposition party to reserve the lecture hall, "denounces the riot & the Unionist papers that instigated it," he added. After four additional days to reflect, his resolve had stiffened, and in a retaliatory spirit, he wrote to William, "The fools. They have helped the cause & the man they hate as no single incident hitherto has." What caused tempers to flare to the extent they did were: consternation over the conditions in camps, which created guilt in the minds of some who had embraced the war; support for the military, which Lloyd George had occasionally criticized; and the fervent gratitude of many in Birmingham for Chamberlain, the Welshman's political but not the personal foe they believed him to be.[35]

The next time Lloyd George spoke in public, every possible measure was taken to insure his safety. Policemen strategically positioned barricades around the perimeter of the building as well as placing a pressure hose on its steps, prepared a contingent for a charge on horseback, and secured all of the entrances, including the windows. In the address, delivered at Bristol six days into the new year, he appealed to the God-given ability of each to use reason instead of physical strength to settle differences, saying that, in spite of danger, he would continue "to stand up for a great principle." Salisbury's last parliamentary session convened later in the month, and Lloyd George gave his final important war speech there on March. He started, opposing martial law against up to four-thousand Boers who were in Britain's Cape Colony, especially without writs of habeas corpus. "The principle" invoked this time was "English law," he stated, under which "every man is assumed to be innocent until he is proved guilty. Martial law says that not only is a suspected person assumed guilty, but he is so guilty that he is sentenced before he has heard the charge." After hearing this, the defender of martial law back-pedaled, stating he had not realized the accused were not informed. Lloyd George went on, "Here are people deported and exiled and sent away hundreds of miles and practically transported, without knowing what the charge against them is, and it is assumed, without any charge being made, that they are guilty." He then criticized Lord Salisbury's statement, "for generations the Boers would be deprived of self-government, and that they would not obtain a shred of independence." Those comments were "calculated to encourage the Boers to resistance," he charged.[36]

Next, Lloyd George blamed Chamberlain for negating peace terms Kitchener had worked out with Botha slightly over a year prior, including funds for rebuilding and indebtedness as well as a council of advisors elected by Boers. The cost to the empire could have totaled £2 million, which the Colonial Secretary rejected outright, along with the council. When the subject was changed by Carnarvon Boroughs's MP to various predictions of how much longer the war would last, a few weeks, a few months, nine months, two more years, and then he alluded to how many battles had been lost, an accuser yelled, "the pro-Boers are pleased at it." Instantly calling it "a perfectly insolent remark," he emotionally responded, "I cannot conceive a more horrible charge than that a number of Britishers rejoiced in the maiming and mutilation of a number of their countrymen." He concluded with the portent that the government's expectation of "absolute surrender" might not achieve peace "for years to come" and that the Boers had not only offered what the war was fought to accomplish, equal suffrage in their states, but also to pay reparations as well as accept British rule in foreign affairs. The following day, he told Maggie he had worked very hard on his debate and it had poured salt on the open wounds of the ministry. Two weeks earlier, he had also written her about the Liberal League, an organization created the month before to make Rosebery the leader of the Liberal Party instead of Campbell-Bannerman. It elected Rosebery as president, Liberal Imperialists were included, Grey as a vice-president, and discontented Liberal Unionists joined its ranks. Lloyd George asked if she had read where Campbell-Bannerman questioned the necessity of the league in a speech, adding that someone "shouted out 'Lloyd George'. It is evidently a league started to keep me down. As usual they are enhancing my power by exaggerating it."[37]

Nine days before Lloyd George's last major comments on the war in

Parliament, he told Maggie that the lower house "presents a thoroughly dejected appearance" due to a "disaster" which "has depressed members. They are beginning to realise in a dim sort of way that things are not all right in Africa. It has caused a good deal of surprise which shows how ignorant even well informed & trained politicians are as to the course of events." Sending her another message later in the evening, he stated that Irish members showed "savage exaltation" when they heard the news of Britain's defeat and had "excited deep resentment" because of it. The news Parliament received was of an embarrassing retreat and surrender at Tweebosch on March 7. A Lieutenant-General, Lord Methuen, had led a search-and-destroy campaign against Boer rebels with twelve hundred irregular troops and raw recruits, who were supposed to be a more rapid deployment force. They were hit first, ran in disarray, and Methuen was shot in the leg. He as well as four artillery pieces were captured, the only general to suffer such a fate during the war, and it was the worst defeat in a couple of years. Lloyd George, referring to his second son in another missive to Maggie, stated he also thought their Gwilym "would have been very delighted at the success of his friends. Did you tell him how the mules ran away when the Boers rushed among them. Then how the cavalry scampered away with the Boers chasing them like deerhounds." He may not have been "savage" in his excitement like the Irish, but he was still cheering for the Boers to a lesser extent. When a leader of the Irish, John Dillon, was suspended during the raging debate for calling Chamberlain "a damned liar" and refused to withdraw it, his fellow Celt voted with the Irishmen against it.[38]

Sixteen days after Methuen's debacle, half a dozen political and military leaders of Boers began talking among themselves on a train to Pretoria about how to bring the war to an end. To Maggie, a day later, Lloyd George conveyed his "doubts as to anything coming of the new peace movement" and intended to speak publicly on his ideas for peace a day later until he was advised not to do so by two other Liberal members. The train arrived on April 11, and their first proposal to Kitchener was flatly rejected by Brodrick because it did not accept annexation of the republics as crown colonies. When amnesty was offered six days later, though, they asked for a cease fire to go and talk to their men who were still fighting. The day after, Lloyd George wrote his wife, "The news from South Africa today is very promising," speculating that it would take three weeks for Boers to achieve their task, adding, "the proposals we have now made are much more liberal & that as far as money for restocking farms is concerned they were fairly lavish. I wish peace would come so long of course as it brings fair treatment to those gallant chaps in the field."[39]

It turned out to be four more weeks before ten times as many Boer representatives, chosen by guerrillas, met in Vereeniging and settled on five leaders to negotiate for them. The delegates were three generals, the Transvaal's state lawyer, and the Orange Free State's judge. Botha was one general, and the lawyer was Jan Smuts, who later joined Lloyd George's War Cabinet. Talks resumed in Pretoria four days later, and they proposed domestic autonomy under the auspices of the United Kingdom but agreed to relinquish all their foreign affairs. The British response was to accept the negotiators as official governmental representatives of the respective republics, which had been expunged by Britain in 1900, but to also require all Boers to acknowledge Edward VII as their sovereign. Alfred Milner, High Commissioner for South Africa, who later also served as a member of Lloyd George's War Cabinet, was most responsible for the response, but only when attorneys for both sides produced a copy of the details was an agreement reached. Just one final statement was added before it was sent to England on May 21.[40]

Lloyd George submitted the following assessment to his spouse two days later: "People very excited here about the prospects of peace. The general opinion is that it is coming off. I earnestly hope so for the sake of Liberalism." As he had pointed out earlier, Liberals would only be returned to power when the war was over and voters wanted social reform. Expressing those sentiments to Maggie one day, he told his younger brother the next he was "apprehensive" about the remaining "details," fearing Chamberlain's "greed may yet upset a settlement." In fact, the Colonial Secretary not only accepted the £3 million debt assistance for the Boers, but also chided Milner when the latter would have possibly ruined the agreement on the point. To his credit, Chamberlain also wanted to give the natives in South Africa the vote at the same time that all whites received it but acquiesced to Milner's wording that it would be up for discussion after the Boer republics achieved self-government. The High Commissioner knew neither state would grant it.[41]

The letter to William also addressed the issue of the Liberal League once more, observing that Rosebery "wants now a fusion & not expulsion of the Pro-Boers. We have beaten him inside the party & the Liberals in the country are with us." The peace treaty was returned to the Boers for an up or down vote with no more negotiations, and fifty-four of sixty representatives agreed to it on the last day of May. Lloyd George heard church bells, shots, and cheering after going to bed the next night and knew the war was over. He exclaimed to Maggie the following day the terms ended up, "Much better than those we offered them 15 months ago—after spending £80,000,000 in the meantime!"

The topic of amnesty for captured commandos in Cape Colony and Natal was not specifically mentioned in the treaty but was granted to all except certain rebel leaders. None of them was executed, but all were forbidden to vote for life. The Transvaal as well as Orange Free State were given civil autonomy by Liberals in 1906 and 1907, respectively. In 1910, they, along with Cape Colony and Natal, became the Union of South Africa as members of the British Commonwealth. Botha served as its first prime minister.[42]

11

Diplomacy and World War, 1902–1916

"I am not against war a bit."

EXACTLY SIX WEEKS AFTER the Boers approved peace terms with the United Kingdom, Arthur Balfour became its prime minister. Salisbury, his uncle, resigned the previous day, July 11, 1902. For the next year and a half, opposing Balfour's Education Act was Lloyd George's primary interest and extension of it to Wales was delayed until February 1904. The Russo-Japanese War began the same month, and William received three letters by mid-April, detailing Japanese naval successes but also Lloyd George's desire for England to stay "out of it." He sent another one day after Japan won at Mukden, the biggest land battle ever, penning, "This will I hope bring peace." Peace talks did not start, however, until Russia's fleet was destroyed by Japan at Tsushima Strait. April of 1904 was also when Britain and France signed the Entente Cordiale, ending the colonial disputes between the two empires over Africa six years after the Fashoda Crisis. On the very day of the signing, Lloyd George got the news at Rosebery's house and expressed delight that the nations' differences had ceased. Before 1904 closed, he said the entente had improved humanity. He did not look at it with an anti-German eye until 1911, when the Second Moroccan Crisis heightened tensions in Europe.[1]

The First Moroccan Crisis started on March 31, 1905, almost resulting in warfare between Germany and France over the next fourteen months. During the year plus, it became abundantly clear that Britain would side with the latter if hostilities commenced. Indeed, the crisis was intended to test the strength of the Entente Cordiale. Germany's Kaiser Wilhelm II personally appeared in Tangier, ostensibly to champion Morocco's independence because

France had insisted on putting its supervisors in charge of the Moroccan army, police, and trade. The entente had agreed that France could intervene in Morocco to bolster the authority of the sultan as well as restore law and order, which had been lacking for some time. Consequently, the kaiser's intrigue led to an international conference at Algeciras, Spain, consisting of thirteen nations. Germany was only able to get two supporters on a mere vote concerning procedure, and when it ended, just Austria-Hungary was on its side. The one restriction placed on France was that it had to include Spain in regulating the police, under a neutral Swiss administrator. By the time the conference met on January 16, 1906, the Liberals had been back in power for over a month, with Campbell-Bannerman as Prime Minister, Edward Grey as Foreign Secretary, and Lloyd George as President of the Board of Trade.[2]

Britain's representative at the Algeciras Conference was Arthur Nicolson, its ambassador to Spain, who followed Grey's orders. His effectiveness in defending the entente caught the attention of a Russian delegate, who communicated to his superiors how supportive Britain would be as an ally. Having lost a fleet in the Russo-Japanese War, but gaining a constitution and representative assembly because of a revolution it spawned, Russia was willing to end its conflicts with Britain in Persia, Central Asia as well as Afghanistan, in return for British naval protection of its coasts. Grey invited Count Alexander Benckendorff, Russia's ambassador to the United Kingdom, for a meeting on his third day in office, expressing desire for the problems between the two empires to be settled. Nicolson was transferred as an ambassador from Spain to Russia during the Algeciras Conference and two months after it ended started talks with its foreign minister. By the time the next month ended, so had the first Duma, Russia's legislature, and another one was dispersed two months before an entente was sealed. Discussions went on regardless, especially when Nicolson extended the carrot of possible access to the Dardanelles for Russia's navy, if other accords were reached. On August 31, 1907, the Anglo-Russian Entente was signed, emphasizing that Afghanistan and Tibet would still be buffers between the two empires, China would oversee Tibet, and Persia would have three spheres: a northern one for Russia, a southern one for Britain, and a neutral one between them. Persia's independence, not included in the talks, was reaffirmed, but the empires were now free to acquire whatever they could politically and economically at its expense. Since Russia agreed to relinquish Afghanistan, Britain allowed its tradesmen to deal with the Afghans, and like the other entente, nothing was said about mutual defense or opposition to the Germans.[3]

In the parliamentary debates about the two ententes, Lloyd George did not comment. His eminent biographer stated during the entente negotiations that he simply wanted peace with whoever would concur, including Germany, and with British concessions when possible. Grigg added for the next three years that he still gave little notice to diplomacy but did put general European harmony over balance of power between entente nations and the central continental alliance. Admittedly, he remained privately and publicly silent in both periods, but another explanation is how busy he was with domestic affairs. In 1904, he was the leading opponent of the enforcement of Balfour's Education Local Authority Default Bill, which threatened to remove government funding for the non-Anglican schools in areas not complying with Balfour's 1902 act. At the Board of Trade until 1908, his hands were full preventing a rail strike and getting the Merchant Shipping Act, Patents and Designs Act as well as the Port of London Act passed. He was kept even busier from 1908 to 1911, the first half of his term as Chancellor of the Exchequer, with the Old Age Pensions Act, National Insurance Act for health as well as unemployment, and the Parliament Act, which stripped the House of Lords of its veto power.[4]

Lloyd George visited Germany in August of 1908 to investigate its government pensions and healthcare programs, but he also addressed the growing arms race between the two countries, saying there would never be an entente between them as long as it continued. He had talked with Germany's ambassador to England twice the month before and proposed it should only build two ships for every three the British constructed. He told his brother the results of their first meeting two days later: "I met Count Metternich the German ambassador at Sir Edward Grey's house for lunch on Wednesday. Very remarkable talk. Gave him my mind freely about the competition in armaments. Grey said he was very impressed & that he will report every word to the Emperor." A day after a second luncheon, by themselves, he further reported, "The Metternich lunch was I believe a historical one. I believe it will end in our understanding with Germany." Even before Lloyd George left Germany, Metternich communicated his comments to Wilhelm II, who called them "the insolent demands of the English Ministers to make their peacefulness dependent on the diminution of our sea force." Being much more emphatic, the emperor then said, "I do *not* wish a good understanding with England at the expense of the extension of the German fleet... this is an excessive impudence, which contains a great insult for the German people and its Kaiser." In spite of caustic words to Metternich in private, Wilhelm II intended to invite Lloyd

George to his court but was dissuaded by his Imperial Chancellor, Bernhard von Bülow, who feared they would have a heated exchange. Lloyd George told his uncle from Carlsbad a day before Metternich saw Wilhelm II: "had a long talk with Clemenceau. I thought him on the whole the biggest man I had met in politics since Gladstone. He is very anti-German but he always has been pro British."[5]

The previous month, a revolution occurred in the Ottoman Empire and was ostensibly instigated for a democracy with a constitution. Three months later, Austria-Hungary annexed the Balkan state of Bosnia-Herzegovina, expecting a better relationship with Young Turks than the Ottoman ruler. Officials for the sultan objected to unilateral annexation because thirty years earlier the Congress of Berlin had allowed Austria-Hungary to occupy the state only under a sultan's sovereignty. No change in status was to occur without first consulting the Ottomans and the other signatories. On Britain's input, Lloyd George formulated a solution satisfactory to the Turks and the Cabinet for H. H. Asquith, who had succeeded the ailing Campbell-Bannerman as prime minister six months before. On October 12, 1908, half a dozen days after Emperor Francis Joseph had announced the annexation, William read his brother "had the honor of making the suggestion which the Cabinet eventually accepted for dealing with the Turkish situation. They were in a great fix, had refused Grey's proposal & we were about to part without agreeing to anything which would have solved the difficulty & Grey was in despair. He was delighted with this idea which I put forward & the Cabinet agreed to it." The Cabinet was willing to support the burgeoning Turkish democracy by delaying longer a repeated request from Russia to have access to the Dardanelles for its warships. To also keep Russia content, though, the Cabinet complied with its insistence on an international conference to discuss the Bosnian Crisis, which Austria-Hungary and Germany rejected. Instead, the Austro-Hungarians made a financial settlement with the Turks, but when Serbia still objected sent an ultimatum to accept or face war. Germany stated it would back its partner if Russia sided with Serbs. Russia had not recovered from Japan, so it and Serbia relented in March of 1909.[6]

A month later, Lloyd George introduced his first budget as Chancellor of the Exchequer, which provided for building fewer warships than the First Lord of the Admiralty or the First Sea Lord wanted but promised more than they asked for the following year. Reginald McKenna was the civilian who had just been appointed to the former office under Asquith, and Sir John Fisher was the admiral in charge of the navy. Fisher, who had occupied his post since 1904, developed the first dreadnought, which was launched two years after. Both he and McKenna had requested six more dreadnoughts. They only received enough funds to start four in 1909, but buying parts for four more, to begin in 1910, was also authorized. Indeed, Richard Burdon Haldane, Secretary of State for War, and Fisher had relinquished monies from the army and navy to help defray part of the cost for pensions in 1908. The result was two dreadnoughts built that year, not four. One each had been scrapped the two previous years under Asquith also. Lloyd George wanted to get more revenue from them, but a scare over Germany's naval buildup forced him to compromise.[7]

The chancellor had intended from the moment he began planning for old age pensions to exhaust "all means of reducing expenditure," informing his brother that he meant "to cut down army expenditure" and that "Sir Guy Fleetwood Wilson one of the chief war office men" was helping him. Wilson was Assistant Under Secretary of State for War in Haldane's office and was in charge of funding. Presenting his budget, Lloyd George said eight dreadnoughts could be finished in three years, "without resorting either to additional taxation or to the vicious expedient of a loan." Yet, it would be "an act of criminal insanity," to spend more for "giant flotillas to encounter mythical Armadas," when so many other social programs needed financing. "[W]e cannot afford to build navies against nightmares . . . to appease an unreasoning panic," he added. At the same time, he used patriotic rhetoric in assuring the continued protection of the country "against every possible invader," "the menaced liberties of Europe from an impending doom," and "the vital interests of Western civilisation."[8]

McKenna, Fisher, Conservatives, economists, the press, the people, Liberal radicals, and even the prime minister were not pleased with the compromise, but generals apparently liked it. Lloyd George told Richard Lloyd the Inspector-General of the Army, John French, was "a great admirer of the Budget," and he as well as other generals "got up a great show especially for me." He deduced from the ensuing maneuvers they were "delighted" to see him. On the other hand, he was not delighted when he met Kitchener for the first time less than two years later. After a meal he chaired, at which Kitchener sat on his right, William got the following letter: "Great driving force but no mental power—that is my reading of him. Hard eyes—relentless—without a glimmer of human kindness." Possibly the generals were pleased because Lloyd George was able to keep from raising taxes for the navy by offsetting its three-million pound additional expenditure with the same amount from a sinking fund. The overall budget, however, did necessitate in excess of thirteen-million pounds from increases on existing taxation and also some new tax legislation.[9]

Army leaders also may have been thrilled because of inter-service rivalry, but more likely, it was because they already had what they wanted. Haldane had reformed the army beginning in 1906, and the end result was an expeditionary force of 160,000 men that could be mobilized and in place on the continent in twelve days. Britain now had twice as many soldiers as when he had come to the War Office, translating to a total of six infantry divisions and almost two cavalry. A territorial force of non-professional soldiers was also established, with fourteen divisions each of infantry and artillery as well as fourteen cavalry brigades. Lloyd George had opposed the cost of those reforms but as chancellor focused on the navy. One week after he granted royal approval to the 1910 budget, which included no new taxes, Edward VII died. His funeral was the final event for which European rulers kin to Queen Victoria by blood or marriage met prior to World War I. Lloyd George considered the king's death to be a "catastrophe" because he was hopeful Edward VII would create more peers to stop the upper house from vetoing his social reforms, Irish home rule, and the Parliament Bill to strip it of veto power. "It never entered into our calculations," he wrote Maggie. "What insolent creatures we all are. We reckoned without taking the Great Ruler into account." Edward VII's son, George V, did promise to add to the House of Lords if Liberals won a big enough majority in new elections scheduled for December 1910. They did win, with a 126 margin, all Irish or Labour members, and eight months later the Parliament Bill was enacted. Irish home rule had to wait until 1914 and was vetoed twice by the upper house before passing its third reading in the lower. It became statute law because a possible world war was looming.[10]

Seven weeks prior to the House of Lords losing its veto power and slightly more than one year after Edward VII's funeral, the Second Moroccan Crisis began. On July 1, 1911, a German gunboat, the *Panther*, steamed into the Moroccan port of Agadir to test whether the British would protect France's authority there. The French had deployed troops to the capital city of Fez in order to protect Europeans being threatened by native tribes. Because the agreement at Algeciras allowed any European power to provide security for its people if they were endangered in a foreign land, Germany justified its involvement. Two days later, Lloyd George tersely wrote his brother, "Moroccan affair serious." The following day, he elaborated on the discussions of it in the Cabinet and then confidently proclaimed, "I had a plan which was finally adopted against Grey's. Grey's plan was a halting one & would have landed us in mischief—with no purpose."[11]

Grey's advice was to send a warship to the port, though in the past he had recommended international conferences to settle disputes. Apparently, Lloyd George persuaded the Cabinet to not only acknowledge Britain's continued support of the Entente Cordiale but also German rights in Morocco, which had been internationally recognized based on possession being nine-tenths of the law. This time, Grey saw Metternich the same day the Cabinet met and emphatically relayed to Germany's ambassador that Britain was going to uphold France's position in northwest Africa. He also told the French ambassador that his nation could be required to give the Germans something. No official response from the kaiser's government was forthcoming, so Grey decided to wait until July 21 before informing Metternich that the British insisted on being involved in the conflict and were prepared to deploy a ship to Agadir. Before he did, Lloyd George told him he would be dealing with the subject the same night in the annual address on the state of Britain's economy, given by the Chancellor of the Exchequer at Mansion House, official residence of London's Lord Mayor.[12]

In his address, Lloyd George talked about the British maintaining their place in the world to support liberty, having done so repeatedly on the continent, and they would not be regarded as "of no account" among the nations' peoples. He stressed how far he was willing to go to support peace but made it clear that peace which ignored the British, diminishing their "great and beneficent position . . . would be a humiliation intolerable for a great country like ours to endure." Ending his remarks, he emphasized that national honor and international economic security were not "party" questions. A week after the speech, most of which concerned foreign affairs, he wrote at the top left of a letter to William: "Foreign Office say I have saved peace of Europe." Four months later, twenty-three days after the crisis ended with France secure in Morocco but with Germany getting much of French Congo, he added that Grey took full responsibility in the House of Commons for his comments on Germany, saying, "he P.M. & I had agreed upon its being said by me." There was also "great cheering," he volunteered, and even Bonar Law, the new leader of Conservatives who had replaced Balfour, "approved." Indeed, except for "the extreme men," the "House as a whole approves." Those he labeled extreme were the remaining pacifists among Liberal radicals.[13]

Obviously, Germany did not approve either, expressing its anger through

Metternich, who met again with Grey four days after Lloyd George's speech. He said Lloyd George's words were more likely to cause violence than anything else, that his nation was great also, and almost no regard was being afforded it. Later in the day, Grey told Lloyd George that he feared the British fleet could possibly come under attack. McKenna overheard the statement and quickly left to warn the navy, including battleships based at Gibraltar. The Cabinet, however, had previously opposed France's idea of Britain sending a vessel to Agadir. After another two days, Metternich returned to Grey's office to announce that his country would not threaten British interests in Africa, German and French holdings there were the only ones under consideration, and Britain could help facilitate agreeable settlement by publicly announcing how pleased the government would be if a peaceful end to the crisis was realized. Asquith made the very statement to the House of Commons the same day but also stipulated that it remained to be seen if British interests were going to be endangered, and Britain would still get involved if the matter did not come to a mutually acceptable conclusion.[14]

Afterwards, it was up to the two continental countries to successfully negotiate. Six days following the signing of a Franco-German accord, Lloyd George insincerely expressed sympathy for the German chancellor in a letter to William: "Poor old Bethmann Hollweg trying to explain his Moroccan downfall. Turns on him to turn the stream of German wrath on to me." Hollweg had tried to justify the settlement with France in the Reichstag but was greeted with raucous and harsh ridicule, his detractors lamenting Germany's shame at the hands of Britain. Earlier, Lloyd George told his wife that the Germans were "blustering a good deal about my speech," and after they started "climbing down," he interjected, "they are very angry with me. They tried to induce the Government to repudiate me. Grey lost his temper with them & now they are all honey." When tensions had neared their worst, he even unequivocally asserted, "People think that because I was a pro-Boer I am anti-war in general; and that I should faint at the mention of a cannon. I am not against war a bit."[15]

In August, Lloyd George and Winston Churchill, Home Office Secretary, were invited by the prime minister to their initial joint participation in the Committee of Imperial Defense. Lloyd George had first attended it in May 1908, but only sat in on one more session over the next three years, though he shared responsibilities in subcommittees of it. The meeting including Churchill the first time convened to discuss Britain's contingencies for supporting France, if war broke out between it and Germany. It led to the conclusion that the navy was not prepared to assist the army in putting troops on the continent, and to Lloyd George's decision to recommend that Churchill replace McKenna. Churchill had earlier backed Lloyd George's naval estimates, but McKenna stood by the Board of Admiralty, which was apathetic about British soldiers entering France early in a war and was resting on its laurels. In October, Asquith had Churchill and McKenna swap places.[16]

Three months later, a British railroad financier and German shipbuilder proposed getting Churchill invited to a meeting in Berlin with Alfred von Tirpitz, the admiral of Germany's fleet, for discussions on naval arms limitation. Churchill presented the proposal to the Cabinet, which agreed for the financier, Ernest Cassel, to go to Berlin and pursue it with his counterpart, Alfred Ballin. Ballin introduced Cassel to Wilhelm II, and Cassel handed the kaiser a written offer from the Cabinet. It asked for a reduction in German dreadnought construction plans, in exchange for official recognition of Britain's superior numbers on the high seas, no interference with Germany building an overseas empire, and an agreement not to employ their respective alliance systems in any aggression against each other. Before the meeting ended with an open invitation to a Cabinet member, Bethmann-Hollweg and Tirpitz were in attendance. The former gave Cassel a detailed written explanation of their naval plans, in addition to telling him they were not likely to change. Instead of the Cabinet sending Churchill or Grey, it chose Haldane, who was instructed to ask the Germans to spread out their shipbuilding over several more years. On January 31, Lloyd George wrote his brother that he had had breakfast with Cassel and Churchill "to hear very important news." After listening to Cassel, he shared, "Peace & good will are within reach—but Grey wont reach I fear. He is timid & slow—both fatal defects in this matter."[17]

Lloyd George was correct, but the reason Grey refused to reach was that Haldane had returned to England not only with German acquiescence on its timetable for building battleships but also with naval plans. They forecasted increases for seamen, cruisers, destroyers, and submarines. Haldane had not bothered to read them, but the Cabinet did. As a result, Grey rejected Haldane's understanding of what he thought had been reached, especially when Bethmann-Hollweg added that Britain should promise neutrality if Germany went to war. After the collapse of the effort, which began with the private citizens, Churchill decided to deploy some British ships in different waters than the French. He could then establish a home fleet and avoid too much duplication of entente defenses in the future. The second was not officially stated. In a letter to his wife after Churchill initially learned he would be the First Lord of the Admiralty, Lloyd George stated Churchill was "so happy" and grateful, "at least for the moment—to me for fighting his cause."[18]

Lloyd George's words proved to be prophetic when, after initially accepting them, he then unsuccessfully opposed Churchill's naval estimates in December 1913 and January 1914. The First Lord had already tried twice to get Germany to accede to a naval holiday, during which time neither nation would build new warships. The kaiser and Bethmann-Hollweg, though, refused to put limits on their naval capabilities. They faced another embarrassment, too, when Italy invaded Libya as the Second Moroccan Crisis was winding down. The war pitted the third member of the Triple Alliance against the Ottoman Empire, a favorite trading partner and possible future ally of the other two. The Italian government had informed its fellow alliance members of its intentions as well as Britain and France, but the Germans and Austro-Hungarians disagreed on what should be done about those aims. Francis Joseph's heir, Archduke Francis Ferdinand, along with Chief of the General Staff, Field Marshal Conrad von Hötzendorf, actually wanted to take advantage of Italy by attacking its forces from the rear during its invasion at Tripoli and Benghazi. Their goal was to precipitate a war against Italy because they believed it could not be trusted as an ally in a probable war with Russia. Both men also hoped to acquire another multi-ethnic empire to lessen the likelihood of revolt at home. The emperor overruled and authorized Hötzendorf's removal.[19]

Two years to the month prior to invading Libyan cities, Italy signed a threefold agreement with Russia: respect national identities in the Balkans, no solitary power should control the area, and both of them would have to concur before accepting any changes to the status quo there. The Italians had declared war against the Turks on September 28, 1911, and put armed forces in North Africa a week later. Provinces around Tripoli and Benghazi were annexed the following month, but the war did not officially end until October 18, 1912. It lasted so long mainly because neither side took the war or a peace treaty very seriously, and each wanted the greater powers of Europe to stay out of it. Germany remained neutral but also used its power and influence to get the same posture from Vienna. Russia and France secretly agreed that Italy be left alone to obtain what it could at the expense of the Turks. Most interestingly, and possibly prejudicially, Britain did not express concern over an Italian presence next to Egypt, like it had Germany's in Morocco. Two months after the war finally concluded, the Triple Alliance was confirmed for a sixth time.[20]

Italy's victory prompted some Balkan states to also go to war with the Turks, and fifteen days before the Italo-Turkish War ended with a treaty in

Lausanne, Switzerland, Lloyd George wrote to William he had just been to the Foreign Office, learning, "War inevitable in the Balkans." The First Balkan War began five days later, and reminiscent of Gladstone's feelings for Bulgars, Lloyd George confided to his brother by writing, "I am frankly delighted. I wish for the moment I were a Bulgar or a Montenegrin. Shame on these greedy suspicious cowardly powers—had they an ounce of chivalry or Xianity in their rotten carcasses this war would have been unnecessary & the Turk would long ago have been swept out of Europe into the Bosporus or Gehenna." Russia as well as Austria, on behalf of the greater powers, warned against a war with the Turks this time, but their counsel reached the Balkan League of Montenegro, Bulgaria, Serbia, and Greece on the very day war was declared by the first of the four. The league was also fearful of intervention.[21]

Germany was strengthening its economic ties with Turks by building a Berlin-to-Baghdad railroad, Austria-Hungary did not want to see Serbia advance, Russia opposed Bulgaria's control of Constantinople, and France would only enter to counter any German action. Twenty days after his scathing rebuking of the Continental powers, Lloyd George updated William, "The Turk is crumbling—the Lord be praised for that. He is a horrid beast. I hope the govt will see to it that those little Powers reap the full reward of their heroism. I mean to put in a good fight for them inside." Two days later, with Grey's approval, he met the minister from Bulgaria, sharing with his brother the foreign diplomat was "anxious to enlist my help for the Balkan states. . . . They are apprehensive of European intervention to rob them of their blood earned spoil." Following the meeting, he also revealed to William that the man had "two sons at the front. For all that his sole anxiety was for his country—not for its victory—of that he was assured but for the fruits of victory. I reassured him on this point as far as our govt was concerned." This letter began in a similar fashion to other ones: "The Turk is tumbling into Gehenna. Courage is always the last virtue to flee—& the Turk has lost that." Clearly, he had hated the Ottoman Empire ever since it massacred the Bulgars, and only a dozen days after it entered the First World War, he described it to a Free Church group as "a human cancer, a creeping agony in the flesh of the lands which they misgovern, rotting every fibre of life." To his credit, though, he emphasized that the United Kingdom was not anti-Muslim or Arab.[22]

Bulgarians reached Constantinople on November 3, 1913, Greeks marched into Salonika after five more days, and twenty from then, Serbs occupied Durazzo, a port on the Adriatic Sea. Five days later, the Ottomans requested an armistice, and an international conference suggested by Grey started a week after in London. The Turks agreed to let go of what had been taken from them militarily, but when asked to relinquish the historic city of Adrianople to the Bulgars, they declined, and war resumed until they again petitioned for it to cease. The Treaty of London was then signed on May 30, granting Adrianople to the Bulgarians and Salonika to the Greeks. Also, an independent Albania was drawn from the area around Durazzo after Russia coerced Serbs into vacating it. Russians acted because Austria-Hungary had demanded Durazzo be made a free city or returned to Turks. Russia pressured Montenegro into giving up Scutari for the same reason.[23]

Just seventeen days after the Treaty of London was signed, the Second Balkan War began primarily because Bulgaria, Serbia, and Greece could not concur on how to divide Macedonia or Thrace. For the Balkan states and Rumania, which had invaded Bulgaria for territory, it ended on August 10 with the Treaty of Bucharest. On September 29, the Bulgarians and Turks made peace in the Treaty of Constantinople. Bulgaria had started the conflict but was accosted from all sides, only walking away with western Thrace and one portion of Macedonia. The rest of Macedonia's south remained in Greek hands, and the north stayed under Serbia's control. To the Rumanians, Bulgaria also lost southern Dobruja, an area between the Danube River and Black Sea. Eastern Thrace, the region where Adrianople is located, went to the Ottoman Empire. When Rumanians threatened Bulgaria's capital of Sofia, Bulgarians requested the assistance of Russia to mediate a settlement. Then, the Turks took eastern Thrace, and Russia warned it would send ground troops through the Caucasus as well as warships to Constantinople. The latter portent prompted Britain to get involved, and an international agreement was brokered.[24]

Bulgaria's losses in the treaties turned it against Russia, but Serbia was emboldened by its successes to strive for more Balkan territory in a quest for Pan-Slavism on the peninsula. Serbia was also now Russia's only remaining ally in southeastern Europe. On June 28, 1914, a Bosnian-Serb trained by Serbia's military, assassinated Archduke Francis Ferdinand and his wife, Sophie, in Sarajevo, Bosnia's capital. After conferring with its German ally, which gave it a blank check to proceed, Austria-Hungary issued an ultimatum to Serbia on July 23. When it was not entirely accepted, war was declared five days later. Two days following, Russia mobilized its military to support little brother Serbian Orthodox Slavs, and after two more days, Germany declared war on Russia. Because of French mobilization, and the Schlieffen Plan, Germany also went to war with France forty-eight hours later. Germany's violation of

Belgian neutrality, however, to invade the French more rapidly, brought the British into the war the next day as the guarantors of Belgium.[25]

Lloyd George started writing his wife about the events on the continent just one day prior to Austria-Hungary's war declaration, complaining, "Crisis upon crisis." Labeling the Irish crisis as "serious," he then added, "but Austria-Servia is pandemonium let loose." On the day war was loosed, he mused to her, "No one can tell what will or will not happen. I still believe peace will be preserved. The Great Powers will hesitate before they plunge their countries into the hell of war." Only a day after did he seem to consider the possibility it would be something other than another short war over the Balkans, worrying, "Foreign outlook most menacing." The day before Britain entered the fray, he acknowledged his view on war was changing: "I have fought hard for peace & succeeded so far in keeping the Cabinet out of it but I am driven to the conclusion that if the small nationality of Belgium is attacked by Germany all my traditions & even prejudices will be engaged on the side of war." He went on in a more dramatic, personal fashion, penning, "I am filled with horror at the prospect. I am even more horrified that I should ever appear to have a share in it but I must bear my share of the ghastly burden though it scorches my flesh to do so." The word "traditions" must refer to his pacifist heritage, though he was never a thoroughgoing one, and "prejudices" surely means his empathy for smaller nations like Israel, God's chosen in the Old Testament. Moses called them "the fewest of all people" (Deuteronomy 7:7, KJV).[26]

Reflecting on his "burden" three months later, to the aforementioned Free Church as well as Welsh assembly at the City Temple in London, Lloyd George justified involvement in the war as being "from motives of purest chivalry to defend the weak . . . a poor little neighbour whose home was broken into by a hulking bully." Then, he added, "we are all looking forward to the time when swords shall be beaten into ploughshares." Isaiah prophesied this concerning Judah and Jerusalem (Isaiah 2:1–4, KJV). Michael Fry rightly observes Lloyd George had "a romantic, even spiritual, sympathy with Zionism" but also he "was neither indifferent nor hostile to Arab aspirations and rights." The cooperation representatives from Lloyd George's church fellowship, however, had met in Wigan for their annual conference the day Britain declared war, drafting a resolution which they telegraphed to him, Grey, and Asquith. It expressed gratitude for all their previous attempts to stay out of the conflict but also beseeched them for the nation's welfare to remain completely neutral.[27]

Lloyd George had exercised extensive sway on nonconformists generally since the death of Gladstone. He must have also had an even greater impact on members of Churches of Christ specifically, most of whom ultimately left pacifism to support the war. In 1915, a list of serving members was made, and within another year "many hundreds" had "gone forth at the call of duty to take their part in the defence of principles held supremely dear." The yearbook naming those in uniform, though, also contained grave concern for brothers "suffering imprisonment and other disabilities" because of conscientious objection. In fact, certain Church of Christ leaders, elders included, chaired tribunals that rejected the objectors and participated in magistrates' hearings that turned them over for punishment. At Leicester, particularly known for its objectors, sixteen-thousand men ultimately received papers exempting them, after being arrested, court-martialed, and/or incarcerated. Seven Church of Christ members there, who asked for exemption, had their cases dismissed when two leaders from their fellowship opposed each other at their hearing. In contrast, one-tenth of more than twelve hundred members in Wigston and Leicester had enlisted by May 1916, the year conscription began. Nationwide, sixty-one members were arrested, forty-nine court-martialed, and/or twenty-nine incarcerated, one of whom died from sickness. In a later case, a death sentence was reversed, and the brother was given ten years in prison.[28]

One week following Great Britain's declaration of war, Lloyd George reassured Maggie about the decision, explaining, "We are keeping the sea for France—that ought to suffice here for the moment especially as we are sending 100,000 men to help her to bear the first brunt of the attack. That is all that counts for Russia will come in soon. I am dead against carrying on a war of conquest to crush Germany for the benefit of Russia. Beat the German Junker but no war on the German people &c." Restoring her confidence was apparently necessary because he had also shared with her four days earlier, "the fleet had not done well. The way they allowed the Goeben to escape is disgracefully inefficient." The *Goeben* was a German battle cruiser that had slipped unnoticed from the Adriatic Sea on its way to Constantinople. It later became the Turkish navy's leading ship, helping Ottomans control the Black Sea once they entered the war on October 29.[29]

Though the news of the British Mediterranean fleet was a disappointment, Lloyd George also let his wife know Belgium had initially fared well against the kaiser's forces at Liège; Erich von Ludendorff finally did take the city the same day the letter was sent, however. "The German defeat although greatly exaggerated in the extent by the papers is in its effect greater than they portray. It has delayed by days the blow against France & given the French time to perfect their arrangements," he wrote. He then extrapolated, "still more it has bucked them up tremendously & that counts more with Frenchmen than with any nation except the Welsh." By the time he got in touch with his brother on August 25, it was abundantly clear France had not enjoyed a perfect foray into the fighting. "The French have made a bad start," he began. "For the moment it looks as if they were outclassed in shere [sic] brain power. Still it may not be fair to judge them on the result of a single action. Our news does not give me the impression of a serious attack upon us by the Germans," he added. "It looks much more like an effort to occupy us whilst the French were being furiously assailed. The Germans are showing better leadership up to the present—& even more heart." He ended by reiterating that Belgium was the reason he had altered his thinking about war, also admitting now it was going to "be a long job. I entered into it most reluctantly. Nothing but Belgium would have induced me to throw in my lot with the war party—but now we are in it we must go through with it whatever the cost to us all."[30]

It should be noted that in his diary, C. P. Scott later recorded Lloyd George as having said he would still have been opposed to war if Germany had simply invaded Belgium by way of the Ardennes. That was a possible circumstance mentioned in the Committee of Imperial Defence session during the 1911 Second Moroccan Crisis and in a Cabinet meeting on July 29, 1914. At the latter, Lloyd George even demonstrated the presumed path it would take on a map. In fact, the Cabinet agreed that day that there was no ironclad British commitment to go it alone on behalf of Belgium but changed its opinion 180 degrees after three more days. Lloyd George disingenuously made the same argument the day Great Britain declared war, apparently deluding himself in one last-ditch effort because of his pacifist traditions and prejudices in favor of small nations. He had already learned the invasion of Belgium by Germany was all-out.[31]

The fighting between British and Germans Lloyd George described for his brother was at Mons, near Belgium's southwestern border with France. The British under John French had just arrived there on August 22, and the next day their four divisions, one corps of which was led by Douglas Haig, fought six German divisions under General Alexander von Kluck along a twenty-mile stretch of canal. All British divisions held, largely due to the Royal Irish Rifles, but when France's General Charles Lanrezac decided to withdraw on August 24 and left their right flank exposed, the British retired also. There were sixteen-hundred casualties for Britain, compared to roughly five thousand on the German side. The departure of British troops from Mons continued for

a fortnight and ended just outside the French capital. Five days into the retreat, Lloyd George reported to his brother, "No news from front which is
good news. The Germans tried a Sedan on us but were beaten off." Then, on
September 5, the day the Battle of the Marne started, he wrote Maggie and
noted both "French & English have turned on the Germans & there is fierce
fighting going on along the whole line. So far going well. Kitchener thinks
Joffre's plan clever."[32]

Kitchener was now the Secretary of State for War, and Joseph Joffre was
the Chief of the French General Staff. The latter's plan, known as Plan XVII,
was to combine Allied forces in an offensive action against Germans, with the
flexibility of striking them where it was deemed best instead of implementing a preconceived strategy. Britain's Expeditionary Force did exactly that as
part of thirty-six divisions facing less than thirty for the Germans. Before
that fighting ended, Lloyd George mailed three more letters to his wife, the
first one positive about France's progress but cautious regarding the outcome,
the second positive in general but cautious too, and the third positive just
for Britain. The first also specifically noted what he considered was the "best
news" concerning the French, that they "cashiered three of their generals &
put better men in." Newly promoted generals in place by the time the engagement started included Henri Pétain, Ferdinand Foch, and Franchet d'Esperey,
the last having replaced Lanrezac. The third letter included more specifics:
"The enemy there getting demoralized. We picked several of them up drunk."
In fact, Helmuth von Moltke the Younger was removed as German Chief of
Staff because the Schlieffen Plan had failed, though the generals in charge on
the field were von Kluck, Karl von Bülow, and Baron Max von Hausen. Erich
von Falkenhayn, Prussian Minister of War, now became the new supreme
commander, but the change was not publicly announced for four months.
His desire to have an official report printed was flatly refused by Bethmann-
Hollweg later that September.[33]

As Germans were the ones to pull back this time, Allied forces pursued
them to the Aisne River, succeeding in crossing to the north side of it in
places. Open-field combat now turned into trench warfare. For two weeks,
September 13 to 27, all armies there moved into position, including the Belgians on the last day of the fighting. After both sides had entrenched, there
was a contest to control the land between the river and the English Channel.
Lloyd George updated William on British efforts during their maneuvering
along the Aisne but was still tentative in his assessment. "Good news from

French today," he reported first, "but everything depends on the fighting now going on." He then mentioned a "bad" naval disaster of the previous day, referring to the sinking of three cruisers by a German submarine near the coast of Holland. *Aboukir*, *Cressy*, and *Hogue* had been blockading when the first was torpedoed. The others two tried to save victims but were also struck. Over fourteen-hundred men expired, and Britain then put nets around its Home Fleet. Also, the losses inspired Lloyd George to get Cabinet authorization on September 28 for the use of nonconformist as well as Anglican chaplains in the military, against Kitchener's objection.[34]

The next German offensive began on October 20 at Ypres, west Belgium, where twelve days earlier British forces had started arriving to support the French. The same day the Germans attacked, Lloyd George told Maggie that he had made it back from the European mainland alive. He revealed he had gone "right to the front—the Germans were shelling the village close by. We got into the French trenches which were not being shelled at that moment. . . . The German trenches were 1400 to 1500 yards from the spot we got to." After glowing words for Joffre and Foch, he dealt with the British, stating, "I went to the English headquarters. Had a great time. Gave me a new idea of what is happening. It is *stalemate*. We cannot turn them out of their trenches & they cannot turn us out. They can only frighten Belgians—French & English stand their ground." He had gone to the continent after being put "on a War Office Committee as to guns. I raised it," he wrote his brother, "having discovered that the provision made was ludicrously inadequate."[35]

The Battle of Ypres would drag on until November 22, but a week into it, Lloyd George gave his wife some "distinctly good" news. "Just had a wire in from Sir John French that Joffre hopes to attack them today & tomorrow. They think the Germans are discouraged by the last few days fighting. They have suffered frightful losses. So have we," he admitted, "but the French are bringing reinforcements up but the Germans are for the moment doing badly in the East & cannot spare men." After another week, he wrote, "Hot fighting at the front. By no means decided. We are hard pressed." Germany used recent high school graduates and university students, who had only been trained for a couple of months, to attack part of the British line. They were massacred. However, the larger German force was able to clear a path between British forces on the outskirts of Ypres and almost took the town but were too worn out to follow through. The British used six divisions from India, and the Indians in them fought courageously but were totally unaccustomed to winters in

Europe. British marksmanship and firing rapidly more than made up for their being outnumbered. Nevertheless, the weather and fatigue ultimately led to a cessation of hostilities by both sides, along a front sixty-two miles in length.[36]

The entire western front extended approximately 470 miles, from the coast of Belgium to the Swiss Alps, but Britain was eventually responsible for only fifty of them. There were fifty-thousand British casualties at Ypres and one-hundred thousand German. Two days after the First Battle of Ypres ended, Lloyd George confided in his brother, "P.M. has appointed a *secret* War Council to consider all questions bearing on the war. I am on it. Glad of that." As 1914 drew to a close, he addressed the conflict in Flanders, a region of Belgium which includes Ypres and where so many of the flower of British youth would die during the war. His sons, Richard and Gwilym, volunteered for the territorial forces, getting officers' uniforms on October 2. Twenty-six days later, he won another Cabinet battle with Kitchener and got a distinct Welsh division. Dick, twenty-five, and Gwilym, twenty, left for the 38th Welsh Army Corps on December 10.[37]

Writing William again eleven days prior to Christmas, when both sides agreed on a truce for the holiday, Lloyd George shared the last telegram received from the western front: "Fighting going on in Flanders today," it read, "French & English both engaged." Now, Germans attacked the Allies at the city of Nieuport, the westernmost point of the front, but before that day ended, a counter-attack extended the fighting the length of it to below Ypres. British ships opened fire on enemy positions near the port, and three barges, equipped with machine guns, assisted along the Yser River, taking the villages of St. Georges and Lombartzyde. At another village southeast of Ypres, Wytschaete, two Scottish battalions, the Royal and Gordon Highlanders, initially captured two trenches on the west but were not able to hold them. The ground of the area had no covering due to winter conditions, and the troops bogged down because it had temporarily thawed. Later named the First Battle of Artois, these indecisive contests ceased Christmas Eve.[38]

New Year's Day, Lloyd George provided the War Council with a written critique of the strategy that had resulted in stalemate and stressed that a conclusive victory had to be won sometime, somewhere. A week later, he called for an invasion of Austria-Hungary from the south but was outvoted. Two days before, Maggie was told, "The usual thing is happening. The generals have fallen out (K. & F.) & the Admiralty & War Office are quarrelling," An offensive to knock the Ottoman Turks out of the war began the next month, however, and he informed his brother of its progress after only six days: "The

Dardanelles campaign has been suspended because of a strong gale." The Turks had invaded the Caucasus, and Russia had asked the other entente powers to create a diversion to keep them occupied. Ottoman forces were diverted to some extent, as their forts were blasted, mines detonated, and Royal Marine raiders landed. The initial foray, though, was not able to neutralize all movable shore batteries or clear enough of the mines, so a month later more mine-sweepers, destroyers, cruisers, and sixteen battleships started into the strait.[39]

The assault stalled when one of four French battleships hit a mine and sank while trying to get out of the way of its own minesweepers. The Turks had secretly placed additional mines near the coast after the Allied campaign began. Significantly greater numbers of ground troops were then added in April, including New Zealanders and Australians. However, the Turks kept them pinned down on the beaches at Gallipoli until the following January, when the combined Allied forces had to ignominiously withdraw. More than 250,000 of the commonwealth servicemen perished. Four British battleships were also sunk, two each by mines and German submarines. Fisher, who had again become First Sea Lord the last day of October in 1914, resigned in May, 1915, because he opposed using so much sea power at the expense of the North Sea fleet. Churchill had to resign later in May too, after a Cabinet crisis over the debacle.[40]

The crisis in the Cabinet led to the first British coalition government in time of war, with Asquith remaining prime minister, McKenna temporarily serving in the post of Chancellor of the Exchequer, Lloyd George acting as Minister of Munitions, and Balfour moving to the Admiralty. In a series of letters to Maggie, Lloyd George indicated that Conservatives had alternately expressed a desire for him to be Secretary of State for War, instead of Kitchener, or the prime minister, but he had declined both. They wanted either the Treasury or Munitions, both of which he opposed, and insisted that Bonar Law get the former if McKenna permanently replaced him. Neither his wife nor Uncle Lloyd favored him stepping down as chancellor. He had been on the guns committee for seven months, though, and had deduced, "in order to attack highly developed trenches protected by barbed-wire entanglements, shrapnel is useless and high explosive shells indispensible [sic]." On the committee the ten days prior to his new post being announced, he told William the day of Fisher's resignation, "Next week I run through the engineering towns up the north to arrange for shells! What a mission for me." To Frances Stevenson, he humbly petitioned, "God help me."[41]

Lloyd George's mission was now to increase the industrial output of arms, and he was so successful during his thirteen-month stint in munitions that no shortage remained. By August, he reported to Maggie he was holding "a series of conferences with Shell Committees from different areas. Most useful." The same month, he gave an accounting to some in the Cabinet of the War Office's delay in sending necessary armaments to the western front, a concern he had repeatedly voiced to the body and to Kitchener in particular over the previous five months. That issue had been a lesser factor in causing the Cabinet's May crisis, but Kitchener was initially unwilling to work with Lloyd George because he viewed it as unnecessary intervention by another sovereign office like his. He had not responded to French's calls for additional munitions either, beginning months prior to May, which Lloyd George learned from subordinates of French. Lloyd George also foretold disaster for Russians during a Cabinet meeting, having recorded in July their loss at Gorlice-Tarnow for his brother; 325,000 ultimately became prisoners. Two more August letters to his wife referenced the ongoing battle at Gallipoli, and he specifically noted the participation of the 38th Welsh Division there. He stated how anxious they both would be if their sons were still "in the Territorial regiments." The nonprofessional forces "were in the fighting & horrible fighting it has been," he continued. The Welsh Division was "rather badly cut up" and "did not do well. Had a fool for a general. So glad & thankful boys have left it."[42]

A month later, Lloyd George was turning his attention to the western front again, because British forces were experiencing a bit of temporary success but very heavy casualties in the Battle of Loos, south of Ypres, in France's northernmost region. "The victories are good but not quite as good as the papers imply," he conveyed to William. "They have broken through the *first* line of German defenses but that will avail but little unless the Germans are forced to retreat." Three days later, he sent him an update, predicting no farther advance. "Not very hopeful of breaking through. Enormous losses. The attack was I fear premature. We were not ready for it. We shall gain a few miles here & a few kilometers there. Just enough ground to bury the dead who won it." The next German line of defense did hold, but the British had gained a two-mile strip when the offensive stopped on October 13, costing them forty-one thousand casualties, many from new volunteer divisions Kitchener raised.[43]

Lack of munitions was one factor in Douglas Haig's inability to break the second German line, but inexperienced men, withering fire from enemy machine guns, and the ineffective use of chlorine gas also contributed. The gas either stayed in the air over the area between the opposing armies or blew back on the attackers. Poison gas had first been introduced into war by Germany on April 22 at the Second Battle of Ypres but was followed by other powers. As a consequence of the large number of casualties at Loos, in addition to the untenable situation at Gallipoli, French was replaced by Haig. Furthermore, Kitchener's role diminished considerably when Sir William Robertson was appointed Chief of the Imperial General Staff before 1915 ended. Another outcome was Lloyd George's decision to insist on conscription in order to properly man Britain's war effort. Asquith, supported by other Liberals in the Cabinet like McKenna, Grey, the Home Secretary John Simon, and Walter Runciman, President of the Board of Trade, resisted. Eleven Labour members of the House of Commons and the Irish also opposed it.[44]

As early as October 15, only two days after the offensive stopped at Loos, William got a letter about the controversy over conscription, claiming that Asquith "has muddled everything up to the present. I fear a great split in the Cabinet." Had all four Liberals resigned, it would probably have led to new elections and a new government, but only Simon left when Asquith finally did agree three days before the new year that married men should be drafted. In another letter to his brother on November 21, Lloyd George again conveyed concern about the "precarious" situation in the Ottoman Empire, and this time he also included Serbia, which Germans and Austrians had invaded forty-five days earlier. Bulgaria also attacked the Serbs after four more days and stopped an Anglo-French force consisting of only one division each coming to Serbia's aid. The Allies withdrew to a base at Salonika, Greece, remaining in trenches there for a year before beginning another offensive. "Fear tragedy developing in that quarter—Servia & Gallipoli," Lloyd George warned his brother. "After that we shall in my opinion have touched bottom."[45]

Interestingly, Serbia had survived to this point partly because the Dardanelles campaign kept Germany busy, and the two Allied divisions had actually arrived from Gallipoli. Also, Italy had entered the war on the side of the entente powers the previous May and had temporarily tied the Austrians down. A much more personal entry into combat occurred on December 30, when Lloyd George's older son went "into the firing line for the first time" as an officer of the Royal Engineers. "He was quite cool," even though his troops were shelled from 150 yards away. No one was injured. "He placed his men, gave them orders & carried out his work calmly and efficiently," the proud father told the boy's mother. Both sons had written "cheerily from France" that month, he also shared with William. The younger was an aide-de-camp to General Ivor Philipps, the first commander of the 38th Welsh Division. Philipps served briefly under Lloyd George as liaison to the War Office for the munitions ministry before leading the Welsh soldiers into France. When Lloyd George went to the western front again on the last weekend of January and met Haig at his headquarters, he was also greeted by both sons, who had been transferred to see him, Dick from the trenches. In a subsequent letter to Haig, he expressed genuine appreciation for "great courtesy" and "a feeling that everything which the assiduity, the care, and the trained thought of a great soldier can accomplish is being done." His sincerity was evident in correspondence with his brother a week before writing Haig. "The new Commander in Chief very hospitable," he wrote. Haig, however, was extremely critical of Lloyd George in his diary, labeling him "shifty and unrealiable" [sic].[46]

On February 3, Lloyd George reported to William how he had just seen "some interesting experiments with a new trench machine," and, "The Zeppelins narrowly missed hitting some of our most important factories." The machine was the tank, and unlike Kitchener, he appreciated its worth. He also understood that more machine guns would be needed than were recommended by Kitchener, increasing the number by sixteen and saving a lightweight mortar the military did not want to implement. This was the third time Lloyd George had mentioned zeppelins in his letters. The first was to Maggie thirteen months earlier on news "a great Zeppelin raid" was coming. It did come above Sheringham and Yarmouth fifteen days later, raining death down on four people. The second was to his youngest daughter, in which with clear trepidation of the airships he wrote, "Tonight I dine with Lady Randolph Churchill. As it is so cloudy I mean to risk the Zeps."[47]

A month after the war began, London started dimming lights and drained an identifiable lake. By the next June, two Zeppelin attacks per month was the average. The worst of 1915 was on the night of October 12–13, causing just under two hundred casualties in London, Suffolk, and Norfolk. Zeppelins attacked Britain fifty-one times in all, from when Lloyd George sounded the alarm to his wife until April 1918. Over nineteen-hundred casualties were inflicted. At first, the Germans only had eleven they could use, but two had begun tracking the movements of Russians five days after Britain entered the war. Also, airplanes played increasingly important roles other than reconnaissance as the war progressed. Fifty-seven sorties raided the British Isles between December 1914 and June 1918, resulting in another twenty-nine hundred casualties plus. A new German monoplane, the Fokker, was employed at the Battle of Verdun in early 1916 and temporarily won control of the skies, but France had the most planes at the outset of the war.[48]

Lloyd George referred to Verdun eight days after it commenced, writing his brother on February 29, "Fight at Verdun going well. Joffre very confident. Thinks he has got them well under his thumb & that they cannot get any farther." The next day he wrote again, beginning the same positive way, though adding, "it is still very much in the balance. If the Germans are checked it will be the most serious defeat yet inflicted on them." A third successive letter in as many days contained a note of caution: "French generals I hear are very pleased with position. Hope they are not oversanguine." On March 11, he shared one particular remaining concern: "Verdun not altogether satisfactory. Still anxious. Don't like the way the Germans are thumbing the French from point to point." His last letter to William on the subject, dated March 24, simply recorded: "Verdun serious." Germans did not break the French line but pressed the battle nonstop for five months before spending another five defending themselves and retreating. When it ceased, there were eight-hundred thousand casualties evenly divided between the two. Pétain became the hero of Verdun, and Falkenhayn was replaced by Paul von Hindenburg in August.[49]

The Battle at Verdun actually interfered with plans the Allies were devising for a twenty-five mile offensive, extending across the Ancre River, south of Loos, to below the larger Somme River it feeds. Those plans had originated in the last month of 1915 but for the British included marshaling roughly five-hundred thousand soldiers, one-hundred thousand horses, and necessary munitions. As a result, the conscription agreement reached by the Cabinet on December 28 and enacted a month later fell short of garnering enough troops to keep the existing quota of 340,000 men, much less the additional forces required for the offensive. Lloyd George started pushing for universal conscription then and was eventually successful by May for all the British Isles except Ireland. In a series of five letters during the previous month, he kept his brother abreast of what was happening and its possible impact on the war effort. "Things critical in Cabinet," he began, "I am afraid we are blundering into defeat. Blunder after blunder. There is no handling of the situation. Our chief has no decision or drive."[50]

The chief, Asquith, bore the brunt of Lloyd George's criticism, but the only Labour MP in the Cabinet, Arthur Henderson, President of the Board of Education, also got some of the blame. "Henderson is holding out," he continued informing William. "If he accepts—it goes through—if he refuses I don't know what will happen." After depicting the dispute as a fight, he confidently relayed, "Victory in the war might very well depend on my taking a bold line now. I am forcing their hands." When he did win, he simply wrote, "It means compulsion in a month" and quickly turned his attention to the issue of supply: "Am now endeavouring to clear up arrears that have accumulated here." His final note indicated urgent implementation, stressing, "Cabinet decided for *immediate* general compulsion" and followed by "Kut surrendered." Kut, northwest of Basra, is where an Anglo-Indian Expeditionary Force landed in 1914, pushing to twenty-two miles from Baghdad before being effectively challenged by Turks. After pulling back to Kut, the force was enveloped, and floods isolated it. Ten thousand capitulated due to hunger, 40 percent dying.[51]

Before the Battle of the Somme started, two very significant events occurred at sea. On the last day of May and the first in June, the Battle of Jutland positioned the British Grand Fleet against the German High Seas Fleet in the North Sea. When it ended, the British had lost more sailors and ships, but the ratio of stronger vessels shifted more in their favor. Almost sixty-one hundred British to twenty-five hundred Germans died, but fifteen ships to eleven were sunk. The British, led by Admiral John Jellicoe, were viewed as the victors because the German fleet under Admiral Reinhard Scheer never ventured beyond Norway again. Lloyd George sent two letters to his brother concerning the outcome of the battle. "Great fight in North Sea," the first one started, "Germans ran away but did us much damage." One day later, his assessment read, "Naval news bad but not so bad as it looked at first sight. The greatest damage has been to our prestige & not to our fleet." Three days after that he noted Kitchener's death from drowning after his ship hit a mine: "What a tragedy! Poor K. Died at best moment & best way for him." He wrote the same first two lines to Frances Stevenson also.[52]

Eleven days after Kitchener died, Lloyd George expressed his opinion of the War Office to William. "I don't think I can leave munitions just yet. The demands here are urgent in view of the great battle. Everything depends on my supplies being kept up for the next few weeks." Then, he compared his current position to the one he might be taking: "I can exercise a greater influence in the conduct of the war here than in the War Office. There I should be tied hand & foot by the military & that would not suit me. In fact it is full of peril." In a more personal vein, he reflected, "It broke poor Kitchener's heart. He had no powers—they were taken from him one by one & he became a miserable & abject figure quite pathetic to contemplate. I would rather be where I am than do that. Here I have full powers & I love the office." A day before, he had said if he took it, he would be the foreman. John French actually begged Asquith to add the job to his, telling him it would be in the army's best interest. One month afterward, Lloyd George became Secretary of State for War, five days after the Somme offensive got underway. Prior to changing jobs, though, he mentioned unfinished work in munitions and forecast the Somme offensive.[53]

"The great attack has commenced," Lloyd George's report to his brother started the first day of the Somme campaign. "After a week's terrible bombardment the infantry attacked at 7:45 this morning. So far the fight is in our favour but it is by no means over," he continued to detail. "There will be heavy fighting today & tomorrow. As far as I can find out our boys are not in the big battle. They are holding the line higher up." The fighting was heavy indeed, particularly on the first day, as twenty thousand of Britain's first one-hundred thousand men to charge perished. An accurate accounting of the wounded men was not even possible for three more days because so many of them could not be removed safely until then. By July 3, Lloyd George was guardedly adding, "Heavy fighting still going on & we seem to be making progress but you cannot tell for some days what the result will be." He ended that day's news, "Haig is satisfied so I learn." On the fourth day, he was also thinking about supplies and boasted, "The fight getting on steadily. Ammunition doing splendidly."[54]

After another week, Lloyd George discussed Welsh troops with William, specifically his sons, who were clearly involved to some extent. "The Welsh Division are doing brilliantly," he gladly related. "They have just captured the Mametz Woods which had defied all attacks up till yesterday. They got one big & three field guns & 400 prisoners. Unfortunately the General has broken down in health & he returned home last night," he then shared, "bringing with him his A. D. C Lieut Gwilym Lloyd George. Dick is A¹ —engaged for the moment in making roads for the artillery & ammunition to pass along to the front." It had rained so much during the first ten days of the battle that the trenches dug along Mametz Woods were flowing with mud. Both of Lloyd George's sons were promoted to the rank of major by the end of the war, Richard from a captain. Following the Battle of the Somme, Gwilym spent the rest of the conflict as a battery officer. The Somme offensive stopped because of a severe snowstorm on November 19. When it was finally over, there were almost four-hundred and twenty-thousand British killed, wounded, or missing.[55]

Dick told his mother who told Uncle Lloyd that he had survived the Battle of the Somme, "Thanks to Providence," referring to God's care. Two sons of a deacon at the Criccieth Church of Christ were not so blessed. One was killed in the weeks leading up to the battle and the other in mid-July. Their father, G. P. Williams, was a close friend of Lloyd George, gave him a knife for Christmas when he was fifteen, attended Sunday singing meetings with him, provided funds for him to go to London for his final law exam, and supported him for Parliament. On June 13, Lloyd George told William he had "written poor G. P." following the first son's death and added four days later, "I shall think a great deal about him during his first summer of grief." After the second son perished, too, he had no words: "I have not yet written poor G. P. I really don't know what to say to him or to the stricken mother. From what you tell me they are behaving in a way which does honour to the memory of their heroic boys." He had learned of their second son's death three days earlier and groaned that it "has knocked us all to pieces. I only heard of it late last night when the list was brought to us. There are so many tragedies in this war that one can hardly grasp their full meaning."[56]

Lloyd George blamed the extent of those tragedies at the Somme on ineptness. Returning from a conference on the war with French Premier Aristide Briand in Paris a day before the battle ended, he also informed his brother, "Most satisfactory as a conference. But execution is what is most needed in this War—prompt efficient. Perhaps above all Vision. Without vision the people perisheth," he ended with a verse from King Solomon (Proverbs 29:18, KJV). Actually, he did not get what he wanted at the conference, a major campaign in the Balkans, though all politicians attending were critical of the generals. Haig was deemed ineffective in use of manpower because he continued to throw more and more soldiers into a virtual stalemate. When he saw how upset Lloyd George was, however, he rejoiced he had been "crushed." The tank was finally introduced into warfare on September 15 at the Battle of the Somme. Some were equipped with cannons or machine guns, making a thirty-five hundred yard advance possible. Nearly all thirty-six proved to be deficient, though, stalling on rugged terrain or from mechanical failure. One very efficient weapon was the German fighter, the Albatross, which could time the firing of two guns between its propeller and almost equaled British air supremacy.[57]

Lloyd George mailed William five more very brief, general messages about the Somme offensive from July 17 to 29, recording "another push forward," "things going well," "getting on slowly," "no news," and "quite a good telegram from the front." He sent nothing else about the tank, but his next appraisal of the fighting was posted less than two weeks after its initial use in war. "The news from the front today is excellent," he conveyed more optimistically. "We have made real progress and the Germans must be getting a little anxious. But the end is not yet." In the last three months of 1916, he continued to ask his brother how "G. P." was too. However, by late October, he shifted his attention to the eastern front, specifically Rumania, which entered the war two months earlier because of the success of the Russians under Aleksei Brusilov. The only time he had even mentioned Rumania before was in a list of countries, including France, Russia, and Serbia, wanting to borrow money in mid-December 1914. On that occasion, he approached it about entering the war on the side of the Triple Entente, thinking he had persuaded them. He had always wanted the eastern front to be foremost in British strategy, to win early victories for morale, deter a trench war, and prevent excessive loss of life.[58]

Rumania was now attacked by Germans, Austro-Hungarians, Bulgarians, and Turks. He wrote William that it needed help he had "begged" the General Staff and the War Committee to send for the previous two months. Germans had taken a "great railway bridge," and he "felt certain" they "meant to crush Roumania." Only at that critical juncture was the assistance provided, but ten days later, he reported, "Roumanians just holding their own. But anxious. The soldiers have rather bungled the Roumanian business. Russia as usual is playing up." In fact, Rumania's entry lengthened the Russian defensive line, already the longest in the war by far. After six more days, he tried to stay positive, stating, "News from East still anxious but by no means devoid of good hope." However, on November 25, he shared, "Roumania bad—muddled," and three days after he reported the Germans were advancing toward Bucharest. It fell a week later, but Rumanians were able to take refuge in Moldavia, with the help of the Russians and the winter. After losing at both Tannenberg and Masurian Lakes, Russians had halted the Triple Alliance's forces around Lemberg and defeated them at Warsaw. No longer were they just playing up.[59]

After Lemberg, Lloyd George described Russia's success in 1914 to his brother as "only middling," but when the enemy failed to take Warsaw, he stated it had "done very well." In the 1916 letter that mentioned the German advance on Rumania's capital, he also communicated, "Aeroplane over London this morning. Two Zepps down. That is the talk." He did not give the type of plane it was, but five weeks later told William to let Dick know Lord Cowdray had been appointed air minister. Dick had begun as a recruiter under Cowdray, who replaced Lord Curzon less than a month following Asquith's fall. By the time Cowdray left the air ministry ten months later, seventy times as many planes were produced as the first year of the war, and the Royal Air Force was created in five additional months. More important news than planes, though, at least politically, was whether Asquith would remain the prime minister. As early as March 21, after having led the lower house for an ailing Asquith, Lloyd George confided to his brother, "General dissatisfaction with Ministry—especially I fear with Chief. It will pass when victory shines on us—but that will not come just yet. There are trying months in front of us."[60]

The concern at that point was universal conscription, which Asquith survived like he had controversy over the same issue for married men. As late as October 11, Lloyd George continued to refer to Asquith affectionately, calling him a "very touching poor old boy." He probably used those words with William because Asquith's eldest son had been killed less than a month before and sympathy was expressed after he had spoken in Parliament. This letter also contained Lloyd George's exultation after having commented in the lower house the same day: "Just had a 'little go' at the Crautes [sic]. Gave them 'one in the jaw.'" During Asquith's speech, he had defended a statement he made to an American journalist for the United Press in an interview published two weeks prior. Reiterating it, he unapologetically proclaimed, "My declaration was that we should tolerate no intervention until the Prussian military despotism is broken beyond repair." After his comment appeared in print, the analysis he offered for his brother was, "The American interview is more opportune than the public know—although they suspect. 11 hrs created a great stir."[61]

Lloyd George had been accused of acting on his own, but the prime minister had said the same thing another way. Also, the rest of the Cabinet, War Committee, and military advisers had all agreed. Referring to a Cabinet speech Asquith made the following month, Lloyd George then characterized him and asked William to let Uncle Lloyd know, "P. M. got on very well. Never better. Most happily. Agreed in all things. He is alright as long as you can get him away from sinister & malevolent surroundings." The Cabinet had debated a proposal from Lansdowne, the coalition's only Minister without Portfolio, to consider if Britain would be able to enforce its will at peace talks when the war was over, or should it negotiate with the Central Powers now. By the first day of December, Lloyd George's characterization of Asquith had significantly changed. He wrote to his brother, "London is seething with unrest & discontent with the direction of the War by the Government. Not surprised. Asquith is a paralytic. He has to be wheeled along any road."[62]

The next day, Lloyd George threatened to resign, dramatically commencing a missive for William, "*Crisis*. We are muddling the War & I have given notice that I shall stand it no longer & that unless Asquith puts things right *I go*. Go to tell the public all about it. He is hopeless." Then noting that three-fourths of the press was on his side, he concluded, "Asquith is showing signs of yielding but I am not sure he will go the whole way & half measures in war are fatal. I have stood it too long & the country will blame me for sinning against the light," invoking a scripture once again (Job 24:13, KJV). His biblical allusions seemed to always crown his most emotional utterances, but after three more days, he really did resign this time. He wrote his brother, "P. M. gone back on all his proposals. So I am out & glad of it for things are going badly & the present regime cannot pull us through. I can do more good out. I am much better out. I cannot forecast what will happen but they are fools not to take my plan *& they will rue it.*" His plan was to have a war committee of four civilians, including Asquith as president, himself as chairman, and two ministers without portfolio. Bonar Law and Edward Carson, of Ulster, were clearly his choices, but his proposal did not specify any names for the other two positions.[63]

Asquith did not want Carson on the committee because he thought he was not capable, he was the ministry's leading critic in the House of Commons, and it would look like an attempt to pay him to keep quiet. Carson had served as the Attorney General for five months after the May crisis but disagreed with the conduct of the war, called for the smallest feasible war committee to be formed, and resigned. He was also, however, the one who had offered sympathy for Asquith. Balfour and Bonar Law left the very day Lloyd George did, so Asquith recommended George V ask Bonar Law to form a government, though he would not agree to serve in it. Bonar Law also refused to become prime minister without Asquith. Therefore, late on December 6, Lloyd George was called to establish another ministry. He then informed William that he was unwilling to become prime minister, but Bonar Law insisted that he do so.[64]

12

Victory and Peace,
1916–1922

"I am getting America at last to do something."

TWO DAYS AFTER HE WAS commissioned to form a government, Lloyd George wrote William on picking a Cabinet: "Almost completed my list of names. Getting on well." Haig sent a letter by a royal family officer to George V the same day, expressing genuine fear that Lloyd George would waste British manpower on the eastern front, specifically the Balkans. He considered it a minor diversion endangering his plan to rid German submarine capability from the coast of Belgium. A day later, Lloyd George finished manning his Cabinet, "except one or two small jobs," he told his brother. On the next, he then confirmed for him, "Presided over my first War Cabinet. Found it embarrassing to be addressed as 'Prime Minister' by all the members." They consisted of Bonar Law, now Chancellor of the Exchequer, Curzon, new Lord President of the Council, Henderson, Labour Minister without Portfolio, and Conservative Minister without Portfolio, Viscount Alfred Milner, former High Commissioner for South Africa. Milner was also the founder of the British Workers' National League, approximately seventy chapters of imperialistic and patriotic workers who expressed pro-war sentiments. Balfour, Grey's successor as Foreign Secretary, was allowed to attend meetings any time he desired. Other Cabinet members and specialists on certain foreign issues could be invited when necessary. Carson assumed Balfour's position as First Lord of the Admiralty. Two days before Christmas, Lloyd George lamented to William his having to miss it at Criccieth: "I am so disappointed not to be able to join you all Xmas day. It would have been such a happiness to me . . . But I am not the only one deprived of that joy by this cruel war."[1]

Before the first month of 1917 was over, Lloyd George noted for his brother the grief of another colleague: "Poor Walter Long lost his son." Long, who had been President of the Local Government Board under Asquith, was now Colonial Secretary in the new Cabinet. His sorrow was sadly soon felt by even more parents, however, due to Germany's declaration of unrestricted submarine warfare on February 1. It had established an unrestricted zone around Britain with its submarines two years to the month earlier but to little effect, but after Americans perished on the *Lusitania* and the *Arabic*, the United States threatened war. Consequently, six months following its first underwater campaign's start, Germany stopped attacks by U-boats on all ships in the zone. Eight days after a second German unrestricted submarine campaign was proclaimed to the world, Lloyd George told William, "Submarines are troublesome but I feel confident they will not get us under." Approximately eighty U-boats surrounded Britain this time, but Lloyd George and John Jellicoe reimplemented the convoy system to counter their impact. Naval convoys had been used by the English as early as the seventeenth century. A day after telling William of the submarines, Lloyd George reported some encouraging news directly related to Germany's policy: "American ambassador just left me. He is very hopeful of America coming in. But he is a partisan." Walter Hines Page was the ambassador and an Anglophile, the latter apparently causing Lloyd George to take him a little less seriously.[2]

As the Minister of Munitions, Lloyd George had told his brother about "a most important interview" on June 2, 1915, "with Colonel House (President Wilson's confidante)." He believed from the interview, less than a month after the sinking of the *Lusitania*, America would enter the war. The two men had first met the year before, but House's opinion of the then-chancellor was not favorable. Their second meeting was ten days following the loss of nearly thirteen hundred lives from a German torpedo, 10 percent of them Americans. Nothing came of that encounter, mostly due to Cowdray, another attendee and petroleum magnate who wanted to talk about oil in Mexico. Four more times in early 1916, Lloyd George and Rufus Isaacs dined with House, twice also including others. On those occasions, Wilson's special advisor wanted the British and Germans to discuss their objectives in the hope of a conference with the other Allies that might lead to peace. Lloyd George wrote to William on February 12, stating that House "had just returned from Berlin & Paris" the previous day. "He was very interesting." For the munitions minister's part, the notion of a conference was a non-starter unless America showed a willingness to deploy a huge arsenal to bring Germans to the table for Wilson to arbitrate. House was unhappy because he wanted Lloyd George to be prime minister. Even though he believed Lloyd George did not understand United States politicians or their policies, he lunched with him alone before going home, discussing both Asquith's lack of engagement and whether Lloyd George desired the premiership. When he left, it did not seem to matter that an Irish Unionist liaison with America or an American expatriate Privy Councillor of Asquith had told him that Lloyd George was "ineffective, shifty, without integrity, and a brilliant but cheap opportunist who would do virtually anything for personal advancement."[3]

Before the end of March in 1917, three times as many British vessels were being sunk by submarines as had been during Germany's first U-boat campaign, and ultimately, a fourth of all British ships leaving port were lost, on average one every couple of days. Foodstuffs diminished to a six-week supply before the convoy system, mines, nets, depth charges, hydrophones, and air attacks significantly reversed the U-boat threat. The initial convoy lasted for thirteen days in late April and early May without one ship sunk. However, the United States started losing merchant ships on March 15, and by April 2, Wilson was asking for a declaration of war against Germany. Congress authorized it four days later. American destroyers began arriving to assist Britain on May 4. Another major development had occurred on the Ides of March with the abdication of Czar Nicholas II as a result of the February Revolution. A provisional government was commissioned to call for the election of a constituent assembly, and Russia became a republic for the next eight months. Only a day after the czar stepped down due to the popular revolution for food, fuel, and the reluctance of troops to return to the front, Lloyd George in proud democratic terms succinctly summarized its significance for his brother: "Russia is triumphant. Worth the whole war & its terrible sacrifices."[4]

Years later, when Lloyd George was writing a chapter on Russia for his war memoirs, he told Sylvester, his secretary, that the first 1917 Russian Revolution "was the greatest development in the world since the Crucifixion," but to state such publicly would be too alarming. One historian of British diplomacy has appropriately described Lloyd George as the first democratic statesman. Russia becoming a constitutional government had also influenced Wilson to enter the war on the side of the Allies. On March 30, Lloyd George turned his attention to the fighting in the Middle East, sharing military progress with William, which made him rejoice politically and religiously: "Then comes the news from Palestine, which is thoroughly cheerful. We are not far from Jerusalem, and although it is not going to fall just yet, I am looking forward to my Government achieving something which generations of the chivalry of Europe failed to attain." British forces had finally taken Kut in February and moved into Baghdad on March 11. After that, their targets were Palestine, Gaza, and Syria, from El Arish on Sinai's northeastern coast. As casualties grew, Sir Edmund Allenby was charged to take Jerusalem before Christmas. He did so two weeks early.[5]

None of Lloyd George's remaining letters to his brother mentions specifics of the war, but on April 1, 1918, he generalized, "We are just holding our own but the gale is not over." Actually, he did not write any letters to William from November 26, 1918, to June 26, 1939. In addition, he wrote no more letters to Frances about the war or Paris Peace Conference after he became prime minister because they were almost always together, and stopped writing her entirely from July 13, 1919, until August 1921. He did, though, continue to regularly write his wife. A letter to her the same day as the above to William noted "the battle," Germany's Spring Offensive that began on March 21. He continued to update her on the course of the war from August 1917 through July 1918 and, of course, talked about it in many of his speeches in Parliament or elsewhere. As one example of the latter, on June 29, 1917, he delivered an address in Glasgow entitled, "When the War will End." In it, he lauded the successes of British and French soldiers on the western front the previous fall, plus more recent Alpine victories by Italians against Austrians. He also praised the Russians for their democratic revolution, noting how he had prophesied following their defeat at Gorlice-Tarnow that Germany was "unshackling" them, describing their loss as "the beginning of the end for autocracy." Calling America "the mainstay and the hope of freedom," he discussed the economic impact of German submarines next.[6]

Flattering his audience, Lloyd George then stated, "You might be driven to eat less wheat and more barley and oats, the food of the men and women who made Scotland. Yes, and my little country, too," he added. "I am running the war on the stock of energy which I accumulated on that fare when I was young, and I am not going to weep over the hardships of a country which is driven back to oats and barley. We were never able to aspire to those luxuries in Wales. We never got further than a bannock." Playing off of the word bannock, he mentioned Bannockburn, where the Scots had won their freedom from the English. Analogously, he also alleged for there to be peace as Wilson "set out recently," the Central Powers would have to free Belgium, Serbia, Mesopotamia, and Armenia, "a land soaked with the blood of innocents massacred by the people who were their guardians." They would have to pay indemnities too. He closed his presentation with apocalyptic imagery, tasking, "we should continue to fight for the great goal of international right and international justice, so that never again shall brute force sit on the throne of justice, nor barbaric strength wield the sceptre of right."[7]

Wilson had "set out" his views in a Flag Day oration only fifteen days earlier, as the first of two million Americans under General John J. Pershing were on their way to France. June was also when Lloyd George created a subcommittee of the War Cabinet to supervise the overall war strategy, composed of Curzon, Milner, and Jan Smuts. Ironically, Smuts not only had led Boers but also the Union of South Africa's defense forces who had helped defeat Germans in southwest Africa and ultimately drove them out of East Africa. Only eight days after the new subcommittee had its opening session, Haig met with it and proposed a new offensive to take the highest points above Ypres in what became known as the Battle of Passchendaele. Lloyd George wanted to help the Italians against Austria rather than backing a new campaign in Flanders but acquiesced to the military. He especially yielded to the Chief of the Imperial General Staff, Sir William Robertson, who supported the lesser of the two evils put forth. Interestingly, though, Robertson did not want him as the Secretary of State for War in 1916, even using his clout with the monarch, council of the army, and newspapers to try to stop him from getting the position.[8]

The British opened fire with artillery on July 16, and confidently, Lloyd George appointed Churchill Minister of Munitions two days later. Their ground offensive started the last day of the month but had to be stopped temporarily due to German counter-attacks and such heavy rain that one battery commander recorded mud ten feet deep. Twice the normal August amount fell. Lloyd George wrote Maggie about their younger son a day before the advance halted, commiserating, "Gwilym left this morning in excellent spirits, not at all sorry to join his battery—& come what may I would rather have him there where so many gallant boys are risking their lives for their country than have him here in safety. So would you I know." Haig's goal was realized after the offensive resumed August 16, but the cost was almost 250,000 casualties. The ridge crest of Ypres was taken, and Canadians secured the village of Passchendaele, but the battle lasted until November 10. It ended because of looming winter weather and the deployment of five divisions southwest of Caporetto to shore up the Italian front against a combined Austro-German attack that had begun on October 24. France got some relief after Passchendaele, or the Third Battle of Ypres, its mutinies ceased because half of the German Army in the west had to be used, and it sent six divisions to Italy. More than a quarter of a million Italian troops surrendered at Caporetto nine days after the Third Battle of Ypres was over.[9]

The same day Haig had renewed the offensive, Germans hit Langemarck, where so many of their inexperienced youth had died in the First Battle at Ypres and poison gas was first used by them in the second. A second lieutenant, Edwin Vaughan, who kept one of the best diaries of the first month's fighting at Passchendaele, noted Langemarck in his entry for August 27, stating to a friend he was "going to eat" some "cold cooked" rabbit "on Langemarck Ridge." By 6:30 in the evening, British artillery guns had ceased firing beyond the ridge and were now hitting it because the Germans had stopped them short of it. "Then I returned to the CO and we waited on and on; the shells continued to crash around us, the sky clouded and rain began to fall. Time after time he sent out runners to find out what the position was, but none returned." Vaughan finished that paragraph by writing, "a runner arrived with a report" at headquarters "the attack was completely held up: 'casualties very heavy.'"[10]

The same month the campaign ended, the Bolsheviks under Nikolai Lenin came to power in Russia and began conversing unilaterally with Germans in December to leave the war, after an agreement for a cease fire. Lloyd George delivered a public speech at the Trades Union Congress shortly after the new year began, in which he observed that peace could be negotiated with Germany if it would free conquered lands exclusive of consideration for Russia. The official stance of the government was that he was encouraging laborers with the suggestion, as more workers would have to be drafted, but a concern over Russia's departure from the Allies was more prominent in War Cabinet talks. He commenced his speech by stating that "nothing else" than "the conscience of the nation" would be able to "sustain the effort which is necessary to achieve a righteous end to this war." He had "taken special pains to ascertain the view and the attitude" from talking to the representatives "of all sections of thought and opinion in the country." He specifically reiterated freedom as well as reparation for Belgium, in addition to "the restoration of Serbia, Montenegro, and the occupied parts of France, Italy, and Rumania."[11]

Addressing Russia directly, Lloyd George then asserted, "The present rulers of Russia are now engaged, without any reference to the countries who Russia brought into the war, in separate negotiations with their common enemy." Consequently, he determined, "Britain cannot be held accountable for decisions taken in her absence, and concerning which she has not been consulted or her aid invoked." He further cautioned that if those rulers did act independently of the Allies, "we have no means of intervening to arrest the catastrophe which is assuredly befalling their country. Russia can only be saved by her own people." The only stipulation he mentioned for territory in Russia taken by Germans was that "an independent Poland" was considered "an urgent necessity for the stability of Western Europe," also one of Wilson's Fourteen Points listed three days later. He referenced Mesopotamia as well as Armenia again but now also included Syria, Palestine, and Arabia as having the right to their own national identities. The future of German colonies would have to be discussed at a peace conference. "The general principle of national self-determination is therefore as applicable in their cases as in those of occupied European territories," he judged.[12]

Self-determination of peoples was another of Wilson's future points, and as Lloyd George concluded, he noted a third one, what became the League of Nations. In it, he also foreshadowed the need for weapons limitations such as those reached at the Washington Naval Conference in 1921. His proposal stated, "we must seek by the creation of some international organisation to limit the burden of armaments and diminish the probability of war." In fact, before he spoke, he wanted to know what Britain's limits were militarily, asking Robertson if it could win the war after another year of fighting. Robertson would not hazard an opinion, however, educated or otherwise. Lloyd George knew Wilson wanted more liberal terms and Georges Clemenceau, France's new premier since November, more conservative ones, but entitled his speech, "The War Aims of the Allies." Nevertheless, Smuts had already secretly approached Austrians concerning a separate treaty with them. Austria refused. Germany would too, both Lloyd George's and Wilson's similar offers.[13]

Lloyd George described his position within British politics "as being caught between the 'extravagance of the Jingo and the cantankerousness of the pacifist.'" The same thing seemed to be true in foreign politics, especially since the Bolsheviks were recommending no reparations or acquisitions of territories. When he wrote his wife about his Trades Union address, he called it "the most important speech I have yet made" and "a carefully prepared statement on War aims." Most of the speech was actually composed by Smuts and Robert Cecil, acting foreign secretary for the ailing Balfour. Three days afterward, he told Maggie, "The speech is still the sensation. It has rallied the Allies but it does not mean peace. Never thought it would. It has just placed us on the sound footing for war. It may weaken Austria." A month after his presentation, however, he depicted the military staff as "sulky," and six days later alerted her, "Revolution going on here. Robertson sent off to Versailles & Wilson brought here as Chief of the Staff. 'Wully' kicking hard. But I had had enough of him for a long time. He was in constant intrigue with Asquith."[14]

Wully was Robertson's nickname, and even though Lloyd George mentions his plotting on Asquith's behalf, it was mostly his dilatoriness and support of Haig's unconscionable sending of so many men to their deaths at Passchendaele that resulted in his replacement. Henry Wilson, who had devised the most rapid, effective way to deploy British troops to the continent and had served as deputy chief, was not only more decisive but also easier to control. Robertson wanted to be assigned to the Supreme War Council in Versailles as Britain's adviser on military affairs, but he did not want to give up his post as chief. The next month saw the start of Germany's last offensive on the western front, during which it pulled ten divisions a month off the eastern front because the Treaty of Brest-Litovsk had been signed with Russians on March 3. When Germans attacked, they numbered twenty divisions more than the Allies. The entire first line of the British twenty-eight-mile front was pushed back by the end of day one.[15]

The day after the collapse of the British first line, Lloyd George relayed to Maggie, "We are all here full of anxiety about this terrible battle—undoubtedly the greatest the world has ever seen. So far nothing much has happened. We have been forced to retire from our front lines but that always happens in an attack of this kind. It will go on for weeks & might well end the war." Clearly, he was trying to reassure himself as well as her, but he shared again four days later how anxious he was and how desperate things had been: "Have had 3 or 4 days of the most worrying time of my life." He did see some hope for the British because Germans were "making for Paris. That gives us at any rate some breathing space. Our fellows have been fine," a clear reference to their two sons. However, the following day he wrote, "Just holding our own. Next three days—in fact next week most critical. If they get Amiens we shall be in the tightest place we have ever yet been in." On March 30, he confided that things were still critical but he was "engaged in waking up the Americans—with some success." He also mentioned the United States on the first day of April, claiming, "I am getting America at last to do something. Hope God it is not too late."[16]

The Americans were possibly sending up to four-hundred thousand soldiers to help until July, Lloyd George elaborated for his wife the next day and accurately predicted the battle would last that long. He then went to France, had a conference with Clemenceau and Foch in Beauvais, but returning quickly informed Maggie, "Haig more anxious. I am still more anxious after seeing

Haig and his Chief of Staff—both of them very second rate men." Six days later, he referred to the British generals the same way, now adding for her they were "fighting first class brains." Of the prime minister, Haig was later quoted as saying the forces he commanded "were at the mercy of an 'Organizer of Defeat.'" In the previous discourse with his wife, Lloyd George also mentioned another conscription bill that provided for drafting the Irish for the first time, noting, "If we fail to carry it we should have to resign or dissolve— the latter is very difficult in the middle of a great battle." Two weeks afterward, he related that there had been "just a little 'biff' south of Amiens," the "naval news" was good, but "the air quarrel" was "a nasty situation." By July 30, he was passing on "very good" news and relief as well: "Believe the German offensive this year is broken."[17]

Following Lloyd George's comment on Germans moving toward Paris, the resulting clash with the French became known as the Second Battle of the Marne. The Germans did not actually begin a concerted effort to take the French capital until May 27, but their farthest incursions were stopped in ten days with the help of Americans at places like Chateau-Thierry and Belleau Wood. They ultimately did advance four miles across the river on July 15 before again being driven back three days later, not to return. Amiens became the German's objective against Britain, after they were unable to fold them back to the English Channel and encountered fierce opposition at Arras. With French assistance and under unified leadership by Foch, designated as the Supreme Allied Commander on April 3 with Haig's approval, the Germans, who had gone the wrong way, were halted five miles from their goal. Pétain had been unable to send help as far north as the British were but recommended Amiens as the place to prepare next for a German assault, even though it was twenty miles farther west in northern France than they had penetrated. Haig and Wilson had engaged in heated disagreements with Pétain over the issue before relenting to Foch's command, which is presumably why Lloyd George labeled them both as second rate.[18]

Wilson considered Lloyd George a machinator, especially when the prime minister, while visiting France, petitioned King George V to encourage Haig to ask for no less than ten divisions of American soldiers. Wilson quickly recorded for his diary, "Of course this is not cricket." The "biff" below Amiens was a tank incursion by the Germans, something they seldom did, but better and more numerous British tanks drove them back. Ironically, the "naval news" pertained to the *Moltke*, a German battle cruiser torpedoed near the northwest coast of Germany, although it made its way back to base. It had already suffered internal damage as part of a High Seas Fleet attempt to surprise a convoy leaving the Scandinavian waters a day later than thought. The "quarrel" over planes got "nasty" because the government established the Civil Aerial Transport Committee, and private entrepreneurs were hawking their own schemes for non-military flights. The committee's chairman was Lord Northcliffe, the most powerful British newspaperman and the brother of Lord Rothermere, Cowdray's replacement as air minister. More important news was of Baron Manfred von Richthofen's death in battle three days earlier, after he had racked up eighty kills.[19]

The Spring Offensive of Ludendorff caused nearly a million casualties for the Germans as well as roughly half a million each for the French and the British. Slightly less than ten thousand Americans were killed, wounded, or missing. Allies countered at Amiens on August 8 and along the Meuse-Argonne front seven weeks later. British forces under Haig broke the defensive line of the Germans on September 29, a day after Ludendorff advised Hindenburg to pursue an armistice. The two German generals had been serving as military governors for Kaiser Wilhelm II since the previous November. He forced Ludendorff's resignation on October 26, but refused Hindenburg's and abdicated two weeks later, accepting political exile in The Netherlands. On November 9, the kaiser fled, and a new German government, the Weimar Republic, was proclaimed. It authorized Matthias Erzberger to sign the armistice two days later. The following month, a general election derogatorily dubbed the "coupon election" by Asquith, gave the existing coalition government in Britain a majority in excess of 250 seats.[20]

Lloyd George and Bonar Law had signed a letter endorsing the coalition's return, mailed to every candidate in favor as an acknowledgment of government approval to be redeemed at the election. Balfour also agreed that the Conservatives should continue to support it, telling Bonar Law of Lloyd George, "Our friend is, I think, the most remarkable single figure produced by the Great War." The Conservatives had predicted over two hundred, but Lloyd George told Maggie, "I shall be surprised if we don't get a majority of over 100. If it is over 120 then I shall be content. If it is under that I shall be disappointed." While he was campaigning, he voiced strong positions on the Germans paying for the entire war and on the kaiser being tried for murder. As he fleshed out the reparations, however, he stressed they should not go beyond what Germany was realistically able to pay or in any way hamper British trade. Concerning Wilhelm II, he most likely knew Holland did not intend to turn him over for prosecution. On January 11, 1919, Lloyd George arrived for the Paris Peace Conference, which officially began one week later, the forty-eighth anniversary of the first kaiser's coronation in the Hall of Mirrors at Versailles following the Franco-Prussian War. It ended in just five months, on the fifth anniversary of Archduke Francis Ferdinand's assassination. Balfour had accompanied Lloyd George as part of a delegation of 207.[21]

The conference's multifarious details were meticulously recorded by British diplomats as well as secretaries at the time and have been thoroughly analyzed by numerous academic scholars since, but certain points related to the present thesis should be stressed. Lloyd George was the one who finally got the Big Four talking seriously about peace terms for Germany on March 25, after a delay of more than two months mainly due to Wilson heralding a League of Nations. On that day, he presented his Fontainebleau Memorandum, advocating temperate terms for Germany in regard to reparations and settling its frontiers. He received so much nationalistic furor from conservative British interests, however, especially newspapers, that after turning the final determination over to a commission to avoid criticism, he later advocated adding military pensions to the total Germany had to pay. Concerning the allocation of Germany's borderlands, he opposed the French desire to separate the Saar and Rhineland, though they were given control of the former's mines for fifteen years. He did support putting the Rhineland within the League of Nations' purview for that same amount of time. Also, he wanted Poles to be given less than the other Allies were willing to cede due to his belief that Bolshevism there and nationalism in Germany would both grow. Two days after making his moderate offer, he told his wife, "I am very hard pressed with the most important discussions of the Conference. Papers all going for us." The papers he alluded to were in Britain, primarily *The Times* and the *Daily Mail*, which Northcliffe owned. By April, he had talked Wilson into making Germany pay for pensions as well as civilian damages and the military cost of the war. Also, he, with Clemenceau, had succeeded in getting a war guilt clause and agreement to try the kaiser, against Wilson's objections, but the president got his goal of a League of Nations.[22]

Interestingly, when the terms for the Treaty of Versailles with Germany were made public, many in Britain and the British delegation felt they were too severe. Lloyd George tried to change the terms accordingly with Clemenceau and Wilson, except the reparations because Parliament as well as the press still clamored for more indemnities. Both men opposed him. After resignations in the German government, the Weimar Republic nevertheless reluctantly accepted the terms, except the war guilt clause, but had to sign anyway because it could not risk a resumption of war. Lloyd George then left France, but the specifics of the treaties with Austria, Hungary, Bulgaria, and the Turks remained to be settled. The Austro-Hungarian Empire had collapsed, and both parts became republics. Austria signed the Treaty of Saint-Germain in September 1919, but the Treaty of Trianon was not given to Hungary until it was more stable nine months later. Bulgaria's kingdom submitted to the Treaty of Neuilly in November 1919, and the Ottoman Empire received the Treaty of Sèvres the following August. Of particular importance to Lloyd George and Balfour were the Jews in Palestine as well as Arabs throughout the Middle East. In 1923, Lloyd George stated most plainly his view of racism against the Jews: "Of all the bigotries that savage the human temper," he said unequivocally, "there is none so stupid as the anti-Semitic. It has no basis in reason; it is not rooted in faith; it aspires to no ideal; it is just one of those dank, unwholesome weeds that grow in the morass of racial hatred."[23]

Lloyd George also used the Old Testament, specifically its references to Jehovah's chosen nation of Hebrews, to support Zionist ambitions, and he believed God's plan was unfolding in the endeavors of outstanding leaders as well as nations. As early as 1892, he had written in his diary, "Israel—a peculiar people—God still selects nationalities to be the missionaries of his ideas." John Clifford, the leading Baptist sage, visited him at Criccieth in the fall of 1919 and went to a Sunday evening worship service at Berea, where Lloyd George used a biblical analogy in a short message on Christian nations cooperating to make lives better for all: "I speak as one standing high on the watch tower," comparing himself to one chosen by God or the prophets (Ezekiel 3:17, Isaiah 21:5, KJV). "What the need of this land is today is not material, but spiritual," he declared, "and I hail any movement advancing the great spirit of brotherhood. The one need of England and France is the spirit of brotherhood. That is still the healer of the world."[24]

The letter Lloyd George wrote to Maggie after presenting his Fontainebleau Memorandum contained a reference to Lieutenant-Colonel Arnold Wilson, Britain's commissioner in Baghdad, who "lunched with me today. Full of admiration for Tom. He is very popular with the high class Arab & Jews & would make money if he settled down there." Tom was T. E. Lawrence, who had taken Aqaba from the Turks during the war as well as territory to the Dead Sea and had organized Arabs to proclaim their independence from the Ottoman Empire. He even accompanied the Emir Feisal, one of their leaders who represented them at the Paris Peace Conference. In the early years of the war, Britain had contributed to another of their leaders also, the Sharif of Mecca, before he became King Hussein of the Hedjah or Saudi Arabia, believing it would endorse the creation of a united Arab nation, the capital of which would be Damascus. The British soldiers under Allenby, Lawrence, and Feisal aiding with Arab rebels, conquered the city on October 1, 1918, but two days afterward, Feisal raised an Arab flag over it. Hussein had begun the Arab rebellion in May 1916, and the Jews were promised a homeland in Palestine eighteen months afterward by Lloyd George in the Balfour Declaration of his Secretary of State for Foreign Affairs.[25]

What muddied the water was the Anglo-French, Sykes-Picot Agreement, the same month the Arab revolt started, which provided for dividing the Arab portions of the Ottoman Empire as well as the Turkish mainland by Britain, France, and Russia. It stated what ultimately did happen, to the chagrin of the Arabs. France would receive Syria as well as Lebanon, while Britain was to get Palestine, Transjordan, and what became Iraq. Russians were to gain Armenia and Kurdistan but after leaving the war got neither, though they took the former, which the peace conference had proclaimed independent, in 1920. Kurdistan, where people were supposed to have a plebiscite for independence or autonomy, was kept by the Turks, who never formally consented to the Treaty of Sèvres. The conflict between what Britain had agreed to with France and what the Arabs thought they were promised was not resolved until April 1920, at another conference in San Remo, Italy. Composed of prime ministers from Britain, France, Italy, and Japan, it established mandates for Palestine, Syria, and Mesopotamia but did not stipulate boundary lines for the various areas. The Balfour Declaration was also officially recognized. Lloyd George did not believe Syria should be granted to France, as British forces had captured it and faith would be lost with the Arabs. His lack of success at two other conferences during early 1922 even weakened his hold on the British coalition government. At both Cannes and Genoa, he was unable to gain acceptance for his plans to reconstruct Germany's economy for the good of Europe and the world, mostly Britain, or for *de jure* recognition of the Soviet Union approved by his own Cabinet.[26]

In Lloyd George's letters to his mistress, who also served as his private secretary in Paris, he was brutally honest in describing his attitudes toward the various powers represented at Genoa. He used such caustic words as "Damn German stupidity," Russian "fanatical Orientals," and in a sweeping indictment, "The Russians difficult—hesitating-with their judgment warped in doctrine. The French selfish—the Germans impotent—the Italians are willing but feeble—the little countries scared." His opinion of the Bolsheviks was not that they were being deceitful but that they were positioning for whatever advantage they could gain. Curzon and the most staunch Conservatives in the Cabinet, though, were convinced that the Soviets were totally untrustworthy. It does seem that Lenin's government made statements the more practical Cabinet members would like, particularly Lloyd George, who wanted trade with Russia reestablished to help alleviate increasing joblessness in Britain but was considered by Bolsheviks to be weaker than his Conservative counterparts, and likely to be outvoted on economic or any other relations with Russia. Lloyd George had given the Bolsheviks some respectability at home and abroad by his attempts to negotiate with them, but he also realized that "unemployment, after all, was 'a far more formidable peril than all the lunacies of Lenin.'"[27]

The failures in Lloyd George's international diplomacy, along with accusations of scandal over honors and his belligerent attitude concerning a struggle between Greeks and Turks, soon led to his downfall. The signs of his decreasing effectiveness with the most conservative members of the coalition also manifested as he considered precipitating another election four times in 1922. In late August and September, correspondence with his wife revealed the rapid decline of his ministry. Expressing concern, he wrote, "I am worried by much bigger issues which may alter the whole course of things. The Coalition is breaking up over the Tory revolt." Honors bestowal, which for two centuries had been common practices by prime ministers, caused part of the revolt because Conservatives had not been getting half of them. Even though there were more of them in his government, the money received was finding its way into his reelection coffers. As early as January 1921, Bonar Law was told about the inequity, especially at the lowest rank where except for military leaders Conservatives only received five out of nineteen baronets, and fourteen were knighted compared to nineteen Liberals. Bonar Law resigned for health reasons two months later, having served as the Lord Privy Seal since the last election, after which Austen Chamberlain became Chancellor of the Exchequer. Conservatives also considered Lloyd George's list of those to be honored too lengthy, again because the money was going into his political chest. He told his wife he had lunch with Bonar Law on September 6, 1922, and that the former Leader of the House of Commons stated, "as to the political situation it was so bad as to be quite irretrievable. I don't like the outlook & as I am not clear what to do I am worried and unhappy."[28]

In that letter and another twenty-two days later, Lloyd George referred to

Greece, initially just noting, "The Greek situation," but the other stating, "The Greek Revolution has changed the situation. I think it just possible God may now take a hand. It looks like it." The first "situation" mentioned was the defeat of the Greeks by the Turks at Smyrna, after which the latter also moved toward British troops stationed at Chanak. That "& the political situation at home have occupied me very much," he told Maggie. The second "situation" regarding Greece was a bloodless revolt that prompted the abdication of King Constantine of the Hellenes. The conflict between the two countries, which had lasted well over two years, was the more immediate cause of a revolt against Lloyd George in England. In the Treaty of Sèvres, Greece got Smyrna, and Constantinople as well as the Dardanelles were demilitarized under Allied occupation. Allied troops had been positioned on the Asian side of the strait, but even when Greece decided it wanted Constantinople plus Smyrna, Lloyd George, Balfour, now Lord President of the Council, and Curzon, newest Foreign Secretary, were in favor. Lloyd George favored it to champion a small people for a third time in hopes they could help stabilize the Balkans, Balfour to get the Turks off of European soil, and Curzon to aid the Greeks who were so patriotic during the war. The majority in the Cabinet disagreed.[29]

The cooperation between the Ottoman government and the Allies at Versailles, in addition to the Greeks taking Smyrna, had led to a successful revolution among Turks for a republic under Mustafa Kemal instead of a sultanate. Afterward, France signed a treaty with the sister republic, not only stopping its support of the Greeks but also providing Turks with guns and planes, potentially putting them at military odds with Britain. Italy also ceased its backing of the Greeks and, like France, its military presence in the Chanak area. When the Turks then threatened Britain's outpost at Chanak, F. E. Smith, now Lord Chancellor as well as Earl of Birkenhead, and Churchill joined Lloyd George in persuading the Cabinet to authorize sending a telegram to commonwealth nations requesting their military assistance, Birkenhead because the Greeks were Christians but Churchill for the prestige of the British Empire. All the dominions except New Zealand and Newfoundland rejected the request. Parliament, the press, and the people were overwhelmingly opposed too, but Lloyd George persisted, thinking a war would unite the Conservatives around him once more and restore him to a strong leadership position. Before any military action was taken, Curzon asked to go alone to France to see if Raymond Poincaré would agree to work with the British to end the crisis through negotiation. At that juncture, Max Aitken, Lord Beaverbrook and former Minister

of Information, decided to approach Bonar Law to issue a press statement to
the same effect, which Law did on October 7. Beaverbrook had helped Law become Conservative leader and as the owner of the *Daily Express* championed
working-class conservatism. In a Conservative MPs meeting at the Carlton
Club on October 19, 187 of 276 voted for Law to govern. Lloyd George tried
to keep a coalition as prime minister or Lord President but knowing he had
lost majority support resigned that day.[30]

Conclusion

THE MAIN OBJECTIVE of this book has been to connect Lloyd George's religious convictions on subjects stressed in his diaries to domestic and foreign policies he championed as a politician. A secondary goal has been to let him speak as much as possible for himself from his own private letters and public speeches to Parliament or the country. So much vitriol has been published on him, it is high time for him to defend himself. Bitter members of the Liberal Party were the first to castigate him, blaming him for causing it to fall. Then, many biographers and historians, who could not research official public archives, his diaries, or most importantly, the letters to his brother, made flawed presumptions or incorrect judgments. As a result, they drew unbalanced final assessments. Government documents were not released for thirty years, and private papers only became available at the discretion of the donor. More recently, and worst of all, several sensationalistic authors have propounded irresponsible, unsubstantiated speculations about his personal morality. Unconscionably, in 2018, the latest goes so far as to depict him as "a sexual predator" and "a sex-pest," with no concrete evidence for such scathing indictments.[1]

It is abundantly clear from sources not cited anywhere else that Lloyd George was always a believer in God, providence, a divine plan for humanity, and Jesus as a real, historical, perfect example to be emulated. The article by Harold Begbie settles once and for all that Lloyd George was talking about the teachings he received at the Church of England school when he repeated to private associates as well as journalists the destruction of a temple of faith he had come to realize was false, although never blaming David Evans, his beloved teacher. Evans had actually wanted him to become a pupil-teacher for the school, which required being a member of the state church, and helped him to prepare for a legal career by spending extra time instructing him in arithmetic, geometry, or Latin. Lloyd George's love for neighbors, the second greatest commandment, was also palpable, and he spent himself in their service. Like far too many Christians, he was guilty of living a secret life for

years, but his flaws never deterred him from his mission to redress the grievances of the poverty-stricken, oppressed, and marginalized. That he did not
agree precisely with every religious doctrine he was taught manifests not only
that he was a free thinker but also that his faith was his own. His consistency in pursuing changes he felt so strongly about in his teens and twenties,
from when he was first elected until he fell from power, is astounding and a
testament to the genuineness of his convictions. He was not another unscrupulous politician, simply going whichever direction the winds were blowing
for selfish aggrandizement, but an egalitarian social reformer who improved
democracy in Britain and through it the rest of the world.[2]

Lloyd George continued to work for more land reform even after he resigned from office, and in 1929 published a pamphlet entitled *We Can Conquer Unemployment*, based heavily on an inquiry into Britain's industrial capability the previous year, to which John Maynard Keynes had contributed.
It proposed a type of British "new deal" three years before Franklin Roosevelt
was elected president of the United States, and six years later Lloyd George
used the actual words in another political campaign. Failing to regain power
in 1929, he told Frances on May 18, 1935, that he was planning "a meeting with
heads of Nonconformists to arrange a campaign." Rhetorically, he wanted a
nonpartisan group to influence the economic and foreign platforms of candidates in the next general election. Funded by £400,000 of his money, ministers from the National Council of Free Churches would primarily lead it,
many of whom signed a manifesto titled *A Call to Action* he published in June.
Then, all prospective members of the new organization were summoned to a
National Convention on Peace and Reconstruction in July, the major concerns to be acted upon. Over twenty-six hundred representatives agreed to
attend, and eighty-two MPs in addition to 445 preachers from every denomination responded to the invitation. Lloyd George's manifesto and a name he
recommended for the body, Council of Action, were approved.[3]

Stevenson's diary specifically mentions two clergymen and one layman as
performing the most crucial functions for the effort, John Scott Lidgett, S. W.
Hughes, and Robert Wilson Black, respectively. Lidgett, a Methodist, was
the secretary for public questions at the National Council, Hughes, a Baptist,
served as its general secretary, but Black, one of its treasurers, younger brother
of Sydney, and a Baptist after 1931, provided a building for its headquarters as
well as substantial monetary support from his real estate developments. Lloyd
George had hoped to get a post in the Cabinet of Ramsay MacDonald's coalition National Government after 1931, but MacDonald, the Labour prime

minister, and Neville Chamberlain, the Conservative Chancellor of the Exchequer, did not want him. Stanley Baldwin, Conservative Lord President of the Council, feigned interest but ultimately opted not to include him after becoming prime minister once MacDonald resigned on June 7, 1935. Labour members, especially George Lansbury, who refused to join the 1931 coalition but became party leader the next year, genuinely desired an association with him. Lloyd George expected enough Labour MPs to win in the next election for as few as twenty Liberals to make a majority coalition of which he could be the real power under Lansbury's leadership. In a letter to a former Labour MP on August 20, he made a very interesting religious statement from his roots but applied to partisan politics: "I am against confessions of faith in religion. They are crutches for people whose limbs are whole. They impede movement instead of facilitating it. As long as you insist on signing on the dotted line for all those who are anxious to help you, your party will always be a futile minority." Ironically, his nonconformist help began dwindling eight days later, and inconsistent candidate choices had little effect in a November election too early for him.[4]

Concerning Lloyd George's differences with some of the teachings and certain aspects of worship in the Church of Christ at Criccieth, his nephew, W. R. P. George stated that Richard Lloyd was more McLeanist in his thinking, while the nonsectarian interpretation of scripture Campbell espoused had a greater influence on Lloyd George. Mclean was too strict, to the extent that he would not attend services at other nonconformist chapels and gave fifteen rules to be obeyed. Campbell stressed each congregation's autonomy, with no external organizations or controls, much less the internal dictates of individuals. Richard Lloyd and his foster son disagreed on the Welsh Revival of 1904–1905, too, because the former thought it was not based on the intellect but too emotional. Furthermore, Lloyd George's nephew said he attended Castle Street Welsh Baptist Chapel simply because the sermons were in Welsh and Welsh hymns were sung. Born in 1912, he remembered communion at Berea being open but conjectured that Uncle Lloyd probably would have been opposed to it. Interestingly, and not referenced by any other published secondary sources, Lloyd George's nephew also mentioned that he was instrumental, with J. Saunders Lewis, in getting Welsh religious services on broadcasts from Sheffield in the late 1930s. Lewis and two other Welsh nationalists had burned a Royal Air Force bombing school's hangers in 1936, were put on trial, judged guilty, and sentenced to nine months' imprisonment. This made Lloyd George furious, since Baldwin's government was doing nothing about Hitler or Mussolini. Lewis voluntarily turned himself in to local authorities, but Lloyd George thought he should have made London officials come for him and that Welsh MPs ought to have caused an uproar in Parliament. A year later, he called Welsh nationalists "a lot of second-rate cranks."[5]

Lloyd George relayed the statements about Lewis in a letter to Megan, his youngest child, on December 1, adding that the change of the trial's venue "is an outrage what makes my blood boil. It has nothing to do with my views as to the merits of the case. It will reinforce the pacifist movement in England," which he was obviously against. Ironically, he had gone to Germany the week prior to the Welsh nationalists' actions and ever since has been criticized for what appeared to legitimize Hitler. He did want to meet Hitler but also desired to see how the German economy compared to the economic plans he had put forth for Britain. Hitler respected him for attempting to moderate Germany's punishments at Paris, but Lloyd George related to his modest upbringing, original economic ideas such as the Autobahn or other projects that created jobs, and his supreme confidence in dealing with German elites. Lloyd George got into Berchtesgaden on September 3, where he was greeted at the Grand Hotel by Joachim von Ribbentrop, the German ambassador to Britain. He had discussions with Hitler over the next two days at his Bavarian alpine house, "The Berghof." Hitler brought up the danger posed by the Soviet Union, but Lloyd George talked even longer about Germany's infrastructure. They shared war memories and stroked each other's ego, too. The problem was that Lloyd George was the highest ranking former or current British politician to visit Hitler. However, Lord Lothian, appeaser in the House of Lords, Anthony Eden, Foreign Secretary for Baldwin as well as Chamberlain, and John Simon, Baldwin's Home Secretary, had already. Greater difficulty occurred, though, when Lloyd George praised Hitler in Britain's press as Germany's George Washington but admitted to his concentration camps and Jewish oppression.[6]

In addition to Lloyd George's comments to Megan on the need for Baldwin's ministry to do something about Hitler and Mussolini, he wrote in a 1937 notebook, whose contents never having been published prior, "France concerned—Italy & Germany openly contrived infractions" to enter action against Spain's Popular Front. He specifically recorded, "women & children of Guernica were blown to pieces" and that "German aeroplanes dipped over the streets at Guernica to bomb churches." He also added they "lowered machine guns over homeless poor sleeping in the streets of Bilbao." Other references to Spain's Civil War include "Food for Spain Society," "Leaflet pro Franco," and "Neville dined at Claridge with Duke of Alba." Chamberlain succeeded Baldwin as prime minister in May, and Franco appointed Alba as Britain's representative for the Nationalists in November. Spain's prime minister invited Lloyd George to his nation to encourage republican forces. Lloyd George also noted Baldwin, Lothian, Eden, Simon, now as Chancellor, and Samuel Hoare, new Home Secretary, but elaborated on Chamberlain more. "Neville beating the drum to call attention to the number of teeth he has drawn painlessly. Kingsley Wood with his triangle." He compared MacDonald's coalition government to France's Popular Front of Leon Blum, too: "Two of the three progressive countries of the world have progressive governments when Labour & Liberal or Radical & Socialist are corporate. Both came after a period of either reactionary or sluggish & sloppy government by the right." Two spiritual sentiments were expressed as well in the notebook, further verifying continued religious convictions in his final years. After citing the scripture, "Psalms 92:14," he quoted it in Welsh and then English, "In old age they shall be fat & flourishing." He also contemplated, though, "Had I God's heart—how I would alter things."[7]

After less than three years as prime minister, Chamberlain resigned two days after a fiery speech by Lloyd George denouncing Britain's feeble and abortive attempt to aid the Norwegians against conquest by Germany. The Conservative Party's baton was handed to Winston Churchill, who offered Lloyd George a seat on his War Cabinet, but only with the approval of Chamberlain, now Lord President of the Council. Lloyd George refused the position, though Chamberlain did finally agree to it the next month. Six months later, Churchill asked him to be ambassador to the United States, which he also declined due to his age, having to move, and the travel involved. As for his religious identity, it remained the same regardless of changing political fortunes. In 1936, he unequivocally stated that he would always be a Church of Christ member, the spiritual fellowship in which he had been brought up. When he died nine years later, Aneurin Bevan, Welshman and the Labour Party member of the House of Commons most responsible for founding the National Health Service in 1948, eulogized, "We have lost our most distinguished member and Wales her greatest son. He was, like the Prime Minister, a most formidable and even terrifying debater, but he also possessed what the Prime Minister possesses—the generosity of greatness. We have lost in death the most iridescent figure that ever illuminated the British political scene." Some Welsh hymns were sung at his funeral by hundreds on the road from his house to the Dwyfor River, and along its banks, but his favorite song, "Guide Me, O Thou Great Jehovah" by William Williams, was sung in English. He was a pilgrim through this barren land, and may he live in the hope that he wanted all God's offspring to find.[8]

The best way to characterize David Lloyd George seems to be with contrasting words that bring his thoughts and actions into clearer focus. He was a democrat not a socialist, rational not dogmatic, a reformer not a revolutionary, egalitarian not elitist, a humanitarian not a communist, spiritual not sectarian, a liberator not a secularist, nationalist not jingoist, pragmatist not pacifist, a realist not an idealist, principled not opportunistic. The first ten characteristics connect to those subjects dealt with in the chapters, respectively, but the last one overlaps with them all and refutes the most often published criticism of him. He was not a politician who arbitrarily vacillated between parties just to promote himself but a scrupulous mediator for what he sincerely believed were the inalienable rights of those who were less able to get them guaranteed in law. What too frequently sounds like an egotist in his private statements or an obstructionist in his public speeches is more determination than conceit and defiance, as he realized all his God-given talents had to be used to secure for his fellow human beings the blessings they were supposed to enjoy. As God's servant on a mission, he became a blessing to millions because his works done in the Lord follow him.[9]

Worshipping at a Welsh Baptist congregation in London after he was elected to Parliament rather than at one of the Church of Christ assemblies in the metropolis caused some exclusivists in his fellowship to disregard Lloyd George as a true Christian devoted to heartfelt religious beliefs. His adultery, had it been known by Church of Christ members, would have been considered a sin by all regardless of how he might have rationalized it in his own mind. If he repented or not once he married Frances only God knows, but the historical archives are replete with references to his spiritual acumen and his determination to use Christian principles to help society. This book has convincingly demonstrated that he was a lifelong member of the Church of Christ, and his religiously worded statements, whether public but especially when private, should not be casually dismissed. He did learn democracy from Campbell, whose Christian unity movement coincided with the age of Jackson, and Lincoln, a hero he tried to emulate, whose government of, by, and for the people also influenced him. Campbell's Lockean as well as the Scottish common sense approach to the scriptures had an impact on him too, and Garfield's plans to reform government services instilled in him the goal to do likewise. Though a Welsh radical who fought for the causes of his own and other small nations, he never joined the socialists in the Labour Party, agreed with anti-Christian revolutions, supported communist class struggle, or accepted blind patriotic imperialism. He did not believe in religious dogmatism, sectarianism, or any established state church, but neither was he secular in his thinking. Religious, social, or economic elitism always raised his ire, too, but he was a benevolent advocate for the freedoms of all the downtrodden, not just the lower classes.[10]

NOTES

Introduction

1. Bentley B. Gilbert, *The Evolution of National Insurance in Great Britain: The Origins of the Welfare State* (London: Michael Joseph, 1966), 345; Peter Rowland, *Lloyd George* (London: Barrie and Jenkins, 1975), 459.
2. Patricia Lee Sykes, *Presidents and Prime Ministers: Conviction Politics in the Anglo-American Tradition* (Lawrence: University Press of Kansas, 2000), 94–114; Lord Riddell, *More Pages from My Diary, 1908–1914* (London: Country Life, 1934), 152; Rowland, *Lloyd*, 268.
3. William George, *My Brother and I* (London: Eyre & Spottiswoode, 1958), 4, 155, 205, 220, 251, 295; Rowland, *Lloyd*, 3, 371–73, 586–87, 796; Bentley Brinkerhoff Gilbert, *David Lloyd George, A Political Life: Organizer of Victory, 1912–1916* (Columbus: Ohio State University Press, 1992), 419.
4. Jerry L. Gaw, "A History of Churches of Christ in the United Kingdom to 1867," (Master's thesis, Northwestern State University, Natchitoches, Louisiana, 1983); A. C. Watters, *History of British Churches of Christ* (Indianapolis: Butler University School of Religion, 1948), 76.
5. Brief descriptions of all the subjects analyzed and interpreted in the twelve chapters that follow, respectively.
6. Quoted in Herbert Du Parcq, *Life of David Lloyd George*, 4 vols. (London: Caxton Publishing Company, Limited, 1913), 1:33–34; Frances Stevenson Diary, April 8, 1915, Frances Stevenson Papers, Historical Collection 195, House of Lords Record Office, London (hereafter cited as HLRO); A. J. P. Taylor, ed., *Lloyd George: A Diary by Frances Stevenson* (London: Hutchinson, 1971), 41–43; W. R. P. George, *The Making of Lloyd George* (London: Faber & Faber, 1976), 125–26; John Grigg, *Lloyd George: From Peace to War, 1912–1916* (Berkeley: University of California Press, 1985), 70–72; quoted in J. Graham Jones, "Lloyd George and the Suffragettes at Llanystumdwy," *Journal of Liberal Democrat History* 34/35 (Spring/Summer 2002): 3, 7–9; Arthur Marwick, *The Deluge: British Society and the First World War* (New York: W. W. Norton & Company, 1965), 203; Timothy Larsen, *Christabel Pankhurst: Fundamentalism and Feminism in Coalition* (Woodbridge, UK: The Boydell Press, 2002), 67, n.62.
7. J. Graham Jones, *Lloyd George Papers at the National Library of Wales and other Repositories* (Aberystwyth: The National Library of Wales, 2001), 9–10, 15, 32–35, 40–41, 54–55, 70–72, 74–76; Kenneth O. Morgan, ed., *Lloyd George Family*

Letters, 1885–1936 (Cardiff: University of Wales Press, 1973); Lucy Masterman Diary, Charles F. G. and Lucy Masterman Archive, University of Birmingham Library, Birmingham; A. J. P. Taylor, ed., *My Darling Pussy: The Letters of Lloyd George and Frances Stevenson, 1913–41* (London: Weidenfeld and Nicolson, 1975), 19, 25–26, 30–31; Richard Lloyd George, *Lloyd George* (London: Frederick Muller Limited, 1960); Lady Olwen Carey Evans, *Lloyd George Was My Father* (Llandysul, UK: Gomer Press, 1985).

8. Letter from J. Graham Jones, Senior Archivist and Head of the Welsh Political Archive at the National Library of Wales, Aberystwyth, to the author, dated March 3, 1994.

9. Personal conversations with a taxi driver in Merthyr Tydfil on July 1, 1995, a B&B owner of Criccieth on July 15, 1995, and a great-grandson at Criccieth cemetery on April 15, 2006.

10. Lloyd George Diaries, June 17, 1880, February 16, 1881, October 29–30, 1882, January 31, August 25, 1886, William George Papers, National Library of Wales, Aberystwyth (hereafter cited as NLW); David Lloyd George to Margaret Owen, July 17, 1887, Lloyd George Papers, NLW; Rowland, *Lloyd*, 84–87, 93–94, 125–31, 226–27; Travis L. Crosby, *The Unknown Lloyd George: A Statesman in Conflict* (London: I.B. Tauris, 2014), 39–41, 361–64, 377–78; Taylor, ed., *My Darling*, 1–2; George, *My Brother*, 194–203.

11. Taylor, ed., *My Darling*, 1–4, 11; David Lloyd George to Frances Stevenson, August 23, 1915, Frances Stevenson Papers, HLRO; Taylor, ed., *Diary*, x, 1–2, 23–24, 214–15, 259–60; Stevenson Diary, January 21, 1915, May 9, 1921, March 10, 1934, Frances Stevenson Papers, HLRO; David Lloyd George to William George, January 5, February 12, 1908, August 1, 1911, William George Papers, NLW.

12. David Lloyd George to Margaret Lloyd George, May 27–28, June 3, August 6, 11, 19, 21, 1897, Lloyd George Papers, NLW, in Morgan, ed., *Family Letters*, 110–12; Colin Cross, ed., *Life with Lloyd George: The Diary of A. J. Sylvester, 1931–45* (New York: Barnes & Noble, 1975), 169; E. T. Raymond [pseud.], *Mr. Lloyd George* (New York: George H. Doran Company, 1922), 26, 235; John Grigg, *The Young Lloyd George* (Berkeley: University of California Press, 1973), 34; Sykes, *Conviction Politics*, 70–71, 99, 111; W. C. R. Hancock, "No Compromise: Nonconformity and Politics, 1893–1914," *The Baptist Quarterly* 36 (April 1995): 59–60.

13. A. J. Sylvester, *The Real Lloyd George* (London: Cassell and Company, 1947), 5.

Chapter 1

1. Bentley Brinkerhoff Gilbert, *David Lloyd George: A Political Life: The Architect of Change, 1863–1912* (Columbus: Ohio State University Press, 1987), 36; Don M. Cregier, *Bounder from Wales: Lloyd George's Career before the First World War* (Columbia: University of Missouri Press, 1976), 13.

2. T. Witton Davies, "The McLeanist (Scotch) and Campbellite Baptists of Wales," *Transactions of the Baptist Historical Society* 7, nos. 3,4 (1921): 166, 176; George, *My Brother*, 3–5, 21; Alexander Campbell, *The Christian System* (Pittsburgh, PA: Forrester and Campbell, 1839; reprint ed., Nashville, TN: Gospel Advocate Company, 1974), xiii; Gilbert, *Architect*, 22; David M. Thompson, "Churches of Christ in the British Isles," *The Journal of the United Reformed Church History Society* 1 (May 1973): 27; C. Melling, ed., "Churches of Christ in Former Years," *The Scripture Standard* 33 (January 1966): 7–8.

3. David M. Thompson, ed., *Nonconformity in the Nineteenth Century* (London: Routledge & Kegan Paul, 1972), 7; David M. Thompson, *Let Sects and Parties Fall* (Birmingham, UK: Berean Press, 1980), 32; Gaw, "United Kingdom," 34–35; quoted in James B. North, *Union in Truth: An Interpretive History of the Restoration Movement* (Eugene, Oregon: Wipf & Stock, 2019), 89, 161, 164–65; Romans 16:16, Matthew 16:18, Ephesians 1:22, KJV.

4. North, *Union in Truth*, 162, 323; James L. Gorman, *Among the Early Evangelicals: The Transatlantic Origins of the Stone-Campbell Movement* (Abilene, TX: Abilene Christian University Press, 2016), 13–23; Cregier, *Bounder*, 4; T. M. Bassett, *The Welsh Baptists* (Swansea: Ilston House, 1977), 69, 73–77.

5. Joshua Thomas, *A List of the Particular Baptist Churches in the Principality of Wales* (London: n.p., 1795), 17–24, 177–81; Bassett, *Welsh Baptists*, 27, 120–21, 284; J. Hugh Edwards, *The Life of David Lloyd George: With a Short History of the Welsh People*, 4 vols. (London: The Waverley Book Company, Limited, 1913–1918), 2:57–62; S. S. Lappin, "Passing of David Lloyd George," *Christian Standard*, April 7, 1945, 6; Diaries, August 13, 1882, William George Papers, NLW.

6. Quoted in Davies, "McLeanist," 155, 163–64, 166.

7. William Braidwood to John Jones, September 12, 1796, in Gilbert Y. Tickle, ed., "The Origin and Progress of the Churches in North Wales. No. II," *The Christian Advocate* 3.s., no. 3 (October 1881): 431–33.

8. Archibald McLean to J. R. Jones, December 12, 1796, in Gilbert Y. Tickle, ed., "The Origin and Progress of the Churches in North Wales. No. III," *The Christian Advocate* 3.s., no. 4 (February 1882): 58–62.

9. Davies, "McLeanist," 155–58, 165–66; Thompson, *Sects and Parties*, 18; Archibald McLean to J. R. Jones, October 1803, in Gilbert Y. Tickle, ed., "The Origin and Progress of the Churches in North Wales. No. VI," *The Christian Advocate* 3.s., no. 4 (May 1882): 195–99; Archibald McLean to J. R. Jones, October 1805, in Gilbert Y. Tickle, ed., "The Origin and Progress of the Churches in North Wales. No. VII," *The Christian Advocate* 3.s., no. 4 (June 1882): 239–41; Edwards, *David Lloyd George*, 2:60–62.

10. Davies, "McLeanist," 170–72; Douglas A. Foster, *A Life of Alexander Campbell* (Grand Rapids, MI: William B. Eerdmans Publishing Company, 2020), 69.

11. B. A. Abbott, ed., "Z. T. Sweeney and Lloyd George," *The Christian-Evangelist*, 1 November 1923, 1392–93.

12. Alfred T. Davies, *The Lloyd George I Knew* (London: Henry E. Walter, 1948), 66; Hans Rollmann, "Lloyd George and Immersion," *Stone-Campbell Archives*, Abilene Christian University, June 11, 1999.

13. Lappin, "Passing," 6; Thompson, *Sects and Parties*, 89–94, 115–16, 203; Watters, *British Churches*, 90–92, 94–96; David King, ed., "Church Intelligence, etc.," *The Bible Advocate* 2 (May 1891): 138; David Lloyd George to William George, June 25, 1898, William George Papers, NLW; Thos. J. Ainsworth, *Sydney Black: Preacher and Social Reformer* (London: Book & Tract Depot, 1911), 82–134; W. M. Jacob, *Religious Vitality in Victorian London* (Oxford: Oxford University Press, 2021), 165–66; Thomas J. Ainsworth, "Letters to Editor," *The Bible Advocate* 24 (May 1913): 317.

14. John R. Jones to Archibald McLean, February 5, 1806, in T. Witton Davies, "John Richard Jones," *The Baptist Quarterly* 1 (April 1922): 88–94.

15. William Braidwood to J. R. Jones, December 21, 1812, in Gilbert Y. Tickle, ed., "The Origin and Progress of the Churches in North Wales. No. IX.," *The Christian Advocate* 3.s., no. 4 (August 1882): 329–30; William Braidwood to J. R. Jones, August 7, 1818, in Gilbert Y. Tickle, ed., "The Origin and Progress of the Churches in North Wales. No. X.," *The Christian Advocate* 3.s., no. 4 (September 1882): 371–77.

16. Lynn McMillon, *Restoration Roots: The Scottish Origins of the American Restoration Movement* (Henderson, TN: Hester Publications, 1983), 81–82; Gorman, *Among*, 117–18; Louis Billington, "The Churches of Christ in Britain: A Study in Nineteenth-Century Sectarianism," *The Journal of Religious History* 8 (June 1974): 22–23; M. M. Davis, *The Restoration Movement of the Nineteenth Century* (Cincinnati, OH: The Standard Publishing Company, 1913), 55–56; Robert Richardson, *Memoirs of Alexander Campbell*, 2 vols. (Indianapolis, IN: Religious Book Service, 1897–98), 1:179–81; Walter Wilson Jennings, *Origin and Early History of the Disciples of Christ* (Cincinnati, OH: The Standard Publishing Company, 1919), 96.

17. McMillon, *Roots*, 85; William Braidwood to J. R. Jones, February 22, October 31, 1808, in Gilbert Y. Tickle, ed., "The Origin and Progress of the Churches in North Wales. No. VIII.," *The Christian Advocate* 3.s., no. 4 (July 1882): 281–85; D. B. Murray, "The Scotch Baptist Tradition in Great Britain," *The Baptist Quarterly* 33 (October 1989): 189–90; John Owston, "The Scotch Baptist Influence on the Disciples of Christ," *Leaven* 5 (Winter 1997): 40–42.

18. Gorman, *Among*, 142, 147; Jennings, *Origin*, 97; Richardson, *Memoirs*, 1:47, 59–60, 64–66, 71, 82, 186–87.

19. Robert Frederick West, *Alexander Campbell and Natural Religion*, Yale Studies in Religious Education, vol. 21 (New Haven, CT: Yale University Press, 1948), 225; Foster, *Campbell*, 36–37.

20. West, *Natural*, 225; Foster, *Campbell*, 37–38; Lester G. McAllister, *Alexander Campbell at Glasgow University, 1808–1809* (Nashville, TN: Disciples of Christ Historical Society, 1971), 4; B. B. Tyler, *History of the Disciples of Christ*

(New York: The Christian Literature Co., 1894), 41–43; Richardson, *Memoirs*,
1:148–49; Alexander Haldane, *Memoirs of the Lives of Robert Haldane of Airthrey, and of His Brother, James Alexander Haldane* (New York: Robert Carter &
Brothers, 1853), 322.

21. Sydney E. Ahlstrom, *A Religious History of the American People* (New Haven,
CT: Yale University Press, 1972), 447.

22. Richardson, *Memoirs*, 1:189–90; Eva Jean Wrather, *Alexander Campbell:
Adventurer in Freedom: A Literary Biography*, 3 vols., ed. D. Duane Cummins
(Fort Worth, TX: TCU Press and the Disciples of Christ Historical Society,
2005), 1:91; Foster, *Campbell*, 40–42.

23. Alexander Campbell, ed., "Preface," *The Christian Baptist* 7 (August 1829; repr.,
Nashville, TN: Gospel Advocate Company, 1956): 4, 6; George, *Making*, 17, 27.

24. Alexander Campbell, ed., "Reply," *The Christian Baptist* 3 (April 1826; repr.,
Nashville, TN: Gospel Advocate Company, 1955): 182–84; quoted in Z. T.
Sweeney, "Sweeney Visits Criccieth," *The Christian-Evangelist*, July 24, 1913,
997; Earl West, "Strange Twists in One Life," *Gospel Advocate*, April 17, 1986,
238, 242.

25. B. A. Abbott, ed., "Hon. Loyd [*sic*] George in St. Louis," *The Christian-
Evangelist*, October 25, 1923, 1354, 1383.

26. David King, ed., "The Editor of the 'British Harbinger' to the Disciples of
Christ in America," *The British Harbinger* 5.s., no. 21 (October 1868): 336–39;
Richardson, *Memoirs*, 1:21–22, 2:180–81; Gilbert Y. Tickle, ed., "The Origin and
Progress of the Churches in North Wales. No. XI.," *The Christian Advocate* 3.s.,
no. 4 (October 1882): 427, 431.

27. J. R. Jones to John Roberts, January 17, 1806, in Owen M. Edwards, ed., "Two
Letters," *Wales* 3 (June 1896): 274–75; Davies, "McLeanist," 163, 178.

28. Tickle, ed., "Origin and Progress, No. XI.," 431; Bassett, *Welsh Baptists*, 225–28,
231; T. R. Roberts, *Eminent Welshmen*, vol. 1 (Cardiff: The Educational Publishing Company, 1908), 88–89, 571; John Thomas Jones, "Ellis, Robert," *The
Dictionary of Welsh Biography*, 1959, NLW; Thompson, *Sects and Parties*,
24–25.

29. Bassett, *Welsh Baptists*, 149, 225; Campbell, *System*, 2–3; Watters, *British
Churches*, 28; Thompson, *Sects and Parties*, 21.

30. Watters, *British Churches*, 29–32, 80–82, 121–23; George, *Making*, 26–27;
quoted in Lappin, "Passing," 6.

31. Thompson, *Sects and Parties*, 19–25; Foster, *Campbell*, 57–60; George M.
Marsden, *Fundamentalism and American Culture* (Oxford: Oxford University
Press, 1980), 49–50, 146.

32. Quoted in Sylvester, *Real*, 237–38; Michael W. Casey and Douglas A. Foster,
eds., *The Stone-Campbell Movement: An International Religious Tradition*
(Knoxville: The University of Tennessee Press, 2002), 18–21, 36; Marsden,
Fundamentalism, 49; J. Hugh Edwards, "The Story of a Great Life," *Christian
Standard*, March 9, 1912, 4.

33. George, *Making*, 26–27; Edwards, *David Lloyd George*, 2:62–63; Tickle, ed., "Origin and Progress, No. XI.," 427–31.

34. William Jones, "Tremadoc," *The Christian Messenger and Family Magazine* 1 (June 1845): 95–99.

35. George, *My Brother*, 21; George, *Making*, 27; James Wallis, ed., "Report of General Meeting," *The British Millennial Harbinger* 3.s., no. 11 (September 1858): 457; Edwards, *David Lloyd George*, 2:69.

36. Diaries, January 20, February 16, November 5, 1886, William George Papers, NLW; William George, "Baptists in Wales," *The Christian Advocate*, April 21, 1945, 122.

37. Thompson, "Churches of Christ," 23–25; John Frost, "Meeting of Messengers," *The Christian Messenger and Reformer* 6 (October 1842): 279–84; S. Mottershaw, *A History of the Church of Christ Meeting in Long Hedge Lane, Nottingham* (Nottingham: "Daily Express" Company, Limited, 1886), 14–15.

38. Quoted in Peter Stephen, "Co-operation Meeting at Chester," *The Christian Messenger and Family Magazine* 3 (November 1847): 494–500; George, *Making*, 26–27; McMillon, *Roots*, 93; Robert Morgan, "Welsh Baptists," *The Millennial Harbinger and Voluntary Church Advocate* 2 (May 1836): 325–26; James Wallis, ed., "Report of the General Meeting," *The British Millennial Harbinger* 3.s., no. 6 (September 1853): 221; William Jones, "Portmadoc," *The British Millennial Harbinger* 3.s., no. 12 (September 1859): 468; Cregier, *Bounder*, 4.

39. Diaries, January 24, 1880; May 8, October 10, 1881; April 30, September 5, 1882, William George Papers, NLW; George, *Making*, 119–21; quoted in David King, ed., "Intelligence of Churches," *The Ecclesiastical Observer* 6.s., no. 36 (June 1883): 152; Thomas Armitage, *A History of the Baptists*, Rev. ed. (New York: Bryan, Taylor, & Co., 1890), 607–08.

40. David King, ed., "Annual General Meeting," *The British Harbinger* 5.s., no. 19 (September 1866): 320; Richardson, *Memoirs*, 1:189–90; Wrather, *Adventurer*, 1:88–91; Foster, *Campbell*, 41–42.

41. David King, ed., "Annual General Meeting," *The British Harbinger* 5.s., no. 20 (September 1867): 313, 325–26; Watters, *British Churches*, 51–52, 55, 74–76, 78; J. George Rotherham, comp., *Reminiscences* (Cincinnati, OH: The Standard Publishing Company, 1922), 9, 32–34; Alan Betteridge, *Deep Roots, Living Branches: A History of Baptists in the English Western Midlands* (Leicester, UK: Matador, 2010): 264–66; David King, ed., "Intelligence of Churches," *The Ecclesiastical Observer* 6.s., no. 39 (June 1886): 94; Wallis, ed., "General Meeting" (September 1858): 465.

42. Diaries, July 24–25, December 10, 1878, June 12, 19, 1881, June 7, 14, 18, 21, 25–26, 1882, July 18, 1883, June 1, July 1, 1884, William George Papers, NLW.

43. Diaries, August 7, 1878, April 22, 1883, William George Papers, NLW; David Lloyd George to William George, June 25, 1898, William George Papers, NLW; Thompson, *Sects and Parties*, 203; D. R. Daniel Memoir, vol. 2, 137, D. R. Daniel Collection 2913, NLW; Gilbert, *Architect*, 57.

44. Diaries, December 16, 1883, May 30, 1886, William George Papers, NLW; George, *My Brother*, 78; *South Wales Daily News*, October 19, 1909, Lloyd George Papers, C/33/2, Historical Collection 192, HLRO.

45. Quoted in A. J. Sylvester Diary, September 12, 1935, A. J. Sylvester Papers, NLW; "Mr. Lloyd George's Foster Father," *The Liverpool Daily Post and Mercury*, October 20, 1911, in Daniel Memoir, vol. 1, D. R. Daniel Collection 2912, NLW.

46. Frank Dilnot, *Lloyd George: The Man and His Story* (New York: Harper & Brothers Publishers, 1917), 27.

47. Gilbert, *Architect*, 37–38, 43; Diaries, July 12, 1878, December 1, 4, 1880, May 12, 14, 1882, William George Papers, NLW; Davies, "McLeanist," 176–77.

48. Diaries, September 22, 1881, May 27, 1882, William George Papers, NLW; quoted in Sylvester Diary, February 12, 1931, A. J. Sylvester Papers, NLW; W. R. P. George, *Lloyd George: Backbencher* (Llandysul, UK: Gomer Press, 1983), 22–30, 51–55, 353–62.

49. *The Birkenhead News*, February 6, 1892, Lloyd George Papers, A/7/1, HLRO; *The Brecon and Radnor Express*, September 30, 1898, Lloyd George Papers, A/8/4, HLRO; David Lloyd George to William George, February 21, April 21, 1901, William George Papers, NLW.

50. David Lloyd George to William George, May 6, 1908, September 11, 1910, December 17, 1912, March 4, 1914, November 18, 1916, William George Papers, NLW; Michael Llewellyn Smith, "Venizelos' Diplomacy, 1910–23: From Balkan Alliance to Greek-Turkish Settlement," in Paschalis Kitromilides, ed., *Eleftherios Venizelos: The Trials of Statesmanship* (Edinburgh: Edinburgh University Press, 2006), 134, 148; Stevenson Diary, November 22, 1915, Frances Stevenson Papers, HLRO; Taylor, ed., *Diary*, 76; Gilbert, *Architect*, 271.

51. "North Wales Calvinistic Methodists," *Carnarvon and Denbigh Herald*, August 28, 1903, 8, Lloyd George Papers, A/11/2, HLRO.

52. *British Weekly*, April 16, 1908, in Daniel Memoir, vol. 2, NLW; "The Modern Neglect of Religion," *Manchester Guardian*, September 24, 1908, in Daniel Memoir, vol. 1, NLW; quoted in *South Wales Daily News*, October 19, 1909, Lloyd George Papers, C/33/2, HLRO.

53. "The World Getting Better," *South Wales Daily News*, June 26, 1911, Lloyd George Papers, C/35/1, HLRO.

54. Diaries, August 19, 22, 1882, William George Papers, NLW; *South Wales Daily News*, December 30, 1911, Lloyd George Papers, C/35/1, HLRO; Kenneth O. Morgan, *David Lloyd George: Welsh Radical as World Statesman* (Cardiff: University of Wales Press, 1963), 6.

55. Quoted in Sylvester, *Real*, 4–5; Ignatius Jones, "Forty Unbroken Years," *The Christian-Evangelist*, July 10, 1930, 912; James F. Sennett, "Providence," in *The Encyclopedia of the Stone-Campbell Movement*, ed. Douglas A. Foster, et al. (Grand Rapids, MI: William B. Eerdmans Publishing Company, 2004), 613–14; Kenneth O. Morgan, *Lloyd George* (London: Weidenfeld and Nicolson, 1974), 206.

56. Crosby, *Unknown*, 23–25; William Abraham, interview in *Y Cymro* (The Welshman), January 5, 1921, John Herbert Lewis Papers, D30/121, NLW.

Chapter 2

1. Quoted in Martin Gilbert, ed., *Lloyd George* (Englewood Cliffs, NJ: Prentice-Hall, 1968), 128–31.
2. George, *Making*, 16–17, 26–29, 62–66, 70–71, 78–80, 84–86, 96–98, 116, 149–51; Edwards, *David Lloyd George*, 2:6; Tickle, ed., "Origin and Progress, No. XI.," 425–32; D. W. Bebbington, "Baptist M.P.s in the Nineteenth Century," *The Baptist Quarterly* 29 (January 1981): 11; George, *My Brother*, 20–21.
3. George, *My Brother*, 39–44; Edwards, *David Lloyd George*, 2:8, 10–16, 18–21; George, *Making*, 72–76.
4. George, *My Brother*, 74–75, 272; Gilbert, *Architect*, 36.
5. Frank Owen, *Tempestuous Journey: Lloyd George, His Life and Times* (London: Hutchinson, 1954), 30–31; Morgan, *Lloyd George*, 22, 32; Rowland, *Lloyd*, 13–14; Cregier, *Bounder*, 13; Martin Pugh, *Lloyd George* (London: Longman, 1988), 2–8; Stephen Constantine, *Lloyd George* (London: Routledge, 1992), 13–16; Hugh Purcell, *Lloyd George* (London: Haus Publishing Limited, 2006), 11–13; Roy Hattersley, *David Lloyd George: The Great Outsider* (London: Little, Brown, 2010), 12–13, 23.
6. George Allardice Riddell, *Lord Riddell's Intimate Diary of the Paris Peace Conference and After, 1918–23* (London: Victor Gollancz, 1934), 123; J. M. McEwen, ed., *The Riddell Diaries, 1908–1923* (London: The Athlone Press, 1986), 12.
7. Grigg, *Young Lloyd*, 33–35; letter to author from John Grigg, dated July 31, 1996.
8. Gilbert, *Architect*, 57; letter to author from Prys Morgan, dated April 18, 1995; Owen, *Tempestuous*, 31; D. Hugh Matthews, *Castle Street Meeting House-A History* (Swansea: John Penry Press, 1989), 29–31.
9. Translation of D. R. Daniel Memoir, vol. 1, 8–10, D. R. Daniel Collection 2912, NLW, graciously included in April 18, 1995, letter to author from Prys Morgan.
10. Lucy Masterman Diary, TS, August 1911, 14, 18, Charles F. G. and Lucy Masterman Papers, University of Birmingham Library, Birmingham; Lucy Masterman, *C. F. G. Masterman: A Biography* (London: Nicholson and Watson, Limited, 1939), 209; Lucy Masterman, "Recollections of David Lloyd George, Part II," *History Today* 9 (April 1959): 274, 277.
11. Quoted in George, *Making*, 108–10.
12. Masterman, "Recollections," 278; George, *My Brother*, 217–18; John W. Derry, *The Radical Tradition: Tom Paine to Lloyd George* (London: Macmillan, 1967), 376; Gilbert, *Architect*, 36.
13. Stevenson Diary, September 28, 1914, February 14, 1915, Frances Stevenson Papers, HLRO; Taylor, ed., *Diary*, 3–4, 31–32.

14. Stevenson Diary, November 22, 1915, Frances Stevenson Papers, HLRO; Taylor, ed., *Diary*, 75–78.

15. Frances Lloyd George, *The Years that are Past* (London: Hutchinson, 1967), 19; Robert Winnett, "David Lloyd George: the Religious Factor," *The Epworth Review* 14 (September 1987): 83; quoted in Sylvester, *Real*, 165–66; George, *My Brother*, 79; Daniel Lleufer Thomas, "Evans, Evan Herber," in *Dictionary of National Biography, Supplement*, ed. Sidney Lee (London: Smith, Elder & Co., 1901), 619–20.

16. Quoted in Du Parcq, *Life*, 1:45, 20–21; Thompson, *Sects and Parties*, 102–05; Watters, *British Churches*, 104–07; Alexander Campbell, ed., "Catechisms," *The Millennial Harbinger* 1 (January 1830): 31–35; Alexander Campbell, ed., "Creeds," *The Millennial Harbinger Extra* 3 (August 1832): 344–47, 598–604; Campbell, *System*, vii–x, 84–89, 196–97; Alexander Campbell, ed., "Sermon on the Law," *The Millennial Harbinger* 3.s., no. 3 (September 1846): 493–521.

17. George, *Making*, 72–76; quoted in Edwards, *David Lloyd George*, 2:17–18.

18. Richard Lloyd George, *Lloyd George*, 20, 22.

19. Sylvester, *Real*, 237, 284–86; Sylvester Diary, January 15, October 23, 1936, A. J. Sylvester Papers, NLW; Cross, ed., *Sylvester*, 77, 129; Frances Lloyd George, *Years*, 19; Winnett, "Factor," 89; quoted in Basil Holt, "David Lloyd George Was a Disciple!", *The Christian-Evangelist*, May 11, 1949, 460.

20. Edwards, *David Lloyd George*, 2:24; Du Parcq, *Life*, 1:21; Owen, *Tempestuous*, 19; "Seiat," in *A Dictionary of the Welsh Language*, ed. Gareth A. Bevan and Patrick J. Donovan, 4 vols., University of Wales Centre for Advanced Welsh and Celtic Studies (Aberystwyth: NLW, 2002), 4:3207; telephone conversation with W. R. P. George on January 18, 1996, in which he told the author that seiats were on Thursday nights.

21. Lancelot Oliver, ed., "Church Intelligence, etc.," *The Bible Advocate*, February 7, 1896, 70–72; Lancelot Oliver, ed., "The Temperance Conference," *The Bible Advocate*, August 26, 1898, 535–36; Bartley Ellis, "A Visit to Criccieth," *The Bible Advocate*, October 27, 1911, 678–79.

22. Grigg, *Young Lloyd*, 27; George, *Making*, 24; Diaries, March 24, 1882, William George Papers, NLW.

23. Sylvester Diary, July 30, 1936, A. J. Sylvester Papers, NLW; Cross, ed., *Sylvester*, 143–44; George, *Backbencher*, 416, 457n.4; George, *My Brother*, 293.

24. Quoted in Donald McCormick, *The Mask of Merlin* (London: Macdonald, 1963), 300–01; Rowland, *Lloyd*, 803; Winnett, "Factor," 89; Diaries, January 24, 1880, May 8, 1881, William George Papers, NLW; George, *Making*, 78–79.

25. Diaries, May 8, 1881, March 2, 1884, William George Papers, NLW; George, *Making*, 110.

26. Diaries, October 12, 1884, William George Papers, NLW; George, *Making*, 110; David Lloyd George to Margaret Lloyd George, August 13, 1890, Lloyd George Papers, NLW, in Morgan, ed., *Family Letters*, 35; Sylvester, *Real*, 294–97, 310.

27. Jones, "Portmadoc," 468; Diaries, October 10, 1881, April 30, September 5, 1882, William George Papers, NLW.

28. Diaries, January 24, 1886, January 8, 1888, William George Papers, NLW; David Lloyd George to Margaret Owen, Undated Letter 65, March 27, 1887, Lloyd George Papers, NLW.

29. Diaries, December 16, 1883, July 13, August 26, 1884, William George Papers, NLW; George, *My Brother*, 78–79; George, *Making*, 87; obituary of John Page Hopps, *The Christian Register*, April 27, 1911, 471; Ronald Bayne, "Farrar, Frederic William," in *Dictionary of National Biography, Supplement, 1901–1911, vol.2*, ed. Sidney Lee (London: Smith, Elder & Co., 1912), 9–12.

30. Diaries, May 30, July 25, September 4–5, 26, November 20, 1886, William George Papers, NLW; obituary of Robert Davies Evans, *The British Medical Journal*, August 16, 1924, 301; George, *Making*, 125, 129–30; Edwards, *David Lloyd George*, 2:26.

31. Diaries, November 12–13, 1881, August 13, 1882, William George Papers, NLW; Lloyd George Diaries, August 28, 1887, Lloyd George Papers, NLW.

32. Diaries, November 17, 1880, April 17, 1881, William George Papers, NLW.

33. Diaries, August 13, 1878, December 12, 1880, February 5, May 1, September 4, 21, 1881, May 14, 1882, William George Papers, NLW; Gilbert, *Architect*, 37–38, 43; Owen, *Tempestuous*, 21–22.

34. David Lloyd George to Margaret Owen, November 7, 1886, Lloyd George Papers, NLW; Diaries, October 4, 1880, August 31, 1884, William George Papers, NLW.

35. Diaries, January 3, 1884, William George Papers, NLW; George, *My Brother*, 78; Hugh Chisholm, ed., "Harrison, Frederic," *The Encyclopaedia Britannica*, 11th ed., vol. 13 (New York: The Encyclopaedia Britannica Company, 1910), 23; James McMullen Rigg, "Congreve, Richard," in *Dictionary of National Biography, Supplement*, ed. Sidney Lee (London: Smith, Elder & Co., 1901), 476–77.

36. Diaries, February 27, May 12–14, 1882, William George Papers, NLW; quoted in George, *Making*, 106–08.

37. Diaries, September 14, October 12, November 2, 1881, January 24, March 7, May 13, June 6, November 21, 1883, July 2, 1884, William George Papers, NLW; quoted in Du Parcq, *Life*, 1:45.

38. Diaries, November 1, 5, 16, 19, 1880, February 15–16, 18, 20, 23, 1881, William George Papers, NLW; David Lloyd George [A Welsh Brother], "An Appeal to the Churches of Christ in Wales," *The Christian Advocate* 3.s., no. 4 (October 1882): 463, 465; *The Christian Advocate*, January 26, 1945, 32; B. A. Abbott, ed., "Hon. Loyd [*sic*] George in St. Louis," *The Christian-Evangelist*, October 25, 1923, 1354, 1383.

39. David Lloyd George, "An Appeal," 463, 467; Diaries, September 1–2, October 28–29, 1882, William George Papers, NLW; Alexander Campbell, ed., "Letter to William Jones," *The Millennial Harbinger* 5 (December 1834): 586.

40. Diaries, June 10, 1884, August 25, 1886, William George Papers, NLW; David Lloyd George to Margaret Owen, August 28, 1886, Lloyd George Papers, NLW, in Morgan, ed., *Family Letters*, 16, n.1; George, *Making*, 136, 140; J. Graham Jones, "David and Maggie," *Journal of Liberal History* 63 (Summer 2009): 24–25.

41. David Lloyd George to Margaret Owen, September 25, 1886, Lloyd George Papers, NLW, in Morgan, ed., *Family Letters*, 16; David Lloyd George to Richard Lloyd, January 4, 1907, William George Papers, NLW; George, *Making*, 137, 147–48; Olwen Carey Evans, *My Father*, 6, 10–11, 17; David Williams, "Church News," *The Bible Advocate*, October 7, 1910, 637–38.

42. Diaries, August 31, September 1, 5, 1882, William George Papers, NLW; David Lloyd George, "An Appeal," 465; George, *My Brother*, 76; James Wallis, ed., "Criccieth," *The British Millennial Harbinger* 3.s., no. 11 (September 1858): 465; Jones, "Portmadoc," 468.

43. Diaries, October 28–31, 1882, February 25, 1883, William George Papers, NLW.

44. Thompson, *Sects and Parties*, 86, 118–19, 202–03; Watters, *British Churches*, 51, 81–82; Diaries, May 29, 1881, William George Papers, NLW; Gilbert Y. Tickle, ed., "The Editor in North Wales," *The Christian Advocate* 3.s., no. 3 (June 1881): 265–67.

45. Masterman Diary, 14, Charles F. G. and Lucy Masterman Papers, University of Birmingham Library; Masterman, *Masterman*, 209; Masterman, "Recollections," 277; Thomas Carlyle, *Sartor Resartus*, 2nd ed. (Boston: James Munroe and Company, 1837), 201, 221; Diaries, October 31, 1880, William George Papers, NLW.

46. Diaries, July 17, 1881, August 26, 1883, April 30, 1884, William George Papers, NLW; David W. Bebbington, *The Dominance of Evangelicalism: The Age of Spurgeon and Moody* (Downers Grove, IL: InterVarsity Press, 2005), 40–42.

47. Stevenson Diary, November 22, 1915, Frances Stevenson Papers, HLRO; Taylor, ed., *Diary*, 77–78; Diaries, February 23, 1881, January 18, 1886, William George Papers, NLW; Hugh Chisholm, ed., "Renan, Ernest," *The Encyclopaedia Britannica*, 11th ed., vol. 23 (New York: The Encyclopaedia Britannica Company, 1911), 93–95.

48. William T. Stead, ed., "Mr. Lloyd George: Chieftain of Wales," *The Review of Reviews* 30, no. 178 (October 1904): 372; David Lloyd George to Margaret Lloyd George, April 18, 1912, Lloyd George Papers, NLW, in Morgan, ed., *Family Letters*, 162, n.1.

49. Edward J. Wheeler, ed., "The Fighting Conciliator of the Present British Ministry," *Current Literature* 44, no. 1 (January 1908): 38.

50. Harold Begbie, "Life Story of Lloyd George," *The Otago Witness*, April 5, 1911, 89, National Library of New Zealand; Alexander Campbell, ed., "Abuses of Christianity," *The Christian Baptist* 1 (November 1823; repr., Nashville, TN: Gospel Advocate Company, 1955): 96–104; Bebbington, *Dominance*, 21, 62; Cregier, *Bounder*, 13.

51. George, *Backbencher*, 138 and 177n.2; quoted in Thomas Jones, *Lloyd George* (Cambridge, MA: Harvard University Press, 1951), 8–9.

52. Stevenson Diary, November 22, 1915, Frances Stevenson Papers, HLRO; Taylor, ed., *Diary*, 78; Daniel Memoir, vol. 2, 137–38, NLW.

53. Diaries, August 28, September 4, November 6, 1887, Lloyd George Papers, NLW; Matthews, *Castle Street*, 27, 29, 31; David Lloyd George to William George, October 4, 1906, William George Papers, NLW.

54. Diaries, September 26, October 1, 1886, William George Papers, NLW.

55. William George, "Churches of Christ," *The Bible Advocate*, October 20, 1911, 657–58.

56. David Lloyd George to Margaret Owen, July 29, December 8, 1886, Lloyd George Papers, NLW; Morgan, ed., *Family Letters*, 15, 17; Diaries, November 23, 25, William George Papers, NLW.

57. Richard Lloyd George, *Dame Margaret: The Life Story of His Mother* (London: George Allen & Unwin, 1947), 26, 40–41, 72–73; David Lloyd George to Margaret Owen, October 13, December 11, 1886, July 17, 1877, Lloyd George Papers, NLW; Diaries, September 27, October 1, November 13, 15, December 10, 1886, William George Papers, NLW; Jones, "David and Maggie," 25–26.

58. Diaries, October 1, 1886, William George Papers, NLW.

59. George, *My Brother*, 98; General Assembly, *The History, Constitution, Rules of Discipline, and Confession of Faith of the Calvinistic Methodists in Wales* (Salford, UK: John Roberts, 1877), 66–67; Diaries, February 12, 1888, William George Papers, NLW.

60. Diaries, February, 15, November 7, 13, 1886, William George Papers, NLW; George, *Making*, 139; David Lloyd George to Margaret Owen, Undated Letter 64, Lloyd George Papers, NLW; Morgan, ed., *Family Letters*, 18–19.

61. David Lloyd George to Margaret Owen, Undated Letter 61, Lloyd George Papers, NLW; Diaries, June 17, 1880, William George Papers, NLW; George, *Making*, 144–45; Jones, "David and Maggie," 26.

62. Taylor, ed., *My Darling*, 1–2; John Straiton, "The Hon. David Lloyd-George," *Gospel Advocate* 80 (October 1938): 941; John Straiton, "Lloyd George's Religious Position," *Christian Leader* 32 (November 1918): 16; Leslie W. Morgan, "Organizing Victory," *The Christian-Evangelist*, August 5, 1915, 999.

63. T. B. Larimore, "The Lindbergh Religion," *Gospel Advocate*, December 22, 1927, 1210; B. C. Goodpasture, ed., "Passing of David Lloyd George," *Gospel Advocate*, April 12, 1945, 202; Stevenson Diary, February 9, 1917, Frances Stevenson Papers, HLRO; Taylor, ed., *Diary*, 12, n.2, 142–43; Malcolm Thomson, *David Lloyd George: The Official Biography*, with an introduction by Frances Lloyd George (London: Hutchinson & Co., 1948), 56.

64. Jones, *Lloyd George*, 276; Morgan, ed., *Family Letters*, 7; Pugh, *Lloyd George*, 5, 19; Frederick D. Kershner, ed., "Secret of Lloyd George's Greatness," *The Christian-Evangelist*, September 23, 1915, 1204.

65. Grigg, *Young Lloyd*, 34; John Grigg, "Lloyd George," *New Statesman*, October 16, 1981, insert.; telephone conversation between author and John Grigg on September 11, 1995; Gilbert, *Architect*, 36–37.

Chapter 3

1. Diaries, July 29, August 30, 1878, February 8, August 26, November 6, 1880, William George Papers, NLW; George, *My Brother*, 24–25; Grigg, *Young Lloyd*, 37.

2. Diaries, November 29, December 1, 1880, February 19, April 18, July 25, August 9, 28, September 13, December 27, 1881, February 5, 1882, William George Papers, NLW.

3. Diaries, May 24, June 11, 1881, March 27–28, June 8, September 29, November 21, 1882, William George Papers, NLW; George, *Making*, 104–05; Gilbert, *Architect*, 43; Thomson, *Official*, 63; P. T. Winskill, *The Temperance Movement and its Workers*, vol. 1 (London: Blackie & Sons, Limited, 1891), vi, 210.

4. W. R. Lambert, "The Welsh Sunday Closing Act, 1881," *The Welsh History Review* 6 (1972–73): 161, 163, 174; John Davies, *A History of Wales* (London: Allen Lane The Penguin Press, 1993), 446–47; Gilbert Y. Tickle, ed., "Sunday Closing in Wales," *The Christian Advocate* 3.s., no. 3 (June 1881): 258; Diaries, August 26, 1881, February 5, March 18, 20, 28, 1882, William George Papers, NLW.

5. Diaries, May 13–14, June 25–27, August 6, 12, 1882, William George Papers, NLW; George, *Making*, 104.

6. Diaries August, 17, 25, November, 27, 30, December, 1, 2, 16, 19, 23, 1882, William George Papers, NLW.

7. George, *Making*, 111–12; Davies, *History*, 421–27.

8. Diaries, March 1, September 28, October 4, 1883, June 15, 1884, William George Papers, NLW.

9. Diaries, October 5–6, 1883, William George Papers, NLW; Du Parcq, *Life*, 1:17; Grigg, *Young Lloyd*, 35–36; Gilbert, *Architect*, 41; George, *Making*, 72–77.

10. Diaries, June, 4, 7–8, 21, 23, 28, July 3, 12, 23, 27, 30, August 3, 7, 10, 17, 30–31, September 1, 3, 1884, William George Papers, NLW.

11. Diaries, September, 2, 6, November 14, 18, 21, 28, 1884, William George Papers, NLW; "Criccieth," *The North Wales Express*, September 12, 1884, 6; George, *Making*, 137, 147–48.

12. Quoted in Du Parcq, *Life*, 1:44–45, 47.

13. Diaries, September 21, 1882, June 23, August 30, 1884, William George Papers, NLW; quoted in Du Parcq, *Life*, 1:45; D. W. Bebbington, *The Nonconformist Conscience: Chapel and Politics, 1870–1914* (London: George Allen & Unwin, 1982), 47; McCormick, *Merlin*, 35; Gilbert, *Architect*, 50–51.

14. Quoted in Du Parcq, *Life*, 1:44, 46–47, 50; Grigg, *Young Lloyd*, 40; Diaries,

January 8, February 9, 1886, January 20, 1888, William George Papers, NLW; Diaries, September 19, 1887, Lloyd George Papers, NLW.

15. Diaries, June 1, 1888, William George Papers, NLW; Gilbert, *Architect*, 75, 78–80; Grigg, *Young Lloyd*, 96–98; David Lloyd George to Richard Lloyd, May 16, 1890, William George Papers, NLW.

16. Gilbert, *Architect*, 82, 86; quoted in Grigg, *Young Lloyd*, 99; Lilian Lewis Shiman, *Crusade Against Drink in Victorian England* (New York: St. Martin's Press, 1988), 238; House of Commons Debates (3rd series) June 13, 1890, vol. 345 cc872–74 (hereafter cited as HC Deb).

17. David Lloyd George to William George, January 31, 1891, William George Papers, NLW; HC Deb (3rd series) March 18, 1891, vol. 351 cc 1341–42; G. O. M. stood for Grand Old Man, a title for William Gladstone but applied here, along with Governor, to Richard Lloyd.

18. David Lloyd George to Thomas Edward Ellis, April 11, 1891, Thomas Edward Ellis Papers, NLW; Edwards, *David Lloyd George*, 3:89–90; Grigg, *Young Lloyd*, 122–23; Gilbert, *Architect*, 103–04; quoted in Du Parcq, *Life*, 1:123–25.

19. George, *Backbencher*, 76; Diaries, June 5–9, 12–14, 22–24, 1892, William George Papers, NLW; Gilbert, *Architect*, 98–99, 101–02; *North Wales Observer*, August 19, 1892, Lloyd George Papers, A/7/1, HLRO.

20. Grigg, *Young Lloyd*, 132–34; HC Deb (4th series) March 15, 1893, vol. 10 cc117–22; James Nicholls, *The Politics of Alcohol: A History of the Drink Question in England* (Manchester: Manchester University Press, 2009), 136.

21. Grigg, *Young Lloyd*, 90, 141–50; quoted in Nicholls, *Alcohol*, 130; Du Parcq, *Life* 1:162–63; Gilbert, *Architect*, 111–13, 115.

22. Grigg, *Young Lloyd*, 151–53, 156–58, 166–71; Gilbert, *Architect*, 117–19, 126–28, 134–39, 145–47; Du Parcq, *Life*, 1:165–66.

23. Quoted in Du Parcq, *Life*, 1:125–26; HC Deb (4th series) July 7, 1896, vol. 42 c964; Grigg, *Young Lloyd*, 203–05, 212–13; Gilbert, *Architect*, 151–55, 159; Constantine, *Lloyd*, 18; Ian Packer, *Lloyd George* (Houndmills, UK: Macmillan Press, 1998), 14.

24. Gilbert, *Architect*, 173; David M. Fahey, "The Politics of Drink: Pressure Groups and the British Liberal Party, 1883–1908," *Social Science* 54 (Spring 1979): 79; Shiman, *Crusade*, 224.

25. "What About Local Option?", *The Christian World*, January 27, 1898.

26. Morgan, ed., *Family Letters*, 13; David Lloyd George to William George, February 8, 1898, William George Papers, NLW; *The Brecon and Radnor Express*, September 30, 1898, Lloyd George Papers, A/8/4, HLRO.

27. David Lloyd George to William George, June 25, July 20, 1898, William George Papers, NLW; Henry Townsend, *Robert Wilson Black* (London: The Carey Kingsgate Press Limited, 1954), 19, 22; William Webley, "The Temperance Meeting," *The Bible Advocate*, August 26, 1898, 536–38; Lancelot Oliver, ed., "The Temperance Conference," *The Bible Advocate*, August 26, 1898, 535–36;

Lancelot Oliver, ed., "Letters to the Editor," *The Bible Advocate*, October 28, 1898, 685; Total Abstainer, "The United Kingdom Alliance's Memorial," *The Bible Advocate*, October 28, 1898, 717; Lancelot Oliver, ed., "Death of Bro. Joseph Collin," *The Bible Advocate*, November 30, 1917, 571.

28. Shiman, *Crusade*, 236–38; Nicholls, *Alcohol*, 144; Fahey, *Pressure*, 81.

29. David Lloyd George to William George, June 6, November 22, 1899, William George Papers, NLW; James Ramsay MacDonald, "Wallace, Robert," in *Dictionary of National Biography, Supplement*, ed. Sidney Lee (London: Smith, Elder & Co., 1901), 1376; Nicholls, *Alcohol*, 137–38, 142–43; Fahey, *Pressure*, 81; Shiman, *Crusade*, 107–09, 214, 216, 229–30, 236; G. I. T. Machin, *Politics and the Churches in Great Britain, 1869–1921* (Oxford: Clarendon Press, 1987), 229.

30. David Lloyd George to William George, December 5, 1899, William George Papers, NLW; Gilbert, *Architect*, 140–41; Shiman, *Crusade*, 83, 223, 285; Nicholls, *Alcohol*, 135–36; Davies, *Lloyd George I Knew*, ix, 23–24; David Lloyd George to Margaret Lloyd George, October 21–22, 1890, Lloyd George Papers, NLW, in Morgan, ed., *Family Letters*, 37–38.

31. Gilbert, *Architect*, 187, 195–96, 210–15; Grigg, *Young Lloyd*, 286–88; John Greenaway, *Drink and British Politics since 1830* (Houndmills, UK: Palgrave, 2003), 75–77; Bebbington, *Conscience*, 48; David W. Gutzke, *Pubs and Progressives: Reinventing the Public House in England, 1896–1960* (Dekalb: Northern Illinois University Press, 2006), 30–31, 104–06; Fahey, *Pressure*, 81; David Lloyd George to William George, October 5, 1902, William George Papers, NLW.

32. Gilbert, *Architect*, 241–42, 266–68, 278–79; David Lloyd George to William George, December 31, 1903, April 12, 1904, William George Papers, NLW; Roy Jenkins, *Churchill: A Biography* (New York: Farrar, Straus and Giroux, 2001), 65; Greenaway, *Drink*, 79–81; Nicholls, *Alcohol*, 146–48; Gutzke, *Pubs*, 26.

33. R. J. Q. Adams, *Balfour: The Last Grandee* (London: John Murray, 2007), 177–78; Greenaway, *Drink*, 80; HC Deb (4th series) April 20, 1904, vol. 133 cc744–48; David Lloyd George to William George, April 20, 1904, William George Papers, NLW; Nicholls, *Alcohol*, 142–44; Bartley Ellis, "The Government Licensing Bill," *The Bible Advocate* May 13, 1904, 305–06.

34. Greenaway, *Drink*, 81; David Lloyd George to William George, June 30, July 13, December 12, 1904, William George Papers, NLW; quoted in John Grigg, *Lloyd George: The People's Champion, 1902–1911* (Berkeley: University of California Press, 1978), 71–72.

35. Adams, *Balfour*, 226–27; Grigg, *People's Champion*, 91–92; Gilbert, *Architect*, 263, 282–83; Nicholls, *Alcohol*, 154; David Lloyd George to William George, December 8, 1905, William George Papers, NLW; quoted in Emyr Price, *David Lloyd George* (Cardiff: University of Wales Press, 2006), 186.

36. Quoted in Grigg, *People's Champion*, 153; Graham Neville, *Radical Churchman: Edward Lee Hicks and The New Liberalism* (Oxford: Clarendon Press, 1998), 141; Fahey, *Pressure*, 82.

37. Greenaway, *Drink*, 81; Gilbert, *Architect*, 77, 111, 335; Nicholls, *Alcohol*, 150; David Lloyd George to William George, February 19, March 28, April 2, 1908, William George Papers, NLW; Lancelot Oliver, ed., "Church Intelligence," *The Bible Advocate*, May 8, 1908, 303.

38. Greenaway, *Drink*, 81–83, 89; Fahey, *Pressure*, 82–83; Grigg, *People's Champion*, 172–73; Gilbert, *Architect*, 335–36.

39. David Lloyd George to William George, November 27, 1908, William George Papers, NLW; Adams, *Balfour*, 233–36; quoted in Chas. Bailey, "Richard Lloyd-Shoemaker Disciple," *Christian Standard*, June 26, 1909, 4; Nicholls, *Alcohol*, 151.

40. Grigg, *People's Champion*, 158–62, 170–81, 190–201; Gilbert, *Architect*, 336–43, 368–79; Ian Packer, *Liberal Government and Politics, 1905–15* (Houndmills, UK: Palgrave Macmillan, 2006), 136–37; HC Deb (5th series) April 29, 1909, vol. 4 cc520–23; HC Deb (5th series) May 11, 1909, vol. 4 cc1688, 1692, 1710, 1729, 1735.

41. David Lloyd George to William George, May 24, September 28, 1909, William George Papers, NLW; David Lloyd George to Richard Lloyd, September 3, 1909, William George Papers, NLW; David Williams, "Church Intelligence," *The Bible Advocate*, August 20, 1909, 560; William Webley, "Home Fields," *The Bible Advocate*, April 19, 1912, 246; Thompson, *Sects and Parties*, 115; Grigg, *People's Champion*, 244–56; Gilbert, *Architect*, 404–10.

42. David Lloyd George, *War Memoirs of David Lloyd George, 1914–1915* (Boston: Little, Brown, and Company, 1933), 285–89; David Lloyd George to William George, March 29–31, 1915, William George Papers, NLW; George, *My Brother*, 249–50.

43. David Lloyd George to William George, April 1, 7–8, 30, 1915, William George Papers, NLW; Gilbert, *Organizer*, 151–71; Grigg, *Peace*, 215, 229–36; David Lloyd George to Margaret Lloyd George, April 16, 19, 1915, Lloyd George Papers, NLW, in Morgan, ed., *Family Letters*, 176–77; Stevenson Diary, April 4, 1915, Frances Stevenson Papers, HLRO, in Taylor, ed., *Diary*, 38–41.

44. Quoted in Greenaway, *Drink*, 91–97; Lloyd George, *Memoirs*, 285, 289–90, 296–97; Nicholls, *Alcohol*, 154–55; Grigg, *Peace*, 236–37; Stuart Mews, "Urban Problems and Rural Solutions: Drink and Disestablishment in the First World War," in Derek Baker, ed., *The Church in Town and Countryside* (Oxford: Basil Blackwell, 1979), 455, 467, 471–73; David Lloyd George to Frances Stevenson, April 6–7, 1915, Frances Stevenson Papers, HLRO, in Taylor, ed., *My Darling*, 6–8; McEwen, ed., *Riddell*, 1, 104.

45. David Lloyd George to William George, May 7, 12, 1915, William George Papers, NLW; Grigg, *Peace*, 236–37; Greenaway, *Drink*, 97–107; Gutzke, *Pubs*, 50–51, 54, 65; Nicholls, *Alcohol*, 155–56.

46. John Turner, "State Purchase of the Liquor Trade in the First World War," *The Historical Journal* 23 (September 1980): 607–13; Nicholls, *Alcohol*, 154;

McEwen, ed., *Riddell*, 104; Lloyd George, *Memoirs*, 284–87; quoted in Mews, "Urban," 473–76.

47. Michael Duffy, "Vintage Audio-Lloyd George's Beer," 2000–2009, http://www.firstworldwar.com/audio/lloydgeorgesbeer.htm.

48. David Ritchie, "Whisky allowed in the forward trenches," Email in H-Albion, June 14, 2008; Greenaway, *Drink*, 124–25; Fahey, *Pressure*, 83; Gutzke, *Pubs*, 109; R. J. Q. Adams, *Arms and the Wizard: Lloyd George and the Ministry of Munitions, 1915–1916* (College Station: Texas A & M University Press, 1978), 207; quoted in Nicholls, *Alcohol*, 130, 159; Olwen Carey Evans, *My Father*, 70; Sylvester, *Real*, 4–5, 163, 297; Anna Rothe, "Lloyd George of Dwyfor, David Lloyd George, 1st Earl," *Current Biography* 5 (1944): 419–23.

49. Grigg, *Young Lloyd*, 43, 201–03, 297–98; Gilbert, *Architect*, 142, 167–73, 263–66, 359–60.

Chapter 4

1. Diaries, January 28, November 1, 5, 16, 19, 1880, 4–5, 18 (misdated), February 20, 1881, William George Papers, NLW; Brutus [pseud.], "The Marquis of Salisbury," *The North Wales Express*, November 5, 1880, 4; Brutus [pseud.], "A Contest in Carnarvonshire," *The North Wales Express*, November 19, 1880, 5; Brutus [pseud.], "Irish Grievances," *The North Wales Express*, February 18, 1881, 6; Du Parcq, *Life*, 1:34–39, 53–56; George, *My Brother*, 260; Alvin Jackson, *Home Rule: An Irish History, 1800–2000* (Oxford: Oxford University Press, 2003), 40–43.

2. Roy Douglas, *Land, People & Politics: A History of the Land Question in the United Kingdom, 1878–1952* (New York: St. Martin's Press, 1976), 24–35; Catherine B. Shannon, *Arthur J. Balfour and Ireland, 1874–1922* (Washington, DC: The Catholic University of America Press, 1988), 7–24; Jackson, *Home*, 18, 37–44; George, *Making*, 113.

3. Jackson, *Home*, 44–46; George Dangerfield, *The Damnable Question: A Study in Anglo-Irish Relations* (Boston: Little, Brown and Company, 1976), 17–21; Thomas E. Hachey, Joseph M. Hernon, Jr., and Lawrence J. McCaffrey, *The Irish Experience* (Englewood Cliffs, NJ: Prentice Hall, 1989), 121–22; George, *Making*, 113–14; Douglas, *Land*, 34–36; Shannon, *Arthur*, 7, 20–23.

4. R. Dixon, ed., *Ireland and the Irish Question* (New York: International Publishers, 1972), 331–32; "Portmadoc," *The North Wales Express*, February 3, 1882, 8; Du Parcq, *Life*, 1:40–42; Diaries, January, 21, 23, 25, February 3, October 24, November 2, 1882, William George Papers, NLW; quoted in George, *My Brother*, 117–18, 128–29; George, *Making*, 113.

5. Jackson, *Home*, 45; quoted but misdated in George, *Making*, 113–14.

6. Diaries, January 9, February 12–13, 1886, William George Papers, NLW; quoted in Du Parcq, *Life*, 1:76–77.

7. Brian Tierney, Donald Kagan, and L. Pearce Williams, *Great Issues in Western Civilization*, vol. 2. 4th ed. (New York: McGraw-Hill, 1992), 432–34; Diaries, April 24, June 2, July 8, 1886, William George Papers, NLW; George, *Making*, 131–32, 166; Grigg, *Young Lloyd*, 55–56; Gilbert, *Architect*, 71–72; quoted in Du Parcq, *Life*, 1:86–89.

8. David Lloyd George to Thomas Edward Ellis, November 27, 1890, Thomas Edward Ellis Papers, NLW; David Lloyd George to Margaret Lloyd George, November 25, 27, December 3, 1890, in Morgan, ed., *Family Letters*, 38–39; George, *My Brother*, 261–62; Jackson, *Home*, 74–75; Gilbert, *Architect*, 89–90.

9. David Lloyd George to Margaret Lloyd George, November 28, December 3, 1890, in Morgan, ed., *Family Letters*, 39–40; George, *My Brother*, 261–64; Jackson, *Home*, 75–76; Gilbert, *Architect*, 90–91.

10. David Lloyd George to William George, November 25, 27, 1890, William George Papers, NLW; Jackson, *Home*, 76; George, *My Brother*, 262–63.

11. David Lloyd George to William George, Misc. Letter 79, 1890, William George Papers, NLW; Jackson, *Home*, 76–79; David Lloyd George to Thomas Edward Ellis, January 24, 1893, Thomas Edward Ellis Papers, NLW.

12. Grigg, *Young Lloyd*, 87–89, 129–31; quoted in Du Parcq, *Life*, 1:158.

13. Grigg, *Young Lloyd*, 143–44, 156–57; Gilbert, *Architect*, 112–13, 136–37.

14. Quoted in Edwards, *David Lloyd George*, 3:105, 126–48, 159–64; Du Parcq, *Life*, 1:169–71, 175–76; Bebbington, *Conscience*, 137–38; Gilbert, *Architect*, 151–55; Grigg, *Young Lloyd*, 203–05, 212–13.

15. Quoted in Edwards, *David Lloyd George*, 3:166–169; Grigg, *Young Lloyd*, 215; Gilbert, *Architect*, 150, 154–58; David Lloyd George to William George, March 9, 1898, William George Papers, NLW.

16. Gilbert, *Architect*, 157, 201, 206–07, 216; Grigg, *People's Champion*, 21, 24, 31–32; Garret Fitzgerald, "Lloyd George & Ireland: How Ireland came to be divided," in *David Lloyd George-The Llanystumdwy Lectures, 1990–1996*, ed. Ann Rhydderch (Gywnedd: Gywnedd Council & the Criccieth Arts Association Festival, 1997), 56.

17. Adams, *Balfour*, 76–86; Shannon, *Arthur*, 118–26; Douglas, *Land*, 126–30; Jackson, *Home*, 89–91.

18. Jackson, *Home*, 90–95; David Lloyd George to William George, February 16, July 13, 1904, February 15, December 4, 8, 1905, William George Papers, NLW.

19. David Lloyd George to William George, July 4, 10, 1906, William George Papers, NLW; Du Parcq, *Life*, 3:474–77; Batsell Barrett Baxter, *Neither Catholic, Protestant, nor Jew* (Nashville: Church of Christ, 1960), 1–13.

20. Quoted in Du Parcq, *Life*, 3:477.

21. Gilbert, *Architect*, 403–05, 427–28; Grigg, *People's Champion*, 251–56, 277–80, 286; David Lloyd George to William George, September 28, 1909, William George Papers, NLW.

22. David Lloyd George to William George, September 28, 1909, April 13, 1910,

William George Papers, NLW; Gilbert, *Architect*, 405–10; Grigg, *People's Champion*, 246–49, 286–90.

23. David Lloyd George to William George, January 31, 1912, William George Papers, NLW; J. Graham Jones, trans., David Lloyd George to William George, February 7, 1912, in "Catalog of Letters between Lloyd George and William George," William George Papers, NLW; Grigg, *Peace*, 17–19, 113–14; Ronan Fanning, *Fatal Path: British Government and Irish Revolution, 1919–1922* (London: Faber & Faber, 2013), 54–59, 63; Jackson, *Home*, 115, 118–19; Shannon, *Arthur*, 165, 168–69, 171; R. J. Q. Adams, *Bonar Law* (Stanford, CA: Stanford University Press, 1999), 97–102.

24. Grigg, *Peace*, 114; Shannon, *Arthur*, 165, 173–74; David Lloyd George to Margaret Lloyd George, April 11, 1912, in Morgan, ed., *Family Letters*, 161; Jackson, *Home*, 109–11; Adams, *Law*, 102–07.

25. Quoted in Grigg, *Peace*, 114–16; Shannon, *Arthur*, 175–78; Jackson, *Home*, 118, 122–23; Adams, *Law*, 107–17.

26. David Lloyd George to William George, November 11, 1912, William George Papers, NLW; John Charmley, *A History of Conservative Politics since 1830*, 2nd ed. (Houndmills, UK: Palgrave Macmillan, 2008), 89–90; Gilbert, *Organizer*, 95–96; Grigg, *Peace*, 116.

27. Alan J. Ward, *The Easter Rising: Revolution and Irish Nationalism* (Wheeling, IL: Harlan Davidson, 1980), 87–88; Jackson, *Home*, 120; Shannon, *Arthur*, 178–89; Adams, *Law*, 123–44; Gilbert, *Organizer*, 96–98.

28. Grigg, *Peace*, 115–17; Gilbert, *Organizer*, 97–99; Shannon, *Arthur*, 188–89.

29. David Lloyd George to William George, February 9, 16, 28, 1914, William George Papers, NLW; Fanning, *Fatal*, 101–02; Grigg, *Peace*, 118; Gilbert, *Organizer*, 101–02; Adams, *Law*, 151–52.

30. David Lloyd George to William George, March 4, 1914, William George Papers, NLW; Fanning, *Fatal*, 105–06; Grigg, *Peace*, 118; Gilbert, *Organizer*, 102–03; Shannon, *Arthur*, 194–97; Jackson, *Home*, 127–29; Adams, *Law*, 152–53.

31. Quoted in Grigg, *Peace*, 118–20; David Lloyd George to William George, March 16, 1914, William George Papers, NLW; Jones, trans., David Lloyd George to William George, March 17, 1914, in "Catalog," William George Papers, NLW; Fanning, *Fatal*, 106–07.

32. Shannon, *Arthur*, 198–99; Ward, *Easter*, 87; Grigg, *Peace*, 120–21; Jackson, *Home*, 129–33; Gilbert, *Organizer*, 103; Jones, trans., David Lloyd George to William George, March 23, 1914, in "Catalog," William George Papers, NLW; David Lloyd George to William George, March 23–24, 28, 1914, William George Papers, NLW.

33. Shannon, *Arthur*, 199–201, 204–05; Ward, *Easter*, 87–88; Grigg, *Peace*, 121; Jackson, *Home*, 133–34; Dangerfield, *Damnable*, 111–12.

34. David Lloyd George to Richard Lloyd, May 7, 1914, William George Papers,

NLW; David Lloyd George to William George, May 15, 1914, William George Papers, NLW; Gilbert, *Organizer*, 104–05; Grigg, *Peace*, 122–24; Jackson, *Home*, 137–39.

35. David Lloyd George to William George, July 16, 17, 1914, William George Papers, NLW; Fanning, *Fatal*, 123–26; Jackson, *Home*, 137–38; Adams, *Law*, 162–65; Gilbert, *Organizer*, 104–05; Fitzgerald, *How*, 62; Grigg, *Peace*, 15; Grigg, *People's Champion*, 61.

36. Gilbert, *Organizer*, 104–05; Grigg, *Peace*, 124–25; David Lloyd George to William George, July 18, 1914, William George Papers, NLW; Adams, *Law*, 165–66; Adams, *Balfour*, 283–84; Fanning, *Fatal*, 126–28; Jackson, *Home*, 125, 138–41; Ward, *Easter*, 90–92; Fitzgerald, *How*, 62; quoted in Shannon, *Arthur*, 48, 171, 204–05, 208.

37. Gilbert, *Organizer*, 104–06; Grigg, *Peace*, 121, 124–26; Shannon, *Arthur*, 182, 208–09; Jackson, *Home*, 135–41; Ward, *Easter*, 88–92; Dangerfield, *Damnable*, 98; Fitzgerald, *How*, 62; George Dangerfield, *The Strange Death of Liberal England, 1910–1914* (New York: Capricorn Books, 1961), 416–21; Fanning, *Fatal*, 128–29.

38. Dangerfield, *Strange*, 421–23; Grigg, *Peace*, 126; Gilbert, *Organizer*, 106, 160; Adams, *Balfour*, 284–85; Shannon, *Arthur*, 208; Jackson, *Home*, 135–37, 141; Dangerfield, *Damnable*, 128; Ward, *Easter*, 92.

Chapter 5

1. Grigg, *Peace*, 35; Dangerfield, *Damnable*, 115–16, 121–22; quoted in Shannon, *Arthur*, 189–90, 206, 209–10; Patricia Jalland and John Stubbs, "The Irish question after the outbreak of war in 1914: some unfinished party business," *The English Historical Review* 96 (October 1981): 786.

2. John Stevenson, *British Society, 1914–45* (Harmondsworth, UK: Penguin Books, 1984), 53–54; Jalland and Stubbs, "Irish question," 786; Grigg, *Peace*, 157, 210n.1, 230–37, 342; David Lloyd George to William George, May 6, 1915, William George Papers, NLW; Stevenson Diary, May 10, 1915, Frances Stevenson Papers, HLRO; Taylor, ed., *Diary*, 48–49, 329.

3. David Lloyd George to William George, May 17, 22, 24-25, 1916, William George Papers, NLW; Gilbert, *Organizer*, 98, 320–23; Grigg, *Peace*, 116, 349–50.

4. Ward, *Easter*, 3–6; Grigg, *Peace*, 342–45; Dangerfield, *Damnable*, 165–69, 173–75, 186–88; Gilbert, *Organizer*, 318–19.

5. Ward, *Easter*, 5–11; Jackson, *Home*, 151–53; Dangerfield, *Damnable*, 175–83; Grigg, *Peace*, 343–46.

6. Jackson, *Home*, 153–55; Grigg, *Peace*, 346–49; Fitzgerald, *How*, 63; Dangerfield, *Damnable*, 198–99, 207–11; Ward, *Easter*, 12–15, 109–12.

7. Gilbert, *Organizer*, 319–25; quoted in Grigg, *Peace*, 318–19, 349–52; Shannon, *Arthur*, 213–17; Fitzgerald, *How*, 63–64; Jackson, *Home*, 155–61.

8. Grigg, *Peace*, 249–53, 352–53; David Lloyd George to William George, June 20, 23, 1916, William George Papers, NLW; Gilbert, *Architect*, 422; Gilbert, *Organizer*, 324–32; Jackson, *Home*, 161–67; Shannon, *Arthur*, 217–22; Adams, *Balfour*, 313–14; Adams, *Law*, 215–16; Fitzgerald, *How*, 64–65.

9. David Lloyd George to William George, June 28, 1916, William George Papers, NLW; Jones, trans., David Lloyd George to William George, June 27, 1916, in "Catalog," William George Papers, NLW; Grigg, *Peace*, 253, 352–53; Gilbert, *Organizer*, 311, 333; Jackson, *Home*, 167–68; Shannon, *Arthur*, 222–23; Adams, *Law*, 217–19; Adams, *Balfour*, 315; Fitzgerald, *How*, 65.

10. Gilbert, *Organizer*, 102–03, 320–22, 333–34; Grigg, *Peace*, 350–55; Shannon, *Arthur*, 224–25; Jackson, *Home*, 168–74; Fitzgerald, *How*, 63, 65.

11. Stevenson Diary, April 25, 1917, Frances Stevenson Papers, HLRO; Taylor, ed., *Diary*, 155–57; Shannon, *Arthur*, 225–36; Jackson, *Home*, 177–85; Dangerfield, *Damnable*, 254–58.

12. Quoted in Ward, *Easter*, 113–19; Adams, *Law*, 241; quoted in Fitzgerald, *How*, 66–68.

13. Adams, *Law*, 266–68; Jackson, *Home*, 99–100, 183, 185–86, 192; Shannon, *Arthur*, 236–39; Dangerfield, *Damnable*, 268–79.

14. Dangerfield, *Damnable*, 260–63, 279–81, 284–92, 295–98; Ward, *Easter*, 116, 119–20; Shannon, *Arthur*, 239–41; Jackson, *Home*, 186; A. J. P. Taylor, *English History, 1914–1945* (Oxford: Oxford University Press, 1965), 6–12, 45–47.

15. Ward, *Easter*, 120–22; Fitzgerald, *How*, 68–69; Dangerfield, *Damnable*, 298–99, 300–01; Shannon, *Arthur*, 242–44; Jackson, *Home*, 186; Constantine, *Lloyd*, 61; Fanning, *Fatal*, 194.

16. Dangerfield, *Damnable*, 301–04; Ward, *Easter*, 123–24; Fitzgerald, *How*, 69–70; Shannon, *Arthur*, 242–44; Jackson, *Home*, 199.

17. Jackson, *Home*, 195–99, 204–05; Shannon, *Arthur*, 244–48; Dangerfield, *Damnable*, 308–15; Ward, *Easter*, 124–25, 131–32; Fitzgerald, *How*, 70; Pugh, *Lloyd George*, 146–47; Taylor, *English*, 156.

18. Fitzgerald, *How*, 70–71; quoted in Fanning, *Fatal*, 215–16, 294.

19. Fitzgerald, *How*, 71–72; Jackson, *Home*, 199–200, 207–10; Shannon, *Arthur*, 250–57; Dangerfield, *Damnable*, 314–19, 322–23; Ward, *Easter*, 125–27; Taylor, *English*, 155; Pugh, *Lloyd George*, 147; Constantine, *Lloyd*, 65.

20. Quoted in Fitzgerald, *How*, 72; Dangerfield, *Damnable*, 318, 320, 322–27; Ward, *Easter*, 126–27; Shannon, *Arthur*, 271–73; Taylor, *English*, 155; Pugh, *Lloyd George*, 147; David Lloyd George to Margaret Lloyd George, September 2, 11 1920, in Morgan, ed., *Family Letters*, 192–93.

21. Ward, *Easter*, 132–34, 136; Fitzgerald, *How*, 72–74; Dangerfield, *Damnable*, 327–30; Shannon, *Arthur*, 273–75, 277–78; Taylor, *English*, 156–57.

22. Stevenson Diary, July 14, 1921, in Taylor, ed., *Diary*, 227–28; Fitzgerald, *How*, 74–75; David Lloyd George to Margaret Lloyd George, August 13, 1921, in Morgan, ed., *Family Letters*, 194.

23. Dangerfield, *Damnable*, 330–32; David Lloyd George to Margaret Lloyd George, September 29, 1921, in Morgan, ed., *Family Letters*, 194; Ward, *Easter*, 134.

24. Dangerfield, *Damnable*, 332–35; Stevenson Diary, July 18, November 6, 1921, in Taylor, ed., *Diary*, 228–30, 234–35; Fitzgerald, *How*, 76–77.

25. Quoted in Fitzgerald, *How*, 77–79; McEwen, ed., *Riddell*, 10, 355–56; Dangerfield, *Damnable*, 335–36.

26. Stevenson Diary, November 14, 23, 1921, in Taylor, ed., *Diary*, 237–38; David Lloyd George to Margaret Lloyd George, November 24, 1921, in Morgan, ed., *Family Letters*, 194–95.

27. Dangerfield, *Damnable*, 336–38; Fitzgerald, *How*, 79–81; Shannon, *Arthur*, 278–79.

28. Fitzgerald, *How*, 79–80; Dangerfield, *Damnable*, 336, 338–39; Ward, *Easter*, 134–36; quoted in Gilbert, ed., *Lloyd George*, 114–15.

29. Dangerfield, *Damnable*, 339, 341–44; Taylor, *English*, 157–61; Adams, *Law*, 302–05; Pugh, *Lloyd George*, 147–48; Constantine, *Lloyd*, 65; Charmley, *Conservative*, 97.

Chapter 6

1. Diaries, April 7, 1880, William George Papers, NLW; Douglas, *Land*, 97; Masterman Diary, 17, Charles and Lucy Masterman Papers, University of Birmingham; Lucy Masterman, "Recollections of David Lloyd George: I," *History Today* 9 (March 1959): 163; Gilbert, *Architect*, 18, 463–64.

2. Diaries, February 2, 17, 24, 1883, January 14, 1884, William George Papers, NLW; Henry George, *Progress and Poverty* (New York: Robert Schalkenbach Foundation, 1990), 433.

3. Du Parcq, *Life*, 1:46–47; George, *Making*, 125–30; Douglas, *Land*, 52–53; Davies, *History*, 445–46, 454; Diaries, January 9, 1886, William George Papers, NLW; "Mr. Michael Davitt in Wales," *The Cambrian News*, February 19, 1886, 7.

4. Douglas, *Land*, 98–99; Cregier, *Bounder*, 24–25; George, *Making*, 129–31; quoted in Du Parcq, *Life*, 1:76–77; Diaries, February 12–13, 1886, William George Papers, NLW.

5. Quoted in Du Parcq, *Life*, 1:76–77; Diaries, January 27, 1886, William George Papers, NLW; Roy Jenkins, *Gladstone: A Biography* (New York: Random House, 1997), 542.

6. Diaries, January 27–29, 1886, William George Papers, NLW; Douglas, *Land*, 103–04; Ian Packer, *Lloyd George, Liberalism and the Land: The Land Issue and Party Politics in England, 1906–1914* (Woodbridge, UK: The Boydell Press, 2001), 12–15, 20; Jenkins, *Gladstone*, 540–42; George, *Making*, 129–30.

7. Diaries, February 1, March 20, 1886, William George Papers, NLW; George, *Making*, 130; Grigg, *Young Lloyd*, 95–96; Cregier, *Bounder*, 24–26.

8. Jenkins, *Gladstone*, 551–60; Douglas, *Land*, 99–102, 104; Cregier, *Bounder*, 26–28; quoted in George, *Making*, 163.

9. George, *Making*, 164; Diaries, February 10, 1888, William George Papers, NLW; Douglas, *Land*, 100–02, 105–06; Grigg, *Young Lloyd*, 106–07; Gilbert, *Architect*, 84–85; Cregier, *Bounder*, 41; Packer, *Liberalism*, 20–22.

10. Packer, *Liberalism*, 22–27; J. Graham Jones, "Select Committee or Royal Commission?: Wales and 'The Land Question,' 1892," *Welsh History Review* 17 (December 1994): 211–29; George, *My Brother*, 161–65.

11. David Lloyd George to Richard Lloyd, March 27, 1896, William George Papers, NLW; Lloyd George, Speech to the House of Commons, March 30, 1896, Parliamentary Debates, Commons, 4th ser., vol., 39 (1896), cols. 496–501, 503–04.

12. Grigg, *Young Lloyd*, 203–05; Douglas, *Land*, 120–23; Packer, *Liberalism*, 24–26; Gilbert, *Architect*, 151–54.

13. Constantine, *Lloyd*, 18; David Lloyd George to William George, April 30, 1896, William George Papers, NLW; David Lloyd George to Richard Lloyd, May 21, 1896, William George Papers, NLW; Quoted in D. W. Bebbington, "The city, the countryside and the social gospel in late Victorian nonconformity," in *The Church in Town and Countryside*, ed. Derek Baker (Oxford: Basil Blackwell, 1979), 418–19; David Thompson, "John Clifford's Social Gospel," *The Baptist Quarterly* 31 (January 1986): 204–05.

14. Gilbert, *Architect*, 151–54; Grigg, *Young Lloyd*, 203–05; David Lloyd George to William George, July 2, 1896, William George Papers, NLW; Packer, *Lloyd George*, 14.

15. Lloyd George, Speech to the House of Commons, April 30, 1896, Parliamentary Debates, Commons, 4th ser., vol., 40 (1896), cols. 241–42; quoted in Du Parcq, *Life*, 1:171; Packer, *Lloyd George*, 14; Douglas, *Land*, 123; Gilbert, *Architect*, 152.

16. Lloyd George, Speech to the House of Commons, April 30, 1896, cols. 237–42.

17. Lloyd George, Speech to the House of Commons, July 1, 1896, Parliamentary Debates, Commons, 4th ser., vol., 42 (1896), cols. 505–07.

18. Douglas, *Land*, 123; Packer, *Liberalism*, 25–26; Travis L. Crosby, *Joseph Chamberlain: A Most Radical Imperialist* (London: I.B. Tauris & Co., 2011), 101–05, 158.

19. Du Parcq, *Life*, 1:168–69; Grigg, *Young Lloyd*, 169; David Lloyd George to William George, April 26, May 5, 1899, William George Papers, NLW.

20. David Lloyd George to William George, May 9, June 13, 22, 1899, William George Papers, NLW; Du Parcq, *Life*, 2:214.

21. Gilbert, *Architect*, 175–76; David Lloyd George to William George, June 24, 1899, William George Papers, NLW; Grigg, *Young Lloyd*, 216–18; Du Parcq, *Life*, 2:214–15.

22. Du Parcq, *Life*, 2:215; David Lloyd George to Margaret Lloyd George, July 21, 26, 1899, Lloyd George Papers, NLW, in Morgan, ed., *Family Letters*, 117–18.

23. David Lloyd George to William George, July 25–26, 1899, William George Papers, NLW; quoted in Grigg, *Young Lloyd*, 218; Gilbert, *Architect*, 176–77.

24. David Lloyd George to William George, October 18, 1899, William George Papers, NLW; Cregier, *Bounder*, 64, 68; Edwards, *David Lloyd George*, 4:43–47.

25. Lloyd George, Speech to the House of Commons, May 22, 1903, Parliamentary Debates, Commons, 4th ser., vol., 122 (1903), cols. 1546–48; Adams, *Balfour*, 212–20.

26. Lloyd George, Speech to the House of Commons, May 22, 1903, cols. 1541–43, 1548.

27. Lloyd George, Speech to the House of Commons, May 22, 1903, cols. 1543–45; Adams, *Balfour*, 220–25; Gilbert, *Architect*, 287–91, 336–37.

28. Grigg, *People's Champion*, 91–92, 132–34, 158–59; Gilbert, *Architect*, 282–84, 330–32, 337–38; H. H. Asquith, Speech to the House of Commons, April 18, 1907, Parliamentary Debates, Commons, 4th ser., vol., 172 (1907), cols. 1190–91, 1211.

29. Cregier, *Bounder*, 114; David Lloyd George to William George, May 6, 8, 12, 1908, William George Papers, NLW; George, *My Brother*, 220–21; Du Parcq, *Life*, 3:508–09.

30. David Lloyd George to William George, May 16, 28, June 3, 9, 11, 15, 1908, William George Papers, NLW.

31. David Lloyd George to William George, June 16, 25, 1908, William George Papers, NLW; Gilbert, *Architect*, 338–39; Grigg, *People's Champion*, 159–61; Du Parcq, *Life*, 3:508–09; Cregier, *Bounder*, 114–15.

32. David Lloyd George to William George, June 25, 30, 1908, William George Papers, NLW; George, *My Brother*, 221; Du Parcq, *Life*, 3:509–11; Grigg, *People's Champion*, 161.

33. David Lloyd George to William George, July 1–2, 1908, William George Papers, NLW; Grigg, *People's Champion*, 61–62; Gilbert, *Architect*, 340–42.

34. David Lloyd George to William George, July 20–21, August 1, September 15, 1908, William George Papers, NLW; George, *My Brother*, 221; Grigg, *People's Champion*, 162–64, 313–15; Gilbert, *Architect*, 337, 342–43, 349–50, 353–55.

35. Gilbert, *Architect*, 355–56; Hancock, "No Compromise," 62; quoted in Beriah Gwynfe Evans, *The Life Romance of Lloyd George* (Utica, NY: Thomas J. Griffiths, "Y Drych" and "The Cambrian," 1916), 143–45; David Lloyd George to William George, October 2, 1908, William George Papers, NLW.

36. David Lloyd George to William George, October 11–12, 16, 1908, William George Papers, NLW; M. A. Crowther, *The Workhouse System, 1834–1929* (Athens: The University of Georgia Press, 1981), 85; Grigg, *People's Champion*, 91, 164, 331; Du Parcq, *Life*, 3:509; Gilbert, *Architect*, 357; Cregier, *Bounder*, 163–69.

37. David Lloyd George to William George, October 19, 25, 27, November 1, 21, 1908, William George Papers, NLW; George, *My Brother*, 222.

38. David Lloyd George to William George, November 17, December 1, 1908, William George Papers, NLW; Grigg, *People's Champion*, 314, 316–17.

39. Gilbert, *Architect*, 356–59.
40. Gilbert, *Architect*, 359; Grigg, *People's Champion*, 317; David Lloyd George to William George, February 25, March 5–6, 1909, William George Papers, NLW.
41. Grigg, *People's Champion*, 197–200; David Lloyd George to William George, May 14, June 22, 26, July 15, 1909, William George Papers, NLW; Cross, ed., *Sylvester*, 143; Du Parcq, *Life*, 3:532–34; George, *My Brother*, 248–49.
42. Grigg, *People's Champion*, 203–05; Gilbert, *Architect*, 384–86; Cregier, *Bounder*, 127–28; Du Parcq, *Life*, 3:537–40.
43. Grigg, *People's Champion*, 203, 205–11; David Lloyd George to William George, July 31, 1909, William George Papers, NLW; Du Parcq, *Life*, 3:540; Gilbert, *Architect*, 386–87; Cregier, *Bounder*, 128–29; George, *My Brother*, 228–29.
44. David Lloyd George to William George, May 5, July 13, August 3–4, 1909, William George Papers, NLW; George, *My Brother*, 228, 230; Grigg, *People's Champion*, 205.
45. David Lloyd George to William George, August 4, 17, 26, 1909, William George Papers, NLW; George, *My Brother*, 230; H. V. Emy, "The Land Campaign: Lloyd George as a Social Reformer, 1909–14," in *Lloyd George: Twelve Essays*, ed. A. J. P. Taylor (New York: Atheneum, 1971), 42–44.
46. Emy, "Campaign," 44–45; Grigg, *People's Champion*, 176–77; Gilbert, *Architect*, 368–70; David Lloyd George to William George, January 3, March 26, May 24–25, September 1, 1909, William George Papers, NLW.
47. David Lloyd George to William George, September 25, October 2, 4–5, 1909, William George Papers, NLW; George, *My Brother*, 229–31; Cregier, *Bounder*, 121–24, 130; Morgan, ed., *Family Letters*, 160n.1.
48. Quoted in Grigg, *People's Champion*, 222–29, 248; Gilbert, *Architect*, 393–96; David Lloyd George to William George, October 22, 1909, William George Papers, NLW; George, *My Brother*, 232.
49. George. *My Brother*. 232–33; David Lloyd George to William George, November 17, 24 1909, William George Papers, NLW; Cregier, *Bounder*, 130–31; Du Parcq, *Life*, 3:541–42; David Lloyd George to Margaret Lloyd George, November 16, 1909, Lloyd George Papers, NLW, in Morgan, ed., *Family Letters*, 151–52; Grigg, *People's Champion*, 198–200.
50. David Lloyd George to William George, November 25, 1909, February 23, 1910, William George Papers, NLW; George, *My Brother*, 233; Cregier, *Bounder*, 131–33; Gilbert, *Architect*, 288–89, 400–03; Grigg, *People's Champion*, 230–32, 235–40.
51. David Lloyd George to William George, February 25, March 4, 1910, William George Papers, NLW; Gilbert, *Architect*, 403–06; Grigg, *People's Champion*, 233–35, 244–51.
52. Gilbert, *Architect*, 406–09; Grigg, *People's Champion*, 251–53; Dangerfield, *Damnable*, 114, 258; David Lloyd George to William George, April 11, 1910, William George Papers, NLW.

53. David Lloyd George to William George, April 13–14, 1910, William George Papers, NLW; H. H. Asquith, Speech to the House of Commons, April 14, 1910, Parliamentary Debates, Commons, 5th ser., vol., 16 (1910), cols. 1547–48.

54. Gilbert, *Architect*, 409–10; William O'Brien, Speech to the House of Commons, April 18, 1910, Parliamentary Debates, Commons, 5th ser., vol., 16 (1910), cols. 1739–51, 1834–37; Grigg, *People's Champion*, 253–56; Morgan, ed., *Family Letters*, 162n.1; David Lloyd George to William George, May 11, 1910, William George Papers, NLW.

55. David Lloyd George to William George, June 17, 21–22, July 16, August 28, September 11, October 6–7, 17, December 19, 30, 1910, William George Papers, NLW; Grigg, *People's Champion*, 237.

56. David Lloyd George to William George, July 16, August 28, 1910, William George Papers, NLW; Emy, "Campaign," 46.

57. Emy, "Campaign," 46–47; Packer, *Liberalism*, 48–53, 60–64; Grigg, *People's Champion*, 240–42.

58. Grigg, *People's Champion*, 240; David Lloyd George to William George, September 11, October 6–7, 17, 20, 1910, William George Papers, NLW.

59. Quoted in "Mr. Lloyd George on Destitution," *The British Weekly*, October 20, 1910; "Mr. Lloyd George on Social Waste," *The Christian World*, October 20, 1910, 4.

60. Grigg, *People's Champion*, 262–77; Gilbert, *Architect*, 411–27; Adams, *Balfour*, 244–47; David Lloyd George to William George, November 3, 11, 1910, William George Papers, NLW.

61. Grigg, *People's Champion*, 146–48, 278–85, 321; Gilbert, *Architect*, 427–29; David Lloyd George to William George, December 19, 30, 1910, William George Papers, NLW.

Chapter 7

1. Adams, *Balfour*, 238–40; Gilbert, *Architect*, 426; David Lloyd George to William George, February 7, 1911, William George Papers, NLW; Grigg, *People's Champion*, 272, 317; Roy Hattersley, BBC Radio 3, Arts & Ideas, Night Waves, September 14, 2010.

2. David Lloyd George to William George, February 28, 1911, William George Papers, NLW; Grigg, *People's Champion*, 317–21; Gilbert, *Architect*, 417–20.

3. Grigg, *People's Champion*, 285–86, 321, 323; David Lloyd George to William George, March 3–4, 10, 16, 24, 28–29, 1911, William George Papers, NLW.

4. David Lloyd George to William George, April 3–4, 6–7, 1911, William George Papers, NLW; Gilbert, *Architect*, 428–29, 434; Lloyd George, Speech to the House of Commons, May 4, 1911, Parliamentary Debates, Commons, 5th ser., vol., 25 (1911), col. 609.

5. Lloyd George, Speech to the House of Commons, May 4, 1911, cols. 609–15.

6. Lloyd George, Speech to the House of Commons, May 4, 1911, cols. 615–22; Grigg, *People's Champion*, 324–28; Gilbert, *Architect*, 434–35.

7. Lloyd George, Speech to the House of Commons, May 4, 1911, cols. 622–27.

8. Lloyd George, Speech to the House of Commons, May 4, 1911, cols. 628–31; Alva W. Taylor, "Department of Social Service," *The Christian-Evangelist*, June 1, 1911, 764; Grigg, *People's Champion*, 326.

9. Lloyd George, Speech to the House of Commons, May 4, 1911, cols. 631–32.

10. Lloyd George, Speech to the House of Commons, May 4, 1911, cols. 633–39; Lloyd George, Written Answers to the House of Commons, May 22, 1911, Parliamentary Debates, Commons, 5th ser., vol., 26 (1911), cols. 98–99W; Gilbert, *Architect*, 434.

11. Lloyd George, Speech to the House of Commons, May 4, 1911, cols. 639–43, 655–56.

12. Lloyd George, Speech to the House of Commons, May 4, 1911, cols. 644, 649; David Lloyd George to William George, May 4, 1911, William George Papers, NLW; Grigg, *People's Champion*, 330.

13. Morgan, ed., *Family Letters*, 157n.2; David Lloyd George to William George, May 15, 18, 24–25, 30, 1911, William George Papers, NLW; Grigg, *People's Champion*, 346–51.

14. Lloyd George, Speech to the House of Commons, May 4, 1911, cols. 624–26, 632, 637; Grigg, *People's Champion*, 328–35; Gilbert, *Architect*, 434–40; David Lloyd George to William George, June 28–29, 1911, William George Papers, NLW.

15. David Lloyd George to William George, July 3, 5, 11, 1911, William George Papers, NLW; Lloyd George, Speech to the House of Commons, August 1, 1911, Parliamentary Debates, Commons, 5th ser., vol., 29 (1911), cols. 317–19; Grigg, *People's Champion*, 332.

16. David Lloyd George to William George, August 1, 1911, William George Papers, NLW; David Lloyd George to Margaret Lloyd George, August 10–11, 1911, Lloyd George Papers, NLW, in Morgan, ed., *Family Letters*, 157,ns.3, 4, 158; Gilbert, *Architect*, 440–41; Grigg, *People's Champion*, 286–88.

17. David Lloyd George to Margaret Lloyd George, September 16, October 9, 11, 1911, Lloyd George Papers, NLW, in Morgan, ed., *Family Letters*, 158–60.

18. Grigg, *People's Champion*, 341–45; David Lloyd George to Margaret Lloyd George, October 16, 1911, Lloyd George Papers, NLW, in Morgan, ed., *Family Letters*, 160; David Lloyd George to William George, October 22, 1911, William George Papers, NLW.

19. David Lloyd George to William George, October 23, 26, November 2, 4, 14, 1911, William George Papers, NLW; William O'Brien, Speech to the House of Commons, November 14, 1911, Parliamentary Debates, Commons, 5th ser., vol., 31 (1911), cols. 212–22.

20. David Lloyd George to William George, November 6, 27–29, December 2, 1911,

William George Papers, NLW; Crowther, *Workhouse*, 96; Gilbert, *Architect*, 444–46; Cregier, *Bounder*, 183.

21. David Lloyd George to William George, December 4–5, 7–8, 1911, William George Papers, NLW; Du Parcq, *Life*, 3:579, 581–82; H. W. Forster, Speech to the House of Commons, December 6, 1911, Parliamentary Debates, Commons, 5th ser., vol., 32 (1911), cols. 1419–33, 1528–29.

22. David Lloyd George to William George, December 11, 16, 18, 1911, May 3, 6, 1912, William George Papers, NLW; David Lloyd George to Richard Lloyd, July 22, 1912, William George Papers, NLW; Grigg, *People's Champion*, 345.

23. David Lloyd George to Margaret Lloyd George, January 12, 1912, Lloyd George Papers, NLW, in Morgan, ed., *Family Letters*, 160–61, 161n.1; Grigg, *People's Champion*, 345–46; David Lloyd George to William George, March 7, May 7, 10, 30, 1912, William George Papers, NLW.

24. David Lloyd George to William George, June 8, 12, 26, 28, July 12, 1912, William George Papers, NLW; Grigg, *Peace*, 67–69.

25. Gilbert, *Architect*, 417; Grigg, *People's Champion*, 317–18; David Lloyd George to William George, July 24, 1912, William George Papers, NLW; Gilbert, *Organizer*, 29; David Lloyd George to Margaret Lloyd George, July 29, 1912, Lloyd George Papers, NLW, in Morgan, ed., *Family Letters*, 162–63.

26. Gilbert, *Organizer*, 30–31; Grigg, *Peace*, 68–69, 69n.1; David Lloyd George to Margaret Lloyd George, August 14, 1912, Lloyd George Papers, NLW, in Morgan, ed., *Family Letters*, 163, 222.

27. Grigg, *Peace*, 69n.1; David Lloyd George to William George, October 5, 23, November 25, 1912, William George Papers, NLW; Lloyd George, Speech to the House of Commons, October 23, 1912, Parliamentary Debates, Commons, 5th ser., vol., 42 (1912), cols. 2188–90.

28. David Lloyd George to William George, December 17, 1912, January 1, 5–7, 11, 1913, William George Papers, NLW; Gilbert, *Organizer*, 30–31; Cregier, *Bounder*, 186.

29. Dangerfield, *Strange*, 258–59, 299–307; Grigg, *Peace*, 20–25, 38–41; Cregier, *Bounder*, 187–89, 197–99; David Lloyd George to William George, June 11, 16, 21, 28, July 3, 1912, William George Papers, NLW; Gilbert, *Organizer*, 58, 238; Packer, *Liberalism*, 78–82; Emy, "Campaign," 47–49.

30. Grigg, *Peace*, 41–43; Cregier, *Bounder*, 199–200; Gilbert, *Organizer*, 58–61; Packer, *Liberalism*, 82–87; Emy, "Campaign," 49–51; David Lloyd George to William George, July 8, 1912, William George Papers, NLW.

31. Douglas, *Land*, 156–58; Packer, *Liberalism*, 81–82, 86–87; David Lloyd George to Margaret Lloyd George, August 12, October 16, 1912, Lloyd George Papers, NLW, in Morgan, ed., *Family Letters*, 163–64, 164n.1; Grigg, *Peace*, 42–43; Lloyd George, Speech to the House of Commons, October 15, 1912, Parliamentary Debates, Commons, 5th ser., vol., 42 (1912), cols. 1193–96.

32. Douglas, *Land*, 158–59; Emy, "Campaign," 48–51; David Lloyd George to

William George, November 11, 1912, February 10, 1913, William George Papers, NLW.

33. Gilbert, *Organizer*, 61; David Lloyd George to William George, January 17, February 12, March 12, William George Papers, NLW.

34. David Lloyd George to William George, March 19, 1912, William George Papers, NLW; quoted in Grigg, *Peace*, 45–47; Grigg, *People's Champion*, 27.

35. David Lloyd George to William George, March 25, 31, April 9, June 9, 14, 17, 21, 1913, William George Papers, NLW; Gilbert, *Organizer*, 32–52; Cregier, *Bounder*, 200–12; Grigg, *Peace*, 47–56.

36. Lloyd George, Speech to the House of Commons, March 11, 1913, Parliamentary Debates, Commons, 5th ser., vol., 50 (1913), cols. 81, 132–47.

37. Grigg, *Peace*, 90–93; Lloyd George, Speech to the House of Commons, April 22, 1913, Parliamentary Debates, Commons, 5th ser., vol., 52 (1913), cols. 279–80; Gilbert, *Organizer*, 60–61; David Lloyd George to William George, May 12, 1913, William George Papers, NLW.

38. Packer, *Liberalism*, 87, 100, 118; Emy, "Campaign," 52–57.

39. David Lloyd George to Margaret Lloyd George, September 10, 1913, Lloyd George Papers, NLW, in Morgan, ed., *Family Letters*, 165, n.1; Packer, *Liberalism*, 87–89; Emy, "Campaign," 57; Grigg, *Peace*, 93.

40. Quoted in Packer, *Liberalism*, 88, n.83, 90–91; Emy, "Campaign," 57–58; Douglas, *Land*, 159–60.

41. Packer, *Liberalism*, 91–94.

42. Bentley B. Gilbert, "David Lloyd George: The Reform of British Landholding and the Budget of 1914," *The Historical Journal* 21 (March 1978): 122–26; Cregier, *Bounder*, 215–16; Grigg, *Peace*, 93–96; David Lloyd George to William George, October 10, 1913, William George Papers, NLW.

43. David Lloyd George to William George, October 13–15, 1913, William George Papers, NLW; Gilbert, "Landholding," 126; Packer, *Liberalism*, 76, 119–20.

44. Packer, *Liberalism*, 119–120; David Lloyd George to William George, October 16, 24, 27, 29, 1913, William George Papers, NLW; Gilbert, "Landholding," 126–27; Cregier, *Bounder*, 216–17; Grigg, *Peace*, 98; Emy, "Campaign," 58–59; Douglas, *Land*, 160.

45. David Lloyd George to William George, October 30, November 6, 11, 1913, William George Papers, NLW; Gilbert, *Organizer*, 64–65.

46. Dangerfield, *Damnable*, 99–106; quoted in Gilbert, "Landholding," 127, n.29; Grigg, *Peace*, 98–101; Cregier, *Bounder*, 217.

47. Grigg, *Peace*, 99–101; David Lloyd George to William George, November 24, December 5, 1913, William George Papers, NLW; Cregier, *Bounder*, 217–18; Packer, *Liberalism*, 30, 100.

48. J. Graham Jones, *David Lloyd George and Welsh Liberalism*, The Welsh Political Archive (Aberystwyth: The National Library of Wales, 2010), 286–87; David

Lloyd George to William George, December 11, 13, 1913, William George Papers, NLW; Packer, *Liberalism*, 56–57, 85; Emy, "Campaign," 59.

49. Emy, "Campaign," 59–61; Grigg, *Peace*, 101–02; Douglas, *Land*, 160–62; Packer, *Liberalism*, 86; Gilbert, "Landholding," 128–29.

50. Gilbert, "Landholding," 130; Lloyd George Speech to the House of Commons, February 12, 1914, Parliamentary Debates, Commons, 5th ser., vol., 58 (1914), col. 338W; David Lloyd George to William George, February 19, 1914, William George Papers, NLW.

51. Lloyd George, Speech to the House of Commons, February 19, 1914, Parliamentary Debates, Commons, 5th ser., vol., 58 (1914), cols. 1176–87.

52. David Lloyd George to William George, February 26, April 30, 1914, William George Papers, NLW; Grigg, *Peace*, 102–03; Emy, "Campaign," 60–61; Packer, *Liberalism*, 100; Gilbert, "Landholding," 131; Douglas, *Land*, 162; Cregier, *Bounder*, 219.

53. Packer, *Liberalism*, 101–14.

54. Douglas, *Land*, 162–66; Emy, "Campaign," 61–62; Grigg, *Peace*, 103.

55. Lloyd George, Speech to the House of Commons, May 4, 1914, Parliamentary Debates, Commons, 5th ser., vol., 62 (1914), cols. 60–65, 68–75, 85–87, 90–91.

56. Lloyd George, Speech to the House of Commons, May 4, 1914, cols. 104–08; David Lloyd George to William George, May 6, 1914, William George Papers, NLW; Gilbert, "Landholding," 131–34, 136–37; Packer, *Liberalism*, 148–52; Grigg, *Peace*, 103–05; Emy, "Campaign," 62–64; Douglas, *Land*, 166; Cregier, *Bounder*, 219–20, 235–36.

57. David Lloyd George to William George, May 21, 1914, William George Papers, NLW; Gilbert, "Landholding," 137–40; Packer, *Liberalism*, 152–55; Emy, "Campaign," 64–66; Douglas, *Land*, 166–67; Cregier, *Bounder*, 220, 236–37.

58. David Lloyd George to William George, July 7, 1914, William George Papers, NLW; Gilbert, "Landholding," 140n.67; Grigg, *Peace*, 105–07; quoted in Bentley Brinkerhoff Gilbert, "David Lloyd George: Land, the Budget, and Social Reform," *The American Historical Review* 81 (December 1976): 1058–66.

59. John Campbell, *Lloyd George: The Goat in the Wilderness, 1922–1931* (London: Jonathan Cape, 1977), 16–17, 184–85; Marwick, *Deluge*, 207, 239–42, 274–77, 312; Stevenson, *Society*, 207, 221–22, 297–98; Kenneth O. Morgan, *Consensus and Disunity: The Lloyd George Coalition Government, 1918–1922* (Oxford: Clarendon Press, 1979), 86–102; W. R. Garside, *British Unemployment, 1919–1939* (Cambridge: Cambridge University Press, 1990), 37–38.

Chapter 8

1. Diaries, November 16, December 2, 1883, November 24, 1885, William George Papers, NLW; George, *Making*, 148–49.

2. Du Parcq, *Life*, 1:44–48, 203; Diaries, February 13, 1888, William George Papers, NLW; Diaries, January 20, 22, 24-26, 1889, Lloyd George Papers, NLW.

3. Du Parcq, *Life*, 1:154; Gilbert, *Architect*, 75, 78–80, 86; Grigg, *Young Lloyd*, 96–99, 100.

4. Gilbert, *Architect*, 80–81, 100; Grigg, *Young Lloyd*, 99–100; David Lloyd George to William George, April 21, 1890, William George Papers, NLW; David Lloyd George to Richard Lloyd, May 16, 1890, William George Papers, NLW.

5. Gilbert, *Architect*, 84–87; David Lloyd George to William George, August 12, 1890, William George Papers, NLW.

6. Grigg, *Young Lloyd*, 106; Jackson, *Home*, 74–75; Du Parcq, *Life*, 1:116–17; Gilbert, *Architect*, 89–90, 146; David Lloyd George to William George, Misc. Letter 85, 1890, William George Papers, NLW.

7. David Lloyd George to William George, Misc. Letter 85, 1890, William George Papers, NLW; David Lloyd George to Richard Lloyd, June 20, 1890, William George Papers, NLW. Grigg, *Young Lloyd*, 96.

8. Du Parcq, *Life*, 1:121–22; David Lloyd George to John Herbert Lewis, February 16, 1891, John Herbert Lewis Papers, NLW; Grigg, *Young Lloyd*, 118–19; David Lloyd George to Thomas Edward Ellis, April 11, 1891, Thomas Edward Ellis Papers, NLW.

9. David Lloyd George to William George, February 2, 18, 1891, William George Papers, NLW; Du Parcq, *Life*, 1:122; Grigg, *Young Lloyd*, 93–94.

10. Gilbert, *Architect*, 98–100; Grigg, *Young Lloyd*, 94–95, 109–10; Du Parcq, *Life*, 1:127–29; *The Birkenhead News*, February 6, 1892, Lloyd George Papers, A/7/1, HLRO.

11. David Lloyd George to Margaret Lloyd George, July 30, 1891, March 30, 1892, Lloyd George Papers, NLW, in Morgan, ed., *Family Letters*, 43–44, 46–47; *Carnarvon and Denbigh Herald*, April 8, 1892, 3, Lloyd George Papers, A/7/1, HLRO; Gilbert, *Architect*, 98–99, 101–02; Grigg, *Young Lloyd*, 116–17.

12. Gilbert, *Architect*, 102–03; Grigg, *Young Lloyd*, 117–18; quoted in Edwards, *David Lloyd George*, 3:91–92.

13. Edwards, *David Lloyd George*, 3:91, 93–95; David Lloyd George to Margaret Lloyd George, August 11, 1892, July 5, 1893, Lloyd George Papers, NLW, in Morgan, ed., *Family Letters*, 56, 60; Grigg, *Young Lloyd*, 115–16, 122, 126–27, 131; Gilbert, *Architect*, 107–08.

14. Edwards, *David Lloyd George*, 3:89–90; Grigg, *Young Lloyd*, 122–24; Davies, *History*, 463–64; Gilbert, *Architect*, 103–05.

15. David Lloyd George to Richard Lloyd, February 6, 1893, William George Papers, NLW; Grigg, *Young Lloyd*, 90–92.

16. Grigg, *Young Lloyd*, 132–34; Gilbert, *Architect*, 110; David Lloyd George to John Herbert Lewis, December 1, 1893, John Herbert Lewis Papers, NLW; David Lloyd George to William George, January 4, 1894, William George Papers, NLW.

17. David Lloyd George to Margaret Lloyd George, January 1, 3–4, 6, 1894, Lloyd George Papers, NLW, in Morgan, ed., *Family Letters*, 65, n.1, 66–67; Gilbert, *Architect*, 110–11; Machin, *Churches*, 228.

18. David Lloyd George to Margaret Lloyd George, May 18, 1894, Lloyd George

Papers, NLW, in Morgan, ed., *Family Letters*, 71–72; Gilbert, *Architect*, 110; Grigg, *Young Lloyd*, 136–39.

19. David Lloyd George to William George, March 5, 1894, William George Papers, NLW; Grigg, *Young Lloyd*, 139–49; Gilbert, *Architect*, 111–16; Du Parcq, *Life*, 1:160–61.

20. Grigg, *Young Lloyd*, 149–51; Gilbert, *Architect*, 115–16; Du Parcq, *Life*, 1:161–63; David Lloyd George to Margaret Lloyd George, April 27, May 3, 1894, Lloyd George Papers, NLW, in Morgan, ed., *Family Letters*, 69–70; David Lloyd George to William George, May 2, 1894, William George Papers, NLW.

21. Quoted in Grigg, *Young Lloyd*, 147–49, 151–53; Gilbert, *Architect*, 117–18; Evans, *Life Romance*, 100–01.

22. Grigg, *Young Lloyd*, 153–55; Gilbert, *Architect*, 126–28; David Lloyd George to Margaret Lloyd George, February 8, 1895, Lloyd George Papers, NLW, in Morgan, ed., *Family Letters*, 79–80; David Lloyd George to William George, March 1, 1895, William George Papers, NLW; D. Lloyd George, "Our Case: Welshmen on Welsh Disestablishment," *The Christian World*, March 21, 1895.

23. Du Parcq, *Life*, 1:164–66; David Lloyd George to William George, May 10, 1895, William George Papers, NLW; Grigg, *Young Lloyd*, 156–58; Gilbert, *Architect*, 133–34.

24. David Lloyd George to William George, May 17, 28, 1895, William George Papers, NLW; Grigg, *Young Lloyd*, 158–60; Gilbert, *Architect*, 128–33.

25. Gilbert, *Architect*, 134–39; Grigg, *Young Lloyd*, 156–58, 166–71; Du Parcq, *Life*, 1:168–69.

26. David Lloyd George to William George, Misc. Letter 364, December 13, 1895, William George Papers, NLW; David Lloyd George to Thomas Edward Ellis, November 4, 1895, Thomas Edward Ellis Papers, NLW; Gilbert, *Architect*, 142–45; Grigg, *Young Lloyd*, 220–21.

27. Julia Neuberger, *Lloyd George's Disestablishment Legacy: Reaching for Egalitarianism* (Caernarfon: Cyngor Gwynedd Council, 2000), 9.

28. Gilbert, *Architect*, 145–47; David Lloyd George to William George, May 8, 1896, William George Papers, NLW; Grigg, *Young Lloyd*, 205–06; Du Parcq, *Life*, 1:173–74.

29. Machin, *Churches*, 228; David Lloyd George to William George, Letter 486, August 1897, February 8, 15, March 22, 1898, William George Papers, NLW; Gilbert, *Architect*, 172–73; Grigg, *Young Lloyd*, 218–20.

30. David Lloyd George to William George, March 31, May 24, July 20, 1898, November 10, 1899, William George Papers, NLW; quoted in *The Brecon & Radnor Express*, September 30, 1898, Lloyd George Papers, A/8/4, HLRO; David Lloyd George to Margaret Lloyd George, July 21, 26, 1899, Lloyd George Papers, NLW, in Morgan, ed., *Family Letters*, 117, n.1.

31. James Bentley, *Ritualism and Politics in Victorian Britain: The Attempt to Legislate for Belief* (Oxford: Oxford University Press, 1978), 45; Machin, *Churches*, 4,

229, 242–44; quoted in Du Parcq, *Life*, 1:193; David Lloyd George to William George, February 6, March 18, 1899, William George Papers, NLW.

32. Gilbert, *Architect*, 181, 185–87, 195–97; David Lloyd George to William George, December 2, 1899, February 9, April 7, 1900, William George Papers, NLW.

33. David Lloyd George to William George, February 21, April 21, July 17, 1901, July 13, 1904, William George Papers, NLW; George, *Backbencher*, 328; Gilbert, *Architect*, 197, 214–15; Grigg, *Young Lloyd*, 270; quoted in *Eastern Daily Press*, April 21, 1903, Lloyd George Papers, A/11/1/32, HLRO.

34. Grigg, *People's Champion*, 94–97; Gilbert, *Architect*, 287–89; Du Parcq, *Life*, 3:447–49.

35. Gilbert, *Architect*, 173, 303–04; Grigg, *Young Lloyd*, 198–99; David Lloyd George to William George, December 9, 1905, William George Papers, NLW.

36. Gilbert, *Architect*, 304–08; David Lloyd George to William George, March 6, 7, 1906, February 2, 1907, William George Papers, NLW; Machin, *Churches*, 298–99; Neil Purvey-Tyrer, "Lloyd George, the Bishop of St. Asaph and the Disestablishment Controversy," in *The Life and Times of David Lloyd George*, ed. Judith Loades (Bangor, UK: Headstart History, 1991), 153–57; Grigg, *People's Champion*, 150.

37. David Lloyd George to William George, June 11, 1907, William George Papers, NLW; Gilbert, *Architect*, 309–12; Grigg, *People's Champion*, 151.

38. Gilbert, *Architect*, 330; David Lloyd George to William George, July 17, 1908, April 21, 1909, William George Papers, NLW; Machin, *Churches*, 299–301.

39. Machin, *Churches*, 301–03.

40. David Lloyd George to William George, October 18, 26, 1910, William George Papers, NLW; Gilbert, *Architect*, 411, 415–16, 422, 426–28; Machin, *Churches*, 303–05.

41. Machin, *Churches*, 305–07; quoted in Kenneth Rose, *King George V* (New York: Alfred A. Knopf, 1984), 47–49, 130–31.

42. P. M. H. Bell, *Disestablishment in Ireland and Wales* (London: S.P.C.K., 1969), 244, 250–52, 255–56; Cregier, *Bounder*, 189–90.

43. Bell, *Disestablishment*, 245–46; Machin, *Churches*, 306.

44. David Lloyd George to William George, March 6, November 11, 14, 1912, William George Papers, NLW; Gilbert, *Organizer*, 100.

45. Morgan, ed., *Family Letters*, 143n.1; Grigg, *Peace*, 26–28; Gilbert, *Organizer*, 100–01; David Lloyd George to William George, November 15, December 6, 10, 1912, William George Papers, NLW.

46. David Lloyd George to William George, December 13, 18, 1912, William George Papers, NLW; Machin, *Churches*, 307–08.

47. Machin, *Churches*, 308–09, 309n.81; David Lloyd George to William George, January 10, February 12, 1913, William George Papers, NLW.

48. Bell, *Disestablishment*, 248–49, 257, 262; Gilbert, *Organizer*, 100; Cregier, *Bounder*, 190.

49. David Lloyd George to William George, April 24, 1913, William George Papers, NLW; Grigg, *Peace*, 27–28; Cregier, *Bounder*, 190; Machin, *Churches*, 309–10.

50. David Lloyd George to William George, May 19, 1914, William George Papers, NLW; Bell, *Disestablishment*, 249, 297–99; Adams, *Law*, 133–34; Gilbert, *Organizer*, 159; S. Maccoby, *English Radicalism, 1886–1914* (London: George Allen & Unwin, 1953), 478, n.1.

51. Machin, *Churches*, 309–10; Bell, *Disestablishment*, 249–59.

52. Bell, *Disestablishment*, 297–98; Gilbert, *Organizer*, 159; Davies, *History*, 507; Neuberger, *Legacy*, 11.

53. Gilbert, *Organizer*, 159–60; Bell, *Disestablishment*, 299–301; Machin, *Churches*, 313.

54. David Lloyd George to Margaret Lloyd George, March 12, 15, April 14, 1915, Lloyd George Papers, NLW, translated and quoted in Morgan, ed., *Family Letters*, 176, ns.1, 3; Stevenson Diary, April 4, 1915, Frances Stevenson Papers, HLRO; Taylor, ed., *Diary*, 39–40.

55. Bell, *Disestablishment*, 301, 303–07.

56. Gilbert, *Organizer*, 160; Machin, *Churches*, 313–15.

57. Bell, *Disestablishment*, 307–11, 315, 383n.72; Adams, *Law*, 67, 277–79.

58. Machin, *Churches*, 315–16; Quoted in Winnett, "Factor," 88; David Williams, *A History of Modern Wales*, Rev. ed. (London: John Murray, 1965), 266–68.

Chapter 9

1. Bebbington, *Conscience*, 34; Constantine, *Lloyd*, 9; Donald Richter, "The Welsh Police, the Home Office, and the Welsh Tithe War of 1886–91," *The Welsh History Review* 12 (June 1984): 50–52, 55–58, 69.

2. Bell, *Disestablishment*, 239–40; Davies, *History*, 452–53; W. Watkin Davies, *Lloyd George, 1863–1914* (London: Constable & Company, 1939), 77–79; Cregier, *Bounder*, 28.

3. "The Anti-Tithe Agitation," *The Llangollen Advertiser*, June 3, 1887, 3; "Scenes At Meifod," *The Cambrian News*, June 3, 1887, 7.

4. "The Tithe Agitation In Wales," *The Cambrian News*, June 24, 1887, 2; Gilbert, *Architect*, 50; Grigg, *Young Lloyd*, 49–50; Richter, "Police," 50–52, 55–57, 59–62, 65, 71, 75; Davies, *History*, 452–53.

5. Gilbert, *Architect*, 50–51; Constantine, *Lloyd*, 10–11; Richter, "Police," 58; Cregier, *Bounder*, 27–28; Grigg, *Young Lloyd*, 93; David Lloyd George to Thomas Edward Ellis, May 19, 1887, Thomas Edward Ellis Papers, NLW; Diaries, June 27, 1887, Lloyd George Papers, NLW; *hywl* is Welsh for "a sail" and refers to a speaker "driven along like a ship in full sail by uncontrollable forces," translated in Du Parcq, *Life*, 1:45n.2

6. Quoted in Du Parcq, *Life*, 74–75, 201–04.

7. Diaries, August 20, 28, September 7, October 31, 1887, January 22, 24–26, 1889, Lloyd George Papers, NLW; George, *Making*, 151–53.

8. Richter, "Police," 54, 56, 67; John Grigg, *Lloyd George: War Leader, 1916–1918* (London: Allen Lane, 2002), 129–32; "The Anti-Tithe Agitation in Wales," *The Spectator*, January 4, 1890, 18–20.

9. Maccoby, *Radicalism*, 78–80; Edwards, *David Lloyd George*, 3:43–44; Du Parcq, *Life*, 1:75, 121; Gilbert, *Architect*, 84.

10. Gilbert, *Architect*, 84–85; David Lloyd George to Richard Lloyd, June 22, 1890, William George Papers, NLW; David Lloyd George to William George, Misc. Letter 79, November 27, December 3, 1890, William George Papers, NLW.

11. David Lloyd George to William George, January 27, 31, February 6, 1891, William George Papers, NLW; HC Deb (3rd series) January 26, 1891, vol. 349 c1056; Du Parcq, *Life*, 1:122–23; Gilbert, *Architect*, 84–85; Grigg, *Young Lloyd*, 106–07.

12. David Lloyd George to William George, February 11, 1891, William George Papers, NLW; Du Parcq, *Life*, 1:121–23; Gilbert, *Architect*, 91–92; Grigg, *Young Lloyd*, 93–94, 106–07.

13. Robert Brown, Jr., "Tithes in England and Wales," *Political Science Quarterly* 7, no. 2 (June 1892): 257; Richter, "Police," 66, 68; Douglas, *Land*, 99–103; Neil Daglish, *Education Policy-Making in England and Wales: The Crucible Years, 1895–1911* (London: The Woburn Press, 1996), 13.

14. Quoted in Du Parcq, *Life*, 1:121–23, 130–32; George, *Backbencher*, 58–61; David Lloyd George to William George, December 3, 1890, February 11, 1891, William George Papers, NLW.

15. David Lloyd George to Thomas Edward Ellis, April 11, 1891, Thomas Edward Ellis Papers, NLW; Grigg, *Young Lloyd*, 108–09; David Lloyd George to William George, June, 16, 22, 24, 30, July 7, 13, 1891, William George Papers, NLW; George, *Backbencher*, 61–62; Du Parcq, *Life*, 1:120–21.

16. Quoted in Du Parcq, *Life*, 1:126–27; Maccoby, *Radicalism*, 106–07, 451, 458; Gilbert, *Architect*, 92–93; David Lloyd George to Richard Lloyd, August 14, 1891, William George Papers, NLW; David Lloyd George to William George, Letter 237, February 1894, William George Papers, NLW; Donald P. Leinster-Mackay, "Diggle, Joseph Robert (1849–1917), in *Oxford Dictionary of National Biography*, ed. Brian Harrison, 60 vols. (New York: Oxford University Press, 2004), 16:174–75; Jacob, *Vitality*, 166, 278.

17. Daglish, *Education*, 52–56, 64–66; Gilbert, *Architect*, 154–55; David Lloyd George to Margaret Lloyd George, June 11, 1896, Lloyd George Papers, NLW, in Morgan, ed., *Family Letters*, 104; Bebbington, *Conscience*, 137–39; David Lloyd George to Richard Lloyd, January 22, 1897, William George Papers, NLW; "The New Education Bill," *The Christian World*, February 4, 1897, 4; quoted in "The Sectarian Five Shillings," *The Christian World*, February 18, 1897; "The Bad Bill's Second Reading," *The Christian World*, February 18, 1897, 1.

18. George, *Backbencher*, 261–62; Machin, *Churches*, 228; David Lloyd George to William George, Letter 486, August 1897, William George Papers, NLW; William McGuire King, "Hugh Price Hughes and the British 'Social Gospel,'"

Journal of Religious History 13 (June 1984): 66, 75, 79; Diaries, January 29, 1888, William George Papers, NLW.

19. David Lloyd George to William George, March 22, 31, 1898, William George Papers, NLW; George, *Backbencher*, 264–66; Jones, trans., David Lloyd George to William George, Letter 635, June 25, 1898, in "Catalog," William George Papers, NLW; Gilbert, *Architect*, 175; *The Brecon & Radnor Express*, September 30, 1898, Lloyd George Papers, A/8/4, HLRO.

20. *Brecon & Radnor*, September 30, 1898; "Grand Liberal Meeting At Pontypridd," *The Pontypridd Chronicle*, January 15, 1892, 6, Lloyd George Papers, A/7/1, HLRO; a vaccination bill passed in 1898 prohibited maintaining them by arm-to-arm transfers, Jerry L. Gaw, "Edward Jenner 1749–1823," in *Research Guide To European Historical Biography*, ed. James A. Moncure, 8 vols. (Washington, DC: Beacham Publishing, 1993), 6:3420.

21. Daglish, *Education*, 3–5; quoted in George, *Backbencher*, 246–48; Hugh Chisholm, ed., "Forster, William Edward," *The Encyclopaedia Britannica*, 11th ed., 10 (New York: The Encyclopaedia Britannica Company, 1910), 675–77.

22. *Manchester Guardian*, November 9, 1898, Lloyd George Papers, A/8/4, HLRO; Du Parcq, *Life*, 1:190; Maccoby, *Radicalism*, 276–78.

23. Quoted in Du Parcq, *Life*, 1:204–08; George, *Backbencher*, 267–68; Grigg, *Young Lloyd*, 216; Gilbert, *Architect*, 177; Douglas, *Land*, 122–23; Maccoby, *Radicalism*, 316–17, 485.

24. Bebbington, *Conscience*, 141–42; Daglish, *Education*, 128–29, 142, 144, 151; Grigg, *People's Champion*, 23–24, 31–33; Gilbert, *Architect*, 216–19; George, *Backbencher*, 353–54, 361–62; Maccoby, *Radicalism*, 336–39.

25. John Crockatt and Thomas J. Ainsworth, "The Education Bill," *The Bible Advocate*, May 23, 1902, 335; Thompson, *Sects and Parties*, 90–92, 94.

26. Thomas J. Ainsworth, "Shall We Pay," *The Bible Advocate*, November 28, 1902, 763–64; Thompson, *Sects and Parties*, 203; Gilbert, *Architect*, 224–34; Daglish, *Education*, 167–68, 172–95; Thompson, "Social Gospel," 206; Grigg, *People's Champion*, 25–28, 37–39; Adams, *Balfour*, 168–69; George, *Backbencher*, 354–58; David Lloyd George to Margaret Lloyd George, March 24, 1902, Lloyd George Papers, NLW, in Morgan, ed., *Family Letters*, 131–32; David Lloyd George to William George, July 22, 31, 1905, William George Papers, NLW.

27. Watters, *British Churches*, 83; John Mason, "Cheshire and North Wales Division," *The Bible Advocate*, January 9, 1903, 30.

28. Mason, "Cheshire," 30–31; Watters, *British Churches*, 52, 55, 74–76, 78; Diaries, July 25, 1878, June 20, 1880, June 12, 19, 1881, June 4, 7, 14, 18, 21, 1882, July 18, 1883, William George Papers, NLW.

29. George, *Making*, 127; quoted in George, *My Brother*, 166–67; David Lloyd George to William George, June 21, 1902, William George Papers, NLW; Grigg, *People's Champion*, 21–25, 42–44; Gilbert, *Architect*, 240–41; Daglish, *Education*, 255–60; Adams, *Balfour*, 168–70.

30. *Eastern Daily Press*, April 21, 1903, Lloyd George Papers, A/11/1/32, HLRO; Grigg, *People's Champion*, 42–43; "North Wales Calvinistic Methodists," *Carnarvon and Denbigh Herald*, August 28, 1903, 8, Lloyd George Papers, A/11/2/10, HLRO; George, *Backbencher*, 386–87; David Lloyd George to John Herbert Lewis, January 25, 1904, John Herbert Lewis Papers, NLW.

31. Gilbert, *Architect*, 245–49; Grigg, *People's Champion*, 21–22, 33–35; Du Parcq, *Life*, 2:370–81; Pugh, *Lloyd George*, 27–29; David Lloyd George to William George, October 30, 1903, William George Papers, NLW; George, *Backbencher*, 384–85.

32. Grigg, *People's Champion*, 34–35, 41–42, 44–48; George, *Backbencher*, 365; Du Parcq, *Life*, 2:369–70, 381–84; quoted in "From our own Correspondents. Wales," *The British Weekly*, December 23, 1903; George, *My Brother*, 167–69; Gilbert, *Architect*, 245; David Lloyd George to William George, February 11, 1903, William George Papers, NLW.

33. Grigg, *People's Champion*, 28–31, 35, 41–42, 47, n.2, 48; Gilbert, *Architect*, 263–64; Pugh, *Lloyd George*, 29; George, *Backbencher*, 358–59, 370, 372–74; Du Parcq, *Life*, 2:360–61, 366–67; Daglish, *Education*, 255–57; Machin, *Churches*, 267–68; quoted with italics in George, *My Brother*, 169; David Lloyd George to William George, February 18, 1903, January 13, 1905, William George Papers, NLW.

34. George, *Backbencher*, 446–52; George, *My Brother*, 87–89; Grigg, *People's Champion*, 90–91; Gilbert, *Architect*, 263; David Lloyd George to William George, Letter 1736, December 4, 1905, William George Papers, NLW.

35. David Lloyd George to William George, December 5, 7–9, 1905, William George Papers, NLW; quoted in George, *My Brother*, 89–90.

36. Translated in George, *Backbencher*, 452–54; David Lloyd George to William George, December 13–14, 18, 1905, William George Papers, NLW; Gilbert, *Architect*, 258, 263; Grigg, *People's Champion*, 47, 91–94.

37. Gilbert, *Architect*, 263–64, 287–89; George, *Backbencher*, 454–56; Daglish, *Education*, 276–77, 285–87, 289, 379; Grigg, *People's Champion*, 52, 94–98, 149, 151; Du Parcq, *Life*, 2:384.

38. David Lloyd George to William George, March 9, 30, June 11, July 8, 26, 1906, William George Papers, NLW; Daglish, *Education*, 289–90, 292, 294–310, 316, 318; J. E. Stephen, "Church Intelligence," *The Bible Advocate*, April 27, 1906, 267.

39. Gilbert, *Architect*, 292–301; David Lloyd George to William George, July 26, September 11, December 19, 1906, William George Papers, NLW; Grigg, *People's Champion*, 151–52; quoted in Rowland, *Lloyd*, 188–89; Adams, *Balfour*, 235.

40. Daglish, *Education*, 315–16, 318–22, 366–70; Gilbert, *Architect*, 301–03.

41. Grigg, *People's Champion*, 152–53; Stevenson, *Society*, 207–08.

42. Daglish, *Education*, 322–24, 379–83; Stevenson, *Society*, 244.

43. Emy, "Campaign," 50; Daglish, *Education*, 401, 446; Grigg, *Peace*, 495–96; Gilbert, *Architect*, 302–03; Dennis Dean, "The Dilemmas of an Academic Liberal Historian in Lloyd George's Government: H. A. L. Fisher at the Board of Education, 1916–1922," *History* 79 (February 1994): 57–63, 69–74, 78–79; Bell, *Disestablishment*, 306, 317.

Chapter 10

1. Diaries, July 12, 1878, April 5, 1880, William George Papers, NLW; R. W. Seton-Watson, *Disraeli, Gladstone, and the Eastern Question* (New York: W. W. Norton & Company, 1972), 435–40, 446, 457–59, 507–08, 537–38, 545–50; Peter Stansky, *Gladstone: A Progress in Politics* (New York: W. W. Norton & Company, 1979), 126–41.

2. Diaries, November 1, 5, 16, 19, 1880, February 18, 20, 1881, June 23, 26–27, 1882, William George Papers, NLW; Brutus, "The Marquis of Salisbury," *The North Wales Express*, November 5, 1880, 4; Brutus, "A Contest in Carnarvonshire," *The North Wales Express*, November 19, 1880, 5; Brutus, "Irish Grievances," *The North Wales Express*, February 18, 1881, 6; Michael G. Fry, *Lloyd George and Foreign Policy: The Education of a Statesman: 1890–1916* (Montreal: McGill-Queen's University Press, 1977), 24–27; Du Parcq, *Life*, 1:34–39, 53–56.

3. Diaries, June 26–27, 1882, William George Papers, NLW; George, *Making*, 16–17; quoted in Tickle, ed., "Origin and Progress, No. VI," 198–99; Alexander Campbell, "An Address on War," *British Millennial Harbinger* 12 (November 1848): 489–506; Lappin, "Passing," 6; Foster, *Campbell*, 293–94, 297–98; J. Caleb Clanton, *The Philosophy of Religion of Alexander Campbell* (Knoxville: The University of Tennessee Press, 2013), 6, 119.

4. Diaries, July 11, 27, November 13, 1882, William George Papers, NLW; quoted in Fry, *Foreign*, 22–23, 31; Byron Farwell, *Queen Victoria's Little Wars* (New York: W. W. Norton & Company, 1972), 253–54, 269; Stansky, *Progress*, xx, 155; Du Parcq, *Life*, 1:40–42; "The Late War In Egypt," *The North Wales Express*, November 24, 1882, 6; Grigg, *Young Lloyd*, 44.

5. Diaries, January 24, 1883, William George Papers, NLW.

6. Diaries, March 9, 22, April 21, 1883, August 5–6, 1884, William George Papers, NLW.

7. Jenkins, *Gladstone*, 509–16, 539–62, 577–89; Stansky, *Progress*, xxi, 155–66, 169; Charles Chenevix Trench, *The Road to Khartoum: A Life of General Charles Gordon* (New York: Carroll & Graf Publishers, 1989), 290–91; Diaries, May 4, 1885, William George Papers, NLW; Morgan, ed., *Family Letters*, 120; Howard Jones, *The Course of American Diplomacy* (New York: Franklin Watts, 1985), 207–13; Fry, *Foreign*, 33–34.

8. Fry, *Foreign*, 33–34; Morgan, ed., *Family Letters*, 120; quoted in Grigg, *Young Lloyd*, 222–23; David Lloyd George to William George, September 5, 1898,

William George Papers, NLW; Philip Warner, *Kitchener: The Man Behind the Legend* (New York: Atheneum, 1985), 88–99, 101–04; David Levering Lewis, *The Race to Fashoda* (New York: Weidenfeld & Nicolson, 1987), 7–9, 27, 30–31, 137–38, 222–30.

9. David Lloyd George to William George, September 2, 18, 1899, William George Papers, NLW; George, *My Brother*, 177; David Lloyd George to Margaret Lloyd George, September 27, 1899, Lloyd George Papers, NLW, in Morgan, ed., *Family Letters*, 122.

10. David Lloyd George to William George, October 16–17, 1899, William George Papers, NLW; George, *My Brother*, 177.

11. David Lloyd George to William George, October 18, 20, 23, 1899, William George Papers, NLW; Thomas Pakenham, *The Boer War* (New York: Random House, 1979), 127–52; David Lloyd George to Margaret Lloyd George, October 23 (two), 1899, Lloyd George Papers, NLW, in Morgan, ed., *Family Letters*, 123.

12. David Lloyd George to William George, October 23, 25–26, 1899, William George Papers, NLW.

13. David Lloyd George to William George, October 28, 1899, William George Papers, NLW; Pakenham, *Boer*, 35, 154–55, 262.

14. David Lloyd George to William George, October 21, 1899, William George Papers, NLW; Robert I. Rotberg, *The Founder: Cecil Rhodes and the Pursuit of Power* (New York: Oxford University Press, 1988), 37, 116, 339–76, 450–87, 546, 609–13, 684–85; George, *My Brother*, 61.

15. David Lloyd George to William George, November 2–3, 1899, William George Papers, NLW; George, *Backbencher*, 293–94; Pakenham, *Boer*, 155–59.

16. David Lloyd George to William George, November 2, 1899, William George Papers, NLW; Pakenham, *Boer*, 145–51; David Lloyd George to Margaret Lloyd George, November 2, 1899, Lloyd George Papers, NLW, in Morgan, ed., *Family Letters*, 124–25; Gilbert, *Architect*, 182–83.

17. Pakenham, *Boer*, 95, 155–59; David Lloyd George to William George, October 30–31, 1899, William George Papers, NLW; George, *Backbencher*, 293.

18. David Lloyd George to William George, March 7, 1900, William George Papers, NLW; George, *My Brother*, 178; Cregier, *Bounder*, 66; quoted in Du Parcq, *Life*, 2:224–25.

19. David Lloyd George to William George, April 4, May 19, 1900, William George Papers, NLW; George, *My Brother*, 179–80, 182, 187; George, *Backbencher*, 311–14; Gilbert, *Architect*, 178, 181, 187–88; Grigg, *Young Lloyd*, 266; Cregier, *Bounder*, 65–67; Du Parcq, *Life*, 2:226–27, 232.

20. David Lloyd George to William George, May 19, 26, 1900, William George Papers, NLW; George, *My Brother*, 181–82; George, *Backbencher*, 314; Pakenham, *Boer*, 34, 173, 176, 399–400.

21. David Lloyd George to William George, June 27, 1900, William George Papers, NLW; George, *My Brother*, 182; George, *Backbencher*, 315–16; David Lloyd

George to Richard Lloyd, July 18, 1900, William George Papers, NLW; Grigg, *Young Lloyd*, 89–90, 168–69, 216–18, 263; Farwell, *Little*, 348–53; Pakenham, *Boer*, 152–59, 254–55, 343–45, 382–86, 391–93, 438–40, 452–60.

22. David Lloyd George to William George, July 6, 1900, William George Papers, NLW; George, *Backbencher*, 317; Lloyd George, Speech to the House of Commons, July 25, 1900, Parliamentary Debates, Commons, 4th ser., vol., 86 (1900), cols. 1199–1212; Du Parcq, *Life*, 2:232–37; Grigg, *Young Lloyd*, 266–67; Gilbert, *Architect*, 189–90.

23. Pakenham, *Boer*, 490–91, 499–501; David Lloyd George to William George, September 1, 1900, William George Papers, NLW; George, *My Brother*, 182; quoted in Grigg, *Young Lloyd*, 277–78.

24. Grigg, *Young Lloyd*, 267–70, 274–76, 281; Pakenham, *Boer*, 484, 492–93, 512–13, 522–23, 618; Warner, *Kitchener*, 124–30; Lloyd George, Speech to the House of Commons, March 19, 1901, Parliamentary Debates, Commons, 4th ser., vol., 91 (1901), cols. 473–75; George, *Backbencher*, 288–89.

25. Lloyd George, Speech to the House of Commons, February 18, 1901, Parliamentary Debates, Commons, 4th ser., vol., 89 (1901), cols. 397–405; George, *Backbencher*, 329–30; Robert Lloyd George, *David & Winston: How the Friendship Between Churchill and Lloyd George Changed the Course of History* (Woodstock, UK: The Overlook Press, 2008), 3–5; Warner, *Kitchener*, 127.

26. Fry, *Foreign*, 50–51; Quoted in Pakenham, *Boer*, 533–39.

27. Lloyd George, Speeches to the House of Commons, June 14, 21, 1901, Parliamentary Debates, Commons, 4th ser., vol., 95 (1901), cols. 409–10, 1055; David Lloyd George to William George, Misc. Letter 1142, 1901, William George Papers, NLW; George, *My Brother*, 182.

28. Lloyd George, Speech to the House of Commons, June 17, 1901, Parliamentary Debates, Commons, 4th ser., vol., 95 (1901), cols. 573–83; Pakenham, *Boer*, 539–40; Fry, *Foreign*, 51–52; David Lloyd George to William George, June 18, 1901, William George Papers, NLW; George, *Backbencher*, 332–35; Du Parcq, *Life*, 2:326–31.

29. St John Brodrick, Speech to the House of Commons, June 17, 1901, cols. 590–97.

30. Quoted in Du Parcq, *Life*, 2:257; Fry, *Foreign*, 25; Pakenham, *Boer*, 540.

31. Grigg, *Young Lloyd*, 282, n.2; Pakenham, *Boer*, 549; Fry, *Foreign*, 55; David Lloyd George to William George, July 6, 1901, William George Papers, NLW.

32. Du Parcq, *Life*, 2:258–60; David Lloyd George to William George, July 3, 1901, William George Papers, NLW; Grigg, *Young Lloyd*, 283–86, 288–92.

33. David Lloyd George to William George, November 7, 1901, William George Papers, NLW; quoted in Grigg, *Young Lloyd*, 285–86.

34. Du Parcq, *Life*, 2:278–94; Gilbert, *Architect*, 210–14; Grigg, *Young Lloyd*, 286–87; George, *My Brother*, 183–85; George, *Backbencher*, 339–42.

35. David Lloyd George to William George, December 19-20, 24, 1901, William

George Papers, NLW; George, *Backbencher*, 342–44; Du Parcq, *Life*, 2:278–79, 294–96; Grigg, *Young Lloyd*, 278–80, 287–88; George, *My Brother*, 184–85.

36. Quoted in Grigg, *Young Lloyd*, 288, 292; Lloyd George, Speech to the House of Commons, March 20, 1902, Parliamentary Debates, Commons, 4th ser., vol., 105 (1902), cols. 638–42.

37. Lloyd George, Speech to the House of Commons, March 20, 1902, cols. 642–58; George, *Backbencher*, 347–49; David Lloyd George to Margaret Lloyd George, March 6, 21, 1902, Lloyd George Papers, NLW, in Morgan, ed., *Family Letters*, 128, 131; Grigg, *Young Lloyd*, 283–84, 291–92.

38. David Lloyd George to Margaret Lloyd George, March 11 (two), 12, 20, 1902, Lloyd George Papers, NLW, in Morgan, ed., *Family Letters*, 129–30; Pakenham, *Boer*, 582–83; John Dillon, Speech to the House of Commons, March 20, 1902, cols. 591–93.

39. Pakenham, *Boer*, 583–86; David Lloyd George to Margaret Lloyd George, March 24–25, April 18, 1902, Lloyd George Papers, NLW, in Morgan, ed., *Family Letters*, 131–32, 134.

40. Pakenham, *Boer*, 596–97.

41. David Lloyd George to Margaret Lloyd George, May 23, 1902, Lloyd George Papers, NLW, in Morgan, ed., *Family Letters*, 136; David Lloyd George to William George, May 24, 1902, William George Papers, NLW; Pakenham, *Boer*, 597–99.

42. David Lloyd George to William George, May 24, 1902, William George Papers, NLW; Pakenham, *Boer*, 603–04; David Lloyd George to Margaret Lloyd George, June 2, 1902, Lloyd George Papers, NLW, in Morgan, ed., *Family Letters*, 136–37; Grigg, *Young Lloyd*, 292–94.

Chapter 11

1. Fry, *Foreign*, 34–35; Adams, *Balfour*, 100–02, 186–89; Grigg, *People's Champion*, 56, 69, 305–12; David Lloyd George, *Memoirs*, 3; Gilbert, *Architect*, 449–58; David Lloyd George to William George, February 9, April 13–14, 1904, March 11, 1905, William George Papers, NLW; Hugh Seton-Watson, *The Russian Empire, 1801–1917* (Oxford: Oxford University Press, 1967), 591–92, 595–97; Robert K. Massie, *Dreadnought: Britain, Germany, and the Coming of the Great War* (New York: Random House, 1991), 344–50.

2. Massie, *Dreadnought*, 353–67; Grigg, *People's Champion*, 91–92, 308; Gilbert, *Architect*, 282–84, 449; Robert A. Kann, *A History of the Habsburg Empire, 1526–1918* (Berkeley: University of California Press, 1974), 411.

3. Harold Nicolson, *Portrait of a Diplomatist* (Boston: Houghton Mifflin Company, 1930), 170–88; Massie, *Dreadnought*, 594–601; Seton-Watson, *Russian Empire*, 679–82.

4. Grigg, *People's Champion*, 21–48, 103–22, 159–62, 306–08, 327–38, 341–45; Fry,

Foreign, 64–67; Gilbert, *Architect*, 313–19, 323–29, 336–43, 429–46; Edwards, *David Lloyd George*, 4:144–66; Adams, *Balfour*, 235.

5. Du Parcq, *Life*, 3:514–16; Cregier, *Bounder*, 115–17; Gilbert, *Architect*, 347–52; Grigg, *People's Champion*, 306–07; Fry, *Foreign*, 94–103; David Lloyd George to William George, July 17, 29, 1908, William George Papers, NLW; quoted in Lloyd George, *Memoirs*, 11–28; David Lloyd George to Richard Lloyd, August 13, 1908, William George Papers, NLW.

6. Kann, *Habsburg*, 279, 412–14; Massie, *Dreadnought*, 602–08; Seton-Watson, *Russian Empire*, 689–91; David Lloyd George to William George, October 12, 1908, William George Papers, NLW; Philip Magnus, *King Edward the Seventh* (New York: E. P. Dutton & Co., 1964), 413–17; Fry, *Foreign*, 119.

7. Gilbert, *Architect*, 342–47, 364–68; Massie, *Dreadnought*, 609–18; Grigg, *People's Champion*, 174–76, 190–94; Fry, *Foreign*, 107–16; Richard Burdon Haldane, *Viscount Haldane: An Autobiography* (New York: Doubleday, Doran & Company, 1929), 193–96; Stephen E. Koss, *Lord Haldane: Scapegoat for Liberalism* (New York: Columbia University Press, 1969), 38–40.

8. David Lloyd George to William George, May 12, 1908, William George Papers, NLW; Lloyd George, Speech to the House of Commons, April 29, 1909, Parliamentary Debates, Commons, 5th ser., vol., 4 (1909), cols. 478–81.

9. Massie, *Dreadnought*, 615–18, 655–57; Gilbert, *Architect*, 367–68, 400–11; David Lloyd George to Richard Lloyd, September 7, 1909, William George Papers, NLW; David Lloyd George to William George, June 15, 17, 1911, William George Papers, NLW; Grigg, *People's Champion*, 176–77, 251–56, 258, 261.

10. Viscount Haldane, *Before the War* (London: Cassell and Company, 1920), 28–35; Koss, *Haldane*, 46–50; Haldane, *Autobiography*, 196–202; Magnus, *Edward VII*, 456; Cregier, *Bounder*, 171–77; David Lloyd George to Margaret Lloyd George, May 8, 1910, Lloyd George Papers, NLW, in Morgan, ed., *Family Letters*, 152; Gilbert, *Architect*, 411–13, 427–28, 437–46, 449–58; Grigg, *People's Champion*, 286–90, 308–12, 315–16, 327–31, 341–44; Grigg, *Peace*, 113–26.

11. Massie, *Dreadnought*, 719–43; David Lloyd George to William George, July 3–4, 1911, William George Papers, NLW.

12. Fry, *Foreign*, 131–42, 147–50; Grigg, *People's Champion*, 308–10; Gilbert, *Architect*, 449–50, 460–61; Massie, *Dreadnought*, 729–33.

13. Quoted in Walter Roch, *Mr. Lloyd George and the War* (London: Chatto & Windus, 1920), 45–46; Lloyd George, *Memoirs*, 39–43; David Lloyd George to William George, July 28, November 27, 1911, William George Papers, NLW; Christopher Clark, *The Sleepwalkers: How Europe Went to War in 1914* (New York: Harper, 2013), 209–11, 328–29; Adams, *Law*, 54–65.

14. Gilbert, *Architect*, 453–54, 459; Massie, *Dreadnought*, 733–38, 741–43; Cregier, *Bounder*, 171–77; Nicolson, *Portrait*, 249–54.

15. David Lloyd George to William George, November 10, 1911, William George Papers, NLW; David Lloyd George to Margaret Lloyd George, July 26, 28, 1911,

Lloyd George Papers, NLW, in Morgan, ed., *Family Letters*, 155–56; Quoted in Fry, *Foreign*, 141–47.

16. Jenkins, *Churchill*, 154–57, 203–06; Fry, *Foreign*, 87–92, 156–57; Gilbert, *Architect*, 451, 453–59; Massie, *Dreadnought*, 768, 792, 794, 802–05, 807–12; Robert Lloyd George, *David*, 86–87; Cregier, *Bounder*, 177.

17. Haldane, *Before*, 55–62, 160; Nicolson, *Portrait*, 263–64; Cregier, *Bounder*, 221–22; David Lloyd George to William George, January 31, 1912, William George Papers, NLW.

18. Massie, *Dreadnought*, 812–17, 823–28, 838; Haldane, *Before*, 59–60, 63–67, 71–72; Nicolson, *Portrait*, 260–62, 264–67, 270–71; Fry, *Foreign*, 157–61; Jenkins, *Churchill*, 211–12, 227; David Lloyd George to Margaret Lloyd George, October 10, 1911, Lloyd George Papers, NLW, in Morgan, ed., *Family Letters*, 160.

19. Cregier, *Bounder*, 222–28; Robert Lloyd George, *David*, 90–91; Seton-Watson, *Russian Empire*, 692.

20. Barbara Jelavich, *A Century of Russian Foreign Policy, 1814–1914* (Philadelphia: J. B. Lippincott Company, 1964), 268–70; Seton-Watson, *Russian Empire*, 691–92; Nicolson, *Portrait*, 262–63.

21. Fry, *Foreign*, 153–54; David Lloyd George to William George, October 3, 8, 1912, William George Papers, NLW; George, *My Brother*, 248; Cregier, *Bounder*, 240–41.

22. Nicolson, *Portrait*, 276–77, 280–82; David Lloyd George to William George, October 28, 30, November 1, 1912, William George Papers, NLW; George, *My Brother*, 248; Cregier, *Bounder*, 241; quoted in Fry, *Foreign*, 154–55, 256–58.

23. Massie, *Dreadnought*, 838–39; Seton-Watson, *Russian Empire*, 692–93.

24. Jelavich, *Century*, 270–72, 276–79; Kann, *Habsburg*, 416–20; Seton-Watson, *Russian Empire*, 693–97; Nicolson, *Portrait*, 282–83; Fry, *Foreign*, 155–56; Massie, *Dreadnought*, 839.

25. Nicolson, *Portrait*, 296–309; Massie, *Dreadnought*, 858–60, 864–69, 874–908; Cregier, *Bounder*, 241–54; Haldane, *Autobiography*, 287–300; Bernadotte E. Schmitt and Harold C. Vedeler, *The World in the Crucible, 1914–1919* (New York: Harper & Row, Publishers, 1984), 6–8, 35–36.

26. David Lloyd George to Margaret Lloyd George, July 27–29, August 3, 1914, Lloyd George Papers, NLW, in Morgan, ed., *Family Letters*, 166–67.

27. Quoted in D. Densil Morgan, "'Christ and the War': Some Aspects of the Welsh Experience, 1914–1918," *The Journal of Welsh Religious History* 5 (1997): 74; Fry, *Foreign*, 184–87, 193–96, 204–207, 258–61; W. Crosthwaite, ed., *For His Name's Sake: Being a Record of the Witness given by Members of Churches of Christ in Great Britain against Militarism during the European War, 1914–1918* (Heanor, UK: W. Barker, 1921), 9; Peter Ackers, "Who Speaks for the Christians? The Great War and Conscientious Objection in the Churches of Christ: A View from the Wigan Coalfield," *The Journal of the United Reformed Church History Society* 5 (October 1993): 156, 166–67; Watters, *British Churches*, 109.

28. Morgan, "Christ and the War," 74–75, 77, 83–84; quoted in Watters, *British Churches*, 109–10; Crosthwaite, ed., *Sake*, 9–11, 21–25, 35–36, 65–69, 71–76; Malcolm Elliott, "Opposition to the First World War: The Fate of Conscientious Objectors in Leicester," *Transactions of the Leicestershire Archaeological and Historical Society* 77 (2003): 85, 87; Ackers, "Speaks," 154, 157, 159, 164; Thompson, *Sects and Parties*, 123–24; Fry, *Foreign*, 197–204.

29. David Lloyd George to Margaret Lloyd George, August 7, 11, 1914, Lloyd George Papers, NLW, in Morgan, ed., *Family Letters*, 168–69; Robert K. Massie, *Castles of Steel: Britain, Germany, and the Winning of the Great War at Sea* (New York: Random House, 2003), 226–55; Schmitt and Vedeler, *Crucible*, 98–100, 119–20; John Keegan, *The First World War* (New York: Alfred A. Knopf, 1999), 216–17; Gilbert, *Organizer*, 139–40.

30. David Lloyd George to Margaret Lloyd George, August 7, 1914, Lloyd George Papers, NLW, in Morgan, ed., *Family Letters*, 168–69; Holger H. Herwig, *The Marne, 1914: The Opening of World War I and the Battle That Changed the World* (New York: Random House, 2009), 105–14, 152–56; Keegan, *First*, 81–86; David Lloyd George to William George, August 25, 1914, William George Papers, NLW.

31. Clark, *Sleepwalkers*, 211, 494, 654n.20; Fry, *Foreign*, 207–13.

32. Keegan, *First*, 27, 38, 88–89, 94–101; David Lloyd George to William George, August 29, 1914, William George Papers, NLW; David Lloyd George to Margaret Lloyd George, September 5, 1914, Lloyd George Papers, NLW, in Morgan, ed., *Family Letters*, 172.

33. Keegan, *First*, 110–22; Herwig, *Marne*, 240–303; Schmitt and Vedeler, *Crucible*, 47–51; David Lloyd George to Margaret Lloyd George, September 8, 10–11, 1914, Lloyd George Papers, NLW, in Morgan, ed., *Family Letters*, 172–73.

34. Keegan, *First*, 123–28, 214; Schmitt and Vedeler, *Crucible*, 51–53, 121; David Lloyd George to William George, September 23, 1914, William George Papers, NLW; Massie, *Castles*, 128–39; Arthur Herman, *To Rule the Waves: How the British Navy Shaped the Modern World* (New York: HarperCollins Publishers, 2004), 495; James L. Stokesbury, *Navy and Empire* (New York: William Morrow and Company, 1983), 316; David Lloyd George to Margaret Lloyd George, September 28, 1914, Lloyd George Papers, NLW, in Morgan, ed., *Family Letters*, 173, n.2.

35. Keegan, *First*, 129–35; Schmitt and Vedeler, *Crucible*, 53–54; David Lloyd George to Margaret Lloyd George, October 20, 1914, Lloyd George Papers, NLW, in Morgan, ed., *Family Letters*, 173; David Lloyd George to William George, October 13, 1914, William George Papers, NLW; Grigg, *Peace*, 178–81; Gilbert, *Organizer*, 124–26.

36. Schmitt and Vedeler, *Crucible*, 53–55; Keegan, *First*, 130–32, 135–37; David Lloyd George to Margaret Lloyd George, October 27, November 3, 1914, Lloyd George Papers, NLW, in Morgan, ed., *Family Letters*, 174.

37. Keegan, *First*, 135–37; Schmitt and Vedeler, *Crucible*, 55; David Lloyd George to William George, October 2, 5, November 24, December 10, 1914, William George Papers, NLW; David Lloyd George to Margaret Lloyd George, October 28, 1914, Lloyd George Papers, NLW, in Morgan, ed., *Family Letters*, 174; Stevenson Diary, October 30, November 2, 1914, Frances Stevenson Papers, HLRO, in Taylor, ed., *Diary*, 7–9; Grigg, *Peace*, 177–78, 198–99; Gilbert, *Organizer*, 128–30.

38. David Lloyd George to William George, December 14, 1914, William George Papers, NLW; Francis J. Reynolds, Allen L. Churchill, and Francis Trevelyan Miller, *The Story of the Great War* (New York: P. F. Collier & Son, 1916), 183–84; Keegan, *First*, 179–81, Schmitt and Vedeler, *Crucible*, 55, 70.

39. David Lloyd George to Margaret Lloyd George, January 6, 1915, Lloyd George Papers, NLW, in Morgan, ed., *Family Letters*, 175, n.1; Fry, *Foreign*, 275–76; Keegan, *First*, 221, 225–26, 234–38; Schmitt and Vedeler, *Crucible*, 77, 105–07; David Lloyd George to William George, February 22, 1915, William George Papers, NLW; Ellery Sedgwick, ed., "'A Paper of the Highest Importance': Mr. Lloyd George's Plan to Win the War in 1915," *The Atlantic Monthly* 138, no. 1 (July 1926): 21–28; Lloyd George, *Memoirs*, 322–30; Massie, *Castles*, 426–61; Herman, *Rule*, 498.

40. Keegan, *First*, 238–49; Schmitt and Vedeler, *Crucible*, 107–17; Herman, *Rule*, 497–99; Massie, *Castles*, 287–99, 461–91; Fry, *Foreign*, 277–78.

41. Grigg, *Peace*, 248–53; quoted in Gilbert, *Organizer*, 177–79, 192–207; Jenkins, *Churchill*, 269–76; Adams, *Law*, 177–92; Lloyd George, *Memoirs*, 196–207; David Lloyd George to Margaret Lloyd George, May 20–21, 24–26, 1915, Lloyd George Papers, NLW, in Morgan, ed., *Family Letters*, 177–79; Adams, *Munitions*, 28–37; David Lloyd George to William George, May 15, 1915, William George Papers, NLW; David Lloyd George to Frances Stevenson, April 6, 1915, Frances Stevenson Papers, HLRO, in Taylor, ed., *My Darling*, 6–7.

42. George, *My Brother*, 250–51; David Lloyd George to Margaret Lloyd George, August 10–11, 16, 18, 1915, Lloyd George Papers, NLW, in Morgan, ed., *Family Letters*, 179–80; Lloyd George, *Memoirs*, 208–308; Adams, *Munitions*, 62–64; Gilbert, *Organizer*, 154–58, 171–79; Grigg, *Peace*, 239–44, 278–79; Keegan, *First*, 229–31; David R. Woodward, *Lloyd George and the Generals* (Newark: University of Delaware Press, 1983), 50–51.

43. David Lloyd George to William George, July 24, September 27, 30, 1915, William George Papers, NLW; Keegan, *First*, 200, 202; Schmitt and Vedeler, *Crucible*, 80–81.

44. Adams, *Munitions*, 153–54; Schmitt and Vedeler, *Crucible*, 78, 81–82; Keegan, *First*, 197–99, 201–02, 286, 288; Gilbert, *Organizer*, 280–82; Grigg, *Peace*, 325–30.

45. David Lloyd George to William George, October 15, November 21, 1915, William George Papers, NLW; Grigg, *Peace*, 330–32; Gilbert, *Organizer*, 282–85; Keegan, *First*, 250–56; Schmitt and Vedeler, *Crucible*, 96–98.

46. Keegan, *First*, 249–50; Schmitt and Vedeler, *Crucible*, 96; David Lloyd George to Margaret Lloyd George, October 20, 30, November 2, 1914, January 12, December 30–31, 1915, Lloyd George Papers, NLW, in Morgan, ed., *Family Letters*, 174–75, 181; David Lloyd George to William George, December 13, 1915, February 1, 1916, William George Papers, NLW; George, *My Brother*, 253; Lloyd George, *Memoirs*, 220–21; Adams, *Munitions*, 48–49; Gilbert, *Organizer*, 117, 130; Woodward, *Generals*, 84–85; quoted in Grigg, *Peace*, 259–60, 282, 377, 402–03.

47. David Lloyd George to William George, February 3, 1916, William George Papers, NLW; Adams, *Munitions*, 161; Woodward, *Generals*, 48, 54; David Lloyd George to Margaret Lloyd George, January 4, 1915, Lloyd George Papers, NLW, in Morgan, ed., *Family Letters*, 175; Marwick, *Deluge*, 44; David Lloyd George to Megan Lloyd George, September 14, 1915, Lloyd George Papers, NLW, in Morgan, ed., *Family Letters*, 180.

48. Marwick, *Deluge*, 37, 44, 136–37, 197–98; Alistair Horne, *The Price of Glory: Verdun, 1916* (Harmondsworth, UK: Penguin Books, 1962), 54–55; Schmitt and Vedeler, *Crucible*, 30, 33, 56–58, 126; Keegan, *First*, 144–50.

49. David Lloyd George to William George, February 29, March 1–2, 11, 24, 1916, William George Papers, NLW; Horne, *Glory*, 79–91, 145–54, 169–70, 337; Schmitt and Vedeler, *Crucible*, 124–30; Keegan, *First*, 278–86.

50. Schmitt and Vedeler, *Crucible*, 131–32, 162; Grigg, *Peace*, 253, 333–41; Gilbert, *Organizer*, 305–14; David Lloyd George to William George, April 15, 1916, William George Papers, NLW.

51. David Lloyd George to William George, April 18–20, 28, 1916, William George Papers, NLW; Keegan, *First*, 300–01.

52. Massie, *Castles*, 579–657; Keegan, *First*, 270–74, 294, 311; Schmitt and Vedeler, *Crucible*, 131–32, 138–47; David Lloyd George to William George, June 2–3, 6, 1916, William George Papers, NLW; George, *My Brother*, 254; David Lloyd George to Frances Stevenson, June 6, 1916, Frances Stevenson Papers, HLRO, in Taylor, ed., *My Darling*, 16–17.

53. David Lloyd George to William George, June 16–17, 1916, William George Papers, NLW; Woodward, *Generals*, 100; Gilbert, *Organizer*, 335–48; Grigg, *Peace*, 256–61.

54. David Lloyd George to William George, July 1, 3–4, 1916, William George Papers, NLW; Lyn MacDonald, *Somme* (New York: Atheneum, 1989), 54–65; Keegan, *First*, 290–97; Schmitt and Vedeler, *Crucible*, 132–33.

55. David Lloyd George to William George, December 10, 1914, July 11, 1916, William George Papers, NLW; George, *My Brother*, 255; MacDonald, *Somme*, 116–18, 133; Schmitt and Vedeler, *Crucible*, 133–38; Keegan, *First*, 297–99; Grigg, *Peace*, 403–04.

56. Quoted in Grigg, *Peace*, 403; George, *My Brother*, 83, 255; Diaries, December 25, 1878, March 5, 19, 26, April 23, September 10, November 12, December 31,

1882, William George Papers, NLW; Diaries, January 3, 1889, Lloyd George Papers, NLW; George, *Making*, 86–87, 133, 159; David Lloyd George to William George, June 13, 17, July 19, 21, 1916, William George Papers, NLW.

57. David Lloyd George to William George, November 18, 1916, William George Papers, NLW; George, *My Brother*, 255; Keegan, *First*, 297–98, 306–308; Schmitt and Vedeler, *Crucible*, 134–38, 151–52, 159–60; quoted in Woodward, *Generals*, 121–22; Adams, *Munitions*, 160.

58. David Lloyd George to William George, December 15, 1914, July 17–18, 26, 29, September 28, October 3, December 9, 1916, William George Papers, NLW; George, *My Brother*, 257; Fry, *Foreign*, 278–80; Woodward, *Generals*, 27–28.

59. David Lloyd George to William George, October 25, November 4, 10, 20, 25, 28, 1916, William George Papers, NLW; Keegan, *First*, 138–50, 155–68; 306–08; Schmitt and Vedeler, *Crucible*, 56–62, 151–52, 159–60; Seton-Watson, *Russian Empire*, 700–03, 718–19; Kann, *Habsburg*, 483–87.

60. David Lloyd George to William George, October 13, November 6, 1914, March 21, November 28, 1916, January 2, 1917, William George Papers, NLW; George, *My Brother*, 257; David Lloyd George to Margaret Lloyd George, October 20, 1914, Lloyd George Papers, NLW, in Morgan, ed., *Family Letters*, 173; Gilbert, *Organizer*, 117; Grigg, *Peace*, 481–83; Adams, *Munitions*, 181–82, 214n.3.

61. Grigg, *Peace*, 325–32, 423–30, 439–40; David Lloyd George to William George, September 30, October 11, 1916, William George Papers, NLW; Gilbert, *Organizer*, 368–74, 389, 411–12, 417–18; Lloyd George, Speech to the House of Commons, October 11, 1916, Parliamentary Debates, Commons, 5th ser., vol., 86 (1916), cols. 134–35; Fry, *Foreign*, 232–36.

62. Lloyd George, Speech to the House of Commons, October 11, 1916, cols. 135–36; David Lloyd George to William George, November 22, December 1, 1916, William George Papers, NLW; George, *My Brother*, 256; Gilbert, *Organizer*, 374 77, 389 93; Grigg, *Peace*, 253, 430–32, 446–52; Adams, *Law*, 220–29.

63. David Lloyd George to William George, December 2, 5, 1916, William George Papers, NLW; George, *My Brother*, 256; Gilbert, *Organizer*, 393–403; Grigg, *Peace*, 452–62; Adams, *Law*, 229–35.

64. Grigg, *Peace*, 251, 316–17, 447, 449, 462–74, 481–84; Gilbert, *Organizer*, 197–98, 269–73, 403–12; Sir Edward Carson, Speech to the House of Commons, October 11, 1916, cols. 104–07; Adams, *Law*, 235–41; David Lloyd George to William George, December 6, 1916, William George Papers, NLW; George, *My Brother*, 256–57.

Chapter 12

1. David Lloyd George to William George, December 8–9, 23, 1916, William George Papers, NLW; George, *My Brother*, 257; Woodward, *Generals*, 129–30; Grigg, *Peace*, 484–87, 491; Gilbert, *Organizer*, 412–18; Adams, *Law*, 241–43.

2. David Lloyd George to William George, January 29, February 9–10, 1917, William George Papers, NLW; George, *My Brother*, 257; Stokesbury, *Navy*, 63–64, 316–18, 325–27; Herman, *Rule*, 240, 402, 495–97, 511–13; Massie, *Castles*, 528–52, 728–33, 737–38; Schmitt and Vedeler, *Crucible*, 201–02, 238–43; Keegan, *First*, 265, 350–55.

3. David Lloyd George to William George, June 2, 1915, February 12, 14, 1916, William George Papers, NLW; Gilbert, *Organizer*, 209, 293–96; quoted in Fry, *Foreign*, 217, n.6, 218–21, 224–28, 230–31.

4. Stokesbury, *Navy*, 326–27; Herman, *Rule*, 511–13; Schmitt and Vedeler, *Crucible*, 163, 188–90, 197, 238–41; Keegan, *First*, 332–37, 341, 352, 354; Seton-Watson, *Russian Empire*, 723–27; David Lloyd George to William George, March 16, 1917, William George Papers, NLW.

5. Quoted in Cross, ed., *Sylvester*, 138; David Lloyd George, *War Memoirs of David Lloyd George, 1916–1917* (Boston: Little, Brown, and Company, 1934), 481–516; Michael Graham Fry, *And Fortune Fled: David Lloyd George, the First Democratic Statesman, 1916–1922* (New York: Peter Lang, 2011), 105–06, 125–27, 139–40; N. Gordon Levin, Jr., *Woodrow Wilson and World Politics: America's Response to War and Revolution* (New York: Oxford University Press, 1968), 40–43; David Lloyd George to William George, March 30, 1917, William George Papers, NLW; George, *My Brother*, 258; Keegan, *First*, 415; Schmitt and Vedeler, *Crucible*, 280.

6. David Lloyd George to William George, April 1, 1918, William George Papers, NLW; Taylor, ed., *My Darling*, 19, 29–31; David Lloyd George to Margaret Lloyd George, April 1, 1918, Lloyd George Papers, NLW, in Morgan, ed., *Family Letters*, 187; Mr. Lloyd George, *When the War will End* (London: Alabaster, Passmore & Sons, 1917), 3–5 [copy of original in the author's possession].

7. Mr. Lloyd George, *When*, 7, 9–13; Fry, *Fortune*, 147–48.

8. Arthur Roy Leonard, intro., *War Addresses of Woodrow Wilson* (Boston: Ginn and Company, 1918), 51–60; Schmitt and Vedeler, *Crucible*, 253–54; Keegan, *First*, 211, 299–300, 357–58, 372–73; Woodward, *Generals*, 98.

9. Keegan, *First*, 343–50, 358–69; Schmitt and Vedeler, *Crucible*, 176–82, 184–88; Jenkins, *Churchill*, 323–24; David Lloyd George to Margaret Lloyd George, August 3, 1917, Lloyd George Papers, NLW, in Morgan, ed., *Family Letters*, 184–85.

10. Keegan, *First*, 130, 133, 198, 362–64; Edwin Campion Vaughan, *Some Desperate Glory* (New York: Henry Holt and Company, 1981), 220, 222–23.

11. Keegan, *First*, 339–43; Schmitt and Vedeler, *Crucible*, 196–99; David Lloyd George, *The Great Crusade* (New York: George H. Doran Company, 1918), 251–58; David R. Woodward, "The Origins and Intent of David Lloyd George's January 5 War Aims Speech," *The Historian* 34 (November 1971): 22–39; Fry, *Fortune*, 148–52; Marwick, *Deluge*, 216–17.

12. Lloyd George, *Crusade*, 258–63; Woodward, "War Aims," 22, 33, 35, 38.

13. Lloyd George, *Crusade*, 264–66; Woodward, "War Aims," 28, 31–32, 36; Fry, *Fortune*, 152–53, 333–39.

14. Quoted in Woodward, "War Aims," 27, 31, 33, 38; David Lloyd George to Margaret Lloyd George, January 5, 8, February 5, 11, 1918, Lloyd George Papers, NLW, in Morgan, ed., *Family Letters*, 185–86; Adams, *Balfour*, 324–25.

15. Roch, *Lloyd George and the War*, 200–02; Keegan, *First*, 44–45, 103, 392–402; Schmitt and Vedeler, *Crucible*, 188, 257–59.

16. David Lloyd George to Margaret Lloyd George, March 22, 26–27, 30, April 1, 1918, Lloyd George Papers, NLW, in Morgan, ed., *Family Letters*, 186–87.

17. David Lloyd George to Margaret Lloyd George, April 2, 4, 10, 24, July 30, 1918, Lloyd George Papers, NLW, in Morgan, ed., *Family Letters*, 187, n.1, 188; quoted in Woodward, *Generals*, 289–90.

18. Keegan, *First*, 402–10; Schmitt and Vedeler, *Crucible*, 259–66; Massie, *Castles*, 764–68.

19. Quoted in Woodward, *Generals*, 339n.59; Grigg, *Peace*, 15, 68, 378, 379n.1, 499; Marwick, *Deluge*, 233; Keegan, *First*, 405–06; Massie, *Castles*, 102, 748–49.

20. Massie, *Castles*, 766, 768; Schmitt and Vedeler, *Crucible*, 266–73, 285–95; Keegan, *First*, 410–14, 416–20; Marwick, *Deluge*, 262–66, 282.

21. Quoted in Adams, *Balfour*, 339–43; David Lloyd George to Margaret Lloyd George, December 13, 1918, Lloyd George Papers, NLW, in Morgan, ed., *Family Letters*, 188–89; Campbell, *Goat*, 14–15; Harold Nicolson, *Peacemaking 1919* (New York: Grosset & Dunlap, 1965), 19–23, 44–48; Sally Marks, *The Illusion of Peace: International Relations in Europe, 1918–1933* (New York: St. Martin's Press, 1976), 10–12.

22. Fry, *Fortune*, 228–30, 232–33, 235–43, 411–59; Marks, *Illusion*, 8–16; Levin, *Wilson*, 144–46, 151–52, 159–161; Nicolson, *Peacemaking*, 51–52, 58–64, 90–91, 209–10; A. Lentin, *Lloyd George, Woodrow Wilson and the Guilt of Germany* (Baton Rouge: Louisiana State University Press, 1984), 46–55, 57–72, 76–80, 96–98; Margaret Macmillan, *Paris 1919: Six Months That Changed the World* (New York: Random House, 2001), 37–38, 83–97, 162–65; David Lloyd George to Margaret Lloyd George, March 27, 1919, Lloyd George Papers, NLW, in Morgan, ed., *Family Letters*, 190, n.1.

23. Lentin, *Guilt*, 3, 81–104; Macmillan, *Paris*, 137–38, 245–46, 259, 448–49, 459–83; Marks, *Illusion*, 6, 16–20; Fry, *Fortune*, 79–80, 274–84; Cross, ed., *Sylvester*, 154n.17.

24. Diaries, January 10–14, 1892, William George Papers, NLW; quoted in Hugh Wentworth Crawford, ed., "Lloyd George on the Watch Tower," *The Northern Advocate*, October 28, 1919, 6, National Library of New Zealand.

25. David Lloyd George to Margaret Lloyd George, March 27, 1919, Lloyd George Papers, NLW, in Morgan, ed., *Family Letters*, 190; Nicolson, *Peacemaking*, 140–44; Schmitt and Vedeler, *Crucible*, 280–85; Fry, *Fortune*, 137–44; Keegan, *First*, 414–15.

26. Macmillan, *Paris*, 366–80, 381–426, 427–55; Marks, *Illusion*, 6, 19–20, 42–47; Adams, *Balfour*, 330–35; Alan Sharp, *David Lloyd George: Great Britain* (London: Haus Publishing, 2008), 158, 163–64, 177–78, 246; Carole Fink, *The*

Genoa Conference: European Diplomacy, 1921–1922 (Chapel Hill: The University of North Carolina Press, 1984), 162–97, 203–80; Fry, *Fortune*, 461–505.

27. David Lloyd George to Frances Stevenson, March 15, 17, 21–22, 24, April 19, 30, May 2–4, 7, 9, 1922, Frances Stevenson Papers, HLRO, in Taylor, ed., *My Darling*, 35–41, 43–51, 54; quoted in Victor Madeira, "'Because I Don't Trust Him, We are Friends': Signals Intelligence and the Reluctant Anglo-Soviet Embrace, 1917–24," *Intelligence and National Security* 19 (Spring 2004): 30–31, 34–35.

28. Marks, *Illusion*, 47–48; Adams, *Law*, 305–08, 311–12; David Lloyd George to Margaret Lloyd George, August 29, September 6, 1922, Lloyd George Papers, NLW, in Morgan, ed., *Family Letters*, 195–96; Campbell, *Goat*, 18–19.

29. David Lloyd George to Margaret Lloyd George, September 6, 28, 1922, Lloyd George Papers, NLW, in Morgan, ed., *Family Letters*, 196, ns.2, 4; Lord Beaverbrook, *The Decline and Fall of Lloyd George* (New York: Duell, Sloan and Pearce, 1963), 152–54, 158–59, 203–04; Adams, *Law*, 280–81, 292–93, 296–97, 314; Fry, *Fortune*, 591–624; Marks, *Illusion*, 20–21, 47–48.

30. Beaverbrook, *Decline*, 149–203; Adams, *Balfour*, 343–44; Adams, *Law*, 281–82, 309–29, 343–44, 355; Marks, *Illusion*, 20–21, 47–48; Fry, *Fortune*, 624–42; Campbell, *Goat*, 12, 18, 28–31; the Greeks and Turks signed a truce on October 4, an armistice was accepted one week later, but on July 24, 1923, the Treaty of Lausanne superseded the Treaty of Sèvres, restoring eastern Thrace, Smyrna, and a couple of Aegean islands to Turks, cancelling pay for war damages, but keeping the demilitarized zone, all negotiated on behalf of the Allies by Curzon.

Conclusion

1. Michael Bentley, *The Liberal Mind, 1914–1929* (Cambridge: Cambridge University Press, 1977), 107–11; Charles Mallett, *Mr. Lloyd George: A Study* (London: Ernest Benn Limited, 1930), 303–13; John Campbell, *If Love Were All . . . The Story of Frances Stevenson and David Lloyd George* (London: Jonathan Cape, 2006), 21–22; Ffion Hague, *The Pain and the Privilege: The Women in Lloyd George's Life* (London: HarperPress, 2008), 124; Richard Wilkinson, *Lloyd George: Statesman or Scoundrel* (London: I.B. Tauris, 2018), 4–5, 11.

2. George, *Making*, 72–77.

3. Campbell, *Goat*, 97–99, 119–28, 197–201, 224–39; Rowland, *Lloyd*, 711, 713–21; Stephen Koss, "Lloyd George and Nonconformity: the last rally," *The English Historical Review* 89 (January 1974): 77–90; Stevenson Diary, May 18, 23, July 1, 13, 16, 1935, Frances Stevenson Papers, HLRO; Taylor, ed., *Diary*, 309–12; "The 'Council of Action,'" *The Times*, July 3, 1935, 9; Jones, *Welsh Liberalism*, 390–409; Crosby, *Unknown*, 357–59.

4. Stevenson Diary, July 17, 22, 29–30, August 12, 28, September 9, 26, October 11, 23, November 17–18, 1935, Frances Stevenson Papers, HLRO; Taylor, ed.,

Diary, 312–20; Koss, "Nonconformity," 80, 90–108; Townsend, *Black*, 51–54, 71; quoted in Rowland, *Lloyd*, 721–23, 731; Jones, *Welsh Liberalism*, 408–22; Crosby, *Unknown*, 359–60.

5. Personal invitation to the house of W. R. P. George, Garthcelyn, in Criccieth, Wales, on July 15, 1995; telephone call to W. R. P. George on January 18, 1996; conversation with W. R. P. George after services at Berea Chapel on April 16, 2006; Rowland, *Lloyd*, 739; Jones, *Welsh Liberalism*, 360; Cross, ed., *Sylvester*, 184–85.

6. David Lloyd George to Megan Lloyd George, December 1, 1936, Lloyd George Papers, NLW, in Morgan, ed., *Family Letters*, 212–13; Stella Rudman, *Lloyd George and the Appeasement of Germany, 1919–1945* (Newcastle upon Tyne, UK: Cambridge Scholars Publishing, 2011), 220–27; Crosby, *Unknown*, 365–70.

7. David Lloyd George private notebook, 1937, in the author's possession; R. A. C. Parker, *Chamberlain and Appeasement: British Policy and the Coming of The Second World War* (New York: St. Martin's Press, 1993), 80–93; "Franco Sends Envoy To Britain," *The Straits Times*, November 24, 1937, 9; Bernhard Dietz, *Neo-Tories: The Revolt of British Conservatives against Democracy and Political Modernity (1929–1939)*, trans. Ian Copestake (London: Bloomsbury Academic, 2018), 175–76, 188; Cross, ed., *Sylvester*, 185, n.22.

8. Quoted in Rowland, *Lloyd*, 769–76, 780–81, 804; Crosby, *Unknown*, 374–76, 379; Sylvester Diary, July 30, 1936, A. J. Sylvester Papers, NLW; Cross, ed., *Sylvester*, 143–44; George, *My Brother*, 295–96; Henry R. Luce, ed., "Lloyd George Dies," *Life*, April 16, 1945, 34–35; Acts 17:24–28, KJV.

9. Crosby, *Unknown*, cites Trevor Wilson, Richard Toye, and George H. Cassar as examples of this criticism of Lloyd George, 283, 373, 380; Gilbert, ed., *Lloyd George*, 140–44; Revelation 14:13, KJV.

10. Nathan O. Hatch, *The Democratization of American Christianity* (New Haven, CT: Yale University Press, 1989), 7–11, 67–69; Clanton, *Philosophy*, 13–19; Rowland, *Lloyd*, 10, 15, 19, 384, 438, 550–51, 600–01, 677–78.

BIBLIOGRAPHY

Primary Sources

Government Documents

House of Commons
   Hansard Archives
      Historic Hansard Debates

Manuscript Collections

House of Lords
   Record Office
      Lloyd George Papers
      Frances Stevenson Papers
National Library of Wales
   D. R. Daniel Collection
   Thomas Edward Ellis Papers
   William George Papers
   John Herbert Lewis Papers
   Lloyd George Papers
   A. J. Sylvester Papers

Society Holdings

Disciples of Christ Historical Society
   Archives

University Archives

Abilene Christian University
   Brown Library
      Special Collections and Archives
Harding School of Theology
   Graves Memorial Library
      Meredith Restoration History Archive

Lipscomb University
  Beaman Library
    Special Collections
Milligan College
  The Seminary Library
The University of Birmingham Library
  Charles F. G. and Lucy Masterman Archive

Newspapers, Magazines, Journals, Encyclopedias, Dictionaries

The Birkenhead News
The Brecon and Radnor Express
The British Medical Journal
The Cambrian News
Carnarvon and Denbigh Herald
Dictionary of National Biography
Eastern Daily Press
The Encyclopaedia Britannica (1911)
Life
The Liverpool Daily Post and Mercury
The Llangollen Advertiser
Manchester Guardian

The North Wales Express
North Wales Observer
The Northern Advocate
The Otago Witness
The Pontypridd Chronicle
South Wales Daily News
The Spectator
The Straits Times
The Times (London)
Wales
Y Cymro (The Welshman)

Religious Periodicals

The Bible Advocate
The British Harbinger
The British Millennial Harbinger
*The British Millennial Harbinger
  and Family Magazine*
The British Weekly
The Christian Advocate
The Christian Baptist
Christian Leader
*The Christian Messenger and
  Family Magazine*

The Christian Messenger and Reformer
The Christian Register
Christian Standard
The Christian World
The Christian-Evangelist
The Ecclesiastical Observer
Gospel Advocate
The Millennial Harbinger
*The Millennial Harbinger and
  Voluntary Church Advocate*
The Scripture Standard

Published Autobiographies, Biographies, Diaries, Histories, Letters, Memoirs, Quarterlies, Reviews, Transactions

Ainsworth, Thomas J. *Sydney Black: Preacher and Social Reformer.* London: Book & Tract Depot, 1911.

Armitage, Thomas. *A History of the Baptists*, Rev. ed. New York: Bryan, Taylor, & Co., 1890.

Assembly, General. *The History, Constitution, Rules of Discipline, and Confession of Faith of the Calvinistic Methodists in Wales*. Salford, UK: John Roberts, 1877.

Beaverbrook, Lord (William Maxwell Aitken). *The Decline and Fall of Lloyd George*. New York: Duell, Sloan and Pearce, 1963.

Brown, Robert, Jr. "Tithes in England and Wales." *Political Science Quarterly* 7, no. 2 (June 1891): 244–57.

Campbell, Alexander. *The Christian System*. Pittsburgh, PA: Forrester and Campbell, 1839; repr. ed. Nashville, TN: Gospel Advocate Company, 1974.

Carlyle, Thomas. *Sartor Resartus*. 2nd ed. Boston: James Munroe and Company, 1837.

Cross, Colin, ed. *Life with Lloyd George: The Diary of A. J. Sylvester, 1931–45*. New York: Barnes & Noble, 1975.

Crosthwaite, W., ed. *For His Name's Sake: Being a Record of the Witness given by Members of Churches of Christ in Great Britain against Militarism during the European War, 1914–1918*. Heanor, UK: W. Barker, 1921.

Davies, Alfred T. *The Lloyd George I Knew*. London: Henry E. Walter, 1948.

Davies, T. Witton. "John Richard Jones." *The Baptist Quarterly* 1 (April 1922): 88–94.

———. "The McLeanist (Scotch) and Campbellite Baptists of Wales." *Transactions of the Baptist Historical Society* 7, nos. 3, 4 (1921): 147–81.

Davies, W. Watkin. *Lloyd George, 1863–1914*. London: Constable & Company, 1939.

Davis, M. M. *The Restoration Movement of the Nineteenth Century*. Cincinnati, OH: The Standard Publishing Company, 1913.

Dilnot, Frank. *Lloyd George: The Man and His Story*. New York: Harper & Brothers Publishers, 1917.

Du Parcq, Herbert. *Life of David Lloyd George*. 4 vols. London: Caxton Publishing Company, Limited, 1913.

Edwards, J. Hugh. *The Life of David Lloyd George: With a Short History of the Welsh People*. 4 vols. London: The Waverley Book Company, Limited, 1913–1918.

Evans, Beriah Gwynfe. *The Life Romance of Lloyd George*. Utica, NY: Thomas J. Griffiths, "Y Drych" and "The Cambrian," 1916.

Evans, Lady Olwen Carey. *Lloyd George Was My Father*. Llandysul, UK: Gomer Press, 1985.

George, Henry. *Progress and Poverty*. New York: Robert Schalkenbach Foundation, 1990.

George, William. *My Brother and I*. London: Eyre & Spottiswoode, 1958.

George, W. R. P. *Lloyd George: Backbencher*. Llandysul, UK: Gomer Press, 1983.

———. *The Making of Lloyd George*. London: Faber & Faber, 1976.

Haldane, Alexander. *Memoirs of the Lives of Robert Haldane of Airthrey, and of His Brother, James Alexander Haldane*. New York: Robert Carter & Brothers, 1853.

Haldane, Richard Burdon. *Before the War*. London: Cassell and Company, 1920.

———. *Viscount Haldane: An Autobiography*. New York: Doubleday, Doran & Company, 1929.

Jennings, Walter Wilson. *Origin and Early History of the Disciples of Christ*. Cincinnati, OH: The Standard Publishing Company, 1919.

Jones, Thomas. *Lloyd George*. Cambridge, MA: Harvard University Press, 1951.

Leonard, Arthur Roy, intro. *War Addresses of Woodrow Wilson*. Boston: Ginn and Company, 1918.

Lloyd George, David. *The Great Crusade*. New York: George H. Doran Company, 1918.

———. *War Memoirs of David Lloyd George, 1914–1915*. Boston: Little, Brown, and Company, 1933.

———. *War Memoirs of David Lloyd George, 1916–1917*. Boston: Little, Brown, and Company, 1934.

———. *When the War will End*. London: Alabaster, Passmore & Sons, 1917.

Lloyd George, Frances. *The Years that are Past*. London: Hutchinson, 1967.

Lloyd George, Richard. *Dame Margaret: The Life Story of His Mother*. London: George Allen & Unwin, 1947.

———. *Lloyd George*. London: Frederick Muller Limited, 1960.

Mallett, Charles. *Mr. Lloyd George: A Study*. London: Ernest Benn Limited, 1930.

Masterman, Lucy. *C. F. G. Masterman: A Biography*. London: Nicholson and Watson, Limited, 1939.

———. "Recollections of David Lloyd George: I." *History Today* 9 (March 1959): 160–69.

———. "Recollections of David Lloyd George: Part II." *History Today* 9 (April 1959): 274–81.

McEwen, J. M., ed. *The Riddell Diaries, 1908–1923*. London: The Athlone Press, 1986.

Morgan, Kenneth O., ed. *Lloyd George Family Letters, 1885–1936*. Cardiff: University of Wales Press, 1973.

Mottershaw, S. *A History of the Church of Christ Meeting in Long Hedge Lane, Nottingham*. Nottingham: "Daily Express" Company, Limited, 1886.

Nicolson, Harold. *Peacemaking 1919*. New York: Grosset & Dunlap, 1965.

———. *Portrait of a Diplomatist*. Boston: Houghton Mifflin Company, 1930.

Owen, Frank. *Tempestuous Journey: Lloyd George, His Life and Times*. London: Hutchinson, 1954.

Raymond, E. T. [pseud.]. *Mr. Lloyd George*. New York: George H. Doran Company, 1922.

Reynolds, Francis J., Allen L. Churchill, and Francis Trevelyan Miller. *The Story of the Great War*. New York: P. F. Collier & Son, 1916.

Richardson, Robert. *Memoirs of Alexander Campbell*. 2 vols. Indianapolis: Religious Book Service, 1897–98.

Riddell, George Allardice. *Lord Riddell's Intimate Diary of the Paris Peace Conference and After, 1918–23*. London: Victor Gollancz, 1933.

———. *More Pages from My Diary, 1908–1914.* London: Country Life, 1934.

Roberts, T. R. *Eminent Welshmen.* Vol. 1. Cardiff: The Educational Publishing Company, 1908.

Roch, Walter. *Mr. Lloyd George and the War.* London: Chatto & Windus, 1920.

Rothe, Anna. "Lloyd George of Dwyfor, David Lloyd George, 1st Earl." *Current Biography* 5 (1944): 419-23.

Rotherham, J. George, comp. *Reminiscences.* Cincinnati, OH: The Standard Publishing Company, 1922.

Sedgwick, Ellery, ed. "'A Paper of the Highest Importance': Mr. Lloyd George's Plan to Win the War in 1915." *The Atlantic Monthly* 138, no. 1 (July 1926): 21-28.

Stead, William T., ed. "Mr. Lloyd George: Chief of Wales." *The Review of Reviews* 30, no. 178 (October 1904): 368-79.

Sylvester, A. J. *The Real Lloyd George.* London: Cassell and Company, 1947.

Taylor, A. J. P., ed. *Lloyd George: A Diary by Frances Stevenson.* London: Hutchinson, 1971.

———. *My Darling Pussy: The Letters of Lloyd George and Frances Stevenson, 1913–41.* London: Weidenfeld and Nicolson, 1975.

Thomas, Joshua. *A List of the Particular Baptist Churches in the Principality of Wales.* London: n.p., 1795.

Thomson, Malcolm. *David Lloyd George: The Official Biography, with an Introduction by Frances Lloyd George.* London: Hutchinson & Co., 1948.

Tyler, B. B. *History of the Disciples of Christ.* New York: The Christian Literature Co., 1894.

Vaughan, Edwin Campion. *Some Desperate Glory: The World War I diary of a British officer, 1917.* Introduction by Robert Cowley. New York: Henry Holt and Company, 1981.

Wheeler, Edward J., ed. "The Fighting Conciliator of the Present British Ministry." *Current Literature* 44, no. 1 (January 1908): 37-40.

Winskill, P. T. *The Temperance Movement and its Workers.* Vol. 1. London: Blackie & Sons, Limited, 1891.

Secondary Works

Articles

Ackers, Peter. "Who Speaks for the Christians? The Great War and Conscientious Objection in the Churches of Christ: A View from the Wigan Coalfield." *The Journal of the United Reformed Church History Society* 5 (October 1993): 153–67.

Bebbington, D. W. "Baptist M.P.s in the Nineteenth Century." *The Baptist Quarterly* 29 (January 1981): 3–24.

Billington, Louis. "The Churches of Christ in Britain: A Study in Nineteenth-Century Sectarianism." *Journal of Religious History* 8 (June 1974): 21–48.

Dean, Dennis. "The Dilemmas of an Academic Liberal Historian in Lloyd George's

Government: H. A. L. Fisher at the Board of Education, 1916–1922." *History* 79 (February 1994): 57–81.

Elliott, Malcolm. "Opposition to the First World War: The Fate of Conscientious Objectors in Leicester." *Transactions of the Leicestershire Archaeological and Historical Society* 77 (2003): 82–92.

Fahey, David M. "The Politics of Drink: Pressure Groups and the British Liberal Party, 1883–1908." *Social Science* 54 (Spring 1979): 76–85.

Gilbert, Bentley Brinkerhoff. "David Lloyd George: Land, the Budget, and Social Reform." *The American Historical Review* 81 (December 1976): 1058–66.

———."David Lloyd George: The Reform of British Landholding and the Budget of 1914." *The Historical Journal* 21 (March 1978): 117–41.

Grigg, John. "Lloyd George." *New Statesman,* October 16, 1981.

Hancock, W. C. R. "No Compromise: Nonconformity and Politics, 1893–1914." *The Baptist Quarterly* 36 (April 1995): 56–69.

Jalland, Patricia, and John Stubbs. "The Irish question after the outbreak of war in 1914: some unfinished party business." *The English Historical Review* 96 (October 1981): 778–807.

Jones, J. Graham. "David and Maggie." *Journal of Liberal History* 63 (Summer 2009): 18–31.

———. "Lloyd George and the Suffragettes at Llanystumdwy." *Journal of Liberal Democrat History* 34/35 (Spring/Summer 2002): 3–10.

———. "Select Committee or Royal Commission?: Wales and 'The Land Question,' 1892." *Welsh History Review* 17 (December 1994): 205–29.

Jones, John Thomas. "Ellis, Robert." *The Dictionary of Welsh Biography.* Aberystwyth: National Library of Wales. 1959.

King, William McGuire. "Hugh Price Hughes and the British 'Social Gospel.'" *Journal of Religious History* 13 (June 1984): 66–82.

Koss, Stephen. "Lloyd George and Nonconformity: the last rally." *The English Historical Review* 89 (January 1974): 77–108.

Lambert, W. R. "The Welsh Sunday Closing Act, 1881." *The Welsh History Review* 6 (1972–73): 161–89.

Madeira, Victor. "'Because I Don't Trust Him, We are Friends': Signals Intelligence and the Reluctant Anglo-Soviet Embrace, 1917–24." *Intelligence and National Security* 19 (Spring 2004): 29–51.

Melling, C., ed. "Churches of Christ in Former Years." *The Scripture Standard* 33 (January 1966): 7–8.

Morgan, D. Densil. "'Christ and the War': Some Aspects of the Welsh Experience, 1914–1918." *The Journal of Welsh Religious History* 5 (1997): 73–91.

Murray, D. B. "The Scotch Baptist Tradition in Great Britain." *The Baptist Quarterly* 33 (October 1989): 186–98.

Owston, John. "The Scotch Baptist Influence on the Disciples of Christ." *Leaven* 5 (Winter 1997): 38–43.

Richter, Donald. "The Welsh Police, the Home Office, and the Welsh Tithe War of 1886–91." *The Welsh History Review* 12 (June 1984): 50–75.

Thompson, David M. "Churches of Christ in the British Isles." *The Journal of the United Reformed Church History Society* 1 (May 1973): 23–34.

———. "John Clifford's Social Gospel." *The Baptist Quarterly* 31 (January 1986): 199–217.

Turner, John. "State Purchase of the Liquor Trade in the First World War." *The Historical Journal* 23 (September 1980): 589–615.

West, Earl. "Strange Twists in One Life." *Gospel Advocate,* April 17, 1986, 238, 242.

Winnett, Robert. "David Lloyd George: the Religious Factor." *The Epworth Review* 14 (September 1987): 83–91.

Woodward, David R. "The Origins and Intent of David Lloyd George's January 5 War Aims Speech." *The Historian* 34 (November 1971): 22–39.

Books

Adams, R. J. Q. *Arms and the Wizard: Lloyd George and the Ministry of Munitions, 1915–1916.* College Station: Texas A & M University Press, 1978.

———. *Balfour: The Last Grandee.* London: John Murray, 2007.

———. *Bonar Law.* Stanford, CA: Stanford University Press, 1999.

Ahlstrom, Sydney E. *A Religious History of the American People.* New Haven, CT: Yale University Press, 1972.

Bassett, T. M. *The Welsh Baptists.* Swansea: Ilston House, 1977.

Baxter, Batsell Barrett. *Neither Catholic, Protestant, nor Jew.* Nashville, TN: Church of Christ, 1960.

Bebbington, David W. "The city, the countryside and the social gospel in late Victorian nonconformity." In *The Church in Town and Countryside*, edited by Derek Baker, 415–26. Oxford: Basil Blackwell, 1979.

———. *The Dominance of Evangelicalism: The Age of Spurgeon and Moody.* Downers Grove, IL: InterVarsity Press, 2005.

———. *The Nonconformist Conscience: Chapel and Politics, 1870–1914.* London: George Allen & Unwin, 1982.

Bell, P. M. H. *Disestablishment in Ireland and Wales.* London: S.P.C.K., 1969.

Bentley, James. *Ritualism and Politics in Victorian Britain: The Attempt to Legislate for Belief.* Oxford: Oxford University Press, 1978.

Bentley, Michael. *The Liberal Mind, 1914–1929.* Cambridge: Cambridge University Press, 1977.

Betteridge, Alan. *Deep Roots, Living Branches: A History of Baptists in the English Western Midlands.* Leicester, UK: Matador, 2010.

Campbell, John. *If Love Were All . . . The Story of Frances Stevenson and David Lloyd George.* London: Jonathan Cape, 2006.

———. *Lloyd George: The Goat in the Wilderness, 1922–1931*. London: Jonathan Cape, 1977.

Casey, Michael W., and Douglas A. Foster, eds. *The Stone-Campbell Movement: An International Religious Tradition*. Knoxville: The University of Tennessee Press, 2002.

Charmley, John. *A History of Conservative Politics since 1830*. 2nd ed. Houndmills, UK: Palgrave Macmillan, 2008.

Clanton, J. Caleb. *The Philosophy of Religion of Alexander Campbell*. Knoxville: The University of Tennessee Press, 2013.

Clark, Christopher. *The Sleepwalkers: How Europe Went to War in 1914*. New York: Harper, 2013.

Constantine, Stephen. *Lloyd George*. London: Routledge, 1992.

Cregier, Don M. *Bounder from Wales: Lloyd George's Career before the First World War*. Columbia: University of Missouri Press, 1976.

Crosby, Travis L. *Joseph Chamberlain: A Most Radical Imperialist*. London: I.B. Tauris & Co., 2011.

———. *The Unknown Lloyd George: A Statesman in Conflict*. London: I.B. Tauris, 2014.

Crowther, M. A. *The Workhouse System, 1834–1929*. Athens: The University of Georgia Press, 1981.

Daglish, Neil. *Education Policy-Making in England and Wales: The Crucible Years, 1895–1911*. London: The Woburn Press, 1996.

Dangerfield, George. *The Damnable Question: A Study in Anglo-Irish Relations*. Boston: Little, Brown and Company, 1976.

———. *The Strange Death of Liberal England, 1910–1914*. New York: Capricorn Books, 1961.

Davies, John. *A History of Wales*. London: Allen Lane The Penguin Press, 1993.

Derry, John W. *The Radical Tradition: Tom Paine to Lloyd George*. London: Macmillan, 1967.

Dietz, Bernhard. *Neo-Tories: The Revolt of British Conservatives against Democracy and Political Modernity (1929–1939)*. Translated by Ian Copestake. London: Bloomsbury Academic, 2018.

Dixon, R., ed. *Ireland and the Irish Question*. New York: International Publishers, 1972.

Douglas, Roy. *Land, People & Politics: A History of the Land Question in the United Kingdom, 1878–1952*. New York: St. Martin's Press, 1976.

Emy, H. V. "The Land Campaign: Lloyd George as a Social Reformer, 1909–14." In *Lloyd George: Twelve Essays*, edited by A. J. P. Taylor, 35–68. New York: Atheneum, 1971.

Fanning, Ronan. *Fatal Path: British Government and Irish Revolution, 1910–1922*. London: Faber & Faber, 2013.

Farwell, Byron. *Queen Victoria's Little Wars*. New York: W. W. Norton & Company, 1972.

Fink, Carole. *The Genoa Conference: European Diplomacy, 1921–1922*. Chapel Hill: The University of North Carolina Press, 1984.

Fitzgerald, Garret. "Lloyd George & Ireland: How Ireland came to Be Divided." In *David Lloyd George-The Llanystumdwy Lectures, 1990–1996*, edited by Ann Rhydderch, 55–83. Gywnedd: Gwynedd Council & the Criccieth Arts Association Festival, 1997.

Foster, Douglas A. *A Life of Alexander Campbell*. Grand Rapids, MI: William B. Eerdmans Publishing Company, 2020.

Fry, Michael G. *And Fortune Fled: David Lloyd George, the First Democratic Statesman, 1916–1922*. New York: Peter Lang, 2011.

———. *Lloyd George and Foreign Policy: The Education of a Statesman: 1890–1916*. Montreal: McGill-Queen's University Press, 1977.

Garside, W. R. *British Unemployment, 1919–1939*. Cambridge: Cambridge University Press, 1990.

Gaw, Jerry L. "Edward Jenner 1749–1823." In *Research Guide To European Historical Biography*, edited by James A. Moncure, 6:3414–27. Washington, DC: Beacham Publishing, 1993.

Gilbert, Bentley B. *David Lloyd George, a political life: The Architect of Change, 1863–1912*. Columbus, OH: Ohio State University Press, 1987.

———. *David Lloyd George, a political life: Organizer of Victory, 1912–1916*. Columbus, OH: Ohio State University Press, 1992.

———. *The Evolution of National Insurance in Great Britain: The Origins of the Welfare State*. London: Michael Joseph, 1966.

Gilbert, Martin, ed. *Lloyd George*. Englewood Cliffs, New Jersey: Prentice-Hall, 1968.

Gorman, James L. *Among the Early Evangelicals: The Transatlantic Origins of the Stone-Campbell Movement*. Abilene, TX: Abilene Christian University Press, 2016.

Greenaway, John. *Drink and British Politics since 1830*. Houndmills, UK: Palgrave, 2003.

Grigg, John. *Lloyd George: From Peace to War, 1912–1916*. Berkeley: University of California Press, 1985.

———. *Lloyd George: The People's Champion, 1902–1911*. Berkeley: University of California Press, 1978.

———. *Lloyd George: War Leader, 1916–1918*. London: Allen Lane, 2002.

———. *The Young Lloyd George*. Berkeley: University of California Press, 1973.

Gutzke, David W. *Pubs and Progressives: Reinventing the Public House in England, 1896–1960*. Dekalb, IL: Northern Illinois University Press, 2006.

Hachey, Thomas E., Joseph M. Hernon, Jr., and Lawrence J. McCaffrey. *The Irish Experience*. Englewood Cliffs, NJ: Prentice Hall, 1989.

Hague, Ffion. *The Pain and the Privilege: The Women in Lloyd George's Life*. London: HarperPress, 2008.

Hatch, Nathan O. *The Democratization of American Christianity*. New Haven, CT: Yale University Press, 1989.

Hattersley, Roy. *David Lloyd George: The Great Outsider*. London: Little, Brown, 2010.

Herman, Arthur. *To Rule the Waves: How the British Navy Shaped the Modern World*. New York: HarperCollins Publishers, 2004.

Herwig, Holger H. *The Marne, 1914: The Opening of World War I and the Battle That Changed the World*. New York: Random House, 2009.

Horne, Alistair. *The Price of Glory: Verdun, 1916*. Harmondsworth, UK: Penguin Books, 1962.

Jackson, Alvin. *Home Rule: An Irish History, 1800–2000*. Oxford: Oxford University Press, 2003.

Jacob, W. M. *Religious Vitality in Victorian London*. Oxford: Oxford University Press, 2021.

Jelavich, Barbara. *A Century of Russian Foreign Policy, 1814–1914*. Philadelphia: J. B. Lippincott Company, 1964.

Jenkins, Roy. *Churchill: A Biography*. New York: Farrar, Straus and Giroux, 2001.
———. *Gladstone: A Biography*. New York: Random House, 1997.

Jones, Howard. *The Course of American Diplomacy*. New York: Franklin Watts, 1985.

Jones, J. Graham. *David Lloyd George and Welsh Liberalism*. The Welsh Political Archive. Aberystwyth: The National Library of Wales, 2010.
———. *Lloyd George Papers at the National Library of Wales and other repositories*. Aberystwyth: The National Library of Wales, 2001.

Kann, Robert A. *A History of the Habsburg Empire, 1526–1918*. Berkeley: University of California Press, 1974.

Keegan, John. *The First World War*. New York: Alfred A. Knopf, 1999.

Koss, Stephen E. *Lord Haldane: Scapegoat for Liberalism*. New York: Columbia University Press, 1969.

Larsen, Timothy. *Christabel Pankhurst: Fundamentalism and Feminism in Coalition*. Woodbridge, UK: The Boydell Press, 2002.

Leinster-Mackay, Donald P. "Diggle, Joseph Robert (1849–1917). In *The Oxford Dictionary of National Biography*, edited by Brian Harrison, 16:174–75. New York: Oxford University Press, 2004.

Lentin, A. *Lloyd George, Woodrow Wilson and the Guilt of Germany*. Baton Rouge: Louisiana State University Press, 1984.

Levin, N. Gordon, Jr. *Woodrow Wilson and World Politics: America's Response to War and Revolution*. New York: Oxford University Press, 1968.

Lewis, David Levering. *The Race to Fashoda*. New York: Weidenfeld & Nicolson, 1987.

Lloyd George, Robert. *David & Winston: How the Friendship Between Churchill and Lloyd George Changed the Course of History*. Woodstock, UK: The Overlook Press, 2008.

Maccoby, S. *English Radicalism, 1886–1914*. London: George Allen & Unwin, 1953.

MacDonald, Lyn. *Somme*. New York: Atheneum, 1989.

Machin, G. I. T. *Politics and the Churches in Great Britain, 1869–1921*. Oxford: Clarendon Press, 1987.

Macmillan, Margaret. *Paris 1919: Six Months That Changed the World*. New York: Random House, 2001.

Magnus, Philip. *King Edward the Seventh*. New York: E. P. Dutton & Co., 1964.

Marks, Sally. *The Illusion of Peace: International Relations in Europe, 1918–1933*. New York: St. Martin's Press, 1976.

Marsden, George M. *Fundamentalism and American Culture*. Oxford: Oxford University Press, 1980.

Marwick, Arthur. *The Deluge: British Society and the First World War*. New York: W. W. Norton & Company, 1965.

Massie, Robert K. *Castles of Steel: Britain, Germany, and the Winning of the Great War at Sea*. New York: Random House, 2003.

———. *Dreadnought: Britain, Germany, and the Coming of the Great War*. New York: Random House, 1991.

Matthews, D. Hugh. *Castle Street Meeting House-A History*. Swansea: John Penry Press, 1989.

McAllister, Lester G. *Alexander Campbell at Glasgow University, 1808–1809*. Nashville, TN: Disciples of Christ Historical Society, 1971.

McCormick, Donald. *The Mask of Merlin*. London: MacDonald, 1963.

McMillon, Lynn A. *Restoration Roots: The Scottish Origins of the American Restoration Movement*. Henderson, TN: Hester Publications, 1983.

Mews, Stuart. "Urban Problems and Rural Solutions: Drink and Disestablishment in the First World War." In *The Church in Town and Countryside*, edited by Derek Baker, 449–76. Oxford: Basil Blackwell, 1979.

Morgan, Kenneth O. *Consensus and Disunity: The Lloyd George Coalition Government, 1918–1922*. Oxford: Clarendon Press, 1979.

———. *David Lloyd George: Welsh Radical as World Statesman*. Cardiff: University of Wales Press, 1963.

———. *Lloyd George*. London: Weidenfeld and Nicolson, 1974.

Neuberger, Julia. *Lloyd George's Disestablishment Legacy: Reaching for Egalitarianism*. Caernarfon: Cyngor Gwynedd Council, 2000.

Neville, Graham. *Radical Churchman: Edward Lee Hicks and The New Liberalism*. Oxford: Clarendon Press, 1998.

Nicholls, James. *The Politics of Alcohol: A History of the Drink Question in England*. Manchester, UK: Manchester University Press, 2009.

North, James B. *Union in Truth: An Interpretive History of the Restoration Movement*. Eugene, OR: Wipf & Stock, 2019.

Packer, Ian. *Liberal Government and Politics, 1905–15*. Houndmills, UK: Palgrave Macmillan, 2006.

———. *Lloyd George*. Houndmills, UK: Macmillan Press, 1998.

———. *Lloyd George, Liberalism and the Land: The Land Issue and Party Politics in England, 1906–1914*. Woodbridge, Suffolk: The Boydell Press, 2001.

Pakenham, Thomas. *The Boer War.* New York: Random House, 1979.

Parker, R. A. C. *Chamberlain and Appeasement: British Policy and the Coming of The Second World War.* New York: St. Martin's Press, 1993.

Price, Emyr. *David Lloyd George.* Cardiff: University of Wales Press, 2006.

Pugh, Martin. *Lloyd George.* London: Longman, 1988.

Purcell, Hugh. *Lloyd George.* London: Haus Publishing Limited, 2006.

Purvey-Tyrer, Neil. "Lloyd George, the Bishop of St. Asaph and the Disestablishment Controversy." In *The Life and Times of David Lloyd George*, edited by Judith Loades, 153–61. Bangor, UK: Headstart History, 1991.

Rose, Kenneth. *King George V.* New York: Alfred A. Knopf, 1984.

Rotberg, Robert I. *The Founder: Cecil Rhodes and the Pursuit of Power.* New York: Oxford University Press, 1988.

Rowland, Peter. *Lloyd George.* London: Barrie and Jenkins, 1975.

Rudman, Stella. *Lloyd George and the Appeasement of Germany, 1919–1945.* Newcastle-upon-Tyne, UK: Cambridge Scholars Publishing, 2011.

Schmitt, Bernadotte E., and Harold C. Vedeler. *The World in the Crucible, 1914–1919.* New York: Harper & Row, Publishers, 1984.

"Seiat." In *A Dictionary of the Welsh Language*, edited by Gareth A. Bevan and Patrick J. Donovan, 4:3207. University of Wales Centre for Advanced Welsh and Celtic Studies. Aberystwyth: The National Library of Wales, 2002.

Sennett, James F. "Providence." In *The Encyclopedia of the Stone-Campbell Movement*, edited by Douglas A. Foster, et al., 613–14. Grand Rapids, MI: William B. Eerdmans Publishing Company, 2004.

Seton-Watson, Hugh. *The Russian Empire, 1801–1917.* Oxford: Oxford University Press, 1967.

Seton-Watson, R. W. *Disraeli, Gladstone, and the Eastern Question.* New York: W. W. Norton & Company, 1972.

Shannon, Catherine B. *Arthur J. Balfour and Ireland, 1874–1922.* Washington, DC: The Catholic University of America Press, 1988.

Sharp, Alan. *David Lloyd George: Great Britain.* London: Haus Publishing, 2008.

Shiman, Lilian Lewis. *Crusade Against Drink in Victorian England.* New York: St. Martin's Press, 1988.

Smith, Michael Llewellyn. "Venizelos' Diplomacy, 1910–23: From Balkan Alliance to Greek-Turkish Settlement." In *Eleftherios Venizelos: The Trials of Statesmanship*, edited by Paschalis Kitromilides, 134–92. Edinburgh: Edinburgh University Press, 2006.

Stansky, Peter. *Gladstone: A Progress in Politics.* New York: W. W. Norton & Company, 1979.

Stevenson, John. *British Society, 1914–45.* Harmondsworth, UK: Penguin Books, 1984.

Stokesbury, James L. *Navy and Empire.* New York: William Morrow and Company, 1983.

Sykes, Patricia Lee. *Presidents and Prime Ministers: Conviction Politics in the Anglo-American Tradition.* Lawrence: University Press of Kansas, 2000.

Taylor, A. J. P. *English History, 1914–1945.* Oxford: Oxford University Press, 1965.

Thompson, David M. *Let Sects and Parties Fall.* Birmingham, UK: Berean Press, 1980.

Thompson, David M., ed. *Nonconformity in the Nineteenth Century.* London: Routledge & Kegan Paul, 1972.

Tierney, Brian, Donald Kagan, and L. Pearce Williams. *Great Issues in Western Civilization.* Vol. 2. 4th ed. New York: McGraw-Hill, 1992.

Townsend, Henry. *Robert Wilson Black.* London: The Carey Kingsgate Press Limited, 1954.

Trench, Charles Chenevix. *The Road to Khartoum: A Life of General Charles Gordon.* New York: Carroll & Graf Publishers, 1989.

Ward, Alan J. *The Easter Rising: Revolution and Irish Nationalism.* Wheeling, IL: Harlan Davidson, 1980.

Warner, Philip. *Kitchener: The Man Behind the Legend.* New York: Atheneum, 1985.

Watters, A. C. *History of British Churches of Christ.* Indianapolis: Butler University School of Religion, 1948.

West, Robert Frederick. *Alexander Campbell and Natural Religion.* Yale Studies in Religious Education. Vol. 21. New Haven, CT: Yale University Press, 1948.

Wilkinson, Richard. *Lloyd George: Statesman or Scoundrel?* London: I.B. Tauris, 2018.

Williams, David. *A History of Modern Wales.* Rev. ed. London: John Murray, 1965.

Woodward, David R. *Lloyd George and the Generals.* Newark: University of Delaware Press, 1983.

Wrather, Eva Jean. *Alexander Campbell: Adventurer in Freedom: A Literary Biography.* 3 vols. Edited by D. Duane Cummins. Fort Worth: TCU Press and the Disciples of Christ Historical Society, 2005.

Theses

Gaw, Jerry L. "A History of Churches of Christ in the United Kingdom to 1867." Master's thesis, Northwestern State University, Louisiana, 1983.

Websites

Duffy, Michael. "Vintage Audio-Lloyd George's Beer." 2000–2009. http://www.firstworldwar.com/audio/lloydgeorgesbeer.htm.

Hattersley, Roy. BBC Radio 3. Arts & Ideas. Night Waves, September 14, 2010. https://www.bbc.co.uk/schedules/p00fzl8t/2010/09/14

Ritchie, David. "Whisky allowed in the forward trenches." Email in H-Albion, June 14, 2008. https://networks.h-net.org/h-albion

INDEX

Acts of Parliament: Agricultural Holding (1900), 135; Agricultural Rating (1896), 94–95, 192, 209; Allotments (1887), 130; Arrears of Rent (1882), 89; Children's (1908), 246; Coercion (1881), 88; Criminal Law and Procedure (1887), 96; Education (1870), 235, 241; Education (1902), 239–40, 269; Education (1918), 246; Education Local Authority Default (1904), 240, 271; Education Provision of Meals (1906), 245; Elementary Education (1891), 232–33; Finance Act (1910), 150; Finance Act (1914), 195; Government of Ireland (1920), 120–21; Home Rule (1914), 113, 115, 119; Housing and Town Planning (1919), 196; Irish Church (1869), 87–88, 215; Irish Free State Agreement (1922), 125; Land Law (1881), 88; Landlord and Tenant (1870), 87–88; Local Government (1888), 231; Licensing (1921), 86; Merchant Shipping, (1906), 271; National Insurance (1911), 178–79, 271; Old Age Pensions (1908), 141, 271; Parliament (1911), 98, 215–16, 218, 271; Patents and Designs, (1907), 271; Poor Law (1834), 143, 192; Port of London, (1908), 271; Reform (1884), 3, 128; Representation of the People (1918), 3; Restoration of Order in Ireland (1921), 121; Riot (1715), 226–27; Suspensory (1914), 108, 219; Tithe (1918), 246; Tithe (1936), 246; Tithe Commutation (1836), 225; Tithe Rent-Charge Recovery (1891), 230–31; Tithe Rent-Charge Recovery (1899), 236; Unemployment Insurance, (1920), 196; Voluntary Schools (1897), 233–34; Welsh Church (1914), 219–21; Welsh Church Temporalities (1919), 223; Welsh Intermediate Education (1889), 231; Welsh Sunday Closing (1881), 64–65, 73, 106

Adrianople, 279–80

Afghanistan, 247–48, 250, 270

Africa: Congo, 275; East, 303; Egypt, 247–49, 258–59, 278; Libya, 278; Morocco, 269–70, 274–76, 278; North, 278; Northwest, 275; South, 95–96, 138, 247, 251–69, 299, 303; Southwest, 303; Sudan, 250–51

Agnosticism, 32

Ahlstrom, Sidney, 16

Albania, 280

Alcoholic beverages, 2–3, 26–27, 39, 63–86, 99, 110, 146–48, 171, 198

Allotments, 129–30, 180, 220

Anglicanism, 28, 201, 206, 210, 213, 216–17, 219–20, 232–33, 235, 245; Apostles' Creed, 32, 38, 67; Ash Wednesday, 32, 38; Book of Common Prayer, 38; Catechism, 32, 38, 53, 67, 235; festival days, 32, 38; prelates, 235

Arabia, 305

Armed forces: 22nd Cheshire Regiment, 226–27; 38th Welsh Army Corps, 286, 288–90; Anglo-Indian

Armed forces (*continued*)
Expeditionary Force, 292; British
Expeditionary Force, 274, 283–84;
German Army, 284–85, 303, 306;
Gordon Highlanders, 251–52, 286;
Grand Fleet, 292; Home Fleet, 277,
285; High Seas Fleet, 292, 307–8;
Hussars, 252, 254; Irish Citizen Army,
111; Irish Republican Army, 120; Irish
Volunteers, 101, 107, 112, 117, 119;
Mediterranean Fleet, 282; National
Volunteers, 112; Royal Air Force,
295, 317; Royal Engineers, 289; Royal
Highlanders, 286; Royal Irish Rifles,
283; Territorial Force, 274, 286, 288;
Ulster Volunteer Force, 104, 107
Armenia, 263, 302–3, 305, 311
Associations: "approved societies," 173,
179–80; British Medical Association,
176, 181; Carlton Club, 314; col-
lecting societies, 173, 175; Criccieth
Debating Society, 3; Cymdeithas
Cymreigyddion, 20–21; Fabian
Society, 142–43, 237; friendly societ-
ies, 135, 143–45, 173–76, 181; Gaelic
League, 59, 112; Irish Reform Associ-
ation, 96–97; National Liberal Club,
190–91, 211; National Reform Union,
259; Oxford Union Society, 190;
Portmadoc Debating Society, 34–35,
65, 89, 197, 248–49; Positivist Society,
46; School Canteen Committees, 245
Astor, Waldorf, 178–79
Atheism, 32–35, 41, 48, 51–52, 210–11
Australia, 115–16, 122, 287
Austria-Hungary, 83, 107, 109–10,
180–81, 270, 272, 279–81, 286, 289,
302–3, 305, 310

Balfour, Alexander; 67
Balfour Declaration, 311
Balkans, 247, 272, 278–81, 294, 299, 313

Ballantine, William, 15, 18
Ballin, Alfred, 277
Baptism, 13–15, 19, 21–22, 24, 35–36,
40–45, 54–56
Baptists, 19–20, 22, 24, 42–44, 48, 57,
59, 72, 132, 237, 310, 316; Leicester, 43;
Llanelly, 42, 49; Particular, 9, 11–13,
21, 23, 55–56, 248; Popular, 18–19;
Scotch, 9–15, 18–19, 21, 42, 248;
Welsh, 3, 11, 19, 21, 27, 32–33, 59, 317,
320
Bath, 23
Battles: Alexandria, 248–49; Bannock-
burn, 302–3; Benghazi, 278; Bilbao,
318–19; Durazzo, 279–80; Guernica,
318–19; Khartoum, 250–1; Mukden,
269; Omdurman, 250–51; Salonika,
279–80; Smyrna, 312–13; Tripoli, 278;
Tsushima Strait, 269
Battles (Second Boer War):
Bloemfontein, 256–57; Dundee,
252–54; Elandslaagte, 252; Glencoe,
251–52, 254; Johannesburg, 256–57;
Kimberley, 253, 256–57; Ladysmith,
252–54, 256–57; Mafeking, 251, 255–
57; Nicholson's Nek, 254; Pepworth
Hill, 254; Pretoria, 256–57, 266–67;
Rietfontein, 252, 254; Talana Hill,
251–52, 254; Tweebosch, 266
Battles (World War I): Aisne, 284–85;
Amiens, 306–8; Ancre Offensive, 291;
Aqaba, 310; Ardennes, 283; Arras,
307; Artois, 286; Belleau Wood, 307;
Caporetto, 303–4; Chateau-Thierry,
307; Dardanelles Campaign, 286–89;
Gorlice-Tarnów, 288, 302; Jutland,
292; Langemarck, 304; Lemberg,
295; Liège, 282–83; Lombartzyde,
286; Loos, 288–89, 291; Macedonian
Front, 289; Mametz Woods, 293;
Marne, 284, 307; Masurian Lakes,
295; Mesopotamia Campaign, 279,

292, 302, 305, 310–11; Meuse-
Argonne Offensive, 308; Mons, 283–
84; Nieuport, 286; Passchendaele,
303–4, 306; Sinai-Palestine Cam-
paign, 301–2, 310–11; Somme, 291–
95; Spring Offensive, 302, 308; St.
Georges, 286; Tannenberg, 295;
Verdun, 290–91; Warsaw, 295;
Wytschaete, 286; Ypres, 285–86,
288–89, 303–4; Yser, 286
Begbie, Harold, 53–54, 315
Belfast, 97, 100, 104, 107, 110, 117, 119, 121
Belgium, 107, 280–83, 285–86, 299, 302–4
Benckendorff, Alexander (Count), 270
Berchtesgaden, 318
Berghof, 318
Berlin, 247, 272, 277, 279, 300
Biographers of Lloyd George: Adams,
R. J. Q., 81, 86, 339n48; Aitken,
William Maxwell, 313–14, 372n29;
Campbell, John, 352n59, 372n1;
Constantine, Stephen, 330n5;
Cregier, Don M., 54, 324n1; Crosby,
Travis L., 324n10; Cross, Colin, ed.,
324n12; Davies, Alfred T., 76, 245,
326n12; Davies, W. Watkin, 356n2;
Dilnot, Frank, 24, 329n46; Du
Parcq, Herbert, 260, 323n6; Edwards,
J. Hugh, 20, 38, 202, 325n5; Evans,
Beriah Gwynfe, 142, 203, 206,
346n35; Evans, Olwen Carey, 4,
43–44, 49, 324n7; Fry, Michael
Graham, 248, 281, 360n2, 370n5;
George, William, 3–4, 26, 55–56,
239, 241–42, 323n3; George, W. R. P.,
4, 17, 40, 60, 66, 89, 317, 323n6,
329n48, 373n5; Gilbert, Bentley
Brinkerhoff, 60–61, 95, 133, 147, 245,
323n3, 324n1; Gilbert, Martin, ed.,
330n1; Grigg, John, 6, 33, 60, 93–94,
112, 137, 169, 184, 190, 195, 204, 271,
323n6, 324n12, 337n34, 357n8; Hague,

Ffion, 372n1; Hattersley, Roy, 169,
330n5; Jones, J. Graham, 4, 351n48;
Jones, Thomas, 59–60, 334n51; Lloyd
George, Frances, 37, 331n15; Lloyd
George, Richard, 4, 38–39, 49, 286,
293, 324n7, 334n57; Loades, Judith,
ed., 355n36; Mallet, Charles, 372n1;
McCormick, Donald, 69, 331n24;
Morgan, Kenneth O., ed., 29, 60,
323–24n7, 329n54, 330n55, 352n59;
Neuberger, Julia, 209, 354n27;
Owen, Frank, 330n5; Packer, Ian, 133,
336n23, 338n40, 344n6; Price, Emyr,
337n35; Pugh, Martin, 60, 330n5;
Purcell, Hugh, 330n5; Raymond, E. T.
[pseud.], 6, 324n12; Rhydderch, Ann,
ed., 340n16; Roch, Walter, 364n13;
Rowland, Peter, 323n1; Sharp, Alan,
371n26; Spender, Harold, 13; Sylvester,
A. J., 6–7, 24, 28, 39–40, 144, 301,
324n13; Taylor, A. J. P., ed., 323n6,
324n7, 347n45; Thomson, Malcolm,
39, 59, 334n63; Wilkinson, Richard,
315, 372n1
Birkenhead, 23, 201, 313
Birmingham, 23, 191, 263–64
Black, Robert Wilson, 75, 316
Black and Tans, 120
Bloody Sunday, 120
Blue Ribbon pledge, 65–67
Booth, Charles, 139
Bosnia-Herzegovina, 272, 280
Bosporus, 279, 313
Braidwood, William, 11–12, 14–15
Brailsford, H. N., 54
British Commonwealth, 122–23, 268,
287, 313
British Guiana, 250
British Rulers: Edward the Confessor,
44; Edward VII, 82, 147–150, 152, 251,
258, 267, 274; George V, 16, 82–83, 101,
103, 105–6, 115, 121–22, 147, 152–53,

British Rulers (*continued*)
176, 215–16, 221, 274, 297, 299, 307;
Henry VIII, 188; Queen Anne, 219–
20; Queen Victoria, 199, 232, 256–57,
274; William the Conqueror, 44
Brugha, Cathal, 119
Bulgaria, 279–80, 289, 295, 310
Burke, T. H., 88

Cabinet members: Addison,
Christopher, 196–97; Balfour,
Arthur James, 299; Beauchamp,
Lord (William Lygon), 188; Birrell,
Augustine, 102, 105–7, 111, 113, 243–
45; Bright, John, 176, 242; Brodrick,
St, 259–61, 266; Burns, John, 142–43,
171, 189; Carson, Edward, 113–14,
297, 299; Cavendish, Frederick,
88; Chamberlain, Austen, 124, 312;
Chamberlain, Joseph, 71, 90–91, 95,
129–30, 136–38, 236, 256–58, 261, 263–
67; Chaplin, Henry, 132–33, 135–37;
Crewe, Lord (Robert Milnes), 106;
Curzon, George Nathaniel (Lord),
295, 299, 303, 312–13, 372n30; Eden,
Anthony, 318–19; Fisher, H. A. L.,
246; Gladstone, Herbert, 73–75,
80; Grey, Edward, 102, 270–72,
274–77, 279–81, 289, 299; Haldane,
Richard Burdon, 142, 153, 182, 186,
189, 273–74, 277; Harcourt, William,
72, 93–94, 131, 133, 135, 176, 205, 209,
233; Henderson, Arthur, 291–92, 299;
Hoare, Samuel, 319; Isaacs, Rufus, 153,
182, 189, 300; Lansbury, George, 25,
317; Lansdowne, Lord (Henry Petty-
Fitzmaurice), 81, 106, 114–15, 296;
Law, Andrew Bonar, 222–23, 287,
297, 299, 308, 312; Long, Walter,
114, 119, 300; McKenna, Reginald,
216–21, 245–46, 272–73, 276–77,
287, 289; Milner, Alfred, 13, 267, 299,
303; Morley, John, 79–80; Ridley,

Matthew White, 132; Runciman,
Walter, 189, 245–46, 289; Samuel,
Herbert, 170, 184; Selborne, Lord
(William Palmer), 114–15; Simon,
John, 289, 318–19; Smith, F. E.,
113–14, 313; Smuts, Jan, 303, 305;
Wood, Kingsley, 319; Wyndham,
George, 96–97
Cadbury, George, 184, 264
Calvinism, 11, 13, 48–49
Calvinistic Methodists, 26, 39, 42–43,
48, 66, 197, 205, 239–40
Cambridge, 10, 212
Canada, 13, 15, 116, 122, 251, 263
Cape Colony, 253–54, 257–58, 264–65,
268
Carlsbad, 271–72
Casement, Roger, 111–12
Cassel, Ernest, 277
Casson, Randal, 63–64, 66, 249
Catholicism, 16, 40, 88–89, 95–97, 107,
110, 114, 116–17, 180, 210, 216, 219, 231,
235, 244; Popery, 16, 116, 235; "Rome
Rule," 91, 117
Caucasus, 280, 286–87
Cecil, Hugh, 145, 216, 219, 222–23
Cecil, Robert, 216, 219, 305
Central Asia, 270
Chalmers, Robert, 153
Chapels: Berea Church of Christ/Welsh
Baptist (Criccieth), 21, 31–32, 39–40,
47, 49, 82, 238, 310, 317; Capel Mawr
Calvinistic Methodist (Criccieth), 64,
197; Capel Seion Calvinistic Meth-
odist (Criccieth), 49; Capel Seisnig
English (Criccieth), 67–68; Capel
Uchaf, Penymaes, Particular Baptist/
Scotch Baptist/Church of Christ
(Criccieth), 9–12, 17, 20–23, 31–32,
34, 40–45, 49–50, 65, 248; Castle
Street Welsh Baptist (London), 3,
27–28, 29, 33, 55, 58–59, 317; Chelsea
Congregational (London), 211; City

Temple Congregational (London), 152, 281; Fetter Lane Moravian (London), 44; Fulham Cross Church of Christ (London), 14, 27, 74–75; Hope Church of Christ (London), 44; Metropolitan Tabernacle Baptist Union (London), 51, 198; Moriah Calvinistic Methodist (Llanystumdwy), 39; Penmachno Scotch Baptist/Church of Christ (Penmachno), 21, 25, 46–47, 65; Penmount Calvinistic Methodist (Pwllheli), 26–27, 239; Portmadoc Church of Christ (Portmadoc), 22, 41–42, 45, 49–50; Salem Congregational (Carnarvon), 37; Tabernacle Calvinistic Methodist (Portmadoc), 64; Westbourne Park Baptist Union (London), 132–33, 237–38; Whitefield's Tabernacle Methodist (London), 176–77

China, 270

Christ, 3, 11–12, 20, 26–27, 32, 35, 49, 52–53, 55, 61, 184, 210–11, 234

Church of Christ; 2, 5, 9–10, 12–15, 17–18, 20–25, 27–29, 32, 38–40, 44–49, 53–56, 58–61, 74–75, 78, 82, 97, 237–38, 244, 248, 282, 293–94, 317, 319–20

Church of England, 3, 18, 24–25, 32, 34, 64–65, 72–73, 76, 87–88, 94–95, 198, 201, 204, 206–7, 210, 213–18, 222–23, 225–26, 228–29, 231, 236, 240–41, 246, 315, 321

Churchill, Lady Randolph, 290

Collins, Michael, 119, 123–25

Commissions: boundary, 119–20, 123–25; Ecclesiastical, 201–2, 219–20, 226–28; Land, 186, 189; licensing, 75–76; National Insurance, 179, 243; pensions, 135; Welsh Church, 55–56, 213; Welsh Land, 131–35, 225, 229, 231

Committee of Imperial Defence, 276–77, 283

Communion, 11, 15–16, 21–23, 40–41, 44, 55–59, 241, 317

Communist, 320–21

Companies: De Beers Mining, 253; London and North-Western Railway, 207, 209; Marconi Wireless Telegraph, 184–85; Prudential Insurance, 180; Welsh National Press, 203

Concentration camps, 95–96, 258–59, 318

Conferences: Anglesey and Carnarvonshire Nonconformist, 202; Anglican and Free Churchmen, 28; British Medical Association, 175; Buckingham Palace, 105–7; Calvinistic Methodists, 26–27, 239–40; Constitutional, 153, 169; Liberation Society, 198, 204; National Council of the Evangelical Free Churches, 76; Northern Counties Education League, 235–36; Temperance Jubilee, 69; Ulster Nationalists, 114; Welsh Land League, 129–30; Welsh Liberal, 240–41; Wesleyan Methodist, 234

Congregational Church, 176–77, 210–11

Congreve, Richard, 46

Connolly, James, 111–12

Conscription, 116–18, 282, 289, 291, 296, 307

Constables; 120, 151, 226–27, 231, 255, 264

Constantinople; 279–80, 282, 313

Conventions: Irish (1917–18), 116; National Convention on Peace and Reconstruction (1935), 316; Trade Union, 304–5; Welsh Church (1917), 221–22; Welsh National (1907), 213–14

Conviction, 1–3, 7, 13, 24, 26–27, 31–32, 35–36, 50, 54–55, 57–59, 61, 133, 241, 260, 315–16, 319

Cooperation meetings, 14, 38, 44–45, 50, 237–38, 282; Birmingham (1867), 23; Chester (1847), 22;

Cooperation meetings (*continued*)
Edinburgh (1842), 9–10, 21–22;
Liverpool (1878), 24; London (1898),
14, 24, 74–75; Newcastle (1870),
9–10; Nottingham (1866), 22–23;
Wigan (1914), 281
Cornwall, 192, 257
Councils: army, 303; Barry County,
243; Central Land and Housing,
191; Council of Action, 316; Council
of Ireland, 102, 119–20; county, 26,
70, 173, 206–7, 211, 216, 220, 231,
238, 240–41; local, 187, 214, 236–37;
London County, 26; Merionethshire
County, 243; Montgomeryshire
County, 243; national, 93; National
Council of the Evangelical Free
Churches, 76, 234, 236–37, 241, 244,
316; National Liberal Council for
Wales and Monmouthshire, 74, 210,
234–36; Portmadoc County, 238;
Privy, 145, 221, 299, 301, 313, 317, 319;
Supreme War, 306; War, 286; Welsh
National, 200, 207–8, 214, 240, 244
Cowdray, Lord (Weetman Pearson),
295–96, 300, 308
Creeds, 3, 32, 38–39, 55–58, 67, 211, 234,
249
Cymru Fydd, 130, 198, 208–9
Cyprus, 247

Dail Eireann, 90–1, 100, 116–19, 121–125
Dangerfield, George, 104–5
Daniel, D. R., 24, 33–34, 52–55, 223
Dardanelles, 270, 272, 286–87, 289, 313
Davidson, Randall (Archbishop of
Canterbury), 213, 215, 220, 241, 244
Davies, John Hugh, 129
Davies, J. T., 5–6
Davitt, Michael, 88–90, 92, 128–30, 136
Deism, 32, 41, 60
Democracy, 2–3, 18, 21, 25–29, 72, 187,
195, 211, 237, 250, 272, 301–2, 316, 320

Dervishes, 250–51
Diggle, Joseph R., 232–33
Diplomacy, 2–4, 149, 221, 260, 271, 279,
301, 309, 312
Diplomatic alliances: Allies, 286, 289,
291, 300–301, 304–6, 308–9, 313,
372n30; Anglo-Russian Entente,
270–71; Balkan League, 279; Central
Powers, 271, 296, 302–3; Entente
Cordiale, 269–71, 275, 277, 287;
Franco-Russian Entente, 271, 277;
League of Nations, 222–23, 305, 309;
Triple Alliance, 271, 278, 295; Triple
Entente, 271, 289, 295
Direct Veto, 70, 76–77, 200–201
Disciples of Christ, 9–10, 17, 20
Disendowment, 3, 18, 72–73, 197, 204–6,
216–17, 219–20, 223, 229–30
Disestablishment, 3, 18, 64–65, 72–73,
87–88, 91–92, 97, 101, 131, 197–223,
227–30, 250
Distraint, 226, 230–31, 239
Dobruja, 280
Dogmatism, 1, 53–54, 57–58, 61, 233,
239–40, 320–21
Dominion status, 18, 116, 118–19, 121–24,
313
Dreyfus, Alfred, 251
Dublin, 89–91, 100, 102, 104, 107, 111–13,
117–18, 120–25, 190
Duma, 270, 301

Ecclesiastical Commissioners, 219–20,
226, 228
Edinburgh, 10, 12, 15, 21–22, 43, 76
Education, 3, 6–7, 25, 32, 34, 54, 73,
77–80, 94–95, 138, 143, 146, 179, 185,
192, 206, 209–13, 231–47, 271, 291
Edwards, A. G. (Bishop of St. Asaph/
Archbishop of Wales), 198–99, 207,
212–13, 215–16, 218–19, 221–23, 228,
233, 241–42
Edwards, Owen M., 245

Egalitarianism, 3, 20, 29, 57–58, 68, 147, 202, 212, 221, 223, 239, 316, 320

Egotism; 320

Elections: 1868, 127; 1880, 25, 127; 1885, 129, 250; 1886, 128, 130, 250; 1890, 2, 25, 92, 198, 229; 1892, 71–73, 91–92, 135, 208, 250; 1895, 73–74, 94, 135, 208, 232–33; 1900, 77, 98–99, 135, 137–38, 211–12, 243–44, 257; 1906, 6–7, 79–80, 98, 139, 212, 243–44; 1910 (January), 101, 148–49, 214–15; 1910 (December), 101, 153, 215, 274; 1918, 101–2, 118, 183, 195, 223, 308, 312; 1922, 312–14; 1929, 316–17; 1935, 316–19

Elitism, 320–21

Ellis-Nanney, Hugh, 38, 67, 131 198, 208, 228

England, 2, 11, 22–23, 44, 75, 86, 93–94, 96, 98, 119–20, 122, 124, 128, 132–33, 136, 141, 152, 187, 210, 220, 231, 235, 237, 239, 247, 252–53, 262, 267, 269, 271, 277, 310, 313, 318

English Channel, 284, 307

Erzberger, Matthias, 308

Evangelists: Ainsworth, Thomas, 14, 237–38; Black, Sydney, 14, 74–75, 233, 316; Campbell, Alexander, 9–10, 15–29, 46–48, 59, 248, 317, 320; Campbell, Thomas, 10, 15; Carson, Alexander, 14–16; Clifford, John, 132–33, 237–38, 244, 310; Crockatt, John, 237; Davies, J. G. 205; Ellis, Robert, 19; Evans, Christmas, 11; Evans, Edward, 23, 65, 238–39; Evans, Herber, 37–38; Evans, John, 19; Ewing, Greville, 15–16; Haldane, James Alexander, 14–16; Haldane, Robert, 14–16; Hopps, John Page, 43; Horne, Silvester, 176–77; Hughes, Hugh Price, 233–34; Hughes, S. W. 316; Jones, John Richard, 11–12, 14–15, 18–22; Jones-Lewis, T., 67; Jones, W. S., 43; Jones, William, 18–21;

Jones, William (Church of Christ), 22, 41–42, 49–50; King, David, 23; Larimore, T. B., 59; Lidgett, John Scott, 210, 316; Lloyd, David, 9, 11–12, 20–22; Lloyd, Richard, 4, 9, 11, 14, 21–22, 24, 31–32, 36–37, 39–40, 45, 49–51, 54, 69–70, 89, 105, 131–32, 174, 179, 181, 200, 230, 232–33, 243, 248, 254–55, 257, 273, 287, 293, 296, 317 ; McLean, Archibald, 11–15, 20–21, 25, 317; Morgan, Herbert, 33, 55, 59; Rotherham, Joseph Bryant, 23; Spurgeon, Charles, 51, 132–33, 198; Stone, Barton W., 10, 17; Wallis, James, 19–20, 22–23; Webley, William, 13–14, 82; Williams, John, 19; Williams, William (Church of Christ), 14, 22, 43, 50, 59

Evans, David, 315

Evans, R. D., 43–44

Fanning, Ronan, 118

Feisal, Emir, 310–11

Fels, Joseph, 186

Ferdinand, Francis, 278, 280, 308–9

Flanders, 286, 303

Fontainebleau Memorandum, 309–10

Forward Movement, 13–14, 237

Foster, Douglas A., 17

France, 109, 269–70, 275–83, 290, 303, 307, 310–11, 313, 318

Franco, Francisco, 318–19

Free Church, 28, 76, 234, 236–37, 241, 244, 279, 281, 316

Gee, Howell, 226

Gee, Thomas, 130, 225–26, 228, 234

Gehenna, 279

George, Elizabeth (mother), 31

George, Mary Ellen (sister), 9, 58, 82

George, William (brother), 9, 26, 55–57, 239, 241–42

George, William (father), 31

Germany, 83, 104, 109–11, 138–39, 141, 143, 195, 269–83, 285, 288–89, 300–302, 304–9, 311, 318–19

Gibraltar, 276

Glasgow, 15–16, 23, 191–92, 254–55, 302–3

God, 6, 17, 20–22, 29, 32–35, 38–41, 45–46, 49–50, 52–53, 57–58, 61, 82, 110, 132, 145–47, 206, 208, 216, 221, 225, 237–38, 249, 255, 264, 281, 287, 293, 306, 310, 312–13, 315, 319–20

Gooch, G. P., 189

Goodpasture, B. C., 59

Gore, Charles (Bishop of Oxford), 218

Greece, 26, 279–80, 289, 312–13

Guerrillas, 119–21, 258–60, 262, 267

Hague, the, 252–53

Heath, J. St G., 191

Higher criticism, 6–7, 37–38, 52

Hobhouse, Emily, 259

Holy Spirit, 13, 21

Home rule, 2–3, 71–74, 87–91, 93–110, 113–15, 117–20, 125, 128, 130–31, 138, 153, 177, 183, 192, 198–99, 202, 205, 209, 212, 215–19, 222, 250, 274

House, Colonel (Edward), 300–301

Housing, 2–3, 80, 134–35, 140–41, 182, 187–91, 193, 195–96, 222, 228 Hugo, Victor; 36

Humanitarianism, 27, 38–39, 46, 50–51, 53–55, 70, 90, 98, 129, 152, 172, 247, 251–53, 260–61, 269, 273, 279, 310, 315, 320

Hyslop, R. M., 39

Hywl, 227, 356n5

Idealism, 54, 209, 310, 320

Imperialism, 98–100, 103–4, 107, 121–123, 185, 247–48, 251, 253, 256–63, 265, 272, 276–77, 283, 289, 299, 303, 320–21

India, 79–80, 106, 122, 263, 285–86, 292

Insurance, 1–3, 18, 99, 138–44, 147, 151, 153, 169–71, 173–84, 189–90, 196, 243, 271

International conferences: Algeciras, 269–70, 274–75; Beauvais, 306–7; Berlin, 247, 272; Cannes, 311; Genoa, 311–12; Hague (1899), 253; London Peace (1912–13), 179–80; Paris Peace, 9, 18, 118–19, 222–23, 302, 308–10; San Remo, 311; Third Chantilly, 294; Washington Naval, 305

International crises: Bosnian (1908), 272; Chanak (1922), 312–14; Curragh, 104; Easter Rising, 2–3, 110–13; Fashoda (1898), 250, 269; First Moroccan (1905), 269–70; Irish (1914), 107–8; Larne, 104–7; Second Moroccan (1911), 269, 274–75, 278, 283; Venezuelan (1896), 250

Investiture, 199, 202–3, 218

Iraq, 311

Ireland, 2–3, 14–16, 18, 71, 87–89, 91–93, 95–106, 108–25, 136, 141, 145, 177, 218, 245, 250, 263, 291

Irish Republic, 87–88, 111–12, 117–20

Italy, 242, 278–79, 289, 303–4, 311, 313, 318 Japan; 269–70, 272, 311

Jingoism, 249, 252–53, 305, 320

Jones, Edwin, 207

Jones, Hugh, 22

Jones, John Thomas, 197

Jones, Michael, 128–29

Kemal, Mustapha (Atatürk), 313

Kew Gardens, 41–42

Keynes, John Maynard, 316

Khaki, 98–99, 137–38, 211–12, 257

Kurdistan, 311

Land Reform, 1, 73, 127–29, 133–35, 151, 169, 183, 189–90, 209, 316

Larkin, James, 189–90

Lawson, Harry, 180–81
Lawson, Wilfrid, 77
Lebanon, 311
Lever, William, 182
Lewis, J. Saunders, 317–18
Liberal League, 265, 267
Liberalism, 38, 55, 142, 176, 179, 191, 208–9, 267
Licensing, 2–3, 63, 65–66, 69, 75–82, 86, 110, 197–98, 213
Liverpool, 12, 18, 24, 67, 102, 118, 174, 215
Lloyd, Daniel Lewis (Bishop of Bangor), 228
Lloyd, Rebecca, 31
Lloyd George, David: backbencher, 73; baptism, 9, 32; birth, 2; childhood, 13, 19, 31–33, 59–61, 63–64; church service, 40, 46–47; death, 31, 40, 319–20; Earl of Dwyfor, 2; education, 32, 37–39, 52–54, 315; family, 9, 31–32, 49; funeral, 319–20; law practice, 22, 41, 48, 51, 57–58, 63, 69, 130, 227, 294, 315; legacy, 184, 316, 320; marriages, 5, 48–49, 57–58, 197, 234, 315–16; mistress, 4–6, 36, 58–59, 83, 110, 221, 311, 320; on clergy, 25–26, 34, 38–39, 48, 67–68, 74, 114, 129, 135, 197–98, 201–2, 205–6, 227–28, 230–32, 234–36, 239–40, 243; on dukes, 145, 147–48; on investitures, 199, 312; on landowners, 32, 67, 74, 87, 89, 95, 127–29, 131–35, 145–46, 151–52, 179, 183–84, 186–89, 191–92, 194–95, 231–32, 236; on Lords, 18, 80–81, 141–42, 146–49, 213–17, 244, 271. *See also* Lloyd George, David, offices held*;* Lloyd George, David *on specific topics; and* Lloyd George, David, speeches of
Lloyd George, David, offices held: Chancellor of the Exchequer, 1–2, 5–6, 17–18, 27, 81–83, 98, 139, 143–44, 150, 174, 177, 180–81, 189, 192, 218, 221, 243, 245, 271–75, 287, 300; Minister of Munitions, 1–2, 82–84, 110–11, 196, 287–90, 292–93, 300–301; President of the Board of Trade, 2, 27, 79, 97, 139, 142, 270; Prime Minister, 1–2, 6, 9, 18, 29, 75, 84–86, 115, 120, 125, 222, 246, 287, 297, 299, 301–2, 307, 311–14; Secretary of State for War, 1–2, 84, 115, 287, 292–93
Lloyd George, David, on military leaders: Allenby, Edmund, 301–2, 310–11; Fisher, John, 272–73, 287; French, John, 273, 283–87, 292–93; Gordon, Charles, 250–51; Gough, Hubert, 104; Haig, Douglas, 85, 283, 288–90, 293–94, 299, 303–4, 306–8; Jellicoe, John, 291, 300; Kitchener, H. H., 250, 258–60, 265, 273, 284–90, 292; Lawrence, T. E., 310–11; Methuen, Paul, 266; Philipps, Ivor, 289–90; Roberts, Frederick, 256–61; Robertson, William, 289, 303, 305–6; Seely, J. E. B., 104; White, George, 251–54; Wilson, Arnold, 310; Wilson, Henry, 305–7
Lloyd George, David, on non-English peoples: Afghans, 247–48; Africans, 122, 263, 269; Arabians, 305, 311; Arabs, 279, 281, 310–11; Armenians, 263, 302–3, 305, 311; Australians, 115–16, 122, 263, 287, 313; Austro-Hungarians, 278, 281, 286, 289, 295, 302–3, 305; Belgians, 29, 107, 280–83, 285–86, 299, 302–4, Boers, 1, 29, 95–96, 98–99, 122, 135–37, 209, 211–12, 236, 239, 251–61, 263–67, 269, 276, 303; Bulgars, 248, 279; Canadians, 13, 15, 116, 122, 251, 263, 303; French, 122, 251, 269, 282–84, 302, 304, 309–11; Germans, 18, 141–42, 269, 275, 282, 305, 308–11, 318–19; Greeks, 26, 289, 312–13; Indians, 122, 263, 285–86, 292; Irish, 87, 89, 91–92, 95, 97–99, 103–5,

Lloyd George, David on non-English
     peoples (*continued*)
     110–11, 113–14, 116, 118–25, 263, 291;
     Italians, 242, 278, 289, 302–4, 311,
     313, 318; Japanese, 269, 311; Jews, 281,
     310–11; Mesopotamians, 302–3, 305,
     311; Montenegrins, 248, 279, 304;
     Muslims, 250–51, 279; New Zealand-
     ers, 263, 313; Palestinians, 305, 311;
     Poles, 304–5, 309; Rumanians, 295,
     304; Russians, 270–1, 282, 295, 301,
     304–5, 311–12; Scots, 42–43, 76, 122,
     201, 247, 302; Serbs, 279, 289, 295,
     302–4; Syrians, 305, 311; Turks, 247,
     272, 279, 287–89, 310–13; Welsh,
     2–3, 18, 44, 54–56, 70–74, 79–80,
     90–91, 94–95, 122, 129–31, 135, 180,
     198, 200–206, 209–10, 214, 217,
     229–31, 234, 240, 242–43, 245, 250,
     263, 283, 286, 317, 319–21; Zulus,
     247–48
Lloyd George, David, on party leaders:
     Asquith, H. H., 102–6, 109–11, 113,
     115, 139–40, 143, 145, 147–50, 153, 182,
     200, 207–8, 214, 272, 281, 289, 291,
     295–97, 306, 308; Baldwin, Stanley,
     316–19; Blafour, Arthur James, 54,
     77–78, 80–81, 109, 113–14, 141, 153,
     169, 212, 215, 238–39, 244–45, 269,
     271, 287, 297, 299, 309–11, 313;
     Campbell-Bannerman, Henry,
     79–80, 209, 214, 262; Canning,
     George, 247; Carson, Edward, 100–
     107, 109, 113–15, 145, 189–90, 297,
     299; Chamberlain, Joseph, 77–79,
     89–91, 93–95, 129–30, 136–38, 144,
     232–33, 236, 256–59, 263–66, 286–87;
     Chamberlain, Neville, 20, 318–19;
     Churchill, Winston, 31, 78, 99, 102–4,
     124, 141–43, 153, 170–71, 182, 276–78,
     303, 313, 319; Craig, James, 104, 106,
     113, 119–21, 123–25; Dillon, John, 88,
     95–97, 102–3, 106, 111–13, 116–18, 266;

Disraeli, Benjamin, 247; Gladstone,
     William, 27, 87–89, 129, 150, 176, 200,
     202–3, 247–50, 272, 279–81; Grey,
     Earl, 212; Henderson, Arthur, 291–92,
     299; Lansbury, George, 25, 317; Law,
     Andrew Bonar, 99, 105–6, 113–14,
     153, 170–71, 184–85, 223, 275, 297,
     299, 308, 312; MacDonald, Ramsay,
     174, 316–17, 319; Morgan, George
     Osborne, 203, 205, 210; O'Brien,
     William, 88, 99, 111, 149–50, 177;
     Parnell, Charles Stewart, 89–93,
     199–200; Peel, Robert, 75; Redmond,
     John, 95–96, 99, 102–3, 106, 109–13,
     115–16, 149–50; Rendel, Stuart, 80,
     203–45; Rosebery, Lord, 72–73,
     93–94, 148, 176, 205–9, 215–16, 262,
     265, 267, 269; Salisbury, Lord, 130,
     133, 209, 219, 247–48, 250, 264–65;
     Thomas, Alfred, 210
Lloyd George, David, speeches of, 3,
     27–28, 54, 60, 68, 70, 73–74, 76–77,
     80, 89, 97, 128–29, 132, 140, 175–76,
     181, 188–91, 194–95, 198–99, 203,
     221, 227, 230, 258, 264–65, 319–20;
     Bangor, 231, 240–41, 255, 257; Belfast,
     97–98; Birkenhead, 201; Birming-
     ham, 263–64; Blaenau Ffestiniog,
     68; Bristol, 264; Cardiff, 79, 91,
     213–14; Carnarvon, 206; Conway,
     202, 257–58; Glasgow, 191–92, 254–
     55, 302–3; Leigh, 263; Limehouse,
     145–48; Liskeard, 257; London, 152,
     214, 261, 304–5; Manchester, 70;
     Mansion House, 275–76; Newcastle,
     147–48; Newport, 209; Oxford, 190,
     244; Portmadoc, 68, 89; Sheffield,
     199; Swansea, 142
Lloyd George, Gwilym, 49, 266, 286,
     293, 303
Lloyd George, Mair, 5–6, 49
Lloyd George, Margaret Owen, 5–6,
     42, 197

Lloyd George, Megan, 5, 39, 49, 58, 290, 318

Lloyd George, Robert (great-grandson), 362n25

Lloyd-Jones, Austen, 153

Lloyd-Jones, John, 67

Local option, 66, 68, 70–75, 77, 80–81, 250

Local veto, 70–71, 75, 77, 80

London, 3, 5–6, 14–15, 18, 24, 26–27, 33, 41–41, 44, 46, 51, 53, 58–59, 71, 74, 76, 93–94, 102–5, 107, 116, 120, 122–25, 144, 148–49, 152, 171, 181–82, 198, 206–8, 212, 214, 233–34, 237, 242, 255, 258, 261, 264, 271, 275, 279–81, 290, 294–96, 317–18, 320

Lothian, Lord (Philip Kerr), 318–19

Luther, Martin, 16–17

Macedonia, 280

MacMillan, Margaret (great-granddaughter), 371n22

MacNeill, Eoin, 112, 119

Macpherson, Ian, 119

Mahdi, 250–51

Manchester, 2, 23, 70, 73–74, 78, 107, 183, 212, 217, 236, 238

Marienbad, 180–81

Marsden, George, 20

Masterman, Lucy, 34–36, 50–54, 127

Mayne, Ernie, 84–85

McCalla, W. L., 19

McMillon, Lynn, 15

Mecca, 310–11

Medical care: asylums, 192; doctors, 69, 86, 143, 172, 175–76, 179–82, 242; hospitals, 143; infirmaries, 143; medicine, 43; sanitaria, 172, 177–78

Members of Parliament: Abraham, William, 29, 199; Acland, Arthur, 200; Acland, Francis, 110; Balfour, Gerald, 96; Bevan, Aneurin, 319; Caine, W. S., 74–75; Collings, Jesse,

129; Courtney, Leonard, 255; Cox, Harold, 142; Davies, David, 190–91; Devlin, Joseph, 110, 113–14; Edwards, Frank, 205, 208; Ellis, Thomas E., 71–72, 91–93, 130–31, 200–201, 203, 205–9, 227, 232; Evans, Samuel T., 200–201, 203, 212–13, 230–32; Forest, Maurice de, 182–83, 186; Forster, H. W., 178; Forster, W. E., 89, 235, 241; Gladstone, W. G. C., 218; Griffith, Ellis, 212–13; Hemmerde, E G., 186–87; Holland, Lionel, 136; Illingworth, Perce, 189; Lecky, W. E. H., 137; Lewis, John Herbert, 54, 132–33, 200, 203–5, 233, 240; Lowther, J. W., 106, 259, 261–62; Markham, Arthur, 170; Masterman, Charles, 34–35, 50–54, 127, 153; Morton, E. J. C., 77–78; O'Connor, T. P., 59; Phillips, Wynford, 201; Raffan, P. Wilson, 191; Redmond, William, 88, 136, 149; Reed, Edward, 203; Roberts, John Bryn, 130; Saunders, W. B., 191; Thomas, D. A., 201, 205, 208–9, 212, 229; Usborne, Thomas, 133; Wallace, Robert, 76

Mesopotamia, 302–3, 305, 311

Metternich, Paul von Wolff (Count), 271–72, 275–76

Middle East, 301–2, 310

Millennialism, 10, 14, 19–20, 23; amillennial, 20; postmillennial, 20, 184; premillennial, 12, 20

Moldavia, 295

Montenegro, 279–80, 304

Morant, Robert, 179, 240, 243, 246

Morgan, Prys, 330nn8–9

Murray, Alexander (Master/Baron of Elibank), 106, 177

Natal, 254, 257, 268

National Eisteddfod, 241

National Government, 316–17

National Health Service, 319
National Liberal Federation, 263
National Library of Wales, 4, 216, 220
Nationalism, 72, 79–80, 207, 209, 309
Naylor, R. A., 212
Netherlands, the, 285, 308
New Deal, 316
New Zealand, 313
Newcastle, 9–10, 147–48, 202–3
Newfoundland, 13, 313
Nicoll, William Robertson, 221
Nicolson, Arthur, 270
Non-British military leaders: Botha,
    Louis, 256–58, 265, 267–68; Brusi-
    lov, Alexsei, 295; Bülow, Karl von,
    284; d'Espèrey, Franchet, 284;
    Falkenhayn, Erich von, 283, 291;
    Foch, Ferdinand, 284–85, 306–7;
    Hausen, Max von, 284; Hindenburg,
    Paul von, 291, 308; Hötzendorf,
    Conrad von, 278; Joffre, Joseph,
    85, 284–85, 291; Kluck, Alexander
    von, 283–84; Lanrezac, Charles,
    283–84; Ludendorff, Erich von, 282,
    308; Marchand, Jean-Baptiste, 250;
    Moltke, Helmuth von, 284; Olivier,
    J. H., 256; Pershing, John J., 303;
    Petain, Hénri, 284, 291, 307; Scheer,
    Reinhard, 292; Smuts, Jan, 116,
    121–22, 267, 303, 305; Tirpitz, Alfred
    von, 277
Non-British prime ministers:
    Bethmann-Hollweg, Theobald von,
    141, 276–78, 284; Blum, Leon, 319;
    Briand, Aristide, 294; Clemenceau,
    Georges, 272, 305–6, 309; Poincaré,
    Raymond, 313; Venizelos, Eleftherios,
    26
Non-British rulers: Constantine I,
    313; Hitler, Adolf, 317–18; Hus-
    sein, King, 310–11; Joseph, Francis,
    272, 278; Lenin, Nikolai, 304,

311–12; Mussolini, Benito, 317–18;
    Nicholas II, 301; Wilhelm I, 308–9;
    Wilhelm II, 269–72, 277, 308
Nonconformists, 3, 6, 25, 27, 33, 40, 54,
    60, 66–67, 74, 76, 78, 95, 142, 190,
    199, 202–4, 206, 209–14, 216, 219,
    221, 223, 225, 227–28, 233–35, 237–41,
    243–45, 281–82, 285, 316–17
Norfolk, 187, 290
North Wales Liberal Federation, 198,
    205
Northcliffe, Lord (Alfred Harmsworth),
    106, 146, 308–9
Northumberland, 23
Norway, 292

Obstructionism, 73, 81, 132, 201, 203,
    206, 209, 229, 320
Orange Free State, 256, 267–68
Orangemen, 97
Orphans, 13–14, 79, 145, 169–70
Ottoman Empire, 247, 272, 278–80, 289,
    310–11
Owen, John (Bishop of St. David's), 216,
    220–21, 241–42
Oxford, 190, 218, 226, 228, 244, 246

Pacifism, 248, 250, 275, 281–83, 305, 318,
    320
Page, Walter Hines, 109
Pakenham, Thomas, 253
Palestine, 301–2, 305, 310–11
Pankhurst, Christabel, 3
Pan-Slavism, 247, 280
Paris, 9, 18, 32, 118–19, 222–23, 294, 302,
    308–10
Pasha, Arabi, 248–49
Pasha, Tewfik, 249
Passive Resistance, 180, 237–38, 245
Pearse, Patrick, 111–12, 119
Pearse, William, 112
Peel, Arthur (Viscount), 75–76

Pensions, 1–3, 18, 70, 135–42, 144, 170, 174, 192, 236, 271, 273, 309

Percival, John (Bishop of Hereford), 79, 218

Persia, 270

Platt, Henry, 211

Plender, William, 180

Popular Front, 318–19

Philosophers: Bacon, Francis, 16; Bernstein, Eduard, 141–42; Campbell, Alexander, 16–17, 320; Carlyle, Thomas, 50–54; Comte, August, 46; Congreve, Richard, 46; George, Henry, 127–28; Godwin, William, 16; Harrison, Frederic, 46; Hume, David, 16; Locke, John, 16, 320; Newton, Isaac, 16; Reid, Thomas, 16–17, 320; Renan, Ernest, 51–52, 54; Rousseau, Jean Jacques, 16; Voltaire (Francois-Marie Arouet), 34–35; Webb, Beatrice, 142–43; Webb, Sidney, 142–43

Poland, 305

Political parties: Conservative, 94, 96, 256, 319; Home Rule, 87; Irish National Land League, 87; Irish National League, 88–89; Irish Parliamentary, 88; Labour, 25, 148–49, 174, 176, 189, 245–46, 319–21; Liberal, 71, 73, 77–80, 90–91, 138–39, 141, 147, 202–3, 214, 243, 262–63, 265, 315; Liberal Unionists, 71–73, 78, 90, 93–94, 114, 208, 214, 232–33, 243–44, 256, 263, 265; Radical, 319; Sinn Féin, 116–19, 121, 124; Socialist, 319

Pragmatism, 1–2, 209, 250, 320

Prayer, 6, 33, 37–41, 45–48, 55, 57, 235, 243

Presbyterians, 13–16, 19, 22–23, 42–43, 96, 99

Presidents: Cleveland, Grover, 250; Garfield, James A., 18, 20, 25, 320; Griffith, Arthur, 117, 123–25; Jackson, Andrew, 320; Johnson, Lyndon, 20; Kruger, Paul, 251–53, 256; Lincoln, Abraham, 18, 320; Reagan, Ronald, 20; Roosevelt, Franklin, 316; Steyn, Marthinus, 256; Washington, George, 318; Wilson, Woodrow, 109, 115, 120, 300–303, 305, 309; Valera, Eamon de, 112, 117–19, 121–25

Principles, 2, 14, 17, 20–21, 27–29, 43, 49, 54, 61, 90–91, 169, 204, 234–35, 238, 253, 264–65, 282, 305, 320

Pro-Boers, 211–12, 255, 259, 265, 267, 276

Protestants, 88, 97–99, 101, 107, 110, 116, 119, 231

Prothero, R. E., 228

Providence, 28–29, 48, 52, 145, 147, 243, 293, 315

Prussia, 143, 294, 296, 308–9

Pryce, John, 207

Publicans, 65–67, 70, 80, 227

Puleston, John, 202

Radical Programme, 129

Rationalism, 10, 24, 43, 54, 60, 84, 128, 149, 234, 261, 320

Realism, 59, 320

Reichstag, 276

Religious societies: American Christian Missionary Society, 17–18; Band of Hope, 38–39; Christian Socialist Brotherhood, 132–33; Christian Socialist League, 132–33; Church of England Temperance Society, 76; Evangelical Alliance, 53; Liberal Christian League, 152; National Council of the Evangelical Free Churches, 76, 234, 316; National Society of the Established Church, 240–41; Particular Baptist Foreign Missionary Society, 12

Republicanism, 15–16, 21, 24–25, 87–88, 111–12, 116–20, 123, 202, 319

Restoration movement, 10, 17, 21, 25–26, 48, 55–56

Revolutions: 1905, 270; Atatürk's, 313; Bolshevik, 304–5, 311–12; February, 301–2; French, 16, 210–11, 248; Greek, 312–13; Young Turk, 272

Rhineland, 309

Rhodes, Cecil, 253

Rhondda, 199

Ribbentrop, Joachim von, 318

Richardson, Robert, 16–17

Richthofen, Manfred von, 308

Riddell, Lord (George Allardice), 1, 32–33, 83, 123

Ritualism, 38, 68, 210–11

Rivers: Afon Dwyfor, 41–42, 319–20; Aisne, 284; Ancre, 291; Danube, 280; Marne, 307; Nile, 250; Somme, 291; Thames, 41–42; Vaal, 256; Yser, 286

Roberts, Henry, 66–67

Roberts, John (deacon), 24–25, 45–46, 49–50, 87, 90, 247

Roberts, John (translator), 18–19

Rothermere, Lord (Harold Harmsworth), 106, 308

Rothschild, Nathaniel Mayer (Baron), 107, 144–45

Rowntree, Seebohm, 26, 182, 187, 191

Rumania, 280, 295, 304

Russia, 270, 272, 278–82, 287, 295, 301, 304–5, 312

Saar, 309

Sarajevo, 280

Saudi Arabia, 310–11

Schlieffen Plan, 280–81, 284

Schools, 151, 214, 232, 238–41, 244–45; Anglican, 3, 25, 32, 34, 37–40, 52–53, 65, 67, 94–96, 129, 198, 228, 232–34, 236–37, 239–41, 243, 315; Board, 67–68, 228, 232–33, 235, 238, 241; bombing, 317; British, 228, 235; Catholic, 95–96; clerical, 239; day, 234; elementary, 235, 245–46; Foreign, 235; high, 285; intermediate, 231, 246; national, 32; nonsectarian, 95, 271; public, 15, 245–46; secondary, 231; sectarian, 95; secular, 233, 238; state, 97, 241; Sunday, 12, 27, 39, 41–44, 46–47, 54–55, 57, 73, 80, 235, 238, 244; technical, 70; university, 95, 285; Voluntary, 134–35, 232–33, 235, 238, 241, 244–45

School boards, 228, 236–38; Carnarvon, 232; Criccieth, 26; London, 233; Portmadoc, 238

Scorched-earth policy, 257

Scotland, 10, 12–13, 16, 23, 42–43, 75, 84, 94, 122, 152, 170, 190, 201, 302

Scott, C. P., 107, 183–84, 217, 235–36, 238, 283

Scruples, 67, 222, 316, 320

Scutari, 280

Seas: Adriatic, 279, 282; Aegean, 372n30; Black, 280, 282; Dead, 310; Mediterranean, 282; North, 287, 292

Sectarianism, 3, 17, 22, 48, 60, 95, 97, 223, 234, 244–45, 317, 320–21

Secularism, 60, 214, 216, 220, 233, 238, 320–21

Seiat, 39, 331n20

Self-determination, 116, 305

Serbia, 107, 272, 279–81, 289, 295, 302–4

Shakespeare, Geoffrey, 125

Shannon, Catherine B., 109

Sheffield, 199, 246, 317

Sheringham, 290

Smallholdings, 129, 135, 187

Smyrna, 312–13, 372n30

Snowden, Philip, 147

Socialism, 6–7, 55, 132–33, 141–44, 148, 152, 191, 234, 237, 243, 319–21

Socioeconomic leagues: Anti-Tithe League, 69, 130, 226–28, 231; British and Foreign School Society, 235; Independent Order of Good Templars, 66–70, 75–76; Land Nationalisation Society, 151; Liberation Society, 198–99, 203–4; National Temperance League, 76; Northern Counties Education League, 235–36; Parliamentary Land Values Group, 151; United Kingdom Alliance, 64, 68–71, 75–77, 80–81, 83; Welsh Land, Commercial, and Labour League, 130

Sofia, 280

South Wales Liberal Federation, 208–9

Southern Unionists, 116–17, 121

Spain, 95–96, 259, 269–70, 318–19

Spender, J. A., 191

Stamfordham, Lord (Arthur Bigge), 215

Stead, William T., 52, 150

Stephen, Peter, 44–45, 238–39

Stevenson, Frances, 5–6, 26, 36–39, 51–52, 54, 58–59, 61, 110, 115–16, 122, 124, 287, 292, 302, 316, 320

Straiton, John, 58–59

Stuart, Jacobo Fitz-James (Duke of Alba), 318–19

Suez Canal, 248–49

Suffolk, 290

Suffrage, 1, 3, 19, 142, 145, 152, 179–80, 192, 265

Sullivan, A. M., 89

Sweeney, Z. T., 17–18

Syria, 302, 305, 311

Temperance movement, 2–3, 25, 64–66, 69–70, 72, 75–76, 79–80, 82–83, 85

Temple, Frederick (Bishop of London/Archbishop of Canterbury), 76, 208, 210–11

Tenants, 18, 64–65, 87–89, 94, 96, 100, 127–31, 133–35, 151–52, 186–88, 192–93, 206, 225–32

Thompson, David M., 10

Thrace, 280, 372n30

Tibet, 270

Tickle, Gilbert Y., 50

Tithes, 2–3, 64–65, 71, 90, 129, 131, 135, 205–7, 209, 212–13, 217, 220, 222, 225–31, 236, 246

Torr, H. J., 204–5

Town hall meetings: Birmingham, 263–64; Bristol, 264; Glasgow, 254–55; Inverness, 122; London, 145; Manchester, 70; Portmadoc, 68; Queen's, 214, 261; Ulster, 97–98

Trade unions, 117, 141–43, 179, 181, 304–5; British Workers' National League, 299; Cambrian Miners' Federation, 199; Irish Transport and General Workers Union, 190; National Farmer's Union, 192; Rural Labourer's League, 129; South Wales Miners' Federation, 199

Transjordan, 311

Transvaal, 136, 253, 256, 258, 267–68

Treaties: Anglo-Irish, 121–25; Ankara, 313; Brest-Litovsk, 306; Bucharest, 280, 295; Constantinople, 280, 313; Franco-German Accord, 274–76; Lausanne (1912), 278–79; Lausanne (1923), 372n30; London (1913), 279–80; London (1915), 289; Neuilly, 310; Racconigi Bargain, 278; Saint-Germain, 310; Sèvres, 310–11, 313, 372n30; Sykes-Picot Agreement, 311; Trianon, 310; Vereeniging, 267–69; Versailles, 305–9, 313

Treves, Frederick, 176

Ty Newydd, 40

Ulster Unionists, 115–16

Unemployment, 1–3, 18, 99, 120, 140–45, 147, 151, 171–74, 196, 271, 312, 316

United States, 9, 13, 15, 17–20, 22–23, 26, 28, 48, 53, 59, 88, 109, 113, 115, 120,

United States (*continued*)
127–28, 185, 250, 296, 300–303, 306–8, 316, 319
University of Wales, 216, 220

Vaughan, Edwin, 304
Venezuela, 250
Vincent, H. C., 148–49

Walton Heath, 186
Warner, Philip, 259
Wars: American Civil, 20, 120; Anglo-Egyptian, 248–49; Anglo-Irish, 2–3, 118–21; Anglo-Zulu, 247–28; Crimean, 256; First Balkan, 278–80; First Boer, 251; First World, 1, 18, 82, 86, 108, 144, 279; Franco-Prussian, 308–9; French Revolutionary, 16, 210–11, 248; Greco-Turkish, 312–13; Irish Civil, 101, 105, 109, 120, 125; Italo-Turkish, 278–79; Mahdist, 250–51; Napoleonic, 248; Russo-Japanese, 269–70; Second Afghan, 247–48; Second Balkan, 280; Second Boer, 1, 77, 95–96, 98–99, 135–37, 209, 211, 236, 239; Second World, 184, 319; Spanish Civil, 318–19
Weapons: airplanes, 290, 295–96, 307–8, 313, 318; artillery, 84, 113, 248, 254, 266, 274, 293–94, 303–4; battleships, 276–77, 287; bullets, 252–53; cavalry, 104, 251–52, 266, 274; convoys, 1, 300–301, 307–8; cruisers, 277, 282, 285, 287, 307–8; depth charges, 301; destroyers, 277, 287; dreadnoughts, 145, 147, 273, 277; gunboats, 274; guns, 102, 104, 106–7, 285, 287, 313; hydrophones, 301; infantry, 254, 274, 293; machine guns, 111, 252, 286, 288, 290, 294, 318; merchant ships, 18, 271, 301; mines, 287, 301; minesweepers, 287; nets, 285, 301; poison gas, 288–89,

304; rifles, 107, 111, 283; shells, 84, 113, 252–54, 285, 287–89, 304; submarines, 1, 83, 111, 277, 285, 287, 299–302; tanks, 290, 294–95, 307
Weimar Republic, 308–10
Welsh cities: Bangor, 19, 21, 37, 148, 206–7, 211, 228, 231, 240–41, 255, 257; Cardiff, 79, 91, 198–99, 210, 213–14; Newport, 209; Swansea, 142
Welsh counties, 128, 208, 226–27, 241; Anglesey, 11, 202, 212; Breconshire, 234; Cardiganshire, 231; Carnarvonshire, 18, 25, 53, 67, 69, 94, 130–31, 197, 202, 211–12, 225–27, 232; Denbighshire, 18–19, 46, 203, 226–27, 231; Flintshire, 54, 201, 226; Glamorganshire, 200–201; Merionethshire, 11, 67, 130, 227, 243; Monmouthshire, 73–74, 202–3, 210, 234–36, 245; Montgomeryshire, 23, 67, 190–91, 203, 205, 226, 243; Pembrokeshire, 214; Radnorshire, 234
Welsh Education Department, 240, 243
Welsh Revival, 10, 55, 317
Welsh towns: Aberystwyth, 128; Barmouth, 205; Barry, 243; Blaenau Ffestiniog, 43, 68–69, 128, 130; Carnarvon, 19, 28, 37, 69, 127, 202, 206, 232, 265; Conway, 202, 249, 257–58; Criccieth, 3–6, 9, 12–14, 18, 20–23, 26, 31–32, 37, 39–42, 45, 49–50, 53, 64, 66–67, 69, 82, 128–30, 197, 228, 238, 255, 257, 293–94, 299, 310, 317; Dolgelley, 12; Harlech, 12, 21; Llandudno, 249; Llanelly, 42, 49; Llanfair Caereinion, 21; Llanidloes, 21, 23; Merthyr Tydfil, 23, 49–50, 201; Newtown, 23; Portmadoc, 22, 34, 41–42, 45, 48–50, 63, 65, 68–69, 89, 197–98, 238, 248–49; Pwllheli, 69, 202, 227, 239; Tredegar, 19; Wrexham, 11–12, 21

Welsh villages: Aberdaron, 227; Garn
Fadryn, 227; Glyn Ceiriog, 12, 19;
Llan Haiarn, 228; Llannefydd, 18;
Llanystumdwy, 3–4, 31–32, 36–37,
39, 41, 63, 66–67, 188, 228; Ramoth,
12, 21; Rhos, 19, 21; Rhyl, 82–83, 241;
Sarn Mellteyrn, 197–98, 227; Talys-
arn, 128; Tremadoc, 22
West, Earl Irvin, 18
Williams, G. P., 43, 293–95
Williams, H. J., 64, 67–68
Williams, Vaughan, 213
Williams, William (songwriter), 319–20

Wilson, Guy Fleetwood, 273
Women: divorced, 5, 91, 177, 199; married, 5–6, 31, 56–58, 61, 140, 172, 177,
197, 204, 289, 296, 320; pregnant, 4,
144, 172; single, 3; suffragette, 3, 142,
145; widowed, 3, 31, 78, 81, 131–32,
144–45, 169–70
Wrather, Eva Jean, 17

Yarmouth, 290

Zionism, 281, 310